MW00627463

THE
SHAHNAMEH
VOLUME II

THE
SHAHNAMEH

VOLUME II

Hakim Abul-Ghassem Ferdowsi

Translated by Josiane Cohanim

GIROUETTE BOOKS

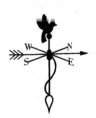

Girouette Books

New English translation copyright © 2023 Josiane Cohanim
Published in the United States of America
By Girouette Books
Santa Monica, California

Paperback ISBN 978-1-7349661-2-1
Ebook ISBN 978-1-7349661-3-8

girouettebooks.com

Cover art by ZariNaz Mottahedan
Cover design by Talia Cohanim
Typesetting and layout design by Sepehr Aziz

"As the golden sun pulls apart the indigo folds of night,
The sound of trumpets rises from Rostam's pavilion.
The hero dresses in his battle armor,
Sits on his charger reminiscent of a mountain,
And commands the army to load the provisions."

CONTENTS
VOLUME TWO

PREFACE

PART EIGHT

The Tale of Siaavosh

1.	The Beginning of the Story	27
2.	The Tale of Siaavosh's Mother	28
3.	The Birth of Siaavosh	31
4.	Siaavosh Returns From Zabolestan	33
5.	The Death of Siaavosh's Mother	36
6.	Sudaabeh Falls in Love With Siaavosh	37
7.	Siaavosh Visits Sudaabeh	39
8.	Siaavosh's Second Visit to the Women's Chambers	43
9.	Siaavosh's Third Visit to the Women's Chambers	47
10.	Sudaabeh Betrays Kay Kaavoos	48
11.	Sudaabeh Conspires With a Witch	51
12.	Kaavoos Inquires After the Infants' Birth	53
13.	Siaavosh Walks Through Fire	56
14.	Siaavosh Asks His Father to Grant Sudaabeh Mercy	60
15.	Kaavoos Learns of Afraasiyaab's Approach	63
16.	Siaavosh Prepares the Army for War	65
17.	Siaavosh's Letter to Kaavoos	68
18.	Kaavoos's Reply to Siaavosh's Letter	69
19.	Afraasiyaab Has a Frightening Dream	71
20.	Afraasiyaab Asks His Wise Men to Interpret His Dream	73
21.	Afraasiyaab Holds Counsel With His Men	75
22.	Garsivaz Travels to Siaavosh	77
23.	Siaavosh Draws Up a Treaty With Afraasiyaab	79
24.	Siaavosh Sends Rostam to Kaavoos	81
25.	Rostam Gives His Account to Kaavoos	83
26.	Kaavoos Sends Rostam to Sistan	85
27.	Kaavoos Replies to Siaavosh's Letter	86
28.	Siaavosh Consults With Bahraam and Zangueh	89
29.	Zangueh Goes to Afraasiyaab	93
30.	Afraasiyaab's Letter to Siaavosh	96
31.	Siaavosh Hands Over the Army to Bahraam	98
32.	Siaavosh Meets With Afraasiyaab	104
33.	Siaavosh Exhibits Prowess Before Afraasiyaab	106

34. Afraasiyaab and Siaavosh Go Hunting 111
35. Piran Offers His Daughter to Siaavosh to Wed 112
36. Piran Speaks to Siaavosh on the Subject of Faranguis 114
37. Piran Confers With Afraasiyaab 116
38. The Engagement of Faranguis and Siaavosh 119
39. Afraasiyaab Gives a Province to Siaavosh 121
40. Siaavosh Builds Gang-Dej 124
41. Siaavosh Speaks to Piran on Various Matters 128
42. Afraasiyaab Sends Piran to Various Lands 131
43. Siaavosh Builds Siaavosh-Guerd 132
44. Piran Visits Siaavosh-Guerd 133
45. Afraasiyaab Sends Garsivaz to Siaavosh 135
46. The Birth of Foorood, Son of Siaavosh 137
47. Siaavosh Plays Polo 139
48. Garsivaz Returns to Court and Slanders Siaavosh 144
49. Garsivaz Returns to Siaavosh 149
50. Siaavosh's Letter to Afraasiyaab 155
51. Afraasiyaab Leads a Campaign Against Siaavosh 157
52. Siaavosh's Dream 159
53. Siaavosh Conveys His Last Wishes to Faranguis 169
54. Siaavosh Falls Into Afraasiyaab's Hands 163
55. Faranguis Weeps and Pleads With Afraasiyaab 170
56. The Murder of Siaavosh by Garooy of Zerreh 172
57. Piran Rescues Faranguis 177

Kay Khosrow

1. The Birth of Kay Khosrow 180
2. Piran Hands Over the Care of Young Khosrow to Shepherds 183
3. Piran Introduces Kay Khosrow to Afraasiyaab 185
4. Kay Khosrow Travels to Siaavosh-Guerd 189

PART NINE

The Events Following the Slaying of Siaavosh: Kay Khosrow's Departure for Iran-Zamin

1. Ferdowsi's Grievance With Old Age 193
2. Kaavoos Learns of the Fate of Siaavosh 194
3. Rostam Travels to Kay Kaavoos 195
4. Rostam Kills Sudaabeh and Prepares for Battle 198
5. Faraamarz Kills Varaazaad, King of Sepanjab 200
6. Sorkheh Sets Off to Fight Rostam 202
7. Afraasiyaab Sets Off to Avenge His Son 208
8. Rostam Kills Pilsam 210

9. Afraasiyaab Flees From Rostam   214
10. Afraasiyaab Sends Kay Khosrow to Khotan   216
11. Rostam Governs Tooran-Zamin for Seven Years   219
12. Zavaareh Checks Out Siaavosh's Hunting Reserves   221
13. Rostam Destroys Tooran-Zamin   222
14. Rostam Returns to the Land of Iran   224
15. Goodarz Dreams of Sooroosh   226
16. Giv Travels to Tooran-Zamin in Search of Kay Khosrow   228
17. Giv Finds Kay Khosrow   232
18. Giv and Khosrow Travel to Siaavosh-Guerd   237
19. Kay Khosrow Adopts Behzaad   238
20. Faranguis Departs With Kay Khosrow
and Giv for Iran-Zamin   241
21. Golbaad and Nastihan Take Flight Before Giv   242
22. Piran Pursues Kay Khosrow   245
23. The Battle of Giv and Piran   248
24. Giv Captures Piran   251
25. Faranguis Frees Piran From the Hands of Giv   254
26. Afraasiyaab Encounters Piran on the Road   256
27. Giv Argues With the Tax Inspector   259
28. Kay Khosrow Crosses the Jayhoon   260
29. Kay Khosrow Arrives in Isfahan   263
30. Kay Khosrow Reaches Kay Kaavoos   266
31. Tous Disobeys Kay Khosrow   270
32. The Anger of Goodarz for Tous   273
33. Goodarz and Tous Ask Kaavoos
About the Line of Succession   274
34. Tous and Fariborz Attack the Castle of Bahman   278
35. Kay Khosrow Seizes the Castle of Bahman   279
36. Kay Khosrow Returns Victorious   283
37. Kaavoos Places Kay Khosrow on the Imperial Throne   284

PART TEN

The Sixty-Year Reign of Kay Khosrow

1. The Beginning of the Story   289
2. Noblemen Pay Homage to Kay Khosrow   290
3. Kay Khosrow Makes the Rounds of His Empire   292
4. Kay Khosrow Promises Vengeance   294
5. Kay Khosrow Reviews the World Heroes   298
6. Kay Khosrow Distributes Wealth   300
7. Kay Khosrow Sends Faraamarz to India   306
8. Kay Khosrow Puts Order to the Army   308
9. The Tale of Foorood, Son of Siaavosh   316
10. Tous Enters the Land of Turkestan   316
11. Foorood Learns of the Arrival of Tous   321

12. Foorood and Tokhaar Review the Iranian Army   324
13. Bahraam Climbs the Mountain to Foorood   327
14. Bahraam Returns to Tous   331
15. Foorood Kills Rivniz   333
16. Foorood Kills Zarasp   334
17. The Battle of Foorood and Tous   335
18. The Battle of Foorood and Giv   338
19. The Battle of Foorood and Bijan   342
20. The Death of Foorood   344
21. Jarireh Kills Herself   349
22. Bijan Kills Palaashan   352
23. The Iranians Suffer From the Snowfall   355
24. Bahraam Captures Kaboodeh   357
25. Tajov Battles the Iranians   359
26. Afraasiyaab Learns of Tous's Presence   363
27. Piran Surprises the Iranians   365
28. Kay Khosrow Summons Tous   368
29. Fariborz Proposes an Armistice to Piran   372
30. The Iranians Are Crushed by the Turks   374
31. Bahraam Returns to the Battlefield   381
32. Tajov Kills Bahraam   385
33. Giv Executes Tajov   388
34. The Iranians Return to Kay Khosrow   392

PART ELEVEN

The Story of Kaamoos of Kushan

1. The Beginning of the Story   397
2. Kay Khosrow Condemns Tous   398
3. Kay Khosrow Forgives the Iranians   400
4. Kay Khosrow Sends Tous Back to Tooran-Zamin   402
5. Piran Sends a Message to the Iranian Army   404
6. Afraasiyaab Sends an Army to Piran   405
7. Tous Fights Arjang   408
8. The Battle Between Hoomaan and Tous   409
9. The Second Battle of the Two Armies   415
10. The Tooranians Use Magic Spells to Overcome the Iranians   420
11. The Iranians Withdraw to Mount Hamaavan   423
12. The Tooranians Surround Mount Hamaavan   425
13. Piran Pursues the Iranians   430
14. The Iranians Attack   432
15. Kay Khosrow Receives News of the Army   437
16. Fariborz Asks for the Hand of Faranguis   441
17. Tous Dreams of Siaavosh   444
18. Afraasiyaab Sends Aid to Piran   446
19. The Emperor of Chin Approaches Mount Hamaavan   449

20. The Iranians Hold Counsel   451
21. Goodarz Learns of Rostam's Approach   452
22. The Emperor of Chin Reviews the Iranian Host   457
23. Fariborz Arrives at Mount Hamaavan   460
24. Piran Holds Counsel With the Emperor of Chin   461
25. The Battle of Giv and Tous Against Kaamoos   465
26. Rostam Unites With the Iranians   468
27. Preparations Made by the Hosts   472
28. The Battle of Rostam With Ashkeboos   477
29. Piran Asks About Rostam's Arrival   481
30. Iranians and Tooranians Form Their Lines of Battle   484
31. Kaamoos Kills Alvaah   486
32. Rostam Kills Kaamoos   488

PART TWELVE

The Battle of Rostam With the Emperor of Chin

1. The Emperor of Chin Learns of the Death of Kaamoos   493
2. The Battle of Changgesh With Rostam   495
3. The Emperor of Chin Sends Hoomaan to Rostam   497
4. Piran Holds Counsel With Hoomaan and the Emperor of Chin   500
5. Piran Goes to Rostam   503
6. The Tooranians Hold Counsel on the War With the Iranians   508
7. Rostam Addresses His Army   514
8. The Iranians and the Tooranians Form Ranks   518
9. Rostam Admonishes Piran   519
10. The Battle Begins   522
11. Shangal Battles Rostam and Flees   524
12. The Battle of Rostam With Saaveh   526
13. Rostam Slays Kahaar   528
14. The Emperor of Chin Is Captured   530
15. The Defeat of the Tooranian Host   535
16. Rostam Distributes the Spoils of War   536
17. Rostam's Letter to Kay Khosrow   542
18. Kay Khosrow's Reply to Rostam's Letter   544
19. Afraasiyaab Learns of His Army's Defeat   547
20. Rostam's Battle Against Kaafoor, Man-Eater   550
21. Afraasiyaab Receives News of Rostam's Arrival   556
22. Afraasiyaab's Letter to Poolaadvand   562
23. Poolaadvand Battles Giv and Tous   565
24. The Battle of Rostam and Poolaadvand   567
25. Rostam and Poolaadvand Fight Hand to Hand   571
26. Afraasiyaab Flees Before Rostam   574
27. Rostam Returns to the King's Court   576
28. Rostam Returns to Sistan   578

PART THIRTEEN

The Story of Akvan Deev

1.	The Beginning of the Story	583
2.	Kay Khosrow Asks Rostam to Battle Akvan Deev	584
3.	Rostam Searches for the Deev	587
4.	Akvan Deev Tosses Rostam Into the Sea	588
5.	Afraasiyaab Arrives to Observe His Horses, and Rostam Kills Akvan Deev	592
6.	Rostam Returns to Iran-Zamin	594

PART FOURTEEN

The Story of Bijan and Manijeh

1.	The Beginning of the Story	601
2.	The Armanians Ask Kay Khosrow for Protection	603
3.	Bijan Fights the Boars	607
4.	Gorgeen Betrays Bijan	609
5.	Bijan Sees Afraasiyaab's Daughter Manijeh	611
6.	Bijan Presents Himself at Manijeh's Tent	613
7.	Manijeh Takes Bijan to Her Palace	614
8.	Garsivaz Takes Bijan to Afraasiyaab	617
9.	Piran Asks Afraasiyaab to Have Mercy on Bijan	621
10.	Afraasiyaab Sends Bijan to Prison	624
11.	Gorgeen Returns to Iran and Lies About Bijan	626
12.	Giv Takes Gorgeen to Kay Khosrow	631
13.	Kay Khosrow Sees Bijan in the World-Reflecting Chalice	634
14.	Khosrow's Letter to Rostam	635
15.	Giv Carries Khosrow's Letter to Rostam	637
16.	Rostam Prepares a Feast for Giv	641
17.	Rostam Travels to the Court of Kay Khosrow	642
18.	Kay Khosrow Celebrates With the World Heroes	646
19.	Rostam Asks the King to Pardon Gorgeen	648
20.	Rostam Organizes His Procession of Troops	650
21.	Rostam Visits Piran in Khotan	652
22.	Manijeh Arrives at the Side of Rostam	655
23.	Bijan Divines Rostam's Approach	658
24.	Rostam Pulls Bijan Out of the Pit	662
25.	Rostam Leads a Night Attack on Afraasiyaab's Palace	665
26.	Afraasiyaab Attacks Rostam	668
27.	The Iranians Defeat Afraasiyaab	670
28.	Rostam Returns to Kay Khosrow	673
29.	Khosrow Celebrates With a Feast	675

Appendix

1. Glossary of Names   681
2. The Kianian Kings: Line of Succession   695
3. The Iranian Heroes: Line of Succession   696-697
4. Tooranian Kings and Warriors: Line of Succession   698-699
5. Glossary of Geographical Markers   701
6. Map of the World of Shahnameh   710-711
7. Glossary of Persian Words   710

PREFACE

"I am Rostam, lion vanquisher,
Champion and distributor of crowns!...
The Creator gave me strength and victory,...
The world is my slave, Rakhsh is my throne,
My ring is my mace, and my helmet my crown.
My spear's point and my colossal mace
Are my dearest companions...
With my sword, I shine light upon dark night.
I spin heads and make them fly across the battlefield.
I was born free; I am a slave to no one.
I am merely the servant of the Divine Creator.
Brave men of Iran have called me to the crown.
They have offered me throne and diadem,
But I did not desire kingly authority.
My eyes are fixed on my path and my duties,
And, above all, my eyes are fixed on world order." (Volume I)

Though the title of Ferdowsi's poem refers to the rule of kings, it has
been argued that it could just as well be titled the "Book of Heroes" or
the "Epic of Heroes." Volume One made clear that the hero warriors,
or *pahlavans*, play roles as significant as those of the kings they serve.
The descendants of Garshaasp–Nariman, Saam, Zaal, and Rostam–
are devoted protectors of king and kingdom. They slay dragons and
undergo various trials and tribulations to protect and maintain the
kingdom's order. Their bold, heroic deeds often overshadow those of
their rulers. Ferdowsi focuses on the ideal state of heroism, which he
conceives as a perfect balance of valor, nobility, and wisdom. He gives
us an ideal of how to live our best lives.

The perfect hero warrior is embodied by Rostam, a most loyal
guardian of kingly values, introduced in Volume One. During the
reign of Manoochehr, Saam abandons his infant son, Zaal, in the
desert for the simple reason that Zaal is born with white hair. The

baby is spotted by the magical bird Simorgh and raised with her winged offspring in a nest on top of Mount Alborz. As an adult, Zaal falls in love, sight unseen, with Rudaabeh, a descendant of Zahaak. Together they have Rostam, whose birth is surrounded by the most fascinating, fantastical circumstances. From early childhood, Rostam exhibits a superhuman nature and an indomitable strength. As an adult, he will obey his superior, the king, no matter what, even when he strongly disagrees or disapproves. He will fortify himself by surmounting the Seven Stages of his Quest to liberate his ruler. This is evident in the episodes relating to Kay Kaavoos in Mazandaran and later in Haamaavaran. In both cases, Rostam risks his life. Furthermore, he does not hesitate to compromise the lives of his family members to protect kingship, as in the conflict with his son Sohraab. Sohraab dreams of a world where his father, the ultimate warrior, ascends the throne, but Rostam subconsciously cannot accept such a world and ultimately discovers that he is responsible for his son's death.

In Volume Two, during the turbulent years of the rule of Kay Kaavoos and the birth of his son Siaavoosh, the relationship between king and hero is further sealed. One wonders what Kay Kaavoos represents, a king so capricious that he thoughtlessly seeks to assert his power and often deserts his throne in pursuit of new thrills. Yet Ferdowsi assigns him a strong presence that stretches his one-hundred-fifty-year reign across three volumes. Throughout, Rostam's commitment is unwavering, first to Kay Kaavoos, then to his son, Siaavoosh, and his grandson, Kay Khosrow. Rostam has a chance to influence a future king when he offers to raise and educate Siaavoosh, acting as a father to him. This will not only affect the kind of prince that Siaavoosh becomes, but will be passed on eventually to Siaavoosh's son, Kay Khosrow. As an adolescent, Siaavoosh must endure the flirtatious advances of his stepmother, Sudaabeh, in her attempts to trick him into amorous submission. When she fails to win him over and her scheme of tricks to punish him is exposed, he resolves to exile himself rather than to sentence her to death. He finds shelter in Tooran-Zamin and marries King Afraasiyaab's daughter, who brings Kay Khosrow into the world. At a later point, Kay Khosrow praises Rostam and says,

"Fortunate is the land of Zabolestan,
Whose milk nourishes such brave heroes.
Fortunate is the land of Iran and its warriors,

Who are blessed with a leader like you.
But the most fortunate of all is the king
Whose throne is served by a hero
Of your ability and high standing." (Volume II)

Where thus far the action has been driven by the heroic feats of the
family of Saam, Zaal, and Rostam, Volume Two recounts the rise of
other valorous characters, such as the members of Goodarz's family,
including his sons Giv and Rohaam, and his grandson Bijan. The two
families eventually merge when Rostam marries Goodarz's daughter,
and their daughter later weds Giv.

We see the emergence of a powerful Tooran-Zamin and an intricate
web of strategic plots, seemingly led by King Afraasiyaab but
crafted behind the scenes by two conniving driving forces: Piran and
Garsivaz. At some point, Afraasiyaab fears that Siaavoosh and Kay
Khosrow pose a threat to his throne and crown and subjects them to
life-threatening challenges. Not satisfied with the slaying of Siaavoosh
by the wicked Garsivaz, the malevolent king attempts to capture
and kill Khosrow and Faranguis, his grandson and his daughter.
After seven years of intense searching, Giv finds the two and helps
them escape to Iran, where Kay Khosrow finally accedes to his
grandfather's throne. He rules with justice but with only one goal in
mind: to avenge the death of his father.

This volume concludes with the touching story of Rostam's grandson,
Bijan, suffering years of bitter imprisonment for falling in love with
Manigeh, Afraasiyaab's daughter. Once again, Rostam comes to the
rescue, and freeing Bijan, he returns him to the King of Iran, who
blesses his union with Manigeh.

Ferdowsi's sources come from both oral and written traditions. He
frequently refers to the stories as either having been found in an
ancient book, perhaps the *Khodaay Nameh*, a collection compiled in
Sassanian times and adapted to Arabic by Ibn al-Muqaffa (d. 759), or
as having been related to him by a poet bard or *dehghan*. The *dehghans*
belonged to an ancient Persian nobility, a class of well-educated
landowners, who were often the keepers of oral and written history.
Ferdowsi himself was affiliated with this class of landed gentry. Here
are the poet's words in relation to the battle between Rostam and
Kaamoos, the ruler of Kushan:

"I shall recount his battle ... as told in an ancient book,

But I shall do so by means of my own words,
Borrowed from the writings of a poet bard.
Pay attention to what this worldly man once said."

Ferdowsi borrows the stories from another era and weaves them into his beautiful rhymes. At times he infuses them with a very personal voice, relating his sentiments on life and his emotional state at the time of writing. The narrator repeatedly opens or closes his episodes by reminding us of the fickleness of human existence and its fleeting nature, of our interconnectedness, and advising us on how to live our best lives by wrapping ourselves in the cloak of truth and joy:

"Such is the way of the world:
It takes with one hand and gives with the other.
Its duperies and deceits plague us, afflict us.
We are placed up so high, then brought down at once.
If your heart succeeds on the road to happiness,
Try to maintain eternally a state of joy." (Volume II)

About This Translation

This translation is based on two editions of *The Shahnameh*: the original Persian text edited by Dr. Seyed Mohammad Dabir Siaghi (2007), and a French edition, *Le livre des rois*, translated by Mr. Jules Mohl (1878).

Although Ferdowsi uses the past tense for his stories, it seemed more natural to narrate the English translation in the present tense. This provides a sense of continuity and permanence, as if the values he upholds cannot be constricted into a specific time frame.

Spelling and Pronunciation

In order to transfer text from Persian to English, we have used a simple form of transliteration. While it may vary from the more common methods, it makes sense to us and, we hope, will to the reader. In this approach, names of characters and places are spelled based on their pronunciation in Persian, rather than on their Romanized equivalent. For example, Zoroaster is *Zartosht*, Alexander is *Eskandar*, China is *Chin*, and Rome is *Rum*.

Most of the sounds for long syllables are pronounced as in English:
1. Aah sounds, as in "fall," are spelled *aa*, as in *Zaal* or *Rudaabeh*, except when a word ends in *ah*, as in *shah*, or *an*, as in *Iran, Tooran*, or *Nariman*. Some exceptions include *Baarmaan* and *Hoomaan*. One phonetic exception is in the second syllable of *Ghaaran* which has the *a* sound as in "fan."

2. Oo sounds as in "fool" are most often spelled *oo*, as in *Tooran* or *Fereydoon*. A few exceptions are *Zu* and *Tous*.

3. Ee sounds, as in "feel," are spelled *ee* as in *beed* and *deev*. At times we revert to -*i*- as in *Giv*.

Persian Words

The Persian language offers a unique perspective that requires careful consideration when translating into English. Finding an accurate English equivalent is often a daunting task. A number of words, such as *farr, kherrad*, and *ayeen*, are almost impossible to translate accurately. We have attempted to provide corresponding English words in footnotes and in the glossary; however, these may not completely capture the essence of the original words.

The absence of pronouns in Persian can lead to the use of vague terms such as "it", "this", or "that" to refer to a person or an object. This translation avoids pronouns when it comes to Yazdan, the divine Creator, and Sooroosh, the archangel. In the case of Simorgh, the mystical bird, we chose feminine pronouns to convey nurturing and maternal qualities.

VOLUME TWO

From the Tale of Siaavoosh
to the Story of Bijan and Manijeh

PART EIGHT

The Tale of Siaavosh

The Birth of Kay Khosrow

1 | The Beginning of the Story

Now peasant bard,[1] fable weaver of awakened mind,
Recount to me a tale, a sweet and pretty one,
For when words match the functions of Eternal Wisdom,
The poet's soul is transported into the heights of bliss.

On the other hand, if thoughts are bitter,
Wisdom will be destroyed, as will reason,
Leading to contempt and self-flagellation.

Still, few people ever discern their own shortcomings,
And most people regard themselves as flawless.

If you seek truth, compose your story.
Divulge it to the wise, for truth lives on forever.
Should the wise deem it praiseworthy,
The waters of your life's stream will flow free and clear.

Do lend an ear once again to the poet bard.
Listen to his words as I renew for you the primordial times,
For our story is an ageless, ancient one.

However long my life, I shall pursue this sweet labor.
I wish to leave behind a fertile, lofty tree,
With abundant fruit to scatter upon the orchard floor.

Anyone who has lived fifty-eight years has seen
Many a strange sight, but the accession of years
Fails to wipe out passion and greed,
And even the aging one continues to seek opportunity
In calendar years as well as in chance.

What does the religious leader say on this subject?
"Anything that gains in age may not be renewed.

Continue to speak words of wisdom for as long as you live.

◇◇◇◇◇◇◇◇◇◇◇◇◇
1 Peasant bard or dehghan: Keeper of land and crops, of rain and sun, and all that grows; keeper of ancient wisdom, poet and bard.

Be a world seeker. Remain aware and kind.
When you die, your fate, happy or sad,
Will remain in Yazdan's hands.

Remember, you will reap the seeds you sow.
The answer reveals itself in accordance with the wager.
A man of sweet words need not ever hear unkind speech.
Mark your wages with kindness as often as possible.

Now listen to this story woven long ago,
Brought to us by way of ancient tales.

2 | The Tale of Siaavosh's Mother

The poet bard relates that one day
At the hour when the rooster sings,
Tous happily exits the court
Escorted by Giv, Goodarz, and several other men.
They set off joyously toward the plains of Daghooy,
Eager to hunt deer with falcons and cheetahs,
And raring to hound their prey.

They run along the river's edge,
Chasing and pouncing on wild beasts.
In this way, they kill many, pursuing others,
Collecting food to last for forty days.

Near these parts lives a Turk
Whose tents obscure the land.
The hunters come across a forest stretching far
Beyond to the border of Tooran-Zamin.
Tous and Giv, along with a few brave men, advance
Through the forest, pleasantly occupied with the chase.

At once they come upon a woman with pretty cheeks.
The two heroes dash over to her with smiles on their lips.

Nowhere does there exist a woman
With such loveliness, a beauty so perfect.
She bears no trace of the slightest flaw.
In stature, a cypress tree, in appearance the moon.
So beautiful is she one dares not allow a glance

To linger at length upon her figure.

Tous is the first to address her:
"Enchanting moon, pray tell me,
What are you doing so deep in the woods?"

She replies, "Late last night, my father beat me
After he returned drunk from a festival.
As soon as he saw me from afar, his anger grew.
He drew his shining dagger
And sought to cut off my head.
I left my home, fled across the land,
And made my way here."

The brave hero inquires after her origins, and soon
She recounts everything from beginning to end.

She adds, "I belong to the family of Garsivaz
And can trace my origins to the noble Fereydoon.
I had no choice but to enter this forest on foot."

Tous says, "How did you find your way
Without a mount or a guide escorting you?"

She replies, "I left my horse behind.
So weary was he, he collapsed beneath me.
I had countless jewels and immeasurable gold,
A golden diadem set upon my head,
But a group of men robbed me
And struck me with the flat of their swords.
Fearful, I bolted away,
And now I find myself alone in the woods,
Shedding abundant tears of blood.
When my father regains awareness,
He will for sure send riders to search for me,
And my mother will not wish
To see her daughter abandon her land."

The hearts of the world heroes soften for this beauty.
The head of Tous, son of Nozar, fills with compassion.
The prince says, "I am the one who found her.
It is for her sake that I rushed forth."

Giv retorts, "Royal leader, you are not my equal
When you cannot rely on my army."

Tous argues, "Do not speak nonsense.
I surpassed you by far in the heat of the hunt."

Giv replies, "I was the one who arrived here first.
Do not attempt to lie to win over a young woman,
For you are not brave enough to prevail in an argument."

Their quarrel grows more heated and more fierce,
So fierce one might fear they may sever the moon's head.
As their debate drags out for some time,
One of the brave warriors intervenes and says,
"Why don't you take her to the King of Iran
And accept his decision, whatever it may be?"

They heed this advice
And march with her to the royal palace.

The moment Kaavoos sets eyes on the young woman,
He smiles and bites his lips.
Addressing his two army leaders, he says,
"You haven't been on the road for very long,
And yet you only manage to bring me a lovely gazelle.
It is indeed a big game hunt,
A hunt that can only be affiliated with a world king.
We shall pass the day listening to the tale of how
Our world heroes were able to capture this lovely sun."

Then the monarch asks the young woman,
"O fairy-faced beauty, what is your birth?
Please oblige me with an answer."

She replies, "On my mother's side, I am a princess.
On my father's side, I come from the race of Fereydoon;
Granddaughter of Garsivaz, army leader,
Whose tents wrap around this very border.
He is a descendant of Toor and a relative of Afraasiyaab."

The king asks, "How could you give
These beautiful locks to the wind
And surrender your face and your high birth?

Perhaps I shall house you in my golden harem.
Perhaps I shall name you queen and have you rule
Over the world's moon-faced women."

She answers, "As soon as I laid eyes on you,
I selected you from among men of high stature."

The king gives each world hero ten noble chargers,
A throne and a crown.
He asks the beauty to enter the women's chambers.
There she takes her place on an ivory throne.
On her head is a golden crown inlaid
With stones of turquoise and ruby.
Her robes are woven with yellow brocade,
Ruby, turquoise and lapis lazuli.
The king's offerings are worthy of such beauty,
As she herself is a flawless, untouched ruby.

3 | The Birth of Siaavosh

Some time passes.
Radiant spring paints its brilliant hues upon the earth.
The sky revolves uninterrupted,
And upon nine months passing,
A child is born, a child bright as the sun.

Kay[2] Kaavoos is told,
"You have taken pleasure in the beauty of fortune's path,
And she has given birth to a noble child.
You must now raise your throne higher than the moon,
For yours is a fairy child whose face
Resembles that of a fair beauty idol."

The world fills with rumors about this blessed son,
For no one will ever see such a face or such hair.

The ruler names him Siaavosh
And gives thanks to the revolving dome.

◇◇◇◇◇◇◇◇◇◇◇◇◇
2 Kay: Meaning king.

FERDOWSI: THE SHAHNAMEH

VOLUME II

Those with the ability to calculate the sky's rotations
And foresee good and ill fortune
Suspect the stars to be inauspicious to this child.
They find themselves saddened by the fact
That luck will turn its back on him.
They see his strengths and weaknesses as reasons to grieve,
And in deference to him, they take shelter in Yazdan.
They divulge to the king his son's fate
And point out to him the way to deal with it.

After some time passes,
Rostam presents himself before the shah and says,
"I must hold in my arms this lion child.
There exists none so eminent
For you to entrust with the care of your son.
He will never find in the world
A more suitable nurse than I."

The king thinks at length, and, in the end,
Rostam's words do not displease him.
He hands over his heart and his eyes,
This well-loved child destined one day to be world king.

Rostam carries the boy to live in a palace
In Zabolestan within a rose garden,
Where he raises him and coaches him.
He trains him in the arts of horsemanship,
Noose, bow and arrow, rein and stirrup,
And anything else his heart desires.
He presents to him an assembly hall, with wine,
Dining companions, falcons, gyrfalcons, and cheetahs.

He teaches him to distinguish between right and wrong,
Instills in him all the virtues,
A sense of duty for crown and throne,
Coaches him on the art of war and of conversation.
Rostam dedicates himself to these tasks
With much pain and effort.
Ultimately, his labor bears fruit.
Siaavosh becomes a man like no other.

Time passes. He gains strength.
He learns to pounce on lions and catch them in his noose.

32

Then one day he says to the noble Rostam,
"I wish to see my father, the king.
You have set forth much effort for me,
And I have given you no cause to worry.
You have taught me kingly virtues.
It is now time for my father to set his sight on me
And assess what I have learned from the warrior hero."

Rostam of lion heart makes preparations for travel.
On all sides he sends messengers.
He searches through the world to obtain the goods
He fails to possess, such as horses and slaves,
Gold and silver, pearls, swords, casks, seal and belt,
Rich carpets and lush fabrics.

He prepares Siaavosh in such a manner that the army
And the world cannot detach their eyes from him.
Then together they set off
In the direction of the royal court,
Hoping the king will find no cause for discontent.

The people of the land arrange formal feasts,
For they wish to please the world hero.

They decorate walls and doors. From high rooftops,
They pour gold mixed with amber
Over noblemen's heads and toss silver coins
Beneath the hooves of Taazian steeds.
A blend of musk, wine, and saffron
Saturates the horses' manes.
The world is decked with all
That is prized and filled with joy
As sadness is banished from the land of Iran.

4 | Siaavosh Returns From Zabolestan

Upon hearing of the approach of Siaavosh,
With great pomp and circumstance,
King Kaavoos orders Giv and Tous to meet up with him,
With a procession of clarions and kettledrums,
And a few select troops.

Noblemen join the prince. On one side stands Tous,
On the other the one of elephantine size.
They set off, proud of stride, toward the king,
For they bring to him a young tree heavy with fruit.

Siaavosh approaches Kay Kaavoos's palace.
A loud clamor rises, and the crowd parts.
Servants holding incense come to greet him,
Full of fragrance and scent, arms crossed at their chests.

In the court's four corners,
Three hundred more servants stand,
And the noble Siaavosh marches in their midst.
They pour much gold and jewels over him.
They sing his praises, clear and joyous.

At the sight of Kaavoos upon the ivory throne,
Wearing a shining crown of ruby,
Siaavosh approaches him with deference,
Head low to the ground as he pronounces blessings.

King Kaavoos embraces him and holds him close.
He asks after Rostam graciously and respectfully.
He gestures to his son to take a seat
Upon a throne inlaid with stones of turquoise.

He is taken aback at the vision of Siaavosh
And periodically summons divine blessings upon him,
Upon his stature, his noble mien, his head and shoulders,
For he notices in him many worthy qualities.

He sees in this child such intelligence that one would
Conclude Eternal Wisdom itself has nurtured his mind.
Kaavoos continues to praise Yazdan, divine Creator.
He rubs his forehead humbly to the ground and says,
"O Creator of earth and sky, Master of love, life,
And Eternal Wisdom, O Source of worldly pleasures,
Everything that is good in the world is a gift from you.
I beseech you to care for my son above all."

Noblemen of Iran-Zamin appear in joy before the king,
Bearing gifts and offerings, in awe at the sight
Of the grace and splendor of the prince.

PART EIGHT

They acclaim him endlessly.

The king commands the army's noblemen to appear
Before him dressed in garments of revelry and feast.
The large group gathers in joy, takes the path
Of court and palace, meeting halls and gardens.

Everywhere banquets are spread, everywhere
Wine is poured, music and song are played.
No earthly prince has ever summoned
Such a lavish spread.

For seven days they revel in this manner,
Engaged in feast and celebration.
On the eighth day, the king opens his treasury's door,
Giving wealth to Siaavosh in abundance:
Pearls and swords, thrones, helmets and seals,
Taazian horses with saddles and strappings
Of leopard skin, coats of mail and rich brocade,
Tens of thousands of silver coins,
Gold and jewels, large and small.

He gives Siaavosh everything but a crown,
For he is still too young for one.
The king hands the gifts over to the prince,
Honoring him with a hopeful and tender expression.

Then for seven years he puts him to the test
To determine if he is able to tackle
Every obstacle before him with caution and purity.

In the eighth year, Kaavoos asks for a golden throne,
A golden necklace and a golden belt.
He requests an inauguration be drawn up
In the manner of brave men and in the custom of kings.

Kaavoos Shah offers Siaavosh the land of Kohistan,[3]
A land worthy only of the master of throne and crown.

◇◇◇◇◇◇◇◇◇◇◇◇◇◇
3 Kohistan is the ancient name for today's Transoxiana.

5 | The Death of Siaavosh's Mother

Once all this is achieved in accordance to royal wishes,
Siaavosh's mother leaves this world.

Abruptly her son abandons his throne.
He sends a deev-like cry of anguish high into the sky.
He claws at his body, tears at his royal robes,
Shrouds his head and face with black dust.
Mourning for his mother affects his sweet soul,
Rendering him fierce and wild.

He sobs uncontrollably. His gentle heart,
Tortured day and night and for many days,
He remains unable to part his lips into a smile.

For one month, he maintains a state of intense distress,
His heart an open wound.
For one month, he does not seek relief from his grief.

Great leaders, sons of famed heroes and kings,
Tous and Fariborz, Goodarz and Giv,
Are made aware of his dire state of being.
They approach their grieving prince.

At the sight of them, Siaavosh's mourning resumes.
His heart exhales its anguish,
Reopening the door to distress.

A troubled Goodarz weeps over the state of Siaavosh.
He says, "O great prince, listen to my counsel
And make every attempt to ignore your pain.
Anyone born from a mother has no choice but to die.
We have knowledge of no one in the world
Able to steal his life from the hand of destiny.
However dear your mother was,
She now dwells in heaven.
You may cease to weep for her."

In this way, with a hundred consoling words of advice,
He is able to calm the heart of the royal prince.

6 | Sudaabeh Falls in Love With Siaavosh

Some time elapses,
And the heart of the king rejoices for his son.

One day, Siaavosh is in the presence of Kay Kaavoos
When Sudaabeh, Kaavoos's queen, makes an entrance.
Her eyes, unaware, fall on the young prince.
She goes deep into thought, her heart beating madly.
She falls into a state of softness,
Akin to a shard of ice placed before a flame.

She summons a servant to approach Siaavosh.
She says, "Go quietly to him,
And tell him that no one will be surprised
To catch sight of him in the women's chambers."

The envoy departs to carry out his mission,
But the famed Siaavosh is disturbed and responds,
"I am not the kind of man who makes it a habit
Of entering the king's night quarters.
Do not come back to find me,
For I care not one whit for your lies and deceit."

The next morning, Sudaabeh quickly finds her way
To the Shah of Iran and says to him,
"O army King, neither sun nor moon has ever
Laid eyes on a ruler of your might and standing,
And no one on the earth is equal to your son.
May the world rejoice in an alliance with you!
Send him to your women's chambers,
Send him to your sisters and to your favorites.
Tell him,
      'Enter the women's quarters,
      Find your sisters and go often.
      Our veiled women's hearts are full of love for you.
      Their cheeks are drenched with tears.'
We shall greet him, lavish him with gifts,
We shall produce fruits on the tree of reverence."

The king replies, "Your words are reasonable,
And your affection is equal to the love

Of one hundred mothers."

Kaavoos then calls Siaavosh and says to him,
"The blood flowing through arteries and love cannot hide.
Yazdan, pure and perfect, has fashioned you in such a way
That whoever sees you has no option but to love you.
Yazdan has proffered upon you an unpolluted birth,
And never has a mother borne a son more chaste.
How can those close to you by blood think they are your kin
If they have only caught sight of you from afar?
Behind the shades of the women's chamber live your sisters,
And Sudaabeh is for you a most devoted mother.
Go to visit these veiled women,
Spend some time with them, so that they may
Lavish upon you abundant divine blessings."

At the king's words, Siaavosh sends a troubled look his way.
He reflects at length and attempts to banish
From his heart the deep concerns that are taking root.
He thinks his father wishes to further test him,
For he knows Kaavoos to be a cunning man,
Cautiously perceptive, suspicious, and sweet of speech.

Siaavosh recoils in his seat
And reflects on the consequences of this act.
"This cannot be a good sign," he thinks.
"Sudaabeh is the one who conceived this scheme.
If I succumb to it and show myself in the female quarters,
I will fall subject to humiliation and shame."

He answers his father, "The king has given me
Not only an order but also the crown and throne.
From the moment the glorious sun ascends
Over the mountains to light up the world
Until the time it sets beyond the horizon,
There is no king of your stature in the world, no one
Comparable in kindness, wisdom, custom, and guidance.
Instead of sending me to the women's chambers,
May I visit with the wise and noblemen and warriors,
The men of spear and mace, bow and arrow?
For I wish to fling myself upon the enemy.
I must have throne and royalty, pomp and court,

Feast and wine, as well as company.
What is there for me to learn in the women's chambers?
Are women meant to guide us down the path of wisdom?
Yet, if such is the king's desire,
My duty will always press me to obey him."

The king says, "May you remain in high spirits, my son!
May you always uphold the voice of reason!
Seldom have I heard such wise words,
And your wisdom will only develop further.
Since you've already understood this, deflect
Dark thoughts that may cause your heart to go amiss.
Be happy and cast out grief and worry.
Go at once and see these children,
So that they may rejoice for some time.
Behind the veil, you have a number of sisters,
And Sudaabeh bears motherly affection for you."

Siaavosh replies, "Tomorrow I shall leave
To carry out his majesty's wishes.
I stand before you, having surrendered
My heart and soul to your command.
I shall go as you order, for you are my king,
Ruler of the world, and I am your servant."

7 | Siaavosh Visits Sudaabeh

There lives a man named Hirbad,
Pure of heart, mind, and soul.
He never leaves the idol's temple
And holds the key to the women's chambers.

The King of Iran says to this wise man,
"As soon as the sun reveals its rays,
You will go to Siaavosh and do as he commands.
You will ask Sudaabeh to prepare gifts, jewels,
Musk, and scents, and to have her servants and sisters
Shower Siaavosh with emeralds and saffron."

One night passes thus.
The sky completes its rotation.

As soon as the sun reveals
Its radiant face over hill and mountain,
Siaavosh meets with the king, who calls blessings
upon him and speaks to him in hushed words.

At the conclusion of their conversation,
Kaavoos calls Hirbad and in turn confers with him.
He tells Siaavosh, "Follow Hirbad and rejoice,
For you are about to see your relatives and sisters."

The two march away, lighthearted and free of worry.
When Hirbad pulls aside the chamber drapes,
Siaavosh senses a pang of foreboding in his core,
Although the women cheerfully greet him,
Ready to play instruments and music.
The house is full of musk, dinars, and saffron.
They toss silver coins, gold, and jewels at his feet.
The floors are covered in colorful Chini silk, and
Scattered around are numerous precious ocean pearls.
The chambers are decked like paradise,
Full of abundance and fairy-faced women,
Lively with wine, fragrance, and the voices of singers.
On every head is a jewel-encrusted crown.

Upon his arrival, Siaavosh is dazzled by
A golden throne trimmed with stones of turquoise,
Its cushion upholstered in royal silk.
Seated on it like paradise is Sudaabeh,
Full of color and scent.
She resembles the star of Canopus,
Her hair cascading in waves
And a tall crown on her head, with panels
That hang down to the ends of her black hair.
One of her chambermaids is at her side,
Head bowed low, holding a pair of golden slippers.

As she spots Siaavosh by the parted drapes,
Sudaabeh quickly climbs down from her throne
To approach him and praise him.
She holds him in her arms for some time.
She kisses his face and eyes at length,
Untiring at the sight of him.

She says, "I thank Yazdan one hundred times
That there does not exist a son like you.
Not even the king has such a lofty stature.
Night and day, I pray and express gratitude for you."

Siaavosh senses that her affection is far from motherly.
It is a sort of affection that is in no way
Compatible with the divine path and modesty.
Realizing that he cannot stay there,
He quickly approaches his sisters.
They praise him and seat him on a golden chair.

He remains with the sisters for some time,
Then returns to his throne.

The women's chambers fill with rumor and cheer
For a prince so full of splendor and grace,
Who exudes such wisdom, such knowing.
It is as if he were not even a member of the human race.

Siaavosh nears his father and says,
"I have seen the women's chambers.
All that is good in the world is on your account.
We must not stray off the divine path.
Your sword, army, and treasury are more valuable
And more cherished than those
Of Jamsheed, Fereydoon, and Hooshang Shah."

The king appreciates these words.
They prepare the hall like spring, full of color and scent.
With wine and harp, they free their hearts from worry.

At nightfall, Kay Kaavoos appears at the chambers.
He tells Sudaabeh,
"Reveal all your secrets regarding Siaavosh.
Talk to me of his mind and wisdom, speech and stature.
How did you find him? Was he wise?
Was he better than rumors spread on his account?"

Sudaabeh replies,
"The world has never seen such a prince.
No one exists of your son's prestige.
This fact must not be concealed from the world."

The king says, "Once he reaches manhood,
Let us hope he is never touched by the evil eye."

Sudaabeh says, "If he accepts my words
And agrees to my point of view,
I will provide him a wife from his own lineage
And not from noble families unrelated to him.
May she deliver a child to him that resembles him!
I have daughters from our pure alliance.
In addition, there are beautiful young women
From the lineage of Kay Aarash and Kay Pashin.
Whoever he desires, he may select to unite with in joy."

The king replies, "This is also my most heartfelt wish.
Such a union will bring us grandeur and fame."

At dawn, Siaavosh nears the king and praises him.
Father and son converse discreetly.
Kaavoos tells his son, "From the World Creator,
I only have one wish, a secret wish,
That a prince of your lineage be born,
That your name may remain in the world forever.
Just as I am thrilled by your presence,
May you gain such happiness
From the presence of your own sons.
The wise astrologers have looked into your stars
And predicted that you will have a son,
A prince whose name will echo throughout the world.
Go and select a mate to your liking
From the daughters of Kay Pashin and Kay Aarash."

Siaavosh says, "I am merely your slave.
The king commands and I shall obey.
Anyone you choose for me, I shall accept gratefully.
Don't allow Sudaabeh to hear our conversation
Or to decide otherwise.
Let us abstain from sharing this matter with her.
I have no more business visiting her chambers."

The king laughs at Siaavosh's words.
He is not fully aware of his son's misgivings.
He says, "You are the one who must make the selection.
Beyond that, there is no need to concern yourself

42

With Sudaabeh and her entourage.
Whatever she tells you comes from her love for you,
As she cares deeply for you and worries about you."

Siaavosh is happy to hear the king's words.
His mind slightly free from prior thoughts and trepidation,
He bends low before Kaavoos to praise and bless him.
Yet secretly he feels suspicious of Sudaabeh.
It is clear to him that his father is under her influence
And that he is conforming to her wishes and her dictates.
This fact only intensifies his resentment toward her.

8 | Siaavosh's Second Visit to the Women's Chambers

One night passes over our story and over the dark earth.
Sudaabeh happily takes her royal seat,
A golden crown of ruby on her head.
She calls to her side all the daughters
And assembles them around her on golden thrones.
With the beauties encircling the queen,
You would think this is not a hall but paradise itself.

She summons Hirbad and says to him,
"Go to Siaavosh and tell him,
        'Make the effort to come to our chambers,
        To grace us with your cypress-like stature.'"

Hirbad swiftly approaches Siaavosh to deliver
A message that leaves the prince quite unsettled.
He asks the Creator for help out of his predicament.
Unable to think of a way out, he remains tense and shaky.
Harried and staggering,
He slowly makes his way to Sudaabeh's throne,
Where she sits, a crown over her head.
She rises and advances to greet him,
Her forehead and hair covered with gems.

Siaavosh sits on a golden throne while Sudaabeh
Stands before him, arms crossed at her chest.
She shows the young heir the young beauties,
Flawless, unpierced pearls, and says,

43

"Look at these servants of golden crown.
They are young women from Taraaz[4]
To whom Yazdan has proffered charm and modesty.
Look at their demeanor, review their stature.
Tell me which among them pleases you most."

Siaavosh surveys each of these beauties,
But none of them dares return his gaze,
For these moons whisper to each other,
"It is not proper to glance at a future king."
They retire to their respective thrones,
Each murmuring to herself and weighing her chances.

Once they are alone, Sudaabeh says,
"What is your secret?
Why do you conceal your thoughts?
I am listening, ready to fulfill your longing.
I see the grace of fairies shine on your face,
And, for that reason, whoever beholds you from afar
Loses consciousness and falls in love with you.
Survey these beauties with wisdom's eyes,
And decide which one merits to unite with you."

Siaavosh is silent, confounded, unable to respond.
He reflects on his pure soul:
"It is better for me to refrain from marriage
Than to select a wife from among my adversaries.
I have heard from a nobleman tales of Haamaavaran.
How its ruler brutalized the King of Iran,
Forcing the dust of army leaders to rise to the sky.
Sudaabeh, full of deception, is his daughter.
This family is lacking both mind and reason."

Siaavosh refrains from responding.
In response to his silence,
Sudaabeh lifts her veil to reveal her face and says,
"When the sun and the new moon share the sky,
One is only able to discern the dazzling sun.
It is no wonder you did not notice the moons
Since you have a resplendent sun

◇◇◇◇◇◇◇◇◇◇◇◇◇◇
4 Taraaz: Or Taraz, a city in ancient Turkestan famous for its beautiful women; also a
river in today's Kazakhstan.

PART EIGHT

Sitting on the ivory throne before you,
A diadem of ruby and turquoise on her head.
I have a daughter not yet of age to be wedded.
If you agree, if you do not take back your word,
I will make her kneel at your feet as a slave.
Commit yourself in a pact with me.
Agree to never stray from my command.
When the king passes on,
You will represent him at my side.
You will not tolerate to endure my suffering.
You will cherish me as much as
You cherish your own flesh and blood.
I am offering you my body and my soul.
I am willing to satisfy your every wish
And never attempt to free
My neck from your noose's knot."

She takes Siaavosh's head into a tight embrace
And brazenly places her lips on his cheek to kiss him,
Having lost all sight of shame and virtue.

Siaavosh blushes deeply with embarrassment,
And his eyelashes flood with warm tears of blood.
He reflects in his heart and silently prays,
"O Creator, protect me from this evil deev.
I neither wish to betray my father
Nor to unite with Ahriman.
If I speak coldly to this woman of immodest eyes,
Her heart will simmer and her wrath will be set ablaze.
She will secretly stir up some spells that will cause
My father to obey and conspire with her.
It is best to address her with sweet words
And expressions of flattery." ·

Siaavosh says to Sudaabeh,
"No woman exists in the world
To match your grace and splendor.
Your beauty is comparable only to the moon,
And none other but the king is worthy of you.
It is comfort and joy enough for me
That you are willing to offer me your daughter,
And I shall never look at or have any other woman.

45

But while you maintain your intention,
Speak to the King of Iran and consider his reply.
I shall ask for your daughter's hand in marriage.
I shall wed her, and as guarantee I give you my word
That I shall never think of any other woman
Until the day your stature reaches mine.

"Also, you have spoken of my face.
You have allowed love to enter your heart.
By the grace of Yazdan, I was created as I am,
More noble and striking than others.
Keep your secret, reveal it to no one. That is all I ask.
You are the head of all women, and you are queen.
I consider you as a mother."

He speaks, then takes leave of Sudaabeh,
Whose evil heart is filled with love for him.

When Kay Kaavoos enters the female chambers,
Sudaabeh rushes to him to give him the good news.
She speaks at length of Siaavosh: "He has come,
He has seen the palace filled with dark-eyed beauties.
It was as if the moon lavished the earth with love.
But he set his sights only on my daughter.
No other maiden was worthy of him."

The king is so thrilled by these words that you
Would think he's holding the moon in an embrace.
He opens the doors to his treasury
And takes out badges of power:
Jewels, golden fabrics and golden belts,
Bracelets, crowns and rings, thrones and torques,
Objects to be worn by bold and brave men.
He spreads out all sorts of riches compiled over time,
And the world appears full of precious things.

Then he says to Sudaabeh, "Keep all this for Siaavosh,
And when he needs it, give it to him and tell him
That it is not much and that he must be given
Two hundred times more riches of this magnitude."

Sudaabeh looks at it with an expression of awe.
She recites many spells in her heart and thinks,

"If Siaavosh does not act according to my wishes,
I resign myself to the fact that my heart will break.
I shall make use of every wile that exists in the world,
Openly or secretly, and if he turns his head away from me,
I shall complain publicly about him to the world king."

9 | Siaavosh's Third Visit to the Women's Chambers

Sudaabeh sits on her throne decked in earrings,
Her head bearing a golden crown.

She summons Siaavosh to discuss these matters:
"The king has selected for you a vast treasure,
More valuable than all the crowns and all the thrones.
It contains all that your heart desires, and in great quantity.
Were you to transport it, you would require
Two hundred elephants to bear the load.
I wish to give you my daughter,
But take a look at my features, my forehead,
My crown, and tell me why you reject my love.
Why do you distance yourself from my face and body?

"Since the day I laid eyes on you, I live as if in death.
I grieve as I feel restless, wretched and miserable.
My pain is such that I see neither day nor night.
It feels as if the sun has entered into an eclipse.
For seven years now, my love provokes
Blood tears to streak my cheeks.
Make me happy only once, secretly.
Gift me one day with your youth, and I shall gather
For you more bracelets, crowns, and thrones
Than the king can offer you.
However, should you attempt to disobey me,
Should your heart reject me,
Should you refuse to heal my grief,
I shall deprive you of this empire.
I shall render dark before you
The shining sun and midnight moon."

Siaavosh replies, "May I never throw my head
Into the wind for the longings of my heart.

Would I ever betray my father so?
Am I capable of rejecting wisdom and virtue?
You are the king's wife, the sun that lights his throne,
And you suggest that we commit such a prodigious sin?"
Outraged, he rises from his seat.

Sudaabeh quickly seizes his hand and says,
"I have confided in you my heart's deepest secret,
And you have kept your ill thoughts concealed.
In your madness, you wish to denounce me,
To disgrace me, and to make me appear
Frivolous in the eyes of wise men!"

10 | Sudaabeh Betrays Kay Kaavoos

Sudaabeh abruptly tears her clothing,
Deeply scratches her cheeks with her fingernails,
And her wails resound across the chambers' halls
Loud voices and much clamor arise from the palace,
As if the night of resurrection had arrived.

The commotion reaches the king's ear.
He climbs down from the imperial throne
And worriedly dashes to the women's chambers.
He finds Sudaabeh, her face scratched up
And the palace in a state of turmoil.
Heart constricted, he questions each person he meets.
Never does he suspect ill-will from his heartless woman.

Sudaabeh runs to him, wailing and hollering,
Shedding blood tears, pulling her hair, and screaming:
"Siaavosh crept on my throne and placed his hands on me.
He grabbed me by force and said,
        'My heart and soul are full of love for you.
        Why do you, O dear beauty, resist me?
        From the beginning, I desired only you.
        The time is here for me to tell you so.'
He threw the diadem off my head of musk.
See for yourself how he tore off my dress
And exposed my breast."fThe king is lost in thought
And asks Sudaabeh all sorts of questions.

He thinks, "If she speaks the truth,
If this is not meant to slander him,
I must sever Siaavosh's head.
In this way, I shall avoid the fate evil has cast on me."

The wise man will now presume this story's
Gentle twists will lead to bloodshed.
Those present in the women's chambers
Are too sensible and too wise to speak.

The king sends everyone away.
Once alone in his palace, he calls Siaavosh
And speaks to him with measure:
"You must not keep this secret from me.
It is not you who has done wrong.
Misfortune follows us
Because of me and my foolish speech.
Why did I have to send you to the women's chambers?
This action has caused me deep shame
And triggered in you sorcery spells.
Tell me the truth; recount to me what happened."

Siaavosh recounts where he went, what was said,
And the consequences of Sudaabeh's secret love.

Sudaabeh exclaims, "This is an outright lie!
From among the beauties, he sought
To force me to possess my body.
I told him what the world king intended
To offer him in public and in secret:
My child, throne and jewels, gold and vast treasure.
I told him I would add just as much.
I would give him my daughter and my possessions.
"He replied,
        'I do not desire your wealth,
        Nor do I wish for your daughter.
        I only long to possess you,
        And no treasure or woman will satisfy me.'
He made every attempt to bend me to his wishes.
He seized me with two hands more dense than rocks.
Because I resisted him, he pulled my hair
And violently scraped my face.

From your lineage, O world King,
I carry your baby and child.
But Siaavosh nearly killed him, so roughly
Did he treat me, rendering the world
Narrow and dark before my eyes."

The king says to himself, "Their excuses do not
Help me to reach a suitable conclusion on this matter.
I must not act in haste,
For my distress may distort sound judgment.
My heart will be my guide once it settles.
I shall see which of the two is the offender
And ought to suffer the scorpions of punishment."

He then seeks a way to determine the truth
And begins by sniffing Siaavosh's hands,
His chest, face, his entire body from head to toe.

Kaavoos perceives on Sudaabeh
The scents of wine, musk, and rosewater
But finds Siaavosh free of these odors.
He appears free of the slightest trace of betrayal
Of any sign of contact with her.

Overwhelmed by anger,
The king treats Sudaabeh with contempt.
His heart full of sadness, he reflects, "I must
Have her cut to pieces with the sharpest sword."

Then he remembers the battles in Haamaavaran
And the threats he suffered.
He remembers when they held him hostage in chains.
He had no one around him, neither friend nor relative.
Sudaabeh served him day and night as his nurse,
Never tiring and never complaining.

He thinks that she has a heart full of love
And that he should spare her temptations to act poorly.
Finally, he remembers the small children
He has from her and how one must not
Take lightly the pains of childbirth.

In the end, Siaavosh is deemed innocent.

Recognizing his sound judgment,
The king says to his son,
"No longer give a thought to this sad affair.
Arm yourself with sense and care.
Do not speak of it to anyone, not a word,
For this adventure must not be heeded."

11 | Sudaabeh Conspires With a Witch

Once Sudaabeh realizes she's been defied
And that the king's heart is no longer tied to hers,
She seeks to extract herself
From an embarrassing situation and cultivates,
Once again, the tree of vengeance.

She has in her chambers a crafty woman
With knowledge in the art of sorcery,
A witch who finds herself with child,
The weight of her pregnancy
Making it difficult for her to walk.

Sudaabeh confides in her,
Asks her for a way out of her situation.
But first she demands a binding oath
From her in which she swears to obey the queen,
No matter the outcome.
The woman gives her word and pledges allegiance.

Sudaabeh rewards her with much gold,
Then she says to her,
"You must tell no one of this matter, not a word.
Prepare a potion that will produce a miscarriage.
I hope that your aborted child will help me
Reverse the fate cast upon me,
As well as the slander I must otherwise face.
I shall tell Kaavoos that this dead child was mine
And that he has been killed by the cruelty of Ahriman.
Perhaps this will suffice to destroy Siaavosh.
We must now find a way to execute this plan.
If you obey me in this matter,
His honor will wane before the king,

And he will be barred from the throne."

The witch replies, "O queen, I am your slave.
I have relinquished my head to submit to your wishes."
As soon as night falls, she takes the drug
And gives birth to two deev infants,
Children of Ahriman, and how could it be otherwise
From the breed of a witch?

Out of sight from her slaves,
Sudaabeh picks a golden tray.
She secretly places Ahriman's babies on it.
Then the witch disappears,
And Sudaabeh flops herself on the bed,
Screeching and screaming so piercingly
Her cries are heard throughout the night chambers.

All the female slaves in the palace rush to her side.
They take note of the two dead babies on the tray,
And their laments rise above palace and court,
All the way to Saturn.

Kaavoos shivers in his sleep,
Wakes up to the commotion.
He inquires as to what is happening,
And is told that the moon-faced Sudaabeh
Has suffered grave misfortune.

The king despairs, finding it hard to breathe.
At dawn he rises and, forlorn,
Walks to his women's apartments.
He finds Sudaabeh in bed, the entire house in a daze,
Two dead infants tossed on a golden tray,
As if two contemptible things.

Sudaabeh sheds abundant tears and says,
"Look at the sun, so bright and pure.
I told you how he hurt me,
Yet you blindly refused to believe me."

The king's heart fills with doubt and worry.
He leaves her side, reflecting at length,
"How can I find a resolution to this sordid affair,

For it is not to be taken lightly?"

12 | Kaavoos Inquires After the Infants' Birth

King Kaavoos looks around him
And summons sages familiar with the stars.
He inquires after their health
And invites them to sit upon golden chairs.
He tells them endless stories relevant to Sudaabeh,
How she suffered during the war in Haamaavaran,
In order for them to understand her position
And accurately evaluate her poor actions.

Then he carries on about the children
She allegedly bore and reveals the secret
That, he insists, must be kept.
The world fills with spells and sorcery.
The astrologers take out their astrolabes and spend
Seven days engaged in readings and calculations.

In the end they say to Kaavoos,
"How can you expect to find wine
In a cup that you have filled with poison?
The two babies come from a different lineage.
They were not spawn of the king and the fair Sudaabeh.
Had they been of royal birth,
We would have easily seen them on our tablets.
But know that the sky does not reveal its mysteries,
And the key to this puzzle cannot be found on earth."

With the royal court free of council and assembly,
They give the king information about the impure woman.
Kaavoos refrains from divulging the matter to anyone.

Sudaabeh despairs, pleading for justice.
She demands that the ruler restore her reputation:
"I have been the king's loyal companion at the time
When he was wounded and had lost his crown.
My heart grieves for my babies' deaths,
And on occasion I lose all sense and reason."

The king says, "Woman, be at peace.
Do not simply fixate on this day,
But think of the end result."

Kaavoos orders his palace guards to set out
To search the towns and neighborhoods,
And to find the evil woman, accomplice to his wife.
They find the witch's trail close by
And pursue her tracks as men of experience.
They close in on the woman sitting on the ground.
Condemning her and holding her down,
They drag her and present her to the king.

For many days, Kaavoos interrogates the witch warmly,
Giving her a sense of hope, making her promises.
But she refuses to comply or confess,
Leaving the illustrious king quite dispirited.

He then commands her to be taken away,
Makes use of all sorts of cunning ways,
Threatens to cut her in two with a saw
Should she refrain from confessing.

I know with certainty that this course of events
Fits within the ways and customs of the period.

They take the wretched woman away from court,
Hanging over her head the threat
Of death by sword or gallows,
But she continues to proclaim innocence:
"I truly have nothing to confess to the eminent king.
I know not what to tell you other than utter nonsense."

Her response is then related to Kaavoos Shah,
Who is told that the Creator alone knows the truth.
The king summons Sudaabeh.
The astrologers repeat their notion that the infants
Belong to the sorceress, that they resembled Ahriman,
And for that reason, sprang from his seed.

Sudaabeh replies,
"It is not your men's wisdom that has dimmed
But the secret reason why they dare not tell the truth.

That reason is because they deeply fear Siaavosh.
They are terrified of him
And of the hero of elephant stature.
He makes everyone shudder with dread,
Even a pride of lions, for he has the strength
Of eighty elephants and, if he wished,
The ability to suspend the course of the River Nile.
By his side is a host of one hundred thousand troops
Ranked for battle who would run from him in an instant.

"How could I resist Siaavosh?
I have no choice but to spend the rest of my days
Bathing my eyes with blood-red tears.
How could an astrologer dare speak against his orders?
If you have no compassion for your children,
Then what is to become of me?
I have no other relations but the ties that unite us.
Still, if you believe the futile words
Of these men over mine, I have no choice but to call
Upon the other world to implement proper justice."
As she speaks, she sheds more tears than the sun
Can absorb from the flows of the Nile River.

The king, saddened by her speech, sobs bitterly.
Then he sends her away, heartbroken.
In the end he says, "I shall pursue this matter
Without rest until I come up with a solution."
He calls the wise men from the border to his side
And speaks to them at length of Sudaabeh.

One of the wise men responds to the king,
"Your pain cannot remain a mystery.
If you wish to extract truth from contradictions,
You must strike the pitcher with a rock.
You must take a risk and strike hard,
No matter how dear your son is to you.
Your heart suspects him of wrongdoing,
And, as a consequence, you suffer.
On the other hand, you are full of doubt
Regarding the daughter of Haamaavaran.
Since you have come here with both,
One of them must pass the test and cross over fire,

For the desire of the glorious sky
Is that the innocent may not perish in the flames."

The king summons Sudaabeh, offers her a seat,
Wishing to debate with Siaavosh to see which
Of the two is willing to come face to face with danger.
He tells them, "My heart and my shining soul will
Never trust either of you unless the scorching fire
Reveals the truth and points to the guilty one."

Sudaabeh replies,
"I shall answer your questions with utmost honesty.
I have shown the king the two aborted infants.
No one can find in me a hint of wrongdoing.
Siaavosh must clear himself, for he is at fault.
He is the source of his own downfall."

The world king asks Siaavosh,
"What is your view on this?"

Siaavosh responds, "Hell is a milder fate
Than the one I must endure right here, right now.
Should there be a mountain of fire,
I shall crush it beneath my feet,
And I would rather die than be subjected
To a most distressing and agonizing shame."

13 | Siaavosh Passes Through Fire

King Kaavoos grows increasingly worried
About his beloved son and the deceptive Sudaabeh.
He says, "If either one is guilty, who will ever again
Call me king, for this concerns son and wife?
Who in the world is a more wretched man than I?
Yet I should relieve my heart of vindictive doubt
And not resort to such painful means.
What did the king say, the one of sage advice?
        'One cannot exercise kingship with a virulent heart.'"

Kaavoos orders the caravan leader to fetch camel drivers
And one hundred dromedaries from the desert,

PART EIGHT

And to proceed to search for abundant wood.

Everyone in the land of Iran gathers at court.
One hundred caravans of red-furred camels,
Full of zeal, carry piles of wood to stack up
Into two lofty mountains that rise to the firmament.
Its mass is so large it exceeds human calculation.

The pyre could be seen from two farsangs[5] away.
People say, "The key to this mystery is to be revealed."
Each person wishes to see how truth
Comes into the light, though he knows
This trial is all deception and lies.

Once you have listened to this tale to the end,
You would be wise to guard yourself against women.
Only select a virtuous wife, for a wicked one
Will undoubtedly cover your head in shame.
An evil woman should be viewed
On the same plane as a dragon.
Both are better off beneath the dust of earth.
The world is a purer place
Without these fraudulent, corrupt beings.

On the plain, two mountains of logs are raised,
And men come from near and far to witness this sight.
In between is left a path so narrow
An armed horseman could barely fit through it.

The king commands black tar be poured over the logs.
Two hundred men come forth to set fire to the mounds.
They blow on them, and it is as if night
Is pushing away day, for their efforts
Yield at first only to dark, black smoke.
Soon, long tongues of fire pierce through and lick the air.
The earth is now infinitely brighter than the sky.
People cry out in alarm
From the intense heat of flames thrusting forth.

Siaavosh nears his father, a golden helmet on his head.
Clad in all white, he is calm and smiles, hopeful.

◇◇◇◇◇◇◇◇◇◇◇◇◇
5 Farsang: Ancient unit of measure equivalent to 6.24 kilometers or 3.88 miles.

He sits proudly on a black steed
Whose hooves send dust flying to the moon.
He pours camphor on himself, as is customary
When preparing a body for the coffin.
It is as if he is on his way to heaven
Rather than the blaze of an inferno.

Everyone fosters a sense of pity for him,
Sobbing at the sight of his trusting, cheerful visage.

He approaches Kay Kaavoos,
Dismounts to greet his father respectfully.
Kaavoos's cheeks are flushed with shame.
He addresses his son with sweet words.

Siaavosh tells him, "Father, have no fear.
This is the wish of the revolving dome.
My head is now obscured by shame and disgrace.
If I am innocent, liberation will be mine.
But if I am guilty, then the Creator will dismiss me.
Thanks to the strength given to me by the divine,
My heart will not waiver before this blazing fire."

He nears the pyre and adds,
"Yazdan pure and perfect, above all need,
Allow me to pass through this mountain of heat.
Release me from the humiliation
I suffer before my father's eyes."
Having thus exhaled his pain,
He charges his black horse, as swift as smoke.

A cry rises from plain and town,
And the earth is seized in the grips of despair.
At the sound of the shouts,
Sudaabeh climbs up to the palace rooftop
From where she can observe the scene.
She wishes great misfortune on Siaavosh.
She cries bitterly, condemns and curses him.

Everywhere, men fix their gaze on Kaavoos,
Mouths full of bane, hearts trembling with fury.

Siaavosh plunges his black stallion into the blaze.

PART EIGHT

You would think the flames are the strappings,
So closely they lunge at him and engulf him.

Bystanders can no longer distinguish
The horseman, his helmet, or his horse.
The entire field is covered with weeping men
Who are trying to see, with much anxiety,
If the prince would emerge from the fire.

And then he does.
The glorious young man materializes out of the flames,
With a smile on his lips and rose petals on his cheeks.

At the sight of him there resounds a common cry:
"The young king has emerged out of the fire!"

Horse, rider, and gear appear fresh.
You would think he carries a lily on his chest.
Were he to cross the sea he would not even be damp,
And his garb would be completely free of moisture.
When Yazdan, pure and perfect, commands,
The fire's breath and the eluding air coalesce.

At the sight of Siaavosh rising
Out of the sea of flames, people cheer,
Echoes reverberating over town and field.
The army's riders rush toward him,
And people toss silver coins in his path.
Joy pulsates through men great and small.
They give each other the good news:
Yazdan, Justice Giver, has spared the innocent prince.

Meanwhile, Sudaabeh pulls at her hair,
Sheds copious tears to bathe her face.

Siaavosh, the virtuous, approaches his father
Without a trace of either smoke or fire, ash or dust.
Kaavoos climbs down from his mount,
And the entire army follows suit.

Having escaped the mountain's flames,
Having evaded his foe's wicked schemes,
Siaavosh arrives before the world master

59

And bows down at his feet, forehead to the ground.

The king says to him, "O my son,
O brave young man of pure and virtuous race,
You are endowed with a shining soul,
You are as you should be.
You are the son of a holy mother.
You are born to be world ruler."

He holds Siaavosh close to his chest
And begs forgiveness for having doubted him.
Then he goes to his palace and sits with his heart's bliss,
The Kianian crown upon his head.
He bids wine be brought forth and musicians,
And grants Siaavosh all that his heart desires.

In this manner, he spends three days in feast and drink
While his treasury's door holds neither seal nor key.

14 | Siaavosh Asks His Father to Grant Sudaabeh Mercy

On the fourth day,
Kaavoos climbs on the Kianian throne,
Holding in his hand a bull-headed mace.
In a state of fury, he summons Sudaabeh.

He reprimands her for her actions:
"You are a brazen, shameless woman.
Your wicked deeds have deeply saddened my heart.
What game have you played to the end,
Conniving and conspiring against my son,
Forcing him into the fire and bewitching him?
Remorse no longer has the power to serve you.
You have no choice but to resign yourself
To relinquish life and prepare for death.
You have not the option to remain on earth.
The noose at the gallows awaits you,
A just reward for your evil acts."

Sudaabeh responds, "O King,

PART EIGHT

Do not rush me into the folds of fire.
If you must cut off my head to top the misfortunes
That have befallen me, then command.
I resign to my fate and no longer wish
For your heart to remain filled with resentment.
Siaavosh will end up telling the truth in this matter.
He will extinguish in the king's heart the flares of anger.
With Zaal's magic spells, he was able to evade the fire,
Able to block the flames from consuming him."

Then she turns to Siaavosh and says,
"Until now, you have prevailed with sorcery.
Will the back of your insolence never bend?"

The king asks the Iranians,
"How shall I make her atone?
How shall I punish her for guileful crimes?"

Everyone invokes Yazdan's grace upon the king
And says, "Her sentence can only be a sure execution.
She must writhe in pain as penance for her misdeeds."

The king then addresses the executioner:
"Bind her to the gallows on the main road.
Leave her there, and walk in the other direction."

When Sudaabeh is dragged away,
Her women sob in grief.
The king attempts to conceal his heart full of rancor,
But his pale cheeks betray his state of mind.

The group gathered at the palace turns the other way
As Sudaabeh is taken from the court in humiliation.

Siaavosh contemplates her exit and tells his heart,
"The king will regret executing Sudaabeh.
He will point to me as the source of his suffering."
He turns to address Kaavoos:
"O Father, do not afflict yourself with this affair.
Grant Sudaabeh forgiveness for her crimes.
Perhaps from now on she will pursue better guidance
And choose to follow a righteous path."

The king, who only wished for a pretext
To absolve his wife for her crimes,
Replies to Siaavosh, "I agree to forgive her
For the sake of your purity and virtue."

Siaavosh kisses his father's throne,
Rises, and takes his leave.

On the king's order, Sudaabeh is returned to the palace.
All the women rush to greet her
And, one after the other, pay her homage.

After some time, the king's affection expands even more.
So full of love is he that he cannot take his eyes off her.

Once again, she secretly engages in witchcraft,
Strategizing by and by against Siaavosh,
Acting as one would expect of a person of a vile nature.
Her words begin to elicit doubt in the king's mind.
Kaavoos's position is such that he lacks
Common sense and wisdom, compassion and justice.

It is only when man fears Yazdan that all things
Happen in accordance to his heart's wishes.
Do not foolishly expect to drink a wholesome drink
From a cup laced with poison.
If you are disappointed in the world,
You need not be harsh.
The revolving dome acts in a way
As to never reveal its true face to you.

A wise man once studied this matter and concluded
That there is no greater love than the bond of blood.
Should you have a worthy son,
Discard a woman's affections,
For her tongue does not adequately
Reflect her heart's nature.
In one's search for a head, one may stumble upon feet.

15 | Kaavoos Learns of Afraasiyaab's Approach

The world king, thus occupied with his love,
Hears the news of what is happening:
Afraasiyaab is on his way to Iran-Zamin,
Escorted by one hundred thousand Turkish troops
Carefully selected and counted.

The land fills with talk of the approach.
Kaavoos's heart clenches
For he must give up joy and feast to engage in war.
He holds a gathering of Iranians, friends of the Kianians,
And says to them, "Yazdan has not molded
Afraasiyaab out of air, fire, dust, and water.
It appears the revolving dome created his essence
In a different way than from the rest of the creatures.
He swore alliance to us,
Bound himself to us with peaceful words,
Then turned around to make dust
Rise in his longing for war,
Violating his oath and his given faith.

"I must now depart and go to execute vengeance.
I must render dark the shining day for him,
Make his name disappear from the surface of the earth,
Or else he will continue to grow his army,
Like a flying arrow suddenly shot from a bow.
He will come to attack the land of Iran
And lay to waste mountain and plain."

One of the wise men says to him,
"Your host is massive.
Why should you yourself engage in war?
Why should you throw to the wind your wealth
By exposing the contents of your treasury?
Twice you have ceded your glorious throne to your foes.
Find among your world heroes one man
Worthy of war and worthy of avenging us."

The king answers, "I do not see
Among those assembled here a single man
Equal to Afraasiyaab in power and grandeur.

I must myself rush forth like a ship on water.
As for you, do not concern yourself with this affair.
I shall only listen and follow my heart's inclinations."

Siaavosh remains thoughtful.
His heart full of worry by his father's speech,
He reflects, "I shall prepare for a campaign.
I shall speak softly to the king
And listen to his instructions.
I hope the divine Judge guards me from Sudaabeh's
Tricks as well as from my father's suspicions.
Then I shall acquire a name in this battle.
I shall capture this mighty enemy host inside my trap."

He straps his belt tight, approaches Shah Kaavoos,
And says to him, "My rank is such that I am more
Than qualified to fight with the Tooranian Shah
And fling to dust the heads of his leaders.
Perhaps by the plots and devices of destiny,
Yazdan the Creator commanded Siaavosh
To relinquish life in the land of Tooran."

The father consents to Siaavosh's wish to cinch his belt,
Draw his weapons, and engage in war.
He is happy with him and proves it to him
By investing in him a new sense of pride.

He says to his son,
"Your father's treasures lie at your feet,
And you might say the entire army is yours.
Everyone in Iran-Zamin praises your words and deeds."

Then he calls Rostam, the world warrior,
And addresses him with kind words:
"No one, not even the elephant, can match your strength,
And not even the course of the River Nile
Is as powerful and potent as your hand.
There exists in the world no warrior
As skillful, discreet, and humble as you.
You lovingly raised and educated my son.
The sight of you with cinched waist is enough to melt
The iron wrapped around a mine of precious stones.

"Siaavosh has come to me, strapped for battle.
He has addressed me like a mighty lion.
What do you think of this affair?
Is he able to engage in a campaign against Afraasiyaab?
Go with him, do not lose sight of him.
The knowledge that you are watching over him
Will allow me to sleep soundly at night.
When you are laid to rest,
I shall worry and rush to action.
The world trusts your sword and arrow.
The moon and starry sky rise above you."

Rostam replies, "I am your slave.
I applaud all that you have said.
Siaavosh is my heart's refuge,
The top of his crown my firmament."

The king hears him out and praises him,
"May wisdom always be at the service of your soul!"

16 | Siaavosh Prepares the Army for War

The sound of trumpet and timpani rings all around.
Tous, the proud leader, arrives
As troops gather before the royal palace.

Kaavoos opens his treasury door, distributes dinars,
And sends the key to his armory store to Siaavosh
To retrieve sword and mace, helmet and belt,
Headgear and mail, spear and shield.
Along with the key, the king sends a message:
"You are master of the palace and all that it contains.
Outfit yourself as you deem most suitable."

Among the famed Iranian warriors,
The king selects twelve thousand men full of fervor,
World heroes from the lands of Pars, Kooch, Baluchistan,
Warriors from Gilan and the desert of Saroj.[6]

◇◇◇◇◇◇◇◇◇◇◇◇◇
6 Pars, Koch, Baluchistan, Gilan, Saroj: Lands and deserts situated from the border of
the Caspian Sea to eastern Iran and today's Pakistan.

From the same region,
He selects twelve thousand foot soldiers
Armed with weapons and ready for battle,
Sons of heroes, brave and careful men of freedom,
Men of the stature and age of Siaavosh,
Full of good sense, caution, and discretion.

Among them are renowned leaders:
Bahraam and Zangueh of Shaavaran.
Finally, the king selects five wise men
To raise the Kaaviani banner high in the air.

Kaavoos orders the army to march to the plains.
You would think the world is covered
With brave warriors, and not a single space
Is left but for their horses' hooves.

The Kaaviani banner rises to the sky,
Shining among the stars, bright as the moon.

King Kaavoos marches swiftly out of the city
With troops sending a mass of dust flying.
He looks over his host decked like a bride,
Accompanied with elephants and lively timpani.

The glorious king blesses them many times:
"O celebrated warriors of fortunate trails,
May your sole companion be fortune itself!
May the eyes of your enemies dim!
May you depart under a happy star and a healthy body
To return to us joyous and victorious!"

The young leader places timpani upon elephants,
Bids men mount their horses,
And he, in turn, straddles his steed.
Kaavoos accompanies his son on his journey
For an entire day, his two eyes filled with tears.

In the end, they kiss one another, eyes shedding blood
Like clouds pouring rain on a spring day.
Their weeping provokes laments throughout the army,
Their hearts darkened with the sense
That they may not see each other again.

PART EIGHT

Such is the way of fate,
It is at times dipped in honey, at times in bane.

Kaavoos returns to his palace
While Siaavosh travels in the direction of Zabolestan
With his army and with Rostam of elephant stature.
They join Zaal and remain some days with him,
Rejoicing with song and wine.

Siaavosh spends some time with Rostam, cup in hand,
And some time with Zavaareh.
Sometimes he sits joyous upon the throne of Zaal,
And sometimes he roams and hunts among the reeds.
When a month passes, he sets forth with
Rostam and troops, while Zaal remains at court.

Siaavosh is joined with armies from Zabolestan,
Kabol, and India, armies led by world heroes.
Wherever there lives a famous prince,
He beckons him to his side on the plain of Hari.

In this way, he marches with many foot soldiers
Under the command of Zangueh of Shaavaran.

Then he takes the direction
Of Taleghan[7] and the river Marv.[8]
You would think the sky continuously blesses him.

From there he nears Balkh,[9] and the entire way
He does not afflict a soul with a bitter word.

In this region, Garsivaz and Baarmaan
Verge upon the land of Iran,
Swift as wind, with an army led by Baarmaan.
Sepahram in the rear and Baarmaan in the front
Receive news of the young prince from Iran
Arriving with army and army leader.

Immediately, Garsivaz summons an envoy

◇◇◇◇◇◇◇◇◇◇◇◇◇
7 Taleghan: City in the Alborz mountain range.
8 Marv: City oasis in Iran-Zamin, situated in today's Afghanistan.
9 Balkh: City in today's Afghanistan near Amu River in the province of Khorasan.

To Afraasiyaab, on a horse galloping swift as a vessel
Sailing through water, to relay the message:
"There comes a vast host from Iran,
Troops including many world heroes, led by Siaavosh.
Rostam of elephant stature is at the head,
One hand holding a dagger, the other a shroud.
At the king's command,
I shall stop them and engage in war.
You should prepare your host without delay,
For the wind will propel the boat forward."

Once these words are relayed to the envoy,
Garsivaz sends him off on a horse as swift as flame.
At the news, the leaders of Tooran-Zamin feel as if
The key to unravel trouble's knots is in their hands.

On his side, Siaavosh does not pause.
He leads his army to Balkh with the speed of wind.
The Iranian soldiers come so close
The Tooranians finds themselves unable to hold off war.

Garsivaz, the warrior, ponders for some time
But sees no other option but to fight.
When the Iranians besiege his host,
He makes the plan for war at the gates of Balkh.

Two huge battles ensue during the next three days.
On the fourth day, Siaavosh,
Who sheds light upon the world,
Sends to each gate of Balkh a group of foot soldiers
And organizes a huge army.

Sepahram flees to the other side of the river Jayhoon,
Charging with his legion toward Afraasiyaab.

17 | Siaavosh's Letter to Kaavoos

Siaavosh and his troops take possession of Balkh.
He asks a letter be written as suits a king,
With musk, rosewater, and amber upon silk.
He begins in praise of the Creator,

Who proffers victory and good fortune,
Master of the revolving Sun and Moon,
Giver of the glory of crown, throne, and headdress,
Dispenser of might and valor,
As well as adversity and pain.
"Man's wisdom must resign to the fact that one
Cannot see the how or the why of divine commands.
May the just World Ruler,
Creator of all that is revealed and unrevealed,
Endow Kaavoos with happiness until the end!

"I arrived in Balkh joyous and triumphant,
By the grace of the king, master of crown and throne.
The battle lasted three days. On the fourth day,
Yazdan the Almighty presented me with victory.
Sepahram fled to Tarmaz.[10]
Baarmaan left like an arrow shot from a bow.
Now my army stretches to the River Jayhoon,
And the world is subject to my splendid helmet.
Afraasiyaab stands with his host
On the other side of the river in the land of Sughd.[11]
If the king commands,
I shall cross the waters with my troops
And engage the fight against Afraasiyaab."

18 | Kaavoos's Reply to Siaavosh's Letter

Upon receipt of the letter, the Iranian king's
Crown and throne rise all the way to Saturn.
He implores Yazdan, asking good fortune
To rain upon this young tree so that it may bear fruit.

Then, in joy, he writes his reply like a new spring,
Like paradise full of delights:
"May Yazdan, Creator of Sun and Moon,
World Master, Dispenser of crown and throne,
Never cease to grant you happiness,
And hold pain and suffering at bay!

◇◇◇◇◇◇◇◇◇◇◇◇◇
10 Tarmaz: A town on the edge of the Jayhoon River.
11 Sughd: A town in Tooran-Zamin.

May you always be awarded victory,
The crown of power, and the diadem of might!
You have led your troops; you have sought battle.
As your share, you have received
Fortune, courage, and honesty.
The scent of milk is still fresh on your lips,
Already your arrow's shaft splintered in war.
May your body remain in good health
And your shining soul
Always reach the object of its desire!

"Now that you have been granted victory,
You must proceed with caution.
Do not disperse your troops.
Set forth and prepare a place to camp,
For this Turk of vile breed is full of cunning.
He leans on malice for guidance, embodies Ahriman,
Yet he bears the crown and holds immense power.
His head rises above the shining moon and sun.
Do not hasten to attack,
For Afraasiyaab will present himself to fight you.
Should he cross to this side of the Jayhoon,
He will drag your robe's skirt through blood."

Kaavoos affixes his seal upon the letter,
Entrusts a messenger with it, ordering him to speed
Through mount and valley to deliver the message.

The envoy arrives at the side of Siaavosh.
After reading the letter,
The prince bends low to kiss the ground.
He rejoices in his pure heart,
Smiles and brings the letter to his forehead.
Siaavosh follows the order of the prudent king,
In no way wishing to stray from the deference due him.

After these events, Garsivaz of lion heart
Approaches the King of Tooran, swift as lightning,
And recounts bitter tales that greatly displease him:
"The leader Siaavosh reached the gates of Balkh.
His army, led by Rostam,
Consisted of innumerable troops,

Including famed warriors eager for battle.
For each of us, there were more than fifty
Noble Iranians armed with bull-headed mace.
The infantrymen arrived like darting flames,
At the ready with shield and quiver.
No eagle flies like they do,
And sleep has no hold on them.
We were occupied in battle
For three days and three nights,
Expending our brave men and their chargers.
As for the Iranians, if one of them felt
The need to sleep, he distanced himself
From the melee, slept, then rising
Restored and refreshed, resumed the battle."

This account sets fire to Afraasiyaab's heart.
He shouts, "What do you say of sleep and rest?"
He glares at Garsivaz in such a way
You would think he is ready to tear him apart.
He hollers furiously and chases him away,
Unable to master his anger.
Then he summons one thousand noblemen
And asks a grand feast to be set for them.

The entire plain is covered with golden decorations,
And Sughd is decked in the manner of Chin.
Noblemen pass the day in amusement,
And when the shining sun disappears,
When the need arises for rest and sleep,
Afraasiyaab flings himself on his bed.

19 | Afraasiyaab Has a Frightening Dream

As half of the dark night passes,
Out of the chambers of King Afraasiyaab
Resound echoes of feverish discourse,
And this place of rest and sleep is jarred awake.
The Tooranian leader falls off the bed into the dust.

Servants jump to their feet with cries and laments.
Garsivaz is informed that the luster

Of the royal throne has dimmed.
He hurries to the kingly palace and finds Afraasiyaab
Unconscious on the dust at the foot of the bed.

He takes him in his arms and says,
"Tell your brother what happened."

Once alert, Afraasiyaab replies, "Do question me.
Do not address to me a single word.
Allow me a moment to regain my senses;
Just hold me close."

After a while, the king reclaims full consciousness
And finds the world resonant with cries and wails.
Torches are lit and brought to the royal court.
Afraasiyaab sits on the throne,
Trembling like the branch of a willow tree.

Garsivaz, eager for glory, asks him
To share the nature of this strange adventure.

Glorious Afraasiyaab answers,
"Never has anyone experienced such a dream.
Neither young nor old has ever recounted anything
Close to what I witnessed in this dark night.
In dream, I saw a field full of serpents,
The earth, a dry mass, covered with dust,
The sky full of eagles.
You would think the world has never
Shown its face since the beginning of time.
My tent was pitched at the field's boundaries
And surrounded by an army.
A strong gust of wind rose,
Sending dust flying around,
Flinging to the ground my banner.
On all sides, rivers of blood flowed,
Overthrowing my tents and surrounding walls.
I saw a great number of men, heads detached,
Bodies flung foully to the ground.
I saw an army of Iranians rushing like a storm,
Some flaunting spears, others bow and arrow.

"Every stick was spiked with a head,

And every rider held one in his arm.
One hundred thousand armed Iranians,
Dressed in black, attacked my throne.
They tore me off my seat and grabbed me, hands tied.
Many men surrounded me but none of my servants.
A famous and proud hero rushed me to Kaavoos,
Who sat on a throne, face shining like the moon.
Next to him stood a young man with moon-like cheeks.
He did not have more than twice seven years.
And when he saw me bound up before him,
He charged at me like thunder
And split me in two with his blade.
In my fear, I cried and sobbed in pain,
And my own shouts jolted me out of sleep."

Garsivaz says, "The dream of the king
Foretells what all his friends yearn for him.
It foretells the fulfillment of his wishes,
The conservation of crown and throne,
The destruction of his foes' fortune.
We must find someone able to interpret dreams,
One often engaged in such occupation.
We shall call wise men and astrologers
Selected among sages of vigilant mind."

20 | Afraasiyaab Asks His Wise Men to Interpret His Dream

Experts in the art of dream interpretation
Arrive at court, from near and far, to hear him out.
Afraasiyaab assigns them seats close to him,
And confers with each of them, great and small.

He addresses the wise men, sages, and astrologers:
"Should anyone, either in public or in private,
Ever hear of the dream I am about to recount to you,
Should any of you emit a single word of this matter,
I shall instantly cleave his head."

He hands out much gold and silver to them
To prevent them from running off in fright.

Then he narrates his dream.

One of the eminent wise men hears the tale.
Fearful, he asks the king to first make him a promise:
"We shall interpret this dream truthfully,
But the king must make a pact with us
And promise that we shall not suffer consequences."
The king agrees to those terms.

The wise man who speaks is a man of sense,
Able to resolve the most delicate matters.
He says, "We shall decode his majesty's dream.
At this very moment, a vast army
Is on its way from Iran-Zamin, surrounded
By a great number of skilled and aged advisors.
According to the stars, Siaavosh is at the lead,
Hoping to destroy this kingdom.
If your majesty fights with this young prince,
Blood will color the face of the world so that
It will appear shrouded in a covering of crimson brocade.
Siaavosh will not allow a single Turk to survive,
And the king will regret having engaged in war.

"Even if the young prince dies at the hands of the king,
The throne will not remain in the land of Tooran.
The earth will fill with discord, battle, and chaos,
As well as the burning desire to avenge Siaavosh.
That is when you will know the truth of my words,
For the loss of men will level
Your kingdom into a vast wasteland.
Even if the king were to grow wings,
He would not escape a certain war.
Such is the rotation of the revolving dome,
At times full of anger, at times full of love."

At these words, Afraasiyaab is seized with worry.
He does not wish to rush to war.
He reveals his secrets to Garsivaz
And retells the sage's mysterious words:
"If I do not send an army against Siaavosh,
No one will seek to battle against us.
Neither he nor I will have to face a certain death,

And people will be saved from conflict and suffering.
Kaavoos will find it useless to pursue revenge.
The earth will be spared turmoil and chaos.
Instead of striving for war and world ownership,
We must then relentlessly ask for peace.

"I shall send Siaavosh a gift of silver and gold,
Crown, throne, belt, and helmet.
Manoochehr divided the world according to justice,
For he allotted a smaller portion of land to Iran.
The parcel that once was ours,
I am willing now to return to the Iranians in peace.
I hope misfortune will spare me, and the fires of hostility
Will be doused in the waters of the Jayhoon.
Once I have sewn the eye of war with a golden thread,
The sun will have no choice but to spare me trouble.
I wish for no other destiny than the one written,
For everything must flourish as the Creator has sown."

21 | Afraasiyaab Holds Counsel With His Men

As half of the sky's rotation comes to its completion
And the brilliant sun displays its face, noblemen appear
At the king's court, respectful and bearing headdress.

The king holds an assembly of gifted sages,
Addressing them in this manner: "In my entire life,
I have seen only trouble ensue from war.
Great is the number of distinguished warriors
Who succumbed to death at my hands.
Many are the towns turned into abattoirs,
Many are the rose gardens gone to thorns,
And everywhere are signs of my army's presence.
Verdant fields have been converted into barren deserts
Under the weight of our campaigns.

"When the world king acts with injustice,
Things of beauty wither and fade.
The deer no longer roams in the desert,
And the baby falcon finds himself blinded.
The udders of wild beasts dry up of milk,

And water turns black as tar in running streams.
Wells empty the world over, musk loses its fragrance,
Justice flees at the sight of tyranny.
Lies and deceit proliferate the world over.

"My heart is weary of battle and evil.
I wish to seek the way of Yazdan.
Let us return to wisdom and justice.
May peace take the place of worry and pain!
May our wards no longer trouble the world,
And may death no longer surprise innocent men!
Two-thirds of the world population are my subjects.
I hold court in Iran-Zamin as well as in Tooran-Zamin.
Look how many warriors bring me tribute every year.
If you share my view, I shall send a message to Rostam,
Open the door of amity, send Siaavosh lavish gifts."

Wishing for peace and harmony, one after the other,
The noblemen reply, "You are king, we are your slaves.
Our hearts' only desire is to follow your commands."
They set off, their heads full of a yearning for justice,
Their thoughts liberated from the pain and labor of war.

Afraasiyaab contemplates Garsivaz and says,
"Prepare to act. Rush to set out on the road.
Stop for nothing, not even discussion.
Select from your army two hundred cavaliers.
Take a variety of gifts and treasures to Siaavosh:
Taazian steeds of golden bridle,
Indian swords of golden sheaths,
A crown inlaid with stones worthy of a king,
One hundred camels loaded with plush carpets.
Take with you two hundred slaves, boys and girls,
And tell Siaavosh that I wish not to fight with him.

"Ask him a great number of questions.
Tell him that the terrain from Chin
To the River Jayhoon belongs to me
And that I am in Sughd, my distinct kingdom.
Unfortunately, the world was turned upside down
In the era of Toor and Salm, when two mindless men
Unjustly killed the pure and virtuous Iraj.

Before their time, there was no proper separation
Marked as the border of our two lands.
People then knew of neither revenge nor war.
Now we have faith in Yazdan,
Who has brought us happy days,
Who has allowed your birth in the land of Iran,
Who will make you the friend of men of heart.
Thanks to your star, the world will find peace again,
And conflict and wars will come to an end.

"Garsivaz is on his way to you
To light up your deep intelligence.
Let us divide the world as it was parted
For his brave sons by the noble Fereydoon.
Let us return to what was accomplished then,
And let us relinquish war and vengeance.
You are king. Soften the heart of Iran's ruler.
Recount to him my words.
Speak as well to Rostam of colossal stature.
Speak to him on the subject of friendship.
To conclude this affair, you will carry gifts to him,
Similar to those intended for Siaavosh,
Except for the imperial throne, for Rostam is not king,
And a leader is not fit to assume a royal seat."

22 Garsivaz Travels to Siaavosh

Garsivaz carries these offerings,
Returning its gleam to the face of the earth.
He travels quickly to the banks of the Jayhoon.
There he selects one of his men to announce him,
To tell the king that he is nearing in grand ceremony.

Garsivaz crosses the river in a boat on the same day
And marches toward Balkh, impatient of heart.
His envoy arrives at the king's court
And relays the message of the righteous hero.

Siaavosh summons Rostam
And speaks to him at length about this news.

Once Garsivaz approaches the prince,
Siaavosh asks him to draw closer, rises cheerfully,
And, with a smile on his lips, addresses him politely.

Garsivaz kisses the ground from afar,
His cheeks flushed with shame, his heart full of fear.
Siaavosh assigns him a seat below the throne
And fusses over the health of Afraasiyaab.

Garsivaz listens to the young king, observes
The youthful head, the diadem, and the shiny throne.
He turns to Rostam and says,
"As soon as Afraasiyaab heard news of you,
He sent an envoy in haste, a reminder I bring with me."
He then commands the gifts be brought to Siaavosh.

From the walls of the town to the king's palace,
One could only see silver and stallions, slaves and troops.
It is impossible to tell the amount or the number,
Nor could anyone gauge how much gold,
How many crowns and tall thrones,
How many slaves wearing helmets and belts,
How many girls with golden bangles and chains.

Siaavosh admires these gifts for some time, smiling,
While he lends his ear to Garsivaz's message.

In the end, Rostam says, "Before we seek an answer,
Let us engage in feast for one week.
We must reflect and deliberate upon this demand."

Garsivaz of foresight hears these words,
Touches his forehead, and kisses the seat of Siaavosh.
A dwelling is set up for him, decorated with brocade.
Chefs are summoned to cook up tasty dishes for him.

Siaavosh and Rostam, two heroes full of foresight,
Distance themselves from the crowd
And sit to discuss matters, great and small.

Rostam has qualms on the nature of this affair
And questions the purpose of Garsivaz's sudden arrival.
They send out scouts to every corner

And prepare as is suitable for various events.

Siaavosh tells Rostam,
"We must get to the bottom of this.
What is the point of this request for peace?
Look and find the antidote to this bane.
Point out to me one hundred kin of Afraasiyaab,
People who surround his throne, that he may send
As hostages to calm our worried hearts.
Do you not see how he is bothered by fear
And how he beats the drum beneath the coat?
He wishes to hide what cannot be hidden.
When we conclude with him, we shall send to Kaavoos
One of our friends to explain what has transpired
So that the desire for vengeance
Will not inspire him to act rashly and insensibly."

Rostam replies, "We shall proceed as you wish.
Only in this manner will a treaty be sealed."

23 | Siaavosh Draws Up a Treaty With Afraasiyaab

At dawn, Garsivaz arrives at court
Wearing helmet and belt according to custom.
He approaches Siaavosh,
Kisses the ground, and praises the king.

Siaavosh asks him how he spent the night
In the midst of feast and noise.
Then he adds, "We have considered your proposition.
Both of us sincerely wish to expel hatred from our hearts.
Return to Afraasiyaab, and tell him,
        'Withdraw all desire of vengeance, for when
        One sees the end of war, one refrains from battle.
        A heart subject to wisdom is a bountiful treasure.
        If there is no hidden poison
        In your honey-sweet words,
        If your heart is free of hateful emotion,
        If you truly wish to draw up a treaty,
        You must send to me one hundred hostages,
        Bound to you by blood,

Brave men whom Rostam knows, whose names
He will tell you as guarantee of your word.
You must evacuate all parts of Iran under your control,
Return the lands to us, and move back to Tooran-Zamin.
For a long time, abandon thoughts of war and hatred.
Nothing but justice must fill the space between us.
Let us not resort to the antagonism of lions.'
On my end, I shall send a letter to the king
So that he may agree to peace and withdraw his troops."

Garsivaz immediately sends a rider, swift as wind,
And says to him, "Do not allow sleep to overtake you.
Hurry to Afraasiyaab to tell him that we have obeyed.
In return, they have agreed to our conditions.
Tell him that Rostam demands one hundred hostages,
Young men of royal blood, in return for renouncing war."

The rider nears Afraasiyaab and delivers
The message of the prince and the glorious Garsivaz.

When the Tooranian king hears the words of the envoy,
He is agitated, not knowing what action to take.
He contemplates the situation:
"If my court were to lose one hundred of my relatives,
There will be a wide gap on the day of battle.
I shall have no friend left in my land.
But if I tell Siaavosh, 'Do not ask for hostages,'
He will hold all my words for lies.
I must then resort to sending him my men
Since he is not willing to battle without guarantee.
My most fervent hope is to evade misfortune.
Better act as a cautious man than as a foolish one."

He selects close to one hundred relations
From Rostam's list to send to the King of Iran,
Giving them gifts of honorary robes and presents.

Trumpets are sounded, and timpani are struck in his camp.
Afraasiyaab withdraws from Bukhara, Sughd,
Samarkand, Chaadj, Sepijaab,[12] and other lands.

◇◇◇◇◇◇◇◇◇◇◇◇◇
12 Bukhara, Sughd, Samarkand, Chaadj, Sepijaab: Towns in Tooran-Zamin.

He vacates the ivory throne and retreats with his host
To Gang without finding a reason to stay or to stray.

With this withdrawal, Rostam's doubts dissipate.
He runs like flying dust to Siaavosh
And recounts to him all that has occurred.
He adds, "Now that the deed is done,
It is right to allow Garsivaz to leave."

Siaavosh orders a gift be readied, to include
Armor, helmet, a Taazian horse of golden bridle,
An Indian sword of golden sheath, and a belt.

At the sight of the royal offering, you would think
Garsivaz watches the moon tumble down to earth.
He departs uttering blessings, so swift on his charger
It appears that he rolls up the earth beneath him.

24 | Siaavosh Sends Rostam to Kaavoos

Siaavosh sits on the ivory throne
And hangs his crown above his seat.
He selects a man from his army's troops,
A skilled rider of sweet speech, able to adorn his words
With color and scent to complement Kaavoos's temper.

Rostam says to Siaavosh,
"Who would dare carry such a message?
Kaavoos is still the man he has always been.
His sternness, rather than diminish, has increased.
Only I may go to the king, disclose to him the secret.
I shall tread the earth at your command,
And only good will come from my appearance at court,
Which I shall carry out with deference in your honor."

Pleased, Siaavosh rejects the idea of sending an envoy.
He and Rostam sit to confer on matters great and small.

The young prince summons a scribe to record on silk
A letter that he begins with praise of the Creator:
"From Whom comes glory, supremacy, virtue,

Master of Eternal Wisdom, time and power,
Who nurtures our minds and hearts
With just ways that deliver joy and victory.
Eternal Wisdom dwells at the crest of the divine pillar,
The Creator before Whose commands no man retreats,
Else he would find nothing in the world but defeat,
From Whom expansion and joy emanate.
May the Creator of Sun and Moon,
Giver of glory to crown and throne,
Proffer abundant favors upon the king,
World master, elected among noblemen,
Whose mind deepens the good and the bad,
Whose stature is the foundation of wisdom.

"I arrived in Balkh and enjoyed a festive spring.
As soon as Afraasiyaab heard of my arrival,
The sun dimmed before his eyes.
He sensed his position was a tough one.
The world collapsed before him, his fortune weakened.
His brother came to me with gifts and arrayed slaves.
He came to ask for the king's protection
And to concede the crown and throne.
He wishes to settle boundaries for his kingdom
And no longer make claims to what is not rightly his.
He wishes to terminate his intrusion on the land of Iran
And to purify his heart from aspirations to war.
In the end, he sent one hundred relatives as hostages.
Rostam is coming your way to bend you to his demands,
And it is fair and right that you agree to them.
Forgive him, for his face betrays his affection."

Once the letter is sealed,
Rostam leaves with banner and troops
In the direction of the royal court of the King of Iran.

Garsivaz takes off as well but in the opposite direction.
As soon as he approaches Afraasiyaab,
He speaks to him at length of Siaavosh,
Saying he has no equal among kings in beauty,
In looks, valor, prudence, humility, and eloquence,
Stressing his courage, his countenance, his horsemanship,
Saying it appears he cradles wisdom in his arms.

The king smiles and says, "A peaceful outcome
In the face of war is more favorable, my friend.
My heart is weary of this dream.
At the height of my good fortune,
I detected signs of its decline.
Increasingly troubled, I sought a way out.
I opened the doors to my treasury,
And now the conclusion presents itself
Precisely as I had anticipated."

25 | Rostam Gives His Account to Kaavoos

Rostam, the lion, travels as swift as flying dust.
He arrives at the hall of the King of Iran,
Appears before the ruler, arms folded at his chest.

Kay Kaavoos rises from his seat, embraces him and,
As is the custom, asks him all sorts of questions
About his son, the fate of the warriors,
The state of the army, and the reason for his return.

Rostam bows low to honor the king.
He first replies to questions about Siaavosh
With much admiration and then presents the letter.

At the completion of the reading by a famous scribe,
The king's cheeks turn black as tar.
He says to Rostam, "I believe Siaavosh,
Though no longer a child, is young and immature.
You, on the other hand, know the world well.
You have witnessed good and bad
In every shape and form.
You have no equal in the realm.
Lions in battle borrow courage from you.
Have you not seen the way Afraasiyaab tortured me,
How he deprived me of food, rest, and sleep?
I should have left, yet I allowed myself to stay.
Though my head longed for war, I did not engage.
I was constantly told to refrain from battle, to hold off
And allow the young prince to carry weapons.
When the time is ripe for divine vengeance,

Evil must reward evil.

"But you have accepted the treasures of this vile man,
And, in this way, appeased your heart.
The gold Afraasiyaab seized from his ingenuous people
Has diverted your head from the right path.
Do you really believe Afraasiyaab is worried
About one hundred wretched Turks of low birth,
Sons deprived of the knowledge of their fathers' names?
In his eyes, they are nothing but water in a spring.
Even if you have acted foolishly,
I am not one to tire of battle and war.
I shall send to Siaavosh a prudent man to guide him,
And here is the order I shall give my son:
          'Light an enormous fire.
          Tie up the feet of the Turks with heavy chains.
          Throw into the fire the gifts received
          And refrain from touching them.
          Then send me the prisoners,
          For I wish to sever their heads.
          Without delay, lead your army
          To the court of Afraasiyaab.
          Release your troops so that they may
          Advance like wolves pouncing on lambs.
          Make every effort to teach them how to act ruthlessly,
          To provoke the warriors to destroy and burn.
          Then Afraasiyaab will come to fight,
          For rest and sleep will no longer appeal to him.'"

Rostam replies, "O King, do not distress your heart.
Listen first to my words, then do as you please.
The world is at your command.
You asked us to hold tight in the war
Against Afraasiyaab, to maintain our army
On this side of the river until he instigated an attack.
We advanced to the water's edge to entice him,
But he was first to open the doors to peace.
It would not have been right for us to besiege
A man whose only wish was peace, banquet, and feast.

"In the second place, consider that a king
Who revokes the terms of a treaty

Will not be acclaimed or respected by his friends.
Siaavosh departed for battle to claim victory.
What more do you need or wish for?
You have it all: crown, throne, royal seal,
Peace, and the treasures of Iran.
Do not foolishly instigate an unnecessary war.
Do not flood your joyous heart with grief and regret.
If Afraasiyaab secretly intends to violate his word,
We shall not refrain from pouncing on him.
Our swords and lion claws are honed and ready.

"Place yourself on the throne next to the noble Siaavosh.
Maintain your position in your land,
Remain in a state of contentment.
If need be, I shall take a small army from Zabolestan,
Destroy the throne of Tooran with my battle mace,
And dim the light of Afraasiyaab's sun.
He and I have often fought against each other.
It may be that he does not wish to expose himself again.
Do not ask your son to retract his word.
Do not command him to take action
For something that could only be deemed a crime.
Why shall I not express my thoughts openly?
Siaavosh has no wish to violate the treaty.
When he hears of the king's scheme,
Our eminent prince will be struck with dismay.
Do not trouble your son's good fortune, for if you do,
Your heart will never again revel in a moment's peace."

26 | Kaavoos Sends Rostam to Sistan

Kaavoos is most incensed by Rostam's speech
And dares not lift his eyes.
In the end he says to the hero,
"Truth can never remain concealed.
You filled Siaavosh's head with these notions.
You dug up, in his heart, the root of vengeance
And, in so doing, you only considered your well-being,
Disregarding the glory of throne, crown, and seal.
Are you sufficiently pleased with the wealth of gifts
You have received to abandon notions of war?

"Remain here until the leader Tous
Places timpani on the backs of elephants.
I shall send a camel to Balkh to carry a letter
With bitter words to seal the matter.
If Siaavosh disobeys me and escapes his obligations,
He will cede power to Tous and extract
Himself and his friends from the army's ranks.
I shall then show him what he will gain
If he attempts to act as master.
As for you, I no longer call you my friend.
I no longer wish you to defend me or my kingdom."

Rostam's fury escalates, and he shouts at Kaavoos:
"The sky cannot hide my head.
How dare you place Tous, the valiant,
On equal footing with Rostam?
You should know that there are
Very few Rostams in this world!"

He says this, then takes his leave,
Heart full of wrath, face pale with anger.
He marches in haste toward Sistan with his escort.

At the same time, the king asks for Tous,
Hands over to him the letter full of bitter words,
And asks him to deliver it to his son Siaavosh.
 "O brave and noble warrior," Kaavoos says,
"Depart with it. Leave this site boldly like a lion."

Tous commands the army to prepare for the expedition.
Warriors renounce rest and sleep.
Clarions and kettledrums are played as they set forth.

27 | Kaavoos Replies to Siaavosh's Letter

Kaavoos asks for a strapped camel, ready to take off.
Then he calls a scribe and sits him before his throne.
Full of fury and rage, mouth rife with harsh words,
Cheeks flushed a deep red, the color of wine,
Kaavoos asks him to write a letter.

He begins with praise of the Creator,
Master of peace and war,
Master of Mars, Saturn, and Moon,
Master of happiness and gloom, of fame and glory,
Whom the revolving dome obeys,
And Who shines light everywhere.
"O, my young son, may health and fortune,
Crown and throne remain yours forever,
Even if your heart forgets my counsel,
Even if your head is troubled by the spells of youth.
You have heard stories of Afraasiyaab's wicked acts
Against Iran, when he was victorious on battle day.
Do not then foolishly seek his friendship.
Do not contribute to his crown's glory.
Do not deliver your head, unconsciously,
To the designs of ill-intentioned men.

"If you wish to avoid being pitched into the throes
Of affliction, tie up the hostages' hands and feet
And send them to my court.
It is no surprise if Afraasiyaab misleads you.
I judge his past actions, for many times he tricked me
Away from battle with his keen and cunning ways.
Never did I utter the words 'peace' or 'amity.'
You never followed my command.
You have led a happy life in the company of pretty slaves,
And you now cowardly shrink away from battle.
Rostam never grows wary of gifts and treasure.
The desire to access the crown of the King of Kings
Has rendered you sheepish before war.
Yet one must open the door to riches with sword,
And it is through conquest that a king gains grandeur.

"When army leader Tous arrives at your side,
He will set everything straight and in order.
You will then place your hostages upon donkeys.
The secret design of the revolving sphere
Is to endanger and ruin your life with a truce.
The news of such misfortune will fill the land of Iran,
And our days of joy will end.

"Leave, be ready for vengeance and invasion,

87

And do not engage in lengthy discourse on this matter.
When you are ready for fight and the shocks of night,
When you will have lifted black dust from the ground,
Then Afraasiyaab will not allow his head to yield to rest.
He will rush to take up arms against you.
But if you hold affection for me, if you do not wish
To violate the treaty, then give up the army's command.
Surrender it to the renowned Tous and return to me,
For you are neither a man of battle nor a man of fame."

The king's seal affixed to the letter, the camel takes off,
Shredding the road beneath its hooves.
Once in hand, Siaavosh reads the missive.
He calls the messenger, asks him what happened,
And extracts from him the truth.

The envoy relates the exchange between
Kaavoos and Rostam, and how the latter
Grew infuriated with the king and with Tous.

Siaavosh listens to this account,
Unhappy with Rostam and what he has done,
His heart full of worry for his father's actions,
The fate of the Turk hostages, and the matter of war.

He says to himself, "Here are one hundred brave riders,
Relatives of an illustrious king, innocent highborn men.
If I send them to the King of Iran,
He will not question them and without hesitation
Will have them tied alive at the gallows.
How shall I ever ask divine forgiveness?
My father's dealings pour misfortune over my head.
If I contend with the King of Tooran
Without provocation, the World Creator
Will likely frown down at my actions, and the people
Of the land will raise their voices against me.
If I return to the king's court, turning over to Tous
The army's command, I shall equally suffer.
I only see loss right and left, and loss of self.
Furthermore, Sudaabeh will continue to be
A grievous source of suffering.
I have no clue what fate the divine holds for me."

28 | Siaavosh Consults With Bahraam and Zangueh

At this time, Siaavosh calls to his side two
Of the army's brave world heroes to confide in:
Bahraam and Zangueh of Shaavaran.
He sends away everyone else and sits the two leaders
Across from him in the grand hall.
Since Rostam's retreat, they are his secret confidants.

He says to them, "My misfortune attracts hardship.
King Kaavoos's heart, in his affection for me,
Was like a tree laden with fruits and leaves.
But ever since Sudaabeh has gained his confidence,
It is as if his heart has been infected by pure venom.
This woman's chambers have become my prison.
A destiny that once smiled my way withers in her hands.
Such is my fate that the fruits of this woman's love
Affect me like a consuming, destructive blaze.

"I avoid the king's banquets to engage in battle.
I stay away from pleasure and feast
To evade the wrath of the whale.
There was in Balkh a large army led by Garsivaz.
Camped in Sughd was Afraasiyaab, full of hatred,
With one hundred thousand men
Willing and eager to draw their swords.
We plunged into battle unwaveringly.
Once the Tooranians were expelled from provinces,
They sent hostages and gifts.
Sages said that it was preferable to refrain from fight
Rather than engage for the sake of self-glorification.
We have obtained gifts and land from the Tooranian king.
Why should we shed blood needlessly?
Why dim our hearts with the seed of vengeance?

"A king devoid of brain cannot
Differentiate between good and bad.
Ghobaad came and went,
Conferring his empire on Kaavoos.
Since then, all might as well have been squandered.
Kaavoos does not appreciate any of my actions.
He only seeks to cause me pain and suffering

By commanding me to campaign against Tooran.
I fear he has no respect for my promises.
Yet one must not draw back from a divine decree.
One must not stray from one's father's path.
He seeks to lose me in this world and in the other,
Hopes to see me slothful in a lowly state of being,
And that is exactly what Ahriman desires.

"Besides, no one can forecast
Which side will suffer defeat.
O why did my mother have to give birth to me?
Why did not death take me hostage sooner?
When one is forced to bear such suffering,
One feeds only on bitterness and fear.
Life becomes a lofty tree bearing venomous fruit,
Its leaves imparting only damage and destruction.
If, after making such a promise and invoking Yazdan,
I turn away from the right path, all will be ruined.
Rumors will spread throughout the world
That I rescinded the agreement with the King of Tooran.
Men will open their lips to curse me, as I justly deserve.

"How would Yazdan approve?
What would the revolving dome bring upon me?
If I were to go back on my promise and,
In vengeance, rebel against earth and sky?
I shall go far away, seek a distant retreat to end my days.
My name shall remain hidden from Kaavoos.
Then Yazdan's will shall pass on this shining world.
Now, O illustrious Zangueh of Shaavaran,
Prepare yourself for the stringent trials that lie ahead.
Go to Afraasiyaab's court without delay.
Return to him hostages, wealth, gold, crown, and throne.
Recount to him what has transpired here."

Then he says to Bahraam, son of Goodarz,
"I entrust you with this glorious army,
This border, these elephants, and timpani.
You will await the arrival of army leader Tous.
In good order, you will hand over the lot to him,
Troops and treasures, and you will give him
An account of the gold, the crowns, the thrones."

Bahraam's heart shudders with fear at these words
In anticipation of the plan Siaavosh is setting in motion.
Zangueh of Shaavaran sheds tears of blood,
Cursing the land of Haamaavaran.
Both remain seated, looking distraught,
Overcome with pain.

In the end they say to him, "This is not the way to act.
Apart from your father, you are displaced in the world.
Write a letter to the king.
Ask him to send Rostam to you.
If he bids you to make war, then so be it.
This is a matter that will soon come to an end
Unless you select the longer route.
If you prefer rest, there is no problem,
You may ask your father's forgiveness without shame.
If you wish to send me, I shall enlighten his heart.
If your prisoners weigh heavy on you, liberate them.
Wouldn't you then be free to declare war?

"In his letter, Kaavoos only bids you
To enter the campaign. There is nothing in
What he says that does not have a solution.
Let us go to war according to the king's orders.
Let us restrict the earth to our enemies.
Do not open lightly your heart to doubt and suspicion.
Gently wrap your father's head in the folds of your net.
Do not destroy our fortune at the time of harvest.
Do not flood with blood your vision, throne, and crown.
Do not allow the core of the royal tree to wither and die.
How could the crown and throne, army and court,
Camp and audience hall be deprived of your presence?
The head and brain of Kaavoos have become an inferno,
And it is madness to try to argue with him.
I shall be silent now, for the sky has ordered otherwise.
It is then pointless to further discuss this matter."

Siaavosh rejects the advice of the two wise men.
The glorious sky has a different purpose.
He voices his answer, "In my opinion,
The king's order is above Sun and Moon.
But in the eye of Yazdan, nothing is strong,

91

From a blade of grass to the elephant and tiger.
Whoever infringes Yazdan's command
Is foolish, reckless, has lost his way.
We must then extend our hands to smear in blood.
We must fling ourselves into war to avenge two realms.
Even if I were to submit to this,
The king would torment the captives.
He would constantly allude to what I failed to do.
If I leave the battlefield without having
Accomplished the deed, he would express his hatred
And in his heart would smolder
The blaze of his anger to the end.
He speaks to us of this and that,
On subjects that are ancient as well as new.

"If, however, you are disturbed by my actions
And refuse to obey me,
I shall be my own envoy and guide.
I shall abandon my tents in this very desert.
Why should I force those who no longer take
Part in my fortune to take part in my affliction?
I shall release the gifts and hostages,
Send them back to Afraasiyaab."

Upon hearing this,
The souls of these two noblemen recoil.
They weep bitterly for fear of losing Siaavosh.
Consumed as if by fire, their hearts darkened,
Their eyes only perceive trouble
And the final destiny awaiting their master.
Knowing they will not see him again,
They weep for him.

Zangueh says to Siaavosh, "We are your slaves.
Our hearts are filled with love for you.
May our bodies and souls serve as your ransom!
May we remain loyal to you until death do us part!"

The mindful Siaavosh hears this message
From his friend and says to Zangueh,
"Go and tell the king of Turks how from amity
And peace emerged acrimony and strife.

92

What he deems as honey is for me poison.
Tell him that I have not violated our treaty,
Even though the end result is for me
A loss of the throne of power.
Yazdan the Creator is my refuge,
The earth my throne, heaven my crown.
Furthermore, tell him that I shall not return
To Kaavoos Shah until I have completed
The execution of his commands.
May Afraasiyaab open the path so that I may go
To the dwelling Yazdan has designated for me.
I wish to seek upon the earth a land where my name
May remain hidden from Kaavoos Shah,
A place where I may not hear of his ill intentions
And where I may for some time rest
Before the struggles against him are launched."

29 | Zangueh Goes to Afraasiyaab

Zangueh departs with one hundred famed horsemen,
The hostages from the Tooranian king's court,
And the presents, whatever they may be,
That Garsivaz had brought along with him.

Once he enters the city where resides the Tooranian king,
A shout is heard, and the sentinel catches sight of him,
A powerful nobleman whose name is Tevorg, the brave.

As Zangueh of Shaavaran approaches,
The sentinel announces him to the king.
Afraasiyaab rises from his throne,
Receives him graciously, and, holding him
Close to his chest, assigns him a seat of honor.

Zangueh takes his place beside the king
And hands the letter over to him,
Recounting the events point by point.
Afraasiyaab is disturbed by the proceedings.
His heart fills with concern and his head with fear.

The king orders chambers be set up for Zangueh

And asks for him to be treated as his rank demands.
Then, in haste, he summons his leader Piran,
Who swiftly appears before him in court.

The king dismisses everyone to discuss with Piran
Matters relating to the Iranian king: his bouts of rage,
His bad temper, his insistence on the pursuit of war.

Afraasiyaab's expression dims,
And his heart fills with pity for Siaavosh
As he recounts the arrival of Zangueh of Shaavaran
And all that happened, from beginning to end.
Then he asks Piran, "How shall we extract
Ourselves from this humiliating predicament?"

Piran replies, "O King, may your reign last forever!
May you live as long as the world endures!
You have more wisdom and knowledge than any of us.
You are more powerful in treasure and courage.
No one equals you in opinion, advice,
Affection, and consideration.
Your majesty shines light on my ideas.
Whoever holds the power to carry out good deeds,
Openly or covertly, cannot refuse to help the king's son.
No matter what it takes, whether in treasure or labor,
He must be tended to with care and affection
For as long as he wishes to remain by your side.
I have heard it said that among this earth's great men,
He has no equal in stature and beauty,
In judgment and insight, in demeanor, grace, and glory.
His essence and wisdom reach higher than his lineage.
Never before has a queen given birth to such a prince.

"But we shall soon lay eyes on him, which is
More valuable than listening to tales about him.
He is a noble prince, son of a noble king.
Is there a higher merit than breaking paternal bonds
To save the lives of one hundred of our men
Than relinquishing the throne and crown, by humbling
Himself and seeking passage through our lands?

"You must make him one of your kingdom's
Most esteemed men, for he is eager to display his courage.

94

Wise men would not approve of your eminence
If you were to refuse him access through our fields.
Besides, Kaavoos's hair is growing white.
The time is here for him to leave the throne vacant.
On the other hand, Siaavosh is young and illustrious.
He will soon possess royal power and royal throne.
If you reject him, your men will cast blame upon you,
For he will foment discontent with you.

"If the king in his wisdom agrees with my counsel,
He will write a long and thoughtful letter.
He will receive this intelligent young man
As one receives one's beloved and precious son.
He will prepare for him a dwelling in this land,
Treat him as deserved by his rank and his talents.
He would present him one of his daughters
And surround him with attention, kindness, and honor.
If Siaavosh remains in proximity,
He would transform your land into a land of peace,
And were he to return to the King of Iran,
Your fortune could only multiply,
For he would come to your defense before Kaavoos,
And the earth's noblemen would praise him highly.
Indeed, were Siaavosh to wind up our way,
We can only hope to see him succeed in soothing
The hostility that has pervaded our two lands since long ago.
He would be worthy of the Creator's justice
And thus restore peace and happiness on earth."

The ruler listens to Piran's words.
He reflects upon the future for a long time,
Thinking about potential joys and sorrows.

In the end, he replies, "I approve of your suggestions,
And among the elite of experienced men
None compares to you in the world.
Yet I have heard the words of a wise man
That could apply to your advice:
        'If you nurture a lion cub, you will repent
        As soon as his teeth are sharp and cutting.
        The moment he grows claws,
        The moment he is strong enough to leap,

He will not hesitate to pounce on his foster parent.'"

Piran says, "May his majesty dare consult his wisdom.
Why should one attribute cruelty to a man
Who does not exhibit his father's violent nature?
You can see that Kaavoos is now old,
And his old age is a sign that he will soon pass on.
Then Siaavosh will rule over the entire world,
And, as a result, it will be yours to dominate:
Treasures acquired painlessly, grand palaces,
The lands of Iran and Tooran, throne and crown.
One must be fate's chosen one
To be handed over such a vast share of fortune."

30 | Afraasiyaab's Letter to Siaavosh

Hearing these words,
Afraasiyaab adopts a wise position.
He calls a skilled scribe and dictates a letter.

The scribe dips the tip of his reed in amber,
And the king begins the letter with praise of Yazdan,
Giving homage to divine supremacy and infinite wisdom:
"The Creator, pure and perfect, above time and space,
Beyond his servants' power of thought,
Master of soul, mind, and spirit,
Whose justice is the support of wise men.
May divine grace shine upon the king's son,
Master of sword, mace and helmet, pure and just,
The one whose heart repels injustice and tyranny.
I have heard your message from beginning to end,
As related by Zangueh of Shaavaran, your envoy.

"My soul grieves for the secret spite
The world king's heart harbors for you.
Yet is there anything in the world
More worthy than throne and crown?
What more can a man of sense desire,
One on whom fortune shines its light?
These belong to you, whether you have ascended
Or await accession to the throne, to rule one day.

96

The entire land of Tooran wishes to acclaim you,
And I have need for your affection.
You will represent a son to me and I a father to you,
A father who will stand before you as a slave.
Know that not for a single day has Kaavoos
Looked upon you with the same affection
I nurture in my heart for you.
I shall open the doors to my palaces and my treasury.
I shall offer you a throne and crown.
I shall deem you with the same tenderness
A father deems a son, and you shall remain
After I am gone, a memory of me in the world.

"If you travel through my land
To take over another portion of the earth,
All men great and small will hold it against me.
Besides, you would have a hard time finding an exit
On this side unless you are gifted with divine powers.
There are no lands that present a passage out.
You would be forced to cross the Sea of Chin.
May Yazdan guard you from such a thing!
Come, establish your dwelling in our land.
United with the bonds of friendship,
All is yours: my army, my forts, my wealth,
And you shall find no reason to leave my side.

"When you are ready to make peace with your father,
I shall give you crown, throne, and belt so that
You may travel with an army to Iran-Zamin.
I shall escort you with care and compassion.
Your father will not keep up his enmity for long.
He is old and must be growing weary of battle.
The breath of a sixty-five-year-old man is too weak
To adequately stoke the flames of a burning blaze.
Iran-Zamin, its throne and its army, will be yours.
You will travel from land to land to collect crowns.
I have received divine command to spend everything,
My soul and my strength, on you.
I shall never ask you to commit evil acts.
I shall never lead you on a deviating course.
I shall not allow my heart to doubt your loyalty."

The king affixes his seal to the letter
And orders Zangueh, Siaavosh's friend,
To strap himself in haste and prepare for departure.
The king assembles many gifts, gold and silver,
And a horse donning heavy golden strappings.

Zangueh of Shaavaran takes off with great speed.
Once he stands before the throne of Siaavosh,
He relates the questions asked and the replies received.

On one hand, Siaavosh is thrilled,
On the other, he is pained and afflicted.
He needed to convert an enemy into a friend, but how
Could a fresh breeze billow out of an ardent fire?
No matter how good your deeds,
A foe will always be a foe.

31 | Siaavosh Hands Over the Army to Bahraam

Siaavosh writes a letter to his father in which
He communicates the developments and says,
"Despite my youth, I am endowed with wisdom.
I have always turned away from wrongdoing,
But the flare of the king's wrath consumes me.
My first distress came from the women's chambers,
Forcing me to wash my face with my heart's blood.
I leapt fearlessly through a mountain of fire,
Making the desert deer weep bitterly for me.
I engaged in war to escape shame and disgrace.
I marched to battle against colossal whales.
Our two lands rejoiced to see us consummate peace,
But the king's heart is as sharp as a sword of steel.
Nothing I do ever pleases him, and whether
I open or close the bonds, he blames me equally.
Since his eyes are weary and no longer view me
As a bold warrior, I shall not stay at his side.
May joy never vacate his heart!
As for me, I continually risk my life in my suffering
And expose myself to the dragon's breath.
I do not know what destiny the revolving dome
Reserves for me, whether in love or in war."

PART EIGHT

Once these words are spoken, he turns to Bahraam
And commands: "May your name flourish in the world!
I entrust you with crown, camp, treasure, and throne,
My seat, my banner, my riders, elephants, and timpani.
When the leader Tous arrives, hand it all to him,
Just as you have received it from me.
Be cautious, and may your days be happy!"

He selects three hundred horsemen,
Warriors skilled in the art of battle.
He orders silver be brought, as much as needed,
Gold and jewels worthy of a king,
One hundred select stallions of golden bridle,
One hundred slaves of golden belt.
He orders a list be drawn of the items he is seizing:
Weapons, strappings, and belts.

Then he summons noblemen
And addresses them with suitable words:
"Piran is coming to our gathering,
With a secret message that will free you from worry.
I am prepared to meet him on the road.
You remain here and listen to Bahraam, your leader.
Make sure to obey his orders."

The brave men bend low
To kiss the ground by Siaavosh's feet,
Calling down divine grace upon the prince.

As soon as the shining sun disappears
And the sky dons its cloak of darkness,
Making the earth appear rough and rocky,
Siaavosh leads his escort toward the Jayhoon,
His features blurred beneath his tears.

In the land of Tarmaz, he finds the doors,
Balconies, and streets adorned like spring.
Everything is full of scent and color.
Every town, from Tarmaz to Chaadj,[13] appears
As a bride arrayed with collars and crowns.

◇◇◇◇◇◇◇◇◇◇◇◇◇
13 Chaadj: City near today's Tashkent, in Uzbekistan.

At each halt, he finds a warm meal,
A table set, carpets spread.
He continues in this manner to Ghajghaarbaashi,[14]
Where he stops and remains for some time.

Tous, on his end, arrives in Balkh, where
He is made aware of the painful turn of events.
He is told bitter tales of the famous son of King Kaavoos,
Who has taken the road leading to the Tooranian king.
Tous rounds up his army and returns to Iran's court.

Kay Kaavoos's cheeks whiten at the news,
And in his rage against Afraasiyaab and Siaavosh,
He hollers, his heart on fire, his eyes flooding with tears.
He does not know what fate holds in store for him,
Nor does he know whether the sky
Will treat him with compassion or with rancor.

He forgets his anger, his longing for vengeance,
And, from this time on, ceases to speak of war.

Afraasiyaab learns that Siaavosh has crossed the Jayhoon
And is about to reach the border with his escort
And that his envoy has just arrived at the court.
The king orders brave men to greet him,
And they take the road attended by the sound of drums.

Piran selects one thousand men from his tribe
And makes preparations to travel to Siaavosh.
He distributes provisions and gifts to his escort.
On the back of one of four white-strapped elephants,
He places a throne inlaid with stones of turquoise
And a shining banner large as a tree.
The flag is topped with a golden moon,
Its background purple, its center embroidered.

Three more elephants covered
In rich brocade carry golden seats.
One hundred noble horses bear golden saddles
Inlaid with fine stones of every kind.
The entire procession is so beautiful

◇◇◇◇◇◇◇◇◇◇◇◇◇
14 Ghajghaarbaashi: A town in Tooran-Zamin.

100

PART EIGHT

You may think the sky has adorned
The earth with immeasurable love.

Upon hearing of the advancing convoy,
Siaavosh prepares for its arrival.
He catches sight of the banner of Piran the leader.
He hears the sound of his horses and elephants.
He runs toward him, embraces him, and holds him close.

He then asks him for news of his land and master
And says, "O army hero, why do you exert
Yourself to come to my encounter?
My soul's most ardent wish was for my two eyes
To find you well and in good health."

Piran kisses his head and feet,
As well as his beautiful, heart-robbing face.
He says to Siaavosh, "O young ruler, if I had
Only seen in dream a being of such intelligence,
I would praise the Creator for returning youth to me.
Now I see you, bright, able-bodied, and well.
Afraasiyaab will serve as a father to you,
And those dwelling on this side of the river,
Men and women, will happily assist you as slaves.

"I have more than one thousand allies
Under my command who wear the ring of servitude.
All my wealth is yours to have.
May your heart be joyous, your body in good health!
May your soul never desire in vain!
If you wish to receive me as your humble servant,
Despite my advanced age,
I shall strap myself in service to you."

The two joyfully take the road to town,
Engaged in conversation over matters great and small.
People awaken to the sounds of harp and lute.
The earth is fragrant with the scent of musk.
Taazian horses appear to have grown wings.

At such a sight, Siaavosh sheds torrents of tears,
And his thoughts dim, for he remembers a time
When the land of Zabolestan to the edges of Kabol

101

Was adorned for celebration, when he was Rostam's
Guest of honor and the noblemen gathered around him.

He remembers gold and jewels scattered around him,
Musk and amber sprinkled over him,
And these memories set his heart on fire,
Consuming him as an ardent flame.
He cannot help but remember also the land of Iran,
And a sigh of nostalgia escapes his chest.

Siaavosh conceals his face from Piran and turns away,
But the army leader notices the anguish and the pain,
And he can only imagine what ailments afflict the prince.
Aggrieved, Piran bites his lip in sympathy.

At Ghajghaarbaashi, they dismount and stop to rest.
Piran sits, his two eyes fixed in astonishment
On Siaavosh's expression, his shoulders,
His chest and arms, his eloquent speech.
He summons Yazdan's name from time to time.

Then he addresses Siaavosh: "O renowned prince,
You are the heir to the world king.
You possess three things no other possesses:
First, you are from the seed of Kay Ghobaad,
And your majesty is such that you could easily
Be taken for the leader of the Kianian family.
Second, you will soon have your tongue's truth
And need only utter words full of integrity.
Thirdly, your face appears as if it sows
Seeds of love throughout the world.
Your mother is a descendant of Garsivaz.
On both sides, your lineage is noble and distinct."

Siaavosh replies, "Old man of pure, righteous speech,
Renowned in the world for your kindness and good faith,
You are detached from Ahriman and from injustice.
If you wish to form an alliance with me,
I am assured that you will not violate our pact.
Then I shall build a place of rest in this land
For the love and the trust you inspire in me.
If my stay here brings me good luck,
You will not need to deplore your place in it.

If fate chooses otherwise, order me to leave
And bring to light a road that leads to another land."

Piran responds, "Do not distress yourself.
Since you have traveled from Iran-Zamin,
Do not reject an alliance with Afraasiyaab.
There is no need to rush to leave us.
Afraasiyaab has a bad name, but he does not deserve it.
He is a man of faith, of sense,
Of wisdom, caution, and strong will.
He would not throw himself foolishly on a path
Leading to his own downfall and demise.

"Besides, I am his blood relative.
I am not only his warrior
But also his counselor and guide.
He respects me, honors me.
My wealth, thrones, and troops are quite plentiful.
At my command are one hundred thousand horsemen,
Of which twelve thousand owe allegiance to my own tribe
And stand before me day and night.
I own territory, herds and sheep, horses,
Weapons, noose, bow and arrow.
My hidden wealth is so vast that I want for nothing.
It is yours should you wish
To happily establish your home here.
I have received you from the pure Yazdan,
And I shall serve you with my heart and soul.
As much as I can, I shall spare you misfortune,
For no one knows the secrets
Of the most awe-inspiring dome of sky
Unless war is declared and one is forced
To infuse and brew venom with its antidote."

Siaavosh, comforted by Piran's speech,
Banishes dark thoughts from his mind.
They sit together to dine,
Siaavosh the son and Piran the father.

Then they set off, laughing in their heart's joy,
And do not stop for anything

Until they reach the town of Gang,[15]
A beautiful and verdant site resembling
The residence of idols from Chin,
Full of color, wealth, and abundance.

32 | Siaavosh Meets With Afraasiyaab

At the news of Siaavosh's glorious approach,
Afraasiyaab eagerly rushes out of his audience hall.

The moment Siaavosh notices him on foot,
He dismounts and runs to him.
They hold each other in a tight embrace,
Kissing each other on the face and head.

Afraasiyaab says, "The wrong
That afflicted the world has been expunged.
War will no longer give birth to grief
Lamb and leopard will drink from the same source.
The world was thrown into conflict by Toor the brave.
Every year the two lands, full of discord,
Kept their distance from peace.
Now, thanks to you, the earth, weary of battle,
Will cease to be flooded with rivers of blood.
Every town in Tooran-Zamin submits to your will.
Every heart is full of love for you.
Everything I have, my heart and soul, belongs to you,
And the leader, Piran, is yours, mind and body.
I will love you like a father.
My face will always be smiling at yours."

Siaavosh summons blessings on Afraasiyaab
And says, "May joy never leave your side!
Thanks be given to the Creator, source of peace and war.
The sight of you, so glorious, so happy,
Has decidedly banished grief from my heart."

The royal leader holds Siaavosh's hand in his.

◇◇◇◇◇◇◇◇◇◇◇◇◇
15 Gang: May be an ancient city on the edge of the Sayhoon River (possibly Syr
Darya).

He takes his seat on the royal throne,
Looks at the prince's face, and says,
"I know no equal to you on earth,
No man with such features,
With such stature, grace, and dignity."

Then he turns to Piran and says,
"Kaavoos is an aging man with little sense
For allowing his son to leave his side,
And with such indifference, a son like Siaavosh,
So tall in stature, so skilled, so brave in courage!
The sight of him astonished me, and ever since,
My heart is mystified by the deeds of the Iranian king.
How can he allow his eyes to wander the world
And fix on anything else but his son?"

Afraasiyaab selects one of his palaces
Stretched in golden cloth from end to end.
In its great hall, a golden throne is placed
Adorned with legs of buffalo heads,
Covered in lush fabrics of Chini brocade.
They summon furnishings and instruments.
Then the king says to Siaavosh that he is
To make use of throne and residence as he desires
And to settle within at his leisure.

When Siaavosh enters the audience hall,
The archway rises to Saturn,
So honored it is by the arrival of this guest.
He climbs and sits on the golden throne,
And his prudent mind reflects on various matters.

The king's table prepared,
Siaavosh is offered a golden seat.
During the meal, the conversation drifts
From one subject to another,
And the company enjoys the young prince.

As they rise from the king's table, they engage in drink.
The brave leaders gather around singers and musicians,
And sit to enjoy wine until darkness covers the earth
And the heads of guests are foggy with drink.

Siaavosh happily returns to his palace.
In his intoxication he no longer lends a thought to Iran.

Afraasiyaab surrenders his heart and soul to Siaavosh,
Without whose presence he finds himself unable to sleep.
That night in the banquet hall, the king hands out orders.
He says to his son Shiddeh, "As soon as Siaavosh rises
At dawn, when the sun peaks out of mountain and hill,
You will gather my relatives and noblemen,
With gifts and slaves, purebreds in golden strappings,
And you will go to Siaavosh's palace,
Where you will discreetly present yourselves."

The army warriors follow the commands,
Offering Siaavosh gifts, gold and jewels worthy
Of a king, addressing him with friendly words.

For his part, Afraasiyaab sends him many presents,
And thus passes one week.

33 | Siaavosh Exhibits Prowess Before Afraasiyaab

One night the king says to Siaavosh,
"Let us stand ready early tomorrow morning.
Let us journey to the arena with mallet and ball.
We shall play there for some time and give in to joy.
I have always heard that, in your field,
Men dare not look at a mallet to challenge you."

Siaavosh replies, "King, may you always live in joy!
May misfortune's hand be kept at bay!
Rulers look to you as the model to accomplish their feats.
Who in the world would succeed in surpassing you?
Your royal grace shines on me day and night.
All good and bad is handed out by you."

Afraasiyaab adds, "O son, may you always be triumphant.
You carry the grace of Homa.[16]

◇◇◇◇◇◇◇◇◇◇◇◇◇
16 Homa: Large, powerful bird in Persian mythology reminiscent of the griffin or the
phoenix, a symbol of happiness.

You are the Kianian crown, the ornament of the throne,
As well as the army's support."

In the morning, joyous warriors gallop,
Prance, and parade to the field.

The Tooranian king says to Siaavosh,
"Let us select our teammates for the game of polo.
You go to one side while I remain on this side.
Let us divide everyone into two teams."

Siaavosh replies, "Why should I seize ball
And mallet to contest against you?
Such a thing is inconceivable.
Find another challenger in the arena.
Should you deem me worthy,
I shall be one of your players on your team."

The king is thrilled by this response.
Everyone else's words are like gusts of wind.
"By the life and the head of Kaavoos," he says,
"You will be my contender and adversary.
Show your skills before these horsemen
So that they do not say I have chosen poorly,
So that our men can applaud you
And my astonished eyes can feast on your game."

Siaavosh replies, "Your wish is my command.
The riders, the arena, and the mallets are yours."

The king then selects Golbaad and Garsivaz,
Jahn and Poolaad, Piran and Nastihan,
Eager for battle, and finally Hoomaan,
Able to make a ball bounce on water.

On Siaavosh's end, he sends teammates Rooeen
And renowned Shiddeh, Andariman, brave rider,
And Arjasp, bold soldier and brave lion.

Siaavosh says to him, "O King, seeker of glory,
Which one of them would dare challenge your ball?
They are your majesty's friends.
I shall be the lone guardian of mallet.

But if the king commands, I shall lead to the arena
Riders from Iran-Zamin, teammates to play the game,
As dictated by the rules of our two lands."

The king listens to this demand and consents.
Siaavosh selects seven Iranian expert players.
The beat of drums resounds on the field.
Dust rises straight to the firmament.
You would think the ground leaps,
So boisterous is the din of timpani and trumpets.

Afraasiyaab hits a ball over the arena into the clouds.
Siaavosh charges his battle horse as the cries
And the shouts of warriors reach the moon.
He does not let the ball touch the dust.
He strikes it the instant it nears the ground
In a way that makes it completely vanish from sight.

Then the powerful king orders a ball be tossed
To the side of Siaavosh, who takes it and kisses it.
The sound of trumpets and timpani escalates to the sky.

Siaavosh mounts a young stallion, pitches the ball
Into the air, and smacks it so hard with his mallet
That the ball catches sight of the moon.
So high it soars that once again it disappears from sight.
You would think that the dome of the sky roped it in.

In the arena, the warriors watch in astonishment,
Aware that they could never match Siaavosh's skills.

For his part, Afraasiyaab beams
At the sight of the ball vanishing.
When his men's expressions relax a bit,
They announce that never have they seen
A man ride on a saddle like the glorious Siaavosh.

The king declares, "This is the way of a man
Dressed with royal power by Yazdan.
I can see that his beauty and behavior,
His talent and glory by far surpass his reputation."

A throne is placed for Afraasiyaab on the field.

Siaavosh climbs on a seat beside the king,
Who rejoices to have the prince in proximity.
He addresses his host with pride and affection:
"To you belong the field, the mallets, and the ball."

The two sides begin to battle, and the dust rises to the sun.
Each group takes its turn to strike the enemy ball with shouts.
The Turks' frustration mounts, for they wish
To win by any means but find it impossible
As the Iranians seize the ball from them.

Siaavosh, troubled, says in the language of Pahlavi,
"Is this a playing field or a battlefield?
Let us, at times, surrender the ball to them."

From this moment on,
The Iranian riders handle the ball gently
And restrain their horses to ride more leisurely.

The Turks toss a ball and dash forward like flames.
The King of Tooran hears their shouts.
He understands why Siaavosh spoke in Pahlavi.
He says, "One of my friends has confirmed to me
Siaavosh has no equal in the art of archery.
No one compares to him in the world
In the power of his chest and shoulders."

Encouraged in this way,
Siaavosh draws a royal bow from its quiver.
The king asks one of his servants to test it.
Astonished, the warrior examines the bow and utters
Blessings upon any man able to handle such weapons.

Then he gives it to Garsivaz, quick to draw his sword,
And says to him, "Rub the back of the bow and bind it."
Garsivaz extends himself to obey but is unable
To make it yield to fix the arrow to it.
Unsuccessful, he feels greatly debased.

Afraasiyaab drops to his knees, takes possession
Of the bow, rubs it, and binds it, all the while smiling.
He says, "What a powerful bow,
Able to fling a shot to the moon.

I, too, when I was young had a similar bow,
But now a time of rest is upon me.
No man in either Iran or Tooran
Dares handle such a weapon on the day of battle,
Only Rostam of elephantine stature,
Eager to fight Ahriman, and Siaavosh,
With his chest, arms, and shoulders."

They affix a target to a wall on the field, and Siaavosh,
Without addressing anyone, sits on his horse like a deev,
Urges his steed into a gallop, and takes off with a cry.
He aims an arrow and sends it straight to the center
Of the target, where all eyes are fixed.

He adjusts a second arrow to his bowstring,
One made of poplar wood and with four fletches.
He pulls back to the anchor point, aims at the mark,
And releases to pierce the target a second time.

Then he leads his steed to the right, flings another arrow,
Striking the mark a third time exactly where he aimed.
So punched with holes is the board
That it resembles a coarse sieve.
Siaavosh loops the bowstring on his right arm,
Approaches the mighty king, and dismounts.

The king rises and says, "Your exploits
Are proof of your skills and your high birth."

From there they go to the king's tall palace,
Full of joy and mutual affection.
They sit. A feast is set up with wine
And musicians worthy to be heard.
They drink much wine, surrendering to revelry
And toasting Siaavosh's health.

The king asks for many gifts to be placed before the table:
A horse with strappings, a throne and crown,
Cloth so beautiful no one has ever seen such luxury,
Dinars, gold and silver coins,
Small and large stones of ruby and turquoise,
A great number of slaves of both sexes,
And a cup full of shiny rubies.

The king commands the gifts be counted
And transported to Siaavosh's palace.
He orders the Tooranians, members of his family,
And those most entrenched in his good graces
To bring jewels and precious dishes to Siaavosh.

Finally, the king turns to his troops and says,
"You are to obey Siaavosh earnestly,
As a member of a herd obeys its shepherd."

34 | Afraasiyaab and Siaavosh Go Hunting

One day the king says to the prince, "Come with me.
We shall hunt, enjoy ourselves by giving in to pleasures.
Let us allow the chase to clear worry from our souls."

Siaavosh replies, "I shall follow your lead,
Wherever your heart desires."

They march one day to the hunting grounds.
The king takes along falcons, cheetahs, and herds
From Tooran and from Iran, and a host eager to hunt.

Siaavosh spots wild deer roaming the plain.
He launches out of the procession's core swift as wind.
He unleashes his horse's reins, urging him at the stirrups
To gallop through mount and valley.

With his sword, he splits one deer in half, weighing
The two pieces as if his hands are two dishes of a scale
And the creature's quarters are silver coins.
Neither half weighs more to him than a grain of barley.

The king's procession stares with eagerness.
The entire gathering exclaims in one voice,
"What a skilled bowman!" To each other they say,
"The land of Iran has sent us trouble.
Our leaders' names will be disgraced.
We are better off contending with this prince."

Siaavosh dashes through plain and mountain,
Making use of sword and arrow, spear and mace.

On all sides, he single-handedly captures
Enough game to feed the entire company.
Then they return to the king's palace, hearts full of joy.

From this time on, Afraasiyaab,
Whether sad or happy, desires no other
Company but that of the skilled Siaavosh.
He no longer confides in
Or shares his joys with Jahn or Garsivaz,
Or with any of his court's noblemen.
Day and night, he only wishes
For Siaavosh as friend and confidant
And only parts his lips to smile in his presence.

In this way, they pass one year
In common joy and sorrow.

35 | Piran Offers His Daughter to Siaavosh to Wed

One day, Siaavosh and Piran sit
To discuss matters great and small.
Piran says to Siaavosh, "Is there anyone in the world
Of your standing and position in this realm?
It is as if you are preparing to exit our lands.
The affection the king holds for you is such
That he murmurs your name at night in his bed.
Know that you are his happy spring,
His idol, and his comfort in challenging times.
You are the glorious son of Kay Kaavoos.
So high are your deeds your head grazes the moon.

"Your father is old; you are young and untested.
Beware that the crown of kings does not elude you.
You are ruler of Iran and Tooran, a skilled and
Courageous royal heir, a reminder of past kings.
We are not witness to any of your blood relations
Making a display of affection for you.
Among the Tooranians, no one is worthy of your love.
You have neither brother nor sister,
Neither friend nor wife.
You rise as a solitary rosebush in a field of grass.

Rest your eyes upon a woman deserving of you.
Forget the suffering you endured in Iran-Zamin.
After Kaavoos's death, the land, the throne,
The crown of noble world heroes: All will be yours.

"Behind the veil in the king's palace
Live three women decked in jewels.
Were the moon to lay eyes on them on its journey,
It would find itself unable to divert its glance.
Three additional ones live in the harem of Garsivaz.
Highborn on the side of both father and mother,
Granddaughters of Fereydoon and daughters of princes,
They are as graceful as owners of crown and throne.

"Furthermore, within the confines of my own home,
I have four young women, and, should you wish,
They will stand before you as your slaves.
Jarireh is the eldest, a moon shining brightly,
Whose beautiful face finds no equal.
If you desire her, she will be your servant."

Siaavosh replies, "I give thanks to you
For considering me as your son.
Among these beauties, Jarireh suits me best,
For an alliance with you is valuable to me.
She will be the delight of my heart and eyes.
I only ask for her among these young women.
With this marriage, you place on my head
A debt that I will never be able to return."

Piran leaves Siaavosh, speeds to his wife Golshahr,
And says to her, "Prepare Jarireh's bedchamber
In honor of the highborn and illustrious Siaavosh."

Golshahr asks, "O glorious man,
Tell me, what is the reason for such joy?"

Piran replies, "How can we not rejoice today?
The grandson of Kay Ghobaad is to be our son-in-law."

Golshahr summons her daughter.
She places a diadem on her head,
Adorns her like gay spring with brocade and gilt,

Gold and silver, color and scent, and, thus arranged
Like spring, she ushers her at night to the prince.

Piran performs the marital rites,
Sending her to her radiant seat next to Siaavosh.
She gleams like the new moon on her throne,
Inlaid with gold and precious stones.
Such is the wealth no one can estimate its worth.

Before Jarireh's stature and features,
Siaavosh, most pleased, smiles with delight.
He spends day and night in bliss at her side,
The memory of Kaavoos banished from his heart.

In this way turns the revolving dome for some time.
The union serves to bolster Siaavosh's standing,
Making Afraasiyaab shower him
With more and more deference and honor.

36 | Piran Speaks to Siaavosh on the Subject of Faranguis

One day, the cautious Piran says to Siaavosh,
"O noble one, you know that the Tooranian ruler
Raises his crown above the dome of sky.
Night and day, you are his soul's joy,
His heart and strength, his mind and his power.
Once you are bound to him by blood,
You will continue to rise in esteem and majesty.
Although you are my daughter's spouse,
I fret over all matters that concern you.
Although Jarireh is your wife,
Selected from among this court's women,
It would be advantageous for you
To single out a gem from the kingly robe's hem.

"Faranguis is the favorite of the royal daughters.
Nowhere on earth will you find a moon-face like hers.
Her stature is more svelte than a cypress tree,
And her head holds a crown of black musk.
Her virtues and wisdom are incomparable.

114

She commands intelligence like one commands a slave.
There is no one more meritorious of uniting with you.
If you ask the king for her hand,
He will offer you this woman who has
No equal in either Kashmir or Kabol.
With Afraasiyaab as your kin and ally,
Your glory and value will shine brighter.
If you allow me, I shall ask the king for you,
And my esteem in his eyes will increase."

Siaavosh glances over at Piran and says to him,
"One must not repudiate Yazdan's command.
If my fate dictates so, I shall surrender,
For no one knows the secrets of the firmament.
Jarireh is the air I breathe, I wish for no other mate.
I do not seek the acquisition of name or fame.
I do not long for sun or shining helmet.
Let us concede for good and bad
That I wish for no other."

Piran says, "Do not concern yourself.
I will prepare Jarireh to approve of this matter.
Although it will be to my family's detriment,
I only aspire to advance your cause."

Siaavosh says, "O wise old man,
If I must be forced into this affair, do as you see fit.
The revolving dome works at your will.
If I am not meant to return to Iran-Zamin,
If I am to never see Kay Kaavoos again,
Zaal who raised me, or Rostam whom I deem
A jolly spring, Bahram or Zangueh of Shaavaran,
Or any of the heroes, if I must resign myself
To never set eyes again on any of them,
If I establish my residence in the land of Tooran,
Then may you play the role of my father.
Prepare this marriage,
But do keep the affair confidential."

As he speaks, his lashes flood with tears
And a sigh escapes his chest.

Piran says, "The wise man accepts his fate.

You cannot rise above the spinning spheres,
For they affect sleep, battle, and love.
If you had friends in the land of Iran,
You left them under Yazdan's protection.
Your residence is here now,
Your banner is firmly planted here.
Besides, someone else is in possession
Of the throne of Iran."

37 | Piran Confers With Afraasiyaab

Immediately Piran is on his feet
And, joyful, takes the direction of the king's palace.

As he dismounts, the crowd parts to let him pass.
He remains standing before the king for some time.

Afraasiyaab speaks to him with kindness.
"Why do you stand thus before my seat?
What do you desire, what is your goal?
My army, my gold, and treasury are yours.
Your deeds further advance my realm and dominion.
If my holding someone in chains whose freedom
Endangers me goes against your wishes,
I am willing to forgive him this very instant
And set him free, for my anger dissipates like wind
In favor of the affection I bear for you.
Whether great or small, anything you wish,
Of sword or seal, throne or crown, is yours."

The wise Piran replies,
"May the world never be deprived of your presence!
I do not come to you for my own gain and glorification.
None of your noblemen want for anything.
Thanks to your kindness and your high fortune,
I have wealth, army, treasure, sword, crown, and throne.
It is in behalf of Siaavosh that I come,
To relay a secret message into the brave leader's ear.
He said:
        'Tell the Tooranian king that I am happy,
        And I wish to expand my glory.

116

He raised me on his knees like a father
And brought me happiness in times of sorrow.
May he now arrange an alliance for me,
For in good or bad fortune, I need him by my side.
You hold, behind the veil,
A daughter worthy of my palace and throne,
A daughter named Faranguis by her mother.
Nothing would make me happier
Than if you found me to be a suitable
And commendable husband for her.'"

Unease settles within Afraasiyaab, and, tearful,
He replies, "Long ago I spoke of this,
But you were of a different opinion.
Yet a wise man of cautious heart
And elevated mind said,
    'You, who raise the young of a wild lion,
    Why do you tire yourself with this hopeless cause?
    You take great pains, giving courage and skills to him,
    But you will cease to bear fruit once his tree blossoms.
    As soon as he is old enough to wage war,
    He will clutch in his claws
    The head of the one who raised him.'

"Then, aged astrologers, skilled in their arts,
Consulted their astrolabes in accordance with rules,
Confessed the same thing, point by point,
And predicted before my father
Astonishing facts regarding my grandson.
They declared that from the lineage of Toor
And Kay Ghobaad will spring a king full of justice,
A grandson who will act in ways
That will instill in me a deep sense of bewilderment.
They told me that he will destroy everything:
My crown and treasury, my army, land, and throne,
That nowhere on earth will I find shelter.
Nowhere will there be a path of escape for me.
He will seize my kingdoms, one after the other,
And he will burden me with misfortunes.

"I tend to believe in the forecast of these sages,
And on the secret designs of the revolving sky.

117

This couple will bear a son who will seize the world,
Who will destroy Tooran-Zamin by usurping my throne.
Why should I then plant, of my own volition,
A tree that will surely bear poisonous fruits?
Why should I allow venom to run through its roots?
Mixing the lineages of Kaavoos and Afraasiyaab
Is like mixing an ardent flame with ocean waves.
I know not if this child will gaze at us
With good intentions, nor do I know
If he will turn a kinder face toward Iran.
Why should we force ourselves to ingest poison?
Why should we expose ourselves to the serpent's breath?
I shall treat him well, as a brother, as long as he remains.
And when he decides to return to Iran,
I shall equip him for the voyage in a magnificent way.
I shall send him to his father in amity, as wishes Yazdan."

Piran replies, "Your majesty, free your heart from worry.
Do not listen to the words of sages and astrologers.
Confer with reason and consent to Siaavosh's request.
A child from Siaavosh will grow up
Cautious, kind, wise, and discreet.
These two noble crown-bearers will bring forth
A king who will scrape the sun with his head.
He will be master of both Iran and Tooran,
Put an end to conflict between the two lands.
The race of Fereydoon and Kay Ghobaad
Will never see a more splendid offspring.
Even if the secret sky had another design,
Your concerns will not make it more favorable.
What is meant to happen will happen, no matter what,
And your qualms will not curtail what is predestined.
Believe that this alliance will bring you greater glory,
And fortune will grant you your heart's desires."

The king says to Piran,
"Your advice cannot bring misfortune.
I submit to your counsel.
Go make preparations in line with tradition."

Piran bows low, honors the king,
Extols him with praise.

He then returns to the side of Siaavosh,
Where he recounts all that happened.
The two remain seated all night, rejoicing
And alleviating their hearts' burdens in wine.

38 | The Engagement of Faranguis and Siaavosh

As the revolving dome exhibits the sun,
Holding it before its face like a golden shield,
Army leader Piran mounts his horse of speed.
He gallops to Siaavosh's palace and showers him
With a stream of blessings in praise of his glory:
"Be ready today to receive the king's daughter.
Should you allow, I shall put together an escort
Worthy of her place and stature."

Siaavosh's heart fills with reticence,
And his cheeks blush with modesty before Piran,
His father-in-law who holds him close in affection
And treats him as if of his own flesh and blood.
Siaavosh replies, "Go and prepare things as you wish.
You know that I keep no secrets from you."

Piran returns to his palace,
His heart and soul unwavering on this matter.
The hero hands over to his wife Golshahr,
A woman celebrated far and wide,
Gifted with a sharp mind, the key to a room
Holding abundant luxurious fabrics.
They select from their most valued objects:
One thousand cloths woven in gold Chinese thread;
Dishes inlaid with emerald,
Turquoise cups full of pure aloe, pouches of musk;
Two crowns worthy of a king,
Ornate with precious gems; two bracelets,
Two earrings, and one enameled gold chain;
Sixty camels loaded with carpets;
Three wardrobes stitched with golden thread,
With patterns of gold and red embroidery,
And with all sorts of precious stones.

Thirty camels are loaded with gold and silver crockery,
Ten massive trays from the land of Pars,
A golden throne, four lavish seats, and
Three pairs of golden shoes trimmed in emerald.
They add two hundred slaves holding golden cups.
The palace could barely contain all of this.
Still more, three hundred male slaves
With golden headdress,
Nearly one hundred princes related to Piran,
One hundred plates of saffron, one hundred of musk.

Golshahr and her sisters depart in golden litters,
Enveloped in brocade covers and trailed by gift bearers
Who carry one hundred thousand golden coins.
The lot is transported to Faranguis
As everyone utters countless blessings.

Golshahr kisses the ground and says,
"The morning star is now the sun's companion."
Then Piran and Afraasiyaab, in respect for Siaavosh,
Quickly perform engagement rites for Faranguis
In accordance with their customs and ways.

They serve as witnesses to the ceremony,
And, having drawn up the contract and concluded
The wedding, Piran sends an envoy to Golshahr
Flying swift as dust and orders her
To lead Faranguis quickly toward Siaavosh.

Golshahr obeys with joy and tells Faranguis
To meet the young prince on that night
So that the moon may become his palace ornament.

Faranguis is immediately adorned in hair of musk,
Tresses braided to tumble down her rosy cheeks.
Then she presents herself, like the new moon,
Before the young prince worthy of crown.

At the sight of Faranguis' cypress stature, her grace,
Her two black tresses framing her moon-like face,
Her two eyes like stars at the break of day,
Her mouth full of pearls, her lips like agate,
You would think Venus is her companion.

Her words spill out like jewels.
Her character is that of a fairy.
She exudes the fragrance of amber.
Her heart is compassionate and her body loving.
Nothing about her is unappealing.
You would think she is a fairy from paradise.

They remain together, enjoying their happiness.
Siaavosh, the sun, united with Faranguis, the moon.
How splendid when sun and moon join together,
Their love growing from moment to moment.

For seven days, neither bird nor fish can sleep.
No man succumbs to rest as the festivities
And sounds of music convert the earth
Into a garden from end to end.

39 | Afraasiyaab Gives a Province to Siaavosh

Seven days pass in this manner.
Afraasiyaab assembles many gifts:
Taazian horses, herds, armor and helms,
Lasso, sword and mace, gold and silver coins,
Robes and various articles of clothing.

Then he orders a list be drawn up of cities and lands
Between his residence province to the Sea of Chin,
Covering nations more than one hundred farsangs long
And their widths beyond gauge.
In royal fashion, Afraasiyaab sends to Siaavosh
An investiture written on silk of the wide territory.
Along with it are a throne and a golden crown.

Then he orders the square bedecked for feast.
Anyone coming upon this field, from near or far,
Would encounter cooks, wine, and spreads.
Everyone is welcome to enjoy to their heart's desire
And to take away to their home
As much food as they can manage to carry.

In this way, Afraasiyaab celebrates his guests.

He opens his prison doors for seven days,
Making the world happy and living in joy himself.

On the eighth day, at the crack of dawn,
Siaavosh goes to the palace with world hero Piran.
He wishes to ask permission to take his leave
And retreat to his residence.

The two men praise the shah:
"O glorious world King, may your days be happy!
May your enemies' backs stoop!
May your body remain healthy as long as life endures!
May the world stand behind you as your slave!
No king exists of your stature,
And nothing will remain when you are gone."

Piran and Siaavosh happily take the road,
Discussing the king and royal matters.

The revolving dome rotates another year,
Watching over Siaavosh with love and justice.
Then a friend comes to him, sent by Afraasiyaab,
With a message: "The king addresses you and says,
          'Illustrious ruler, do you not miss me?
          Does your place of residence please you well enough?
          I have given you lands that stretch from here to Chin.
          Go on tour and survey these nations.
          Select a town in which to take up residence,
          One where you may find peace,
          A town that pleases you and satisfies your desires.
          Remain there in joy and pleasure,
          And never allow your heart to cast aside happiness.'"

Siaavosh celebrates these words.
He bids trumpets and timpani be played.
He takes with him armor, gem, and golden crown,
Loading luggage and a great number of litters
With adorned beauties to hide behind curtains.
He sits Faranguis with her belongings,
And they depart with Piran and Siaavosh at the lead.

PART EIGHT

They travel together gaily until they reach Khotan,[17]
Where they rest in amity, as it is under the rule of Piran.

Siaavosh remains Piran's guest for one month.
Not one day passes when he does not attend a feast,
Drinking wine, listening to music,
Or participating in a hunt.

At the start of the month, drums echo the rooster's call.
Siaavosh departs in the direction of his kingdom
Preceded by Piran and trailed by his army.

When the inhabitants of the border are summoned,
The noblemen rise in their heart's joy
And march off to greet the son of the King of Kings.
People prepare feasts as custom calls.

At that time, a noise is heard in the kingdom,
As if the earth and sky have entwined.
Sounds of voices, lutes, and flutes bring joy to hearts.

They come upon a beautiful, fortunate site.
On one side is the sea, on the other mountains.
There are hunting preserves, far from dwellings.
The air is balmy, the earth verdant and lush,
With a scattering of vibrant flowers,
Like the hindquarters of a leopard.
Populated with lush trees, it is a site
That runs with lively springs of pure water,
Where the hearts of old men grow young again.

Siaavosh says to Piran, "Here is a fine land.
I shall establish here a magnificent city,
Holding within it many palaces and many gardens.
I shall build a lofty castle to graze the moon,
One worthy of the master of throne and crown."

Piran replies, "O kind and compassionate prince,
Should you allow, I shall build right here, at the site
Where your thoughts linger, a palace tall as the moon.
I do not wish to own land or treasure.

◇◇◇◇◇◇◇◇◇◇◇◇◇
17 Khotan: Town on the southern side of the Silk Road between China and the west.

Because of you, the entire world is irrelevant to me."

Siaavosh says to him, "O fortunate man,
You will plant a tree that will bear fruit.
I owe to you my treasure and my fortune.
What touches me most is the trouble you expend for me.
I shall build myself a city right here
That will be the astonishment of men."

Siaavosh and Piran spend some time
Enjoying their stay in these lovely parts.

40 | Siaavosh Builds Gang-Dej

I shall now open history's gates to our ancestor's
Traditions and tell a story that will leave you,
For some time, in a state of wonderment.
Listen now as I speak of the fortress of Siaavosh,
As I describe this city and report ageless tales.

Glory to the Creator of both the revealed and
The concealed, Master of being and non-being.
Glory to the Creator, who is One, unique and
Inimitable, while every other creation exists in pairs.

Glory to the prophet and to each of his followers.
Everyone departs one day, and you will too,
Since the world witnessed their departure.
Where are the kings, bearers of crown?
Where is the throne of the King of Kings?
Where are the brave men full of heart and nobility
Who executed the mightiest feats?
Where are the sages, wise men, untiring examiners?
Where are the idols full of grace and modesty,
With their kind words and tender voices?
Where are the oppressed who sought refuge
In mountains, deprived of rest, joy, and glory?
Where is he, the hero who raised his head
Above clouds in order to capture his prey?

In the end, they have all laid their heads to rest

On a pillow of dust and a brick of earth.
Fortunate is the one who sows righteous seeds.
We come from dust and to dust we return.
Fear of death is at the source of our troubles.
The world presents to us a lesson on life,
But we remain unaware and refuse to learn.
After searching for sixty-six years for a place of rest,
Your forehead wrinkled from hard labor and pain,
You spread across the world the hand of ambition,
Yet most of your companions have preceded you,
And you shall not remain as their confidant.
You will depart as well
While the world will remain for a long time yet.
You will never become aware of its mysteries.
You came into the world to accumulate wealth,
And as you were doing so,
You witnessed many of your friends pass away.

Listen then to a story drawn from an ancient book
About illustrious men of yore.
In light of their departure, why would you want
To place upon your head the crown of ambition?
They are the ones who made the world flourish
At a time when justice reigned supreme.

Although you may not agree with me on these matters,
I still wish to tell you a story from long ago.
Since the world emptied of so many noblemen,
Why continue to seek excessive power and wealth?
Once justice ruled the world,
And the flow of life ran peaceful and abundant.
Of their treasure, castles, and crowns,
What did they take with them?

I wish to recount the tale of Gang-Dej.
Lend your kind ear; listen to me attentively.
There is no place on earth of equal beauty,
No land to delight the heart so.

Siaavosh built this town, enduring in its labor
The harshest strain and the greatest fatigues.

Once you travel for the duration of one month

Beyond the Sea of Chin, you will see a large dry plain.
You will cross both desert and sea.
You will encounter a vast and expansive field.
Beyond it you will find a land
Within which are all sorts of delightful things.
There you will face a lofty mountain,
Its crest higher than anything you have ever seen.
Halfway up, in the middle, is Gang-Dej.
With this story, learn and remember
To always expand your knowledge.

This fort is safe and protected,
With one hundred farsangs of highland surrounding it.
So elevated is it that you cannot distinguish its crest.
No matter where you turn, around and around,
You will not find a path or a way in.

Around the fort is a basin measuring thirty-three
Farsangs in diameter and surrounded on all sides
By a rampart of heavy rock boulders.
If we were to place five men to defend it,
Not even one hundred thousand enemy troops,
Armed in coats of mail and mounted on dressed horses,
Would succeed in passing through to invade.

Once you bypass this wall of rock,
You will discern a great city with abundant flower beds,
With luscious parks, and bright homes and palaces,
With hot springs as well as freshwater springs.

In every dwelling, you will find song,
Music, scent, and color.
The mountain is populated with wild beasts
And the plain with doe and buck.
Once you discover this paradise,
You will never want to leave.

In the mountain dwell peacock, partridge and pheasant.
The summers are balmy, and the winters are fair.
Everywhere one finds amusement, feast, and rest.
No one is ever afflicted with disease.
All in all, it is a veritable garden in paradise.

The waters running through are limpid and clear,
The fields are dressed in eternal spring.
To measure this space in Persian farsang,
You would calculate thirty in length and width,
And one and a half farsang in height.
So steep is the incline that no man dares venture up.
On the other side, a valley extends far and wide,
Like no other in verdure and vibrancy.

Siaavosh sets foot on this place
And prefers it over the other sites in Tooran-Zamin.
The glorious hero assigns his own name to it
And crowns the surrounding rocks with a wall
Built of marble, stone, plaster, and a certain material
Bearing a name outside the limits of human knowledge.

The height of this wall is more than one hundred arrash,[18]
Its thickness over thirty-five.
One must indeed grasp it with one's own eyes
To truly understand the degree of its inaccessibility.
Neither catapult nor arrow can pierce through,
Neither could they make a dent.
If one speaks of it to someone who has not seen it,
He may not comprehend its scope.
He may grow incensed with the speaker
And his excessive use of superlatives.

There are two farsangs from the rampart's top
To the foot of the boulders.
A moat encircles the mountain.
The eye may not wander beyond its crest,
A crest so high no bird dares fly above.

Siaavosh undertakes much labor on this beautiful site
Where he establishes his power, throne, and crown.
He erects houses, builds a city with palaces and fields.
He plants innumerable trees, rendering it a place
Akin to paradise, with roses,
Hyacinths, narcissus, and tulips.

◇◇◇◇◇◇◇◇◇◇◇◇◇◇
18 Arrash: Unit of measure corresponding to the length of the forearm, from fingertip to elbow.

Siaavosh thinks and reflects at length
As they make their way back from this verdant land.

41 | Siaavosh Speaks to Piran of Various Matters

Siaavosh and Piran, the warrior of the family of Viseh,
Travel to a land so beautiful that the mere sight of it
Is enough to renew one with youth again.
A happy, joyful, verdant place
With abundant wealth, it is a place with palaces,
Worthy of kings and noblemen.

Siaavosh questions the astrologers on his future,
"I have founded here a beautiful city.
Will it contribute to my power and happiness,
Or will it be the cause of deep regret?"

To the world king they respond,
"This foundation does not promise happiness."

Siaavosh grows impatient with the sages,
His heart pained, his eyes filling with burning tears.
He holds his horse's reins limply in his hands.

Piran says to him, "O King, what preoccupies you?"

Siaavosh replies,
"The rotation of the sublime sky troubles my soul.
No matter what treasures I accumulate,
No matter how I multiply decorated palaces,
In the end, it will fall into enemy hands,
To be trampled beneath their feet.
Misfortune upon misfortune will befall me.
There is no place on earth like Gang-Dej,
No city that enraptures the heart so.
Divine grace has been my support,
Caution and fate have watched over me
So that I may build this large city,
Its towers' crests rising to the Pleiades.

"I am now occupied with this city,

Shaping it, embellishing it in all sorts of ways.
Once it is complete, bright and beautiful,
Once it is filled with palaces, treasures,
And precious things, I shall not enjoy it for long
And another will seize my seat.
Neither I nor my children, nor a noble hero
From my kin, will enjoy the fruits of my labors.
I shall not be granted a long life.
Soon I shall need neither palace nor audience hall.
My throne will be the seat of Afraasiyaab.
Death will rush to devour me in my innocence.
Such is the secret of the glorious dome of sky,
One moment showering us with kindness,
Another throwing us into the woes of despair."

Piran replies, "O King, hold your head high.
Do not linger foolishly on these dark thoughts.
Afraasiyaab is your support in times of misfortune,
And you wear the royal seal on your finger.
As long as life flows through my being,
I shall do all in my power not to break our alliance.
I shall not allow a single breeze to pass through you
Or a gust of wind to count the hair on your head."

Siaavosh says, "My only wish is to share your glory.
I entrust you with all my secrets,
For you are a man of saintly body and shrewd spirit.
I shall share the decrees of Yazdan, the illustrious,
As well as the mysteries I have learned from the heavens.
I shall reveal to you the future accurately
The moment I am out of this palace and gardens.
I speak of this now so that later,
When the events unfold, you may not say,
        'How could Siaavosh have ignored his destiny?'
Wise and prudent Piran, lend your ear to my words.
Not much time will pass before the evil, suspicious king
Will send me, despite my innocence, to a cruel death
And another will seize my crown and throne.
Though you will stay loyal to me and take the proper path,
The sky has decided contrary to your desire.
Expressions of slander, as well as my poor fortune,
Will bring upon my innocuous head sadness and adversity.

"As soon as the word spreads to Iran-Zamin, someone
Will come to Tooran and discover the cause of death.
Iran and Tooran will be turned upside down,
And vengeance will be so deep
That life will become a burden for men.
The earth from end to end will fill with gloom,
And the sword of hatred will reign upon the world.
On their way from Iran to the land of Tooran,
You will witness many banners
Yellow, red, black and purple.
A vast destruction will ensue,
The looting of all that is precious
And the clearing of all amassed treasures.

"Great will be the number of lands
To be trampled beneath the horses' hooves,
Lands where the rivers' waters will be disturbed.
The King of Tooran will regret his words and deeds.
But this repentance will not benefit him, for the entire
Inhabited earth will be lost to smoke and devastation.
Cries will rise from Iran and Tooran,
And my blood will send trouble amidst men.

"The Creator's command was written in the firmament,
And divine seeds bear fruit from divine will.
Come let us happily go and generously give,
And when the time of death arrives,
We shall surrender and die.
Why should we tie our hearts to this passing sojourn?
Why should you attach yourself to treasures?
Why resign yourself to the hardship of acquiring?
After us, another man will enjoy these things, and
Why should a wise man tire himself
To empower his mortal enemy?"

Piran listens to him and grows increasingly troubled.
His heart fills with pain at his words.
He thinks, "I have myself attracted this misfortune.
If what he says is true, I shall be responsible
For the destruction of Tooran-Zamin.
I have spread across the world the seed of vengeance,
For it is under my care that he came here.

I gave him land, treasure, and crown,
Although I heard the words of Afraasiyaab,
Who repeatedly predicted a similar consequence."

Then, with tenderness, he further reflects,
"What does he know of the actions of the heavens?
Who enlightened him as to its secrets?
These thoughts came to him because he remembered
A happier time, Iran, Kaavoos and the royal throne.
He must remove them from his memory,
Act like a man of sense."
In this way, Piran pacifies his heart.

They engage in conversation for the rest of the travels,
Their minds preoccupied with thoughts of the future.
Only when they dismount do they cease to speak.
They ask for a spread to be provided,
And they enjoy the night with wine, music, and song.

42 | Afraasiyaab Sends Piran to Various Lands

They give into pleasure and feast for seven days,
Drinking to the health of world kings.

On the eighth day, a letter arrives from Afraasiyaab
Addressed to the leader of the Tooranian army:
"Depart and travel toward the Sea of Chin.
With a host of bold warriors, march to the border of India
And all the way to the Sea of Sindh.
In every land, ask for the tribute due us,
Then deploy your troops to the edge of Khazar."[19]

The leader exits his pavilion.
A roaring sound reverberates through the hall.
The land shakes with the beating of timpani and drums.
From every side, troops approach Piran,
Forming a vast host, eager for battle.

Having thus mobilized Tooranian troops

◇◇◇◇◇◇◇◇◇◇◇◇◇
19 Khazar: Caspian.

Around his palace, Piran prepares to depart
For the lands mentioned by the king.
He offers Siaavosh many precious objects,
Including silver and stallions in strappings.
Then he takes his leave, withdrawing with his host,
Just as Afraasiyaab has commanded.

43 | Siaavosh Builds Siaavosh-Guerd

One night an envoy arrives sent by Afraasiyaab,
Riding a dromedary, a flame in the dark of night.
He brings a letter to Siaavosh, full of affection,
A letter as light and clear as sky, in which the king says,
"Since you have left, I feel no joy,
And sorrow never leaves my side.
Still, I have found a suitable residence
For you in the land of Tooran-Zamin.
Although your dwelling now is charming
And your soul is sheltered from worry,
I bid you to travel to the land I am offering you
And to fling into the dust our enemies' heads."

Siaavosh makes provision as the king commanded
And departs in haste leading one thousand camels
Of reddish fur, loaded with his precious belongings.
One hundred mules bear silver coins,
And forty more with golden coins.
Ten thousand Iranian and Tooranian warriors
Are selected as escort, ready to strike with sword.
This procession is preceded by the king's treasury
And by litters sheltering exquisitely decked women,
With rubies and turquoise worthy of a king,
Gem-encrusted crowns, amber and sandalwood,
Musk and other perfumes, and, finally,
Bolts of brocade and silk from Egypt, Pars, and Chin.

The leader and his glorious convoy
Take the direction of a land fair as spring.
Once in view, Siaavosh points to a site and asks for
A location measuring two farsangs in width and length.

He builds a city with lofty palaces and blooming gardens.
He covers his audience halls with paintings and drawings
Representing kings, battle scenes, and feasts.
Above the throne is a relief of Kay Kaavoos
With crown, seat, bracelet, and mace.
Close by is a representation of Rostam, the brave,
And one each of Zaal, Goodarz, and the world heroes.

On the other side is a painting of Afraasiyaab
With his warriors Piran and Garsivaz, the vengeful.
Throughout Iran and Tooran, men praise this city
Where, from every angle, one discerns
Domes rising to the clouds.
Everywhere are singers and musicians,
Princes and noblemen.

This city is given the name of Siaavosh-Guerd,
And everyone rejoices in his heart.

44 | Piran Visits Siaavosh-Guerd

Upon his return from India and Chin,
Piran hears about the noble city of Siaavosh-Guerd.
A city founded during the auspicious day of Ard,[20]
Its fame has spread throughout Tooran-Zamin.

Every mouth recounts tales of the city,
Its palaces and domes, its gardens and parks,
Its mountains and springs, its valleys and fields.
Piran grows impatient to see what the young ruler
Has accomplished in this beautiful land.

Once the time arrives for him to depart,
Piran takes along his companions,
Men of rank able to participate in feast,
One thousand riders, valiant and vigilant.

As Piran approaches the city, Siaavosh takes
The road with an escort to greet him.

◇◇◇◇◇◇◇◇◇◇◇◇◇
20 Ard: The 29th day of any month is the day of Ard in ancient Iran.

Piran immediately dismounts at the sight of him,
And Siaavosh climbs down from his blue-gray horse.

Siaavosh and Piran fall into a tight embrace.
Then, together, they tour the city from end to end.
Piran finds this place, once a barren desert, charming.
Homes, palaces, and gardens shine like radiant lamps.

The leader visits all the sights and praises Siaavosh.
He says to him, "Had you not been gifted
With power, wisdom, knowledge, and royal majesty,
You would not have found this site to build
The most beautiful city the world has ever seen.
May brave men surround your banner
Until the day of Resurrection!
May your sons, from generation to generation,
Remain in a state of happiness and, like you,
Be world masters, virtuous and victorious!"

After wandering through a part of the city,
Piran enters Siaavosh's palace and gardens.
There, filled with joy and high spirits,
He walks into Faranguis' chambers.

The daughter of Afraasiyaab meets him,
Addresses him with the customary salutations,
And scatters gold coins over him.
Jarireh, sun-like daughter, tall as a cypress tree,
With musk-scented hair, approaches her father.

Piran sits on the throne and sees
A multitude of servants standing before him.
Once again he glorifies Siaavosh
And prays to the Creator, asking for acts of grace.

A feast is prepared with wine and delectable fare,
Singers and musicians. They remain for seven days,
Cup in hand, at times merry, at times inebriated.

On the eighth day, Piran asks that presents be brought,
Offerings worthy of a king, suitable for Siaavosh:
Rubies and jewels fit for a royal,
Brocade, and an ivory crown inlaid with gems,

PART EIGHT

Dinars and stallions, a saddle of poplar wood,
Golden straps, and a cover of leopard skin.

Piran gives Faranguis a diadem and earrings,
Necklaces and bracelets set with precious stones.
Then he departs for Khotan
With a procession of famous heroes.

Happily he travels to his palace,
Steps into his chambers, and says to Golshahr,
"Anyone who has not seen the verdant site
And does not know what the guardian
Of paradise, Rezvan, has planted there
Must instantly visit this splendid city,
Where palace and throne appear
Greater than a magnificent paradise.
They must see Siaavosh, shining like the sun,
Sitting on his seat of power,
Resembling Sooroosh[21] in glory and prudence.
They must travel happily to Siaavosh-Guerd
Where the ruler is so bright it is as if he rises
Like the shining sun from the east.
The lovely Faranguis is at the side of the sun,
Akin to a two-week moon in rank and posture."

Piran takes the direction of Afraasiyaab's court,
Traveling swiftly, like a boat gliding on water.
Once there, he gives the ruler
An account of all that he has accomplished,
Handing over to him the tribute from the provinces.
He tells him about the battles in India and how
He buried the heads of evil men in the dust.
Then he speaks on the subject of Siaavosh
As the king asks about his efforts and exploits,
His new city, his crown, his throne, and his palace.

Piran says, "Anyone who has set eyes
On this joyful city in the month of Ordibehesht[22]
Cannot distinguish it from paradise, nor

◇◇◇◇◇◇◇◇◇◇◇◇◇
21 Sooroosh: Archangel able to hear and relay divine messages.
22 Ordibehesht: Second month of the solar calendar and of spring, corresponding to
April, a time of spring blossoms.

135

Can he distinguish the noble prince from the sun.
There exists no such city in Tooran or in Chin.
So numerous are the citadels, gardens, and running
Springs that you would think to create them
Siaavosh's soul made use of all the world's wisdom,
Transmitted to him in secret messages from Sooroosh.

"When you walk through its halls, fountains,
And verdant grounds, it feels as if
Your wisdom is in communion with your spirit.
From a distance, Faranguis' palace is a mass of jewels,
Shining luminescent like a bright light.
Not even Sooroosh, descending from the heavens,
Would be on equal footing to your daughter's mate
In majesty, glory and foresight, in grace and dignity.
There is nothing to complain about,
Nothing more to want from the universe.
Siaavosh, with his beauty and his faith,
Is as compassionate as your joyous heart wishes.
Besides, the two battling lands now enjoy peace,
Just like a foolish man at once reclaims sanity.
May the hearts of sensible men
And the desire of great ones
Remain thus inclined forevermore."

The king is thrilled by these words,
For he sees that his fecund offshoot is bearing fruit.

45 | Afraasiyaab Sends Garsivaz to Siaavosh

Afraasiyaab gives the news to his brother,
Revealing what Piran shared with him in secret.
The leader says to Garsivaz,
"Go happily to Siaavosh-Guerd,
Observe all that he has done and report back to me.
Siaavosh has placed his heart on Tooran-Zamin
And retains no memory of Iran-Zamin.
He has renounced the throne and crown,
As well as Goodarz, Bahraam, and King Kaavoos.
He no longer wishes to see Rostam, son of Zaal,
No longer reaches for his spear and iron mace.

He has turned a field of weeds
Into a town resembling joyous spring.
He has raised tall palaces for Faranguis
And treats her with utmost affection and respect.

"Rise and go make preparations for your trip.
Present yourself before the noble Siaavosh.
Observe his crown and turquoise throne.
Speak respectfully with words of friendship.
You will defer to his greatness and power,
Whether at hunt or in banquet,
Whether on plain or on mountain.
And when the crowd of Iranians is before you,
You will show admiration to him and to his brave men.
Lavish him with praise and celebrate his glory.

"Gather innumerable gifts: dinars and precious stones,
Horses, golden belts, crowns and thrones of brocade,
Diadem, mace, seal and blade, gold, emerald, and jewels.
Take carpets from your treasury
And any other object of beauty, scent, and color.
Furthermore, take many presents to Faranguis,
And once there, may your tongue be full of blessings.
If your host receives you with honor,
Remain joyously as his guest for two weeks."

The renowned Garsivaz sets his sight
On one thousand Tooranian riders.
He gathers this glorious host and swiftly
Departs toward the city of Siaavosh-Guerd.

When Siaavosh hears the news of his approach,
He instantly sets off toward him with a procession.
The two come face to face, embrace,
And Siaavosh asks Garsivaz for news of the king.
They march to the palace, where Siaavosh calls
For quarters to be prepared for the Tooranian troops.

The next day, early in the morning,
Garsivaz presents the gifts
And relates the message from the king.
Siaavosh blushes like a spring rose.
He climbs upon his horse of speed,

And the Iranian riders gather around him.
He shows Garsivaz the city, street by street,
And from there they enter the palace.

46 | The Birth of Foorood, Son of Siaavosh

At this moment, a cavalier, swift as wind,
Rushes to Siaavosh with good news:
"The daughter of the Tooranian hero has given birth
To a child beautiful as the moon.
This noble child has been named Foorood.
Piran heard the news in the middle of the night.
He ordered me to rush to you with an escort,
O prince, and share with you the happy news.
Jarireh, the greatest Queen of Queens
And blessed mother of this glorious child,
Ordered her slaves, from her bed,
To dip the baby's hand in saffron.
The imprint was then applied to the back of this letter,
And Piran said,
        'Take it to Siaavosh, for his wishes are granted.
        Tell him that, despite my old age,
        Pure divine grace has rendered me ecstatic.'"

Siaavosh replies, "May this child
Never be deprived of the throne of power!"
He gives the messenger so many coins of silver
That the bearer of the load soon tires from its weight.

When word of the birth reaches Garsivaz,
He exclaims, "Piran is today equal to the king!"
Happily they draw near palace of Faranguis,
To whom Siaavosh recounts the good news.

Garsivaz observes Faranguis seated on the ivory throne,
Head covered in a turquoise crown, moon-faced slaves,
Adorned with golden diadems, standing before her.
Faranguis is overjoyed at the sight of her uncle.
She climbs down from her throne and greets him,
Scattering coins over his head and asking after the king
And after the fatigues of his long voyage.

The heart and head of Garsivaz boil with rage,
But he conceals his anger with courtesy and prudence.
He tells his heart, "Not a year will pass before Siaavosh
Will refuse to spare a single person to whom
Belongs royalty and throne, treasury, land, and host."

In his attempts to suppress his soul's secret,
He shakes with anger and his cheeks grow pale.
He says to Siaavosh, "You enjoy the fruits of your labor,
And your heart cheers at the sight of your treasure."

Two golden thrones are placed in the palace,
And the two sit, full of joy and happiness.
Music and song are played before the thrones
Inlaid in precious stones, and the sound of harps,
Flutes, and song delights Garsivaz's heart
And helps him to lose sight of his anger.

47 | Siaavosh Plays Polo

As the shining sun reveals itself
By presenting its face to the world from above,
Siaavosh jockeys onto the field to play polo.

Garsivaz arrives and tosses a ball.

Siaavosh races after it and smacks it with his mallet,
Sending a thick cloud of dust over his adversary.
The ball disappears as if the sky swallowed it.
It bounces back onto the field just as the royal prince
Reaches it to strike it once again.
At the sight, you would think the Turks' souls
Have deserted their bodies.

Siaavosh says to the glory-seeking men,
"The land and field, mallet and ball are yours."

They dash on horseback to the square, and in a moment
Both teams swiftly hurtle after the ball.
The Iranians easily capture the ball from the Turks.

Siaavosh, proud of the Iranians,

Rises tall as a noble cypress tree.
He asks for a golden throne and javelins
To be brought and placed on the field.
The two princes take their seats on the golden throne,
Debating as to which team exhibits more skill.

The riders bolt on, creating a tornado of dust,
Battling with javelins and weapons, Tooranians
And Iranians charging at each other as if at war.

Garsivaz says to Siaavosh, "O courageous prince,
Heir to the King of Kings, rendered even more
Glorious by your valor rather than your birth,
Show these Turks how well skilled you are
In the use of spear tip, in the art of archery,
In the way you handle the reins and conduct battle."

Siaavosh places his hands on his chest in compliance,
Descends the throne, and climbs on his horse.

Five breastplates, each heavy enough
To weigh down the chest of one man,
Are tied together and placed at the end of a wall.
The army looks on to assess Siaavosh's strength.

He takes a spear worthy of a king,
A souvenir from his father, who used it
In the war in Mazandaran to stab lions in the hunt.
He climbs down the fortified wall gripping the spear,
Bolts forward like a drunken elephant,
Strikes the breastplates, and removes them.
Not a single button or a single stitch remains.

Siaavosh returns from his course,
Brandishing his spear high in the air
And scattering the armor into the dust.

Eager for battle, the riders and Garsivaz
Come forth, armed with long spears.
They roam around the breastplates
At length but are unable to lift a single one.

Siaavosh then asks for four shields from Gilan

And two additional ones of solid metal.
He asks for a quiver with arrows of poplar wood,
Places six in his belt, retaining three in his grasp.
He affixes one arrow to his bow
And tightens his stance on the stirrups.
The onlookers' eyes are locked on him,
Steadfast on his every move.

The shaft of the glorious king pierces through
The two metal shields and the other four.
He similarly sends ten more shots
To the acclaim of young and old.
Every single shield is punctured,
And the entire throng hails the great Siaavosh.

Garsivaz says to him, "O prince,
You have no equal in Iran or in Tooran.
Come, let us fight, you and me, before the troops.
We shall hold each other by our belt straps,
Like two battling, brave warriors.
I have no equal among the Turks,
And you will not find many horses such as mine.
As for you, you have no match in the field in Iran,
Whether in strength or in stature.
If I succeed in removing you from the saddle
And fling you to the ground before you expect it,
You will recognize that I am the stronger one,
The better rider, and the more expert player.
If, on the other hand, you throw me to the ground,
I shall never show my face again on the battlefield."

Siaavosh replies, "Do not speak of this.
You are a prince and a lion eager for battle.
Your horse is king to my mount;
Your helmet is as sacred as Aazargoshasp.[23]
Point out to me a Tooranian other than you,
So that he may measure his strength against mine
Without holding a grudge against me."

◇◇◇◇◇◇◇◇◇◇◇◇◇
23 Aazargoshasp: Divine, holy, eternal flame; a revered fire temple for kings and
warriors during the Sasanian times in Azerbaijan.

Garsivaz replies, "O glory seeker,
A game should not incite anger
Just because two men fight together
And hold on to each other by the belt."

Siaavosh retorts, "You are in the wrong.
I cannot fight against you.
A battle between two men,
No matter what battle, generates anger,
Even when they fight with smiles on their faces.
You are the brother of the world king.
You trample the moon beneath your horse's hooves.
I am ready to obey you in all matters.
But on this one, I reject your challenge.
Select among your men a valiant lion.
Have him mount his blazing charger,
And since you wish me to battle,
You will see the highest heads trampled
Beneath the dust at my horse's hooves.
I shall seek to have no cause for shame
Before the king from the outcome of this battle."

Garsivaz, the ambitious, smiles, flattered.
He says to the Turks, "O noble warriors,
Who among you wishes to accede to fame,
To withstand a battle against Siaavosh
And fling into the dust the leader of brave men?"

The Turks appear reticent to reply until
Garooy of Zerreh approaches and says,
"If no contender presents himself,
I am the one worthy of this battle."

At the sound of his words, Siaavosh's
Forehead wrinkles and his cheeks contract.

Garsivaz says to him, "O royal one, there is
No one of his strength and stature in my host."

Siaavosh replies,
"Since I am excused from a fight with you,
I make little case of a match with your men.
May two of them, instead of one, prepare

To measure their strength against mine."

A warrior Turk steps forward,
A brave one named Damoor,
With no equal in strength in all of Tooran-Zamin.
He hears Siaavosh's words,
Runs to Garooy of Zerreh swift as smoke,
And equips himself in haste with weapons.

Siaavosh readies himself for battle.
Damoor and Garooy fall on him.
Garooy seizes Siaavosh's belt
And twists it as if to make a knot,
But Siaavosh grasps him by his belt's strap
And makes him feel the mighty force of his arm.
He removes Garooy from the saddle and flings him
To the ground without the use of mace or noose.

Then he charges at Damoor, grabs him sharply
By the chest and neck, and tosses him off the saddle
So deftly that the troops remain confounded.
He brings him to Garsivaz without hurting him.
You would think he is carrying a hen under his arm.
He dismounts, releases Damoor,
And climbs with a smile on the golden throne.

Garsivaz is furious with Siaavosh's deed,
His heart worried, his cheeks pale.

They leave the golden throne and return to the palace.
You would think they raise their heads to Saturn.
They sit for seven days to dine and feast with wine
And music, with their noblemen of fortunate path.

On the eighth day,
Garsivaz and his men prepare for departure.
Siaavosh, despite all suspicion,
Writes a letter to the king full of expressions
Of subservience and friendly questions.
Then he rewards Garsivaz with many gifts.

The Turks leave this beautiful site in joy,
Speaking at length amongst themselves of the city

And of its ruler's high deeds and splendor.

Garsivaz, eager for vengeance, tells them,
"Great misfortune is ours from the land of Iran.
From there, the king has summoned
A man who makes us wallow in shame,
Embarrassed of our own blood.
Two mighty lions such as Damoor and Garooy,
Two heroes full of fervor for battle, found
Helpless and weak at the hands of a sole rider.
His heart is impure.
The situation the king has brought upon us
Will not conclude peacefully.
It began poorly and will surely end poorly."

48 | Garsivaz Returns to Court and Slanders Siaavosh

Garsivaz returns to the king's court,
His anger depriving him of rest or sleep.
Once in the presence of the Tooranian army leader,
The king asks him all sorts of questions.

Garsivaz answers at length and hands over the letter.
The king reads the message within and rejoices.
The glorious Garsivaz observes
The signs of delight on the monarch's face.
He withdraws at sunset, heart full of hatred.
Through the night and until the first light of day,
He writhes like a serpent rolling in the dust,
Loathing depriving him of sleep.

At dawn, Garsivaz joins Afraasiyaab at court.
They dismiss the visitors to deliberate on matters.

Garsivaz says, "O King,
Siaavosh is indeed not the man he used to be.
Not long ago, he received a secret envoy of Kaavoos
And, soon after, messengers from Rum and Chin.
He drinks to Kaavoos Shah's health.
Gathered around him is a large army and, soon,
You will have to thrash in fear at the sight of him.

If Toor had not sported a fierce heart,
He would not have killed Iraj so unjustly.
But since that time, these two entities,
One water, the other fire, have regarded
Each other with suspicion and resentment.
Today you foolishly wish to form an alliance,
As if you could avert the biggest storm.
To conceal this grave danger from you
Would have brought ruin and dishonor to my name."

The king's heart is aggrieved by these words,
And the idea of a distressing future strikes him hard.
He replies, "It is our brotherly bond and love
That moves me and guides your heart.
Let us spend three days reflecting on this matter.
We shall then be able to make a mature decision.
If I find myself assured of a menacing danger,
I shall seek a remedy to extricate this menace
From looming over our heads."

Three days pass during which Afraasiyaab
Deliberates at length on the unequal levels
Of enmity and unity between the two realms.
On the fourth day, Garsivaz appears at court,
Helmet on his head, belt strapped across his hips.

The Tooranian king speaks to him earnestly
On the subject of Siaavosh: "Son of Pashang,
What do I have in the world besides you?
I must then reveal to you all my secrets.
I must make you see to the bottom of this matter
So that you may give me suitable guidance.
The bad dream I had long ago had me
Worried and abated my intelligence.
I decided then not to engage in battle with Siaavosh.
For his part, he did me no harm.
On the contrary, he renounced the imperial throne.
His life is a vast cloth with intelligence as its framework,
With virtue woven into delicate stitches through it.
Never did he distance himself from my command.
Never did he experience from me anything but kindness.
I have given him land and treasure,

Never did I remind him of the worries
And suffering he inflicted on me.
I offered him an alliance with my daughter,
An alliance that bound me to him.
I refused to take vengeance on the land of Iran.
On his account, I deprived myself of treasure
And of a daughter who is my eyes' most prized delight.

"Now there should rise in the world
A unanimous cry against my person?
How can I think poorly of him
After having bestowed on him kind deeds,
After having shielded him from one hundred hardships,
After having deprived myself
Of kingdom, crown, and treasure?
I have no reason to do him ill, and
I shall be blamed by the Creator and by brave men
For any little grievance he may endure on my account.
I shall be banished from the world.
There is no wild beast with teeth sharper than a lion
Whose heart does not tremble at the sight of a sword.
Yet when he sees his offspring in distress,
He turns a grove into shelter from danger.
The Master of Sun and Moon would not approve
Should we clamp down on an innocent man.
I only know the Siaavosh to whom
I gave the name of son while you were intent
On me sending him back to his father.
If ever he desires throne and seal, it is not my land
He wishes to subjugate and dominate.
He will withdraw from here
And take with him his rancor and hostility."

Garsivaz replies, "O King, I wish
You would not make light of a serious matter.
If ever Siaavosh decides to leave Tooran-Zamin,
If ever he returns to the land of Iran,
Our kingdom will surely be entirely devastated.
Every time a stranger enters your family,
He learns the secrets of your strengths and flaws.
Listen to me, for a wise man said on this subject:
        'A storm that comes from your own house

Can only sweep in pain and worries.
It will scatter your wealth,
And destroy family and glory.'

"When your relatives become outsiders
And are aware of your secrets, great and small,
Guard yourself and remain vigilant day and night.
Once they know everything about you,
Wealth and all, they will seek to hurt your being.
Don't you know that whoever raises a leopard
Can only expect spite and skirmish in the end?"

Afraasiyaab reflects on Garsivaz's words,
Which appear to him as echoes of truth.
He regrets what he wished for and his actions.
He feels that his life and his plans are in disarray.
He responds, "I see that, in this affair, every decision
We make will lead down the path of misfortune.
I shall wait for the secret rotation of the sky
To guide me and determine an outcome.
It is better to stand by than to make haste.
Let us watch the sun rise over darkness
To reveal the Creator's wishes;
Let us see what direction the star
Shining on the spinning spheres will face.
If I summon Siaavosh to my court,
I shall better ascertain his secret intentions.
It will suffice to observe him
And examine the turn of events.
Should he display such perversity as to force my heart
To be unappeasable, then no one will blame me,
For the evil man deserves only punishment."

Garsivaz, the vengeful, replies,
"O perceptive King of just speech, the weapons,
The might, and the power of Siaavosh are such,
The strength given by the divine to his arm,
Sword and mace are such that he will not
Turn up at your court without an army.
His presence will surely darken
For you the light of sun and moon.
He no longer resembles the person you knew.

147

He raises his crown above the sky in the same manner.
Furthermore, you will not recognize Faranguis,
Who appears to have need for nothing in the world.
Your army will drift over to Siaavosh's side,
And I fear you will become a shepherd without a flock.
A host, at the sight of a ruler so intelligent, so joyous,
And fine as the moon, would never settle on a king like you.

"Siaavosh's place would be with ram, yours with fish.[24]
Furthermore, you wish to command him
To leave the city he built and the beautiful land
Of his residence to come here as your slave,
To lower his head humbly and respectfully
Before you, but no one has ever seen
An alliance between lion and elephant.
No one has ever seen fire rise from water.
One might try to set to rest, on a sheet of silk,
A lion cub not yet weaned from its mother's teat.
One might try to gently nourish him with milk
And sugar, and raise him in a close embrace.
Nature will take over as soon as he is grown, and
He would not fear the strength of a mighty elephant."

Afraasiyaab is trapped in the links of this discourse.
He is saddened, and dread has lodged in his heart.
But he prefers to wait than to rush into action,
For the cautious and discerning man prevails
While the one with his head full of wind
Never attracts any praise to himself.

A wise man said on this subject,
"When wind rises unawares,
You can resist its force if you show care.
But a man light of head never will rise to power,
Even a nobleman, even a man of cypress stature."

Afraasiyaab and Garsivaz take leave of each other
In a state of deep worry, mouths full of discourse,
Hearts swelling with frenzied hatred
With remembrance of times gone by.

◇◇◇◇◇◇◇◇◇◇◇◇◇
24 Ram and fish: Reference to the signs of Aries and Pisces, spring and winter.

The cruel Garsivaz returns frequently to court,
Full of pernicious designs and ill intentions.
He continues to communicate all sorts of lies
To the King of Tooran, forcing his heart away
From any affection he may cling to for Siaavosh.

Some time passes in this manner, and the king's heart
Slowly fills with disquiet and contempt.

One day Afraasiyaab determines
That the outsider must exit his land and country.
He opens himself to Garsivaz about
His intentions with Siaavosh, and he says,
"You must go to him, visit him at length, and say to him,
    'Do you never wish to leave this delightful place?
    Yet it is time for you to take the road with Faranguis.
    Visit the Tooranian king who needs to see you.
    He wishes to dwell in the presence of
    Your virtuous heart and your cautious mind.
    You will find in our mountains hunting grounds
    And in our emerald cups milk and wine.
    Let us go for some time and give in to fun and joy.
    When the memory of the town you built awakens,
    You will return cheerfully with song.
    Why should you refuse our wine?
    Allow your heart to forget the Kianian throne.
    Strap your belt in preparation for your departure.'"

49 | Garsivaz Returns to Siaavosh

Garsivaz, the traitor, prepares for his trip,
Heart full of hatred, head full of secret plans.

As he approaches the city of Siaavosh,
He selects a man able of speech from his host
And says to him, "Relay this message to Siaavosh:
    'O noble son born of a noble father, O name-seeker,
    By the soul and head of the King of Tooran,
    By the soul, head, and crown of Kaavoos Shah,
    I implore you not to vacate your throne on my account.
    Abstain from meeting me on the road.

You are spared by virtue of your good fortune,
Your distinction and high birth, your crown and throne.
Though the winds obey you, are you willing
To desert your royal throne on my account?'"

The envoy approaches Siaavosh.
As soon as his eyes fall on him, he kisses the ground
And conveys the message from Garsivaz.

Siaavosh, feeling a tremor of inner worry,
Remains seated at length, immersed in reflection:
"There must be a secret motive behind this.
I have no clue what Garsivaz, who pretends
To be my friend, has told Afraasiyaab on my account."

Siaavosh advances on foot to meet Garsivaz.
He greets him, asks him about his travels,
About the king's health, and about
The state of the army, throne, and crown.

Garsivaz relates the message of the king.

Siaavosh, delighted, replies,
"For love of the king, I shall not hesitate
To expose myself to the sharp-edged metal blade.
I am ready to leave, and my horse's reins
Are joined to your battle steed.
But first, let us sit for three days and drink wine
In this golden pavilion with a floor of roses.
This passing world is full of plight, suffering, and pain.
Unfortunate is the man who wallows in sorrow
As he journeys through these elusive days."

The duplicitous Garsivaz hears the wise prince's reply.
Trembling, he says to his heart,
"If Siaavosh accompanies me to Afraasiyaab's court,
He will crush my thoughts and intentions
With his courage, his strength, and his good sense.
My words will carry little weight,
And my advice will appear perfidious to the king.
I must then find a way to dissuade the prince
From making the journey to the imperial palace."

He remains silent for some time,
His eyes fixed on Siaavosh.
In the end, the yellow tears he sheds
Reveal to him a solution.

Siaavosh sees him sobbing as if shaken by anger.
He says to him in a gentle voice,
"What happened? What distresses you?
Is your anger a result of your dealings with Afraasiyaab?
If that is the case, why must pain dampen your eyes?
Here I am, ready to go with you and fight
Against the leader of the Tooranian host
Until he abandons all desires to persecute you unjustly.

"Why should he treat you as someone of lower status?
If someone presents himself as your enemy,
You must return to him the feelings of hostility.
Here I am, willing to defend you in any way I can.
If your relationship with Afraasiyaab has been tarnished
For no good reason, a fraudulent person must have
Taken your seat next to the king to undermine you.
If the king is the cause of your misfortune and disgrace,
Recount to me all your secrets regarding this matter
So that I may find a way to assuage your suffering.
I shall depart to resolve all your issues
And make the hearts of your enemies tremble in fear."

Garsivaz, the noble, replies, "Glorious prince,
The source of my grief is not my relation with the king,
Nor is it an adversary who cast me in the woes of despair.
My courage and my wealth
Excuse me from seeking the means to a way out.
It is your ascendance that fills me with worry,
And here I must speak to you openly and truthfully:
The wrong first took root at the hands of Toor,
For divine grace was extracted from him.
You have heard of the way he killed the soft-spoken Iraj
At the start of our family's history of hatred.
You know how, from that era until the time of
Manoochehr and Afraasiyaab, peace was upheld
In both Tooran and Iran, how the two peoples
Have never and in no place become entangled.

But ever since that time, they somehow
Distanced themselves from the precepts of reason.

"The leader who governs Tooran-Zamin
Is more vile than his ancestor.
The conclusion to this affair is not yet evident.
We cannot truly assess the king's evil nature.
Wait for some time to pass. Take note of Aghriras,
Who died a miserable death at the hands of Afraasiyaab.
He was his brother from the same father and mother.
He was full of wisdom and innocence,
Yet Afraasiyaab murdered him cruelly
And, in the same manner,
Later executed many great and innocent men.

"I feel apprehensive about your fate,
For you are a kind and brave man,
And never did you seek to harm anyone
Since your arrival to this land.
You have always acted with virtue and humanity.
You have rendered men better by your kind nature.
But Ahriman, who breaks up souls,
Has fueled the king's heart against you
And has filled it with rancor and hatred.
I cannot foresee what the World Creator holds in store.
You know that I am your friend, that in joy and sorrow,
I am genuinely devoted to you.
I do not wish the day to come
When you may be convinced that, despite
Being aware of the king's unjust intentions,
I may not have given you fair warning.
That is why I am confiding in you today.
Think and find a solution to evade a downfall,
And speak only with gentleness and moderation."

Siaavosh replies, "Do not worry,
For the World Creator is my support.
My hope was that the king would convert
My dark nights into bright, happy days.
If he had doubts on my account,
He would not have raised me above his court.
He would not have given me kingdom, crown,

And throne; daughter, treasure, land, and army.
I shall go to the royal palace with you.
I shall return light to his dimming moon.
Anywhere honesty shines, the luster of lies tapers.
I shall show Afraasiyaab that my heart is more pure
Than the light of the brilliant sun shining in the sky.
Restore your joy, and prohibit
Doubt from entering your soul.
A man who does not walk the dragon's path
Will remain aligned with the Creator's path."

The malicious Garsivaz replies,
"Afraasiyaab is not the man you think he is.
When an incensed revolving dome
Frowns deeply and lines its face with wrinkles,
Even the wisest, most informed man may fail
To discern fraud creeping up on the horizon's edge
In time to free himself from its bonds.
Despite your sound judgment and your discerning mind,
Despite your tall stature and your resolve, you cannot
Make the distinction between guile and goodwill.
May ill fortune never have access to you!
Afraasiyaab has enveloped you in cloaks
Woven out of deceit and sorcery.
He has cast a spell upon your discerning eyes.
First he gave you the name of son-in-law,
And the act made you rejoice.
Then he bid you depart, offering you a feast
Attended by the noblemen, and you rejoiced.
Should you speak to him with arrogance,
He would punish you mercilessly.
You are not closer to him in kin than the famed
Aghriras, yet he slashed him, his own brother,
In half with a dagger, sending tremors of fear
Through the hearts of his noblemen.

"I have exposed to you the deep, dark folds of his soul.
Know that it is exactly as I tell you.
You must not trust his deeds or his speech.
I conveyed to you the worries that stir up my heart,
As well as my thoughts and the resources
I have at my disposal.

I have made them clear as sunshine.
You have abandoned your father in another land,
Founded a city in the land of Tooran,
Committed yourself to Afraasiyaab's words.
You enjoy surrounding him with your care,
And yet all you have accomplished is,
With your own hands, planting a tree
Growing venomous fruit and bitter leaves."
Garsivaz speaks thus, his lashes soaked with tears,
His heart full of cunning, his lips expelling long sighs.

Siaavosh looks at him with surprise,
Two streams of tears running down his cheeks.
He thinks of his miserable fate, of the sky
That deprives him of love at the end of his young life.
He thinks about the little time he has left to exist.

His heart filled with grief, his cheeks pale,
His soul distraught, he exhales deeply and says,
"The more I think of this, the more I realize
I do not deserve such a punishment.
Neither my words nor my deeds, nor any part
Of my life has given the world cause to complain.
My hand has been lavished with the king's treasures,
But my heart has suffered greatly.
No matter what misfortune befalls me,
I shall not disobey his order and his wish.
I shall leave with you without an escort, to investigate
This source of ill-will the king is directing at me."

Garsivaz says to him, "O renowned prince,
Do not present yourself before him.
One must neither walk on fire nor trust ocean waves.
You would foolishly fling yourself into trouble,
And your good fortune would instantly vanish.
I can interfere on your behalf and perhaps
Succeed in tossing icy water on the heat of fire.
You must reply to his letter,
Express the good and the bad.
If I see that his head is free of hostility
And you may wish for better days ahead,
I shall send an envoy on horseback, and

I shall return the delight to your afflicted soul.
I hope that the World Creator,
Who discerns both the revealed and the mysterious,
Will help Afraasiyaab choose the right path
And distance himself from injustice and wrongdoing.

"But if I find him further angered,
I shall hasten to send your way an envoy riding a camel.
Now prepare without delay; do not lose any time.
You are not far from leaders and kings in other lands.
You can easily travel from here to Chin with only
A distance of one hundred and twenty farsangs,
Or from here to Iran-Zamin
With three hundred and forty farsangs.
On this side, everyone is your friend and servant.
The army is at your command, as is the town.
In Iran-Zamin dwells your father,
Who longs for your return, along with troops
That stand as slaves to your seal and authority.
Secretly send long letters to these two sides.
Equip yourself and do not remain idle."

Siaavosh allows himself to be persuaded.
In this way, his vigilant mind is led astray.
He replies, "I shall not deviate from the path
Drawn by your words and your advice.
Take responsibility for my demands to Afraasiyaab.
Maintain peace between us, and serve me as guide."

50 | Siaavosh's Letter to Afraasiyaab

Siaavosh summons a scribe and dictates to him a letter
In words clear and bright as gleaming ivory pearls.
He begins in remembrance of the Creator,
Able to unfasten his servants' bonds of suffering.

Then he celebrates eternal wisdom
And invokes blessings on the King of Tooran:
"O victorious and fortunate ruler,
May the time never come when remains
Only the memory of your being!

You called me to your side, and I rejoiced
To see you seated, surrounded by your wise men.
You also called Faranguis, and this action
Filled her heart with love and tenderness,
And with the desire to obey.
But Faranguis is not well at this time.
Her lips decline food, her body refuses to move.
She lingers in bed, hovering between two worlds,
With me held captive at her side.
My heart's fiercest desire is to see you again,
To brighten my soul with your kind words.
As soon as Faranguis is appeased,
She will travel to his majesty's side.
But until then, may my anxiety serve as my excuse.
The secret of this delay lies in her state of affliction
And in the care necessary to relieve her suffering."

Once the seal is imprinted on the letter,
Siaavosh hands it over to the evil Garsivaz.
This offspring of poor ancestry asks
For three speedy horses, then takes off,
Galloping day and night without pausing to rest.
In three days, he completes a long journey,
Most arduous in its ascents and descents.
On the fourth day, he appears at the king's gate,
Lips rife with falsehoods, heart shrouded with sin.

Afraasiyaab asks him many questions
And finds him weary and full of anger.
"Why," he asks, "are you in such a hurry?
How did you so swiftly carry out the excursion?"

Garsivaz replies, "When fortune takes a wrong turn,
There is no time to dawdle or rest.
Siaavosh paid little attention to me,
Refusing to trouble himself to greet me on the road.
He neither listened to my speech nor read your letter.
He made me kneel before his throne and,
Having just received a letter from Iran,
He kept the gates of his city locked,
Refusing passage to our cortege.
I fear armies from Rum and Chin may,

In an instant, cast the earth into a state of turmoil.

"If you remain passive and fail to keep a watch on him,
You will soon hold in your hand nothing but wind.
If you hesitate, he will declare war
And, with his courage, will seize all your provinces.
Were he to travel with his host to the land of Iran,
Would you lead a campaign against him?
Now that I have made you aware of his intentions,
You must pay heed to his schemes,
Or else you will have cause to tremble in fear."

51 | Afraasiyaab Leads a Campaign Against Siaavosh

As Afraasiyaab hears these words,
He feels as if young blood
Has been injected into his old age.
His heart burns, his breast sighs deeply,
And his anger reaches such heights he finds
Himself unable to answer back to Garsivaz.

He orders trumpets and timpani be played,
Along with clarions and bells. he casts aside
The letter, unread, and furiously gathers troops,
Commanding them to prepare to fight.
He departs in the direction of Siaavosh's court
With his animated and buoyant noblemen.
The words of the villainous Garsivaz succeed in planting
Once again the seed for the tree of vengeance.

While Garsivaz, the double-dealer, wearies
The straps of his stirrups on the way to Tooran,
A sad Siaavosh enters the women's chambers,
Heart aflutter and cheeks pale.

Faranguis says to him, "O noble and bold hero,
What has happened? Why so pallid?"

He replies, "O fair-faced woman,
The honor that once embraced me
In the land of Tooran has now tarnished.

I do not know what to tell you, for I myself
Remain rattled and baffled by these events.
If Garsivaz tells the truth, what remains for me
Of life's circle is only its center point."

Faranguis takes the curls of his hair in her fingers,
Scratches her coral face with her nails,
And streaks her musk-scented cheeks with blood.
Her heart is on fire, her face awash with tears
That stream down like torrents
Upon the silver mounds of her breasts.
She bites her tulip lips with her glistening teeth.
She pulls out her hair in despair and sobs
For the words and deeds of her father, Afraasiyaab.

She says to Siaavosh, "O tall and noble King,
What will you do? Hurry to tell me your secret.
Your father's heart is full of wrath.
You dare not speak of Iran-Zamin.
The road to Rum is long and tiresome,
And you will not wish to go to Chin,
For such a thing will bring you shame.
Where can you seek refuge in the world?
Your only saving light is the Master of Sun and Moon.
May those who harbor malicious thoughts
Live in a state of affliction for years to come!"

Siaavosh replies to her, "O moon-faced beauty,
Do not claw your face so desperately.
The only one worthy of our trust is Yazdan,
Whose resolve we may never evade.
The generous Garsivaz, who is my friend,
Will soon return from the king's court,
Bearer of a kind message.
I am sure he will appease the king's hateful heart,
Redirect it to nurture tenderness for me."

He says this and surrenders his trust to the Creator.
But his heart is dim and sorrowful
Due to the harshness of his destiny.

52 | Siaavosh's Dream

Siaavosh spends three days writhing like a snake.
On the fourth night, the prince falls asleep,
Snuggled in the arms of moon-faced Faranguis.
All at once he shudders and awakens from sleep.
He sits up and cries out like a mad elephant.

His fair-faced wife holds him close to her breast.
She says, "O King, in the name of our love,
Tell me what is happening to you."

As he continues to tremble and cry,
Someone lights a torch and burns
Sandalwood and amber around him.

Afraasiyaab's daughter asks him once again,
"Wise King, what did you see in your dream?"

Siaavosh replies, "Do not open your lips to reveal
My dream, not to anyone, O silvery cypress tree!
I had a vision of a massive body of water,
And on the outer bank rose a mountain of fire.
The edge of the river was lined
With a row of shielded and armed horsemen.
On one side was an immense swirling fire
That burned and destroyed Siaavosh-Guerd.
On the other side was the body of water,
And at the forefront sat Afraasiyaab on an elephant.
Once he set eyes on me, his countenance dimmed,
And he further stoked the fire already so ardent.
A fire ignited by the wicked Garsivaz
Ultimately consumed and devoured me."

Faranguis attempts to reassure him:
"Your dream is a sign of happiness.
As long as you take advantage of this very night,
All the misfortune will befall Garsivaz,
And he will die at the hands of the ruler of this land.
Find a state of peace, and do not concern yourself.
This dream can only foretell future blessings."

Siaavosh assembles his troops
And positions them at the gates of the palace.
He arms himself and, blade in hand, climbs
On his horse and launches his host toward Gang.

As two-thirds of this long night passes,
A rider returns from the desert to report that
From afar he spotted Afraasiyaab approaching,
Galloping at high speeds with a vast host.

An envoy arrives, sent by Garsivaz, to say to Siaavosh,
"Equip yourself in ways to save your life.
All my speeches have been in vain,
And this fire has only turned into black smoke.
Reflect on a course of action to take
And a direction to lead your army to safety."

Siaavosh does not suspect Garsivaz of misguiding him.
He continues to believe in the purity of his intentions.

Faranguis says to him,
"O wise ruler, do not pay heed to us.
Climb on a speedy charger;
The land of Tooran is not safe.
I wish to see you remain alive and well.
Go and save your head.
Do not attempt to postpone your departure."

53 | Siaavosh Conveys His Last Wishes to Faranguis

Siaavosh tells his wife, "My dream has been fulfilled,
And now my glory is on the decline.
My life is about to reach its end,
And the anguish of a bitter day is closing in.
Such is the way of the revolving dome of sky.
At times you are happy, at times you are down.
Even if my castle rooftop were to reach Saturn,
I still must drink the poison of death.
Even if my life lasted one thousand two hundred years,
My final dwelling would still be the dark dust of earth.
One man finds his tomb in the jaws of a lion,

Another is devoured by a vulture,
A third one perhaps by a majestic eagle.
But no one, no matter how skilled he may be,
Can convert the darkness of night into shining light.

"You are now five months pregnant.
You will soon bear an illustrious child.
Your body's noble branch will yield a dazzling fruit;
It will give birth to a world king.
Name this child of tall stature Kay Khosrow.
Make him your consolation in times of worry.
Nothing escapes the power of Yazdan, pure and perfect,
From the shining sun to the dark earth,
From a fly's frail wing to the foot of a mighty elephant,
From the source of a stream to the blue swells of the sea.
The dust of Tooran-Zamin will shelter my remains,
Though I am loyal to the dust of Iran-Zamin.
Such are the motions of the revolving dome,
So speedy in its rotation that it will never allow us
To witness ancient lands being renewed.

"From this moment on,
My fortune is obscured at Afraasiyaab's will.
This innocent head will be severed,
And my heart's blood will serve as its diadem.
I shall be given neither casket nor tomb,
Neither shroud nor sorrowful tears.
I shall rest below the ground like a stranger,
Head severed from my body by the sword.
The king's executioners will toss my bare head
And body disgracefully into the dusty road.

"Army leader Piran will appear at the palace gates,
Pleading with your father for mercy on your behalf.
He will appeal vehemently to spare your innocent life.
Piran will offer you shelter,
And in the home of this old man full of virtue,
You will give birth to the noble Kay Khosrow.
A long period of time will pass until the moment
Arrives for your son to rise as world ruler.
At that time, from Iran and by divine command,
A savior will travel, his belt cinched for battle,

A wise, courageous, skillful warrior named Giv,
Who has no equal in Tooran-Zamin.
He will secretly take you and your son
To the shores of the River Jayhoon.
Across the river, your son will sit on the throne
Of royalty, devotedly obeyed by birds and fish alike.

"Once in possession of the Kianian crown,
Kay Khosrow will seek to avenge my death.
As the earth dons a fertile, lush cloak of greenery
And splatters of vibrant tulips erupt in the hills,
The world will fill with chaos and clatter.
Kay Khosrow will bring a vast
And vengeful host from Iran.
This is the way of the revolving dome,
For it never affixes its affection on anyone.
Many warriors will wish to avenge my death.
They will dress in armor and bear shields
To honor my life and death.
Rattled by Kay Khosrow,
The earth will echo with the shouts of men.
Red, yellow, black, and purple banners
Will multiply as they approach
To hover over the land of Tooran.
Rostam's Rakhsh will trample the land,
Deeming Tooranian lives as insignificant.
From that day to the day of resurrection,
You will see nothing but mace and jagged sword
In eager motion to execute retribution."

Having thus spoken, the liberated Siaavosh
Embraces Faranguis and takes his leave,
Saying, "My beautiful mate,
I am about to march to my death.
Never forget my words. Prepare for hardships.
Renounce your idle life, luxury, and throne."

Faranguis tears at her face, pulls out her hair.
She allows a flood of tears to stream down her face.
As Siaavosh says these painful words,
She hangs on his neck, shrieking.

World, I do not know why you raise men
Only to turn them into prey.

Siaavosh emits a scream of anguish
As he exits the palace and marches to his stables,
Face awash with tears, heart pained.
He returns with Behzaad, his black steed
Who on the day of battle rivals the wind in speed.

Sighing, he clutches his horse's head to his breast.
He clears out bridle and reins and whispers
Sadly and quietly in Behzaad's ears,
"Take care and attach yourself to no one.
When Kay Khosrow comes to avenge my death,
Only then will you allow bridle to be strapped.
Renounce the stables forever.
Tread the earth, for your destiny is to transport
The noble Kay Khosrow on the day of vengeance.
Then you shall make use of saddle, crush the world,
Willfully striking it hard with your hooves,
To sweep away my son's adversaries."

He then cuts off the remaining horses' hooves
With his sword, as if he is slicing through reeds.
Everything he owns of brocade and gold,
Pearls and precious stones, helmet and belt,
All his treasures amassed over time, he destroys
And then sets fire to palace and garden.

54 | Siaavosh Falls Into Afraasiyaab's Hands

After that, Siaavosh prepares for departure,
Astonished by the turns of his misfortune.
He climbs on a young horse and commands
The Iranians to take the road leading to Iran.
His cheeks, red with blood tears, are like bitter apple.

Having traveled half of one farsang,
He comes face to face with the King of Tooran
And his troops armed with sword, mace, and armor.
He fastens his coat of mail knot by knot,

163

Thinking, "Garsivaz this time has spoken the truth.
I must not question his honesty on this matter."

At the sight of the Tooranian ruler,
Siaavosh fears for his life, yet he stays put,
Without attempting to find a place to hide.
Soon, Tooranian troops swarm the land,
Closing in on him and blocking
The road for him and for his horse.

The two parties stare each other down.
Never before has Siaavosh felt such hatred.
The Iranians, witnessing his dread, stall for a bit,
Then organize in ranks, ready for bloodshed.
They blame Siaavosh for their predicament,
Feeling that he is wasting time.

From the ranks rises a cry of confusion:
"They are going to kill us, but we must not
Allow ourselves to be tossed into the dust.
Wait until we demonstrate our courage to them
Instead of dismissing them so quickly."

Siaavosh tells them, "You are wrong.
This is not the time nor the place for battle.
I shall today dishonor my birth.
If I offer the king a fight in the place of a gift,
If the turning skies wish, despite my innocence,
To make me perish at the hands of evil men,
On that day, no amount of valor will serve me,
For one cannot go against Yazdan's will.
What did the wise man full of caution once say?
          'The use of force is pointless
              In an attempt to prevail over your ill-fated star.'"

Then Siaavosh turns to Afraasiyaab:
"O brave and skillful King, master of throne and glory,
Why have you marched here with your army?
Why do you wish to kill me, guiltless as I am?
Your actions will spawn hatred between two peoples.
This century and world will fill with strife and setbacks."

The foolish Garsivaz replies, "Such words

164

Are unbefitting, coming from your mouth.
If you claim to be so innocent,
Then why show yourself in a coat of mail?
It is not the proper way to appear before the king.
Bow and armor do not make a worthy offering."

Siaavosh realizes that the troubles stem from
This evil man who instigated the king's anger.
As soon as he hears him out, he cries, "O miserable,
Hateful man, your words have led me astray.
You said that the king was infuriated with me.
Thousands of innocent heads will fall
As a result of your slander.
Your malicious talk has given rise to the king's anger.
You will soon suffer the consequences of your deeds.
You will soon consume the fruit
Of the seeds of evil you have sown."

Then Siaavosh turns to Afraasiyaab:
"His majesty must not, in his fervor,
Kindle a flame to consume his breast.
Shedding my blood should not be deemed a game,
Neither should the hanging of innocent men.
Do not throw to the wind all of Tooran-Zamin
And your life because of lies uttered by Garsivaz,
Who is a progeny of an evil ancestry."

Garsivaz the traitor observes the king and cries out
In a bout of anger, "O brave leader, what is this?
How can you interact with your enemy?
Why do you bother to hang on his every word?"

Afraasiyaab takes into account his brother's speech
At the moment the mighty sun's
First strokes paint the eastern sky.
The king orders his troops to draw their swords
And to cry out shouts to make the earth rattle,
As if the day of resurrection was upon them.

The world is full of clangor, the air full of dust,
One warrior eager for battle,
Another longing for peace.
Siaavosh, loyal to the promise he had made,

165

Does not reach for the hilt of his sword,
And refrains from giving his troops the order of war.

The untamed Afraasiyaab of ill design
Satisfies his rage toward the King of Iran.
He shouts out, "Deliver them, stab them with swords.
Spread the troops one by one on the field of carnage
Like ships gliding over a sea of blood."

The Iranians, numbering one thousand warriors,
Are hit hard, each illustrious one wounded fatally
And wiped out from life on earth.
The land is speckled like a field of red tulips.

At the start of battle, Siaavosh finds himself injured,
His body riddled with punctures of spear and arrow.
He tumbles off his black stallion,
Rolling on the dark ground like a drunken man.

Garooy of Zerieh approaches and seizes him
To fasten his hands tight behind his back.
A noose is clamped around his neck,
Blood streaks down his rose-colored cheeks
And masks the eyes of a young prince
Who rarely had the chance to witness a happy day.

The king's executioners hastily drag him
To his city of Siaavosh-Guerd,
With a large crowd gathering all around him,
Preceding and following the cortege.

The leader of the Tooranian host says,
"Take him from here, far away from the road.
Split his head from his body with a dagger.
Do so in a barren corner
Where no plant has a chance to grow.
Spill his blood on the parched ground.
Do so quickly and without a glimmer of fear."

The entire army replies to Afraasiyaab,
"King, tell us, what wrong has he done to you
That propels you to wash your hands in blood?
Why would you kill someone for whom

The crown and ivory throne will weep bitterly?
Do not plant on the day of prosperity, wise king,
A tree bearing fruits destined to envenom you."

But the evil Garsivaz, in his madness,
Pressures the executioners, for he has wished
To spill Siaavosh's blood ever since hatred for him
Took root in his heart, the day of the polo match.

Now there lives a man, a brother of Piran,
Younger than he and his noble companion.
This valiant hero, named Pilsam, is of shining mind.

Pilsam pleads with the renowned king:
"The tree you have planted with hatred and vengeance
Will only bear fruits of pain and sorrow.
I have heard a wise thinker say in good sense:
        'How can a man who acts slowly and deliberately
        Ever have cause for repentance?
        May the one driven by anger use reason as a cure.
        Rashness and spite are the workings of Ahriman.'
The head of the prince must not be severed so swiftly,
Without proper thought and discussion.
Do not act hastily to renew the old hatred.
Hold him captive until time reveals the outcome.
Wait until the breath of wisdom
Sheds clarity upon your heart,
Then you may take action and cut off his head.

"O wise king, refrain from giving the order.
One must not sever the head of one whose helmet
Will one day be replaced by a royal crown.
Such action will only spawn bitter remorse.
For if you were to execute this innocent man,
Kaavoos and Rostam would rush to avenge his death.
His father is the King of Iran, his foster parent
Is Rostam, who raised him in the practices of virtue.
The consequences of such an action would be manifest:
You would find yourself squirming in a state of turmoil.
Remember the blades that shone bright as diamonds,
Rendering the world red with abundant blood?
Remember the noble leaders of Iran,

And how their fury weighed down on the world?

"Men such as Goodarz, Gorgeen, Farhaad, and Tous
Will tie up timpani to the backs of elephants.
Rostam of colossal stature will rush forth,
Considering us thorns in his side.
Fariborz, son of Kaavoos, lion-like warrior,
Who never grows weary of battle;
Bahraam; Zangueh, son of Shaavaran; Gostaham;
Zavaareh; Gojdaham; Faraamarz; and Zaal,
Son of Saam, will draw swords from sheaths.
The brave warlords of Kaavoos Shah, along
With his world heroes, holders of rank and glory,
Will strap their waists in vengeance,
Filling the fields with spear-holding fighters.
Neither I nor any one of our warriors
Will have a chance against them.
Piran will arrive at the break of dawn to speak
To the king and advise him with his vast wisdom.
Do not unfold a carpet of vengeance upon the world.
Do not command your troops to take in haste
Action that will cause the land of Tooran
To be destroyed and razed into a barren desert."

The leader is shaken by these words,
But his shameless brother Garsivaz,
Remaining unmoved, merciless, and determined
To carry out the deed, stays on his argument,
"O sensible King, do not allow his words
To affect or change your resolve. Do not weaken.
Take swift action; destroy your enemy.
Ignore the words of Pilsam.
The field is strewn with Iranian corpses,
And the air is filled with rapacious vultures.
Do not fear an act of required and just retribution.
If Siaavosh cries for help at the border of Rum and Chin,
The world will fill with sword and mace.
Do not needlessly listen to others' advice.
Complete the action; execute the deed.
After having crushed the serpent beneath your feet,
Wounding its head, now you wish to dress it in silk?
If you show mercy and spare his life,

You will no longer find me at your side.
I shall never again show myself at court.
I shall hide in a corner of the world,
Wishing for my life to quickly reach its end."

Damoor and Garooy appear in fear and anguish
To approach the King of Tooran to say,
"Do not retreat before the death of Siaavosh.
Consider that you will never live in peace.
Listen to the advice of the sage Garsivaz,
Your trusted guide, and destroy your enemy.
You set a trap and captured your adversary in it.
Send him to his death immediately.
Do not dishonor yourself.
You hold in your hands the master of Iran.
Break, once and for all, the hearts
Of those who wish to do you wrong.
You have already slaughtered his noble heroes.
Imagine how their leader will feel toward you?
Even if he is not the first to be wrong,
Do you think you can wash away with water
Such a grave and punishable injury?
The best course of action is for Siaavosh to be
Entirely absent from the visible or hidden world."

The king replies to them,
"I have not seen him commit a single crime.
But, according to the astrologers, he will overcome
Us one day and cause all sorts of troubles.
If in my hatred I shed his blood,
There will rise in the land of Tooran a huge
Cloud of dust that will obscure the sun's light.
On that day, wise men will be mystified.
The misfortune that was predicted is now
Upon my realm, and my worry, my sorrow,
My pain are about to intensify.
Yet, a better course is to kill him
Rather than to restore his freedom.
Although it costs me deep pain to sentence
Him to death, neither the righteous man
Nor the malicious one will ever unearth
The secret intentions of the revolving dome."

55 | Faranguis Weeps and Pleads With Afraasiyaab

At the news of the developments,
Faranguis scratches her cheeks,
Straps herself with a bloody belt, and appears
On foot before the king, beautiful as the moon
But with two cheeks stained with blood tears.

She comes forth full of fear and dread,
Shouting, hollering, scattering dust upon her head.
She says to him, "O King of high merit,
Why do you make me the most miserable person?
Why have you ceded your heart to lies and deceit?
Do you not, from your place high
On a pedestal, see the abyss
In which you may tumble down one day?
Do not sever the innocent head of a crown bearer,
For the Creator of Sun and Moon will not approve.
Siaavosh renounced the land of Iran
To render homage to you as world ruler.
He infuriated his father on our account,
Abandoning crown, royal throne, and treasury.
He arrived here asking for shelter.

"What has he done that makes you
Sever the bonds of affection?
No one can cut off the head of a crown bearer
And then retain for long his own crown and throne.
Do not cause me harm or overburden me;
You know that I am innocent.
This world is nothing but a passing journey,
An illusion full of storms and deep sighs,
Full of meaningless, devious lies.
This world flings an innocent man into a dark well
While it raises a guilty one to sit on the throne.
Sooner or later, though, dust will cover them both,
And the obscure trap of a tomb will pin them down.

"Do not make yourself appear
Despicable in the eyes of the world
By giving in to the advice of the wicked Garsivaz.
People will curse you and disapprove of you

For your remaining days.
Upon your death, your road will lead to hell.
You know how Fereydoon, the hero, dealt
With Zahaak, the Taazian, and how the mighty
Manoochehr Shah handled Salm and Toor.
The Iranian world heroes are still alive and well,
Sitting at the side of Kaavoos Shah:
Zaal and Rostam the avenger;
Goodarz, whose mace, on the day of battle,
Pierces through a lion's heart
And rips to shreds a leopard's skin;
Bahraam and Zangueh of Shaavaran,
Who do not fear the sword of war;
Giv, son of Goodarz, who sends fright
To rattle the earth on the day of vengeance;
Tous, Gostaham, and Gorgeen the lion;
Khorraad and Borzeen, brave heroes;
Rohaam, Ashkesh of sharp claws;
And Shiddush the warlord, bold as a whale.
You are planting a tree into the ground,
Its leaves' veins run with abundant blood,
And its bitter fruit digs its roots in hatred.

"The waters will simmer at the memory of Siaavosh;
The revolving dome of life will curse Afraasiyaab.
You are your own worst enemy.
You will often remember my words.
This is not a hunt where you chase
And slaughter an antelope.
It is a king you are plucking from the throne,
And both the Sun and Moon will despise you for it.
Do not foolishly deliver your realm to the wind.
May you never have cause to repent your actions!"

As she pronounces these words,
She sets her sights on Siaavosh
And cries out, clawing at her cheeks,
"O King, O brave one, O warrior, O lord,
O noble lion, you deserted the land of Iran.
Why did you set your affections on the army
Commander, regarding him as your father?
They bound your hands, dragged you on foot.

171

Where is your crown now?
Where is the throne of brave men?
Where are the king's pledges and oaths,
For now Sun, Saturn, and Moon are shuddering?
Where are Kaavoos and his noble heroes?
May they see you at this moment and in this state.
Where are Giv, Tous, Rostam, Zaal, and Faraamarz?
Where are all the members of Iran's imperial court?

"Once they find out about the crime committed,
Our good fortune will shake from it.
Garsivaz is the one responsible for misguiding you.
May he, Damoor, and Garooy be damned!
May the head of the one who raises a hand
Against you be sundered and flung into dust!
May the Creator temper your suffering
And strike your enemy's heart with terror!
O how I would rather be deprived of my vision
Than witness the sight of you dragged on the road.
How could I ever expect my father
To rip out of my arms the sun
He had given me as a beloved husband?"

As the king hears these words from his daughter,
The world fades before his eyes.
His heart feels for her,
But his mind is closed on wisdom.
He says to her, "Go away! Never return to this hall!
Do you even know the reasons for my actions?"

Afraasiyaab orders his executioners to drag away
Faranguis, to lock her up like a mad person,
In quarters unfamiliar to her.
They shove her into a dark corner
And secure the lock.

56 | The Murder of Siaavosh by Garooy of Zerreh

Garsivaz glances over at the cruel Garooy,
Who does not turn his way. He approaches Siaavosh
And, shedding all pretense of kindness and pity,

172

Grabs the prince by the beard and drags him,
O shame, face down into the dust like a vile thing.

Siaavosh implores the Creator:
"You, who are Master of space and fate,
Find a royal offspring from my seed,
One who shines before his people like the sun,
One who will avenge me of my enemies
And will renew my path and purpose,
One who commands the world beneath his feet
And who shows what can be done
With skill and courage."

Pilsam follows him,
Eyes flooding with blood, heart full of grief.

Siaavosh says to him, "So long, my friend,
May you live forever interlaced with the world!
Express my farewell to Piran. Tell him that fate
Took an unfortunate turn away from our wishes.
I had better hopes from Piran.
But his promises are just like the wind,
And I am nothing but a shivering willow tree.
He promised me one hundred thousand riders,
Sheathed in armor and riding strapped horses.
He promised that on the day of misfortune,
He would offer himself as lush pasture
Where I could peacefully graze.
Now I am forced to walk on foot before Garsivaz,
Gasping for breath, draped in contempt and indignity,
Nursing a grieving heart with not a single friend
By my side to weep over my destiny."

They cross city and army camp,
Dragging Siaavosh bound up through a large plain
Where Garooy seizes the shining blade from Garsivaz,
Ready to pierce the prince and shed his blood.
He continues to haul his captive by the hair,
All the way to the square displaying the target
Into which Garsivaz and Siaavosh, lion vanquisher,
Had competed with arrows on the day of the game.

At the goal, the wicked Garooy of Zerreh,

Whose actions are guided by a perfidious nature,
Flings Siaavosh, mighty elephant,
To the ground without a trace of either pity
For the prince or fear of the divine.

He positions a golden urn before Siaavosh,
Turns his head and neck as one would a lamb,
Then, with a quick slash, he separates the head
From his body, once a silver cypress tree,
And allows the blood to pour into the urn.

Then Garooy takes the urn to the place indicated,
Empties it out into the dust,
And watches as instantly the ground opens up
And a plant takes root at that very spot.

Within an hour, a verdant shrub sprouts.
No one can make sense of this curious phenomenon
Except for Yazdan, the Creator.
Let us promptly point out this plant:
It is the one we call the Blood of Siaavosh.

The head, severed from its cypress body,
Is sent to sleep, a motionless slumber
That spans long periods of time.

A storm bursts out.
Rising black dust dims the sun and moon.
Men are unable to discern one another,
And each one condemns Garooy, saying,
"Now that the royal throne is deprived of a master,
May there be neither sun nor cypress tree!
I turn left, I turn right,
This way and that way in the world,
And I am unable to recognize myself.
One acts in evil ways, and fortune runs before him,
The world his slave.
The other lives only for good deeds,
And yet trouble sears his life.
Do not give a care to the world,
Do not surrender your soul and heart to torment.
The world is unstable, the world is a traitor.
It has been so since the beginning of time.

PART EIGHT

Remember this: Nothing born will stay forever."

From the palace of Siaavosh, a great clamor arises.
Everyone boils with rage toward the evil Garsivaz.
Slaves loosen their tresses.
Faranguis rips out a long strand of her ebony hair
And ties it around her waist.
She scratches her rosy cheeks with her fingernails,
Cursing out loud the soul of Afraasiyaab,
And shedding copious tears.

Moon-faced beauties tear out their hair,
Bloody their cheeks, and maintain a state of shock.

Their bitter moans and curses are heard
By Afraasiyaab, who says to Garsivaz,
"Let that woman of ill words come out of her retreat.
Drag her through the court, stripped of her veil,
Then deliver her to our executioners
So that they may seize her by the hair
And strike her sharp blows with their clubs
Until she spits out onto the earth of Tooran-Zamin
The child of vengeance buried in her bosom.
I wish not for the root of Siaavosh to grow a stem.
I wish for neither its leaves nor its fruit,
Neither its throne nor its crown."

The noblemen curse and damn the king,
One after the other: "No one has ever
Heard a king utter such despicable words
Or a warrior place such judgment."

Pilsam, his two cheeks streaked with blood,
His heart wounded and full of anguish,
Approaches Lahaak and Farshidvard
And tells them all that has occurred, adding,
"Hell is better than the throne of Afraasiyaab.
We must neither sleep nor rest in this land.
Come, let us rush to Piran so that we may
Save the prisoners for whose lives we fear."

They saddle three noble horses and charge forth
As if they are reeling in the earth beneath the hooves.

175

The will of the Creator was to place Piran
On the dusty road before the three cavaliers.
Aware of the conflict between the two princes,
Troubled like a grieving lion, he travels with horse,
Escort, and elephant to Afraasiyaab's court,
Hoping to alter the course of Siaavosh's fate.

The three riders meet Piran,
Cheeks flooding with blood, hearts aggrieved.
They confess to him the king's actions,
The evil means he endorsed to eliminate the prince:
"O army leader, do not expect the king or his brother
To behave in virtuous, honorable ways."

They sob and weep violently, a sight no man,
Great or small, has ever witnessed before.
They add, "Siaavosh was dragged on foot,
His hands tied up behind his back hard as rock,
A noose around his neck.
His head full of dust, his face full of tears,
His body was flung into the dirt shamelessly.
Garooy, himself on horseback, led him
To a concealed spot where he dismounted,
Placed an urn before the prince,
And cut off his head as if it were a lamb's head,
Severing the crown-bearing head from its body.
It was as if he were uprooting a cypress tree
From the verdant ground.
The entire city filled with laments and cries.
Tears flooded down from eyes like a rainstorm.
Shepherds in the fields would not dare
Treat their lambs in such a beastly manner.
No one had ever before witnessed
A more abominable execution."

At this account, Piran falls unconscious off his horse.
Soon after, he is beside himself with grief, tearing
His clothes and hair, and tossing dust over his head.
Yellow tears flood down his cheeks
As he bewails the death of Siaavosh.
He cries out, "Alas, prince worthy of crown,
Never will the ivory throne see a ruler like you!"

Pilsam says to him, "Hurry,
For even graver sufferings are forthcoming.
Faranguis has been snatched off her throne,
Captured, shivering like a leaf on a willow tree.
She was dragged by her hair, treated with contempt,
To be handed over to the king's murderous servants."

57 | Piran Rescues Faranguis

As Piran hears this dreadful account,
He shouts in fury, asking for ten young steeds
From the stables, at ease with riders, to be saddled.

On the road, Piran the brave, Rooeen the warrior,
And Farshidvard send dust soaring to the sky.
They gallop for two days and two nights.

At the royal gates, they observe much turmoil.
They find Faranguis lifeless,
Being dragged by the hair
By executioners, each wielding a sharp sword.
A loud racket is heard in the palace courtyard.
It is as if the day of Resurrection is upon them.

People look on with heavy hearts and tearful eyes,
Tongues full of curses for the wicked Afraasiyaab.

Men, women, and children say to each other,
"It is a cruel and dangerous act to cut Faranguis
In half and send her plummeting to her death.
The kingdom will perish for the violence of this man.
No one will ever wish to call him king again."

At this moment, Piran arrives swift as wind,
And all the men of sense rejoice.

Once the eyes of the noble Faranguis fall upon him,
Tears flood her face as she mutters,
"Why did you entangle yourself in so much trouble?
Why did you fling me alive into the blaze?"

Piran jumps off his horse and into the dust.

He tears his garments off his body.
He lovingly kisses her feet and her head,
His soul burning hard, his face flooding with tears.
He says, "This is not a proper path to take.
How sad that the king's head is devoid of brain.
Was it not enough to uproot the tall cypress tree?
Must he pounce upon a fine and delicate blossom?"

He commands the guards to hold the execution
For a moment while he dashes to Afraasiyaab
With a mournful heart and tearful eyes.
He says to him, "O King, may you live forever!
May the hand of wrongdoing never affect you!
What has happened to you, O gracious master,
That you have resolved to destroy and kill?
How did the evil deev conquer your heart?
Has he erased in you all fear of the divine?
Who enticed you to commit such an act?
May his destiny be driven by misfortune.

"You have slain the innocent Siaavosh,
Dragged into dirt his name and throne.
The news of such a tragedy will reach Iran-Zamin.
Our good fortune will decidedly come to an end.
Tears will be shed for the throne of the King of Kings.
The Iranian warriors will promptly appear on our soil
With vast hosts to exercise the will of vengeance.
The world was once saved from troubles,
The path to the Creator laid wide open,
But a cheating, lying deev slithered out of hell
And perverted the heart of the once noble king.

"May this Ahriman who led you astray be damned!
He caused you to walk down a treacherous path.
You will repent at length for what you have done.
You will spend your remaining days in solitude,
Your soul aflame and consumed by pain.
I do not know who gave you such advice.
I cannot foresee what the Creator will dictate.
But after decapitating Siaavosh,
Must you hurt your own progeny?
Must you clamp down on your own family?

You rise as if you are possessed by a deev
And foolishly scheme calamity upon calamity.
Yet the poor Faranguis asks for neither the honor
Nor the crown and throne of royalty.

"Do not render yourself infamous by your cruelty
Toward your daughter who is with child.
People's curses would weigh heavy on you and
Pursue you to the end of your days.
Upon your death, you can be sure
Your lot will be to face the gates of hell.
If his majesty wishes to bring light to my soul,
May he send Faranguis to my palace,
And if this child worries him,
Although he can give little cause for worry,
May his majesty wait until his mother gives birth.
Then I shall bring the boy to you,
And you will do with him what you please."

The king replies, "Do as you wish.
You have robbed me of the desire to kill Faranguis."

The leader Piran, happy with this decision
And his mind free of the weight of sadness,
Runs to the palace courtyard, cursing the executioners.
Then he peacefully takes Faranguis away to Khotan,
Escorted by joyous cries from the court and the people.

As he enters the palace, he says to Golshahr,
"We must hide this fair-faced woman
Until she gives birth to the world king.
Then I shall find a way to protect them.
Hold yourself before the beautiful queen.
Serve and safeguard her.
I entrust you with her care."

In this way, some time passes,
And Faranguis, who lights up the world, watches
Herself grow heavy with her precious burden.

Kay Khosrow

1 | The Birth of Kay Khosrow

In the middle of one night,
So dark the moon is nowhere to be found,
As birds and wild creatures are fast asleep,
Piran has a dream in which he sees candlelight
Emanating from the sun, and in the midst of it
Sits Siaavosh upon a throne, sword in hand.
He talks to Piran: "Now is not the time to rest.
Shake off your sweet drowsiness;
Reflect on the fate of the world.
Today is a day of glory, a day of feast and celebration,
For tonight witnesses the birth of Kay Khosrow."

The leader trembles in his sweet sleep.
His shivers, awakening sun-faced Golshahr.
He says to her, "Rise and go calmly to Faranguis.
I saw Siaavosh in dream,
More radiant than the disks of the sun and moon.
He said to me,
        'Why are you sleeping? Without delay,
        Present yourself to the feast of Kay Khosrow.'"

Golshahr immediately rises and arrives
By the side of the moon-faced beauty
At the time when she has just given birth.
She observes the prince and returns to her palace,
Filling the halls with joyful cries of awe.

Moved with emotion, she says to Piran,
"You would think the moon has joined with the king.
Go and look for yourself in great wonder,
The magnitude of divine wisdom and power.
His head merits nothing less than the royal crown,
His body nothing less than armor,
Mace, and the spoils of war."

The leader visits the young prince
And praises the Creator for bestowing him
With such stature, such neck and head, arms and legs,
It is as if the span of a year had already passed over him.

He sheds tears at the thought of Siaavosh
And curses Afraasiyaab at length.
Then he says to his illustrious gathering,
"Should I have to sacrifice my life,
I shall not allow Afraasiyaab to touch him,
Even if I were to end my days in the jaws of a whale."

As soon as the sun reveals its rays
And the dark cloud of night dissipates,
Army leader Piran, resolved with fear and hope,
Travels in haste to the king's court.

He sits, waiting for the gathering to disperse.
Then he approaches Afraasiyaab's glorious throne
And says, "O sun-like King, O world master,
Prudent and expert in the arts of magic, last night
A new child servant was added to your court.
You would think he borrows wisdom from the moon.
No being exists with his virtue and splendor.
It is as if the moon itself has reclined in the crib.
Should Toor's life be restored,
He would envy this child's face.
Never has the palace housed such loveliness.
The king's majesty is rendered new again
By his grandson, whose beauty, face,
Hands, and feet remind us of Fereydoon.
Distance your heart from wicked thoughts.
May your crown shine,
And may your soul be lifted from despondency."

With infinite grace and wisdom,
The Creator removes from Afraasiyaab's heart
All thoughts of war, injustice, and vengeance.
The king remembers, in anguish,
The execution of Siaavosh and sighs deeply.
He repents from having committed the crime hastily
And having ruined his own well-being and happiness.

181

Repentance is an ailment for which there is no cure.

He replies to Piran, "I am destined to suffer.
My future is deplorable, filled with misfortune.
This child will cause the rise of noise and clatter.
I clearly remember the advice of wise men about
Two families, descendants of Toor and Ghobaad.
They said the two would produce a king
Whose love will be longed for throughout the world
And who will be hailed in both lands, Iran and Tooran.
Now what is meant to happen will happen, and
No amount of worry can affect the course of events.
Do not raise this child above the crowd.
Send him to the mountains to live with shepherds
So that he may grow up unaware of my existence,
His high birth, and the circumstances surrounding it."

He further reflectson how this ancient world is renewed
And lacks experience. But what can one do?
One does not have the means to subjugate it.
It is vast and will not fall into your traps.
But if the world makes you suffer on one hand,
It teaches you to make good on the other.

Piran, world hero, takes the path to his palace,
His heart full of joy, his mind full of musings.
He yearns for the roots and leaves
Of the young tree to thrive.
He gives thanks to the World Creator.
He praises and blesses the new world king,
Uncertain of what the future may hold
And what conclusion will seal this affair,
Unaware that he will relinquish life for him.
Unaware that the seed he sows today
May have dire consequences in the future.
He plants the germ of virtue into the soil,
Not mindful that the ground is salty or that
He is digging a ditch which he may inhabit one day.

He reflects, "Curse the ill nature of life.
Even more unfavorable than the visible
Are the machinations of the hidden world."

2 | Piran Hands Over the Care of Young Kay Khosrow to Shepherds

Piran summons shepherds from Mount Gholoo[25]
And speaks to them on the subject of the child.
Then he turns over to them the beautiful boy
Who stands before him full of grace,
His eyes' and heart's delight.

"Treat this pure child with tenderness,"
Piran tells the shepherds.
"Treat him as if he were your own.
Protect him from the dust and the wind
And from all sorts of hazards.
Fulfill all his wishes, serve him as his slaves.
May the day never come when he desires
Something that is withheld from him."

They answer in one voice, "We shall obey
And never stray from your commands."

Piran rewards the shepherds with gifts
And sends a wet nurse to them.
In an expression of submission,
Each brings a finger to his eyes and head
Before they set off to climb the mountains
To take shelter with the precious royal child.

In this way the wheel of sky turns for some time.
The cycle of life fills with affection for the prince.
Once the hero of tall stature reaches the age of seven,
He is betrayed by his courage and his royal birth.

He assembles a bow with a stick
And a bowstring with intestines,
Creating knots at the two ends.
Then he crafts an arrow free of feather or steel tip.
He sets out for the desert in preparation for the hunt.

At the age of ten, the young boy

◇◇◇◇◇◇◇◇◇◇◇◇◇
25 Gholoo: Unclear of the location, but in Tooran-Zamin.

Bravely attacks wild boars, bears, and wolves.
From there, he runs after lions and leopards.
He creates a weapon out of his own wooden bow.
After some time, he rebuffs the orders of his teacher.

One day the shepherd travels through
Mountain and plain in search of Piran.
He laments, "I come to the world hero
To complain about the highborn, brave lion.
He began by hunting antelopes,
Avoiding the lion's path and the leopard's fight.
But now he is indifferent to either antelope or lion.
May misfortune never affect him,
For I fear to be bound up by you as punishment!"

Piran listens to him, smiles and says, "High birth
And courage never remain concealed for long."
He climbs upon a fervent stallion and speeds
To the young lion who shines like the sun.
He summons him, watches his stature,
Watches the way he races to him fast as wind.

The prince bounds up to Piran and kisses his hand.
The leader admires his beauty and royal demeanor.
His cheeks moisten with tears,
His heart fills with tenderness.
He holds Kay Khosrow close to his chest
For some time, quietly praying for him.

In the end, he says to him, "O pure, faithful boy,
May you bring joy to Tooran-Zamin,
For whoever knows you will not wish to call you
By any other name but that of compassionate."

Kay Khosrow answers, "O noble leader,
Why did you wish to see me?
Do you not feel belittled by holding
A shepherd's son close to your breast?"

The sage Piran's heart fills with pity.
His cheeks burn like fire as he says,
"O royal heir, worthy of possessing the world,
You have still much to experience and live.

184

You are not a descendant of shepherds or herdsmen.
I have many tales to recount to you
Concerning your true ancestry."

Piran offers the young man a show horse
And plush royal robes and takes him to his palace,
Heart full of bitterness at the memory of Siaavosh.

The leader raises him in his embrace,
Relishing the sight of him.
He loses appetite, rest, and sleep,
So deep is his love for the boy,
So strong his dread for the wrath of Afraasiyaab.

In this way turns the revolving dome of sky,
Having ceded its favors on the young king.
Piran's heart is all affection, peace and serenity.

3 | Piran Introduces Kay Khosrow to Afraasiyaab

In the dark of night, at the time of rest and sleep,
An envoy sent by Afraasiyaab summons Piran.

The world king speaks at length to Piran
Of times gone by and says,
"My agonizing heart writhes with gloomy thoughts,
Unable to lift the weight of worry.
This child of Siaavosh darkens my days.
How can it be wise and proper to allow
A shepherd to raise the grandson of Fereydoon?
If it is written that misfortune will befall me
At his hands, no preventive measure will protect me,
For the source of such bad luck is the Creator.
Should he remain unaware of past transactions,
He can live happily and we too shall be happy.
But should he display an evil character,
I shall cut off his head as I did his father's."

Piran replies, "O King, how can a stupid child
Be aware of what happened so long ago?
No one can live to be your teacher.

A naïve adolescent knows nothing of bygone times.
A child raised by a simple shepherd
High in the mountains is a wild animal.
Who would inform him of past events?
Where would he draw his intelligence?
I heard his foster parent say that,
Although he has the face of a fairy,
He greatly lacks in wisdom and sense.
His features are fair, his stature tall,
Though his head is devoid of brain.
Do not concern yourself, O crown-bearer.
Do not resort to violence, for I can speak on his behalf.
What does he say, the sage wiseman?
        'The one who fosters a child
        Is more worthy than a father.
        This secret is held
        In the bosom of the loving mother.'

"Should the king so desire, I shall immediately
Summon this illustrious young man to his side.
But first set my mind at peace with a solemn oath,
Promised in the manner of kings.
Fereydoon, when he owned glory, throne, and crown,
Always maintained his sights on the absolute truth.
Toor, master of crown and treasure,
Swore to the Creator, Justice Giver.
Your grandfather Zaadsham
Swore to the Master of Mars, Saturn, and Sun."

Piran's words calm the mind
Of the quick-tempered Afraasiyaab,
Who commits to an oath in the manner of kings.
He swears to the bright day and the indigo night,
To the World Creator, Maker of sky, of beasts,
Wild and tame, Maker of our body and soul,
That never would he seek to harm the child
Or to treat him harshly.

Piran kisses the ground and says, "Your excellency,
Giver of law and order, you are at one with justice.
May intelligence be your guide to good deeds!
May space and time be the dust beneath your feet!"

Then he swiftly approaches Kay Khosrow,
Cheeks full of color, heart full of delight.
He says to him, "Banish reason from your heart.
Should the king speak of war,
Reply of feast and festival.
Treat him as a stranger.
Allow your tongue to utter only idiotic words.
Do not exhibit a single hint of reason before him
So that today may pass free of misfortune."

Piran sets a royal helmet upon the prince's head
And straps a royal belt around his waist.
The hero of pure heart climbs on a nimble horse
And urges it forward in a gentle voice.

He takes the direction of the palace with Khosrow.
On the road, men shed tears at the sight of him.
One could hear them say, "Make room.
Here comes the young world hero, crown-seeker."

Kay Khosrow enters the king's court,
Where the leader Piran introduces him.
The prince approaches his grandfather,
Whose cheeks are wet with shameful tears.

Piran shakes like the branch of a willow tree,
Growing hopeless for the life of Kay Khosrow.

The king turns pallid as he observes the prince,
Confounded by his royal stature, his powerful
Hands, his stride, his poise and nobility.
He seeks to remember his oath to suppress his hatred.

He remains in this state for some time.
In the end, his features smooth out,
And fate grants him rising affection for the child.
Afraasiyaab says to him, "Young shepherd,
What do you know of day and night?
What do you do with your flocks?
Have you counted your lamb and sheep?"

Khosrow replies, "There is no prey.
I have neither rope nor bow and arrow."

187

The king questions him on his troops,
On his good and bad fortune.

Khosrow replies, "The leopard's den
Will tear the breast of vengeful fighters."

Afraasiyaab's third question deals with father
And mother, home, Iran-Zamin, peace and rest.

Khosrow replies, "The wild lion will not turn
Into a procession dog's master."

The king asks, "Do you wish to go from here
To the land of Iran to see the king of brave men?

He answers, "A rider spent the night before last
With me in mountain and plain."

The king smiles and blossoms like a rose.
He tells Kay Khosrow in a gentle voice,
"Do you not wish to learn how to read and write?
Do you not wish to chastise your enemy?"

The boy replies, "Oil cannot mix with milk.
I wish to chase shepherds away from the desert."

The king laughs at these words.
He turns to the army hero and says,
"He is mad. I speak of head; he answers with foot.
He is unable to commit any act, either good or bad.
He does not exhibit the manner of a vengeful man.
Go and return him gracefully to his mother.
Put him in the hands of a watchful and kind man
Who will take him to the city of Siaavosh-Guerd.
Chase away from him all bad advisors.
Provide for all his needs: gold and silver,
Horse and servant, and anything else he may desire."

4 | Kay Khosrow Travels to Siaavosh-Guerd

The leader rushes Kay Khosrow away from court.
They take the path leading to his palace.
Joy shines in his eyes as he walks with assurance,
For he successfully banished an imminent threat.

Piran exclaims, "By divine grace,
A new, healthful tree bears fruit in the world."
He opens the doors to ancient treasures,
Furnishes the young king with goods
To meet his needs: brocade and gold,
Blades and precious stones, horses and weapons,
Helmets and belts, thrones and coins,
Carpets, and many other assets.

He asks the lot be brought to Kay Khosrow
And adds abundant blessings to the lavish gifts.
Then he sends him and his mother
To the town built by the kind Siaavosh.
They happily depart toward a city,
Now turned barren, having been laid to waste.

As they reach their destination,
Crowds surround Faranguis and Kay Khosrow.
Men bow low before them,
Touching the ground with their eyes.
Sounds of voices are heard throughout the city,
Praising and blessing them, saying,
"The noble tree that was cleaved
Now sprouts a strong offshoot.
May the evil eye never touch the king!
May Siaavosh's soul shine with light!"

Every thorn in the land turns into boxwood,
Every blade of grass into a proud cypress tree.
A green sapling grows from the ground
At the spot where the blood of Siaavosh spilled.
It rises tall to reach the clouds,
Its leaves bearing the image of the king's face
And emanating scents of musk and love
That drift into the air and envelop everyone.

It blossoms in the midst of winter as if in spring,
And those who mourn for Siaavosh
Pray beneath the shelter of its branches.

Such is the way of this ancient world:
It deprives children of a mother's breast,
Full of rich, nutritious milk.
The one whose heart grows attached
Will be flung unexpectedly into dust.
Should you put up a struggle,
Even greater affliction will plague you.
Ask for only joy in the garden of life.
Refrain from sniffing flowers of concern.
Whether you possess a crown
Or whether you are destitute,
Your life will pass before long.
Do not whine about this dwelling;
It will not be yours forever.
Your final place of rest will be a coffin.
Why would you amass vast wealth?
Sit before the banquet spread;
Trust the Creator's treasures.
Although it grants love to no one,
The world gives you much pleasure.
It raises one to fling him into a ditch.
Such is the way of the great firmament,
Glorifying one, then moving on to another.

PART NINE

The Events Following
the Slaying of Siaavosh:
Kay Khosrow's Departure for Iran-Zamin

1 | Ferdowsi's Grievance With Old Age

I have completed the story of Siaavosh's bloody end.
I shall now recount the way Kay Khosrow
Is delivered from the land of Tooran-Zamin.

As the sword of twice thirty years lowers on one's head,
A man must give up hope of life and living.
Do not serve him wine, for he is intoxicated with years.
Age hands you a stick to replace the reins.
My treasure is gone; good fortune has deserted me.

My two eyes no longer distinguish
A massive host looming on a mountaintop.
Were the tips of enemy spears to reach my lashes,
I would have no power to yank the reins to flee.
The mountain is now capped with a blanket of snow.
The army blames the king for its predicament.
My two legs, once with stallion strength,
Have fallen into the confinement of sixty years.

The poet is weary of song.
The voice of the nightingale
Sounds the same as the lion's roar.
Alas, the rose, the scent of musk,
And once healthy, pearly teeth!
Alas, the salient blade of the Parsi verse!
The pheasant does not circle the narcissus,
For he searches for the blossom
Flowering on the pomegranate tree
As well as the branch on the cypress tree.

I have drunk from the cup of fifty-eight years,
And now I shall think of nothing
But coffin, shroud, and graveyard.
I only ask of the Creator that my life endure
Long enough so that I may leave behind
A story drawn from an ancient, illustrious book.
For whoever speaks eloquently

Bequeaths to the world the gift of a good name.

I have an interpreter in the other world,
Master of pulpit and sharp-edged sword.
I am a slave to the prophet's family.
I am the dust at Ali's feet.

The story of Siaavosh has reached its end.
I wish to launch the story of Kay Khosrow,
Relate to you Rostam's exploits as he avenges
The death of the lion-man in Tooran-Zamin.
Pay attention to the words of the poet bard,
Listen and see what the minstrel has to say.

2 | Kaavoos Learns of the Fate of Siaavosh

Soon after, Kaavoos is made aware
That Siaavosh's life has ceased,
That the King of Tooran has cut off his head
As one severs the head of a bird;
That beasts, wild and tame,
Cry glumly in mountain and plain;
That the nightingale on the cypress branch,
The rooster on the heather shrub,
And the pheasant beneath the rosebush
All sympathize for his fate;
That the entire land of Tooran
Is consumed with pain and sadness;
That the petals of the flower of the pomegranate
Yellow and wither in the forest;
That Garooy placed before Siaavosh a golden platter,
Then wrung his neck like a crushed ram;
That his royal head was sundered from his being
Without a single person coming to his aid,
Without a single person asking for his life to be spared.

Kaavoos's crowned head bends to the dust.
He tears the clothes off his back,
Scratches out his cheeks,
And tumbles down from his high seat.

The Iranian leaders gather, lamenting and crying,
Covered in clothes of mourning,
Eyes full of blood tears, cheeks pallid,
Hearts aggrieved over the fate of Siaavosh.

Here are Tous, Goodarz, and the brave Giv,
Shahpoor, Farhaad, and Bahraam the lion,
Rohaam, Zangueh of Shaavaran, Khorraad of Borzeen,
And all the other warriors:
Gorgeen and Ashkesh, the bold,
Shiddush, a lion equipped for war,
Each dressed in blue and black,
Each with a cap of dust in lieu of headdress.

3 | Rostam Travels to Kay Kaavoos

The news reaches Nimrooz that the world hero,
Light of the world, has perished.
Shouts are heard in the land of Iran,
Bemoaning the rattling of the black earth,
The way Kaavoos has scattered dust
Upon his throne, torn his robes to shreds, because
Siaavosh's head has been shamefully sliced off
And tossed impudently onto the ground.

At the news, Rostam loses sense and reason.
His cries of anguish echo throughout Zabolestan.
Zaal claws at his cheeks with his nails.
He scatters dust over his crown and his body.

Zavaareh and Faraamarz shred their clothing.
Rostam laments,
"The world has never seen a prince like you.
Alas, the land of Iran is left bereft of your presence!
Everyone mourns and weeps over your absence.
Alas, the heart of our spiteful adversary now rejoices!
Alas, how futile the time and effort
Spent in raising Siaavosh!"

For seven days, Rostam is plunged
Into a state of mourning and despair.

On the eighth day, a trumpet blare rises to the sky.
The entire army assembles from Kashmir to Kabol
Before the gates of the hero of elephantine stature.

Rostam marches off toward Kaavoos's court,
Eyes full of blood, heart full of vengeance.

Once in the Iranian capital, he tears off
His world hero garb and swears by the name
Of the Creator, Master of the universe,
"Never shall I shed my war armor!
Never shall I wash the dust off my cheeks,
For I must carry this grief eternally!
A helmet will be my crown,
The sword gripped in my hand my cup of wine,
The noose around my arm a net to capture prey.
I hope to avenge the young king for the pain
Inflicted on him by this Turk, bearer of a dim soul.
I shall allow neither Tooran to remain nor its king.
I shall turn his land into a river of blood.
I shall extract out of this Turk's dark soul
The spike of vengeance for this lost prince.
Tomorrow, as the sun rises, it will be
My mace, the arena, Afraasiyaab, and me.
I shall strike a blow of my powerful mace,
Like the blows delivered by blacksmiths."

Rostam nears the land of Iran.
News reaches the king of great warriors
That the hero has arrived like a cloud,
His head bare, his body stripped of Babreh Bayan.[26]
His face drenched with tears meant for Siaavosh.

Noblemen march on foot to greet him, noiselessly,
In the absence of drum, timpani, and clarion,
Each lamenting and shedding copious tears,
Tongue speaking of king, soul seeking the king.
At the sight of Rostam in the distance,

◇◇◇◇◇◇◇◇◇◇◇◇◇
26 Babreh Bayan: Armor that is to be solely worn by Rostam; there is uncertainty
about its meaning; literally, refers to leopard skin, but some interpretations
suggest beaver skin or dragon skin. In all cases, it is meant to be waterproof and
impenetrable.

It is as if the world howls its outrage,
Bewailing its heartbreak and sorrow.

The noblemen and Rostam catch up with each other.
They question each other, hearts torn apart
By their affliction over Siaavosh.

Rostam bemoans, "O King, world hero, leader of men,
O your majesty, issued from the Kianian lineage,
O ruler of the world and brave warlord,
The sun sheds tears over your agonizing fate.
The moon's chest is consumed with sympathy.
Where is that brave leader with elephant power?
The River Nile has dried up from a sense of affliction.
Blessed was the day we were in the flowering garden,
In the company of the lofty Zaal engaged in feast."

He laments in this way to the gates of the royal palace.
He stands before the throne of King Kaavoos,
Covered in dust from head to toe, and addresses him:
"O King, you allowed your bad nature to win over,
And the seeds you have sown have borne fruit.
Your love for Sudaabeh and your evil weaknesses
Have snatched from your head the royal diadem.
Now it is clear your seat is on ocean waves.
The doubts and passions of this cruel king
Made the land of Iran sustain a grievous loss.
Better for the world king to lie in a coffin
Than to fall prey to the domination of a woman.
It is by a woman's words that Siaavosh has perished.
Happy is the one who is not born from a mother.

"Never has there been a ruler like Siaavosh:
Liberated, steadfast, bold warrior.
Alas, such head and arms, such chest and hands!
Alas, his royal face! Alas, this brave king!
The world will never see one like him.
In feast, he was like the crown of kings.
In war, he was akin to lion, tiger and leopard.
Never has the world experienced sharper claws.
From now on, and for as long as I shall live,
I devote myself wholeheartedly to vengeance.

I shall cast into battle eyes full of tears.
I shall make the world suffer
As I suffer so keenly myself."

4 | Rostam Kills Sudaabeh and Prepares for Battle

Kaavoos observes Rostam's features,
The tears of blood flowing from his eyes,
And his obvious affection for Siaavosh.
Shame prevents him from responding,
And he sheds burning tears.

Rostam leaves the king's side and resolutely
Marches in the direction of Sudaabeh's palace.
He pulls her by the hair from the women's chambers,
Plucking her off the throne of power.
He drags her through blood and pierces her
With his dagger, cutting her in half.

Kaavoos does not shift his position on the throne.

Rostam retires to his palace, anguished and grieving,
Eyes awash with blood tears, cheeks pale.

The entire land of Iran shouts out in desolation.
Brave men in their pain visit Rostam, who remains
Seated in his palace for the duration of seven days,
In mourning and in tears, heart full of sorrow and ire.

On the eighth day, he asks for trumpet and timpani.
The leaders arrive at Rostam's court:
Goodarz, Tous, Farhaad, Shiddush, Gorgeen, and Giv;
Rohaam, Shahpoor, valiant Khorraad, and
Fariborz, son of Kaavoos; Bahraam the lion,
And Goraazeh the brave dragon;
Gostaham, Zangueh of Shaavaran,
Warrior Ashkesh, and Faraamarz, son of Rostam;
And Zavaareh, head of the gathering.

Rostam says to these heroes, "I have surrendered
Heart, soul, and body to this quest for vengeance,

For never again in the world will a rider
Of Siaavosh's competence strap his belt for battle.
This is a venture not to be taken lightly,
A vengeance that must be viewed most earnestly.
You must distance yourselves from any inkling of fear.
You must flood the earth with torrents of blood,
Wide as the River Jayhoon.

"I swear by the Creator that, for as long as I live,
My heart will remain broken,
Filled with grief for Siaavosh.
To appease it, I shall bow low at the barren place,
Where the evil Garooy of Zerreh spilled his blood.
I shall rub in that desolate spot my eyes and face
To alleviate the pain that has lodged in my heart.
Unless my hands are bound with a lasso
And I have a noose around my neck, unless
I am shamefully flung into dust like a lamb,
I shall make the world tremble
At the sight of my mace and my sharp sword,
Like it will tremble on the day of Resurrection!
My eyes will, from now on,
Only fix on the dust of battle, and I shall
Forever renounce the chalice of feast."

The border keeper and the brave men
And world heroes unanimously reply.
You would think the entire field shakes,
And a sound rises from the land of Iran
Toward the sky, as if the earth is a lion's lair.

From atop his elephant, Rostam gives
The signal for departure, and his troops
Draw their swords of vengeance from sheaths.

The sound of trumpets, clarions, and timpani echoes.
The world fills with hatred for Afraasiyaab
To the point that it appears as if ocean water simmers.
No space is left on earth to walk.
The air disappears beneath the tips of countless lances.

Rostam, the army favorite, readies for battle,
And the universe prepares for great ills.

The Iranian warriors strap their belts
And march off, preceded by the Kaaviani banner.

Rostam, master of Zabolestan, chooses
His warriors from the lands of Kabol and Iran,
As well as from the forest of Naarvan.[27]
One hundred thousand warriors assemble,
Ready to strike.

Rostam declares, "I shall make the world
Suffer as I suffer so profoundly myself."

5 | Faraamarz Kills Varaazaad, King of Sepijaab

One young warrior, Faraamarz, Rostam's son,
New army commander, leads the troops
To the border of Tooran.

At this time, Sepijaab is ruled by a king named
Varaazaad, a brave warrior, owner of troops
And treasure, a hero who shines among men
Like a pearl shines in clear waters.

At the sound of trumpets, clarions, and Indian bells,
Varaazaad asks timpani be drummed and sets forth,
Drives his army through the desert onto a battlefield,
Soon to be converted into a sea of blood.
With him are thirty thousand sword-wielding men,
Renowned riders, eager for battle.

Varaazaad emerges from the army's core.
Advancing quickly toward Faraamarz.
He demands, "Who are you?
How dare you come to this side of the border?
Are you here by order of the king,
Or are you sent by the army warrior?
Have you never heard of Afraasiyaab,
Of his nobility, of his throne and his royal crown?
You must identify yourself, for you will fail

◇◇◇◇◇◇◇◇◇◇◇◇◇
27 Naarvan: An area in northern Iran.

In this venture, and I do not wish
To remove your soul from your body
Without first learning your name."

Faraamarz says to him, "Unfortunate hero,
I am the fruit of the tree that bears all world heroes.
I am the son of the one before whom lions tremble,
And who, in his anger, can destroy mighty elephants.
But why should I reply to a man of evil race,
A son of deevs such as yourself?
My father, Rostam, is on his way with a vast host,
Ready to vanquish the enemy.
He is strapped to avenge Siaavosh.
He marches on, drawing near like a fierce lion.
He will bring massive destruction to this border
And throughout Tooran-Zamin.
The air will not venture to disperse
The dust rising from his campaign.
Neither army nor Afraasiyaab will pull through,
Neither harvest nor border, nor shiny water."

Varaazaad realizes that discussion is useless.
He gives his troops the order to move
And to draw their arrows from end to end.

The warriors form ranks on both sides,
Shield their heads with iron helms.
Everywhere the sound of battle echoes,
And the earth rattles beneath the horses' hooves.

At the boom of kettledrums and the blare of trumpets,
Faraamarz's heart drums wildly.
He flings himself into the mix, like a mad elephant,
Lasso on one arm, belt strapped firmly.
In a single assault, he overthrows one thousand men,
An act that determines the outcome of battle.

Faraamarz sprints, spear in hand,
To cut short Varaazaad's retreat and to capture
One thousand two hundred enemy troops.
He says to Varaazaad, "Today is the day of retribution,
The day to suffer the consequences for evil deeds."

The vast host disperses;
Its riders scatter across the plain.
Once Faraamarz's gaze falls on Varaazaad,
He emerges from the army's core,
Bellowing like a fierce lion.
He charges his black steed, and, with a strong grip
On his spear, he strikes Varaazaad at the waist,
Splitting his armor by unclasping its knots.

Then he dislodges him from his saddle
With the ease of someone handling a mosquito.
He heaves Varaazaad to the ground, dismounts,
Blesses the memory of Siaavosh,
And cuts off his opponent's head,
Thus covering his tunic with blood.

Faraamarz exclaims, "Enjoy the fruits of vengeance!
When you sow seeds of hatred,
You reap the harvest of war."

He carries the fire to all the lands,
And smoke rises up to the awe-inspiring sky.

Then he writes a letter to his father about the fate
Of Varaazaad, the one so eager to engage in battle:
"I have opened the door of war and vengeance.
I have removed Varaazaad from his saddle
Of poplar wood, cut off his head, avenged Siaavosh,
And destroyed his kingdom by way of a blazing fire."

6 | Sorkheh Sets Off to Fight Rostam

A messenger takes the direction
Of the Tooranian army leader.
"Rostam is intent on avenging the death of Siaavosh."
He says, "Noblemen from Iran gather in Tooran,
With Faraamarz at the lead, ready to engage in war.
His belt strapped for vengeance,
He shamefully severed Varaazaad's head.
The length of our border surrendered to destruction.
The Iranians ravaged the army, set the land on fire."

These words painfully remind Afraasiyaab
Of the ancient predictions of sages and astrologers.
He summons his prominent men from the provinces.
Distributing coins and treasures, he bids for horses.

Shepherds herd stallions from the plain to the square.

The king opens his stores of mace and horse armor,
Warrior arrows, nooses, and swords.
He asks his minister for the keys to his treasury
And exhibits his pearls and precious stones,
Crowns, bracelets, golden belts.
He unfolds a blanket of coins
Over the palace and the main square.

Once the army is equipped,
Once it has collected the royal gifts,
The king gives the order
For brazen timpani and Indian bells.
The cavaliers assume their positions
And get ready for battle.

Afraasiyaab, the whale, leads his host,
Vast as the sea, out of the city of Gang,
Marching from narrow city streets
Toward the expansive, barren desert.

He speaks at length to Sorkheh about Rostam,
Adding, "Take with you thirty thousand
Sword-bearing warriors keen on fight.
Go swift as wind to Sepijaab,
And abstain from taking part in rest or pleasure.
There you will find Fariborz and his army.
You must capture him and send me his head.
But beware of Rostam, who may threaten your life.
He is the only man able to sustain a battle with you.
You are my son, devoted and loyal to me.
You are the army's pillar and my shining moon.
If you are cautious and diligent,
Who would dare challenge you?
Now take the lead, grasp the circumstance,
And preserve our troops from Rostam's assault."

Sorkheh replies, "O King, I shall eliminate Rostam.
I shall bring Faraamarz, bound hard as stone,
His neck in a yoke, to the court of Afraasiyaab.
The tip of my spear will travel beyond the sun.
At the spot where I am to battle a leopard,
A war dog will not be worthy of a fight."

The ruler of the Tooranian host says,
"O noble war seeker, I wish to relate to you a story
That remains a reflection of this world.
An experienced dog is able to capture the leopard.
A lion, untrained in the skills of war, will fear the fox.
Faraamarz, son of the world hero, is brave,
Vigilant, and from the seed of warriors.
Do not regard him as inconsequential in war,
For he is shrewd, devious, and conniving.
Be bold and prepare to battle them.
Do not allow thoughts of reconciliation
To have access to your mind.

After hearing these words of advice,
Sorkheh leaves his father's side and sets forth.
He leads army and banner through the plain
And takes the direction of Sepijaab in haste,
His head replete with dreams of battle.

At the sight of the dust rising in the distance,
The sentinel in the Iranian camp quickly reports
To Faraamarz, who orders the beating of kettledrums.
The air turns to ebony from dust.
The sound of horse and rider treading on the plain
Rises higher than Venus and the sun.

Swords of steel shine like diamonds.
Tips of spears find warmth in blood.
One would think steam rises from the ground
As the surface of the world is set ablaze from battle.
The corpses of leaders, dispersed here and there,
Form a mountain from one end to another.

Sorkheh observes the battle scene,
Catches sight of the tip of Faraamarz's weapon.
He lets go of his bow to grab his lance

And rushes toward his foe, swift as wind.

Faraamarz springs up out the army's core
In the direction of Sorkheh,
Brandishing his spear of vengeance.
He says to him, "O misfortunate Turkman,
I shall stitch your body to your horse's saddle.
You spilled the blood of Siaavosh
Without fear or consideration for the Creator.
Now it is your turn to fall prey to death,
Right here, on this field."

Sorkheh says to him, "Do not speak thus.
You have no knowledge of what the future holds.
I am Sorkheh; I spring from the seed of Afraasiyaab.
The whale in the waters
Is consumed with panic at the sight of me.
I have come toward this battlefield
To extract your soul from your body."

He says this and strikes Faraamarz's spear,
Shattering it to bits.

But the noble warrior does not shift in the saddle.
He laughs and says, "Look at the elephant strength.
It will cause the world to turn indigo in your eyes."

The leaders of the Tooranian army
Charge forth full of fury and ardor for battle.

Sorkheh realizes, with great disquiet,
That he is the weaker, and he cowers back into retreat.
Faraamarz pounces after him like a mad elephant.
The Iranian riders trail their leader with loud cries.

As soon as Sorkheh is within reach, Faraamarz
Extends his arm abruptly like a nimble leopard,
Grabs him by the belt, lifts him from the saddle,
And tosses him onto the ground.
Then he forces Sorkheh to walk behind him,
Dragging him shamefully in this manner
From the mix of warriors to the Iranian camp.

At this moment, Rostam's banner crops up.
The rumble of his elephants
And approaching host is heard.
Faraamarz rushes toward his father
To announce his victory.

Rostam sees Sorkheh, hands tied,
Injured on the ground.
He sees Varaazaad's severed head and his body.
He sees the valley and plain strewn with corpses.
He sees the enemy's head crushed in battle.

The troops commend the young and glorious hero.
Rostam joins in the praise,
Then engages in distributing vast wealth to the poor.
He regards Faraamarz, as large as a whale,
His head and hands the color of a crimson tulip.

Then he tells a story to his son:
"To raise your head above the crowd,
You must possess both skill and high birth,
Wisdom must be your mate, insight your teacher.
The union of these four assets
And your valor assure you world conquest.
A fire has the ability to lighten the world
As well as to consume and burn its surroundings.
Though full of pride,
Faraamarz did not reveal himself until now.
Though steel is full of fire, its quality appears
Only when it makes contact with hard stone."

Rostam's sight falls on Sorkheh,
Who is a tall cypress in the middle of a field,
His chest like a lion's chest, his face like spring,
Framed by black curls, a drawing on his rosy cheeks.

Rostam commands Sorkheh be taken into the desert,
Where they send executioners with sword and urn.
His hands bound with noose,
He is to be laid down on the ground like a sheep,
His head severed just like Siaavosh's head,
Left disrespectfully to be devoured by vultures.

Commander Tous volunteers and immediately
Proceeds to send Sorkheh to his death.

Sorkheh pleads him, "O eminent prince,
Why do you wish to spill my innocent blood?
Siaavosh and I were friends of the same age.
My eyes cry mourning his loss day and night.
My lips constantly curse the ones
Who cut off his princely head
And hauled the sword and urn to that end.
Forgive my misgivings,
For I am young and of royal strength.
Refrain from having me executed."

Tous's heart feels pity for this man of high rank
Who has fallen so low.
He returns to Rostam and repeats to him
The words spoken by Afraasiyaab's son.

Rostam replies, "If Khosrow finds himself afflicted,
May Afraasiyaab's heart and soul
Eternally remain in a state of torment.
May his eyes continue to shed bitter tears.
In any case, a son from this man of evil race
Would surely strategize new spells and schemes.
Siaavosh was tossed to the ground,
His breast flooding his limbs and hair with blood.
I swear by the life and by the head of the King of Iran,
The noble and renowned Kaavoos Shah,
That as long as I live, I shall sever the head
Of every Turk who crosses my path,
Whether he is a king or a slave."

The hero of lion heart orders his brother Zavaareh
To spill the blood that could not be spared.

Zavaareh takes sword and urn and delivers
The young prince to the executioners,
Who cut off his head with a sharp blade,
Putting a decisive end to Sorkheh's life.

World, what do you want from those you nurture?
What do you want from your slaves?

They break Sorkheh's neck clean
And hang the severed head in a quarry.
The two feet of the dead man are placed above.
In loathing, dust is scattered on the corpse,
And the flesh torn to shreds with a dagger.

7 | Afraasiyaab Sets Off to Avenge His Son Sorkheh

As the Tooranians return home from the battlefield
With bloodstained bodies and dust-covered heads,
They tell tales of the noble Sorkheh
And how his fate was promptly curtailed,
How his head was severed mercilessly,
His blood-soaked body hung by the feet.

The people of Tooran-Zamin stand up,
Arms raised, hearts dark and wounded,
Grieving the death of Sorkheh.

Afraasiyaab lowers his crowned head.
He tears his stately robes to bits,
Screaming and scattering dust over his head.
He cries, "O my dear and noble son,
O leader of brave men, heroes and rulers,
Gone are your rosy cheeks beautiful as the moon.
Gone is your chest, your waist, your royal stature.
Your father shall never enjoy a moment of peace.
He will take his seat on his horse's saddle
To endlessly roam the battlefield."

Afraasiyaab turns to his troops and says,
"One must think of neither food nor sleep.
Let us breathe only for the execution of vengeance.
Let us don armor and coat of mail,
Fill our hearts with a dark form of loathing
To more fiercely engage in battle."

Once the voice of timpani rises on both sides,
A warrior may no longer ask for deferment.
Everywhere resound the clangor of weapons
And the blare of trumpets, clarions, and timpani.

The earth quivers beneath the horses' hooves,
And the drone of war rises to kiss the sky.

Afraasiyaab shouts to his leaders, "O noblemen,
Once the sound of war drums echoes on both sides,
There is no hesitation; we must begin the fight.
Let us fill our hearts with a sense of vengeance.
Let us pierce our enemies' hearts with short spears."

He says this, then asks for the chime
Of Indian bells and the strike of cymbals.
The wail of war horn, trumpet,
And kettledrums reverberates.
The earth trembles beneath the horses' hooves.
The shrieks of the troops reach the clouds.

As the army thus makes the plains' dust rise,
An observer approaches Rostam to tell him,
"The leader Afraasiyaab is on his way in great fanfare,
Escorted by a marching host, like a ship on water,
A host enlisted in vengeance and battle,
With honed claws keen and quick to shed blood."

At the news, Rostam sets off with the Kaaviani banner,
And the air turns purple from the swords of warriors.

On both sides, one hears the clamor of troops.
On both sides, the land fills with men eager for battle.
Day and night blend to be indistinguishable
As the light-shining sun disappears.
You would think the sun and moon are eclipsed
And the stars have dissolved
Inside the jaws of a whale.

The Tooranian leader forms his troops in ranks,
Commanding them to seize mace and spear.
Baarmaan takes the right wing
With a group of restless Turks.
Kohram the hero, ready to strike, takes the left side
While in the center stands the army king.

For his part, Rostam deploys his host,
And the earth disappears beneath heavy dust.

Goodarz, Hojir, and other noblemen take the left.
Giv and Tous, riders escorted
By elephants and kettledrums, take the right.
Rostam, ready for battle and eager for vengeance,
Affirms his position in the center,
Placing Zavaareh in the rear
And Faraamarz at the vanguard.

The horses' hooves color the earth black.
The sky, a stripe of spears, resembles tiger fur.
The tips of flags and blue swords puncture the clouds.
You would think the earth is a mountain of steel,
Its crest covered thickly in armor and helm.

The two hosts collide, equal in might.
Neither side tires,
Neither side is diminished in strength.

8 | Rostam Kills Pilsam

Pilsam arrives at the army's core, his heart
Intent on fight, his face creased with belligerence.
He says to the Tooranian ruler, "O glorious King,
Allow me to seize armor, horse, helmet, and sword.
I wish to assault Rostam, to cover his name in shame.
I shall bring the gift of his head, his mace, and blade,
As well as his horse Rakhsh, to your kingdom."

Afraasiyaab's heart delights at these words.
He raises his spear's tip above the sun and replies,
"O bold lion, may this elephant never vanquish you!
If you succeed in overcoming Rostam,
You will save the world from tyranny.
Your throne and seal, your blade and headdress
Will prevail in the land of Tooran.
You will make my head ascend to the revolving dome.
I shall award you with my daughter and my crown.
Two thirds of Iran and Tooran will be yours,
As well as these two lands' jewels, treasures, and cities."

Piran is aggrieved by these words.

He nears the king on whom fortune shines
And says to him, "This young man is too passionate
And may cause harm to his own life.
If he attacks Rostam, his head will roll in dust.
In my opinion, he will squander his distinction
And cut short his destiny's trajectory.
No one, of his own accord,
Takes the direction of hell or of the jaws of a dragon.
This action will cover the king in shame.
The army will fail, its courage to fight depleted.
You are well aware of the affection
An older brother holds for a younger one."

Pilsam answers Piran: "I do not fear this world hero.
Should I engage in battle with him,
I hope, by virtue of the king's good star,
Never to be a source of shame.
You have watched me conquer four eminent warriors.
Since that time my strength has only increased.
It is not right for you to deprive me of heroism.
I shall carry on and complete this venture.
Do not stir up a star of ill-fortune."

With these words, the king hands over
A battle horse with bard, a sword and spear,
A coat of mail, and a helmet.

Pilsam equips himself for the fight
And charges forth like wind, brave as a daring lion.
His shield on his shoulder, his spear in his hand,
He bolts restless, like a drunken elephant,
Storms onto the battlefield swift as dust,
Shouting, loud as thunder, at the Iranians:
"Where are you hiding Rostam,
The one claimed to be a dragon on the day of war?
Tell him I search for him. Tell him to come and fight.
I am ready to exchange blows with him.
I am ready to wield my sharp claws."

Giv leaps, quick to draw his sword.
He screams, "Rostam will never wish to tarnish
His name by fighting against a single Turk."

211

The two heroes, Giv, son of Goodarz,
And Pilsam, fall on each other.
Pilsam strikes a blow with his spear,
Making Giv's feet lose hold of the stirrups.

At this moment, Giv is in need of a valiant friend.
Faraamarz, witnessing the assault, flies to the rescue.
With his sword, he strikes and shatters Pilsam's spear.
With a second blow on the other's helm,
He breaks it as well.

Pilsam and the two Iranians chase each other
Like mad lions until Rostam spots,
From the army's core, the two brave warriors
Fighting a single man of lion heart
And stirring the dust to soar to the clouds.

Rostam reflects, "I know of only one man
Among the Turks, a man named Pilsam,
Strong enough to fight in this way."

He also heard during his travels through the world
The good and bad predictions of sages and astrologers
Regarding the land of Tooran, and he further thinks,
"If Pilsam is able to overcome the dangers
He is exposed to and gain experience,
He is destined to become a hero such as none
Has lived before, neither in Iran nor in Tooran,
None comparable, the world over.
But I have a feeling his end is near, as I see him
Charging my way with great fury to challenge me."

He turns to his troops and says, "Stay put.
Make no attempts to move out of ranks.
I shall test Pilsam myself
To determine which of us is the stronger."

He takes hold of a mighty spear,
Braces himself on his saddle seat,
Dons his helmet, kicks the stirrups,
And, handling gently the reins,
Raises the point of his spear to eye level.
Incensed, lips foaming,

He springs out of the army center
And rushes to the front of the line of Turks,
Crying, "Renowned Pilsam, here I am,
If you wish to burn me with your scorching breath.
You will now feel the blows of a brave crocodile.
Never again will you lead your horse into a battle scene.
My heart is consumed with pity for your youth.
Alas, why should a world hero like you perish so?"

He says this and spurs his horse,
Rushing to fight like the dome of the turning sky.
He strikes Pilsam at the belt with his spear,
Removing him from the saddle
Like a ball struck by a mallet.
Then he leaps into the center of the Tooranian troops,
Flings Pilsam into their midst as if a vile thing,
Saying, "Envelop this man in yellow brocade,
For my mace has made him the color of lapis lazuli."
Then he pulls the reins in the opposite direction,
Swiftly flying away and back to the heart of his army.

Piran sheds torrents of tears, for the art of medicine
Is powerless to return Pilsam's strength and health.
The Tooranian men, heartbroken,
See the battlefield dim before their eyes.
Everywhere cries mix with the sound of blows
Rising from the two hosts.

The echo of timpani, played from atop elephants,
Fills the air for miles around.
The earth shakes beneath the horses' hooves.
The mountain turns into a sea of blood,
The desert into a mound of corpses.
The sky quakes at the fanfare of trumpets.
Every stone takes on the appearance of coral.
The ground is soaked in blood
As innumerable leaders fall.

You would think blood rain plummets from the sky.
You would think fathers
No longer hold affection for sons.
A violent gust of wind rises above the battlefield,

And a canopy of black dust shrouds the sky.

In this way the two armies fight.
One could hardly distinguish
One combatant from the other.
The world darkens like the darkest night,
And the day dons the color of dusk.

9 | Afraasiyaab Flees From Rostam

Afraasiyaab addresses his troops and says,
"The good fortune that once shone upon us
Has fallen asleep since you battle so meekly.
The time has come for action.
At least for today, you must proceed like leopards.
Overwhelm and assail the enemy on all sides.
Overpower the Iranians.
Raise the tips of your spears high to the sun
And bring them crashing down to earth."

He emerges out of his army's center
And, heart wounded, eager for vengeance,
Throws himself on enemy troops,
Attacking the wing commanded by Tous.
He kills a great number of Iran's leaders
While Tous, fearful of his adversary, takes flight.

A man rushes to Rostam and says,
"Today our glory is lost.
The right wing is a sea of blood,
And the Iranian banner is down."

Rostam advances to the army center,
Escorted by Faraamarz and his men.
He is accosted by relatives of Afraasiyaab,
Armed with shields and furious with him,
Their hearts full of hatred, their heads full of haste.

Rostam kills a great number of them
While Faraamarz and Tous hold their ground.

Once Afraasiyaab makes out Rostam's purple flag
And the Kaaviani banner, he realizes that
There stands the hero of elephantine stature,
The proud descendant of Nariman.
The Tooranian king leaps like a brave leopard,
Strengthens his position on the stirrups,
And bursts out toward Rostam.

When the glorious hero sees the black banner,
He turns loose Rakhsh's bridle
And races forth like a fuming lion.
Simmering with rage, he charges at Afraasiyaab
And strikes him with the tip of his spear,
Making blood flow like water.

Rostam pierces the king's helmet
With an arrow tipped in the shape of a willow leaf,
While Afraasiyaab strikes a blow on Rostam's side.
The spear's point punctures the hero's leather belt
But does not penetrate his armor of Babreh Bayan.

Rostam pounces on the king with renewed fury
And whacks the flank of the royal horse.
The battle steed keels over with intense pain
And tosses the brave king to the ground.

Rostam hopes to seize Afraasiyaab by the belt
In an attempt to rush him toward his death.
Hoomaan, watching the fight,
Raises his heavy mace high to the sky
And smacks Rostam on the shoulder.
The entire army cries out, and Rostam
Pivots around to glower at Hoomaan.

Afraasiyaab seizes the moment to slip away
And climb upon a speedy horse.
Hoomaan rescues him from the dragon's claws
By means of one hundred spells of sorcery.

The vanquisher of lions, donor of crowns, shudders
With anger and launches Rakhsh after Hoomaan.
But despite his speed, despite the fervor of the chase,
He is unable to catch up with him,

215

For fate awards him with a moment of respite.

The cry of the Tooranian warriors reaches the clouds
As they take hold of their heavy maces.

The Iranian troops encircle Rostam to protect him.
The noble Tous asks him if the elephant's shoulder
Felt the blow of the deer.

Rostam replies, "When the arm of a brave man
Brings down the strokes of his heavy mace,
Neither boulder nor anvil is able to resist.
To strike like that, one must have chest and arm.
But when Hoomaan handles his mace,
You would think it is made of wax, not metal."

Afraasiyaab evades Rostam and flees.
The entire army, from end to end, bellows a cry.
Warriors raise their spears toward the clouds.
One can see everywhere corpses and wounded men.
It is as if tulips sprout from a ground of saffron.
Horses and elephants trudge along in blood,
Their soaked limbs tinted scarlet.

The Turks take flight swiftly to fend off Rostam
And to avoid falling prey to his forearm's power.

Rostam rushes after them for three farsangs.
Then he returns, for he knows that the world
Is casting a friendly eye on the Tooranian leader.

Rostam and his men take the path of their camp.
His host's fortune expands by a vast booty.
The entire plain is covered in iron, gold, and silver,
Spear, armor and bridle, helm, shield and belt.

10 | Afraasiyaab Sends Kay Khosrow to Khotan

As the sun reveals its face above the mountain crests,
As it scatters rubies upon the pitch darkness,
One hears the clank of weapons
And the blare of trumpets.

Rostam sets his army into motion.

The Iranians chase after Afraasiyaab, all the while
Shedding tears at the memory of Siaavosh's death.

Afraasiyaab hears of their approach.
Aware that their leader's every move
Is prompted by a fierce longing for vengeance,
The Tooranian king guides his troops to the Sea of Chin,
For the earth's surface is shrinking for him.
He crosses the sea at the exact place he intended.

Then Afraasiyaab turns to Piran and says,
"Give me advice on this blasted,
Senseless son of Siaavosh.
If Rostam is able to reach him,
He will usher him to Iran-Zamin, where
They will crown this deev child and hail him as king.
They will seat him on the new throne,
Place on his head a shining crown.
Now find him and bring him to this side of the sea.
Hurry to faithfully follow my command."

Piran replies, "Refrain from sending him to his end.
I shall take such measures that the king
Will commend his loyal and devoted servant.
We shall bring him here with us,
Consign him to the region of Khotan.
Never should a wicked man rise against the king."

The monarch replies, "Master of wisdom,
You always provide me with worthy guidance.
Immediately make preparations,
For we must overlook nothing in this affair."

Piran sends an envoy, a sensible man of noble birth,
And orders him to fetch the prince.
The messenger takes the road,
Traveling as swift as flying smoke,
Obeying the order just as the leader directed.

He reaches Khosrow, observes his majesty,
Delivers blessings on his person and pays homage,

Holding himself at length with utmost respect.
In the end, he relates the contents of the message.

Khosrow is unsure what to think.
He reveals his secret thoughts to his mother:
"Afraasiyaab sent someone
Who wishes to take me to the seashore.
What shall I do? What remedy shall I seek?
Wisdom may perhaps lend us
A path to safeguard our lives."

Mother and son weigh various options
But find no means to avoid the journey.
They depart against their wishes and in great haste.
They travel, low-spirited, eyes full of tears,
Mouths heavily cursing Afraasiyaab.

In the end, Khosrow arrives at Piran's side.
Upon seeing the prince, Piran immediately
Climbs down from his throne and rushes forward.
He asks him how he bore the hardships of travel,
Praises him at length, receiving him with tenderness
And seating him by his side.

Piran asks for Khosrow's needs to be looked after.
Anything that has to do with food and clothing,
Carpets and tents, and various mounts.
Once the prince's every need is attended to,
Piran presents himself at court and says
To Afraasiyaab, "O wise king, glorious and renowned,
I have brought here the noble child.
What now is your wish and your command?"

The King of Tooran-Zamin replies to Piran,
"You must send him away from the Sea of Chin,
So far away that brave men of Iran
Will never hear of him."

Piran swiftly sends Khosrow away
In the direction suggested by the king,
Like smoke ushered by wind.

11 | Rostam Governs Tooran-Zamin for Seven Years

Rostam travels to Tooran-Zamin,
All the way to the edge of Chin and Maachin,
Capturing Khataah[28] and Khotan
With his sweeping sword.
As he seizes the royal throne and climbs to sit on it,
Afraasiyaab's good fortune decidedly vanishes.

Rostam says on this occasion,
"Great is the man who walks to meet his enemies.
If an ill-wisher comes before him, better he be killed.
If he is a loser, he might as well run off the battlefield."

In the palace, he seeks the king's treasures.
He is led to them, one after the other, in precise order.
He is shown the door to the golden treasury,
Handed golden crowns, brocades and ivory thrones,
Servants, horses, golden strappings,
And slaves of great beauty.
In addition are many jewels, gems, and thrones,
Seized from the treasury of Gang.

He renders wealthy all his army's men,
Giving them bracelets, crowns, and diadems.
He gives Tous the famous ivory throne, bracelets,
One torque, and the rule of the town of Chaadj.
Rostam says to him, "Cut off the head of any rebel
Who continues to lean on Afraasiyaab's authority.
Turn his body into a feast for vultures.
On the other hand, treat with fatherly tenderness
Anyone who submits to you and seeks your protection,
As well as anyone who renounces Ahriman's faith.
Guard him from pain; raise him above all need.
Do not cause affliction to those who are happy.
Never diverge from justice's path or from virtue's path,
For this world is momentary and does not last eternally.
No glory is higher than that of Jamsheed,
Yet the revolving dome beat him down
And delivered the world to other masters."

◇◇◇◇◇◇◇◇◇◇◇◇◇
28 Khataah: A town near Chin.

He gives Goodarz a crown worthy of a king,
Inlaid with precious stones,
A throne, a bracelet, and earrings.
He hands over to him the regions of Sepijaab
And Soghdi[29] with their strongholds,
Offering him much advice
And handing him the investiture of the land.
Rostam lavishes his brave leader with praise
And respect, for he is connected to the holy faith.

Rostam says to Goodarz, "The seal of power
And justice as well as the seal of battle and feast
Have retained a memory of you.
Skill is more valuable than an illustrious birth,
But high birth well suits a warrior.
You are gifted with courage, ancestry, and wisdom.
My mind enjoys dwelling on thoughts of your greatness.
All will end well if you wish to follow my advice,
For you originate from a powerful and noble family.
From Sepijaab to the banks of the Golzarioon,[30]
No one will refuse to obey you."

Then Rostam sends Fariborz, son of Kaavoos,
A golden crown, gold coins, and many jewels,
Along with a message: "You are army leader.
You are a prince and the brother of Siaavosh.
Strap yourself in preparation to avenge your brother.
Maintain your noose upon your saddle's hook.
Never grow weary of tracking down Afraasiyaab.
Release all thoughts of food, sleep, and rest.
Never cease to pursue justice,
For no one ever suffers from being just and fair."

Next he proffers Khotan to Giv, and Khataah
And Chagal[31] to sword-sweeping Ashkesh.
Rumors travel to Chin and all the way to Maachin
That Rostam has assumed the imperial throne.
Noblemen supply offerings and gifts

◇◇◇◇◇◇◇◇◇◇◇◇◇
29 Sepijaab and Soghdi: Lands in Tooran-Zamin.
30 Golzarioon: A fictional river in Tooran-Zamin.
31 Chagal: A city in Tooran-Zamin.

Of silver and jewels worthy of a monarch.
They bring these to him and say,
"We are your servants and slaves.
We live solely to obey your command."
Seeing how prudently they proceed,
He decides to spare their lives.

Rostam engages in the practice of hunting
With cheetah and falcon,
And in this way some time passes.

12 | Zavaareh Surveys Siaavosh's Hunting Preserves

One day, Zavaareh sets out for the hunt,
Taking a Turk with him as guide.

Once he arrives at the designated site,
He perceives a forest in the middle of a large field.
It is as if one could never leave this place,
So beautiful is it in color and scent,
So lush with running water, you would think
The soul itself could take nourishment from it.

At that moment, the Turk carelessly opens his mouth
And says to Zavaareh, "This is the site of Siaavosh's
Hunting preserve, a place he enjoyed above all others
In Tooran-Zamin, a place where he was happy,
While he deemed other grounds as a source of sadness."

These words stir up the memory of what happened.
Zavaareh dismounts and falls unconscious.
After some time, he sits up and releases the falcon
Tied to his fist, allowing it to fly away.
His lashes fill with his eyes' blood tears.

His brave companions find him distraught,
Sobbing and lamenting.
They curse his guide, strike him a hard blow,
And trample him beneath their feet.

Zavaareh, shedding tears of grief,
Takes a great oath and says, "From here on,
I shall allow myself neither to hunt nor to rest.
I shall be relentless in my pursuit of Afraasiyaab.
Nor shall I allow Rostam to rest or sleep.
We must at once prepare to execute vengeance."

At the moment his sight falls on Rostam,
He shouts heatedly: "Have we come for retribution
Or to make this land a better place?
Since the glorious Yazdan gifted you with strength,
Since you have been handed over the sun's sphere,
Why are we not laying waste to this land?
Why do we allow a single man here to live in peace?
Do not forget the vengeance we owe Tooran's king,
For the world will never witness,
Not in one hundred generations, one equal to him."

13 | Rostam Destroys Tooran-Zamin

Zavaareh succeeds in convincing Rostam
And in drawing out this man of lion heart
Who springs into action,
Killing, destroying, disrupting the entire nation.

One could no longer find a single inhabited section,
From the land of Tooran
To the lands of Saghlaab[32] and Rum.
The heads of men are severed, young ones and old.
Women and children are abducted
And forced into servitude. Destruction prevails,
Extending for more than one thousand farsangs.

Noblemen come to Rostam, their heads low.
They tell him, "We have grown weary of Afraasiyaab.
We wish to never set eyes on him again,
Not even in our dreams. None of us ever offered
The smallest advice or the slightest assistance.
Why must you shed innocent blood?

◇◇◇◇◇◇◇◇◇◇◇◇◇
32 Saghlaab: Land beyond Tooran-Zamin and Rum; land of the Slavs.

PART NINE

We are now a scattered people.
We stand by your side as your slaves.
Since you are master, do not kill us.
We are not to blame. Do not put up
A struggle against the revolving dome.
No one knows where the king resides,
Nor do we know if he remains alive.
Perhaps the dragon's tail
Has wrapped itself around him."

Rostam, whose heart is full of wisdom,
Trembles with apprehension at these words.
He hurries to the border of Ghajghaarbaashi[33]
And convenes his army's greatest leaders.

Wise and worldly men gather around him and say,
"Kaavoos, devoid of grace, wisdom, and dignity,
Lingers upon the throne without an advisor.
If Afraasiyaab wished, he could rush his army to Iran.
No matter which road they take,
He would succeed in capturing the aged Kaavoos.
All our victories would be in vain.
Never again would we enjoy peace and rest.
We have stretched the nets of vengeance far and wide.
We have ravaged and consumed in fire
All the cultivated lands of Tooran-Zamin.
Let us now go to the old king, fight for him,
Find a way to regain our strength.

"We spent six years without a day of rest or happiness.
Our thrones, seals, and crowns await us in Iran-Zamin.
We are weary, unhappy.
We sought material wealth, but our minds subside.
If you attach yourself to this ancient world,
It will break you while suppressing the truth from you.
Greed is your enemy. Do not seek to possess it
Unless your heart is veering down the path of Ahriman.
Dress yourself in rich clothing, eat and drink your fill,
And always perform acts of charity.
Such is your role, for this life is a transient state."

◇◇◇◇◇◇◇◇◇◇◇◇◇
33 Ghajghaarbaashi: Situated in today's Turkey.

223

Rostam approves of the words of the sage
And blessed wise man who continues to speak:
"Work to seek glory during this temporary journey.
Once you rest below the ground,
Who will you have as companion?
How long do you wish to weep
For the goods that evaded you in this lifetime?"

14 | Rostam Returns to the Land of Iran

Ashamed to have extended his stay, Rostam feels,
Growing within, an ardent longing to depart.
He summons herds of horses grazing freely
In various fields of Tooran-Zamin.

He gathers ten thousand slaves of both sexes,
Worthy as gifts for the king.
He compiles purses of musk and sable fur,
The pelts of ermine and Siberian squirrel.
He adorns the backs of male elephants
With splendor, coins, and golden covers.
He asks for scores of precious things:
Strappings, fabrics and cloths, gold and silver,
Swords, armor, thrones and crowns, to be loaded
On beasts of burden and taken to Iran-Zamin.

Once everything is arranged,
Rostam leaves Tooran-Zamin and takes the direction
Of Zabolestan and his celebrated father, Zaal.

Tous, Goodarz, and Giv depart for the land of Pars
And for the imperial court, along with brave,
Glorious, and prosperous world warriors.

As Afraasiyaab learns that Rostam and Tous
Have crossed the Jayhoon,
He returns from the east toward the Sea of Gang,
Heart full of vengeance, head keen on battle.
He finds his land devastated,
Men, great and small, dead and gone,
The place cleared of horse and treasure,

Crown and throne, his royal dwellings destroyed,
The trees raided of leaves, men perished in fires,
Homes ravaged by flames.

The king sheds tears of blood and says to his leaders,
"Anyone who chooses to forget
And forgive these acts has forsaken reason.
Fill your hearts with a deep longing for revenge.
May your shields serve as cradles
And your helmets as pillows!
Take hatred and war to Iran-Zamin.
Make the sky tumble down to earth.
Let us avenge our land, our dead, our offspring,
Our pillaged treasure and broken parents.
Let us trample beneath our feet the land of Iran-Zamin.
Let us go to war like mighty lions.
They have conquered us in one campaign,
But we shall not wallow in defeat.
On every side, let us gather weapons and troops
To newly open the road leading to good fortune."

In haste, Afraasiyaab puts together a vast host,
Troops equipped with spear and firmly clothed in mail.
He leads the warriors to Iran-Zamin.
He launches attacks on all points and all sides,
Allowing the Iranian troops neither rest nor reprieve.
He burns harvest and trees, rendering
His enemy's position more and more precarious.

For seven years, the sky remains dry of rain.
Fortune turns against Iran
As its affluence gradually vanishes.
Men complain of pain and hardship.

In this way, a long time passes.
All the while Rostam, hero of elephantine stature,
Holds himself strong and steady in Zabolestan
While the world succumbs to the Turkish leader
And his piercing, striking sword.

15 | Goodarz Dreams of Sooroosh

One night, Goodarz has a dream.
In it, he sees a cloud full of moisture,
Showering down on the land of Iran.
On this rain cloud glides blessed Sooroosh,
Who says to Goodarz, "Lend your ear to me.
If you wish to be free of the evil dragon Turk
And liberate the world from anguish and grief,
There is in Tooran-Zamin an offshoot of the royal seed
Whose name is Kay Khosrow, a prince,
Son of Siaavosh, courageous and illustrious.
On his father's side, he is a descendant
Of the bloodline of Kay Ghobaad.
On his mother's side, his lineage is traced to Toor.
Once his auspicious foot touches the earth of Iran,
The sky will reward him with his heart's desires.

"He will strap himself to avenge his father
And will turn upside down the land of Tooran.
He will make the waters of the Sea of Gholzom[34]
Simmer to a scalding temperature.
Unfailing in his desire to retaliate against Afraasiyaab,
All year he will cling to his vengeful suit of armor
While he maintains himself, day and night,
Lodged in the saddle, ready to engage in battle.
From among Iran's bravest men, only one is destined
To locate him and reach him: the glorious hero Giv.
Such is the wish of the sky in its sweeping justice,
For it holds your son in the deep folds of its affection."

Goodarz awakens from sleep, prays
To the World Creator, distributor of love and justice,
And grazes the dust with his white, aging beard,
Feeling hopeful for the world king.

As the sun breaks through the wings of night's raven,
Rising like a golden light across the skies,
The army leader rests on his ivory throne and places
In the audience hall a seat made of teakwood.

◇◇◇◇◇◇◇◇◇◇◇◇◇
34 Sea of Gholzom: The Red Sea, between Egypt, Saudi Arabia, Sudan, and Yemen.

Heart full of new reflections, he summons Giv
And speaks to him at length of the dream:
"May your blessed footsteps
And your shining star light up the world.
Since your pious mother blessed you with life,
The earth is sanctified with Yazdan's grace.
Sacred Sooroosh appeared to me
In dream by divine command,
Seated upon a moisture-filled, wind-filled cloud
That drifted down to purge the world of grief.
Sooroosh faced me and said,
        'Why are you so dispirited?
        Why are men so full of hatred,
        And the earth barren, devoid of water?
        It is because the king carries neither grace nor dignity.
        He does not go down the path of just rulers.
        When Kay Khosrow turns up in the land of Iran,
        He will burden your foes beneath the weight of wars.
        Among brave world heroes,
        There is only one man able to seek and find him,
        A man named Giv, son of the brave Goodarz.'

"Such is the fate reserved to you by the sky sublime.
You are the one summoned to liberate us from pain
And suffering and from the shackles of chains.
You sought fame in two armies.
Now before you stands eternal glory,
Such glory that will never fade as long
As men and their traditions endure on earth.
This venture, though full of danger,
Will soon be replaced by glory and wealth.
It will culminate in great joy and pride.
Since you cannot remain on earth forever,
Fame is more valuable than this transient dwelling.
You will return a king to the world.
You will make the tree of salvation blossom."

Giv replies, "Dear father, I am your slave.
I shall follow your orders as long as I shall live.
I swear on your renowned name, O my mentor
And guide, that I shall accomplish this task
To the best of my ability."

He returns to his palace and prepares for departure,
Astonished at the scope of his father's dream.

The highest ranking lady of ladies,
Rostam's esteemed daughter Baanoogoshasp,
Who is Giv's wife, hears of his preparations.
She sees her spouse's horse being saddled.
She slowly approaches him and says,
"O noble man, O fame seeker, I hear you are off
To Tooran-Zamin in search of Kay Khosrow.
Should the world hero allow it, I wish to go to Rostam.
I wish to see my father's face, for I miss him dearly
And have not seen him in a long while.
I bid you farewell, O world conqueror.
May you always remain the sustainer of brave men!"

Giv consents to his mate's departure,
And Baanoogoshasp swiftly travels to Sistan.

16 | Giv Travels to Tooran-Zamin in Search of Kay Khosrow

As the shining sun rises to paint the earth in the image
Of a golden rose, Giv emerges into the morning light,
Strapped and ready for battle,
Bestriding his horse of speed.

Goodarz asks him, "Which companion and mate
Do you intend to take on this journey?"

Giv replies, "O brave world hero of shining soul,
You hold your head up high.
I prefer to go alone into the land of Tooran,
Alone with noose and horse.
Should I take an escort,
My identity will be questioned.
I shall be forced to face the enemy
And engage in battle.
A noose will suffice, attached to my saddle,
Along with a speedy horse
And an Indian sword shining silken colors.

Desert and plain will serve as my dwelling.
Should the need arise,
I shall ask assistance from a guide,
But I shall not enter town and city where
I would be recognized and find cause to repent.
I leave, happy and content,
Trusting the good fortune of the world hero,
And I shall return happy and content.
Take in your care my son Bijan.
Protect him from the fate's ambush.
Teach him the art of war, for battle and feast
Are the only occupations that will ever suit him.
Despite his youth, I see in him a certain valor
That has captured my heart.

"Farewell. Soften the affliction caused by my absence.
I do not know whether we shall see each other again.
Only the Creator holds such knowledge.
When you bathe your cheeks to pray,
Remember me in your appeals,
For Yazdan is supreme and above all power.
Ruling kings are slaves to the Creator,
To whose order wheels the revolving dome,
At whose command the sun dips into the horizon,
At whose will we eat and sleep, Creator of the strong
And the weak, Source of hope and fear,
Master of earth, time and space, wind and fire,
Water and dust, my sole Protector, my Guide,
As I make my way to find the glorious king."

The brave father is now an aged man.
His heart full of grief and his face full of tears,
As his young son straps himself,
A lion ready for battle.
Goodarz is pained by the uncertainty of Giv's return
And whether he will set eyes on his dear son again.

Giv dismounts to kiss the hand of his father
Of lion heart, who, in turn, holds him close
And kisses his face and head numerous times.

The aged Goodarz addresses prayers to Yazdan:

"O Justice Giver, come to my aid.
I entrust you with the care of my glorious son.
He is my life and my world. Take care of him
So that he may free our land of persecution.
Then return him to me, O Supreme Being."

Many bear the agony of life in their wish
To acquire power, still they retain no other
Place of repose than the humble cradle of earth.
What remains is lethal poison without its antidote.
Since you hold the knowledge
That your life on earth will not last long,
Why do you display the crown of greed?
You will take it with you to bury beneath the dust
And continue to cling to it inside your casket.

The world offers countless delights.
Why should you exert yourself for someone else?
You work hard, yet another may enjoy
The fruits of your labors without glancing once
In the direction of your coffin. He in turn
Will see his joyous days skid to a quick end.
Dust will soon cover his head as well.
Remember that your days are passing.
Occupy yourself in prayers to the just Creator.
However long your sojourn on earth, in the end,
The path is a one-way road with no point of return.
You might as well engage in good deeds
And take great pains not to trouble anyone.
Such is the path to salvation. Do not surrender
Your heart to love this unstable world,
For it does not belong to you or to anyone for long.
You are here for some time, then you must depart,
And once you do, there will be no point of return.

O wise man of pure heart,
Abstain from drowning in doubt
And remove your foot from this constricted fissure.
Yazdan is your adoptive parent.
You are both slave and divine creature.
Should you choose to burden yourself
With the heavy load of apprehension,

At least believe irrefutably in divine presence.

The one who dwells in denial
Does not deserve food or sleep.
One must not sit beside him, for his heart is blind
And his head is devoid of sense.
Water and earth testify to divine presence.
Do not toss away your heart into dark distress
For the sake of feigned knowledge.

Yazdan is capable of anything,
Knows everything and holds everything.
Yazdan is Creator of mind, wisdom, and soul,
Creator of time and space,
From the tiniest ant to the most colossal elephant.

The King of Tooran, wishing to raise his head
Above all men, killed the young prince to such end.
With this act, he dictated
His own worthless, abysmal fate,
For Yazdan, Justice Giver, allowed to emerge
And grow an offshoot bearing fruit
From the very rib of the King of Turks.
Yazdan would punish Afraasiyaab as he deserves,
Destroying both his power and his palace.

Yazdan is Master of Saturn, Sun, and Moon,
Giver of victory, skill, and power,
Master of existence and justice, Source of greatness
And weakness, of deliverance and all things,
A Being above and beyond need, Creator of world
And love, Venus and the revolving dome.
The true path resides in divine will and command.
The Sun and Moon function as divine implements,
Quiet and blind.

Giv straps his belt by holy command.
Like a wild lion he sets off alone, trusting
The Creator, his being accustomed to opulence.
He gallops until he reaches the border of Tooran.
Every time he encounters a solitary man,
He questions him softly in the language of Turks,
Inquiring after the location of Kay Khosrow.

If the Turk denies knowledge, Giv kills him instantly,
Binds him with his noose, drags him some distance,
Then digs a grave to bury him.
In this way, he allows no one to get word of his secret
Or to learn his name and his arrival in Tooran-Zamin.

Once, he takes as guide a common man.
He follows him prudently and reveals
His secret only a few days later, saying,
"In all confidence, I wish to pose a question to you.
If you act with righteousness,
If you distance falsehood from your heart,
I shall give you all that you want.
I shall refuse you neither my life nor my body."

The Turk replies, "Many things are known,
But the knowledge is widespread among all men.
If I am familiar with the answer to your question,
My tongue will not fail to provide a reply."

Giv asks, "Where is Kay Khosrow?
Respond to me with utmost honesty."

The Turk retorts, "I have never heard such a name.
No one has ever uttered it in my presence."

Upon hearing the reply from the guide,
Giv strikes a sharp blow on the man's head
And with his sword knocks him dead.

17 | Giv Finds Kay Khosrow

For seven years, like a foolish man,
Giv roams around the land of Tooran,
Hoping to find a hint of the prince's whereabouts.
His hips are battered by the rubbing
Of his sword, belt, and straps.

He lives off deer flesh, dresses in its skin,
Feeds on herbs, and, instead of wine,
He drinks brackish water.

In this way, he roams around the land,
Over mountain and plain, exhausted and weary,
Keeping his distance from men.

Meanwhile, at the moment when Rostam
Leads his army to the other side of the river,
Afraasiyaab marches into Gang,
Recapturing Tooran-Zamin.

Afraasiyaab says to Piran, "O wise man,
Summon the cursed Kay Khosrow from Maachin.
Return him to his mother, but block all the roads
To bar him from a possible escape."

Piran immediately sends an envoy on a race camel
To fetch the bright and sensible son of Siaavosh
And hand him over to his mother.

Some time passes.

One day, the valiant Giv, crossing the land of Tooran,
Stands deep in thought before a majestic forest.
He enters the woods mournfully.
Nature is bright and cheerful,
But Giv's heart is burdened with deep sorrow.
He observes the ground lush with greenery,
A gurgling spring carving into it,
And he finds it a pleasant place to rest and sleep.

He dismounts, allows his horse to roam freely,
And lies down on the ground.
But his heart is full of worry as he reflects,
"I am isolated from the world.
I enjoy neither sleep nor feast.
What if it was an evil deev who appeared
Before my valiant father in his strange dream?
I find no signs of Kay Khosrow here.
Why should I drag myself further across this land?
It is as if the prince has never been born
Or, if he has, as if his life has drifted in the wind.
There is no sign of him anywhere.
My army companions are either engaged
In battle or spending their time in feast.

Some seek glory while others delight in revelry.
Meanwhile, fate deprives me of any such joy.

"In vain my days slip away.
My mind folds upon itself like an arched bow.
Perhaps this king is fictitious, dreamed up.
Perhaps he was never even born.
Or perhaps he lived once upon a time,
His life flung aside into the wind by fate.
From this quest, I have gained
Nothing but trouble and pain.
Happy is the one whose life comes to an end
From a drink laced with venom."

The hero in search of the king
Treads through the forest mournfully,
Then he sees from afar a shining fountain.
Beside it stands a young man of cypress stature
Whose mere sight has a calming effect on one's spirit.

The youth holds in his hand a cup of wine.
On his head is a cluster of flowers
Full of color and scent.
His height is imprinted with divine, majestic grace,
His expression claims a wise man's acumen.
It is as if Siaavosh himself sits upon an ivory throne,
A turquoise crown upon his head.
His face exudes the scent of love,
His hair rendered even more gracious by his crown.

Giv says to his heart, "This can only be the king.
One finds such face and features
Only on those deserving of crown and throne."
As he nears the imperial being on foot,
The knots in the rope that for so long had
Closed the doors of hope loosen and unfasten,
And the prize Giv was so vehemently after
Materializes before his eyes.

Kay Khosrow, seated by the spring,
Catches sight of him.
He smiles and his heart leaps with joy.
He thinks, "This brave man can only be Giv.

There is in this land no one of such appearance.
Without a doubt he must be looking for me,
Wishing to acclaim me as King of Iran-Zamin."

Kay Khosrow rises and says, "O Giv, welcome,
Since you are here by divine command.
How did you enter this land?
How did you cross its borders?
What news have you of Tous,
Goodarz, and Kay Kaavoos?
Are they living in joy?
Do they think of me at all?
How is world seeker Rostam of elephant stature,
The one who aspires to world possession?
And how are Zaal and his family?"

Gazing in wonder at him,
Giv speaks the Creator's name.
Then he says to Kay Khosrow, "O blessed prince,
The world longs for your exalted affection.
I think you are the wise son of Siaavosh.
You are Khosrow of Kianian ancestry."

Khosrow says to him, "O noble man,
You are Giv, son of Goodarz."

Giv replies, "Tell me, O leader of the righteous,
Who has spoken to you of the hero Goodarz?
Who made you aware of Kashvaad and Giv?
May happiness, power, and glory be forever yours!"

Kay Khosrow answers, "O lion man,
My mother recounted to me what my father told her
As he expressed his last wishes in the grace of Yazdan.
He said to my glorious mother,
         'No matter what misfortune befalls me,
         Kay Khosrow will soon be born.
         He will be the one holding the key to locked doors.
         Once he has matured into a worthy warrior,
         The skillful Giv will arrive in the land of Tooran.
         He will deliver our son to the throne of Iran,
         Place him in the presence of lion men.
         Khosrow will restore, with immense valor,

235

Prosperity to the world, thus avenging us.'"

Giv says, "Leader of courageous men,
What sign, what proof have you of your high birth?
Siaavosh had on his arm a visible black mark,
The size of a pea against a background of roses.
Expose your forearm, show it to me,
For the mark you bear is known to all."

The king uncovers his arm on which Giv observes
A black design, inherited by the royal family
Since the time of Kay Ghobaad,
Infallible evidence of a descendant of Kianian race.

The moment Giv sees the mark of nobility,
He pays respect to the king,
Embracing and praising him.
He sheds tears and reveals the secret.

Kay Khosrow holds the world leader,
Praising him joyfully.
He asks about Iran and the royal throne,
About Goodarz and Rostam the warrior.

Giv answers him, "O noble world master,
Cautious, aware, and blessed king of the earth,
Everyone's heart will beam with joy at the sight of you.
Though they haven't seen you yet,
They foster in their hearts great love for you.
If the Creator, with the awareness of good and bad,
Had given me the entire paradise
With the seven lands and the world empire,
Along with power and the Kianian crown,
My heart would not rejoice more
Than to have found you here in the land of Tooran.

"No one knows in Iran whether I am dead or alive,
Whether I am beneath the dust or burning
In a blazing fire, whether I have seen Khosrow alive
And have questioned him about his suffering.
Praise be to Yazdan that my star has turned
My deep torment into deep happiness."

The two emerge from the forest, and, during
The journey, Kay Khosrow asks after Kay Kaavoos
And the suffering endured for the past seven years.
He asks Giv how he slept and nourished himself.

Giv tells the king about the designs of the skies,
Goodarz's dream, his own immense ordeal,
The way he ate and dressed himself,
His lassitude, his joy, how Kaavoos, broken by age,
Finds himself meek of body and spirit,
Weakened by the grief of his son's death,
And how the land of Iran has squandered
Its prosperity to be cast out as a wasteland.

Khosrow's heart is consumed with pain.
His cheeks burn as he speaks:
"After these long hardships,
May fate deliver you rest and happiness!
Play the role of father to me. Speak to no one,
And behold the turns of our fortune."

18 | Giv and Khosrow Travel to Siaavosh-Guerd

The royal prince climbs onto Giv's horse
As the hero walks ahead with deliberation,
Indian sword in hand.
Every time the prudent Giv encounters someone,
He strikes him a blow on the neck without hesitation,
Then scatters dust over him.
In this manner, they proceed toward Siaavosh-Guerd.

The two friends combine heart with wisdom,
Taking Faranguis as friend and confidant.
The three decide to run off secretly without
Revealing their plan to warriors keen on battle.

Faranguis says, "If we hesitate and
Take too long, we shall constrict the earth.
Afraasiyaab will suspect something.
He will find a reason to neither eat nor sleep.
He will charge at us like the White Deev,

Leaving us little hope to save ourselves.
None of us will remain alive, either openly or not.
The world is full of foes and ill-intentioned men.
From border to border in this land dwells Ahriman.
If the evil man catches on, he will burn the land.
O noble King, my dear son, listen to my advice.
There is a field not far from here,
Near the road taken by the riders of Tooran.
Go there tomorrow at daybreak,
And take with you saddle and black bridle.
You will see a mountain rising, grazing the clouds.
You will climb and find a field fresh as springtime.
Flowing across it is a source of running water,
The sight of which renews one's soul.

"At the hour when the sun is above the dome of sky,
At the time when one opens the gates of sleep,
Horses in herds found grazing in the plain
Will come to drink at the source.
Show Behzaad saddle and reins.
If he obeys you like a well-bred horse,
Approach him with a smile.
Brush him lovingly with your hand,
For when Siaavosh surrendered hope on his life,
Witness to the dimming of his bright day,
He said to Behzaad, his black horse,
            'From here on, do not even obey the wind.
            Wander through field and mountain
            Until Kay Khosrow comes to find you.
            Allow him to bestride you and lead you.
            You will then strike the earth with your hooves
            And liberate it from our enemies.'"

19 | Kay Khosrow Adopts Behzaad

The next day, Kay Khosrow climbs upon Giv's horse
While the world leader escorts him on foot.
Hurriedly, they take the road of the mountain,
Like men in search of deliverance.

Soon, a herd of stallions appears to drink at the spring.

238

PART NINE

The noble Khosrow dismounts, approaches the water,
And, impatient to accomplish the deed,
Quickly presents saddle and reins to Behzaad.

The steed raises his head, notices the king,
Then draws a deep sigh when his eyes
Fall on Siaavosh's cover of leopard skin,
The long stirrups and the saddle of poplar wood.
Behzaad stands still by the drinking trough
Without attempting to step forward.

Kay Khosrow, taking notice of him at ease,
Slowly walks over with the saddle.
The liberated horse does not shift position.
His beastly eyes fill with emotion, two fountains of tears.

The leader and Giv also weep
With an all-consuming sense of grief.
While their eyes shed tears, their tongues
Utter curses at the wicked Afraasiyaab.

Khosrow strokes Behzaad, brushes his hand
Over the horse's eyes and face, chest and limbs,
And runs his fingers through his thick mane.
He loops the reins on him and adjusts the saddle,
Speaking softly to him of his father.
He mounts the steed, grips his flanks with his knees,
And, on cue, this powerful beast dashes forth,
Leaping like a storm through the air,
Flying and disappearing before Giv's eyes.

Disheartened, Giv utters prayers to Yazdan:
"Ahriman the cunning has taken the shape of a horse
And appeared to us beneath this guise.
Now Khosrow's life and my years of labor
Searching for him are lost to the wind.
What was once my worldly treasure has vanished,
Earning me nothing more than suffering."

After traveling through half the mountains,
The brave king holds Behzaad steadfast by his reins,
Awaits the arrival of Giv, then says to him,
"Would you like me to guess, by my mind's power,

Your secret thoughts and concerns, O world hero?"

Giv replies, "O famed King, with the grace
Of the Creator and the power of the Kianian lineage,
You are privy to all secrets.
You are able to penetrate a single strand of hair
To examine what is contained within."

Kay Khosrow retorts, "O brave hero,
You suspect this horse of noble race,
And this is what you were thinking,
        'Ahriman has come to take away this young man,
        And now my troubles are lost, gone with the wind.
        My heart is full of worry as the evil deev triumphs.'"

Calling blessings upon the king,
The prudent Giv dismounts and gratefully says,
"May your days and nights be blessed!
May your enemies' hearts be torn to shreds!
Yazdan awarded you with power, throne, and crown,
With divine glory, courage, and a noble birth."

They return from mountain to palace,
Heads full of worry, minds searching for a solution.
As they arrive at the side of Faranguis,
They speak of the lengthy road left to travel
And try to find a way to keep
Their venture shrouded in a veil of secrecy.

At the sight of Behzaad,
Faranguis's face dissolves beneath the tears.
She presses her cheeks against the horse's chest
And painfully invokes the spirit of Siaavosh.
Once her eyes' tears are spent,
She quickly accesses her amassed wealth,
A secret treasury she hides in the palace:
A cache of gold and silver, rubies and gems, weapons,
Horse straps, daggers, swords, and heavy maces.

She opens the treasury doors before her son,
Her heart swollen with grief and frayed with worry.
She says to Giv, "You have suffered great pains.
Look at this wealth and take your share.

Take enough gold and gems as deserves a king.
Take rubies and inlaid crowns,
For we are simply the guardians of this treasure.
It rightly belongs to you.
You are the ransom of our lives,
The recompense to our suffering."

The world hero kisses the ground and says to her,
"Queen of Queens, your mere presence
Renders the earth a spring paradise.
By your command, the sky assigns good and ill.
May the earth stand as slave at your son's feet!
May your enemies' heads fall to the ground!"

After glancing at the jewels and riches,
Giv selects the armor of the brave Siaavosh.
They carry with them precious gems in such
Abundance that their backs bend with the weight.
They take helmets, handsome horse straps,
And weapons worthy of a world hero.

Then the king closes the treasury doors
And makes preparations for the desert crossing.

20 | Faranguis Departs With Kay Khosrow and Giv for Iran-Zamin

Once measures are taken,
They saddle fine horses of wind speed.
Faranguis dons her helmet,
And the three furtively take the road to Iran,
As it suits people trapped in a thorny situation.

It does not take long for the news of their secret
Getaway to spread throughout towns and cities.
Someone finds Piran and says to him,
"The noble Giv has traveled from Iran-Zamin.
He has found the wise and brave prince.
The young king and the fierce hero have left
For the land of Iran in the company of Faranguis."

Piran is dismayed at these words.
He quivers like a leaf and thinks,
"Afraasiyaab's predictions are now realized.
What shall I tell him?
My integrity will be tarnished before his eyes."

Among his brave men, he selects Golbaad,
Along with Nastihan, an iron man,
In addition to three hundred Turkish riders.
Piran orders them to lead a campaign, saying,
"Leave at once on horseback without wasting a moment.
Plant the head of Giv at the end of an iron spear.
Lay to rest Faranguis below the ground, and bind
Kay Khosrow, the cursed, for his very footstep
Is the star of misfortune of Tooran-Zamin.
If this doomed man succeeds in crossing the Jayhoon,
What calamities will befall our land?
What hardships will plague our warriors?"

In this way, a battalion of soldiers sets forth
Under the command of two warrior leaders.

Faranguis and her son, exhausted, fall asleep,
For they traveled far through many sleepless nights,
While Giv, worn out but held awake by his bitter anger,
Watches over the king, world seeker.
His eyes are fixed on the road.
He maintains the strappings on his horse
As suits a valiant leader,
His chest still covered in armor, his head in helm,
His heart burning, his body devoted to death.

21 | Golbaad and Nastihan Flee Before Giv

Once Giv sees the dust of the army surging
In the distance, he hurries to rise, extracts his sword,
And shouts a warning cry like thunder
Dropping from clouds, a cry that would make
The brain and heart of a lion shudder with fear.
He boldly rushes to the midst of the warriors.
The earth darkens, recoiling in fear of his fury.

He sends showers of blows with his mighty sword,
Strikes with his mace from atop his horse.
The Tooranian leaders despair from the shock.
The injuries are so deep they lose the desire to fight.

So furious is Giv's heart that the sea appears to him
Like the tiniest pool of water.

Countless Tooranians surround him
While the mad lion is alone and unattended.

The spears turn the battleground into a field of reeds,
Casting a shadow over the sun and moon.
The lion, restlessly and in anger, bustles about,
Painting the ground crimson with heavy bloodshed
As if wine has spilled from a press.
He overturns a great many adversaries.
The warriors in the enemy host find themselves
Engulfed by a deep sense of fear and foreboding.

Golbaad says to the daring Nastihan,
"This man is a boulder with such arms and shoulders.
Know that this turn of events comes
From the glory of Kay Khosrow and not from
The blows of the sword and mace of the brave Giv.
I do not know the fate of this land.
One cannot shrink from Yazdan's secrets.
Stargazers have predicted that ill fortune
Awaits Tooran-Zamin and its leader."

They engage with their army in one last mighty fight.
Blows are dealt, blows are suffered.
The shouts of fighters and the sound of trumpets
Make the hearts of mountains tremble in fear.

Ravines and plains are strewn with cadavers.
The earth is tinted in blood like a blooming rose.
At the sight of the brave Giv, support of armies,
The Tooranians lose their nerve and attempt to flee.
They retreat to the side of the distinguished Piran,
Wounded and defeated.

Giv approaches Kay Khosrow like a fierce lion,

His chest and hands covered in blood,
And says to him, "O King, be happy,
Take wisdom for companion, and rejoice.
An army came to battle with us,
Led by Golbaad and Nastihan,
But the survivors fled and must shed tears
Over the wounds to their chests and arms.
I only know Rostam, brave horseman from Iran,
Who can hold his ground against me."

Khosrow of pure faith is thrilled to hear these words.
He showers Giv with praise
And invokes on him divine grace.

Then they have a meal of this and that,
And hurry on their way,
Avoiding roads well-traveled.

The Turks return to Piran, bruised and distraught.
The brave leader flinches at the sight of Golbaad
And says, "Such an astonishing venture
Must not be kept secret.
What have you done with Giv? Where is Khosrow?
Recount to me with precision the course of events."

Golbaad replies, "O world hero,
If I tell you how the brave Giv treated your men,
Your heart will grow weary of battlefield.
He fought with me in such a way that I believed
My days were numbered and my end was near.
You have often watched me battle.
You have praised and admired my skills.
Well, I struck Giv with my stirrups with a force
You would think would make him collapse.
At the same time, I administered to him
More than one thousand blows of my mace.
But it is as if his head is a block of iron
As strong as an anvil,
His chest and arms as sturdy as an elephant's tusk.

"I have often watched Rostam in battle.
I have heard of the high deeds of other brave men,
But never have I seen anyone with Giv's strength,

244

Anyone resist or remain so calm like him
In the tumults and vicissitudes of battle.
Even if our maces were made of wax
And our spears of leopard skin, his chest, arms,
And hands should have been crushed.
But each of our blows only fueled his anger.
He hollered like an inflamed elephant.
The field turned into a mountain,
Replete with corpses, and so many men
Quailed before the wrath of a single one."

Piran bursts out against him and shouts,
"Enough! It is disgraceful to speak thus.
No matter who is listening,
These are words a warrior must never utter.
You must renounce all consideration of war.
You left with the renowned Nastihan
And with a troop of warriors brave as lions.
Now you have turned Giv into a furious elephant,
Losing your honor among world heroes.
If Afraasiyaab gets news of this,
He will fling his royal crown to the ground
Because two brave heroes on horseback,
Along with a courageous army,
Have taken flight before a single warrior who
Left a great many courageous Turks for dead.
Everyone will laugh. Everyone will mock you,
For you are not worthy of banner, timpani, and mace."

22 | Piran Pursues Kay Khosrow

Piran selects two times three thousand riders,
Brave men suited for battle, and says to them,
"We must quickly seize our chargers' reins.
Night and day, like brave lions,
Without a moment's waste,
We must pursue our enemies' tracks.
Let us not unfasten our warrior belts,
For if Giv and Khosrow reach Iran-Zamin,
The women of that land will convert to lionesses.
What is left of our share of land and sea will be drained.

Afraasiyaab's heart will bleed with despair.
I shall be the one deemed responsible for this flight,
Not the rotation of sun, moon, and stars."

On the order of the renowned hero, the Turks
Raise their heads, mobilize, and take off like a storm.
They rush forth, riding day and night without rest
Until news reaches Afraasiyaab.

On their side, Giv, Faranguis, and the king
Travel at swift speeds until they arrive
At a river that is not very wide,
Yet fairly deep and almost impossible to pass over.
They reach the river crossing
With helmet and shield, and Giv as the king's guide.

This waterway is the Golzarioon River.
In spring it appears to be a sea of blood.
The three make their way to the opposite bank,
Where they seek a moment's respite.
Giv says to Khosrow and Faranguis,
"If the enemy should pursue our tracks,
This river will function as a wall to shield us."

They have a meal composed of remnants of food.
Then the king and Giv fall asleep.
Faranguis is on watch, her eyes locked on the land.
At once, she makes out the banner of Tooran's leader.

Faranguis quickly awakens the two heroes.
She says to Giv in warning,
"No matter how tired you are,
You must rise, brave man, for it is time to flee.
An army is after us, and I fear for our lives.
Look at Piran's banner,
How it casts a shadow over the earth.
If they reach you, they will kill you,
And the pain of your loss will be tragic for us.
They will take my son and me to Afraasiyaab,
Burdened with chains and eyes full of tears.
I don't know what further misfortune will befall us.
Who knows the secrets of the sublime dome of sky?"

Giv replies, "O Queen, why does your heart despair?
Climb with the king upon this narrow height,
And do not fear either Piran or his army.
My deeds have been in favor of Kay Khosrow,
The noble leader of the new world.
The universe will light up with his good fortune.
The earth will be the foundation of his throne.
If the Creator wills it, we shall reach a favorable outcome.
I shall lean on Yazdan and the king's crown
For assistance and harbor not an inkling
Of fear for the Tooranian host.
Climb to the mountaintop, and do not worry.
The Creator is my support, my lucky star is on my side.
By the power given to me by Yazdan, Creator of life,
I shall strike down every rider from his saddle
In recognition of my duty as warrior."

Kay Khosrow replies, "You are always ready for battle.
You have already sacrificed too much for me.
I have been freed by you from the traps of misfortune.
Do not fling yourself into the dragon's maw.
I originate from that pure essence of Siaavosh,
Innocent lion vanquisher from the Kianian lineage.
It is my turn to go on the field, and with my sword
Shed blood to spill all the way to the firmament."

Giv says to him, "O noble King,
The world is in need of your crown.
Your father was a fierce warrior, as I am a warrior,
Waist forever cinched in service to you.
I have seventy-eight brothers,
But the world would end if you were to die.
There are many warriors but very few just kings,
So few that I do not even know of one.
If I die, there will remain other world heroes.
If your crowned head falls,
It will be the end of throne and crown.
If you perish in distant captivity,
I know no one worthy of kingship.
My seven years of pain and hardship will be lost,
And my family's noble line will go down in shame.
Climb up these heights and observe the army from above.

Yazdan the Creator, pure and perfect, will come to my aid.
If I succeed in winning,
It will be because of your good fortune,
For the world subsists beneath your blessed shadow."

23 | The Battle of Giv and Piran

Giv dresses in armor and charges forth
Like a lion atop his fervent steed.
On one side is the leader, on the other the army,
And in between the river cutting the way.

Giv sends out a cry reminiscent of thunder in spring
And asks who is at the head of this vast host.

Piran, angered by him, curses him and says,
"Evil man of evil race, you are alone on the battlefield.
You have come bravely to confront our army.
We shall make you feel the tips of our spears.
We shall give you the claws of birds of prey as a coffin.
Even if you were a mountain of steel, O lone cavalier,
Thousands of adversaries will surround you like ants.
They will shatter this armor that covers your chest,
Sever your head, and bury you like a vile object.
A leaping lion once said:
        'When the time comes for a gazelle,
        Fate counts its breaths,
        And it will run toward my claws.'
In this same manner, providence brings you to me
And before this renowned army."

The fear-inspiring Giv, mighty world hero,
Leader of brave men, shouts a cry of rage.
He says, "O Turk of ill nature, son of a Deev,
May there never remain on earth a leader like you!
You have seen how I avenged Siaavosh,
And without a doubt,
You have approved the blows I have administered.
So many noblemen from Tooran and Chin
Have perished at my hand.
I have left destruction at your palace.

I have afflicted your heart.

"I have taken two of your women captive,
Noble ones from your chambers, from Khotan.
One was your sister, the other your wife.
They trembled in fear for your soul and body.
I came across two desperate Turks
And gave to each of them one of your women.
I am up here, and you are below.
You wish to act in haste,
But I proceed with patience.
You have turned your back like a female.
You fled, moaning and crying.
You seek men weak as women to contend with.
But do not boast of your high deeds
When you are among brave men,
For your great shame will be made
Public with music and song.
The story will go that Giv single-handedly
Freed Kay Khosrow and helped him escape,
And you and your family will be subjects of scorn.

"Do you not know that the world's leaders
Of the likes of the Faghfoor,[35] Emperor of Chin,
The Caesar of Rum, the noblest men of Iran
And the finest relations of Kaavoos,
Many warriors and heroes of golden helmet,
Have asked for the hand of Rostam's daughter,
Have desired her with their heart's fervor?
Tous sent a messenger to ask for her in marriage,
But Rostam only laughed.
He has rejected most alliances,
Having deemed none worthy of her.
He has searched long and hard from end to end
And found no man exceptional enough.
He singled me out for my wisdom, my glory,
My lineage, my integrity, my generosity.
He offered me his most noble daughter,
The one most dear to his heart,
Dearer to him than a crown. The hero who

◇◇◇◇◇◇◇◇◇◇◇◇◇
35 Faghfoor: Title used for the rulers of Chin or China.

Raises his head to the sublime dome of sky
Gave me the hand of his beloved daughter,
Queen of all daughters, Baanoogoshasp, the rider.
This union promoted me to rise in rank and stature.
For he favored me out of the most worthy men.

"As for me, I gave Rostam my sister Shahrbaanoo,
Who has the appearance of a garden in paradise.
Only Rostam of lion heart
Is able to stand against me in battle.
When I join him in the exercise of vengeance,
You will be left to grieve the dead.
This field of war is my festival hall.
My crown is my helmet of steel.
Although I am alone, with my shining sword,
I shall render the world dark as tar before your eyes.
If I allow a single warrior in your host to remain alive,
I shall never again be referred to
As a brave and courageous man.

"I shall guide Khosrow, King of Kings,
To Iran-Zamin and to the ruler of great warriors.
I shall seat him on the glorious ivory throne,
Place upon his head a shining crown,
Able to shed light into obscured hearts.
Then I shall don my famed armor
And obliterate the land of Tooran,
Convert it into a lion's lair.
I come to this land like a fierce lion,
Cinched at the waist to avenge the death of Siaavosh.
I wish to eliminate both Afraasiyaab and his land,
Which I long to turn into a vast sea of blood.

"I am the son of Goodarz,
Son of Kashvaad, leader of brave men.
I am Giv, the liberated, born of noble parents.
You are Piran, the cursed, the Turk of ill fortune.
May you find yourself bereft of land, throne, and crown!
I shall break your neck clean with this Indian blade
So that your shield and helm shed bitter tears for you.
The knot of my noose will expedite your death.
Your helmet and headgear will serve you as shroud."

24 | Giv Captures Piran

Piran's heart is consumed with dread.
His eyes fill with tears as he remains silent and still.
He trembles like the leaves on a willow tree,
Losing hope for his sweet life.
He shouts at Giv: "O lion man, O world vanquisher,
Come, let us wrestle like two lions.
Then we shall see which of us is knocked down."

Giv replies, "O leader of lions, if you wish to fight,
You better come on this side of the river
Where you will witness one skillful man
Overcome your vast army.
You have six thousand troops; I am a lone warrior.
I shall destroy anyone who does not obey.
I shall make all your heads roll in the dust
With my head-smashing mace."

Piran's anger only mounts.
His heart boils with fury. His eyes fill with tears.
He launches his horse forth, clenches his thighs,
And places on his shoulder his heavy mace.
He charges from the river bank into the water,
Like a small boat surrendering to divine force,
The source of all happiness.

Giv does not rush to battle, and when
The Tooranian leader emerges out of the waters,
Giv turns his back to him as if in a show of cowardice.
He runs in the other direction,
Though he is most eager to test himself against him.

His enemy chases after him, closing in,
And the world darkens like a night of ebony.

At a fair distance from the river and from the army,
Giv unties his mace from his horse's saddle
And flings himself on world hero Piran.
You would take him for a furious dragon.

Now it is the turn of Piran, the lion, to bolt

And for Giv to pursue him.
Without the powerful hero noticing,
Giv detaches his noose from his saddle's hook,
Swings his arm numerous times,
And sends the loop flying to entrap Piran.
He effectively captures the head of the world hero
And removes him from the saddle.
Then Giv makes Piran walk shamefully before him,
Moving him away from the river.

There he throws him to the ground,
Ties up his hands, dresses in his armor,
Climbs on his horse, takes his banner,
And returns to the edge of the Golzarioon.

When the Turks see the banner of their leader,
They advance, unsuspecting, with shouts,
Sounding horns, clarions, and Indian bells.

Giv, witness to this, slides into the river,
Like a vessel breaking the waves.
As soon as he reaches the other bank,
He raises his heavy mace above his shoulders.

The entire army glares at him in surprise.
He lets go of his horse's reins
To steady himself on the stirrups.
The warriors panic, gripped by fear.
With sword and stirrup, with shoulder and breath,
Giv knocks the Turks over into the dust.
Soon the plain becomes a mountain of body parts.

The surviving men, fearing his mace,
Turn their backs on him.
Giv does not lose a single hair,
Nor does a single link of his chainmail come undone.
He is like a lion hurling himself in the middle of a herd.
The huge enemy army and its warriors turn
Their backs, showing their steeds' hindquarters,
As they expeditiously take flight.

Giv returns victorious to cross the river once again.
You would think he did not encounter a single enemy,

252

Not even in dream, as he is unaffected and unscathed.
In haste, he returns to Piran's side,
Wishing to sever his head.
He makes him walk shamefully behind him,
Forcing the old man to run
While fear nearly deprives him of reason.

Giv brings him before Kay Khosrow thus humiliated,
Cheeks pale, head bowing low in shame.

Giv dismounts, kisses the ground before the king,
Praises him, and says,
"This traitor was captured in the folds of the dragon's tail.
Your father surrendered his head
Because he trusted this man's words.
He must perish as did Siaavosh."

Piran begins to utter blessings to the king.
He moans, kisses the ground, and says,
"O King, seeker of knowledge,
You shine among the crowd like the glorious sun.
You know the pain I have suffered because of you
And the care with which I have surrounded you.
You know the struggles
I have overcome for you before Afraasiyaab.
If I, your slave, had been present in the king's court,
Siaavosh would not have been killed.
I have rescued you and your mother.
I have plucked you from under the deev's claws
By way of care and cunning.
I surrendered my own life for Siaavosh.
You can ask Faranguis for confirmation.
I hope that through your mercy and good fortune
I shall fend off the dragon's talons."

25 | Faranguis Frees Piran From the Hands of Giv

Meanwhile, Giv observes Kay Khosrow,
Awaiting the orders of the brave king.
He observes Faranguis, her tearful eyes
And her tongue full of curses for Afraasiyaab.

She says to Giv, "O world hero, you have endured
This long, arduous journey on our account.
Know that this old warrior
Is a wise and noble man of shining spirit.
He is the one who kept death at bay for us,
By the command of our Guide and Justice Giver.
His affection has been our shelter against danger.
Now he asks for our protection
As reward for his good deeds.
Grant him mercy, O illustrious world hero,
For he never advised us wrong."

Giv replies, "Queen of Queens,
May the world king maintain his youth.
I have sworn by the moon,
By the throne and crown of the renowned king,
That I shall render the earth red with Piran's blood
Should he fall into my hands on the day of battle."

Kay Khosrow says to him, "O lion world hero,
Do not violate an oath you have made to Yazdan.
Satisfy your heart and complete the deed.
Pierce through Piran's ear with your dagger.
Once his blood spills to the ground, you will fulfill,
In one blow, both vengeance and clemency."

The world hero, seeing the king weaken over Piran's fate,
His royal cheeks' flow of tears betraying his affection,
Says to Kay Khosrow, "O King, maintain joy in your heart.
Give up thinking on this matter.
May there be one hundred thousand men like me,
Willing to sacrifice their lives for you!
May divine wisdom be your cloak of protection!"

The king's face brightens with joy at these words.
He laughs and says, "O kind world hero,
May you rejoice and be blessed with a long life."

Giv pierces Piran's ear with his dagger,
And in this way frees himself from his oath.

Piran then says to the king,
"I cannot reach my army on foot.

Tell him to give me my horse and remember
That I owe him my life as well as all that I own."

Then Kay Khosrow turns to Giv:
"O brave ruler, return his stallion to him."

Giv says to Piran, "O army leader,
How did the battlefields render you so lazy?
You are the one who said that in the world
There is no rider with my skill and ability,
Not even among one hundred gatherings.
You are the leader of Turks and lions.
In battle, you are the nemesis of Iranian troops.
Now you stand before me, eyes closed,
Full of tears, devoid of name, honor, dignity,
Strength, rage, and shame.
You weep like a woman, beseeching me
And pleading with me and with the king.
If you wish to reclaim this horse of winded hooves,
I shall tie your two hands with a sturdy strap.
I shall make you swear an oath to me
To return to your captive body its freedom.
You must agree and swear to allow one person,
Golshahr alone, to unfasten these bonds.
She is the one I select for this exploit,
For she is the first of all your wives,
And nothing of yours remains secret from her."

The world hero submits to this condition
And regains possession of his steed, swearing
To allow no one to untie him during his journey
And to save this action for his wife, Golshahr.

At this time, Giv ties his hands,
Returns to him his horse, and helps him climb upon it.

Faranguis and Khosrow of sweet face hug him tenderly.
Khosrow tells him,
"May you travel in the shadow of the Creator.
You are at one with the world's loom, weave into it.
You are willing to sacrifice your life and soul
In favor of spreading divine justice all around."

Piran departs in one direction,
Praising the king and the world hero, while Khosrow,
Faranguis, and Giv take the opposite direction.

26 | Afraasiyaab Encounters Piran on the Road

Once Afraasiyaab hears of Khosrow's flight,
Sunlight dims before his eyes.
He commands the blowing of trumpets
And the beating of timpani, gathers his army,
And departs from his palace burning with fury.

For each day, he travels the length of two,
Advancing with great urgency,
Flying like an arrow shot from the bow.
He leads his army to the battlefield
Where Golbaad and his troops had fought.

Everywhere, he finds scattered warriors wounded,
Every step of the way, men lying about in the dust.
He asks, "When did the world hero arrive from Iran
With troops to engage in battle here?
None of my warriors has gotten wind
Of a vast host crossing the border.
Who could it be? Who alerted the son of deevs
That we have hidden here a child from Siaavosh?
Oh, why did I not nurse this child into the earth?
Then my two eyes would not witness such calamity."

Sepahram replies, "May your peace be untroubled.
If the idea of an army frightens you,
I shall tell you that Giv, son of Goodarz,
Came unescorted, O King, without a single horseman.
The army is struck with fear
From the assault of a lone man.
Giv, Faranguis, and the king were able to flee."

Afraasiyaab's cheeks pale at these words,
His heart frightened by the fate cast upon him by the sky.
He replies, "I see events unfolding
That had been predicted long ago by the wise man.

A person graced with Yazdan's favors
Climbs on the throne effortlessly."

As he speaks, he spots an army approaching.
At the lead is Piran, whose head, face, and body
Are entirely drenched in blood.

Afraasiyaab believes Piran has successfully found Giv
And that he rushes forth to announce his victory.

The closer Piran moves to the Tooranian king,
The more obvious are his injuries,
Obvious that he is bound firm as rock to the saddle,
And that his two hands are tied behind him with a strap.

At such a sight, Afraasiyaab finds himself
Confounded and deeply saddened.
Full of worry, he questions Piran, who says to him,
"There is neither fierce lion nor wild wolf
Able to achieve what Giv has achieved on his own.
The day Giv appears equipped for battle, the whale
In the deep ocean will be consumed with fear.
He came at me with his heave mace and struck
A powerful blow as if from a blacksmith's hammer.
He overthrew my warriors
With horse, foot, arm, and stirrup.
He wounded and killed all our men,
Taking no account for their lives.
Never has cloud released so many drops of rain
As we dealt blows of mace upon his head.
But he remained sturdy in the saddle, undisturbed
And at peace, as if happy inside a rose garden.
You would think his mace is an extension of himself.

"In the end, the entire army fled
While I remained alone to fight him.
In the act of bolting, he swung his noose in the air,
Flung it far, and captured my head in his knot.
Lightheaded, I fell unconscious to the ground.
He dismounted, tied my two hands,
Made me walk before him
While he climbed back on his horse.
He dragged me shamefully to Kay Khosrow,

Where a new danger threatened me,
As he wanted to cut off my head.
But Faranguis rushed to my aid so that
Instead of killing me, he settled for piercing my ear.
He tied me up while screaming with rage
And making me swear by the life
And by the king's head, by Sun and Moon,
By Yazdan, pure and perfect,
And by the throne and crown, that I will
Maintain these ties all the way to Khotan."

"Seeing how fortune worked against me,
I swore to never ask anyone to untie me
And to continue on home until I reached Golshahr.
The oath I have taken is a noose around my neck.
I do not know the secret wishes of the sky,
For it appears to refuse me its favors.
It delivers my head and arms to enemy straps,
Subjecting me to be constrained by oaths and bonds."

Infuriated, Afraasiyaab's eyes fill with tears.
He shouts and commands Piran to leave his sight.
Trembling, Piran remains quiet.

The king, reassuming his foolish pride, bursts out,
Cursing his enemy: "Even if Giv, son of Goodarz,
And this son of deev were clouds of lightning and storm,
I would pluck them right out of the sky."

He brings his hand to clench his sword and adds,
"I shall destroy them with this steel-piercing blade.
Once I have captured Faranguis,
I shall constrict the earth for her,
Render it black in her eyes.
I shall slice her in two with this sharp sword,
Then cast her out into the sea for fishes to feast on
And shred her into tiny morsels.
I understand why Khosrow wishes to travel to Iran,
But what purpose does Faranguis have in going?"

27 | Giv Argues With the Tax Inspector

Piran dolefully takes the path to Khotan
While the famed king takes
The opposite direction in haste with his unlawful
Leaders until he arrives at the Jayhoon
In great fury and with a deep longing for bloodshed.

Afraasiyaab says to Hoomaan, "Hurry, loosen
Your horse's reins all the way to the river's shore.
If we learn that Khosrow has already crossed,
Our hard work will have been in vain,
Just like the wind blowing across the plain.
I was once warned by wise and truthful men
Who have claimed since ancient times
That a king would rise from the union of two families,
The descendants of Toor and of Kay Ghobaad,
That he would flatten Tooran, turning it into a desert,
That he would not let stand a single city in the empire,
That his heart will turn with affection
Toward the land of Iran and his back
In vengeance toward the land of Tooran."

Meanwhile, Giv and Khosrow reach the river's edge.
They wish to cross without delay.
They argue with the guardian to let them
Navigate on a craft designed for passage,
A swift boat equipped with a new sail,
Worthy of serving Kay Khosrow.

The guardian says to Giv, "What difference
Does running water make for a slave or a king?
If you wished to cross the river,
You should have warned the owner of a boat."

Giv replies, "Ask for payment and take us on board,
For we are pursued by a mighty host."

The guardian becomes even more demanding:
"I shall not ask for monetary compensation.
I shall request one of four things:
Your coat of mail or your black horse,

This lovely slave or this servant
Who shines like the moon."

Giv replies, "Have you completely lost your mind?
How can you make such requests?
Even if you were the ruler of some land
And you demanded tribute from your people,
Your winnings would still not be complete.
Who are you to speak with such insolence,
Making such claims of the king?
Your head must be filled with wind.
How can you equate the king's mother
Or the king's crown to the payment of fees?
Thirdly, how can you ask for Behzaad,
His black steed swifter than the wind?
How foolish of you to wish to collect my coat of mail.
You have not the power to unfasten a single button,
An armor so thick it is impenetrable by water or fire,
A coat of mail that neither spear nor arrow,
Neither sword nor Indian saber is able to pierce.
If you wish payment, take it in the river now,
To us the water and to you the boat,
To us the treasures you request,
To you regret for your stupid demands."

28 | Kay Khosrow Crosses the Jayhoon

Giv says to the king, "If you are Kay Khosrow,
The waters are a source of benefit to you.
Fereydoon crossed the River Arvand
And took hold of the throne of power.
The world obeyed him from end to end,
For he carried himself with grace and clarity.
How can you hesitate
If you are the King of Iran-Zamin?
You are the shelter of warriors and lions of Iran.
How could the water be hostile toward you?
You possess splendor, power, stature,
And are deserving of the throne's grandeur.
If your mother or I drown, do not be concerned.
You are the reason I exist in this world,

PART NINE

For the throne of the King of Kings is now vacant.
I was born from my mother with the single
Purpose of serving and protecting you.
Do not hesitate, for there is no doubt Afraasiyaab is,
In haste, approaching the river's shore.
Should he gain access to us, he will hang me alive,
Cover me with denigration.
As for you, he will throw you into the river
Along with Faranguis, as repast for fish.
Or perhaps he will trample you
Beneath the horses' hooves."

Kay Khosrow replies, "This is the way it is.
I surrender my hopes to Yazdan the savior."
He dismounts, flings himself to the ground,
Face down, and moans,
"You are my support and my shelter.
You are my guide on the path of justice.
You are my rudder and my sail on the water,
My guide across dry, pathless shores.
Spirit and wisdom are your wings' shelter.
What I experience of fortune and misfortune
Stems from your care and compassion."

He speaks, then climbs on his black steed,
His face shining with the light of Venus.
He charges into the water and crosses the river,
Like a boat sailing to reach the opposite bank.

Faranguis and the brave Giv follow close behind,
For the lion does not fear the flows of the Jayhoon.
The three touch ground safe and sound
On the opposite river bank.

World seeker Khosrow washes his head and body.
Then, kneeling by the reeds,
He engages in prayer to honor the divine presence.

The boatman, baffled to see the three of them
Emerge from the waters, exclaims to his mates,
"Never have I seen a more astonishing sight!
With three horses, three armors, three strappings,
They crossed the deepest flows of the River Jayhoon,

With its rushing waters swelling from spring rain.
A man of sense cannot view them as mere humans."

Realizing that he missed the mark,
He feels regretful and ashamed of his rough words.
He then fills his boat with all that is precious,
And the sky's wind swells his billowing sail.

As soon as he touches the bank,
He approaches the king, asks forgiveness,
Depositing at his feet the presents:
A bow, a noose, a helmet.

But Giv cries out, "Foolish dog,
Why did you tell us these waters take away men?
When the glorious, renowned king asked for a boat,
You refused him, and now he rejects your favors.
The era of vengeance will commence,
Then your remaining days will be thrown to the wind.

The boatman returns so fearful he despairs for his life.
The moment he touches the bank,
He spots the Tooranian host charging toward him.

Afraasiyaab stops before the river,
Sees on the water neither boat nor man.
He asks the boatman, screaming with rage,
"How did this deev cross over the waters?"

The boatman responds, "O King, I am the guardian,
And before me was my father.
Never have I seen or heard such a thing,
Someone to make a path of the river's flows.
Right now it swells with spring rains,
And heavy waves abound.
If you enter, your chances for escape are rather slim.
Despite all this, these three riders navigated across.
You would think the air lifted them in invisible arms,
As if they were the storm's offspring
Sent by Yazdan in the guise of men."

Afraasiyaab listens, his cheeks pale.
In his anguish, he sighs,

"Hurry and toss your boat into the flows.
I wish to find these fugitives, check to see
Whether they have left or have stopped to rest.
Do not waste a moment.
Set the sails to catch up with them."

Hoomaan says to him,
"Your eminence must think before acting.
Do not kiss a flame that would consume you.
Do you wish to cross Iran with these cavaliers?
Do you wish to lose yourself to lion claws?
You would have to contend with the likes
Of Goodarz and the colossal Rostam,
Tous, or Gorgeen army-vanquisher.
Are you weary of throne to come here
And place yourself at peril's mercy?
From the edge of this river, all the way to Chin,
The land stands at your command.
Yours are Sun and Moon, Saturn and the Pleiades.
Take care of Tooran-Zamin and your mighty throne.
You have nothing to fear from Iran-Zamin."

The Tooranians return, saddened,
Their hearts surging with the blood of their wrath.
A long time passes in this manner.

29 | Kay Khosrow Arrives in Isfahan

Kay Khosrow arrives in Zam with Giv.
Most of the Iranians receive him in delight,
But a few regard him with caution,
Even with a hint of malice.

Giv sends envoys to all corners with letters
In which he and the noble king announce
That the army chief, from the race of Kay Ghobaad,
Arrives in joy from Tooran-Zamin,
That Kay Khosrow the auspicious, the one
To hold his head high, turned the turbulent flows
Of the Jayhoon into a calm and tranquil surface.

Giv searches for a brave rider as envoy.
He selects among the noblemen of Zam
A cautious one with foresight and devotion.
He shares the state of affairs with him
And adds, "Go to Isfahan, the land of kings,
The seat of great men, and say to Goodarz,
          'World hero, your awakened mind received
          A message from Sooroosh at the time of sleep:
          Now the end of your dream is unfolding
          As the sun is rising over the eastern lands.
          Kay Khosrow has arrived in Zam,
          Untouched by any hostile wind.'"

Then Giv writes a letter to Kaavoos Shah,
And the messenger rises to take his leave.

A camel of swift feet dashes forward.
Giv's envoy of shining spirit reaches the world hero.
He relates the message and hands the letter
To Goodarz, who brings it to his forehead,
Sheds tears at the thought of Siaavosh,
And vociferously curses Afraasiyaab.

Then the envoy takes the direction
Of Kay Kaavoos with such alacrity
Drops of sweat fall off his camel's limbs.
He is met at the royal court with cries of joy.

The king calls the messenger before him,
Scatters precious stones over Giv's letter.
Men in their bliss prepare for feast.
In every palace, in every home,
People call for music and song.

News reaches Nimrooz of the victorious Giv,
The one who shines upon the world,
And his triumphant return to Iran-Zamin
In the company of Kay Khosrow,
Young king of pure faith.
Rostam distributes gold to the poor in gratitude
For the safe return of the brave lion.

Then he bids Baanoogoshasp

To swiftly take presents to Giv, along with
One thousand two hundred warriors of name,
With throne and heavy crowns,
With three hundred female slaves,
And one hundred and twenty male slaves,
Each one of them cradling a golden chalice.

The princess leaves her father's side to rush to Giv,
A bird in flight with open wings.
Giv sends her to Isfahan, where she spreads
Her glory throughout the realm.

The entire world learns that Kay Khosrow,
Son of the king and heir to the throne, is on his way.
On all sides, worldly men travel to Isfahan.

Goodarz furnishes his palace,
Spreads out beautiful brocade,
Adorns the throne with gold and precious stones,
As is due a seat destined for a monarch.
He prepares a torque, bracelets and earrings,
And a crown inlaid with gems worthy of a king.

Goodarz bedecks the city for a grand feast.
Then he mounts his horse as proud noblemen
Come to their feet in readiness to greet King Khosrow.
They travel forth at a distance of seventy farsangs
To receive him solemnly according to custom.

As the king emerges into sight along with Giv,
Brave horsemen dismount.
As soon as Goodarz catches sight of Khosrow
And his son trailing behind, he sheds tears of venom
And laments on the fate of Siaavosh.

The world hero dismounts,
And the young king presses him against his chest.

Goodarz showers blessings upon Khosrow:
"O King of the earth, may your destiny always
Maintain you in a state of awareness and victory!
I would rather see you than possess a kingdom.
May the eye of ill-wishers be blinded!

May light be the share of Siaavosh's soul!
The Creator knows well how the sight of you
Lights up my heart with tremendous joy.
It is a joy greater than if I were to find Siaavosh alive."

Then he kisses Giv on the eyes and forehead
And says to him, "You have brought to light
The deepest secrets of providence.
You are the hero who made my dream a reality.
At the time of need, you are our support and savior,
Able to sit and wait when necessity demands."

The noblemen of Iran bow low to touch
Their foreheads to the ground before Kay Khosrow.
Goodarz the leader continues to rejoice
At the sight of the king and of his own offspring.

They happily return to the city,
Their fortune resplendent.
They arrive at the palace of the world hero,
Hearts full of bliss, souls enlightened.
For seven days, they sit in the banquet hall,
Elated, with their cups in their hands.

On the eighth day, hearts full of joy, they depart
Toward the city and residence of Kay Kaavoos.

30 | Kay Khosrow Reaches Kay Kaavoos

As Kay Khosrow nears the king, the world
Fills with scent, color, and beautiful pictures.
Everywhere is adorned for feast:
Doors, gardens, and walls
Are covered in lush precious fabrics.
Everywhere one hears the sound of singers.
Everywhere one sees rosewater, wine,
And a blend of musk and saffron.
Horses' manes are drenched in musk and wine,
Sugar cubes and silver coins
Are tossed beneath their hooves.

Once Kaavoos lays eyes on Kay Khosrow,
A shower of tears floods his eyes
And streams down his cheeks.
He climbs down from the throne,
Approaches him, and kisses his eyes and face.
The young world seeker king praises him in turn,
And the two take majestic strides to the throne.

The king questions Kay Khosrow at length
On the Turks, their customs,
And on the throne of the King of Tooran-Zamin.

Khosrow replies, "Every breath this foolish king
Takes is to wreak his treachery and his hate.
Why talk to me about this cursed man?
May his dreams never be fulfilled!
May his throne and crown perish!
He is responsible for my father's wretched death,
For the brutal beating my mother sustained
To prompt my early death within the womb.
May he never be free of worry!
Once my holy mother gave birth to me,
This unworthy king sent me to the mountain
Where I shepherded goats, buffalo, and horses,
Where I spent my time counting the days and nights
Completed by the sun's rotations.

"In the end, Piran came to the mountain
And took me to this hateful man.
I feared him, I feared his deeds,
I trembled before his anger and his accusations.
He questioned me, spoke to me at length,
But I hid from him what I consider of sense and value.
When he spoke to me of head, I replied of leg.
When he questioned me on food, I spoke of dwelling.
Yazdan eclipsed his mind full of dark designs
So that he may view me as a mad man.
Thus finding my brain empty of logic,
He sent me to my mother, cursing me all the while.
I could never be the friend of my father's murderer,
Even if the clouds were to shower the earth with jewels."

Kaavoos replies, "O noble one, the world yearns
To see you reign, for you are of Kianian blood,
Worthy of the throne and as wise as the King of Kings."

Khosrow addresses Kaavoos Shah again,
"O master of world and ancient throne,
If I were to recount to you all that Giv has achieved,
You would be astonished, and with good reason,
For you cannot begin to imagine how he suffered.
He searched for me in all of Tooran-Zamin for years,
Overcoming trials and tribulations.
But, in addition, he single-handedly twice defeated
The armies of Tooran-Zamin who assailed us
Like a massive all-consuming blaze.

"I then witnessed such a deed from Giv,
A sight not even beheld by Indians
Watching the most furious elephants,
A sight greater than a whale emerging from the waters.
He sent them all fleeing in battle, two world heroes
Scampering with their troops, young and old.
Piran arrived like a lion armed for war,
Mounting a high-speed horse, consuming the ground.
Giv swung his noose above his head, captured the hero
Around the neck, and dragged him toward me.
With my wounded heart, O mighty king,
I intervened on behalf of Piran.
Giv was about to cut off his head, but I pardoned Piran,
For he had condemned my father's murder
And never voiced malicious words toward me.
So I begged Giv to spare Piran on my account.
He agreed, since Piran is the reason my mother
And I were freed from the eager claws of the lion
Who sought to disconnect my head from my body,
The way he had my father's.

"I have to praise Giv, who neither rested nor slept,
Neither drank nor ate, and fought mightily
With his bull-headed mace until we reached the Jayhoon.
In his rage, he crossed the river without a thought
To whether he was traveling across land or water.
Such a world hero must never cease to be youthful."

Kay Kaavoos is quite pleased at these words,
Which make his heart blossom like a rose.
He takes Giv's head into his hands, presses it
Close to his chest, and kisses his face several times.
Then he praises Goodarz
For his show of loyalty to land and crown.

Kaavoos hands Giv a robe of honor so lavish,
Such as no one, great or small, had seen before.
He orders a certificate be written on silk
By which the king assigns Giv
Governance of Ghom, Rey, Khorasan, and Isfahan.[36]
The world hero's head is thus raised to the sun.

The king says to Giv, "You have deeply suffered.
Now go and enjoy your land and your wealth."

Goodarz and his sons bless and thank the king,
Each bowing low in tribute to Kaavoos's glory.

Then the king asks for a grand palace to be
Refurbished with golden doors, golden thrones,
And Chinese brocade stretched across its walls,
A palace to be bestowed to Faranguis,
Along with a necklace and a pair of earrings.

Kaavoos says to her, "O Queen of Queens,
May you never experience sorrow!
You deserted land and kin to come to ours.
You have suffered grave hardships.
Iran-Zamin is now your home
And your desire is my guide.
You will find me kinder than Afraasiyaab,
For I deem your face as glorious as the sun and moon.
Everything in my possession belongs to you.
In this place, any wish or command you may have
Will be granted expeditiously."

The moon of all women praises the king:
"May time and space never be deprived of your glory!"

◇◇◇◇◇◇◇◇◇◇◇◇◇

36 Ghom, Rey, Khorasan, Isfahan: Cities across Iran; Ghom, Rey, and Isfahan are in
the south-central region, and Khorasan is in the northeast part of Iran.

Kay Kaavoos, Kay Khosrow, and the noblemen
Sit and engage in revelry while musicians entertain.
After feasting, the older king brings the key
To his treasury and passes it on to his young son.

31 | Tous Disobeys Kay Khosrow

Kashvaad has a palace in Estakhr,[37] the glory of Iranians.
As Goodarz and Kay Khosrow leave Kay Kaavoos,
They make preparations to proceed in its direction.

They take the road,
And once they arrive at the golden palace,
Khosrow is asked to sit upon a golden throne.
He is widely hailed as king.

The noble warriors cinch their belts to praise him,
Everyone with the exception of Tous, son of Nozar,
Who feels he is the rightful heir of timpani
And golden shoe, since he has been appointed
To carry the Kaaviani banner.

Goodarz finds himself mocking such pretentious airs.
He prepares a gentle message addressed to Tous.
He calls Giv, world seeker of heroic lion arms,
And tells him, "Speak to Tous, son of Nozar, and say,
        'Do not seek an excuse to quarrel in times of joy.
        Iran's noblemen are here to pay tribute to the king.
        Why are you refusing to present yourself?
        Is this by the deev's command?
        Do you not perceive how Yazdan's grace
        Rests in the being of Kay Khosrow?
        If you refuse to obey, you will entice my aversion.
        I shall be forced to fight you.
        I send Giv to relay this message.
        It contains the order of the royal council.
        O skillful one, pay heed to this advice.'"

◇◇◇◇◇◇◇◇◇◇◇◇◇
37 Estakhr: Ancient city in southern Iran in the Pars province, north of
Persepolis.

Giv leaves his father's side, head full of harsh words.
He marches to army leader Tous and says to him,
"Your behavior is foolish. You conspire with deevs.
You deviate from the path of wisdom."

Tous listens to him and says,
"Unlucky is the one who wishes to trifle with me.
After Rostam of elephantine stature,
I am the one among noblemen,
The most renowned army leader of Iran.
Manoochehr, the valiant king, was my grandfather.
He subjected the world to his sharp sword.
I am the son of Nozar, world king,
Highest in rank and royal blood.
I originate from the seed of Fereydoon.
In war, I am a battle-seeker able
To tear apart the lion's heart
And shred to bits the leopard's skin.
Without me, you wish to organize
The affairs of the kingdom, hold council,
Place a new king on the seat of power?
I shall not consent.
Do not speak to me of Khosrow.
If we place upon the throne a king
From the seed of Afraasiyaab,
Iran-Zamin's good fortune shall fall dormant.
We do not want as king a descendant of Pashang.
A herd may prosper in the presence of a leopard.

"You came, and with great pains,
But your labors are lost,
For Khosrow is young and strong,
While a man who wishes to be world king
Must be skilled, of pure blood, majestic, and with faith.
If we must select a king,
It must be the son of Kaavoos and not his grandson.
Fariborz, whose blood flows pure,
Is worthy of throne and crown.
On neither side is he related to our enemies.
He has dignity and courage; he is just and kind."

Giv jumps to his feet in great fury,

For he does not trust Tous's wisdom and faith.
He says to him, "Brave and renowned leader,
Do not withdraw at the beat of kettledrums
Or when you see the spears of the sons of Goodarz.
Your ambition will be your defeat.
Together we have engaged in many battles,
But now you have thrown memory into the wind.
Had you been a wise man worthy of throne,
We would have had no need
To find a king on Mount Alborz.
If your head is devoid of crown,
It is because you have neither brain nor wisdom.
Yazdan assigns the royal throne
Only to a man worthy of power.
He must be prudent and wise, brave and regal."

After uttering these bitter words,
Giv turns his back on Tous, finds Goodarz,
Son of Kashvaad, and says to him,
"This man has neither dignity nor good sense.
Although he has two eyes, it is as if he is blind.
He appoints Fariborz to be king,
Yet there is in the palace no painting
More beautiful than that of Kay Khosrow
And no king more able and more worthy.
Never has Iran witnessed a rider of his ability.
Never has there been a prince of such beauty
Seated on either golden saddle or golden throne."

32 | The Anger of Goodarz for Tous

Outraged, Goodarz cries,
"May Tous vanish from the company of men!
We shall show him who is worthy of power
And leadership, of the splendor of throne and crown,
Of the favors handed out by good fortune."

Goodarz is blessed with seventy-eight
Grandsons and great-grandsons.
He orders timpani be played,
Proceeds from the palace courtyard to the plain,

Where twelve thousand brave soldiers gather,
Riding horses decked in strappings.

Tous takes the road as soon as he hears
That army vanquisher Goodarz is on his way
With his warrior offspring, preceded by timpani.
Kettledrums are placed atop elephants.
A great number of men take arms,
And the banner of Kaaveh billows above the front.

At the sight of Goodarz and his vast host,
The faces of sun and moon dim before Tous.
He sees a throne atop a bold elephant, shining
With turquoise stones reminiscent of ocean waters.
Seated on the throne, he sees Kay Khosrow,
A prince, a world seeker, worthy of crown,
Cinched at the waist and fully armed.
He is surrounded by two hundred war elephants.
You would think the world itself
Would fail to contain the lot.

Khosrow shines upon his throne like a bright moon,
A sparkling crown of ruby upon his head.
He wears bracelet and torque, and on each ear, a ring.
In his hand is a bull-headed mace.

Disconcerted, Tous reflects,
"If I engage in battle right here, right now,
We shall see massive losses on both sides.
Iran will forever remain a huge battlefield.
Afraasiyaab's wish would then be fulfilled.
The Turks' good fortune would awaken.
The throne of the King of Kings would be captured
By them, and, along with great loss sustained,
We would have squandered our joy and happiness."

He sends a wise man full of good intentions
To Kaavoos Shah to say,
"If a single man upon the battlefield
Affixes an arrow of poplar wood to his bowstring,
An intense struggle will ensue, one that Afraasiyaab
Could never imagine in his wildest dreams."

33 | Goodarz and Tous Ask Kaavoos About the Line of Succession

The moment Kaavoos hears these truthful words,
He summons to his side the two adversaries.

A messenger finds the army leader and says to him
In a soft voice, "O brave lion full of experience,
Do not pour deadly poison in the cup of milk.
Lay down your sword and coat of mail.
Unfasten your warrior belt.
What is to our benefit must not turn to our detriment.
Both world heroes must appear before the king."

Tous and Goodarz present themselves at court
To plead their cases before Kaavoos's throne.

Tous the leader says,
"If the noble king is weary of throne and crown,
Then his son must accede to the empire,
To power, crown, and royal throne.
When a prince has a son,
Why should a grandson succeed him?
Fariborz has majesty, Kianian nobility and lineage.
He is a fierce lion ready for battle."

Goodarz replies, "O foolish one, the wise thinker
Does not regard you as belonging to the race of men.
Never has the world seen someone comparable
To Siaavosh in nobility, splendor, and cordiality.
World seeker Khosrow is his son;
He resembles him in many ways.
You would take him for Siaavosh himself
In stature, face, and demeanor.
On his mother's side, he has ties to Toor.
But on his father's side, he is of royal race
And will not sway from the righteous path.
No man exists of his status in all of Iran and Tooran.
Why speak of him with foolish words?
Your two eyes have never witnessed
A man with such a beautiful face,
Such height, such loving nature.

He crossed the Jayhoon without the use of a vessel
In the example of Fereydoon, who,
Without a boat, crossed the Arvand River,
Then caused the world to blossom.
He put his trust in the splendor of the Kianians
And in the virtue of his intentions.

"By his valor and by divine grace,
Khosrow will subjugate
The heart, the hand, the eye of evil-doers.
Then he will strap his belt and, like a mad lion,
Will strike to avenge his father's blood.
He will purify Iran, wash away all pain.
The cunning Afraasiyaab will shiver with fear.
Blessed Sooroosh revealed to me in dream that,
With his good fortune, he will put an end
To cries of suffering rising from Iran-Zamin.
As master of crown and powerful throne,
He will banish grief and anguish from the world.

"You are Nozar's son and not a stranger,
But your father was ill-tempered
And you have an impetuous nature.
If I had weapons in my possession,
I would assail you with the sword of battle,
Flood your chest and arms with blood,
Without the need to speak meaningless words.
We cannot allow you to cause chaos and destruction
Among the descendants of the Kianian race
And to give into greed and self-indulgence.
Kay Kaavoos knows what he wants.
He will turn over the throne to whoever pleases him,
For he is world master and King of Kings."

Tous replies, "O unfortunate old man,
Your words are worthless and harsh.
You are neither of royal blood nor of noble blood.
Your father, who lived in Isfahan,
Was nothing more than a blacksmith.
Because he was obedient to us, we raised his rank,
Promoting him from metalsmith to army leader."

Goodarz says, "Listen carefully to what I tell you.
You speak to me on equal footing,
But I stand taller than you in stature.
You remain with little knowledge of who I am.
What kind of a speech is this you give
Before the king and before our noblemen?
I suffer no shame for my blacksmith lineage.
O selfish man, one must hold wisdom and courage.
My grandfather was Kaaveh the blacksmith,
Who was holder of glory, stature, and bracelet,
Who tore to shreds evil Zahaak's unscrupulous covenant,
Who founded and raised the Kaaviani banner,
Which you, with your golden boots, boastfully brandish.
Beyond Rostam, Zaal, and the rider Saam,
My forefathers are Nariman and the virtuous Garshaasp.
I am Goodarz, son of Kashvaad, and with my many sons
We have staunchly strapped ourselves in service to Iran."

Tous says to him, "O aged warrior, you speak nonsense.
We are the providers of your rank and glory.
You function to serve us yet act irrationally.
If you are a descendant of Kashvaad and Kaaveh,
I am Tous, son of Nozar, a prince, offspring of a king.
If your blade is laced with anvil,
My spear will pierce the heart of Mount Ghaaf.
If your mace is heavy with stone,
My bow can sew the heart of the sun.
Why should we continue to fight and argue?
The King of Kings knows who is worthy of kingship.
Put a stop to your futile words.
What do you know of king and kingship?"

Goodarz replies, "Do not speak thus,
For I do not recognize such honor in you.
The question should rather be:
What do you know of king and kingship?
Your head is devoid of brain
And empty of knowledge.
Fereydoon's rise to throne, power, and crown
Was by virtue of the rise of Kaaveh.
Afflicted by the evil deeds of Zahaak the sorcerer,
He found himself with no other recourse

276

But to cinch his waist in preparation for battle.
Kaaveh alone could take on the heroic position
As Kianian pillar of support to the Iranian host.
Beyond Kaaveh, there was Ghaaran, my paternal
Uncle, skillful Kashvaad, bearer of golden belt,
Who shed light all around,
Sustaining both loss and profit.
There is no one in the world of the likes
Of the members of the Goodarzian family.
If you think that you stand above us in any way,
You are delusional, for the truth is otherwise.
In courage, in knowledge, in wealth, and skill,
From father to son, we have stood steadfast
As unwavering pillars of Kianian sovereigns."

Then he turns to Kaavoos and says, "Skillful King,
Do not turn your back on ancient customs.
Do not reject the right path.
Call to your side your two noble sons.
Both are young; both deserve the throne.
Determine which one
Is most worthy in power and grace.
If you wish to abdicate, hand over to him the crown
And rejoice to see one of your sons ascend to kingship."

Kaavoos says, "I do not find it a reasonable request.
My two sons are equally dear to my heart.
If I show more affection to one,
The other will feel contempt for me.
I shall find a way to test the two
And thus avoid dissension in this gathering.
My two sons must leave, each escorted by an army.
They must go to Ardabil[38] to defend the border,
Where Ahriman picks a battle with us every year.
He spawns distress among the believers at Fort Bahman,
And no faithful wise man dares stay there.
I shall offer treasure and royal throne to the one who,
Sword in hand, will seize and destroy the fortress."

Pleased by the decision of the mindful king,

◇◇◇◇◇◇◇◇◇◇◇◇◇
38 Ardabil: Ancient city in northwestern Iran.

Tous and Goodarz accept the resolution,
And no one has a wiser story to tell.
They hurry to make preparations.

34 | Tous and Fariborz Attack the Castle of Bahman

As the sun enters the house of lion
And the sky vanquishes remnants of night,
Fariborz, son of Kaavoos, and Tous, son of Nozar,
Hurriedly enter the dwelling of the world king.

Tous says to the king,
"I shall take host, timpani, and elephants.
I shall carry the Kaaviani banner
And render pallid my enemies' ruby cheeks.
I shall strap my Kianian belt, entrusting myself
To the fortunes of Fariborz
And to the value of our noble family."

The king replies, "When you engage in a campaign,
No one takes danger, great or small, more into account.
You can hope to return victorious,
By the will of the Creator of Sun and Moon.
If Fariborz consents, guide your host
And remain at his side.
Destiny carves the path, no matter what is said.
Whether one is ahead or dragging behind,
It matters little, for ultimately
The important thing is victory."

Tous takes off with Kaaviani banner and golden boots,
Leading the troops with elephants and procession.
Fariborz, son of Kaavoos, occupies the army center.

As vengeful warriors advance to Fort Bahman,
The earth exhales scorching flames
That make the tips of spears sizzle.
The warriors smolder in their steel armor.
You would think the earth is ablaze from end to end
And the air is a net stretched out by the rebel Ahriman.
The crests of ramparts are lost in the clouds.

The Iranians seek in vain a way to engage in war.

The army leader says to Fariborz,
"A man can throw his enemy's head into the dust.
He can seek to attack with sword, bow and arrow,
Noose and mace, but no path leads to this castle.
If one exists, no one has knowledge of it.
Our hips burn in armor; our horses' bodies are aflame.
I see no one willing to fight, only blazing fire.
But do not despair, for if you cannot take the castle,
Rest assured that no one else can achieve the feat."

For seven days, they go around and around,
Unable to discover a path to access the fort.
They return discouraged, having gained
Nothing more than a long and exhausting campaign.

35 | Kay Khosrow Seizes the Castle of Bahman

Soon Giv, Goodarz, and members of Kashvaad's family
Learn that Tous and Fariborz are on their way back.
Goodarz thinks, "The time has come for battle."

He sends out his order, the cry of war is heard,
And the young world master's host forms its ranks.
The golden throne, inlaid with emeralds,
Is placed on the back of an elephant.
Brave soldiers with golden boots, torques, and crowns
Inlaid with jewels take position beneath a purple banner.

Goodarz says, "Today is a new day,
The accession to the throne of Kay Khosrow,
The king who yearns to possess the world."

The world seeker climbs on the golden throne,
A crown on his head, a mace in his hand.
In this way, the noble king departs with Giv, Goodarz,
And a vast host, toward the castle of Bahman.

Once close to the fort, Kay Khosrow climbs
Down from the throne to bestride his horse of steel.

He straps his belt and fastens his coat of mail.
He summons a scribe to write in Pahlavi with amber
A gracious letter in the manner of kings:
"This letter comes from the Creator's servant,
From the renowned Kay Khosrow, world conqueror,
The one who escaped the ties of the evil Ahriman,
Who, with divine aid, renounced cruel acts.
O Bahman, dark sorcerer, beware of the World Creator,
Who is supreme, an eternal Guide,
A Giver of our sustenance, Master of Saturn
Mars, and Sun, Master of grace and power,
The One who bestowed upon me Kianian glory,
The body of an elephant and the claws of a fierce lion.

"I rule over the world from end to end,
From Taurus to Pisces. If Ahriman resides
In this fort, he is the Creator's enemy.
In the glory of Yazdan, pure and perfect,
I shall bring his head down from the clouds
To roll onto the dust of the earth.
Should the masters of this castle
Excel in the art of sorcery,
I shall have no need for an army to crush them.
I shall swing my noose to seize the heads of sorcerers.
Even if blessed Sooroosh were to dwell in this place,
An army would still march by divine command.
I am not of the seed of Ahriman;
I possess royal grace and glory.
At the will of the Creator, I shall empty this fort
By imperial wish and command."

Khosrow grabs a long spear, secures the letter to it.
He raises the weapon straight into the air like a banner,
Desirous of only one thing: divine splendor.

Then he orders Giv to approach the wall
With the spear and says to him,
"Take this gallant letter to the castle rampart.
Drop the spear there, utter the name of Yazdan,
And wheel your horse around without hesitation."

Giv takes the spear, ready to obey,

His lips full of praise for Kay Khosrow, divine servant.
Entrusting his fate to the world-seeker prince,
He drops the spear with the letter,
Watches it disappear as he utters Yazdan's name,
Giver of all that is valuable and good.
Giv then retreats on his speedy horse,
Flying away like the wind.

After the king's letter disappears,
A rolling sound is heard. The castle floor rises,
Suddenly and by divine command.
The wall of the castle splits and separates with
A boom that resounds through field and mountain,
Like the roar of thunder in a spring storm.
The world turns dark as ebony.
Sun, Pleiades, and moon immediately vanish,
As if a cloud of gloom envelops the earth.
The skies part much like a lion's gaping jaws.

Kay Khosrow charges his black horse.
He shouts to his troops,
"Send a shower of shots flying over the castle.
Duplicate with your bow and arrow
The fall of a spring deluge."

A cloud of arrows drops a hailstorm of steel
That causes grave injury, death, and destruction.
The arrows kill a great number of deevs
While others find their demise from their deepest fears.

A bright light appears and darkness dissipates.
The world shines like the new moon in the name
Of the World Creator and in the glory of the king.
A kind and gentle wind whirls and whispers.
The face of the earth appears to be smiling.
The deevs leave on the order of the king.

The dust enveloping the army dissolves,
Revealing the face of the castle's gate.
The liberator king crosses the threshold
With the aged Goodarz, son of Kashvaad.
Beyond the gate, he discovers a dazzling city,
Full of gardens, squares, public and private dwellings.

Anywhere light shines, darkness is expelled.
The king commands a temple
Be built on the site of destruction,
A temple crowned with a dome,
Its crest reaching the sky.
The structure is ten kamands[39] in length and width,
Surrounded with tall, vaulted rooms,
A space to span the course
Of a Taazian horse's racetrack.

Kay Khosrow completes it
By lighting a sacred fire of Aazargoshasp.
He entrusts the rooms surrounding the place
To a number of wise men, sages and astrologers.
He remains in this city until he illuminates the temple
With the blaze, scent, and color of his splendor.

A year passes in this manner
After which he orders the departure of his host,
Packs up the load-bearing creatures,
And tells his troops to mount their horses.

36 | Kay Khosrow Returns Victorious

Once word spreads throughout Iran
That the king is victorious by divine grace,
The world stands astonished at the fortune
And the power achieved by Kay Khosrow.
Countless noblemen, bearers of gifts,
Come to pay tribute in joy, one by one.

Fariborz meets Kay Khosrow with a procession,
An army of bold Iranian warriors, vast as a mountain.
As soon as he sees the king,
He descends from Golrang, his rose-colored mount.

In turn, the valiant king dismounts
His night-dark steed, and Fariborz,
His father's brother, kisses him on the face,

◇◇◇◇◇◇◇◇◇◇◇◇◇◇
39 Kamand: Unit of measurement.

Prepares a golden throne inlaid in turquoise stones,
And recognizes him as king by divine will.

Kay Khosrow takes his place upon the golden seat,
A crown ornate with gems upon his head.

Tous approaches the king and places at his feet
The Kaaviani banner, timpani, and golden boots.
Kissing the ground, he says,
"Select a warrior from our host, worthy of timpani,
Golden boots, and Kaaviani banner, valuable objects
That will bring him glory and good fortune.
Give them to someone more deserving than me.
When one makes a mistake, repentance shows its face
In the manner of saving another man's life."

In this way, Tous asks forgiveness for words
He had spoken, pledging to forsaken foolish deeds.

The victorious king greets him graciously,
Smiles at him, and asks him to sit on the throne.
Khosrow says to Tous, "I see no one in the army
Who merits these symbols of power more than you.
Continue to enjoy them; they can only belong to you.
I hold in my heart no enmity.
You have no need to ask forgiveness.
You did not seek to place a stranger upon the throne."

From there, Kay Khosrow takes the road of Pars
To visit the glorious Kay Kaavoos who,
Aware of the approach of his auspicious grandson,
Rises and proceeds, yearning to meet him,
His cheeks colored by joy, his aging heart renewed.
He dismounts gaily, and, with his procession, advances
On foot to present Khosrow offerings and greetings.

From afar, the young king smiles, his heart bounding
With delight at the sight of his grandfather.
He climbs down to pay tribute to Kaavoos.
The older king in turn laughs, presses him
Against his heart, and showers him with praise.

The lion emerges triumphant from battle,

Having blinded his enemies' eyes
And darkened their hearts.
Kaavoos honors him, extols his glory,
His fine-looking face and his unwavering faith,
His tall stature, his divine grace, his wisdom, and
The splendor with which he adorns the royal throne.

Kay Kaavoos says, "O Creator of sky, Moon, and Sun,
You have elevated my status and my name.
My heart beats with joy at the sight Khosrow's face."

Then they leave in the direction of court and palace,
Where the throne of the world master awaits.

37 | Kay Kaavoos Places Kay Khosrow on the Imperial Throne

The two kings dismount and enter the palace,
Mouths and hearts full of benevolent words.
Khosrow comes forward, kisses Kaavoos's hand,
And bows low before the throne.

His grandfather guides Khosrow to his seat.
He concedes his place in joy, utters good wishes
Asks the treasurer to bring the Kianian crown,
Kisses Kay Khosrow
And lowers the crown onto his head.
He climbs down from the glorious throne
To take a seat on an ordinary chair.

Kaavoos calls for an offering of emeralds
To be drawn from his treasury
And a great number of jewels worthy of a king.
He pronounces blessings on Siaavosh,
Whose features shine on the face of Kay Khosrow.

Leaders and the earth's most notable men, travel
From far and wide to pay homage to the new king.
They scatter pearls and precious stones over him.

Such is the way of the world:

It takes with one hand and gives with the other.
Its duperies and deceits plague us, afflict us.
We are placed up so high, then brought down at once.
If your heart succeeds on the road to happiness,
Try to maintain eternally a state of joy.
When you are happy, let your heart revel.
When you are blessed with abundance,
Share with others; contribute to better the world.
Do not torment yourself needlessly.
Use what you have; distribute the superfluous.
You have taken great pains in life.
Do not forsake the fruits of your labor to your foes.

You will lack for nothing, nor will your children,
For we are all offshoots of that ancient root.
Do you not see the world so abundant in wealth?
Do you not see all the blessings of divine grace?
Yazdan's gifts are boundless.
Therefore, restrain your heart
From surrendering to fear and worry.
Maintain yourself in a state of bliss and happiness.

PART TEN

The Sixty-Year Reign of Kay Khosrow

1 | The Beginning of the Story

The poet bard who relates this saga
Shares more than a tale from ancient times.
He relates the story of Kay Khosrow,
The way he sits on the royal throne with the goal
Of sending troops in the direction of Tooran-Zamin.

If the revolving dome wishes to grant me a few more
Years of youth, I shall now speak of this ageless tale.

When in the garden, the cypress tree grows an offshoot,
Its verdant crest rising above the palace roof.
The tree rejoices at such lofty height,
Just as a father delights at the sight of his watchful son,
Knowing his labors will spread joy across the world.
If kingship is in his nature,
He must rule with compassion and benevolence.

Above all else, you must reflect on three attributes:
Acquired virtues, birthright, and a kind nature
That perhaps could be referred to as your essence.
How could we have virtue without a kind nature?
When you possess essence, it will convert into virtue.
Have you ever seen anyone who,
Though deprived of lineage, is full of virtue?
Your nature or essence is given
By the divine grace of the Creator:
It compels you to abstain from lending an ear to evil.
Your birth is a gift handed down as your paternal heritage.
A pure trunk inherently produces pure fruit.
Virtues are acquired in your dealings with others.
They cost much effort and force you
To exert yourself under the weight.

Of these three attributes, linked tightly,
The most important one is essence: a holy bequest.
Once you have acquired the three qualities,
You must develop a fourth one, wisdom,

Which is the ability to discern between good and evil.
A man able to integrate these four attributes
Is able to cope with any challenge,
Overcome most things: greed, suffering, and grief,
With the exception of death, for which there is no remedy,
And which is the most harrowing of all calamities.

Moreover, Kay Khosrow, without question,
Is in possession of all four qualities.
The revolving dome of sky sent him from above
To rule down here on the magnificent earth.

2 | Noblemen Pay Homage to Kay Khosrow

With the ascension to the throne of Kay Khosrow,
The world, from end to end, feels his dominance.
Seated on the imperial throne, the crown of power
On his head, he distributes justice all around,
And digs out and cleaves the roots of crime.

This liberator, master of throne and Kianian lineage,
Places the royal crown upon his head,
An act that exalts both king and kingship.

The world fills with rivers, streams and springs.
Kay Khosrow replaces barren lands with cultivated ones.
He frees the hearts of mourners from sorrow.
Spring clouds rain upon the land
To wash away the rust of grief.
In the aftereffects of his justice and his generosity,
The world prospers like a beautiful paradise,
Filled with wealth, good will, and truth.
Hearts flourish with a sense of hope, joy, and security,
Banishing Ahriman, cutting short his hand,
Rendering it powerless to carry out
Acts of deceit and duplicity.

Just as Jamsheed and Fereydoon long ago,
Khosrow restores peace and harmony to the world.
Messengers travel to the court from various lands:
Noblemen, princes, and warrior heroes.

PART TEN

The whole world flows under his command.

When word reaches Nimrooz and Rostam's court
That the glorious Kianian traveled from Tooran to Iran
To take his seat on the throne of power,
That he strides on the firmament of sovereignty,
Rostam, the world-illuminating hero,
Convenes his troops from all corners of his domain
And equips them to travel to pay homage to the king.

He joyously takes the direction of the royal hall
In pomp and circumstance, escorted by his host
And by his father Zaal, son of Saam of Nariman,
And a number of noblemen of the land of Kabol:
A procession so vast, it turns the field black as ebony.
The blare of trumpets resounds to pierce dim hearts.

In the vanguard are Zaal and his famed convoy.
In the rear is Rostam, carrier of the purple banner.
They follow the road leading to Iran-Zamin,
With Zavaareh, Faraamarz, elephants, and host.

Once the royal court is made aware of the hero's
Ceremonial approach with his renowned noblemen,
Everyone in the land rises to greet him.

The king rejoices and says to Kay Khosrow,
"May Rostam continue to live in good health!
He raised your father, tirelessly spreading
His skills and virtue throughout the world."
The king then commands Giv, Goodarz, and Tous
To take to the road with clarion and timpani.

Drums roll at the palace gates;
Brave warriors don their helmets.
From every corner of the land, men turn out
With banners and drums to greet Rostam.
The world heroes and a huge host trudge for two days.
Once they sight his banner
And his army's dust rising to the sun,
They shout happily, and sound trumpets and timpani.

Giv, Goodarz, and Tous emerge from the army center,

Rush toward Rostam, and embrace the hero,
Vanquisher of lions, who in turn asks after the king.
Hearts radiant with joy, the warriors approach Zaal.
They seek out Faraamarz, rejoicing at the sight of him.
Together they travel to the king's court,
To hail and praise the master of the glorious crown.

Once Khosrow's eyes fall on the mighty hero,
A stream of tears floods his cheeks.
He climbs down his seat to greet Rostam,
Who bows low to kiss the ground before his monarch.

The young king says to Rostam,
"O world hero, may you live in joy!
May your soul forever remain clearsighted!
You are the wisest man in the world.
You served as father to my father Siaavosh."

Then Khosrow kisses Zaal, takes his hand into his,
And raises it to his forehead in remembrance of Siaavosh.
He places the two heroes, Zaal and Rostam,
On the imperial throne, invoking Yazdan's grace.
Rostam examines Khosrow from head to toe,
Observes his manner of seating, speaking, judging.
His heart fills with grief, his cheeks with blood,
As he laments at length the fatal end of Siaavosh.

Finally, Rostam says to the world ruler, "O King,
You are the living memory of your father.
Never have I seen a crown-bearer of such glory,
Nor one who so resembles his predecessor."

Then they rise, ask for banquet and wine,
And the world master remains awake half the night,
Discussing the bygone course of events.

3 | Kay Khosrow Makes the Rounds of his Empire

Once the sun draws out its shining blade,
And the dark night absconds in fear,
The sound of horns is heard at the king's court.

The leaders enter the illustrious royal palace:
Tous, Goodarz, and the valiant Giv;
Gorgeen, Gostaham, and Shahpoor the lion;
Rohaam and Bijan, always ready for war;
Ashkesh the bold, who gained fame in battle;
Fariborz, son of Kaavoos;
And Zangueh, triumphant champion.

The young king addresses his army warriors:
"I wish to see the entire land of Iran secured
From border to border. I wish to engage in the hunt,
Spend some time in diversion and delight."

The noblemen make preparations,
Then depart with the king
To explore and discover new sectors of the world,
With Rostam, famed world hero, at the lead.

A number of warriors bring up the rear,
Including Giv, Goodarz, son of Kashvaad;
Shahpoor, Bahraam, sword brandisher; Gorgeen;
Bijan, skilled archer; Farhaad; Zangueh of Shaavaran;
Goraazeh, the warlord; along with a procession so large,
The polish of swords and armor, arrows and helms
Overshadows the light of the sun and moon.
They kill so many wild beasts that the earth
Is strewn with bodies, similar to a battlefield.

In this way and thus occupied, the king crosses
Lands both inhabited and unsettled in Iran-Zamin.
When he comes across a region that is desolate
Because of some sort of wrong, he makes things right,
Repopulates it by giving abundant coins and dinars,
Never tiring from handing out justice and generosity.

He stops in every city, setting up his throne
As suits a king favored by good fortune.
He draws gold and silver from his treasury,
Wishing to embellish the world.
Then he travels to a new town,
Always engaged in drinking wine,
Seated on his throne with the crown upon his head.

He continues in this manner until he arrives
With his cortege at the land of Azerbaijan[40]
Where he stops to rest, at times drinking,
At times dashing on his horse
To visit the temple of Aazargoshasp
Where he invokes divine grace at the altar
And worships the Creator.

In the end, he returns with his cortege to his land,
Joyously takes his seat at Kaavoos's side,
And abandons himself completely to revelry.

King Khosrow, intoxicated with shining wine,
Quickly surrenders to rest and sleep.

4 | Kay Khosrow Promises Vengeance

Once the resplendent sun brings in the dawn of day
And scatters its rubies across the dim earth,
Khosrow and Kaavoos, two proud rulers
Whose paths bring good fortune,
Sit with Rostam and Zaal.

Kaavoos speaks of various matters to his grandson,
Beginning with the subject of Afraasiyaab,
Flooding his cheeks with blood tears.
He recounts how this Turk treated Siaavosh,
How he destroyed the land of Iran,
Slaying so many world heroes and reducing
Women and children to the depths of despair.

He says to Khosrow, "You will find in Iran
Many towns ravaged by him.
The Creator's affection rests on you.
You are powerful, wise, and valiant.
Kianian good fortune and your lucky star
Have endowed you with attributes
More valuable than any king.
Now I wish to ask you to make a solemn oath

◇◇◇◇◇◇◇◇◇◇◇◇◇
40 Azerbaijan: A region situated in northwestern Iran.

That must be kept scrupulously.
Promise me to fill your heart
With hatred for Afraasiyaab.
Promise me to never allow this blaze
To be extinguished with the waters of oblivion.
Promise me that you will never envisage him kindly
Just because he is your mother's father,
That you will never allow him
To make you bend to his will and that you will
Never listen to favorable accounts of him.
You cannot be seduced by wealth and ambition,
No matter your financial state.
Promise me that whether you are triumphant
Or defeated, neither mace nor sword,
Neither throne nor crown, neither speech
Nor advice will deter you from scorning him.

"I shall tell you how you will swear.
What is better than advice for the mind and soul?
You will swear by the Master of Sun and Moon;
By the crown, throne, seal, and headdress;
By the warrior's sword that holds the glory of war;
By the white day and the indigo night;
By the memory of the just Fereydoon;
By the majesty and the demands of royalty;
By the blood of Siaavosh and by your soul, O King;
By the grace of the Creator and your lucky star,
That you will never lean to commit acts of evil,
That you will never seek other intermediaries
But the double-edged sword and your mace,
That you will act with the respect and pride
That is due your lofty height and stature."

The young king listens to his grandfather,
Then turns toward the flames and,
Shedding copious tears,
Swears by the pure Creator:
"By the brilliant day and dark night;
By the Sun and Moon, by the throne and crown;
By the king's seal, sword, and diadem;
By the acts of sages and warriors;
By the speech of awakened wise men,

Never will I consider Afraasiyaab in a favorable light.
Never will I glance at his face, not even in dream.
I shall never follow the path where he leads,
For his ways and deeds distress my soul.
I shall fight to avenge my father's blood.
I shall adorn my heart with vast hatred.

"I shall cinch my waist toward this aim,
Hoping that the dome of sky
And my good fortune will stand by me.
I shall not stop until the goal is accomplished,
Unless the heavens have other designs for me.
I shall neither revel nor ever take time to rest
As long as he sits on the throne bearing the crown.
I shall relent only when he vacates the earth,
Making the soul of Siaavosh rejoice.
I shall nurse this vengeance toward Afraasiyaab
As long as there is water and mud upon the ground.
I hope you will agree with all my words,
Allow wisdom to rule over all things."

These words, written in Pahlavi with a pen
Dipped in musk, are recorded on a royal scroll.
Zaal, Rostam, and the army leaders inscribe their seals.
This document with its oath is handed to Rostam
To be placed under his watchful eye.

Then they ask for tables and wine,
And form a very joyous assembly.
For seven days, the leaders reside in Kaavoos's palace,
Listening to music and drinking wine.

On the eighth day, the king washes head and body,
Composes his face, and takes the direction
Of the sanctuary, where he appears
Before the Master of the spinning spheres,
Where he exhales piety in veneration.

Khosrow remains there in the dark night until dawn.
With deep sighs and tears in his eyes, he laments,
"O Yazdan, Distributor of justice,
Donor of good fortune and Guide of humanity,
You alone are almighty.

You alone have the power to ease our suffering.
You abandoned me inside the dragon's jaws
In the days of my youth when I was devoid of army.
You know that the master of Tooran-Zamin
Lacks conscience and lacks fear to commit misdeeds.
Lands both inhabited and deserted curse him equally.
The dim hearts of innocent men are filled with hatred.
He has consumed this beautiful land with an intense fire,
Covered the heads of brave men with the dust of worry,
Unjustly spilling the blood of Siaavosh on the earth.
With these actions, he has torn apart our dim hearts.
Kings tremble before him.
You know that his nature is malicious,
That his essence and lineage are vile,
And that he is a contemptible sorcerer.
For the sake of my father's blood and the aged Kaavoos,
Take everyone's hands and forgive them.
He cannot distinguish wisdom from justice.
His path is twisted and devious,
And all his deeds are in favor of destruction.
Hearts have grown weary of his character.
Eyes shed copious tears."

After touching his forehead to the ground
And celebrating the praises of the Creator,
Kay Khosrow returns to his throne
And says to his warriors, "My brave, highborn men,
Always standing at the ready to conquer the world
And strike with your swords, I have trod Iran,
From this border to the temple of Aazargoshasp.
Nowhere did I encounter a happy man, a wealthy one,
Or one whose lands were well cultivated.
Everyone has been affected by Afraasiyaab's wrath.
Hearts are dim with the swelling of blood.
Eyes are flooding with tears of affliction.

"He intensely pained my heart first,
Then my body and soul suffered.
The noble King Kaavoos, my grandfather,
Does not cease to sigh deeply for all his evil deeds.
Afraasiyaab did not take pity on Siaavosh.
He killed him ruthlessly, afflicting his own daughter,

Subjecting his own brother to his dagger's sharp blade.
In addition, he beheaded Nozar, king and liberator.
Throughout the land of Iran, men and women bemoan
The murders, the looting, the wars and destruction.

"Now, since you are my loyal friends, devoted to me,
Let us love one another and unite in avenging my father.
Let us deliver the land of Iran from its ailments
In the battle of heroes. If united, we fight like leopards,
We can convert mountain to plain.
Afraasiyaab will be responsible for the bloodshed.
If one of ours perishes, he will dwell in paradise.
What do you say? What is your answer?
Present me with sensible advice.
Whoever assails us with animosity must be deterred.
Afraasiyaab is the author of these troubles.
We must think of retribution.
Now is not the time to rest."

The leaders rise with bitter hearts and respond,
"Your eminence, may your soul dwell in joy!
May your being be forever immune to pain!
We are devoted to you, body and soul.
We share your sadness in your losses
And your joy in your triumphs.
Our mothers gave birth to us
So that we might die one day.
Though we are free men,
We are your subjects and slaves."

The king's face blossoms with delight at the statements
From Rostam, Tous, Goodarz, and the other heroes.
Khosrow is graced with youth and a burgeoning empire.
He utters blessings upon them: "May the world prosper
Beneath the shelter of my renowned warrior heroes!"

5 | Kay Khosrow Reviews the Warrior Heroes

The sky continues its revolutions until the sun
Presents its face under the house of Virgo.
Khosrow summons his wise men from the provinces

And addresses them with suitable words.

He keeps the audience doors closed for two weeks
To put together a new and extensive list of warriors.
He asks the accountants for the names of the bravest.
A chronicle is drafted, detailing each hero's rank.

First is drawn a list of the members of Kaavoos's family,
Comprising one hundred and ten leaders
Under the command of Fariborz,
Son of Kaavoos, uncle of the young king.
Counted among these are men
From the lineage of Manoochehr,
Devoted, body and soul, to Commander Tous.

Next is a list of eighty descendants of Nozar,
Valiant warriors armed with mace, led by Zarasp,
The most glorious Kianian, son of Tous,
Master of mace, sword, and timpani,
Whose only preoccupation is their well-being.

Next is Goodarz, son of Kashvaad,
Whose guidance maintains order in the army.
His seventy-eight sons and grandsons
Are able horsemen in the mountains
And bounding leopards on the plain.
Carriers of the Kaaviani banner,
They reflect the light of Kianian splendor.

Sixty-three heroes of the race
Of Gojdaham are led by Gostaham.
One hundred riders from the lineage of Milaad
Fall under the command of Gorgeen the victorious,
With eighty-five relatives of Tavaabeh,
Valiant cavaliers, keepers of war and royal treasury.
They are to be led and supported by Barteh.

Thirty-three brave men from the seed of Pashang,
Holders of javelin, stand at the ready.
Rivniz, brave, bold, and wise,
Settles ahead of the drums.
He is protector of the troops and Tous's son-in-law.

Seventy men, relatives of Borzeen, strong as lions,
Are placed under the command of Farhaad,
Who in battle appears as strong as an iron anvil.

Goraazeh supervises over one hundred and five
Members of his family, all courageous warriors.

From the seed of Fereydoon come eighty fighters,
Competent and bright, guarded by the famed Ashkesh.

Finally, there are so many eminent princes and heroes,
So many glorious noblemen and great warriors,
That the wise man finds himself unable
To count each member of the illustrious gathering.

The names are written on parchment for future use.
Then Khosrow commands them to exit the city,
Cross the border, and enter the desert plains.

He says, "At the advent of the new moon,
Sound the drums and Indian bells.
Engage in war against Tooran-Zamin
And regard it as a venture full of pleasure."

The brave men bow low to the ground,
Invoking blessings upon the Creator.
They say, "Glorious and powerful King,
You have returned splendor to the crown and belt.
We stand as your subjects and slaves.
The empire and everything,
From Aries to Pisces, belong to you."

6 | Kay Khosrow Distributes Wealth

The shepherds drive herds of wild horses
From meadows to camp. Khosrow says,
"Whoever displays a brazen figure on the battlefield
May cast his noose into this band of feral steeds
And capture the head of one of winded hooves."

The victorious world master sits on his golden throne,
Hand braced on royal mace, head capped with crown.

He discloses his treasury and says, "It is not agreeable
For brave men to conceal their wealth.
In times of war, vengeance, and battle,
One must distribute dinars and treasures.
I shall bestow upon my warriors
All my fortune and all my thrones.
I shall raise the branch of the imperial tree to the sun.
Why would one absorb himself with the acquisition
Of gold when there are brave men in need?"

He asks his treasurer to bring one hundred cloaks
Of Rumi brocade, embroidered in pure gold
And embellished with precious gems,
As many bolts of beaver skin, sheets of gold,
And one cup full of jewels fit for a king.

The lot is placed before the virtuous Kay Khosrow,
And the world king says to his warriors,
"Here is the prize I offer for the vile head of Palaashan,
The dangerous dragon Afraasiyaab named army leader
And upon whose watch he is able to rest.
Who will, on the day of battle, crush him
And return to me armed with the head, sword,
And steed of this wicked warrior?"

Bijan, son of Giv, rises brusquely
And declares that he is ready to slay the dragon.
He seizes the fabrics and the cup of gems,
Calls on divine grace to shine upon the king,
And says, "May your wishes be granted forevermore!"
He then returns to his seat, golden cup in hand.

The king bids the treasurer to bring two hundred
Robes woven in gold, one hundred silken ones,
As well as brocades and furs of beaver skin,
In addition, two slaves with pink cheeks,
Adorned with magnificent belts.
He says to his gathering, "If someone wishes
To venture forth and return with the crown
That Afraasiyaab bestowed upon Tajov,
His noble son-in-law, I shall give him all these gifts
And grant him innumerable favors."

Bijan, son of Giv, of sharp claws, mighty in war,
A young seeker of name and fame,
Rises once again and, to everyone's surprise,
Accepts slaves and presents, and blesses the king:
"May his majesty make the world flourish!"

Kay Khosrow now demands ten slaves
With splendid belts; ten chargers with golden bridles,
Worthy of a hero; and ten women adorned and veiled.
Then the people's mindful ruler adds,
"These horses and these beautiful women
Are meant for the one who acts upon my command
And makes Tajov of lion heart abscond,
Though he will most likely not resist your efforts.
This warrior is escorted in battle by a sweet slave
Whose voice has the ability of taming a leopard.
Her cheeks are fresh as spring,
Her stature slender as a cypress tree,
Her waist reed-like, and her stride pheasant-like.
This moon-faced woman, as lovely as a fairy,
Bears the name of Aspanooy.
She steals hearts and emits the scent of musk.
Her breast is white as a lily.
Even her name exhales the flower's scent.
The rider able to capture her must not wound her,
For such a beauty must not be pierced by blade.
This man must enfold her in the loop of his noose,
Lift her off the saddle, and pull her onto his lap."

Once again, Bijan brings his hand to his heart,
Approaches the victorious king, vows his loyalty,
And calls upon the help of the World Creator.

The mighty king observes him with joy and says,
"Illustrious hero, may my adversary never have
In his company a warrior of your stature!
May your shining soul never exit your body!"

Then the king commands his treasurer
To draw from the treasury's secret chambers
Ten golden goblets filled with scented pellets,
Along with ten silver cups filled with gems,

PART TEN

A cup made of topaz filled with musk,
One of turquoise and one of lapis lazuli,
Both brimming with stones of garnet,
And emeralds dipped in musk and rosewater.

Next are brought ten slaves adorned with belts
And ten noble chargers of golden reins.
The king addresses the assembly:
"These valuables belong to the one
Who will valiantly battle Tajov
And bring down his head on the battlefield."

Giv, son of Goodarz, raises his hand to his heart
And declares himself ready to fight this dragon.
They turn over to him the pretty slaves,
The gold, and the riches in good order.
He honors the king and exclaims,
"May throne and seal never witness your absence!"

The king then commands his treasurer
To place before the throne ten golden tables
Covered with dinars, musk, and fine gems,
And to organize before the tables
Ten fairy-faced slaves adorned with diadem and belt,
Two hundred furs and bolts of silk brocade,
A royal crown, and ten golden belts.

Then he says, "This gift is for the volunteer
Who never retreats before hardship and exhaustion
When it comes to the acquisition of wealth and fame.
He must go to the edge of Kaasseh Rood[41]
To greet the soul of Siaavosh.
He will find a mountain of timber,
More than ten kamands high, which Afraasiyaab
Gathered at the spot where he sailed across the river.
He did so to prevent others from taking this path
And crossing over from Iran into Tooran-Zamin.
The man who accepts this mission
Is to set ablaze this barrier close to Kaasseh Rood
So that, once we engage in battle, the enemy host

◇◇◇◇◇◇◇◇◇◇◇◇◇
41 Kaasseh Rood: Perhaps a fictional river.

May not have a barrier to hide behind."

Giv volunteers: "This hunt is to be mine!
I shall burn this mountain of wood,
And should the army express opposition,
I shall not fear to fight, destroy,
And invite vultures to feast on their carcasses."

The king hands the goods to Giv and says,
"O glorious army hero, may your sword
Never fail in service to my shining crown!
May you live forever in bliss and happiness!
Where there is idol, there is an idol worshipper.
We must immediately bring, by way of the treasurer,
One hundred pieces of colored brocade.
From my treasury, pick one hundred crystalized pearls,
Which could be mistaken for icy droplets.
In the women's chambers, search for
And find five servants whose curls
Are concealed beneath diadems.
This gift is destined for the one ruled by wisdom;
The one who is brave and cautious,
Graced with a sweet, articulate tongue
But who never turns his back on a fight with lions;
The one who, eyes dry of tears of fear,
Delivers a message to Afraasiyaab
And returns to me swiftly with a reply.
Who among those gathered here
Wishes to embark on this venture?"

Gorgeen, son of Milaad, spreads out his hand
And vows that he is ready to take the road.
The king gives him slaves,
Golden-stitched robes, and royal gems.

Gorgeen, in turn, blesses him: "May wisdom
Always be the mate of Kay Khosrow's soul!
I shall charge forth, deliver the message,
And return swiftly.
I shall disclose all there is to disclose."

The world king, with blazing heart and tearful eyes,
Secretly whispers to Gorgeen, "Travel to Afraasiyaab

PART TEN

And relay to him the entirety of my message:
    'O bloodthirsty, ill-intentioned man,
    No one in the world has acted so maliciously
    To flood the land with a brother's blood,
    To destroy the world from end to end,
    To provoke men and women of Iran to tremble
    In terror and bemoan their fate to the Creator.
    You beheaded the renowned Nozar,
    A vestige of the Kianian race in the world.
    When Rostam and Siaavosh took up arms
    To constrict your world, you misled them
    By opening the doors of your treasury and wealth.
    You sent one hundred members of your family to them.
    Both Iran and Tooran witnessed this undertaking.
    Kaavoos opposed a peace accord,
    Wrongly assuming Rostam was acting out of greed.
    Because of this, the king wrote a letter to Siaavosh,
    Ordering him to kill your relatives.

    'Siaavosh did not obey the king.
    He came in search of your support and protection.
    For your sake, he abandoned his native land of Iran.
    He abandoned its crown and ring, its banner and host.
    He sought your affection, O man of evil lineage.
    May your name disappear from the list of noblemen!
    You recklessly severed the head of this adored leader,
    Like one cuts off the head of a sheep.
    Then you hungered to spill my blood,
    Strategizing my death, though I was not yet born.
    How much longer shall I recount your wicked deeds?
    The only worthy dwelling for you is one in hell!

    'If you wish to appease my mind
    And for me to renounce thoughts of vengeance,
    Send to me three warriors
    So that I may cut off their heads in retribution.
    Send to me Garooy Zerreh, of the seed of Toor,
    The one who breeds chaos throughout the world,
    Along with Garsivaz and Damoor, who, in utter hatred,
    Cinched their waists to slaughter my father.
    Unless I execute vengeance on Afraasiyaab,
    In the name of the pure Yazdan,

In the name of Sun, Moon, and shining flame,
I shall enjoy neither peace nor sleep.'"

Once Gorgeen hears the message,
He takes a step to climb on his horse
And tramples the ground toward Tooran-Zamin.

Meanwhile, the earth turns black as a crow's feather
As the torch of the moon climbs over the mountains.
The king returns to his palace,
Noblemen to their dwellings.
They spend some time in feast and drink.
The king distributes wealth all around.

7 | Kay Khosrow Sends Faraamarz to India

As the rooster's cry rises above the clouds,
Daylight covers the mountains in hues of sandarac
Rostam presents himself at the king's side,
Accompanied by Zavaareh and Faraamarz.
They wish to discuss various matters, great and small,
To speak of ruler, empire, and the land of Iran.

Rostam says to the world king,
"Noble and glorious Shah, long ago Zabolestan
Included a province that belonged to Tooran,
A beautiful, magnificent land
From which Manoochehr banished the Turks.
With Kaavoos growing old and weak,
His worth, dignity, and glory appearing to diminish,
The Tooranians seized the chance to capture that region,
Challenging the Iranians to vacate their homes.
Tributes and taxes are paid to the Tooranian king,
And no one there turns a glance toward the Iranian king.

"The land is rich, full of gardens, parks,
And fertile fields, a land abundant
In wealth, elephants, and troops.
Its border, akin to paradise,
Was named Khargaah by an ancient bard.
On one side, it is flanked by the river Sindh

And by the spreads of Ghennooj and Kashmir;
On the other side, by Chin and Tooran-Zamin.
Its inhabitants are needlessly unhappy,
For they are constantly invaded, pillaged, and killed.
They are, at this moment, ready to rebel
Against the authority of the Tooranian king.
Now to you belong kingship and empire, including
The stretch of Iran-Zamin from border to border,
From the foot of the ant to the lion's claw.
Now is the time to send a vast host,
Under the leadership of a fearless world hero,
So that the people either pay due tribute
To your majesty or present themselves
Before him with heads bowing low.
Once this land falls under our rule,
We shall venture to desolate Tooran-Zamin."

The king replies to Rostam, "May you live forever!
At all times, you provide me with sound advice.
You are the army support and joy.
Estimate the number of troops required,
And make a selection among our glorious host.
A province bordering your land
Is worthy of your coveting it.
Assign a vast host to Faraamarz, one worthy
Of his leadership, one composed of heroic men.
He will lead this mission to an assured victory.
Tell him to strap his belt in vengeance:
He is both world warrior and nobleman.
From Khargaah to the land of India,
From Kashmir to the edge of the land of sorcerers,
May he triumph in his feats;
May the crocodile's jaw catch the bait!"

The world hero's heart swells with joy,
Renewed like fresh grass in the meadow.
He praises the king: "With your pure soul
And vast wisdom, all will be well.
May your crown and throne be victorious!
May the universe serve under your rule!"

Khosrow orders his chamberlain to set up spreads

With food and wine and to summon singers.
He sits to delight in the sweet songs
From their nightingale voices.

8 | Kay Khosrow Puts Order to the Army

Once the sun in all its splendor rises past the mountains
And singers are weary of song, one hears
At the royal gates a call and the beating of drums.
The army forms ranks before the palace.

Brazen timpani hang on elephant's backs,
Trumpets blare, the royal throne is placed
On top of a mighty elephant, and this offshoot
Of the imperial tree begins to bear fruit.

The king arrives, climbs on the elephant,
His head covered with a diadem of gold and gems.
Around his neck is a band of fine, precious jewels.
In his hand is a bull-headed mace.
Hanging from his ears are two rings,
And around his neck a torque of emerald.
His arms dazzle with two bracelets of ruby and gold.
Strapped around his waist is a belt
Adorned with pearls, gold, and emeralds.

He advances at the head of the procession,
Furbished with golden strappings and golden bells,
Moving into the army's core.
He holds in his hand a cup and a ball,
And the army's clamor rises to Saturn.

Once the king places the chalice on the back
Of his war elephant, he throws the ball inside,
And the world fills with human swells
Like waves on the surface of the sea.
The earth is dipped in hues of black;
The sky dims to weigh as a mass of indigo
From the dust swelling from army troops
And from the wielding of sword, mace, and timpani.
It is as if the firmament has been captured in a noose,

PART TEN

As if the heavens have tumbled to the bottom of the sea.

The watcher's eye can no longer discern the world.
The sky and stars can barely see the tips of spears.
The army parades, squadron by squadron,
Like waves tossed by a blustery sea.

Royal tent enclosures are taken from palace to desert.
At the moment the illustrious king flings the ball
Into the cup and straps himself for departure,
The dome of sky is rattled by the sound of weapons.
In every kingdom, the best one can do is to serve the king.

This is the way the glorious Khosrow begins his reign,
Surrounded by the empire's most valiant men.
He holds himself in the large field,
Seated on his elephant as the troops parade before him.

Fariborz is first to show himself at the new ruler's feet.
He holds sword and mace, wears golden boots,
And is shadowed by a banner in the form of a sun.
He is seated on his golden-skinned charger,
His noose tied around his saddle's hook.

As the glorious prince of royal composure, strong body,
And tall stature parades before Kay Khosrow,
With his troops covered in gold and silver,
The world king salutes him and says,
"May you retain power and dignity,
Two attributes that are the privilege of valiant men!
May your fortune always shine!
May each day of your life
Unfold like the festivities of Nowruz!
May you depart in fitness and return to us safely!"

After Fariborz comes Goodarz, son of Kashvaad,
Whose wisdom helps the world prosper.
Behind him rises a banner with the image of a lion
Holding onto a mace and sword with its claws.
To his left marches the brave Rohaam,
To his right, the proud Giv, and behind him
Shiddush with a banner that casts lion shadows
With tints of purple upon the ground.

Following the group are thousands of cavaliers
Armed with long spears.
Behind Giv looms a black standard bearing
The image of a wolf and surrounded by troops.

The tip of the banner of the fervent Rohaam rises
To the clouds, its flag billowing the figure of a tiger.

Goodarz has seventy-eight sons and grandsons,
Armed and valiant warriors, accounted for on the plains.
Each is graced by a distinct banner,
Each clutches a sword and sports golden boots.

You would think Goodarz is world master,
Able to subject the heads of the boldest men to his blade.
As he approaches the king's seat,
He blesses the throne and crown many times,
And the king exults Goodarz, Giv, and their troops.

After Goodarz, Gostaham steps forward,
The son of the watchful Gojdaham,
Whose hand brandishes a spear in battle,
Whose bow and arrow of poplar wood never betray,
And whose arrows pierce through
The thickest boulders and the deadliest anvil.

He advances at the head of numerous troops, armed
With mace and sword, and shielded by precious gear.
He marches beneath a banner with the image
Of the moon, its shining tip grazing the clouds.
He offers homage to Kay Khosrow,
Who returns his attentions, quite pleased.

After Gostaham parades Ashkesh, of piercing spirit,
Wise heart, and tender soul, a mace-wielding hero
Of the family of Ghobaad, proud, calm, and noble,
Who regards the thickest mass of steel
As nothing more than wind,
Escorted with brave warriors from Kooch and Balooch.
As zealous as wild rams and armed to the fingertips,
They have never been known to scamper away.
They carry high a standard depicting
A combative tiger seeming to tear apart the world.

PART TEN

Ashkesh applauds the king on the happy turn of events.
From atop his elephant, Khosrow observes him
And his troops, who cover the space of two miles.
He receives him graciously and blesses this man,
A favorite of good fortune and of his blessed land.

Next rises the renowned Farhaad, army commander,
Who leads troops to battle like a nurturing father.
He walks beneath a banner portraying the image
Of an antelope, its shadow obscuring his face.
Farhaad takes off like a leaping lion with his vast host
And his gigantic, strong elephants.
His brave soldiers, all princes from Ghobaad's race,
Protected by Yazdan's grace and their own virtue,
Are armed with Indian sabers,
Turkish armor, and Sughdi[42] saddles.

Cheeks luminescent like the moon,
They shine bright as the sun on the battlefield.
At the sight of the radiant royal throne,
They acclaim and praise the young king.

Behind Farhaad stands a brave and famed cavalier,
Goraazeh, the leader of the race of Giv.
He advances in leaps, reminiscent of a male lion,
With his family members and skillful warriors,
Nooses' loops hooked to their stallions' saddles.
The king considers Goraazeh with an approving eye.

Eager for battle, Farhaad holds
A banner detailing a wild boar.
He leads combat-ready troops
Skilled with the handling of noose.
Battle riders and brave men on the field
Parade before the king, who applauds them.

Behind Goraazeh is the fierce Zangueh of Shaavaran
At the head of a group of valiant men and fighters.
His banner portrays a royal eagle.
He advances like a mountain of steel, blesses the king,

◇◇◇◇◇◇◇◇◇◇◇◇◇
42 Sughdi: From the region of Sughd in northern Mongolia, near the Chinese border.

Blesses his tall stature, his sword and seal.

Next advance the men from the land of Baghdad,
Armed with spear and sword.
They march beneath the royal eagle banner
And before the king seated on his elephant.

Next is the warlike Faraamarz, armed with mace,
Full of dignity, grace, and glory.
He is trailed by timpani, elephants,
And a vast host full of pride and keen on battle.
They come from Kashmir, Kabol, and Nimrooz,
Heads held high, ready to fill the world with glory.
His banner, akin to his father Rostam's banner,
The most glorious, most indomitable of world heroes,
Displays a dragon with seven heads, as if the creature
Has liberated itself from bonds and chains.

Faraamarz comes forth like a tree heavy with fruit
And gives homage to the king,
Whose heart rejoices at the sight of him.
Khosrow confers on Faraamarz much advice:
"May you live in joy and with foresight!
May your thoughts reflect the crown's glory!
The one raised by the hero of elephantine stature
Must hold his head high in every assembly.
You are the son of Rostam of vigilant mind.
Your lineage is from Zaal, son of Saam of Nariman.
The border of India belongs to you;
From Ghennooj to Sistan, all the lands are yours.

"Do not needlessly engage in war, but if a man
Provokes you, feel free to smash his head into dust.
Do not seek to fight a man who is not cinched for war.
Always remain the poor man's loyal friend;
Always give generously to your people.
Pay close attention to whom you befriend.
Discern those who are guided by wisdom and
Those who have the resources to ease your worries.
Spread your wealth, be active,
And postpone a task for tomorrow.
A man does not have the means

To determine what tomorrow may bring.
I have entrusted you with this power;
You must exercise it.
But never seek a fight when one is not bestirred.
Never be greedy to acquire wealth in your youth,
And never wrong the ones who do not seek to crush you.

"Do not rely on this deceitful world:
One moment it is the color of sandarac,
The next the color of ebony.
Try to leave behind a glorious name.
Pay heed that your heart remains pure in friendship.
My days will end; so will yours.
The turning sky calculates each breath.
Seek to maintain peace in your heart, strength in
Your body, and never lose sight of your life's true goal.
May Yazdan the Creator grant you peace!
May your enemies' heads fill with smoke!"

After hearing the advice of the new world master,
Faraamarz dismounts his blazing steed
And commends the young king, saying,
"May you flourish like the glowing new moon!"
He bows low to kiss the ground,
Then sets out for a faraway destination.

Rostam's heart is overcome with sadness
At the thought of his son's departure.
He accompanies him the distance of two farsangs,
Advising him on war, feast, and proper behavior,
Expressing his hope for fate to favor him.
"O dear warlike son, do not kill needlessly.
You must never ransom justice and integrity.
Should you come across a fame seeker,
Address him with sweet speech.
Remain on the path of justice.
If you may not advance your mission in this way,
Then you may resort to fight.
Pay attention. Maintain your focus on the end result.
If a malicious man places a meal before you,
Beware that it may be a trap.

"Never follow a course of action
That does not conform with your being.
If you do, you will be cursed.
Do not close the door to justice and justice givers.
If someone draws an agreement with another,
Give it ample consideration.
Attempt to deal with good advice.
Just as the Creator spreads affection all around,
You may do so with those who cross your path.
Do not dismiss an adversary,
For at a time of action he will turn into a fierce dragon.
Extinguish a blaze when it is insignificant,
For when it swells it will consume all things.
Put in motion preparations for war in secret.
Guard your enemy from discovering your plans."

He adds, "O renowned warrior,
Remain sensible, mindful, and of clear soul.
Follow the example of our ancestors.
When world owner Garshaasp entered old age,
Nariman took over, inheriting his mace.
When he in turn brandished said staff,
The battlefield emptied of enemy warriors.
In all of Rum, Chin, and India,
There was no fighter of his strength and power.
As long as he was alive in the world,
There was no one able to vanquish him.
When Saam, the brave hero, arrived,
Nariman rejoiced and reveled in feast and wine.
By the time Zaal was born and later cinched his waist
To protect the throne, Saam had grown weary of war.
From father to son, this is the way of the revolving dome.

"My turn came to mount my steed and free my father
From the responsibility of war and grief.
Whether a dragon or a deev challenged me,
I did not hesitate for a moment.
I rushed to slay it with blade or mace.
The time is here for me to slip out of armor and mail.
The time is here for you to feud and vanquish evil ones.
If you can achieve all that you have set your mind
To achieve, your glory will rise to the highest skies."

Rostam further instructs his son on the arts of war
And feast, imparting to him all ways of wisdom.
He expresses his wishes to see him live in happiness.

Finally, they kiss each other and take their leave.
Faraamarz gratefully accepts his father's advice,
Then departs to fulfill his mission.
Rostam, heart full of worry, mind full of thought,
Leaves the desert and takes the direction of his camp.

Once there, he kisses the ground at the king's feet.
Thrilled at the sight of him, Kay Khosrow orders wine.
He empties a large cup and declares,
"O world warrior, spend some time in joy today.
The wise man never speaks of tomorrow.
Where are Salm, Toor, and Fereydoon?
They have disappeared beneath the dust of earth.
Why should we labor, kill ourselves to amass wealth,
And suppress in our hearts any other desire?
In the end, we are left with nothing but a coffin.
Death is a demise no one may escape.
Let us enliven the gloomy night with our goblets,
And when day returns, it will count our footsteps.
Let us convene and converse until Tous
Sounds the trumpets and beats the drums.
Then he will swiftly go to Tooran-Zamin
To wipe out the border of Chin and Maachin.

"We shall see which way in this struggle
The revolving dome turns its affection.
Man may labor, but to what end?
What will manifest is what has already
Been decreed from the beginning of time.
Happiness and sadness pass over our heads,
But why should the wise man worry about his fate?
If Yazdan the Creator comes to our aid,
We shall vengefully annihilate all criminals.
Life has a direction that we cannot alter.
We must not concern ourselves with the outcome.
Whether good or bad, it will pass.
Wise men never waste time in grief and sorrow."

9 | The Tale of Foorood, Son of Siaavosh

A worthy and valiant world owner
Must not entrust the enemy with his army,
Else his eyes will shed tears of jealousy
For which a physician will find no remedy.

An offshoot of a noble race will remain honorable
And never succumb to greed.
When you cannot attain your heart's desires,
You must seek to satisfy other people's wishes.
The army leader displays little wisdom
When he calls a man friend who acts contrary
To his heart and to the needs of another.
If the heavens refuse to grant his dreams,
He will never regard the Creator with affection,
Nor will he envisage others with kindness,
For his heart will be split
And refuse to cast aside his own desires.

A person who is not governed by wisdom
Is not included in the gathering of wise men.
Once you've heard this story to the end,
You will fully understand the nature of evil.

10 | Tous Enters the Land of Turkestan[43]

As the sun exposes itself in all its splendor,
Taking its seat on the expansive throne of sky,
Galloping across the house of Aries,
The world fills with a bright light, clear as golden wine.
The sound of drums, clarions, and timpani
Beats at the doors of Tous's pavilion.

The entire land resounds with tumult.
The air echoes with the boom of voices,
The bucking and the whinny of horses.
The blare of war clarions shakes the earth.

◇◇◇◇◇◇◇◇◇◇◇◇◇
43 Turkestan: Land of Turks; east of Iran. It is interchangeable with Tooran-Zamin.

PART TEN

The faces of the sun and moon dim.
The clink of weapons and the trumpeting of elephants
Ring out like the tide rising on the River Nile.

The air is red and yellow, blue and amethyst,
Resplendent with the billowing of the Kaaviani banner,
Around which assembles the Goodarzian family.

Kay Khosrow appears beneath his pavilion door
Wearing a headdress, holding a mace,
Preceded by the blare of trumpets.
Tous sets off, followed by the Kaaviani banner
And renowned warriors with golden boots.

Brave men from Nozar's family, world conquerors,
Place themselves in the vanguard.
Decked with torques and diadems,
On leaping chargers they approach the king.

Ahead of Tous is the renowned Zarasp,
A young, newly enlisted army warrior.
His banner, sporting the image of an elephant,
Has a golden crest that pierces through clouds.
He is the recipient of deep affection, bestowed
Upon him by the descendants of Manoochehr.

They advance like a black cloud,
Making the sun and moon cease to shine.

Once all the garrisons are near the king,
Marching noisily with banners and helms,
Kay Khosrow orders the army commander
To fetch the famed leader of his troops.

The mindful king says to them,
"You must obey the orders of Commander Tous,
Who will direct the army with honor
And will display on high the Kaaviani banner."

Before the congregation, he hands Tous a seal
And names him chief leader and guide.
"Do not miss your duty toward me," he adds.
"Respect my authority.

Do not stray from my command and my glory.
Do not seek to harm a single soul on the road.
Such is the law of the royal throne and crown.
Do not challenge a farmer, an artisan,
Or anyone ill-equipped for war.
Fight only with those who provoke a fight.
Refrain from injuring when unprovoked,
For this world is fleeting; it remains for no one.
Always nurture the affection of your warriors.
Always address them with kindness and compassion.
No man from the lineage of Afraasiyaab
Must be left thirsty. No man must remain
To reap the benefits of a life of ease.
But listen carefully to me.
In no way must you pass through Kalaat,[44]
For if you take this road, you will deeply suffer.
May the soul of Siaavosh shine like the sun!
May the other world be for him a sojourn of hope!

"He had a son from the daughter of Piran who,
By his father's orders, rarely appeared in public.
He is my brother and resembles me greatly.
He is young, born the same year as I,
And was raised in joy and happiness.
He is a powerful man, full of majesty,
Surrounded by brave and worthy men.
He lives with his mother in Kalaat.
He knows no one in Iran by name.
You must not swing your horses' reins
In the direction of his land.
He prevails over an army and famed warriors,
And resides on a mountain accessed
Only through a narrow, arduous path.
He is a young, brave, and bold rider,
Of generous nature and robust complexion.
You must then take a different direction.
Follow the desert road and thus avoid
Engaging in a brawl with the lion's claws."

Tous says to the king, "May fate never contradict you!

◇◇◇◇◇◇◇◇◇◇◇◇◇◇
44 Kalaat: City in today's Afghanistan.

I shall take the road you prescribe,
For your orders can only lead to triumph and victory."
The leader immediately departs, and the king
Returns to his palace with the loyal Rostam.

Khosrow forms an assembly comprised of Rostam
And other warriors, princes, sages, and wise men.
He confides in them at length
About how he suffered under the unjust Afraasiyaab,
The torments endured by his father
And later by his mother:
"He handed me over to some uneducated shepherds
At a young age, to prevent people from identifying me.
Later, when Giv found me and secretly
Guided my mother and me on the road to Iran-Zamin,
He charged behind us with a vast host,
Ready and willing to kill both my mother,
His own daughter, and me.
The Creator, our Guide, ordained otherwise.
Afraasiyaab's hatred caused me such
A great deal of pain that I never wish
For anyone to praise and acclaim him.
As long as I live, I shall never forget this vengeance.
I am sending Tous and the army, and from now on
You and I will travel and cover ground together.
We shall confine the world for evil men,
Bury his head and his hand beneath a block of stone."

Rostam replies, "You need not worry,
For destiny revolves at your will."

Meanwhile, the army led by Tous
Marches from station to station until it comes
Upon the place where the road splits in two.
One road leads to the arid, waterless desert,
The other to Kalaat and to Jaram.[45]
At this spot, army and loaded elephants
Come to a halt to await the arrival of Tous,
Who will determine which of the two roads to select.

◇◇◇◇◇◇◇◇◇◇◇◇◇
45 Jaram: A city in today's Afghanistan.

The commander approaches at a slow pace.
They speak of the dry and arid road,
And Tous says to Goodarz,
"Even if the dust of this barren desert
Turns into amber and its ground into musk,
We shall nevertheless have much need for water
And for a place of rest after our long journey.
It is therefore wiser for us to march on the road
Leading to Kalaat and Jaram,
Where we shall halt to give our troops a chance to rest.
Left and right, we will find flowing springs and rivers.
Why should we follow the path to the desert
And submit ourselves to utter fatigue and exhaustion?
Once I took the desert road with Gojdaham, my guide,
And this long path brought us nothing but lassitude.
Although there are few climbs and descents,
It is better for the army to take the other road,
Else we shall have no chance
To measure the stretch of the desert in farsangs."

Goodarz replies, "You are elected as army leader.
But I advise you to follow the road the king indicated.
We must not suffer dire consequences from your choice.
The king's heart would be aggrieved,
And the army would suffer from his wrath."

Tous retorts, "Noble hero, do not trouble yourself.
The king will not be displeased.
Do not allow fear to be your heart's companion."
He then commands, "Let us march out!
Let us follow the road to Kalaat and Jaram!
We shall have need to count neither village nor farsang."

Horsemen, elephants, and timpani
Take the road signaled by Tous.
The troops are so numerous that the light of day dims.
They march to Kalaat, crowding the roads and plains.
They set ablaze the villages and cities along the way.

Watch and see what happens when Tous
Gives little consideration to Khosrow's command.
Watch and see what calamitous storm

Is on the verge of churning, swelling, and erupting.

11 | Foorood Learns of the Arrival of Tous

Foorood hears the news that the face
Of the brilliant sun has been dimmed
By the dust raised by camels and war elephants,
Making the earth roll like a sea of indigo.
His brother's vast host is marching from Iran
And has crossed the border into Tooran-Zamin,
A vast host eager to avenge the death of Siaavosh,
Led by a formidable, highborn leader.

The tumult of soldiers on foot and on horseback
Sounds like a boulder splintering on the mountainside.
Everyone is keen on vengeance,
Everyone armed for war.
You would think the sea
Is in turmoil with waves of steel.
They take the road in the direction of Kalaat,
Not knowing where they will engage in war.

At the rumor, the untested young prince's heart
Reels with pain, his mind spinning with concern.
He unlocks the bars that seal the castle gates
And exits to observe the lofty mountain.
He orders his men to gather in camels, horses,
And herds of lambs, empty mountain
And plain of them and of any other wild creature
Freely roaming in the pastures.
Once collected, they take the animals to Mount Sepad.[46]

Then Foorood returns, locks the castle gate,
And climbs onto a speedy horse.

Soon the blare of trumpets resounds from Jaram,
And the world is covered in dust, dark as ebony,
He spots his mother, Jarireh, from the castle tower,
And his heart clamps at the thought of such an army.

◇◇◇◇◇◇◇◇◇◇◇◇◇◇
46 Mount Sepad: Appears to be a fictional mountain in Kalaat.

Jarireh continuously mourns the death of Siaavosh.

Foorood rushes to her and says: "O Queen of Queens,
A vast host is approaching from Iran,
One with elephants and timpani, led by the proud Tous.
What action shall we take to prevent an attack?"

Jarireh replies, "You are always ready for battle.
May you never witness a more unfortunate day!
There is in Iran a new king, your brother,
Kay Khosrow the prudent, world master.
He is aware of your name and your essence,
For you are of the same blood and share the same father.
Siaavosh was a king such as the world has never seen.
May the world never dismiss or squander his memory!

"Piran offered my hand to Siaavosh first,
For he did not wish to unite with any other woman
From the land of Tooran-Zamin.
So you see, you are of illustrious birth,
On your father's side as well as on your mother's.
When your brother undertakes his mission
To avenge Siaavosh and glorify his soul,
You should come to his aid,
Advance ahead of everyone,
Equipped with weapons and with waist cinched.

"Cover yourself in Rumi armor.
Present yourself with heart keen on vengeance,
Head full of passion.
Battle may suit you better than guile when united
In the common goal of punishing his grandfather.
Leopards have cause to moan with our grief.
Whales emerge from the sea, howling and hollering.
Birds in the sky, fish in the ocean: all curse Afraasiyaab.
Never had the world seen a nobler king than Siaavosh.
He was wise and glorious, joyous, just, and generous,
His belt strapped in service to power, heroism, courage,
To fortune, ancestry, splendor, dignity, and divine grace.

"You are the son of such a king and of Kianian seed.
You carry yourself with royal demeanor,
Strapped in readiness to avenge your father.

Show yourself worthy of your race and birth.
Go to this army to evaluate its commander.
Select an individual from your men,
Someone wise and renowned,
Able to speak eloquently and listen accordingly.
Call warriors to display on palace tables
Various swords, helmets, strappings, and coats of mail,
Indian daggers, spears, and dinars,
And other items to present to your brother as gifts.
Your brother is the most valuable possession you have.
Go to him. Do not leave the glory of vengeance
And the status of your position to a stranger.
Go to the leader of this host.
You are a young, avenging man,
And Khosrow is a young king."

Foorood replies to his mother,
"Who shall I first address among the eminent heroes?
Who will back me up on the day of battle?
I know of no one, not even by name.
How shall I send them greetings and messages?"

Jarireh says to her son, "When you see from afar
The dust rising from their troops,
Seek to recognize one of their brave warriors,
Such as Bahraam or Zangueh of Shaavaran.
Ask what marks distinguish these two warriors,
For neither you nor I shall have secrets before them.
May you live forever in full glory!
May the soul of Siaavosh shine eternally!
Bahraam and Zangueh never left your father's side.
They were powerful border guards while he was king.
Go with Tokhaar as your sole escort;
Do not scorn my advice.
The brave Tokhaar will point out to you
The elements that distinguish these leaders.
He is acquainted with the men of Iran, great and small.
He will enlighten you
As to whether one is shepherd or sheep."

Foorood says to her, "Beloved mother,
Your counsel is our family's salvation!"

323

A sentry returning from his post approaches Foorood
And announces that the Iranian army
Is occupying field, mountain, and vale.
The sun is shrouded in dust, and from castle to mountain,
One only perceives flags, elephants, and soldiers.

12 | Foorood and Tokhaar Review the Iranian Army

At the news, Tokhaar and Foorood hit the trail swiftly.
The head of the young prince is troubled,
His heart saddened, for when the revolving dome above
Takes a position so unfavorable,
Neither anger nor affection can keep you safe.
How can a youth who ransoms his life attain old age?

They reach a high mountaintop from which
They have an expansive view of the Iranian host.
The two are astonished to see the swarm of troops
And the countless piles of weapons and war gear.
The youth says to Tokhaar in a sweet voice,
"Do not conceal any answer to my questions.
When you recognize a warrior and his banner,
Or a hero warrior with mace and golden boots,
Immediately reveal to me his name
And point out all the men you are able to identify."

The Iranians, battalion upon battalion,
March to a gorge between the two mountains.
There are so many golden helms and shields,
Maces, and golden belts that you might think
The world's mines have been depleted of gold
And that a thick cloud has emerged
To shower the land with precious gems.

The vulture flying high is deeply startled by
The beat of drums rising between the two mountains.
Thirty thousand men strapped and armed
With shield and sword advance boldly in order of battle.

Once the prince takes his fill of the astounding sight,
He addresses the wise Tokhaar, who replies,

"You may not be aware of the information I disclose.
The blue banner you see sporting an elephant
And the riders in its vicinity belong to Tous, who,
When vengeance stirs him, is determined to battle.
Behind him is another banner shining like the sun,
Adorned with the sign of Gemini.
It belongs to your father's brother,
The blessed leader Fariborz, son of Kaavoos.
Next we have a large banner with the image of a moon,
Surrounded by many valiant warriors.
It belongs to the young Gostaham, son of Gojdaham,
Before whom the elephant shudders
Down to its bone marrow. Further out,
You may see a tall banner painted with a wolf,
Encircled by warlike troops,
Beneath which stands Zangueh,
Son of Shaavaran, the most valiant hero.

"Then we have a banner, beautiful as the moon,
With a crimson backdrop and black fringe.
This one belongs to Bijan, son of Giv,
Who makes his victims' blood gush out to the sky.
The banner sporting a tiger, the sight of which
Will shred a lion's skin, is under the guard
Of the brave Shiddush, able to rip out a mountain.
Behind him is one bearing the image
Of a boar appearing to pierce the sky.
This one belongs to Goraazeh, the world hero,
Who views a brawl with lions as a game.
The banner with the buffalo,
Followed by a group of warriors and preceded
By riders armed with spears, belongs to Farhaad,
The most renowned man of Iran, whose head
Appears to touch and commune with the sky.

"The emblem of a wolf marks the spot
Where Giv, the fierce leader, stands.
The standard with the image of a lion
Embroidered in gold drifts
Above the head of Goodarz, son of Kashvaad.
The one with the image of a leopard belongs to Rivniz.
The one adorned with the figure of a deer

Is raised by Nastooh, son of Goodarz,
And surrounded by his troops.
Finally, the one with the image of a mountain sheep
Is the banner of Bahraam, son of Goodarz of Kashvaad.
All these men that you see upon the field
Are true lions and brave horsemen, but it would
Take too long to enumerate each one of them."

While Tokhaar identifies each heroic banner,
Foorood, the offshoot of royal race,
Keenly observes the army's men, great and small.
His heart rejoices, his features light up, and,
In the end, the young prince says,
"Now it will be easy for me to avenge my father.
If the Creator of the sun is my companion,
I shall no doubt succeed in this venture.
While I pursue this, I shall allow no cavalier
To survive, whether in Chin or in Maachin.
I shall seize the dragon Afraasiyaab
And trample his throne beneath my feet."

Once the Iranians perceive Foorood and Tokhaar
On the mountaintop, leader Tous is seized by fury.
He demands elephants with timpani to halt
Their march and declares: "A cautionary rider
From this glorious army must come out of ranks,
Climb the lofty mountain on horseback,
And find out the identity of these two brave men.
Find out why they stand alone on the boulder's crest.
If they belong to our army, he will inflict
On their heads two hundred blows of the whip.
If they attempt to fight us as our foes, he will tie
Them up and drag them to me face down in the dirt.
If he kills them, let him yank them all the same
Without fearing vengeance from anyone.
If they are spies who wish to secretly assess our army,
He will instantly cut them in two,
Fling them off the mountain, and then return.
And if they are sitting and they are numerous,
He will come back secretly to report
So that we can obliterate boulder and mountain,
And empty the land of their presence."

13 | Bahraam Climbs the Mountain to Foorood

Bahraam, son of Goodarz, says to the army leader,
"I shall shed light on this matter. I shall depart,
Climb the mountain, and execute your orders."
He leaves the army ranks seated upon his charger,
And, thoughtful, he takes the mountain's direction.

Seeing him, prince Foorood says to Tokhaar,
"Who is this man approaching so insolently?
Does he not fear us, so fast he speeds toward us?
He has beneath him a dun-colored steed,
And on his saddle's knob hangs his noose."

The cautious advisor replies,
"We must not mistreat him. I know not his name,
For I do not recognize his distinguishing marks.
But I think he is related to the warlord Goodarz.
When Khosrow left Tooran-Zamin
To go to the land of Iran, he took with him
A royal helm, which the rider is sporting, and
His noble chest is shielded with the matching armor.
We must ask him his identity.
May his trail bring good fortune to our land!"

Reaching the crest, Bahraam raises his voice,
Loud as thunder, and asks, "Who are you?
Why do you stand on a mountaintop?
Do you not perceive this massive army?
Have you not heard the sound of timpani?
Do you not fear Tous, our wise commander?"

Foorood replies, "Do not seek to provoke
When there is no hint of malicious intent.
Speak softly, O experienced man,
And do not offend your lips with icy arguments.
You are not a war lion, and I am not a desert deer.
There is no need to consider us with disdain.
You are in no way superior to me,
Either in courage or in strength.
You are no better in head and feet, brain, heart, hands,
In intelligence, eyes, ears, and eloquent tongue.

Observe me, and if I am indeed endowed with these,
Refrain from menacing me in such a foolish way.
I am going to address some questions to you.
If you wish to answer, I shall be content,
If you wish to listen to the advice of reason."

Bahraam replies, "Speak,
As you are in the sky while I am on firm ground."

Foorood asks, "Who is your army leader?
Who is the battle-seeking challenger?"

Bahraam answers, "Our commander is Tous,
Master of Kaaviani banner and timpani.
Escorting him are warlords Goodarz,
Rohaam, and Giv, Shiddush, Gorgeen,
And the bold Farhaad, Gostaham, Gojdaham,
Chief Goraazeh, Fariborz, Bijan the lion man,
And Ashkesh, the one able to soar to the sky in war.
In addition to these renowned heroes
Is the glorious Zangueh of Shaavaran."

Foorood then says,
"Why do you omit Bahraam's name?
He is a member of the Goodarzian family,
The one we would see most happily.
Why have you not pointed him out?"

Bahraam replies, "Man of lion heart,
Who has spoken to you so honorably of Bahraam?
Who has led you to know Goodarz and Giv?
May you find eternal happiness!
May Yazdan's grace rest upon your being!"

Foorood says, "I have heard stories
On his account from my mother.
She told me that, should an army appear,
I should present myself before its leaders.
I should ask for Bahraam and for Zangueh,
For these two were my father's nursing brothers.
I would delight in receiving news of them."

Bahraam replies, "O fortunate one,

You are the fruit of this royal tree,
Of the innocent Siaavosh who died so brutally.
Are you Foorood, O young prince?
May you live forever! May your soul
Shine brightly for the rest of your days!"

The other confirms, "Yes, I am Foorood,
The offshoot of the uprooted cypress tree."

Bahraam retorts, "Uncover your body,
Reveal to me the markings of your ancestry."

Foorood shows Bahraam his arm and a brown mole,
A stain of amber upon a delicate rose,
One that no painter on earth could reproduce,
Even with the aid of a Chini compass.

Bahraam is then assured that Foorood is indeed
A descendant of Kay Ghobaad and Siaavosh.
He pays due homage to him,
Prostrates low to the ground, then climbs
The narrow path to the mountain crest.

The young prince dismounts, sits on a boulder,
His soul rejoicing, and says to Bahraam,
"O noble, awakened hero, you are a lion in battle.
If I encountered my father alive with my own eyes,
I would not be happier than to see you
So joyous, so brave, and so sensible.
I have come to this mountain crest to ask Tokhaar
Some questions regarding the Iranian warriors.
I wish to learn who is the glorious leader
Driving them to war. I shall muster a huge feast.
I shall contemplate with eagerness the face of the hero,
Distribute in great numbers horse, mace, sword,
And belt, as well as my wealth and my treasure.
I shall spend one week in joy,
Honored by the sight of each of you.

"Then I shall depart proudly at the head of an army
For the land of Tooran-Zamin, for my wounded heart
Is thirsty for the blood of vengeance.
I am worthy of seeking it,

329

For in time of battle and seated upon my horse,
I am all-consuming, like the flame of Borzeen.

"Would you kindly tell the chief hero
To come and see me on this mountain?
We shall spend seven days engaged in discussion
On all sorts of matters, great and small.
On the eighth day, at the thumping of kettledrums,
Commander Tous will climb on his horse.
I shall strap myself in readiness to avenge my father.
I shall lead, with my achingly throbbing heart,
Battles that will recognize the combat lion,
That will show the capability of arrows
Fletched with eagle plumes, for never in the world
Has a brave man been more keen on revenge."

Bahraam replies, "O young and mindful prince,
Skilled and steady horseman,
I shall recount to Tous what you have said.
I shall kiss his hand so that you attain your desire.
But the leader is not a reasonable man.
His head rebuffs sound advice.
He is brave, rich, and of noble birth,
Yet he has not been blessed with good sense.
He never utters his majesty's name.

When Giv returned with Kay Khosrow,
Tous expressed his bitterness
Toward Giv, Goodarz, and the king, insisting
That Fariborz was next in the line of succession.

"Now he continues to boast about his heritage
And the fact that he is the son of Nozar and,
Therefore, most worthy of throne and crown.
It is possible that he may refuse my demands
And violently try to quarrel with me.
If another man approaches you, do not allow him
To set eyes on your head and helmet.
Tous once told me,
        'Go and find out who is on the mountain,
        And when you reach him, do not speak to him.

Do not ask him why he is there.
Only act with mace and dagger.
How is it that someone sits on these heights today?'

"If I am able to soften Tous's heart, I shall return
With good news and lead you in joy to our camp.
But should you discern from afar another man
From our troops approach, do not trust him.
In any case, only one cavalier will advance
To fight against you, such is our leader's rule.
Now beware. Return to your castle.
Leave this place and lock up all the gates."

Foorood draws from his belt a heavy mace,
Its golden handle inlaid with turquoise gems.
He hands it to Bahraam and says,
"Take it as a memory of me. It will serve you well.
If the leader Tous comes to me in friendship,
We shall be happy and full of joy.
I shall distribute gifts worthy of a king:
Horses and saddles, diadems and gems."

14 | Bahraam Returns to Tous

Upon his return, Bahraam says to Tous,
"May wisdom be your soul's mate.
Know that Foorood is the son of King Siaavosh,
The innocent one who was killed so unjustly.
He has shown me the markings of his family,
Confirming his ties with Kaavoos and Kay Ghobaad.
He holds you in high regard and most amicably.
If you see fit, please accept his greetings in joy."

The irrational Tous replies,
"I am master of army, clarions, and timpani.
I told you to bring him without question.
If he is king, then who am I?
What am I doing on this mountainside?
Why does he think he can stop me at this castle?
He originates from the seed of a Tooranian.
How dare he intercept my troops' path

Like a dark crow of ill fortune?
You went on your way to discuss this and that
With him, and return believing that he rules.
You are telling me to entrust him with my troops?
Why should I have any concern
When I have a warrior such as you?
I shall expect more from the stubborn
Members of the Goodarzian family.
You act in ways detrimental to our cause.
You are fearful of a single rider,
As you did not find upon this mountain a fierce lion.
You know that the Turks are despicable and deceitful.
Though they may be intelligent,
They continually entertain evil thoughts.
This Turk is the enemy of Kay Khosrow and our troops.
He has seen our vast army, taken recourse in cunning.
In vain you labored to climb the mountain.
In vain you return to camp with his empty lies."

Then he turns to his warriors: "O noblemen,
I ask for someone desirous to further his glory,
To step forward and volunteer to go after this Turk,
Break his neck clean with his dagger,
And bring his head to me before this gathering."

Rivniz presents himself to the proud Tous,
Strapped and not aware that this bold act
Is about to bring an abrupt end to his life.

Bahraam says to him,
"O warrior, do not foolishly rush to your death.
Draw on the fear of the Creator of Sun and Moon.
You may blush in shame before the king.
Foorood is Siaavosh's son and relative,
An able and illustrious horseman eager for battle.
If you send one hundred warriors to this mountaintop,
None of them will return alive.
Why do you seek to bring grief to our joyous hearts?"

Displeased with Bahraam's words,
Tous orders a few warriors to go and attack Foorood.
Many offer to serve the commander in battle.

The brave Bahraam says to them,
"Do not view this affair as of little consequence.
The man on this mountain is Khosrow's brother,
And a single strand of his hair is more worthy
Than one hundred brave warriors.
Whoever has not laid eyes on the features of Siaavosh
Will stop in his tracks at the sight of Foorood."

Once Bahraam draws this portrait of Foorood,
The brave men march off to retrace their steps.

15 | Foorood Kills Rivniz

Rivniz, Tous's son-in-law,
Upon whose head the sky revolves with scorn,
Takes the road and the direction of Jaram
And Mount Sepad, heart full of courage,
Head full of trepidation.

At the sight of him, from his high position,
Foorood draws his royal bow from its quiver
And says to Tokhaar, experienced warrior,
"Tous despises my words, for here comes
A horseman who does not look like Bahraam.
My heart feels oppressed and deeply troubled.
Observe him and tell me who he is.
Can you guess why he wears steel from head to toe?"

Tokhaar replies, "This brave rider is Rivniz.
He has forty sisters, all beautiful as spring,
But he is his father's only son.
He is a cunning man, deceitful and flattering,
But young and valiant. He is Tous's son-in-law."

Foorood says to his well-informed companion,
"One must not praise the enemy at the time of battle.
If he comes to assail us, I shall have him reclining
Upon the hem of his sisters' dresses.
The mere touch of the wind stirred by my shot's arrow
Is enough to deprive him of existence.
Should he not expire from it, you might as well

Consider him as a being above the human race.
But tell me, O advisor full of wisdom,
Who shall I strike, the man or the charger?"

Tokhaar responds, "Aim your shot at the man.
Perhaps then Tous's blood will boil with fury.
He does not know that your heart is set on affection
After you offered him a peace settlement.
Why does a man like him attack you foolishly?
Why does he want to dishonor your brother?"

As the lion Rivniz draws near, sword in hand,
The brave Foorood binds his arrow and sends it
Flying from above, aimed at the other's head,
Pinning his Rumi helmet to his skull.

Rivniz tumbles down, his horse flees,
And the hero's head is ploughed with dirt and dust.

When Tous looks beyond toward the heights,
His warrior, large as a mountain, has gone missing.

A wise man once proclaimed on this matter,
"An evil character will attract punishment
And will forever dwell in regret."

16 | Foorood Kills Zarasp

Commander Tous then tells Zarasp, "In your fury,
You must toss around flares wrathful as Aazargoshasp.
Don your warrior armor, exercise your force,
And be vigilant, body and soul.
Avenge the illustrious Rivniz,
Or else I shall accomplish the deed myself."

Zarasp immediately reaches for his helmet,
Heart full of hatred, head full of pride.
He emerges from the army's core swift as fire,
Like a wild lion eager to catch its prey.
Hollering, he leaps onto the mountain path.

The young Foorood sees him from afar,
Casts a quick glance in Tokhaar's direction,
And says to him, "Here comes another combatant.
Look at him, O man of experience,
And tell me, who is this Iranian warrior?"

Tokhaar unveils it all: "He is the bold Zarasp,
Son of Tous, a warrior who will never
Turn his horse away in cowardly retreat,
Not even at the sight of a wild elephant.
Rivniz was married to his sister,
And he now comes in retribution.
Once he is close enough to distinguish
Your chest, your arms, your helmet,
Send an arrow straight in his direction
To snag his head, pitch it into dirt.
Let him keel over and fall off his horse.
I am sure that his time is near.
Tous's heart is like a withering autumn leaf.
May the foolish commander learn his lesson,
That we are not here to sustain insults."

The Iranians watch Zarasp approach the mountain.
The fearless Foorood charges his horse,
Strikes Zarasp with an arrow right at his core,
Pinning his armor to his saddle's pommel
And instantly driving his soul out of his corpse.
Zarasp falls off his stallion, who takes off with speed,
Breastplate skimming the ground,
Toward the Iranian camp.

17 | The Battle of Foorood and Tous

A great tumult rises in the Iranian host.
The troops cover their heads with helmets.
Tous's heart is warm with blood, his eyes with tears.
He quickly dons and fastens his armor to his chest,
Lamenting the death of his kin
And trembling like a quivering autumn leaf.
He climbs on his charger, tall as a mountain
Large as a prodigious war elephant.

Fuming, he hurtles after the proud Foorood,
Heart full of vengeance, head clouded with smoke.
He clenches his teeth from anger and confusion.
He is geared for battle, ready to avenge his son,
Ready to make use of his sharp claws.

The eloquent Tokhaar says,
"Ascending toward us arrives a huge mountain,
Chief Commander Tous, to fight with you.
But you may not resist this dangerous whale.
Come, let us shut the castle gates tight.
Let us await the decision of fate.
You have killed his son as well as his son-in-law.
You may no longer have peace of mind.
You may no longer engage in feast."

The young Foorood, infuriated with Tokhaar, says,
"When it comes to fight and battle, what is Tous?
What is an elephant or a mad lion?
What is a belligerent leopard or Babreh Bayan?
You are supposed to empower me and support me.
Why do you discourage me?"

Tokhaar, the experienced, replies,
"Monarchs must not scorn wise advice.
You are a lone warrior, even if you were made of steel.
Even if you could rip out a boulder from its base,
There are thirty thousand renowned Iranians
Who will come to battle you on this very mountain.
They will lay waste to everything
And will allow to stand neither castle nor rock,
Neither grain of dust nor stone.
Were Tous to perish at your hands,
Khosrow would be deeply aggrieved by the loss.
It would affect his purpose of avenging your father,
A wrong he may never make right again.
Turn your bridle, refrain from shooting arrows.
Return to your castle. Renounce a foolish battle."

He abstains from adding more, keeping from him
Part of the truth so that the madness of Tous
Does not rush Foorood to battle and to lose his life.

His dwelling is a secure castle,
The residence of eighty female slaves.
The moon-faced beauties stand at the rampart,
Dressed in Chini silk, chatting and looking beyond.

Foorood is ashamed to retreat before their eyes.
He redirects his horse's reins,
Holds his position on the saddle, and places
On his bowstring an arrow of poplar wood.

Tokhaar tells the combative king,
"If you have resolved to fight the illustrious Tous,
Refrain from killing him.
Seek only to bring down his horse,
For princes do not fight on foot,
No matter how great the humiliation.
You may not kill him with a simple arrow.
As soon as he reaches the mountaintop,
His entire army will be trailing behind.
You will never be able to resist him.
You have never been witness
To the fierce wrinkles that crease his forehead."

Foorood approves of these words,
Fixes an arrow to his bow, pulls back tightly,
And hurls a shot directly at the commander's horse.
The charger lowers its head
And tumbles down, instantly dead.

Tous, heart full of rage, head full of wind,
Returns on foot to camp,
Confounded and covered in dust,
His shield hanging around his neck.

Foorood follows him with scorn.
"What happened to the famed warrior
Who came to fight a lone horseman?
He could not even contend with one man.
Why does he return so proudly to camp?"

Foorood's slaves burst out laughing,
And their voices rise above the sky:
"There goes an old man, rolling down the mountain,

337

So fearful of the arrows of the younger one."

Once the commander returns,
His worried men flock around him.
One after the other, they greet him and praise him:
"O famous warrior, you return to us safe and sound.
We shall have no cause to cry over your fate.
We are so grateful to the Creator, O warrior,
That your soul was not affected by the shaft."

But the respected Giv is ashamed to see
The brave commander return on foot.
He says, "Foorood does not know where
To take his place, and our heroes' cheeks
Have been tarnished by his action.
Even if he were a prince wearing the earring of royalty,
How can he treat this huge army with such contempt?
We must not submit to such pretense.
Perhaps Tous expressed unreasonable fervor for war,
But Foorood fills the world with discord,
Killing two of our mightiest warlords.
We have all devoted our lives
To avenge the death of Siaavosh,
But we must not silently suffer from such disgrace.
The noble Zarasp, brave horseman
From the seed of Nozar, was viciously killed,
As well as Rivniz, who drowned in blood.
What new humiliation awaits us?
Foorood is from the race of Jamsheed and Ghobaad,
But he opened a door, unaware of where it may lead."

18 | The Battle of Foorood and Giv

Having thus spoken, Giv dresses in armor
And charges forth, swift as Aazargoshasp,
Mounted on a battering steed,
Ready to climb the mountain to Jaram.

As soon as Foorood, son of Siaavosh,
Catches sight of him, he inhales deeply and,
Feeling hopeless, he says, "In this valiant army,

No one can distinguish between climb and descent.
Each man appears braver than the last,
Each man, a crown shining over the army's head.
However, their commander is devoid of good sense.
A head deprived of judgment
Is like a body deprived of soul.
I fear they may not successfully execute vengeance
Unless Khosrow himself travels to Tooran-Zamin.
Then he and I together shall attempt to avenge
Our father and trample the enemy beneath our feet.
Tell me the name of this proud cavalier
Who will make his loved ones cry bitterly
For his powerless hand and his unworthy sword."

Tokhaar briefly glimpses from atop the mountain
Down toward the valley and says,
"This fierce dragon, whose breath kills a bird in the air,
Is the same glorious and highborn hero,
Master of mace and sword,
Who tied the hands of your grandfather Piran,
Who fought against two Tooranian hosts.
He is the same man who orphaned many children,
Crossed many mountains, rivers, and plains,
Deprived many fathers of their sons,
Crushed with his foot the neck of innumerable lions.
He is the same man who led your brother to Iran,
Journeyed across the Jayhoon without a boat.
He is an elephant called Giv, who, in battle,
Is as mighty as the waters of the River Nile.

"No matter how tight you string your bow,
Your arrows will not pierce his coat of mail.
Giv, dressed for battle in the armor of Siaavosh,
Does not fear your shot's trajectory and wrath.
Fix your arrow and aim at his horse,
For you may succeed in wounding it.
Finding himself afoot, he will most likely retreat
And cower back, shield loose around his neck,
His tail between his legs, as did Commander Tous."

The intrepid Foorood binds his bowstring,
Places one end on his shoulder,

Rubs the curve with the palm of his hand,
And sends an arrow flying to hit the horse's chest.
Giv is forced off his mount
With the only option to return to camp on foot.

At the sight of him humiliated,
Bursts of laughter resound on Mount Sepad,
The echoes of which trouble Giv.
His brave men reach him and say,
"O noble hero, though your horse is injured,
You return safe and sound.
Thanks to the Justice Giver you are not crushed!"

At this moment, Bijan arrives, swift as wind,
And addresses his father in a disrespectful manner:
"O world hero, vanquisher of lions,
Whose hand is always ready to strike,
Against whom an elephant dares not fight,
How could you turn your back before a lone rider,
You, whose hand has always been the soul of battle?
A Turk wounds your horse and you return
Dazed and dumbfounded like an inebriated man?"

Giv replies, "My charger was injured.
I left him immediately without thinking.
Your behavior is impulsive and unruly,
For you lack experience in the ways of war."
He adds a few harsh words
After which Bijan turns his back on him.

Giv is furious to see his son scorn him.
He strikes him on the head with his whip and says,
"Have you not heard from your master
That while in battle one must reflect and think?
But you lack in brains, in sense and intelligence.
May misfortune fall upon
The one who raises a son like you!"

These angry words fill Bijan's heart with bitterness.
He swears by the Creator, World Master:
"I shall not remove my horse's saddle
Until I avenge the death of Zarasp,
Should I die in the course of doing so."

He presents himself before Gostaham,
Heart full of pain, head longing for vengeance.
"Let me have one of your horses,
One who is passionate and able to carry me
Swiftly and easily up the mountain.
I shall don my coat of mail
And show how a man must act.
There is a Turk stationed on this mountain crest,
And the entire army watches him.
I shall find him and fight him,
For his deeds have deeply distressed my soul."

Gostaham says, "You are not being reasonable.
Do not foolishly sniff the leaf of the tree of misfortune.
Once we set on the road, we shall stumble upon
Many climbs and descents, as well as countless plains.
I have only two steeds able
To carry my weight with armor.
Now if this Turk kills one of them,
I shall not have access to another
Of equal stride, vigor, and stature.
Zarasp, world master, Rivniz and Tous,
And your father, who can crush a wild elephant
And deigns not glance at the turning sphere,
Were either killed or returned
Utterly discouraged from the venture.
No one has been able to attack this tough boulder.
Only the wing of a vulture or an eagle
Can carry someone to this castle."

Bijan replies, "Do not break my heart.
I shall have no recourse beyond my arm's strength.
I have solemnly sworn by the moon,
By the world master, and by the king's crown
That I shall never divert the head of my horse
From this Turk and from this mountain, even if
I were to perish in my attempts to avenge Zarasp."

Gostaham replies, "This is not the way to proceed.
You cannot be effective without drawing on wisdom."

Bijan says, "I have no need for a mount.

I shall go on foot. The time for retribution is now."

Gostaham replies, "I wish not for a single strand
Of your hair to fall off, and even if I had
One hundred thousand horses and the tail of each
Were decorated with precious stones worthy of a king,
I refuse you neither treasure nor life,
Neither horse nor blade.
Go and review all my mounts.
Select the one that best suits your needs,
Have it saddled.
I shall not blame you if this beast is taken down."

Now there is a charger brave as a wolf,
Ardent and strong and of slender neckline.
They prepare it for the young, ambitious world victor.

Giv's heart fills with worry
At the news of Bijan's preparations
For he remembers the skill with which
Foorood extended his bowstring.
He summons Gostaham and speaks to him
At length of his son's youth, then he provides him
With Siaavosh's armor and his royal helmet.

Gostaham takes the armor of battle to Bijan,
Who dresses and arms himself as suits a warrior.
He then takes the road to Mount Sepad,
Determined and eager to seek vengeance.

19 | The Battle of Foorood and Bijan

The young king says to Tokhaar,
"Here comes another renowned horseman.
Observe him and tell me his name.
Who is the one who will shed tears over his death?"

The eloquent Tokhaar replies to the prince,
"This man has no equal in the land of Iran.
He is the only son of Giv,
Brave as a lion and victor in battle.

Bijan is more dear to him than his own sweet life.
You had better aim to strike his horse.
We must not distress the heart of the Iranian king.
Besides, Bijan is wearing Siaavosh's armor and helm.
These are impervious to either spear or arrow.
He may continue to battle you on foot,
In which case you will not be able to win him over.
Look, he holds in his hand
A sword that shines as bright as a diamond.
Do not begin a fight. Follow the path of wisdom,
Or else you will have reason for remorse.
You have killed a number of Iranians.
Refrain from causing harm to befall you."

Giv's son nears him and binds his bow and arrow.
The valiant Foorood sends a shot at Bijan's horse.
The horse instantly falls. It is as if it had never lived.
Bijan untangles himself and walks toward Foorood.
Brandishing his sword, he cries,
"O brave rider, wait for me.
You will then witness a fierce contest between lions.
You will learn how people rush to battle
On foot, sword in hand. The sight of me wrestling
Will make you wish you had not provoked a fight."

Once Foorood realizes that Bijan will not withdraw,
He grows furious and fastens another arrow to his bow.

The world hero protects his head with his shield,
Which the shot pierces without touching his coat of mail.
Bijan continues his uphill climb until he reaches
The steep summit, then immediately draws his sword.

The eminent Foorood fears for his life and rides away
While a cry of distress echoes from the castle ramparts.

Bijan chases him, brandishing his razor-sharp sword.
He strikes the horse's strappings and shreds them,
Making the noble animal fall to the dust.

Foorood flings himself inside the fortress gates.
His brave men rush to quickly secure the bolts.
They send a shower of stones from atop the ramparts,

For now is not the moment to hesitate.

Bijan cries out, "O noble hero,
You ride off in this manner before a man on foot?
Are you not ashamed to flee? Alas, what became
Of the courage and glory of the valiant Foorood?"

He then returns to world hero Tous on the battlefield
And says, "In order to combat this lone brave man,
One would need a famed desert lion.
The army leader must not be astonished
If Foorood's arrows reduce a boulder to water
And open a powerful mine beneath the sea,
For one cannot imagine a more valiant hero."

The commander swears by the Creator and says,
"I shall make the dust of this castle fly to the sun.
I shall lead my army to engage in a prodigious battle
To avenge Zarasp, my dear son.
I shall kill this evil Turk and wash
The very heart of this rock with his blood."

20 | The Death of Foorood

Once the shining sun disappears,
The gloomy night's army of stars invades the sky.
One thousand brave cavaliers enter Kalaat
To form a garrison and barricade the castle door,
Facing in the direction of Jaram.
The jingle of bells hanging on horses' necks resounds.

Jarireh, Piran's daughter and Foorood's mother,
Feels great distress as her heart
Grows more and more tremulous for her son.
She joins him in his chambers and sleeps by his side.
Her companions are the dark night and her pain.

In dream, she sees a giant blaze
Shooting out of the castle and drifting
Toward her dear son in Mount Sepad,
Consuming everything from castle to Foorood's slaves.

Heart afflicted, mind troubled, she stirs awake,
Filled with worry for her cherished son.
She climbs up to the rampart, scans the land below,
And sees the entire mountain
Covered with enemy shields and spears.

Her cheeks flooding with blood tears,
Her heart smoldering, she runs to Foorood
And says, "Wake up, my son.
The stars have sent us grave hardship.
The entire mountain is covered with enemy troops,
And the castle door is fenced in by spear and armor.

The young man replies to his mother,
"Until when do you wish to shed tears of pain?
My life is over.
Do not count it among the finer things.
My father perished in youth,
And I shall perish just like him.
He received death at the hands of Garooy.
Mine is to be administered by the hand of Bijan.
But I shall fight and I shall die a man
Who refuses to beg for mercy.
Life is nothing more than a record of our breaths,
And the ultimate outcome is a certain death."

He equips his troops with armor and mace,
Covers his head with a magnificent Turkish helmet,
His body with a Rumi coat of mail.
Thus equipped, he takes the road,
Wielding a Kianian bow.

As the sun reveals its shining face
And rises with glory in the dome of sky,
The Kianian army marches toward Tous
At the command of leaders, the crash of clubs,
And the thunder of trumpets,
Kettledrums, clarions, and Indian bells.

Commander Tous steps out of his camp,
His heart grieving the deaths
Of both son and son-in-law.
He takes the direction of the mountain with troops,

345

Like wild wolves, full of wrath and hostility.

They surround Foorood's castle like beetles and ants,
Their heavy maces brandished in readiness.
In every direction, the leaders' voices
Rebound and mix with the sound
Of kettledrums, horns, and trumpets.

Foorood exits through the castle doors,
Escorted by Turkish warriors.
The air fills with a shower of blade and mace,
Inducing boulders to bewail their fate.
The dust of riders and their arrows' fletches
Turn the mountain into a sea of tar.

There is no flat surface to fight on,
And horses stumble and slip over mountain rocks.
Cries are heard from here and there.
Each fighter battles with all his strength

Tous leads his host, armed to the teeth,
Clutching a shield in one hand
And a piercing sword in the other.
His warriors surround him on foot.
They turn toward the castle ramparts.

In this way, Foorood's troops battle, losing
Many men until the sun reaches its zenith above.

Turks are killed on mountain heights
And in shallow ravines.
The young hero is witness to his diminishing fortune.
His fearlessness and skills
Make an impression on his foes.
As the battle progresses,
He recognizes his imminent end.

There does not remain a single Turkish rider
Able to bear the weight of battle.
Foorood, alone, turns his reins the other way
And flees to the mountain crest,
Galloping toward his fortress.

PART TEN

Rohaam and Bijan erect an ambush
And agree to attack him at the same time
From the top and the base of the path.

Bijan spots him, takes him from below, launching
His steed and firmly pressing down on the stirrups.

At the sight of Bijan's helmet,
The young Foorood immediately draws
His sword to strike him on the head,
To cleave in one blow the head from the body
Like a wild lion, but he is not cognizant of his fate.

Bijan moans, about to lose consciousness,
As he is weakened by an injury.

But Rohaam falls upon Foorood from behind,
Hollering and wielding his Indian sword.

At that moment, Bijan, son of Giv, deals him
Such a blow of his mace on shoulder and helmet
That it paralyzes the young man, who shrieks in pain.

In this predicament, Foorood reaches his castle.
The gate is about to close when Bijan busts in and,
With a sharp blow, strikes Foorood's horse's leg.
The hero returns on foot,
Along with a few servants dispersed by the battle.
They enter and the doors are closed shut.
Alas, his name and audacious heart!

His mother rushes up to him with her slaves.
The veiled women press him against their breasts
And settle him moaning on the ivory throne.
The noble Foorood is about to expel his last breath
At the very moment he is about to possess the crown.

Jarireh's slaves pluck out their musk-scented locks.
His throne is ringed by curls, his fort hazy with smoke.

One more time, he opens his eyes, exhales a deep sigh,
Turns his face toward his mother and her slaves,
And says, parting his lips with much effort,

347

"I am not surprised that you pull out your hair,
For the Iranians are on their way here,
Determined to vandalize the castle.
They will turn our slaves into prisoners.
They will devastate it all, fort, mount, and bastion.
Go, all of you, whose hearts are consumed for me,
Whose cheeks burn in the grief of losing me.
Climb up to the ramparts and drop down
So that Bijan finds no one here.
I can only survive you by a few short breaths.
Bijan has found a way to break my pure heart.
He is the one who kills me in my time of youth."

Having uttered these words, his cheeks turn pale.
He raises his face toward the sky, despondent with pain.

The celestial sphere, unstable as if intoxicated,
Resembles a player who makes seventy turns
To mock us and use us in its mischievous games,
Drawing on wind or lightning, on dagger or sword,
Or perhaps on an unexpected evil man.
Sometimes this hand extracts you from danger.
Sometimes it gives you throne, crown, and diadem.
Sometimes it burdens you with pain and humiliation,
Weighs you down with chains, propels you into a ditch.

All things that sustain life must submit to its laws.
Take advantage of the things you have.
As for me, my heart is clenched with despair,
And I am left empty-handed.
If a man of sense had not been given life,
He would feel neither heat nor cold in this world.
But once he is born, he faces adversity,
Unable to reach the object of his desires.
One must shed tears on his wretchedness,
For in the end, his place of repose is a bed of dust.
Alas, his heart, his intelligence, his faith!

21 | Jarireh Kills Herself

Once Foorood, son of Siaavosh, leaves this world,
Having failed to attain his goal of fame and glory,
His slaves climb on the castle portal and leap
From its heights to their deaths on the ground.

Jarireh lights a huge fire
In which she burns all the treasures.
She grabs a sword, strikes the doors of the horses'
Stables, slashes their bellies, cuts off their feet,
Flooding her cheeks with sweat and blood.
Then she goes to the side of the noble Foorood,
Next to whom she finds a shining dagger.
She presses her cheek against her son's face
One last time, stabs herself in the abdomen,
And expires, her body stretched next to him.

Meanwhile, the Iranians tear the castle doors
Off their hinges and set about destroying
Everything that gets in their way.
Bahraam approaches the ramparts,
Heart wrenched with grief.
He nears Foorood's bed, cheeks drenched in tears,
Head full of anguish, and says to the Iranians,
"Here is a man whose fate is even more distressing
And more deplorable than that of his father.
Siaavosh did not ask his slaves to perish with him,
His mother did not kill herself on his deathbed.
He did not witness his castle burning around him,
Destroyed and devoured by flames,
His home and all he possessed consumed and gone.
The sky's hand is long enough
To reach and to punish crime.
It does not act with love above the face of injustice.
Are you not ashamed now
To appear before Khosrow
After the clear instructions he delivered to Tous?
He sent you to avenge Siaavosh,
He gave you much advice.
Tous came and first killed the king's brother.
Our commander must be congratulated

For being such a cowardly scoundrel.
Once the king is made aware of his brother's murder,
His love and his favor will vanish.
Rohaam and the quick-tempered Bijan
Can never act according to justice."

At the first beat of timpani, Commander Tous
Begins his march toward Kalaat,
Escorted by Goodarz and Giv,
Powerful army leaders, and a long procession
Of brave men from the land of Iran.
They take the direction of Mount Sepad,
Advancing swiftly, hearts free of worry.

Once Tous stands in front of the deathbed
Of this man so deplorably killed,
Once he sees Foorood and his mother
Lifeless upon the throne,
Bahraam crying on one side, full of anger,
Once he sees Zangueh, son of Shaavaran,
On the other side, leaders around
The deceased prince on the ivory throne,
Handsome like the moon, tall as a cypress tree,
He imagines Siaavosh dressed in armor and belt,
Holding sword and arrow,
Asleep on the golden throne.

Goodarz, Giv, and the warriors shed bitter tears.
Tous himself floods his cheeks with his heart's blood,
Regretting the deaths of Foorood and of his own son.
Eyes full of tears, breaths full of deep sighs,
The Iranians turn to Tous.

Goodarz addresses the commander:
"Violence always brings on the fruits of regret.
Never sow the seeds of hatred in the garden of life.
Making haste does not suit an army leader,
For a man carried away is not fit for command.
A leader of your standing must exhibit wisdom
Rather than fury and haste, which in the end
Only served to bring down this youth of Kianian race,
So majestic and strong, so lean and slender.

Your impulsive ways also caused the deaths
Of Rivniz and your dear son Zarasp,
Leader and grandson of Nozar.
Never has the world witnessed graver misfortune.
Courage and wisdom are in the soul of an angry man,
Like a corroding sword red with rust."

Tous sheds tears at these words and replies,
Forgetting his anger and his violence:
"Misfortune condemns men with pain and hardship."

Then he asks that a royal mausoleum be built
On the mountaintop, in which they place Foorood,
Seated upon the golden throne,
Dressed in golden brocade, strapped with royal belt,
And adorned in kingly insignia.
Rosewater is brought forth with musk and camphor.
The head is embalmed in camphor while the corpse
Is rubbed with myrrh, rosewater, and musk.

Once the body is placed upon the throne,
The others retire, and it all ends
For this renowned prince of lion heart.

The coffins of the proud Zarasp and Rivniz
Are placed beside the prince,
And blood tears stream down Tous's white beard.

Such is our fate that, no matter how long we live,
Neither the powerful elephant nor the fearless lion
Lives to endure and carry on forever.
We are all, young and old, journeying toward our ends.
Death is a lion, and we are each prey to it.
The hearts of stone and anvil have cause to fear,
And neither root nor leaf escapes death's grip.
Nothing remains in this world, whether in pain or joy.
You must hurry to busy yourself with work.

22 | Bijan Kills Palaashan

Once the conflict with Foorood concludes,
Tous descends the mountain, all the while reflecting
On his misgivings and on the grim turn of events:
"Whether one senses fear or one does not,
One has no choice but to withdraw from this land."

He halts for three days in Jaram.
On the fourth day, at the sound of clarions,
The commander sets the army in motion,
Trumpets and timpani resounding as a black dust
Looms above the plain from mountain to mountain.

Each time Tous encounters a Tooranian soldier,
He kills him and dumps him in a ditch.
He proceeds in this manner, laying waste to the border
And marching toward the edge of Kaasseh Rood.
There he stops to allow his army to set up camp.
The surface of the land stretches with tent pavilions.

Word spreads in Tooran-Zamin that an army
Of Iranians has reached the banks of Kaasseh Rood.
Palaashan, a young Turk warrior,
Full of courage and care, takes on
The mission of reviewing the enemy troops
And appraising the banners and tents of its leaders.

In the middle of the camp stands a lofty mountain.
On one side swarm the forces, and above, on its crest,
Giv and Bijan sit, discussing various matters,
When they spot on the road Palaashan's banner.

At the sight of the Tooranian, the brave Giv draws out
His sword and says, "I shall go to meet him
And either cut his throat or drag him as prisoner,
Hands tied, before a gathering of noblemen."

Bijan replies, "O noble one, since I accepted
The king's gifts, I pledged to engage in battle.
I must obey royal command.
I am the one who must attack the brave Palaashan."

Giv says to him, "Do not rush to fight him,
For you may not have the strength to overcome him.
A defeat on your part would curtail my joyous day.
Palaashan is a field lion whose only hunt is warriors."

Bijan replies, "Do not smear my name in shame.
For this fight, allow me to borrow Siaavosh's armor.
You shall then witness a lion crush its leopard prey."

Giv hands to him the coat of mail.
Bijan carefully secures each fastening.
He then climbs upon a blazing horse
And advances on the field, spear in hand.

Palaashan, having just killed a deer,
Roasts its flesh on the fire.
He feasts upon the meal,
His bow still hooked on his upper arm
While his charger is peacefully grazing in the pastures.
As soon as Palaashan's horse
Makes out Bijan's horse from afar,
It shouts a loud whinny, rushing to its master,
Who assumes a rider is advancing, heavily armed.

Palaashan understands that a contender is looming.
He addresses Bijan in a rather brash voice:
"I am destroyer of lions, vanquisher of Deevs.
What is your name?
Your star will have reason to weep over your fate."

The hero replies, "I am Bijan, and in combat
I am a deev of impervious brazen stature.
On the day of battle,
An elephant, a lion, or a bold warrior
Are all one and the same for me.
My grandfather is a lion full of courage.
My father is the brave Giv,
And you shall suffer by the strength of my arm.
You are nothing more to me than a greedy vulture
Feeding on carcasses,
Nourished of smoke, ash, and blood.
It is time for you to lead your army onto the plain."

Without an acknowledgment,
Palaashan launches his horse like a war elephant.

The two horsemen fall upon each other in great fury
Like war lions, raising a thick, black dust.
They battle with spears first.
One warrior is a lion, the other a leopard.
Soon, the tips of their spears splinter,
So they seize swords.
So hard are the blows, blades soon shatter to pieces,
Trembling and tumbling like autumn leaves.
The chargers are awash with sweat,
Their heads in a daze.

These two proud lions, two passionate combatants,
Grab their heavy maces and continue to fight
Until Bijan shouts a cry, raises on his shoulder
His weighty mace, and strikes a blow, injuring
His opponent mid waist, shattering his vertebrae
And forcing him off his horse, his head, his helmet
And his metal armor plunging to the ground.

Swift as a dust tornado, Bijan dismounts,
Ready to behead Palaashan.
He seizes the armor, the head, and the horse
Of the renowned hero and takes the path to his father.

Meanwhile, Giv's heart is full of worry
About the fight and about how the wind of destiny
Would affect the outcome of the day.
He hollers and cries, scanning the horizon,
Hoping to discern the dust raised by Bijan's return.

In the end, his young son appears
With the head, armor, and horse of his challenger.
He places them before his father, who cries out,
"May you always be victorious, my dear son!
Your feats will forever be celebrated by noblemen.
The king's joy will bloom like a spring flower
When he hears of your success!"

They happily return to camp,
Where Bijan hands over to the commander

His opponent's helm-covered head, armor, and horse.

Tous, beside himself with joy, exclaims,
"You are the support of this army,
The leader of brave men, the crown of the king.
May you forever remain happy and prosperous!
May your enemy's hand fall short and powerless!
One must praise Giv, son of Goodarz,

Who raised a son of your strength and stature."

23 | The Iranians Suffer From the Snowfall

Afraasiyaab learns that Tooran's border
Is flooding with Iranian troops, that an army
Approaches Kaasseh Rood, and that the world
Dims with the vengeance of Siaavosh.

The royal leader says to Piran, his army chief,
"Khosrow revealed his secrets, and unless we surrender,
We must depart with banner and drums or else
Iran's army will cast out the light of sun and moon.
Gather troops from every corner of the land,
And let us not waste time on hopeless discourse."

Meanwhile, a violent wind blows in Tooran-Zamin,
A wind so fierce no one can recall such a phenomenon.
Thick clouds envelop the earth,
And the bitter chill freezes warrior lips.
The tents are coated with ice, and snow
Spreads thick, white blankets on mountaintops.
For the duration of seven days,
The land disappears beneath the snow.

There is a shortage of food, sleep, and shelter.
It appears the surface of the earth is a solid rock.

The thought of battle now looms in the distance.
War horses are killed, their flesh to be consumed.
Many soldiers and four-legged beasts perish.
Not even a white battle horse survives the elements.
The hands of brave men grow frozen and numb.

On the eighth day, the sun appears in all its glory
And converts the earth into a vast, flooding sea.

Commander Tous convenes his army chiefs
And speaks at length of future war opportunities:
"Our host has grievously suffered from famine.
It is time for us to leave this camp, this cursed land.
Damn Kalaat, Mount Sepad, and Kaasseh Rood!"

Bahraam, the proudest of the warriors, says to him,
"I must not hide the truth from the commander.
You always wish to silence us with your words.
You drive madness to the point
Of killing the son of Siaavosh.
I warned you to abstain from such an action,
For it was not fair and just.
Look and see how many men we have lost.
Remember the troubles we faced from your deeds.
Think of the misfortunes awaiting you)
This venture is only at its starting point."

Tous replies, "Foorood was no more glorious than
The valiant Zarasp, yet he was not killed so innocently.
It was written and what is done is done.
If Foorood was of royal lineage,
The brave Zarasp did not derive from deevs.
He was also a prince. Observe the army
And tell me if you find a man equal
To Rivniz in height, beauty, and caliber.
He filled my life's chalice with milk and wine.
In stature he was a youth;
In speech he was a wise old man.
Come, let us not speak of the past,
Of whether Foorood was killed fairly or unjustly."

Commander Tous addresses
The noble warriors of glory and justice:
"The time has come to accomplish the deed.
Giv accepted his gifts from the king.
He accepted the mission to burn the mountain
Of wood that barred our way,
To light with this fire the sphere of sky

And free the road for the army's advance."

Giv says, "This venture is not an arduous one,
And even if it were, it is not one without reward."

Bijan is saddened by these words and says,
"I shall not consent to what you say.
It is not suitable for me, a young man, to rest
While you cinch yourself for action in your old age.
I was raised with much trouble for such exploits.
You never found any cause to reproach me."

Giv replies, "I am the one who wished it.
I committed full-heartedly to carry through the task.
The time has come for me to bring it to fruition.
I must equip myself, forgo age and rest.
Do not fear for my fate
Or be chagrined by my departure.
My breath can melt a mountain of granite."

Giv crosses Kaasseh Rood with great difficulty,
For its surface is covered in patches of ice and snow.
At the mountain of wood, he finds himself
Unable to estimate its height and width.
He lights a fire with the aid of an arrow tip
And flings it into the mass of wood, setting fire to it.

For three weeks one cannot cross this brazier
Due to wind, smoke, and the intensity of the flames.
On the fourth week, once the level of water drops
And the fire is extinguished,
The way clears for the troops to cross.

24 | Bahraam Captures Kaboodeh

After passing through the fire and reuniting around
Its commander, the Iranian host sets off
In good order on the road to Gorooguerd,[47]
Covering plain and ravine with masses of tents,

◇◇◇◇◇◇◇◇◇◇◇◇◇
47 Gorooguerd: A province of Tooran-Zamin.

Taking every precaution, sending scouts everywhere.

Gorooguerd is under the rule of Tajov,
A horseman who never fears the lion.
He possesses herds of horses who wander
The plain from one mountain to the other.

Once aware of the approach of the Iranian host,
He feels the need to evacuate his stallions.
He sends a brave warrior named Kaboodeh,
In all haste, to Afraasiyaab's herders.
Kaboodeh is an able, talented man,
For skill is required for such an endeavor.

Tajov says to him, "As soon as darkness descends,
You will depart; allow no one to see you.
Go and assess the number of Iranian troops,
The nature of their leaders,
Carriers of banner and headdress
I wish to ambush them with a night attack.
I wish to convert the plain into a vast sea of blood."

Kaboodeh takes off like a black deev
To approach the Iranians, assisted by the shield of night.

The night watchman is Bahraam, a man who,
With a noose, is able to catch wild elephants.
At the whinny of Kaboodeh's horse,
Bahraam's ears sharpen.
He fixes an arrow to his bow, steadies himself
On the stirrups, and prompts his steed,
Who bears the appearance of a camel.

Without saying a word,
Without distinguishing much in the darkness,
He shoots an arrow straight at the belt.

The Tooranian king's herder turns black with fear.
He tumbles off his mount and begs for mercy.

Bahraam addresses him:
"Speak the truth. Tell me who sent you
And which of our warriors you meant to attack."

Kaboodeh replies, "If you wish to grant me mercy,
I shall answer all your questions.
Tajov, my master, dispatched me.
I am merely one of his servants.
If you choose to let me live,
I shall show you where he dwells.

Bahraam says to him, "Tajov is to me
The equivalent of a cow to a fierce lion."

He slits the neck of Kaboodeh with his dagger
And hangs the head on the rope of his royal saddle.
He carries it to camp and flings it with contempt,
For it is neither the head of a renowned man
Nor that of a brave equestrian.

At the time the rooster and the lark call,
Kaboodeh has still not returned to Tajov.
The ruler, eager for battle, troubled by the absence,
Assumes some misfortune has befallen him.
He gathers nearby troops
And immediately sets out on the road.

25 | Tajov Battles the Iranians

As soon as the sun rises over the plain
And its dagger casts a purple gleam
Over the fleeting darkness of night,
Tajov advances with his army.

The Iranian sentries announce
The approach of a garrison from Tooran-Zamin,
Directed by a leader brandishing
A banner sporting the image of a whale.

Giv and his men leave the Iranian encampment
To meet the challenger on the road.
A furious Giv asks his name and adds, "O war-seeker,
Why are you approaching us with your procession?
Are you here to engage in war or to surrender?"

The brave Tajov replies, "My heart is valiant,
My arm is strong and my hand is a lion's rapacious paw.
I am Tajov, the man-slayer able to behead a war lion.
I originate from an ancient Iranian family,
A family of noblemen from the race of lions.
I sit on this province's throne, guarding its border.
I am the seal of brave men and the king's son-in-law."

Giv says to him, "Do not speak in this manner,
For such words tarnish your honor.
It is hard to imagine an Iranian
Who is willing to settle in Tooran-Zamin,
Unless he is nourished with blood and bitter melon.
If you are the guardian of this land and a royal son-in-law,
Why have you not more numerous troops?
Do not seek war with such a meager host.
Do not walk madly against brave men.
I am a famed hero. I shall trample
Beneath my feet the heads of border guards.

"If you and your host wish to submit,
If you wish to travel to Iran and appear before the king,
Then we must escort you to Commander Tous instantly.
Speak to him, listen to him, and obey his orders.
I shall ask him to give you treasure and robes of honor,
Slaves, and many gilded and adorned horses.
I think, O illustrious man, that this is the way to proceed.
What is your opinion, or shall I engage you in combat?"

The clever Tajov replies, "O world hero,
There exists no one capable of overturning my banner.
The seal and throne of this land belong to me.
I possess horse, sheep, and a vast army.
My master is Afraasiyaab, a king the likes of which
No Iranian has caught a glimpse of, not even in dream.
I have slaves and horses of winded feet
Wandering freely in field and plain.
Do not consider my limited troops.
Observe me, seated on my charger, mace in hand!
Today, with this small army,
I shall treat you in a way that you will
Deeply repent of your belligerence."

Bijan says to his noble father, "O renowned hero,
Always ready for battle, noble, mindful warrior,
You are no longer in old age what you were in youth.
Why do you advise Tajov in this manner?
Why this affection and these offers of alliance?
You must seize mace and sword.
You must pluck out his heart and brain."

Bijan charges his horse. The air resounds with shouts.
Maces and swords are raised, sending to the sky
A dark, black dust that conceals the sun.
The world dims as if beneath a winter cloud,
And the glimmer of stars and moon disappears.

In the middle of the line stands the valiant Giv,
Alone able to obscure the day's bright light.
In the vanguard is the fervent Bijan,
Never delayed in action.

In opposite rank is Tajov, with crown on his head
And able to fight the fiercest lion.
He is surrounded by skilled warriors,
One named Arjang and the other Mardooy the lion,
Who never tire of battle,
Clawing mace and sharp swords.
It does not take long for Arjang the warrior
To meet with his demise on the battlefield.

Two-thirds of the Tooranian troops are killed,
And fortune abandons the vindictive Tajov.
He runs away, and the glorious Bijan chases after him,
Shouting and boiling up with rage, wielding his spear.
You would think he is a wild lion.
His spear strikes Tajov mid-waist,
Depriving him of strength and vitality.
The Tooranian falters, his Rumi armor shattered,
Its buckles snapping undone.

As Bijan sees his enemy escaping battle,
He flings his spear to the ground and fans out his hand,
Just as a leopard unfurls its claws
To catch a mountain ram.
Like a falcon snatching a lark,

He plucks the royal crown off Tajov's head.
This is the crown Afraasiyaab bestowed upon him
And which Tajov never parted with,
Not even at night, at the time of rest and sleep.

Tajov urges his horse toward his castle, followed
By Bijan, bolting like the blaze of Aazargoshasp.
Once he approaches it, Aspanooy appears before him,
Face flooded with tears and bawling: "Tajov,
Where is your army, your strength, your courage?
Why did you leave my side and so shamefully
Abandon me in this castle, turning your back on me?
Allow me to climb behind you on your horse.
Do not forsake me in this fort to fall into enemy hands."

The proud Tajov's heart fills with shame,
His cheeks burning like flames.
He approaches her, helps her climb on his horse,
And hands her the reins.

Aspanooy, moon-faced beauty, settles behind Tajov.
She wraps her arms around his waist.
He rushes forth with her like a dust tornado
In the direction of Tooran-Zamin.

For some time, Tajov's horse sustains the course.
But in the end, man and charger are equally exhausted.
Tajov says to his servant, "My beautiful companion,
Danger is pressing, my horse is spent.
Behind us is the enemy, before us a cavern.
You must find a way to keep the enemy at bay.
If we maintain this pace, we will fall prey to Bijan.
Remain here.
Your life is not at risk since you have no foe.
Allow me to regain the road with my steed."

Aspanooy alights, and the pain of losing her
Causes Tajov to weep.
The horse, relieved of her weight, takes off
With new momentum toward Afraasiyaab's court.

Bijan chases the fugitive with renewed ardor.
Once his eyes fall on moon-faced Aspanooy,

Whose black musk-scented mane cascades to her feet,
He dismounts near her and picks her up gently.
He places her behind him on his horse
And returns to the camp of the brave world hero.

He arrives in joy at the entrance of Tous's pavilion,
Where he is received to the beat of kettledrums,
Like a cautious and brave horseman
Returning proudly from a hunt, loaded with game.

The commander and brave heroes spend time
Vandalizing Tajov's castle, then they go on a search
For herds wandering the plains of Tooran,
Each clutching a noose and handling it skillfully.
The heads of horses are captured in their knots,
And the entire army is equipped with mounts.

Finally, the Iranian horsemen, men full of courage
And wrath, set up camp in Tajov's residence.

26 | Afraasiyaab Learns of Tous's Presence

Tajov appears before Afraasiyaab,
Eyes grieving with tears, and says to him,
"The leader Tous has arrived, with timpani and troops.
The Iranians have kindled a war, making warrior
Heads roll into dust, taking our relatives captive.
Neither castle remains nor border,
Neither horse nor field.
There is no sense for us to remain here,
Since they have laid waste to plain, field, and herds.
Palaashan and all our noblemen
Have been dragged into dust."

Afraasiyaab is dismayed at the news and,
Seeking a remedy for his ailments, snaps at Piran,
"I had ordered you to gather a vast host from all sides,
But your laziness and old age, your foolishness
And indolence made you lose precious time.
Now a great number of my relatives have been killed,
And the star of our fortune has dimmed.

It is not the time to be slow to act.
The world is narrowing for sensible men."

The leader Piran instantly takes leave of Afraasiyaab.
He summons his men of war from every border,
Distributes arms and silver, sets his army into motion.
Once he crosses the border,
He assigns each warrior his rank.
The right wing he hands over to Baarmaan and Tajov,
Riders as powerful as wild elephants.
The left wing goes to Nastihan, a warrior who deems
A wild lion as tame as a feeble lamb.

The world fills with the blast of trumpets
And the chaotic sound of kettledrums and Indian bells.
The air turns yellow, red, and purple from the reflection
Of the vast number of colorful spears and banners.
From sea to sea there is no path, so numerous
Are soldiers, horses, camels, and elephants.

Piran walks in haste to the plain
As Afraasiyaab leaves his palace to count the troops.
He calculates one hundred thousand ardent men.
He is so pleased and full of hope that he blesses the hero
And says, "May you leave victorious and return in joy!
May your eye never witness a moment of misfortune!"

On an auspicious day, Piran departs with his host
While world keeper Afraasiyaab remains behind.
The battalions march forth in succession,
Their motion making mountain and river disappear.

Piran directs the troops: "Avoid major roads,
Take the shorter, more isolated paths.
We must not let the Iranians know of our approach.
I wish to surprise them and make our illustrious troops
Collapse upon their heads to form a huge mountain."

In secret, he sends spies to inquire prudently
On what to expect while advancing with forced steps.
Once he nears Gorooguerd, his spies receive
News of the enemy host and report in secret to Piran:
"The leader Tous is still camped at the same site,

364

And one does not hear the sound of kettledrums.
They are busy drinking and getting drunk.
Day and night, they sit, cup in hand, in the absence
Of watch guards and sentries making the rounds,
For they do not suspect the approach of an army."

Piran summons his men to discuss the enemy.
He exclaims, "Never have we secured a surer victory!"

27 | Piran Surprises the Iranians

From his glorious army, Piran selects
Thirty thousand sword-bearing riders
With whom he departs at midnight.
Silently, free of the beat of drums
And the sound of clarions, the watchful leader
Travels a distance of seven farsangs.

First they reach the herds of horses
Wandering freely through the Tooranian plains.
They capture a great number without mishap.
They kill numerous guardians and herders,
And the Iranians decidedly run out of luck.

From there, they make their way toward the enemy,
Like a sinister, gloomy whirlwind.

The Iranians, unaware, sit in groups,
Drunk, unarmed, and defenseless.
Giv is awake in his tent while Goodarz is vigilant.

The sound of voices and the blow of the axe
Surprise Giv, who rises, always eager for battle.
By his tent stands a horse saddled with strappings.
Like a lion, he dresses in Siaavosh's armor,
Angry at himself for having wasted time on rest.
Giv says to his heart, "What is happening tonight
That my mind is in such a state of torpor?"

He advances, mounts his steed,
And charges, swift as wind.

He notices the sky darkened by both dust and dusk.
He reaches Tous's tent enclosure and calls out, "Rise!
An army is upon us while our men are fast asleep."

Next he rushes to his father,
Bull-headed mace in hand.
He crosses the field with the speed of smoke,
Spurs sober men and scolds them,
Reprimanding Bijan: "Is this the time to sit
Cup in hand or the time of battle?
An army has encircled us, threatening our troops."

A loud clash is heard on the battlefield.
The intoxicated Iranians look around in confusion.
They are stunned and startled by the blows.
A cloud drifts above them with a shower of arrows.
Below their drunken heads are soft cushions
And above, stinging arrow, sword, and mace.

As soon as dawn raises its head in the house of Leo,
The brave Giv observes the plain covered
With lifeless Iranians, the earth soaking in blood,
And recognizes the decline of their fortune.

Goodarz also sees the growing enemy army
And troops equal in number to crawling beetles and ants,
Covering the small space of the camp like a carpet.

Commander Tous looks for his troops
And notices no one standing, neither warrior nor lion,
Only Giv and Goodarz and a few riders fighting hard.
The battlefield is strewn with bodies,
The ground muddied with blood.
Banners are torn to shreds, kettledrums overturned.
The cheeks of Iranian warriors are black with grief;
Sons are deprived of fathers, fathers deprived of sons.
The entire army has been turned upside-down.

Such are the actions of the sky of swift rotations.
At times it hands you happiness,
At times it weighs you down with pain and sorrow.

In their despair, the Iranians turn

And abandon their tents, taking notice
Of neither timpani nor army or gear.
Everything and everyone has been crushed or
Wounded, left and right. In disarray, they march,
Ashamed, to the edge of Kaasseh Rood.

The Tooranian cavaliers pursue Tous,
Hearts full of vengeance, mouths full of scorn.
You would think clouds drop a rain of mace,
Falling from behind and striking armor, helm, and mail.
No one attempts to resist. Everyone seeks refuge.
Horses and men fall from exhaustion,
Unable to maintain a remnant of self-control.

They travel toward the mountain,
Depleted by the carnage and by their long journey.
As soon as Tous exits the plain
And arrives at the mountain base,
He senses that he is safe from battle.

Iranians go missing in vast numbers.
Screams of agony are heard.
The survivors are either wounded or held captive.
It is for them that one must shed tears.
Nothing is left, neither crown nor throne,
Neither tent nor horse, nor warrior, able or not.
No one is left to comfort the wounded
Or to care for them.
No one is left to gather and to bury the dead.
So many fathers weep for sons,
So many injured lie in agony.

Such is the way of this unpredictable world.
It hides what is to come, conceals it out of sight.
It takes your life for a game
And treats you with wrath and utmost disdain.
We are delivered to endless grief.
Dipped in ignorance, we are the slaves of our greed,
Unable and unwilling to fully grasp life's mysteries.
We come from wind, and to dust we shall go.
But until then, what do we know of our destiny?

Two-thirds of the Iranians are dead.

The rest return from battle covered in wounds.
There are no physicians to attend the injured.
Everywhere, one perceives suffering and blood tears.

Such a grievous defeat makes Tous lose his mind,
As it appears devoid and deprived of reason.
The Iranian troops wasted time drinking and resting
When they should have directed their attention to battle.
They slept deeply and peacefully for too long.
Goodarz, the aged warrior, full of skill and experience,
Has lost sons and grandsons. He has lost everything.

The wisest men of the army go to him heartbroken
And surrender to his command.
He places a sentinel on the mountaintop to keep watch.
He sends patrols on all sides to make rounds
In the hopes of finding a solution to his troubles.

Then he orders an envoy to strap himself,
To report to the king the costs of Tous's actions,
To inform his majesty that misfortune and grave loss
Have overcome Iran-Zamin and its leaders.

28 | Kay Khosrow Summons Tous

Goodarz's envoy enters the court of Kay Khosrow
And recounts to him in detail
The circumstances leading to their defeat
And the way the Iranians' bright days dimmed.
The valiant king boils with rage at the news,
And pain overtakes him, inciting his heart to pulsate.
His brother's dismal fate afflicts him deeply,
And his army's misadventures increase his sorrow.

All night long, he curses Tous.
At the rooster's crow, he summons a judicious scribe
And pours out his weary heart
In a letter full of furor and tears to be sent to Fariborz,
Son of Kaavoos, and to army leaders.

As suits custom and faith, he begins the letter

With praise of Yazdan, Creator of time and space:
"In the name of the Master of Sun and Moon,
Who bestows strength in times of adversity and joy,
From Whom comes victory and defeat,
On Whom, in all circumstances,
Are contingent the fulfillment of our innermost desires
And the realization of our achievements:
Creator of world, time, and space,
Creator of the ant's leg as well as massive mountains,
Donor of wisdom, soul, and strong body,
Of eminence, crown, and lofty throne;
The One Who accords some people honor and grace,
And others hardship, need, pain, worry, and grief;
From the shining sun to the dark dust of earth,
Everywhere one finds evidence of pure divine justice.

"Tous left with the Kaaviani banner,
Along with forty brave men fitted with golden boots.
I have sent him with an army to Tooran-Zamin,
And the first thing he manages to accomplish
Is to convert my own flesh and blood, my own brother,
Into a victim of his spite and foolishness.
The land of Iran did not long for such an army leader.
Alas, my young and beloved Foorood,
Chief of brave warriors,
Descendant of renowned lineage!
The fate of my father filled me
With the most intense grief.
For a long time, I have shed bitter tears for him.
Now I find myself weeping for my departed brother.
I no longer distinguish between friend and foe.
I instructed Tous in no uncertain terms:
        'Do not take the road to Jaram.
        Do not approach Kalaat and Mount Sepad,
        For Foorood lives there with his mother,
        And he is an illustrious hero of noble nature.'

"Not aware of the approaching host,
Not knowing why it marched his way,
Foorood battled in the mountain where many perished.
Alas, this brave hero, son of a king,
Whom Tous delivered to the wind!

369

If Tous had rather commanded his army honorably,
The star of Kaavoos would not have slipped away.
He falls asleep in battle and springs up quick to act
Only at the time of reveling in feast and drink.
What good is courage when one is led by him?
Damn his dark, detestable soul!

"When you read this letter,
Renounce food, rest, or sleep.
Send Tous back to me immediately.
Do not disobey me and do not deliberate.
Take command of the host, slip into golden boots,
Advance at the head of the Kaaviani banner.
In all matters, consult the noble Goodarz
And the council of brave men and leaders.
Do not rush to engage in battle.
Abstain from drinking wine. Shun rest and sleep.
Do not allow your rashness to lead you into war.
Before your wounded are healed, entrust Giv
With the army's vanguard, for he is a noble cavalier,
With hands as wide and strong as a leopard's paws.
On all sides, gather the means to continue the war,
And abstain from contemplating the thought of feast."

The king's seal is affixed to the letter.
Khosrow says to the envoy, "Leave right away.
Rest neither by day nor by night,
And at every station take a fresh horse."

The messenger takes the road as commanded.
He arrives at the camp of the renowned world hero,
Approaches Fariborz, and hands over the letter,
Bringing joy and happiness to the leaders.

Fariborz calls to his side Tous and the warriors
And speaks to them at length of what occurred.
He discloses the contents
Of the king's letter to Giv, Goodarz,
And the cavaliers and brave men of this border.
A young tree begins to bear fruit in the world.

Lion warriors of Iran-Zamin hail the king.
Tous asks for noble banner, kettledrums, golden boots,

And elephants, which he gives to Fariborz, saying,
"These honors are worthy of you,
For you are respected.
May your fortune remain victorious!
May your life be a continuous Nowruz!"

Tous departs, along with ardent riders,
From the family of Nozar, eager for battle.
He does not stop until he approaches the king.

He kisses the ground at Kay Khosrow's feet.
The latter does not bother to turn to face him.
In the end, the king opens his mouth to curse him
And humiliate him before the entire court:
"May your name disappear from the list of heroes!
Have you no fear of the pure World Creator?
Do you not blush or tremble before brave men?
I gave you Kianian headdress and belt,
Sent you on your way to battle our foes.
I directed you to stay away from Jaram,
And yet you disobeyed and ended up there,
Hence delivering my heart to immense grief.
Your first act was to spread hatred of me
By reducing the family of Siaavosh when you executed
My dear noble brother, unmatched in the world.
You murdered Foorood, a man against whom
Our fortune would demand an army.
You merit spikes and chains, not crown and wine.
Alas, the innocent Tokhaar, who did not take
These words seriously!
Otherwise, instead of striking Tous's horse,
He would have beaten Tous himself.
The world would be set free from the bondage of Tous.
Damn him, his elephants, and his kettledrums!
You entered the land to fight our adversary,
And while there you only thought of feast and rest.

"There is no place for you in this realm.
A mental asylum is a more suitable home for you.
You have no right to appear among noblemen
For you lack sense and purpose.
The connection you have to Manoochehr Shah

371

And your white beard are the only reasons
You may feel secure and harbor a sense of hope,
For without these I would have given you up
To your enemy, commanding them to sever your head.
Go, and let prison be your everlasting dwelling
And welcome your ill nature as your merited jailer."

He banishes him to be enchained, and with his captivity
Removes any remnant of joy from the heart of Tous.

29 | Fariborz Proposes an Armistice to Piran

As Tous departs swiftly in a state of despair,
Fariborz places the crown on his head,
For he is both army warrior and son of a king.
He orders Rohaam to take on a mission
To aggrandize both his name and his lifeblood,
A mission to travel to the mountain and to Piran,
To speak with him at length and to listen to his reply.

Fariborz says to Rohaam, "Go and meet the leader Piran.
Relay to him a message, and tell him,
        'The revolving dome of sky always treats men
        At times with harshness, at times with tenderness.
        It raises one to the glorious firmament
        To condemn another with misfortune, loss, and disgrace.
        A brave man must not resort to nocturnal battles,
        And heroes handling weighty mace do not plan them.
        If you wish to settle a truce, we are ready to accept.
        If you wish to battle, we shall engage in battle.
        We ask that you consent to a one-month truce
        So that our wounded men have a chance to recover.'"

Rohaam, the bold, takes leave of Fariborz,
Responsible for the message and carrier of a letter.
On the road, he meets a patrol. Its leader spots him,
And asks him for his name and where he comes from.

He replies, "I am Rohaam the warrior.
I am a man of skill, prudence, and discernment.
I come on a mission given to me by Fariborz,

Son of Kaavoos, to relay a message to Piran."

A horseman emerges from the group,
Runs to his leader as fast as a cloud of dust,
And announces that Rohaam, son of Goodarz,
Arrives from the enemy camp to see the army chief.

Piran advances toward him graciously,
Invites him in, treats him with kindness and amity,
And bids him to sit upon the throne.

Rohaam, the spokesman, listens
To Piran's questions and eloquent words,
All the while suspecting him of secretly plotting schemes.
He reveals the undisclosed reason for his visit
And conveys the message of Prince Fariborz.

Piran replies, "You are the ones who kindled the war.
Tous treated us with disregard and disrespect.
In haste, he crossed the border like a wild wolf
And slaughtered without care both weak and strong.
Countless men did he kill, countless more were taken captive,
Without concern for the joys and grief of our land.
He came seeking vengeance for the death of Siaavosh,
To contend with the leader of the Tooranian army.
Ultimately, he slew the son, even more savagely
Than the father had been slain.
May he never lay eyes on either crown or belt.
Today you suffer the consequences for his deeds,
For you are the ones who attacked us unexpectedly.

"Now, as your army's leader, what is your wish?
If you are set on a cease-fire for one month,
Not a single rider from my army will attack you.
If you prefer to engage in battle, so be it.
Then command your troops and send the call to arms.
If you wish peace to reign for the duration of one month,
Take advantage of this delay, withdraw your army,
Abandon the land of Tooran, cross our borders.
Your wise decision will be placed into effect.
Otherwise, expect us to reengage in combat
Without a moment's waste."

He arranges a present worthy of Rohaam's name,
And the valiant hero delivers a letter to Fariborz
With contents similar to the one he relayed to Piran.

Fariborz, receiving the armistice, lowers his hand
Like a rapacious lion in every direction.
He asks his treasurer to unlock silver crates
Brought from all corners of the land,
Containers of spears, arrows, and nooses.
He restores the army losses to the troops
And everywhere asks for reinforcement.
In this way, they equip the army and prepare for war.

30 | The Iranians Are Crushed by the Turks

After one month, the time of battle returns
As the peace treaty comes to an end.
On both sides, one hears the clatter of gear
And armament carried onto the battlefield.

The sky is shaken by the sound
Of kettledrums, clarions, and bells.
All one can see are horses' manes, countless men,
Bridles, spears and maces, bows and arrows.
Not even a mosquito could pass through the mass
Of swords, maces, nooses, and shields.

On his side, Piran assembles his troops,
Raising dust to obscure the revolving dome.
In charge of the right wing is Rooeen the warrior,
With noblemen able in battle.
In charge of the left wing is Lahaak the fighter,
For whom, in war, a lion is as meek as a lamb.
In the center of the army stands Piran,
With Hoomaan and the vengeful Nastihan.

At the sight of the enemy host, Fariborz descends
The mountain and assembles his troops.
You would think the world
Has been swallowed up by a giant dragon
Or that the sky has tumbled upon the ground.

The right wing of the Iranian host
Is under the command of Giv, son of Goodarz,
A powerful lord and governor of the border.
The left wing is under the command of Ashkesh,
Who is quick to strike
And make torrents of blood flow in battle.
At the army core, and with his banner behind him,
Stands Fariborz, son of Kaavoos,
Encircled by brave men.

This prince and leader says to his troops,
"Our value remains hidden for too long.
Today we must fight like lions, constrict the world
For our opponents, or else our maces and Rumi helms
Will mock us until the end of time."

The two hosts fall upon each other,
Each warrior vindictive and vengeful.

The Iranians shower a fierce storm of arrows,
Like autumn rain falling from trees.
It appears the air is made of vultures' wings.
The ground turns a shade of scarlet
Beneath elephant feet.
No bird would dare fly overhead,
For the sky is pierced and intersected
By a multitude of arrows and spears
Flying through the dust stirred by the troops.
In the midst, sharp swords glimmer like hot flames.
You would think the earth is the face of a black man
And the fading hearts of warriors are bright stars.

Countless spears, maces, and double-edged swords
Make the earth quiver as if it is the day of resurrection.

Giv emerges out of the army's core, lips foaming.
He is surrounded by members of Goodarz's family,
On whom depends the battle's gains and losses.
They charge and raid with arrow and spear,
Making flames spew out of metal tips.

Piran assaults Giv, the bold, in such a way
That the world grows dim.

Witness to this and to the noblemen's dusty faces,
Goodarz hurls forward from the army center.
Everyone falls on each other.
Blows are administered this way, that way.
The field of vengeance becomes a sea of blood.
With arrow and spear they strike each other,
Making the metal tips glisten and gleam.

The battle of Goodarz and Piran is a fierce one.
Nine hundred men from the tribe of Piran fall,
But Lahaak and Farshidvard, seeing this vast army
Succumb, direct a sharp attack against Giv
And his mace-bearing warriors.
The leaders let loose a line of shots
On the mail-bound combatants.
Then they lower their bows
And reach for their piercing swords.

Soon the surface of the nation
Disappears beneath the heaps of corpses.
No one wishes to take his eyes off the enemy.
No one wishes to concede his place.

Hoomaan says to Farshidvard,
"We must guide our attack on the army's center
Until Fariborz abandons it
And takes refuge in the rear.
Then we shall easily vanquish the right wing,
And we shall seize loads and weapons."

They fall upon the center
And upon Fariborz, son of Kaavoos.
When Goodarz sees the turn of battle and
The worry on his warrior's faces, he leads an assault
From the army center into the core of the brawl.
This way and that way, blows are dispensed,
The land turning into a sea of blood.

Warrior Fariborz retreats at the sight of Hoomaan,
Causing the Iranian battle line to dissolve and break.
The prideful soldiers cede their positions in surrender.
With no one left to obey, they yield the field.
One no longer distinguishes banner and kettledrums.

PART TEN

Soldiers' faces turn pale, witness to grim developments.
They reverse and retreat, their fists clutching wind.

Banners, spears, and timpani are overturned,
Bridles and reins in a blur, warriors' hearts demoralized,
Plain and mountain soaked in blood.

The enemy advances in great numbers on all sides,
And Fariborz takes shelter on the mountainside.
The surviving Iranians flee.
One must shed tears for those who save themselves.

No one is left but Goodarz and Giv, who,
Surrounded by innumerable renowned warriors,
Are able to maintain their position.

Once Goodarz, son of Kashvaad,
Notices that the banner of Fariborz, son of Kaavoos,
Is missing at the army's center,
Once he sees that so many heroes have disappeared,
His heart is consumed by an intense fire.

He swings the reins to flee, and the riders
Of the Goodarzian family shout a great cry of fear.
Giv says to Goodarz, "O aged leader, you witnessed
Many maces and arrows in your lifetime.
If you recoil before Piran, I shall cover my head in dust.
Neither skilled warrior nor experienced nobleman
Lives in this world forever.
You and I are sure to die, for of all the ailments
Oppressing mankind, death is the most infallible one.
Now, since fate is against us, it is far better
For your rival to see your forehead than your back.
Let us not flee the battlefield.
Let us not dishonor the memory of Kashvaad.
Have you not heard the wise man's ancient saying
About razing a mountain and turning it to dust?
You are here, you have seventy brave sons.
Your family still boasts many elephants and lions.
Let us darken with our daggers enemy hearts.
Let us uproot the mountain at its base."

At Giv's words, Goodarz feels great shame.

He observes the heads and helmets of his relatives,
Regrets having thoughts of retreat.
He then secures himself steadfast on the saddle.

Goraazeh, Gostaham, Barteh, and the brave Zangueh
Emerge to utter a solemn, sacred oath:
"We shall not withdraw from the battlefield,
Even if blows of mace incite torrents of blood.
We shall maintain ourselves back to back,
To reclaim our fallen glory."

They hold their positions,
Fiercely fighting with their maces.
Many renowned Tooranians weaken and collapse,
As fate seems to turn against them.

Goodarz says to Bijan, "Go with mace and arrow.
Turn your horse's reins swiftly toward Fariborz.
Bring me the Kaaviani banner.
Let us paint the earth a deep shade of purple."

Bijan obeys, charging his horse toward Fariborz,
Galloping like the flame of Aazargoshasp.
Bijan says to Fariborz, "Why do you hide here?
Charge your horse as would a brave man.
Emerge from your shelter.
If you do not wish to join us, hand over your banner
And your riders armed with swords."

Bijan's words do not bring Fariborz back to reason.
He shouts a sharp cry of anger at Bijan and cries,
"Go away! You are a novice when it comes to weapons.
You are excessive in your recklessness and impatience.
The king entrusted me with banner, army, and glory.
I am the one with throne and diadem,
And not Bijan, son of Giv, or any other warrior."

Bijan draws his sword and strikes at the standard's pole,
Breaks it in two and grabs the upper portion,
Running off to reunite with his men.

Once the Turks see him coming with the flag,
A great number of men of lion heart, eager for battle,

Fling themselves at Bijan with mace and sword
To quarrel over the Kaaviani banner.

Hoomaan says to them, "It is precisely this purple
Banner that represents the strength of Iran.
If we succeed in seizing it,
We shall limit the world for their king."

Bijan binds his arrow like a mighty world hero
And showers the enemy with a line of shots,
Keeping them at a distance,
Preparing a feast for wolves.

The riders around Giv and Gostaham say,
"The moment has come to attack the Tooranian host
And to seize from them crown and throne,
But first we must await Bijan's arrival with the banner."

The brave Iranians advance, brandishing heavy mace,
And kill many rival cavaliers.
The illustrious Bijan charges as fierce as a lion,
Waving the Kaaviani banner, around which
The army gathers, the dust of their motions
Tinting the surface of the earth in shades of purple.
They shake themselves one more time
And take up the fight on the battlefield.

Rivniz,[48] as dear to Kaavoos as his own life,
Dies at the lead. He was a prince who wore the crown,
Youngest son of Fariborz and a favorite.
His crowned head rolls in the dust,
Causing many brave men to shred their garments.

Giv says in a loud voice, "O renowned heroes
And brave warlords, no one in our camp
Has been so dishonored as Rivniz, son of Fariborz.
The aged Kaavoos, in this land of misfortune,
Sadly loses a son and two grandsons:
Foorood, son of Siaavosh, and now Rivniz.
Never has the world witnessed a greater calamity.

◇◇◇◇◇◇◇◇◇◇◇◇◇
48 Rivniz: Different warrior from Tous's son-in-law who was killed by Foorood in an
earlier battle; this one is Kaavoos's grandson.

If we allow the crown of this young prince,
Full of pearls, rubies, and shining jewels,
To fall prey to our foe, we shall be covered in shame.
Yet, if I throw myself into the fray,
The ranks of Iranians will be defeated.
We must not abandon Riviniz's crown to the Turks,
For its loss would be an even greater indignity
Than the loss of its bearer, which weighs so heavily."

The noble leader Piran overhears Giv's words.
He leads his army to attack anew
In order to seize the illustrious crown.
On both sides, many a brave warrior's fortune dims.
Many Iranians succumb and fall to their demise.

The brave Bahraam springs like a lion
And attacks the Tooranians, spear in hand.
He grabs Rivniz's crown with the point of his spear
And sends both armies into a state of stupor.

The Iranians are beyond themselves with joy
At the sight of the young hero reclaiming the crown.
The battle turns more and more violent.
No one wishes to abandon his post.

The opponents fling themselves upon each other,
Striking heads well into the night, until darkness
Prevents them from making out more than shadows.
Only eight members of Goodarz's family survive.
All the others are sprawled lifeless on the battlefield.
Twenty-five members of the family of Giv,
All worthy of diadem and treasure, have been slain.
Seventy men from the race of Kaavoos have perished,
All able horsemen and valiant lions on the day of battle,
Although I have merely named the brave Rivniz.

Nine hundred relatives of Piran are deceased on this day.
Three hundred members of Afraasiyaab's family
Find their fortunes dimmed.
Still, Piran holds on to the battlefield and honor,
The star of his fortune shining bright upon the world.

The Iranians are left weak and dishonored.

Having aimed for a struggle, they stumble upon defeat.
They pull out of the battlefield,
Abandoning the wounded.

They return to the mountainside,
Hearts full of despair for their losses.
At the moment when fortune turns against them,
Gostaham's bounding horse falls to its death.
The hero retreats on foot, spear in hand,
With armor and helm, staggering like a drunken man.

Once night engulfs the fading light of day,
Bijan presents himself at the side of Gostaham
And says, "Climb up next to me.
No man is dearer to me than you are."
The two continue, saddled upon Bijan's charger.

The Iranians rush to take shelter on the mountainside.
The Tooranian riders, hearts brimming with joy
And free of grief, return to their camp full of pride
And ready to start the battle afresh.

In the Iranian camp, one hears only cries.
Ears turn deaf from the moans and plaints.
Men search the mountains for parents and allies,
Abandoning themselves to weeping and pain.

Such is the way of this ancient world.
One cannot escape the fate dictated by its rotations.
It looks upon no one with care and affection.
It may not make the distinction between friend and foe.
Upon this discovery, with his life on the decline,
Man may fear the rotations of the skies.

31 | Bahraam Returns to the Battlefield

The two armies rest. Part of the dark night passes.
Bahraam rushes to his father and says, "O noble,
Skillful father, the moment I picked up the crown
And raised it to the clouds on the tip of my spear,
I let drop a whip, which I fear

Will be seized by the evil Turks.
Bahraam will be a laughingstock,
And the world will dim before his eyes,
For my name is written on the whip's leather,
And the leader of the Turks will soon reach for it.
He will recognize my name,
Which will tarnish my honor.
I wish to leave right away to retrieve it,
No matter the cost.
I will not allow my unlucky star
To cover my name in shame."

The aged Goodarz replies,
"My son, such action is unwise.
Would you really risk your life, deliver yourself
To the enemy's wrath, for nothing more
Than a piece of wood wrapped in a leather strap?
We may yet have great need for your chivalry.
Why are you opting for a meandering course?"

Bahraam, the warrior, says,
"My life is no more precious than the lives
Of my parents and those who surround me.
One must die when the hour comes.
Why are you pondering over unwelcome thoughts?"

Giv says to him, "O dear brother, do not go there.
I possess many new whips.
I have one with a gold and silver handle,
Another encased in leather embroidered with jewels.
When Faranguis opened the doors to her treasures
And offered me weapons and belts,
I seized this whip, as well as the armor
That I wear and that belonged to Siaavosh.
I abandoned the rest in Tooran-Zamin
Because it was all worthless to me.
Kaavoos gave me yet another whip,
Inlaid with precious stones and shining like the moon.
I own five more ornate in gold and gems,
All quite worthy of a king. I offer you all seven.
But do not leave us to espouse a foolish mission."

Bahraam replies to Giv,
"I cannot judge as slight the shame that will ensue.
Your words are convincing, but my honor is at stake.
I shall retrieve my whip or else, in this venture,
I shall surrender my head to the blades of death."

Yazdan decides otherwise on the fate of Bahraam,
And the wheels of the dome work in opposition to him.
Once your fortune has surrendered to sleep,
Any effort to reawaken it is pointless.

Bahraam strikes his horse
And takes off for the battlefield,
Guided by the light of the moon.
He sheds bitter tears at the sight of the dead,
Whose fortunes have dimmed, bitter tears for Rivniz
As he stumbles across his slumped body,
The split armor sprawled in a pool of blood and muck.

Bahraam, the lion, bemoans,
"Alas, O brave young horseman, once dead,
A man of your stature is but a fistful of dust!
Your family dwells in a palace
While you are sprawled lifeless in a ditch."

One after another,
He finds his brothers dead on the plain.
He comes across an illustrious rider,
Wounded yet breathing.
Moaning, the rider asks Bahraam,
"What is your name?"

"I am Bahraam, O noble one.
Please tell me what you need."

The wounded man says, "O lion, I am still alive,
Although my body lies among the dead for three days,
Exhaling for bread and water and for a bed to lie on."

Bahraam rushes to him,
For he is his brother and friend.
He approaches him, laments, and sits beside him.
In great distress, he rips his tunic to dress the wound

And says to him, "Do not trouble yourself.
It is only a lesion, and your weakness is caused
By the fact that it has not been cleaned and dressed.
Now that I have taken care of it,
Return to the army, and you will be promptly cured."

In this way he takes the other on the road to safety
Without realizing that he is losing his way.

Then he says to the wounded man, "Young man,
Wait here until I return. I shall be quick.
I lost a whip on the field
While reaching for Rivniz's crown.
As soon as I find my whip, I shall leave with you
And return you without delay to the army camp."

They swiftly approach the site of battle.
Bahraam dismounts to search the debris until he finds,
In the midst of a pile of wounded warriors
His whip soiled in blood and brush.

He dismounts and reaches to seize it.
He hears the whinny of horses.
His charger senses his mother's presence.
Consumed like Aazargoshasp, it turns its head
Toward the mares and quickly departs.

Bahraam, astonished, attempts to run after it
Dressed in helmet and armor and soaking with sweat.
Once he reaches the steed, he seizes the reins
And bestrides it, Indian sword in hand.
He kicks his heels, but the horse does not budge.
Horseman and mount soon
Are covered in dirt and drenched in sweat.
In the end, Bahraam succumbs to such despair
That he knocks his horse down
With a blow of his sword,
Striking its head and instantly killing it.

He then returns on foot to the battlefield, swift as wind.
He finds the field, full of corpses, is the color of roses.
He marches on, searching for the wounded man.
He says, "What shall I do now

Without a horse to transport me?"

A few brave Turks observe him.
One hundred riders run from their camp
To capture him and to present him to their leader.

But the lion Bahraam binds his bow
And showers them with arrows,
Determined to resist as long as he has a shot
To place on the string in concern for his brother.
When a world hero affixes a warrior arrow to his bow,
Those around him are sure to disperse and flee.

He wounds and kills a great number of Turks,
Without the urge to yield or retreat,
Although he is on foot.

The riders return to Piran and tell him,
"There is a world warrior out there.
Though he is deprived of a mount and is on foot,
He is skilled and able to fight like a lion."

32 | Tajov Kills Bahraam

At Piran's side, the Tooranian troops
Recount the young man's deeds,
Speaking at length of his courage, of the battle,
And of various matters concerning him:
"A most valiant lion he is,
Tireless in fight, even on foot."

Piran asks, "Who is this man?
What is his name and rank among brave men?"

Someone replies, "His name is Bahraam,
Defeater of lions, a leader in whose presence
The army surrenders in trust."

Piran commands Rooeen, "Promptly take leave.
We cannot allow Bahraam to slip through our fingers.
If you succeed in capturing him alive,
The world will have respite from upheavals.

Take with you as many men as you may need,
For he is a renowned warrior, eager to fight."

Rooeen listens and immediately takes off,
His head full of irate thoughts for his adversary.

Bahraam perceives fresh troops approaching.
Protecting his head with his shield,
He readies his bow and loses a hail of shots
That pierce through the moon's rays.

At the sight of Rooeen struck by an arrow,
His soldiers appear to be at a loss of limbs.
They return to the world hero, weary, troubled,
Overcome by sadness, and say to Piran,
"Never has a man battled like Bahraam.
Never have we encountered so bold a whale."

Piran remains in a state of deep distress.
He shakes like a leaf, then climbs on his fervent horse
And takes off, followed by his warriors.
He approaches Bahraam and says to him,
"O illustrious hero, why are you fighting on foot?
When you escorted Siaavosh into Tooran-Zamin,
You were wise, aware, and reserved.
Once upon a time, you and I dined on bread and salt.
Sitting at the banquet together assured our friendship.
One must not toss into dust
The head of a highborn man.
With your family, essence, and courage,
With your countless skills,
It would be a shame to weep over your death.
Come, so that we may sanction a treaty
With an oath and with your heart's approval.
Then I shall seek an alliance with you,
And once you have entered into my family,
I shall make you a most influential man.
You cannot resist us alone and on foot.
Do not foolishly sacrifice your life."

Bahraam replies, "O discerning and brilliant warrior,
For three days, my lips have been sealed to food.
Yet I continue the battle day and night.

I only ask of you to be kind enough to provide me
With a horse to carry me to my noble friends
And to the aged Goodarz, son of Kashvaad,
Or else a fight will be an undeniable outcome."

Piran says to him, "O name-seeking warlord,
Do you not see how impossible that is?
What I propose to you is worthy of you.
You are a brave man, and you will not stupidly persist.
Will the riders of this army withstand humiliation?
Too many noblemen, princes, and warriors
Have suffered the wounds caused
By your arrows in this unexpected battle.
Which one of us will, from here on,
Cross the border into Iran
Without his head and blood turning to a simmer?
Yet, if I did not fear Afraasiyaab's wrath,
I would surely offer you a horse, dear young man,
To aid you in your return to world heroes."

Piran says this, then leaves,
Heart full of tenderness but head full of caution.
Near the camp, he comes across Tajov,
Strong as an elephant, who approaches him,
Set on vengeance, and asks Piran what he has done.

Piran replies, "Bahraam has no equal among men.
I have given him much advice in friendship.
I showed him the way, offered him a profitable treaty.
But my words did not affect him,
For he insists on returning to his Iranian troops."

The warring Tajov exclaims,
"Affection is not the right course of action!
I shall march against him,
And even if I must fight him on foot,
I shall soon enough plunge him into his grave."

Tajov runs in all haste to the battlefield,
Where he finds the hero Bahraam alone.
At the sight of Bahraam, spear in hand,
Tajov cries out like a drunken elephant,
"You have no chance of survival

In a fight contended by this glorious army.
You will yearn to return to Iran,
To rise once again to your past grandeur.
You have beheaded our famous leaders.
You must stay here, for your final hour has arrived."

He commands his men to attack Bahraam,
To strike him with arrow, javelin, spear, and mace.
A garrison of army leaders surrounds Bahraam,
Who grabs his bow and
Sends enough arrows to dim the world.

Once his shots are spent, he reaches for his spear,
And mount and plain turn to a sea of blood.
Once his spear is no more than a splinter,
He seizes sword and mace and sends a shower of blood,
Like a heavy crimson rain falling from a cloud.

In the middle of this struggle, the world hero is injured
Tajov, seeing him weak and wounded, is unable to resist.
He approaches Bahraam from behind
And strikes his shoulder with his sword.

The brave Bahraam falls face first into the dirt.
His arm cut off, unable to fight,
His fate comes to a brutal end.

Even his cruel enemy is overwhelmed with pity.
His cheek turns red like a sudden flame.
He moves his head away, distressed and ashamed,
And his blood simmers within his heart.

33 | Giv Executes Tajov

Once the shining sun begins its descent,
Giv worries about his brother's fate.
He says to Bijan, "My joy-spreading son,
My brother has not yet returned.
We must go and see what has happened to him,
For we wish not to weep over his passing."

They take the road like a whirlwind of dust.
They examine the wounded and the dead
On the battlefield, searching only for Bahraam.
In the end, they spot him and run toward him,
Shedding copious tears of blood,
For they find him sprawled in a brew of mud and blood,
Left with only one arm in a most desperate state.

Giv falls off his horse, hollering like a lion.
He sheds torrents of tears that drench Bahraam's face,
His heart inflamed, his eyes full of blood,
Such is the excess of his love.

His cries of grief awaken Bahraam who,
Upon gaining consciousness, reels on the ground.
He opens his eyes to see his body drenched in blood.
His heart full of anger and woe, he says to Giv,
"O glory seeker, after you place me inside my grave,
Cover my face with a shroud,
And then you may retaliate against Tajov,
For the bull cannot resist the lion.
Piran caught sight of me and did not seek to hurt me.
He treated me in good faith and amity.
Brave men from Chin did not attempt to harm me.
Only Tajov is guilty for acting with cruel injustice.
In an affront, he slighted my rank and my high birth."

At these words, Giv sheds tears of hatred and swears
By the World Master, by the white day and dark night,
To never remove from his head his Rumi helmet until
He is presented with the chance to avenge Bahraam.
Giv reclimbs quickly on his horse, heart full of pain
And vengeance, firmly grasping his Indian sword.

As night falls, Tajov appears, making the rounds.
The brave Giv sees him from afar,
Tugs at his horse's reins, and breathes
More evenly at the sight of his enemy alone.

Giv detaches his coiled noose from the saddle's hook
And at once captures Tajov's body inside its loop.
He drags him toward him, then swings, plucks him off
The saddle, heaves him despondently to the ground,

Climbs down his horse, and ties up his hands.

Then Giv bestrides his horse
And drags Tajov behind him like an inanimate object.

Tajov implores him, "O world hero, I am spent.
What have I done that out of this huge army
You have singled me out in the dark of night?"

Giv in response belts him on the head
Two hundred times with his whip and says to him,
"This is not an opportune time for you to speak.
Do you not know, you vile and miserable man,
That you planted a tree in the garden of vengeance,
A tree that will one day touch the firmament,
Its trunk filled with blood, and its fruit a dagger?
You sought as victim a man of Bahraam's stature,
But now you will instead have to contend
With the dark, narrow jaws of a whale."

Tajov now comprehends Bahraam's demise
And that Giv's heart is troubled by his death.
He replies, "You are an eagle, I am a lark.
I never wished to cause Bahraam harm.
He did not die at my hands.
When I arrived on the battleground,
Chini riders had already executed him."

Giv says to him, "O guilty man,
You are responsible for Bahraam's death.
No need for lies or useless words.
Retribution is mine."

Giv drags him toward Bahraam, the lion,
And says to him, "Here is this worthless man
To whom I dish out cruelty for cruelty.
I give thanks to the Creator, who gave me life,
For this very moment so that I may, before you,
Pluck out the dark soul of your evil enemy."

Tajov implores him, begging for mercy:
"Even if I were guilty of such an accusation,
What good is there in cutting off my head?"

He drops on the ground and says to Bahraam,
"O young warrior, allow me to be your slave,
Allow me to serve you,
And worship the guardian of your grave."

Bahraam, the bold, says to Giv,
"Whoever is born must die one day.
But just because Tajov hurt me
Does not mean he must drink the poison of death.
Do not cleave his guilty head.
He must live on to suffer."

Giv does not obey,
So sad is he for his brother's state.
He grabs Tajov by the beard
And proceeds to cut off his head.

Bahraam weeps blood tears at the works of destiny.
He screams, "Who has ever seen such a thing?
If I kill or if someone else is killed before me,
The deceased is either my brother or my relative!"
His voice trails off weakly as he breathes his last breath.

Such is the way of this world.
Anyone who yearns for glory and fame
Must wash his hands in blood.
If one kills another or if one is killed in pain,
Do not attach yourself to this world.

Once Giv completes the task,
He approaches Bahraam, the brave.
The valiant Giv howls in grief
At the sight of his departed brother.
He scatters black dust over his head.
He places Bahraam's body on Tajov's horse
And tells Bijan to take him and bury him.

Bijan hollers like a lion and sighs,
"Alas, O brave equestrian!"
He prepares a royal grave for Bahraam,
Fills his brain with musk and amber,
Places a cloth of Chini brocade around his body,
And, in the manner of kings, he sets him to rest

On an ivory throne and hangs a crown next to him.

They close the door to the gravesite in sorrow.
You would think that Bahraam had never existed.
The Iranian troops languish in mourning Bahraam
And the somber twists of his fortune.

34 | The Iranians Return to Kay Khosrow

As the shining sun climbs over the mountains
And the white light of day reveals itself,
The scattered troops congregate to tell their story:
"So many of our warriors have perished,
Our leader's good fortune has been overturned.
Since we have been defeated by the Turks,
We cannot remain here any longer.
We must present ourselves before the king,
Who will dictate our next course of action.
If his heart is set on peace,
You and I shall abstain from battle.

"Sons have lost fathers, and fathers have lost sons.
A great number of Iranians have died,
And the survivors live with broken hearts.
Yet, should the king command us to wage war again,
If he assembles a glorious army to that end,
We shall march off right away,
Breathing nothing but vengeance and conflict,
And we shall limit the earth for our enemies."

In this state of being, shedding copious tears
Over the thought of their fallen brothers,
They cross the border, sighing despondently,
Their hearts clamped in suffering,
Their tongues full of words of bereavement.
They take the direction of Kaasseh Rood,
Bidding farewell to the deceased.

A round of Turks emerges at the Iranian camp.
Finding it empty, they report to Piran
That the enemy host has withdrawn.

PART TEN

At the news, Piran quietly sends spies across the land.

Once assured that the renowned warriors have left,
Once his heart is relieved of doubt and worry,
He marches out with his host in the early morning hour
And inspects the camp to find innumerable tents
Of various sizes in mountain, valley, plain, and ravine.
He hands them over to his troops and keeps a number
For himself, confounded by the uncertainty of his fate.

At times, fortune takes us high; at times, it plunges us low.
At times, we are joyous; at times, most anxious.
We might as well sit with shining cup in hand.

Piran dispatches a camel to Afraasiyaab
With news that renders him happy
And frees him of pain and worry.

The entire army shares his joy.
Brave men raise pavilions on the road,
Cover terraces and doors in silk,
And scatter silver coins on the head of Piran.
In this way, he approaches the royal town.
Afraasiyaab marches out to meet him with a convoy
And praises him after blessing him:
"You truly have no equal among brave warriors!"

For two weeks, the sound of harp and song
Is heard in Afraasiyaab's palace.
At the start of the third week,
Piran joyfully returns home.

The king prepares so many presents for him
You would lose patience were I to enumerate them.
He offers him gold and gems worthy of a king,
Golden belts inlaid with jewels,
Taazian horses of golden bridle,
Indian sabers in golden sheaths,
A magnificent ivory throne detailed in precious wood,
A turquoise throne, a crown inlaid with rubies,
Chini slaves and Rumi ones holding turquoise cups
Filled with amber and musk.

He offers Piran these gifts and much more, saying,
"O great and glorious world warrior,
Surround yourself with wise men and be careful.
Preserve your army from an enemy ambush.
Send on all sides vigilant sentries,
For Kay Khosrow is now master of supremacy.
His justice and kindness make his empire flourish.
You have birth and power, throne and crown.
Do not ask for more. Do not trust the enemy,
For he has retired, and you must discover,
From time to time, his secret strategies.
Keep your eye on the provinces governed by Rostam,
Who will pounce on you at the moment of sleep.
He is the only man who causes me concern.
He only knows and breathes of vengeance.
I always harbor the fear that he will, one day,
Leave his home and invade the land of Tooran."

Piran accepts the king's advice as befits
The army leader, a relative of the king.
Then he departs with his escort to the border of Khotan,
Army and troops speeding joyously ahead.

The story of Foorood here comes to an end.
Now listen to the story of the war of Kaamoos.

PART ELEVEN

The Story of Kaamoos of Kushan[49]

1 | The Beginning of the Story

In the name of the Creator of Sun and Moon,
Whose glory reaches your heart by way of wisdom,
Creator of life and truth, expeller of lies and deceit,
Creator of Mars, Venus, and Sun,
My source of hope, happiness, and fear.

I have no clue how to celebrate,
And when I think of Yazdan, Creator of sky and earth,
My soul is crushed, for I witness divine existence
Inside the foot of an ant and in all the elements.
From the sphere of Sun to the dark earth,
In the air, in fire, in limpid water, everywhere,
I find proof of pure, divine revelation.

Should you have the desire to do so,
You are the only one with the ability
To seek a path leading to the Creator,
Who is above all necessity.
Yazdan demands neither chief nor minister, nor treasurer;
Neither crown nor throne, neither scarcity nor abundance,
Neither fortune nor misfortune.
As for us, we are mere slaves,
Prostrated before divine wish and command.

Since, without a doubt, the Creator is the One
Who created spirit and soul
And revealed the sky with its stars,
Do not assign to another the name of Yazdan,
Source of our joys and sorrows,
Creator of day and night, of the revolving dome of sky,
Of food, sleep, anger, and tenderness.

The celestial dome of speedy rotations
At times brings you joy, at times sorrow.
But in the midst of these changes,
There remains in the world happy stories of Rostam,
And each person's mind recalls his deeds.

Rostam is an example of courage in battle,
Of prudence, wisdom, and dignity,
An elephant on land and a whale in the water,
A wise man of vigilant mind,
A valiant and discerning warrior.

I shall recount his battle with Kaamoos
As told in an ancient book,
But I shall do so by means of my own words,
Borrowed from the writings of a poet bard.
Pay attention to what this worldly man once said.

2 | Kay Khosrow Condemns Tous

Fariborz, Tous, and Giv, vanquishers of armies,
Return from Tooran-Zamin along with their troops.
Overcome with sadness,
Their faces are drenched in tears.
On the path leading to Jaram, with Kalaat
In sight above and the waters of Mayam[50] below,
They halt to remember the battle of Foorood,
And a swelling wave of remorse seizes them
Along with a pang of immense pain.
They grow dim with worry and with fear of the king,
Their eyes wet with tears,
Their hearts trembling with guilt.

In such a state, they return to the royal court,
Shame-ridden, wounded, and repentant
Of the crime of having killed his innocent brother
And having ceded seal and crown to the enemy.
They present themselves before the king,
Hearts aflame and arms crossed in reverence.

Khosrow fires a furious glare their way,
For his heart's distress and his blood-drenched eyes.
He addresses Yazdan: "O Justice Giver,
You have blessed me with throne, fortune, and skill,
And now I appear before you exposed to shame.

◇◇◇◇◇◇◇◇◇◇◇◇◇
50 Mayam: Fictional river or sea.

But you know better than I the cause
For the turn of events and its dire outcome.
Without it, I would have planted
One thousand stakes in this land of worthless men,
And I would have hung from them
Tous and all those who fought with him.
I was eager to avenge my father,
My heart full of pain and passion.

"Now I find myself forced to avenge a new death,
The one of my brother Foorood.
I should seek to roll the head of Tous, son of Nozar,
Into the dust, for I had expressly commanded him
To stay away from Kalaat and Jaram,
Even if he were showered with silver coins and jewels.
I told him Foorood, a brave man of high birth,
Unaware of the identity of the wretched Tous,
Resided there with his mother.
How was Foorood to know the reason
Why such a large host was dispatched?
What would have kept him from descending
The mountain and engaging in battle,
Killing countless men?
Why did Tous, cowardly and foolishly,
Have to spring toward Foorood's fort?
Divine affection was turned away from them.
That is when the Creator abandoned him and his army.
That is when Tous brought misfortune
To the Goodarzian family.

"May he, his elephants, and his kettledrums be damned.
I gave him abundant presents and a wealth of advice,
Yet he left with the design to attack my brother.
May there never live another prince to bear
The slightest resemblance to Tous, son of Nozar!
May there never be a commander of equal nature!
Alas, Foorood, son of Siaavosh!
Even with his strength and courage,
With his skills, sword, and mace,
Innocent as he was, he was killed as was his father,
Put to death with his men by my army chief!
I know no one in the world more vile than Tous.

He is worthy of chain, ditch, and stake.
His head is devoid of brain, his body devoid of heart.
In my eye, the ignoble Tous has nothing over a dog."

The king continues to be distressed over the losses
Of his brother and of a father he longed to avenge.
A deep wound is lodged in his heart.
Blood flows from his lashes and streaks his cheeks.
Banishing his troops, he shuts entry to his court,
His heart torn apart at the memory of his brother.

Iran's noblemen depart in despair,
Taking the direction of Rostam's court,
Telling themselves, "This must be divine will.
Which one of us wished to battle Foorood?
Once the son of Tous fell
And then Rivniz, his son-in-law,
Anguish conquered the heads of our warriors.
Never has the world witnessed such misfortune.
Which one of us was familiar with the markings that
Distinguished Foorood, whose death afflicts the king?
May he intervene on our behalf.
The king is young, and he may yet renounce vengeance.
Was not Rivniz, the son of Kay Kaavoos, killed in battle?
Was he not a brave man, a favorite of the father,
Of our King Khosrow, whose face gleams like the moon?"

Such is the outcome of war: One finds in it a crown
And the other a casket, cramped and confined.

3 | Kay Khosrow Forgives the Iranians

Once the face of the world
Turns golden with the advent of dawn,
It is as if indigo night has fallen captive
To the noose of the sun.

A sound reverberates outside the palace gate.
Rostam presents himself at the king's feet
And says to him, "O glorious Kay Khosrow,
You are the pride and joy of seal, crown, and throne.

The shah is incensed at Tous and at the army.
May he grant them pardon, no matter their wrongdoing.
Once Tous caught sight of his son and son-in-law,
Both dead on the field,
Reason abandoned his heart and mind.
Consider it. He is a violent man,
Devoid of a sense of caution.
The life of a son is not of little value.
One must not be surprised to find him enraged
At the sight of two fallen warriors:
Rivniz and Zarasp, a most noble horseman.

"Besides, the king must not retaliate.
Consider it further. The army was of the belief
That your noble brother was at your majesty's side.
Know also that no one dies before his time.
Do not surrender your heart to remorse.
Whether life flies away on its own or whether
Enemy hands rip it out, it departs nonetheless,
With or without three hundred invocations."

Kay Khosrow replies, "O brave world hero,
My heart is consumed with grief
Over this young man's death.
But I shall allow it to heal with your advice."

Rostam steps forward and
Kisses the ground before the king.

Once the sun shoots darts toward the horizon,
Hastening its climb to expose its robes of turquoise blue
And to reveal its sphere of shining ruby,
Leader Tous, escorted by Giv and Iranian army chiefs,
Presents himself before the sovereign.

He kisses the ground, praises the king adoringly:
"May you prosper in happiness to the end of times!
May the earth be a servant to your throne and crown,
And the firmament the source
Of your glory and good fortune!
My heart is plagued by my deeds,
Crippled by pain and anguish.
My soul languishes in shame before his majesty,

Yet my tongue emits only appeals for forgiveness.
I am consumed by the blaze of remorse,
A blaze as fierce as Aazargoshasp, at the thought
Of the innocent Foorood and my dear Zarasp.
I alone must be blamed before the assembly.
I writhe before you at the mere thought of my actions.
My life is not worth a meager offering
Compared to that of Bahraam and Rivniz,
But if the king wishes to absolve me of my crimes
And forgive this innocent and glorious army,
I shall leave to avenge our shame,
Raise our humiliated heads to be proud again.
Reserve only for me the weariness of the army.
From here on, I shall be indifferent to my own life,
No longer yearn for throne and crown, and my head
Will accept no other headdress than a Rumi helmet."

The king rejoices at these words.
His heart renewed like a spring rose, he holds counsel
With Rostam and noblemen through the night.

Ultimately, Khosrow asks Tous to return to Tooran-Zamin
With horn and timpani, elephants and troops.
At night's end, everyone disperses,
And Rostam takes the road home.

4 | Kay Khosrow Sends Tous Back to Tooran-Zamin

Once the shining sun reappears over the horizon
To brighten the pale face of dawn, the world king
Approaches the leader Tous and the warriors.

Kay Khosrow says to them,
"The scars of vengeance do not heal and disappear,
And never shall we cease to speak of Toor and Salm,
Of the ancient struggle, of bygone days,
And of Manoochehr setting things right again.
But never has an Iranian king been covered in such shame.
Never has the world flooded with so much blood.
The mountain, strapped with a crimson belt,
Is colored in the blood of the sons of Goodarz.

Birds in the sky, fish in the sea mourn bitterly.
The entire land of Tooran-Zamin is spotted
With the heads and hands, feet and waists of our men.
But your new mission gives me joy, and my heart
Shudders with delight at the thought of vengeance."

The brave men, hands crossed at their chests,
Bend low to kiss the dust before the sun-faced king.
Present are Rohaam, Gorgeen, Goodarz, Khorraad, Tous,
Zangueh of Shaavaran, Bijan, Giv, and other warriors.
They say, "O auspicious King of lion heart,
You rend the hearts of lions
With your courage and power.
We stand before you as your slaves,
Heads lowered in reverence.
If your majesty orders us to fight,
We shall surrender our heads on the battlefield.
If the sun and moon do not withhold their faces,
You will have no cause to reproach any of us."

The world leader seats Giv on a noble throne,
Showers him with praise, gives him presents
And the marks of friendship, and says to him,
"You have tirelessly fought in service to your king,
And never have you received any part of my wealth.
The leader Tous must not send to battle timpani
And elephants without consulting you.
Did you witness the assault upon our troops
And the execution of the brave Bahraam?
May his soul rejoice.
Oftentimes, a man covered in glory
Views the world with aversion because of slander.
Though we may not live for long,
It is better for our names to live on than our disgrace."

The king distributes coins
And asks for prayers for the army.
The world hero is appeased to see the troops mobilized.
On a propitious day, he consults with astrologers
To determine the best time to advance.
The king gives Tous elephants, timpani,
And Kaaviani banner with his blessings,

In accordance with Kianian custom.

The sound of weapons is heard.
The earth shakes beneath the horses' hooves.
A black cloud of dust rises from the scuffle,
And trumpets blare.
The world, from end to end, turns purple
With the reflection of armor and Kaaviani banner.
You would think the sun has dipped into the ocean,
And the sky and stars have fallen sound asleep.

The king watches his troops parade before him.
Cushions of brocade embroidered in turquoise
Are placed upon an elephant, and, in a grand manner,
Tous advances all the way to the River Shahd.

5 | Piran Sends a Message to the Iranian Army

At the river's edge, Tous sends an envoy to Piran,
Mounted on a speedy dromedary, with a message:
"I am raising my head once again for battle.
I stand armed and ready at the edge of the River Shahd."

Piran is deeply aggrieved at the news.
With no other option, he dons armor and mail
And takes off with his renowned warriors,
A number of brave riders to whom he says,
"What sort of battle is Tous hoping to wage?
How many heroes are counted among his escort?"

Piran forms his army on the western bank of the river
And bids greetings to Tous who, on his side,
Brings forth troops, imperial banner,
Elephants, and kettledrums.

Piran dispatches a soft-spoken Turk
To speak on his behalf: "At every occasion,
I treated Faranguis and the shah with kindness.
I expelled a deep cry of anguish,
Consumed by grief like an ardent fire
At the sad twist of fate that befell Siaavosh.

But the tree that once held a shield of heat
Now presents us with nothing but poison
And retains for me nothing but pain and suffering.
Nine hundred brave warriors, renowned lion men,
Were killed in the process."

This approach only serves to further stoke Tous's anger,
And his expression clearly reflects his sentiment.
He says to the messenger,
"Return to the fortunate Piran and say to him,
        'If you tell the truth,
        Our quarrel will be inconsequential.
        Free yourself of the yoke you bear.
        Close the door of fear; block the path of evil.
        Present yourself without an army to the King of Iran.
        He will reward you with great deeds.
        He will give you a post of governance in our lands
        And set a royal diadem upon your head.
        Once he recalls all the good you have done,
        His heart will clench for the pain you have endured.'"

Giv, Goodarz, and the leaders confirm these promises.
The envoy listens to the reply and, swift as wind,
Approaches Piran, son of Viseh, to relay to him
What was said by Tous and the illustrious Goodarz.

Piran replies, "I shall praise the leader day and night.
I shall leave for Iran-Zamin with allies and relatives,
All those who have enough sense to hear me out,
For my head is worth more than throne and crown."

But these words do not conform with his schemes,
For he seeks only one goal,
And that is to regain his fortune.

6 | Afraasiyaab Sends an Army to Piran

At the hour of sleep, Piran sends to Afraasiyaab
A messenger riding a camel, and bids him to say,
"There comes, from the land of Iran,
A vast host, along with elephants and kettledrums.

It is led by Giv, Goodarz, Rohaam, and Tous.
I have told the latter many lies
And given him all sorts of misleading advice.
It is time to equip a host with our illustrious warriors,
For we must pluck out the Iranians, uproot them,
Devastate and consume their land with fire,
Or else this army and its king will never, ever
Relinquish the thought of avenging Siaavosh."

Afraasiyaab immediately gathers his army's leaders.
He tells them what is happening, bids them in haste
To prepare for war and depart for revenge.

Numerous troops collect,
And dust rises to obscure the sun.
On the tenth day, this vast host nears Piran,
Raising a cloud over the sun's glorious face.
Once the troops are rested, the balance is paid,
And the luggage loaded,
The riders climb on their horses.
Piran marches in haste to the river's edge
Without lending a thought to the peace treaty.

A guard approaches Tous to advise him to attach
Kettledrums to the backs of elephants.

Goodarz tells Tous, "O world hero, remember this:
Piran only resorts to lies and deceit
When he finds himself in the throes of danger.
The banner of the tyrant has been spotted,
And his troops form ranks on the river's banks."

Tous organizes his armed forces and,
Preceded by timpani, advances on the plain.
On each side a host approaches, large as a mountain.
On one side the Turk warriors,
On the other a mass of Iranians.

The sun is so enveloped in the dust of the infantry
That it seems as if a massive blaze emerges from the sea.

The right wing of the army is led by Bijan and Giv,
While the left wing is consigned to Rohaam.

The center ranks are assigned to Goodarz, Tous,
Gostaham, Shiddush, Farhaad, and Gorgeen,
With Bijan at the lead, fluttering standard in hand.

On the Tooranian side,
Farshidvard commands the right wing,
Hoomaan and Lahaak the left.
The entire plain is filled with a sea of steel.
Piran, son of Viseh, is at the center.

The sparks of swords, spears
And javelins project such reflections,
It is as if the land has sown tulips into the sky.

The movement of so many golden helmets
And golden belts, so many cavaliers of golden shields,
Stirs a cloud of dust the color of sandarac
Dimming the earth. The heads of brave men
Resound beneath the blows of heavy mace,
Like an anvil beneath a blacksmith's hammer.
The flow of blood gives the earth
The appearance of a wine shed.
Spears turn the air into a field of reeds.

Many a head is captured inside a noose's knot.
Many a noble warrior perishes,
His armor serving as his casket,
The blood-infused earth serving as his resting place.
Corpses that once enjoyed the delights of life
Are now ruptured and riddled by sharp blades.

The earth is red, the air black as ebony.
Sky and stars resound with the boom of war.

Whether the seeker wins the crown
Or whether he encounters only dust and battle blood,
Whether his lot is joy or whether it is poison,
I know not what the end will be.
All we can do is weep over unfulfilled dreams.

7 | Tous Fights Arjang

Their lives a mighty Tooranian called Arjang,
Who, in battle, has made for himself
A name that rises to the clouds.
He dashes forth in a flurry of dust
And provokes the Iranians to join in battle.

Commander Tous sees him from afar, shouts a cry,
And, drawing his sword, he says to him,
"What is your name?
Who are your allies among warring Turks?"

The other replies, "I am Arjang the brave, son of Zerreh.
In war, I am a formidable lion.
I hold my head up high,
Knowing when and how to stand by.
I shall make the earth tremble beneath your weight.
I shall fling your head off your corpse,
Toss it like a ball to make it roll on the battlefield."

The son of Zerreh concludes his boast.
The leader of Iran listens, and without bothering
To reply, he strikes him on the helmet
With his hand's shining sword.
You would think Arjang's body never held his head.

The Iranians sound the drums and bells,
And shout out, "Our leader Tous stands triumphant!"

Piran and the Tooranians look on in a state of distress.
The battlefield is abandoned, empty of combatants.
Tooranian warriors and leaders grab sword and mace.
These brave lions address each other,
The sound of their voices booming:
"Let us make every lasting effort!
Let us fight and narrow the world for Tous's heart!"

Hoomaan says to them, "Let us open hostilities.
Let us not be discouraged and shrink away at the sight
Of a famed Iranian emerging from the army to fight.
We shall send against him one of our men,

And we shall see, between the two,
Which one of them is doomed to face his end.
But let us not attack impulsively,
Rather express restraint.
Tomorrow when the army stirs,
When the drums are heard in the confines of tents,
Then we shall flaunt our maces, draw out our daggers,
Advance beyond the river, and,
With the aid of Yazdan and good fortune,
We shall together deliver a fierce battle."

8 | The Battle Between Hoomaan and Tous

Hoomaan climbs on his speedy horse, charging forth.
You would think he rides an iron steed
Or perhaps Mount Alborz braced in armor.
A shiny javelin clutched in his hand,
He emerges from the army to entice the Iranians.

The leader Tous springs up.
The world fills with the blare of trumpets
As he cries out, "From the despondent Viseh,
A cursed tree has grown in the garden of vengeance.
It produces nothing but bruised leaves and fruits,
Which hold no value before renowned men.
I shall uproot this tree, erase it from world history.
I have shown the strength of my arm to Arjang,
The most celebrated among your warriors.
Now you come to fight against me,
Mounted on your charger, grasping a javelin?
I swear on the soul and head of the master of Iran
That if I set aside my armor, mace, and Rumi helm,
If I attack you unarmed and defenseless,
Like a leopard stretches its claws upon its prey,
You will then witness a bold man
Perform the greatest feats on the battlefield."

Hoomaan replies,
"An excess of ambition incites bad luck.
Do not scorn others
Just because you killed one ill-fated man.

409

If Arjang were to battle with me,
He would not dare confront me.
The warriors of Iran have no shame.
Warm blood does not flow through their veins,
For they send their leader to war
While their hands are too feeble to fight.
Where are Bijan and Giv, noble warriors,
Goodarz, son of Kashvaad, world master?
If you consider yourself a world hero,
Why forsake your army's core to fight on your own?
Men of good sense will no longer recognize you,
And sages will refer to you as a stranger devoid of sense.
Go and pick up the Kaaviani banner.
An army leader, in his wisdom, knows better
Than to throw himself into the scuffle.

"Look and see to whom your king has offered gifts
And which among your brave men
Aspires to seal and crown.
Command them to fight like lions and to overcome
Those who, once upon a time, had conquered them.
If you die at my hands, your glorious host
Would find itself lost, deprived of strength and life.
Though they may continue to breathe,
They would feel as if all the troops had perished.
After Rostam, son of Zaal, son of Saam the rider,
I know no man more distinguished than you.
From fathers to sons, you are brave men and princes.
What need is there for an army?
If you wish to battle in person, then leave,
And may one of your brave, glory-seeking men
Present himself to contend with me.
If you still refuse to listen to my advice,
My soul and my heart are witness to my words.
Courageous men who challenge me
Will suffer greatly on the battlefield."

Tous says to him, "O noble man,
I am both army leader and warrior rider.
You are also a brave and noble man,
Though your affinity is with the land of Tooran.
Why show yourself on the battlefield?

410

PART ELEVEN

If you wish to follow my advice,
You would soon seek an alliance with me.
You would hastily travel to the King of Iran
With Piran, your illustrious warrior.
Never will my troops dismiss thoughts of vengeance
As long as one of yours remains alive.
It is to your advantage to abstain from engaging in war.

"Do not expedite the path to your death,
And do not act in a way that will force you
To recall my counsel once it is too late.
Allow the ones destined to perish
To partake in the scuffle, for not
A single guilty man will escape our vengeance.
Prepare yourself to act in accordance with reason.
The King of Iran advised me,
        'Piran must not suffer,
        For he was my guide in childhood.
        He is a man full of wisdom and my loyal friend.
        Do not align yourself with him in this unjust war,
        But try to force him to embrace your advice.'"

Hoomaan replies, "Just or unjust,
Once a king of noble lineage commands,
One must comply without hesitation.
One must absolutely forgo one's needs.
Piran himself does not wish to engage in war.
He is a man with a generous soul,
A noble and benevolent warrior."

While Tous speaks, Giv's face turns red as sandarac.
He exits the ranks, swift as wind,
And says, "O glorious Tous, what secret matter
Does this cunning Turk of spuming mouth discuss
With you in the midst of two hosts awaiting battle?
You must not converse with him unless it is with sword,
And you must refuse to accept a peace accord."

His fury mounting, Hoomaan says to the blessed Giv,
"May Goodarz, son of Kashvaad, perish!
May he be missed among the assembly of free men!
Not long ago, you witnessed my swordsman's skills.

411

Few are the ones from the race of Kashvaad
Who did not pay homage to the edge of my Indian blade.
Your fortune has turned as dark as the face of Ahriman.
Your home echoes with the long wails of the anguished:
Seventy-five men from your family have,
By my hand, either perished or been wounded.
You have seen how, during another battle,
I annihilated countless troops.
If I die at the hands of Tous,
The sound of bell and timpani will not be heard,
And the world will not suffer from my absence.
We must speak words of wisdom in this gathering,
For Piran and Afraasiyaab will survive,
And they will hastily come to avenge my death.
But if Tous succumbs beneath my blows,
No one will return to the land of Iran.
You should shed tears for the deaths of your brothers
Instead of holding quarrel with Tous, son of Nozar."

Giv replies, "O man of insignificant nature,
Why do you speak of past battles,
Ones that clearly show your lack of courage,
For you led a campaign for a night assault?
This does not reflect the feats of brave world heroes,
This is not the action of a battling lion.
You make no mention of Piran and Afraasiyaab.
You seemed to be asleep, always absent from war.
I am the one who crossed the border of Tooran-Zamin
With my merciless sword.
I am the one who led the king into Iran-Zamin.
I pierced Piran's ear with this very dagger.
Listen to what I have to say:
The king and I crossed the Jayhoon River.
In times of war, this is the way
The most courageous men display their skills.
This is the way of things, O suffering Turk.
If Tous allows me to fight against you,
You will witness the extent of my valor.
I shall toss you off your saddle of poplar wood
Into the dust in such a way
That you will never battle again."

Tous says, "Why are you ruining everything?
I am the one who wishes to fight with him.
I shall not allow him to stay alive one more day.
I shall spill his blood to flow over this vast plain.
Come, let us prepare for vengeance.
Let us frown and charge forward."

Hoomaan replies, "Death is our destiny,
Whether our head is covered with crown or with helm.
When one must die, better to do so on the battlefield
And at the hands of a brave horseman, a world hero,
An army leader, a man full of verve and spirit."

They both seize their heavy spears and attack each other.
The earth wheels beneath their feet. The day dims.
Such a cloud of dust rises above the battlefield
You would think night
Surprises them in the midst of day
And that the shining sun has vanished.

The shock of heavy spears makes them bend
Like a curved bow from Chaadj.
Their heads, struck by blows of mace,
Resound like the anvil of a blacksmith.
It is as if their skulls are made of solid stone.
The clash of metal sends shrieks into the sky,
And the squall caused by its motions
Whisks the waters of the River Shahd.
You would think death itself
Fears the gaze of these two heroes.

They reach for Indian swords,
And flames arise from iron and stone.
Sharp blades curve to the strength of the combatants
And break into splinters beneath the pounding.
Their throats dried out,
Their heads powdered with dust,
They seize each other by the belt,
Press against the stirrups with all their might,
But neither one allows the other to throw him down.

Hoomaan's belt is first to split;
He leaps onto a fresh horse.

Tous brings his hand to his quiver,
Reaches for the bowstring,
Adjusts an arrow of poplar wood to it.
He sends a shower of shots toward Hoomaan,
Attacking his riders left and right.

The metal tips and the eagle feathers on the lines
Darken the world as if two nights have fallen at once.
You would think the entire nation
Is enveloped in shimmering diamonds.

Tous strikes Hoomaan's horse
With an arrow of poplar wood.
The charger tumbles to the ground.
Hoomaan trembles like a quivering leaf and reflects,
"I feel as if my fortune has taken a sour turn."
He lifts his shield above to protect his head,
Thus exposing his face.

Once the brave men of Tooran's army see him on foot,
They fear his defeat and bring to him a noble steed.
Hoomaan sits on the saddle with his Indian sword.

Heroes full of courage surround Tous and say,
"The day turns to night. The time of battle is over."

The Iranian soldiers closer to Tous shout in great joy
As the blare of trumpets booms.
They praise Tous: "O chosen leader,
May your being ward off the evil eye!
May the end of this battle be for you a time of feast,
For today you delivered justice on the battlefield,
And the sight of you brings us such delight."

As Hoomaan withdraws from the arena
To present himself before Piran,
His troops ask him about the outcome of battle:
"O warrior, seeker of battle, tell us
What happened when you fought with Tous.
Our hearts remain in a state of grief.
Only the Creator is fully aware
Of the extent of our suffering."

The lion Hoomaan replies to the troops,
"O brave men, you have witnessed many a battle.
When the dark night makes way to light,
Victory will be ours, for the sun shining
Upon the world looks down on us with favor.
You will have cause to revel
As my lucky streak reawakens."

On his side, Tous lets his voice be heard loud
And clear through the night, until the rooster's cry.
Then he says, "Who is Hoomaan to resist me?
I am the rival of the fiercest lions!"

9 | The Second Battle of the Two Armies

The sublime dome of sky crafts its crown of lapis,
Scattering stars and the scent of night flowers
Across the blue firmament.
Sentinels are stationed before tent enclosures.

As the shining sun raises its head
From the house of Cancer
And the world is bright as a Rumi face,
One hears in both camps the beating of drums.
The world fills with the blare of trumpets.
The air clouds over in the reflection of banners
In hues of red, black, yellow, and mauve.

Warriors draw out their swords
And unfasten their maces,
Wrapping their steeds' reins around their palms.
You would think the sky, time, and space
Are braced in a robe of steel.
The radiant sun hides behind a veil of dust.
The sky, fearful of the clatter and the chaos
Produced by the stampede of whinnying horses
And the sound of timpani, appears to be
About to lower itself and sink into the earth.

Hoomaan prances before the army's ranks,
A glistening dagger clutched in his fist.

He says, "When I shout the war cry,
When I charge on my stallion and depart,
Simmering with impatience,
You will all draw out your swords
And protect your heads with your Chini shields.
Maintain your gazes on the manes
And reins of your steeds,
For I do not wish to have recourse to bow and arrow.
We shall make use of spear, sword, and heavy mace.
You shall distribute deadly blows
And perhaps at times receive them,
As it suits in a battle of courageous men.
Let us toss the bridles over the necks of our chargers."

Having thus spoken, Hoomaan, brave equestrian,
Runs like a fierce lion to his brother Piran
And says, "World warrior, open for me
The crates that hold your weighty armor.
Do not bind yourself to silver and treasure.
Do not be tightfisted with your weapons.
Should we return today victorious,
Our lucky star will delight your heart."

Piran, the leader, overjoyed at these words
Remembers the feats of ancient times.

On his side, Commander Tous arrays his army
To shine and glimmer like a rooster's eye.
Brave men bless him and acclaim him as world hero,
Saying, "On the day of battle,
You have been victorious.
Your courage has defeated Hoomaan."

The leader says to Goodarz, son of Kashvaad,
"We must reveal this secret to the world.
If our troops rush to battle, the evil riders will win.
They will raise their hands toward Yazdan in unison.
Let us renounce our positions of superiority
Unless the Creator lends us a hand.
Otherwise, our star will dim,
And our fate will turn sour.

Goodarz replies, "O world hero,

416

Why do you obscure our shining souls?
Do not speak thus,
Do not break our hearts with your words.
If the star of the king shines bright with good fortune,
What do we know of our enemies' victory?
The Giver of all that is good is on our side.
Kay Khosrow is our leader, heart, blade, and banner.
O world hero, do not trouble yourself.
Do not speak of these matters with our warriors."

Tous replies, "O skillful man,
Do you not perceive a looming war?
Furthermore, Hoomaan spoke to Piran
In his Tooranian language about how, tomorrow,
They will enjoy a great victory, how they will conquer
Our army, as a leopard conquers a ram.
We shall kill every one of them without mercy.
Noblemen of golden boots, lift the Kaaviani banner
But do not stray away from the mountain base,
For on this day, one must contain oneself,
And in this spot, one must act with extreme caution.
Moreover, for every one of us,
There are at least two hundred or more enemy troops."

Goodarz says, "If the Creator wishes to avert misfortune,
It is useless to speak of more or less numbers.
Do not trouble the heads and hearts of the Iranians.
If the turning sky, in its rotation, brings us adversity,
Our efforts to assure victory will have been in vain.
Organize your army for battle,
And abstain from tormenting yourself."

Tous activates his army,
Stations his war elephants, his men, and timpani.
He begins his march on foot to the mountainside
With infantrymen and baggage.

The leader Goodarz commands the army's right wing.
The troops form ranks as Rohaam and Gorgeen
Take their places at the head of the left wing.

The sky shakes with the sound of timpani and trumpets.
The heart of the celestial dome tears away,

417

And the mouth of the sun is choked by dust.

The plain disappears beneath the churning sand.
A shower of steel emerges from this dark, murky haze.
Helmets and swords flicker and flash with sparks.
The metal of spears and double-edged swords glows.
Above are the standards.
Below are the pounding heavy maces.
You would think the air is nothing but wood and steel,
And the earth nothing but hooves and armor.

Desert and field form a sea of blood.
The air is heavy as night with gloom.
Swords flare up like torches.
The moan of timpani and trumpets is such
That one could not extricate heads from feet.

Tous says to Goodarz,
"The rotation of the sky brings about darkness.
The astrologer told me at the passing
Of three parts of night, the swords of brave men
Will shed blood upon the battlefield
As profusely as a black cloud sheds rain.
I fear that in the end
Our combative enemy will be the victor."

Shiddush, Rohaam, Gostaham, and Giv,
Khorraad, Farhaad, and Borzeen the brave,
Heroic men and indomitable dragons,
Leave their positions to stand between the two hosts,
Heartbroken and eager for vengeance.
On every front, shouts rise to the sky
Like deev cries piercing the silence of the night.

On the other side, Hoomaan, as vast as a mountain,
Mobilizes his troops, faction by faction.

The time comes to select the fearless ones
And bring them onto the plain.
It is agreed that Goraazeh, head of Giv's family,
Will contest with Nahel,
Two noble warriors of lion hearts.
Rohaam, son of Goodarz, is to measure himself

Against Farshidvard, and Shiddush against Lahaak.
Bijan, son of Giv, is to fight Golbaad,
To stir up beneath their jolts fire and storm.
Two noble warriors, Giv the illustrious and Shitarakh,
Will joust, as will Goodarz with Piran.
Finally Tous and Hoomaan are to fight each other
Without the use of treachery or ruse.

After the selection is made, the blare of trumpets
Echoes menacingly throughout the field.
The brave men fall on each other,
Striking hard with their maces.

Numerous Iranians fall.
Corpses are sprawled on the ground
As their fortunes turn.

Hoomaan cries out, "Today's struggle
Must be different from yesterday's.
Put your lives in the palms of your hands,
And holler and strike with shouts of hatred.
We must free the earth from the grip of these opponents
And render them incapable to reengage in battle.
We must end this conflict once and for all."

Tous advances on foot with elephants and timpani.
The troops form a line before him,
Armed with shields, spear, and javelin.
Tous says to them, "Remain where you are.
Hold tight to shield and spear,
And we shall see how the brave chiefs of Tooran
Will handle their heavy mace in conflict.
Let us see how the revolving dome
Distributes its affection in this battle.
Let us see which side it will choose to steal away."

10 | The Tooranians Use Magic Spells to Overcome the Iranians

There lives among the Turks a man named Baazoor
Who exercises spells in various lands.
He has cultivated the art of cunning and sorcery,
And is articulate in both Pahlavi and Chini.

Piran says to him, "Go to the mountain crest,
Oppress the Iranians with snow, cold,
And a fierce, blustery wind."

The sorcerer climbs its heights and, all at once,
A snowstorm rises, a brutal blizzard
That paralyses the hands of the Iranians on their spears.
In the midst of the glacial winds,
They hear the cry of war
And feel a hail of shots rain down on them.

Piran takes advantage of seeing the enemy, frozen
And incapable of making a display of courage,
To command his host to proceed with an attack.

Hoomaan sends up a cry and, like a male deev,
Pounces with his troops upon the Iranian warriors.
They kill so many of them that a sea of blood
Seeps into the ground,
Deepening the line between the two hosts.
The plain and valley are covered in snow and blood.
Iranian riders are spread and scattered upon the ground.
The corpses are so numerous they constrict the field,
Leaving little room to trudge, to battle, or kill.

Tous and his brave men address their pleas to the sky:
"O Creator above all wisdom, knowledge, and thought,
You cannot be contained in a single place,
For You are everywhere, at all times,
We are each your slave, burdened with many sins.
In our distress, we beg for you to intercede.
You are above sorcery, You are World Owner
And Distributor of justice to just people.
You are the Savior of those who despair,

More powerful than the blazing fire or the bitter cold.
Save us from this glacial wind, for we know no one,
Besides you, able to come to our rescue."

A man of knowledge approaches Rohaam
And points to the mountain height
Where the brave Baazoor stands,
Where he practices magic and intones chants.

Rohaam whirls his horse away from the battlefield
And out of the army's ranks.
He clasps the panels of his coat of mail into his belt
And climbs on foot to the mountaintop.

The sorcerer sees him and rushes to fight him,
A solid mace of Chini steel in his hand.
Once by his side, Rohaam draws his vengeful
Sword of battle and cuts off Baazoor's hand.
At the same time, a tempestuous storm takes shape,
Like the one conjured up on the day of resurrection,
Which lifts the obscure clouds
And makes them dissipate from the sky.

The brave Rohaam, holding in his palm
The sorcerer's severed hand, descends the mountain
And, once back on the plain, climbs on his charger.
The air returns to its windless state,
With the sun shining and the sky a bright blue.
Having reached his noblemen, Rohaam raises his sword
And proceeds to cleave Baazoor's head.

Then he recounts to his father, Goodarz,
Baazoor's cunning tricks and spells,
And how he treated the Iranians on this day of battle.

The king's warriors then survey the battlefield,
A sea of blood, entirely covered with Iranian cadavers,
Bodies without heads, and heads without bodies.

Goodarz says to Tous,
"We have need for neither elephants nor kettledrums.
We must draw our swords and engage in an attack.
Whether we overcome or we perish,

Our end is imminent.
This is not a day where noose and arrow can serve us."

Tous replies, "O aged man full of experience,
The freezing breath of wind has ceased.
Why despair? Our Savior has restored vigor to us.
Do not direct this attack anew.
These brave men surrounding us will lead us in battle.
Do not advance for fear you will succumb,
Do not throw yourself impetuously at the enemy.
Hold yourself for some time, blue sword in hand,
In the army's center, near the Kaaviani banner.

"Giv and Bijan command the right wing,
Gostaham the left.
Rohaam, Shiddush, and Goraazeh,
Whose lips are spewing the foam of rage,
Will take their stands before the ranks.
If I fall on this battlefield,
You will return the army to the king.
I much prefer death to reproaches on the part
Of ill-intentioned men who threaten me on all fronts.
Such is this world: It ceaselessly dispenses pain.
As much as you can, try not to seek grandeur.
It may compensate you one day with all its favors,
But it will not prolong your existence, not for a minute.

The sound of trumpet and Indian bells is heard anew.
The roar of cavaliers eager for battle,
The lightning of swords and hammering of weapons,
The shock of mace, javelin, and arrows,
All make the earth throb and fold into a sea of tar.

The plain is a field of carnage,
Strewn with heads and severed arms.
The whack of mace echoes in everyone's ears.

The Iranians feel the star of their fortune dim.
They turn their backs on the enemy.
Tous, Goodarz, and the brave Giv, Shiddush, Bijan,
Rohaam the lion place their lives in the palms
Of their hands and move to the battlefront.
Brave warriors and governors fight fiercely against Tous.

They shed copious blood at the vanguard,
But those in the rear commit themselves to flight.
At this moment, a wise man calls Tous:
"There are no warriors left behind you.
Do not allow yourself to be surrounded.
Do not imperil the army with the loss of its leader."

Tous says to the brave Giv,
"Our troops have lost their minds.
They abandon us at the most critical time.
Go and lure them back by making them apprehend
The scorn of the enemy and the shame they will feel
Once they are in the presence of the king."

Giv leaves and returns with troops.
At the sight of the plain and dispersed corpses,
The commander says to his men,
"This is a battle and a struggle worthy of army leaders.
But the face of the earth is covered in darkness
As it takes on the appearance of a sea of blood.
We must then find a place of respite.
We must try to rest during this dark night
So that we have the chance to give our dead
A resting place of sand and a cover of dust."

11 | The Iranians Withdraw to Mount Hamaavan

The Iranians retreat from battle,
Heads covered in shame
And heartbroken by the loss of kin.

At the same moment, the moon reveals its face
Above the mountain, resembling a victorious king
Proudly seated on a turquoise throne.

In the Tooranian camp, the leader Piran
Summons his men and says,
"Not many enemy troops remain,
But as soon as the yellow ruby
Spills its waves over the horizon of lapis blue,
I shall kill every survivor with everything I have:

My power, my thoughts, my heroic skills.
Whoever is alive I shall destroy,
And render desolate the heart of the King of Iran."

The Tooranians return jubilant and sit before their tents
Where the sound of harp and lyre
Keeps them awake through the night.

The remaining half of the Iranians
Are plagued by sadness.
Fathers lament, shedding tears for departed sons.
The field is littered with bodies, wounded or dead,
The ground awash with the blood of mighty warlords.
So littered is the field of carnage
With a great many limbs, arms, legs, and feet,
That one can hardly find a way to pass through.

Throughout the night,
The Iranians care for the dead and wounded.
If they come across strangers,
They drop them and abandon them with contempt.
They light fires above the corpses,
Dress the injured and sew their wounds.

Among the members of Goodarz's family,
Some are hurt, others are dead,
And still others are held captive.

Informed of the fate of his kin, Goodarz hollers
A mournful cry that shatters the earth beneath.
The noblemen tear at their robes,
While Goodarz sprinkles dust upon his head.
He says, "Never has a man felt a more earnest grief!
Why should I survive, old and decrepit,
While my precious sons are lifeless upon the ground?
From the day I was born,
I have been vested in armor at all times.
My sons and grandsons have always escorted me in war,
Riding alongside world warriors and famed equestrians.

"Few men of my race survived
The first war against Tooran-Zamin,
For on the day of vengeance, I lost my son Bahraam,

His death dimming the bright light of our sun.
Now I witness a vast number of my children
Killed in the midst of this war.
Once Tous is made aware of Goodarz's dreadful losses,
His eyes will shed blood tears,
His cheeks will blush red as sandarac!"

He shouts a cry of anguish, and his breast floods
With blood tears as he continues to bemoan:
"If Nozar, the holy one, had not planted
The roots of my life in the orchard of existence,
I would not have to endure such hardships in war,
Such deep anguish, such grief, such persecution.
I would not be mourning over precious deceased.
From the moment I first strapped my belt,
My heart has ceaselessly bled,
Though I continue to lamentably exist.

"Now, cover the dead with dust in a hollow place
And set the severed heads beside the bodies.
Then, carry the loads to Mount Hamaavan.
We shall depart with the entire host
To pitch our tents on the mountain.
I shall expedite a messenger on camelback
To carry news of our failures to the king.
His heart will enflame, and he will quickly send us help.
I hope he will command Rostam, son of Zaal,
To take the road, escorted by a vast host."

Goodarz asks his troops to climb on horseback
And to load the luggage,
Continuously speaking of those who perished.
They gallop through the night
With thoughtful heads and scorching hearts.

12 | The Tooranians Surround Mount Hamaavan

As the brilliant sun reveals its crown
And begins to drizzle camphor on its throne of teak,
Tous has already traveled ten farsangs
While his enemy remains in a state of slumber.

425

He continues to stride, night and day, troubled,
Lips deprived of food, eyes filled with blood.

Approaching Mount Hamaavan, he halts the army
At the mountain's foot, consumed by fear and worry,
His heart as dark as a crow's raven plumage.
Commander Tous says to Giv,
"O wise man, brave and illustrious,
You march for three days without food or sleep.
Take care of yourself, nourish yourself and rest.
Restore order to your attire,
For I do not believe Piran is on our trail to resume battle.
Have Bijan take command of the troops least fatigued,
And take the road leading to the mountain."

Giv enters the mountain with the wounded,
Those weary of life and of the world.
He guides them to the castle,
Selects the least weary of them to guard,
And says to them, "Attempt to heal.
This mountaintop is now our dwelling."

Sentries are sent to the desert
To block passage to the enemy.
Such are the cries of sentinels,
Such is the sound of bells
That you might think mountain and boulder holler.

Once the sun appears above Mount Hamaavan,
The hearts of the Tooranian troops feel the urge to act.
A sound is heard from the camp of Piran.
It is as if the dust is violently tossing and turning.

The leader of Tooran brings his army to the battlefield,
Swift as a flame, and says to Hoomaan,
"Today's battle will not be long, for the riders of Iran
Are either dead, desponded, or wounded."

He asks for kettledrums,
Their sound reverberating throughout the plain.
He marches at the head of the army,
And once he and his soldiers arrive on the battlefield,
They find it covered with tents but deserted by the host.

A spy approaches Piran and says to him,
"One cannot find a single man from the Iranian army."

A cry of joy erupts among the ranks of Tooranians.
Then they sharpen their ears to the words of Piran,
Who says to these sensible warriors,
"Renowned and noble wise men, what do you say?
What do you advise now that the enemy has decamped?"

The army's cavaliers, young and old,
Reply crossly to the world hero,
"The enemy has fled before us, vanquished.
The battleground is caked with blood and dust.
This is not the time to fear the adversary.
We must follow its trail and take action.
Leaping into the water to escape the wind
Is a more worthy effort than to remain inactive."

Piran replies, "In war, the one who exercises patience
Exhausts the foot of the one who acts in haste.
The path and way of brave men
Is to conquer the lion with measured self-control.
Afraasiyaab has mustered an army vast as the sea.
Let us wait for this mighty host of valiant men.
Then we shall allow no one in Iran to remain alive.
This surely is wisdom's sound counsel."

Hoomaan responds, "O world hero,
Do not trouble the minds of our troops.
They are skilled riders and warriors
Who make use of noose, mace, and dagger.
The Iranians have left in the direction of their king,
Weak and wounded, weeping and wailing.
This vast enemy host, with once infinite might,
Has departed, leaving behind vacant tent enclosures.
They have withdrawn, cowardly, out of necessity.
We shall wait until they reach Khosrow
And organize fresh troops, at which point
Rostam will rush to engage in a clash with us.
His arrival will make us deplore any delay.
We must at once prepare an assault,
Cleverly devise tricks and strategies.

We can be sure to seize Goodarz and the leader Tous,
The imperial banner, elephants, and timpani.
Such a feat would, undoubtedly,
Be a wiser strategy than waiting here."

Piran praises his brother:
"May you be blessed with clarity and vigilance!
Do as inspired by your lucky star and good sense,
For your stature rises to the dome of sky."

The troops take off on the trail of the Iranian host.
Piran says to Lahaak, "Do not remain here.
Leave at once with two hundred cavaliers.
Maintain yourself strapped to find out
Where the Iranians have taken shelter."

Lahaak presses on, swift as wind,
Without lending a thought to food or rest.
Once half of the dark night elapses,
He perceives Iranian sentinels on the dark plain and,
Booming from the mountain,
The clatter of the army and the jingle of bells.
He does not sense prudence in pausing there.
He retraces his steps to recount to Piran the news:
"They have retreated to Mount Hamaavan.
They are guarding its access against a surprise assault."

Piran says to Hoomaan,
"Make good use of stirrup and bridle.
Take with you a number of warriors,
Brave and renowned cavaliers,
For the Iranians have taken shelter,
With army and banner, behind Mount Hamaavan.
A strenuous battle awaits us.
Reflect and design for us a way out.
If you are able to reach a solution
To seize the vile Kaaviani banner,
The light of the Iranians will turn a dark shade of purple.
If you are victorious, then proceed
To shred their banner with your sharp sword.
I shall follow your trail without delay."

Hoomaan selects, among Tooranian skilled horsemen,

Thirty thousand men armed with shield and sword.

Once the bright sun reveals its face
And spills its affection over the world,
Dust arises in the distance and sentinel shouts echo
As an army of Turks emerges out of a black cloud.

At the commotion, Tous dons his coat of mail.
Clarions and kettledrums resound, and a mass
Of Iranian riders form ranks at the mountain base.

At the sight of the sizable enemy host,
At the sight of its leaders wielding mace and sword,
Leaping and roaring like enraged lions,
At the sight of the Kaaviani banner,
Hoomaan says to Goodarz and Tous,
"You left Iran with elephants and kettledrums.
You vengefully invaded our cities.
You charged this land, occupied it with your troops.
Why then have you settled in the shade
Of a mountain like quivering wild deer?
Are you fearful of the brave warriors of Tooran?
Are you not blushing with shame?
Are you able to find food, sleep, and rest
In the shelter of rocks and boulders?
Tomorrow, once the sun rises above these heights,
I shall turn your entrenchments into a sea of blood.
I shall drag you from this lofty mountain,
Hands bound in the strap of my noose.
I shall take you to Afraasiyaab,
Deprived of food and sleep.
Your retreat will not spare you.
These boulders will make you shed copious tears."

He sends a camel-riding messenger to Piran in haste
And asks him to relay his message:
"This affair has a different outcome from the one
We envisioned when we thought at first of an attack.
The entire mountain is covered with spear and timpani.
Above Goodarz and Tous fly their respective banners.
Once the bright day breaks
And the star shining above appears,

429

Come to this very spot with an army ready to fight.
We shall darken with troops the surface of the field."

The messenger arrives at the side of Piran,
Who is touched by Hoomaan's words.
He leads his troops in the dark, at the hour of sleep,
And they march away, surging like ocean waves.

13 | Piran Pursues the Iranians

Once the sun wearies of its dark veil
And tears it open to reveal itself,
The leader arrives at Mount Hamaavan
And the world disappears beneath the dust of troops.

Piran says to Hoomaan, "Do not pass the battlefield.
Do not allow their army to advance.
I shall assess troops, elephants, and kettledrums.
I shall ask Tous, the chief commander of the Iranians,
Why he plants the Kaaviani banner here,
Who advised him to come to this mount,
And what thoughts and hopes he harbors in his mind."

He approaches the Iranian host, head full of hatred,
Heart full of ill intentions, and cries out,
"O famed Tous, master of elephants, mace, and timpani,
For five months you have sought the exertions of war.
Now the bravest men from the family of Goodarz
Are sprawled headless on the battlefield.
You resort to the fate of a mountain goat,
Prowling in search of shelter between two summits.
Your heart is filled with judgment,
Your head with enmity.
You have fled, and your army has followed you,
But you will not escape the trap we have set for you.
We shall behead you and thus avenge Foorood."

Tous replies, "I chuckle at your denigrations.
You are the one who spread hatred in the world
With the ruthless way you handled Siaavosh.
Have you no shame to utter words in vain?

I shall not fall into your snare
By conceding to your impassioned speech.
May world heroes of your kind
Never live among brave men of lucid minds!
You led Siaavosh to his end with your false promises.
You caused him to part with this world.
It is for you that he stayed in Tooran-Zamin.
Now, because of his demise,
The world falls prey to discord.

"Alas, this great and noble prince,
Whose face and figure filled mankind with joy!
Your weapons of war, your plots and lies
Have not the power to dazzle a levelheaded man.
You fight at times with sorcery, at times with spells.
Yet I shall overcome you in the end
And spill your blood. Being short of food,
I steered my army to Mount Hamaavan.
Now that the world king has been informed,
He will rush to our aid without delay.
His army's most impressive men,
The mighty Rostam and Zaal, have joined forces.
When the world king stirs to move,
There will remain in Tooran-Zamin neither grass nor dirt.
But since you are here, you will witness a genuine fight,
For today we deal with neither ploy nor ambush."

At these words, Piran sends troops everywhere
To occupy the roads leading to the mountain.
On all sides, Tooranian contingents advance
And take hold of the mountain base.

In this manner, Piran closes the road for the Iranians,
Blocking their access to food. For one week,
The Tooranians cinch their waists for revenge.

Hoomaan says to the bold Piran,
"We must take hold of the mountain base.
I shall deliver a battle that will undermine the Iranian
Host, restrain it from girding itself for vengeance."

Piran replies, "The wind is on our side.
Never has anyone sought

431

To fight with an onrushing wind.
Since we have blocked the troops from collecting food,
They will not last long among the boulders.
Brave men will disobey their leaders,
As their sight will dim and blur from deprivation.
One by one, they will come to implore us for protection.
After that, they will relinquish weapons and war.
It is for us to grant them peace and not for them
To assail us and organize in rank for battle.
No one will dare march into Tooran-Zamin,
And no one will remain joyous in Iran-Zamin.
Now is the time for us to settle a peace accord,
Not the time for battle and war."

14 | The Iranians Attack

Once they uncover the plot of the Tooranians,
Goodarz and Tous find themselves troubled.

The aged Goodarz says to Tous,
"Our only way out is to spend our last breath,
For it appears that battle is now inevitable.
Our supplies will last at the most for three days,
While no path is open for us to access more.
We have neither tent nor luggage,
Neither provisions nor food.
Soon our troops will be famished and demoralized.
So when the golden face of the sun
Makes way for the dark veil of night,
We must select brave equestrians
And rush from mountain to plain to wage war.
Let us surprise them with a night assault.
Let us fight with utmost valor
And find out on which side fortune shines.
Either we shall sacrifice our lives or we shall place
On our heads the coronet of celebrated victors.
Such is the outcome of every battle: One ends up
In a dark coffin while another attains fame and glory."

As Tous listens to Goodarz, his heart fills with affliction,
Reviving and stoking the flame of the ancient hatred.

PART ELEVEN

At the advent of night and the departure of the sun,
The world is steeped in darkness.
No one speaks.

Tous prepares for war and summons the warriors.
He commits to Bijan one of the army's wings
While the other is to be led by Shiddush and Khorraad.
He entrusts the auspicious banner to Gostaham,
Giving each of his warlords much counsel and advice.

Tous, along with Giv, Rohaam, and a number of riders,
Hoists his mace onto his shoulders
And takes the direction of the leader Piran's camp.
They fling themselves like a flame into the army's core.

Soon the entire plain surges as a sea of blood,
And a long wail rises from the ground.
The banner of the leader is cut in half.
The hearts of brave men are permeated with fear.

The army's tumult reaches Hoomaan's ears.
He quickly mounts his black Taazian steed,
Rushes forward, and sees countless fallen men
While many others have fled the scene in fright.

With the blood of his eyes running down his chest,
Hoomaan shouts to his troops:
"Were there no guards or sentinels?
Do your heads not harbor any thoughts of vengeance?
We number three hundred troops for every one of theirs.
You must not succumb to sleep on the battlefield.
We must not allow them to consider us helpless or weak.
We must not allow them to trick us in any way.
Do you not understand anything about war?
Who has ever seen a feeble enemy rise to victory?
Let us draw out iron spear and heavy mace,
Pierce our adversaries' eyes with arrows.
Be vigilant. Seize your swords.
Cover your heads with Chini shields.
Block the path to these proud warriors.
With the help of the rising moon,
Not one of them will escape us.
Do not waste any time. Go and suit up in armor."

The blare of trumpets is heard.
Brave warriors begin to stir.
The Iranian riders surround them like fierce lions.
Flares spark from swords and helmets
As if a shower of mace rained through the fog.
The night is dark, and the dust stirred up by the troops
Allows for neither a star to gleam nor the moon to shine.
The shields weigh heavy on them as they make their way
Through a veil of dust so dense it feels as if
They were swimming in a deep ocean of tar.

Hoomaan says to his men,
"Refrain from killing more soldiers.
Bring them to me captive.
Do not wound them with your arrows."

The troops cry out, "Now that we are desperate,
Do not advise us so needlessly.
Let us strike with mace and sword
To place crowns of blood on their heads."

Tous says to Giv and Rohaam,
"We have been bewitched.
If the Creator of the sublime dome
Does not remove this serious threat
From our bodies and our souls,
We shall find ourselves beneath the eagle's wing,
Or perhaps swept up
And drowned by a fierce ocean swell."

The three world heroes mount a common attack,
Like lions leaping in their wrath.
But on the Tooranian side, echoes are heard,
The sound of trumpets, timpani, and Indian bells.
One no longer distinguishes horses' reins and manes.
Such is the scuffle that eyes are blinded by spears.

Hoomaan shouts in a heavy voice,
"You have neither space to fight nor a way out.
Your misfortune forced you out of your camp,
Causing the ill-willed to be doomed."

Tous curses, "O man of evil race,

PART ELEVEN

With our small host we have killed many Tooranians.
We present ourselves here to lead a night attack.
Come and fight with us if you are able."

The three leaders remain on the battlefield
With some weak army splinters.
The name of the triumphant Rostam lingers on their lips.
They speak at length of Shiddush, Bijan, and Gostaham,
For they cannot discern
A single Iranian through the obscurity.
They cry out, "We came here to fight.
We foolishly flung ourselves inside the jaws of a whale.
Alas, what will become of the crown of the world king
If we are to be taken captive?
Rostam is in Zabolestan with Zaal,
And the strength of Iran will be destroyed."

At this time, one hears in the Iranian camp
The clang of mace and the blare of trumpets.
Tous and Giv delay their departure.
Gostaham and Shiddush the lion say to each other,
"The army chief has been missing for some time,
And the war is taking longer than needed."

Goraazeh says to Bijan,
"Our commander is taking too long."

The roll of timpani pierces through the obscurity.
The air is steeped in darkness,
The ground is as black as ebony.
The world heroes depart, using sound as their guide.
They find the field flooding with blood.

They retrieve their heavy maces and, letting go
Of the bridle, they stamp down on the stirrups.
They can barely see before them objects low or high.
The blows administered by warriors
And the sound of bells are so powerful
They would extract the whale from the deep sea.
Everyone is armed with mace and sword.

Hoomaan is soon aware of the riders' approach.
Tous also perceives that help is on the way.

He hollers and cries as loud as the sound of timpani.
Giv and Rohaam, like male lions, find their strength
In the boom of their commander's voice.

The scuffle is fierce until the dawning of the day.
Once the sun shines upon the world,
The heroes withdraw
And return the troops to mountain and rock.

Tous says to his warriors,
"From the rising sun until the hour of its descent,
The evil eye will remain at bay from those
Who are included in the race of noblemen.
May our struggle end up in feast and victory!
Never have I witnessed such acts of valor!
Never have warriors told me such heroic tales!
I pray to the Creator that no harm befalls the army.
I trust that we shall depart from here, hearts full of joy,
In the hopes that, by divine grace and without delay
An army will join us as swift as smoke.
We must write a letter to the king
To inform him of our glorious feats.
Upon receipt of my letter, Kay Khosrow's heart
Will be consumed with newborn passion.
Rostam, the warrior hero, will come to our aid
With an army of bold lions.
Then we shall return contented and triumphant,
Impatient to set our sights on Kay Khosrow.
I shall tell the victorious king all that has transpired,
Whether in the open or in secret.
With his grace, your fate will quench your desires."

Having renounced the fight,
The two armies take time to rest in their tents.
On both sides, they dispatch sentinels to the field,
Where heroes once displayed their skills.

Hoomaan visits the arena, where he has difficulty
Finding a path among the corpses and the waste.
He says to Piran, "Return to camp,
For today the battle did not end to our advantage.
But once my warriors, my noble chargers, and my troops

Have had time to rest, I shall engage in a battle
Such as sun and moon have never witnessed before."

After this speech, they take their leave,
Each to meditate on a strategy of a different sort.

15 | Kay Khosrow Receives News of His Army

Meanwhile, Kay Khosrow learns of Piran's victory
And Tous's retreat toward Mount Hamaavan,
How many brave men have perished,
And how the house of Goodarz, son of Kashvaad,
Has been deprived of its noble and free men.
The king learns that stars shed tears for their losses
And that, in the garden,
The rosebush no longer blooms;
That their deaths make the world
Swell with blood and dust, and, finally,
That Tous's powerful star has collapsed.

Kay Khosrow's noble heart is deeply moved.
He commands Rostam, of elephant stature,
To present himself at court with his assembly.

Warriors and glorious wise men from across Iran
Take off in the direction of Zabolestan to advise
The famous warlord to present himself before the king.

They speak to Rostam of the battle waged
By the Iranian army and say,
"O illustrious world hero,
May your heart remain forever joyous!
We have come on behalf of the king to take you to him.
O noble son of Zaal, prepare to travel to the royal court."

The auspicious Rostam says,
"I sacrifice my life for the king.
I am the devoted servant of his crown and throne!"
He then climbs atop the brilliant Rakhsh
And speeds to the court of Kay Khosrow.

Rostam ceremoniously kisses the ground
And praises the king.
Kay Khosrow addresses the war: "O highborn hero,
I fear that this ancient empire is doomed,
For my soul feels oppressed by so grave a misfortune.
You have sustained both throne and crown.
Providence, world mistress,
Draws its splendor from you.
The heart of the firmament is at the tip of your sword.
The dome of sky, space, and time submit to your rule.
You plucked out the heart and brain of the White Deev.
The world lays its hope at the foot of your compassion.
The earth is slave to the dust rising from the stirrings
Of Rakhsh, your most powerful stallion.
Time is, for you, a loving mother.
The sun retreats at the point of your sword.
Venus weeps at the sight of your arms and shoulders.
Your mace and your arrows' tips make the lion
Repent for his aggression on the day of misfortune.

"Since you set upon your head the manly headdress,
No adversary dares glare in the direction of Iran-Zamin.
But now Tous, Goodarz, and Giv, my army's leaders,
Along with many brave men under my dominion,
Have hearts full of blood and eyes full of tears.
They are fleeing before Afraasiyaab's warriors.
Many members of the Goodarzian family have perished,
Their place of rest being the dust of the battlefield.
Those who survived subsist on Mount Hamaavan,
Wounded, their faces turned toward the sky
And toward the Creator of time and space,
Yearning for you to liberate them on my order,
Aided by the power bestowed on you
By the mighty World Creator.

"It was nighttime when I read the letter,
And since then, my eyes have shed torrents of tears.
For three days I have spoken to no one of the matter
Except to Yazdan the Savior.
I am no longer able to constrain my anguish.
This misfortune exceeds all measure.
Any hope for the army's future rests on your person.

438

May your soul dwell in joy and your health be strong!
May your head retain its youth
And your heart live in peace!
May your body remain pure
And keep evil thoughts at bay!

"Demand the necessary actions of me.
Demand what you require in terms of horses,
Weapons, men, and treasure.
Depart, heart abounding with joy,
Mind solid with certainty, for one must not
Take lightly such a tremendous venture.
You must engage in war
As the Iranians are in a dire state.
No one ever thought we would be reduced to this:
With Tooran the arrow and Iran the target.
Now I can think of no one
Besides you who is able to untie these knots.
No one stands equal in power.
No one is better able to don your armor.
No one can withstand you in battle.
Only you are able to roll your foes' heads into the dust.
Your name alone triggers shudders of fear in everyone."

Rostam replies to the shah,
"May seal and crown never be deprived of your being,
For you are a glorious king, strong, wise, and just!
The dome of sky remembers not a ruler of your stature.
Kay Khosrow has indeed heard that,
Until Kay Ghobaad donned the Kianian crown,
I have stayed in Iran, girded for vengeance,
Without a single day's respite.
I never worried about desert, darkness,
Elephants, or lions, nor did I fear
Witchcraft, brave dragons, or bold fighters,
Whether they came from Tooran or Mazandaran.
I never concerned myself with the advent of night
Or the heavy blows of enemy mace.
I thirsted for long and arduous roads
With the promise of toils and weariness.
Having renounced all pleasure,
I suffered such distress, ran into

Such grave danger that never did I consider,
For a single day, spending a moment reveling in feast.
You are a young king of new path, and I stand
As your slave, belt cinched to obey your command.
May his majesty be consoled for the loss of the deceased!
May the cheeks of your adversaries pale in fear!
I shall go to the leader
And gird myself to avenge the Iranians.
My heart agonizes for the loss of the relatives of Goodarz.
The thought of them dead plunges me into mourning."

Once Kay Khosrow hears these words,
Torrents of tears stream down his cheeks
As he replies, "Without you I do not wish to live on.
I aspire for neither glory nor the Kianian throne.
May the sky be captured in your noose's knots!
May crowned heads remain in your powerful grip!
The world is your treasury
And your sword its treasurer
Heads of world leaders,
Though they may claim high status,
Are positioned well below you."

The royal treasurer brings the key to the treasury,
Containing dinars and wealth, crowns and jewels,
Headdresses, bows and arrows, nooses and belts.
He shatters the lids of silver containers
So that the King of Iran may distribute the lot to Rostam.
Kay Khosrow says, "Leave, swift as wind,
With celebrated Zaboli warlords
As well as bold, Kaboli mace-bearing men,
And do not stop on the way for anything.
Be vigilant, make use of wisdom, and stay the course.
Take with you thirty thousand sword-wielding men,
And select other worthy warriors as escort.
Give a contingent of troops to Fariborz,
Who is consumed by a desire for vengeance.
May he command the vanguard!"

Rostam kisses the ground and says to the king,
"Rein and stirrups are my companions.
I shall urge warriors to action and repudiate

Any thought given to rest and sleep."

Then he distributes silver to his troops
And takes the direction of the plain to prepare for war.

Rostam says to Fariborz, "Leave in the morning
With a division of the host that will form its vanguard.
Keep up a brisk pace, by day and by night,
Until you reach the leader Tous, to whom you will say,
    'Refrain from getting carried away
    And acting rashly out of passion.
    Pay heed to gain time, and do not stray.'
I shall take the road as swift as wind and without delay.
Gorgeen, son of Milaad, a trained man,
Will serve as my adviser in good and ill fortune."

16 | Fariborz Asks for the Hand of Faranguis

Fariborz says to Rostam,
"O giver of crowns, master of coat of mail,
Of mace and Rakhsh, I nurture within me
A desire I dare not mention to anyone but you.
O noblest world hero, worthy of seal, crown, and ring,
You are the army's support and shelter.
Because of your mace, warriors stand proudly.
O renowned warlord of Iran-Zamin,
Know that Yazdan praises you endlessly.
I am the noble Siaavosh's brother.
I am of his lineage, his essence, and his seed.
The woman who survived him is worthy of me.
If you wished to speak to the king on my behalf,
You would place a dazzling crown upon my head."

Rostam says to him, "Your command is mine,
And I shall secure this affair to your liking."

The mighty hero appears before Kay Khosrow:
"O glorious King, I have a request to ask of you.
If granted, my head will rise above the moon's sphere.
Should his majesty grant consent,
It will be a remarkable thing in the eyes of the Creator.

441

Everyone secures a share of your justice and affection.
You are as generous as the firmament itself.
There is no one among world princes
More celebrated than Fariborz, son of Kaavoos,
Who is from the lineage of free men.
He has no equal in valor, skill, or wisdom.
He has a wish that converts a brother into a supplicant.
May he prepare to battle for you
And to return to the Iranians.
He is the guardian of palace and treasury.
He desires to be united with Afraasiyaab's daughter,
In the way the moon unites with the sun."

King Khosrow listens to the words of the wise Rostam
And says: "O warrior, anyone who neglects to heed
Your advice will be trampled beneath destiny's feet.
Your words can only convey good luck.
May you live eternally in grace and glory!
You know that I have no power over Faranguis
And that she will not consent to what you ask.
But if she accepts to listen to me, I shall give her
Some guidance that her wisdom will receive."

Rostam and the king, full of benevolence,
Present themselves before the moon.
Khosrow says to his mother, "In all the world,
You are the only memory I retain of my father.
You are my shelter in good and ill fortune.
You are my ruler while I am merely your border guard.
You know the army's fate, its struggles and conflicts.
You know the number of Iranian warriors who have
Ceded their heads to vengeance in Tooran-Zamin.
I wish to send a host led by Rostam, son of Zaal.
Fariborz, a brave world hero, will stand at its vanguard.
Rostam wishes for you to take Fariborz as spouse.
What do you think? What is your command?
May power and joy be your companions!"

Her son's speech awaken in Faranguis
The sweet memory of bygone times.
Deep inside, she quivers with anguish and wrath.
In the end, she says, while shedding copious tears,

"I feel no resentment toward Rostam.
Even if I did, now would not be the time for it.
When Rostam has a wish,
Not even the sky will resist him."

The brave hero responds, "O Queen of Queens,
Your nature's purity is the object of every tribute.
May your enemy be kept at bay and perish!
Listen to my counsel and my last word of advice:
A woman is never insensitive to the love she inspires.
Which young woman receives coldly a young man,
Especially when he is of Kianian ancestry?
Men are created for women, and it is their position
To ask for their hand in marriage.
The victorious Fariborz, son of Kaavoos,
Is worthy of crown and throne.
He is equal to Siaavosh, his brother in lineage,
As they originate from the same seed.
Two parts of the land of Iran are under his rule,
Whether barren land or lush and populated land.
Upon the advice and wishes of the king,
He will make an agreeable companion for the moon.
What do you say? Will you agree?
Does Fariborz suit you as a mate?
You would do well to listen to me
And follow the orders of the king."

The Queen of Queens remains a long moment
In a state of embarrassment, unable to reply.
She continuously sighs in distress
And maintains silence in shame before her son.

In the end, she speaks to the mighty warrior hero,
"O highest, most able member of our assembly,
I have no free will, for it seems that your words,
O world hero, have tied up my tongue.
Although Fariborz does not have his equal in Iran,
One must submit to the command of the glorious king."
In this manner, the mother of the king consents,
Her cheeks shining like a rose in a newborn spring.

Rostam hurries to conclude the affair

And does not allow it to drag in length.
He calls a wise man to draw up an agreement,
According to form and protocol.
The world hero does not rest
Until the prince and the moon,
Fariborz and Faranguis,
Are joined to form a strong union.

In this way, Fariborz becomes a groom,
Grateful for the authority of Rostam and Kay Khosrow,
Who showers the hero with various honors,
A higher rank, a robe of distinction, and a crown.

Three days pass.
On the fourth day, the affair is concluded,
And Rostam, world hero, takes to the plain,
Marching to war with his bold soldiers.

Fariborz, with a corps of troops, travels ahead of him,
Shining like a star in the sky.

When the sun rises bright in the dome of blue,
Like a beautiful woman whose heart is filled with love,
The blare of trumpets rises on the plain.
Rostam sets his troops in motion.
The king, world master, heart full of worry,
Escorts him for the distance of two farsangs.

Rostam travels each day the distance of two,
Not stopping by day or by night.

17 | Tous Dreams of Siaavosh

One night, at the hour of the drumbeat,
Tous falls asleep with a troubled, wounded heart.
He has a dream, a vision of a shining candle
Rising out of the water, and next to this light
Is an ivory throne on which sits the pure Siaavosh
In vast splendor, wearing a crown on his head.
His lips curled in a smile,
His tongue whispering gentle words,

He turns his sun face toward Tous and says,
"Maintain the troops at their posts,
For you are to be victorious in battle.
There is no need to grieve for the Goodarzian family.
We dwell together in a spring garden, drinking
An endless supply of wine beneath the rosebushes."

Tous awakens in joy, heart free of pain and worry.
He says to Goodarz, "O noble warlord, I had a dream.
Know that Rostam will swiftly arrive at any moment."

He orders trumpets to be blared,
And his host shifts its position on the mountain.
Brave warriors from Iran-Zamin brace for battle,
Flaunting high in the air the Kaaviani banner.

On his side, Piran brings forth his army.
Dust blackens the face of the brilliant sun.
Warrior cries are heard.
A rain of arrows dazzles the sun's eye.
The two hosts remain thus, reluctant to initiate combat.

Hoomaan says to Piran, "Why are you slow to act?
We have not come here to hunt but to engage in war.
Bodies and horses are weighed down by thick armor."

Piran replies, "Do not be so impatient.
We need not act in haste. There is no cause for discord.
Last night three men, with a handful of troops, emerged.
They rushed into our camp like famished lions,
Springing, leaping from the side.
We appeared to them meek as a herd.
We found the entire plain flooding with blood,
Our most skilled and renowned men slain.
They are posted in a barren land with dried up bramble.
Their starving horses sniff the ground as if it were musk.
Wait until they wear themselves out on those rocks.
Once their resources are drained, they will perish.
Let us block the road out of their camp,
Either in the vanguard or at the back.
If we can seize our enemy without war or struggle,
A delay of one day or two is certainly advisable.

"Why should we then provoke a fight?
It will be enough to send ten of our greatest cavaliers
Into this desert field and remain quiet
Until there is a shortage of goods, of bread and water,
Reducing the enemy to being forced to plead for mercy.
Unless they are able to subsist on dirt, dust, and stone,
They will starve to death soon enough."

They retreat into their respective tents
And place sentinels along the army's front.
The heroes remove their belts to eat, rest, and sleep.

Tous also goes to his camp, heart bursting with blood,
Face black as ebony. He says to Goodarz,
"Our affairs have taken the wrong turn.
Iran's fortune is in grave danger of collapse.
We are surrounded by troops,
And our horses can find nothing
But thorns and weeds as a source of nourishment
The army is going to run out of supplies.
Our situation is so dire
That there remains only one way out:
To take hold of clubs and blades,
To draw our swords at daybreak,
And lead our troops into battle along the mountainside.
If our lucky stars favor us, we will be granted victory.
If the Master of sky forces us
To perish at the point of the blade,
We shall find ourselves powerless in the hands of fate.
Do not worry then foolishly.
I would rather die with a glorious name
Than to live in fear and dishonor."

The Iranians concur with the advice
Of their auspicious leader.

18 | Afraasiyaab Sends Aid to Piran

Once the sun displays its beams in the sign of Cancer,
Parting and shredding layers of obscurity,
One of the king's messengers bows before Piran:

446

PART ELEVEN

"There comes an immeasurable army,
Drawn from every side of the empire, an army that
On the day of battle will cover the Sea of Chin
With a layer of dust, converting it into a vast desert.
A brave leader has arrived from the opposite shore.
He has been greeted and praised highly by Afraasiyaab.
His body has the strength of one hundred lions.
He tramples beneath his feet the head of a war elephant.
He stands as tall as a cypress tree,
His face, beautiful as the moon.

"World conqueror, he is esteemed by crown and throne.
A highborn leader from Kushan named Kaamoos,
He will overcome and eradicate Goodarz and Tous.
He brings with him an army drawn from inhabited lands
Situated between the borders of Sepijaab and Rum.
He is under the command of the Emperor of Chin,
To whom the sky serves as crown and the earth as throne.
The brave, sword-wielding Kaamoos has come,
Whose eye has never witnessed defeat,
Who succeeds in his strange ventures,
And whose wrath summons storms and snows.
Furthermore, there is the warring Manshoor,
Whose solid blows smash the heads of contenders."

Piran addresses the Tooranian host:
"O warriors of the king,
You carry yourselves with pride and dignity!
May this royal message make young and old rejoice!
Banish from your hearts darkness and worry,
For I shall destroy all that exists and grows in Iran.
Afraasiyaab no longer fears revenge,
For we are prepared.
We lead campaigns full of fight and fatigue.
The lands and the waters of both Iran and Tooran
Will never see any other rule
But that of Afraasiyaab's will."

New army envoys continue to arrive at the side
Of the illustrious leader Piran, to whom they say,
"O noble warrior, may you live forever in clarity and joy!
May the sight of kings make your heart rejoice!

447

May your soul be free of impure thoughts!
From Kashmir to the edge of the River Shahd,
One detects only flags, troops, elephants, and howdahs.
From Saghlaab[51] arrives Kondor of lion heart,
The one who decides the outcome of war.
From Kaat[52] arrives Bivard,
To whom the sky is a battleground.
From the land of Sagsaar[53] rushes Ghorcheh,
And from India, Shangal, who fills the air with banners
And covers the earth with shining swords.
From Chaghan[54] comes Fartoos, the army's glory,
And from Kahan[55] comes Kahaar,
Destroyer of bold warriors.
The world renowned Shamiran from Shakni,
Spreads poison upon sword and spear.
Carry yourself tall, surrender to joy,
For this message brings ancient wisdom to a youth."

The heart and soul of Piran light up.
You would think he is resurrected from the dead.
He says to Hoomaan, "I shall go and meet this army.
These fighters come from afar,
Full of zeal and eager for battle.
Their status is not below that of Afraasiyaab,
For they are favored by fortune, wealth, and honor.
I shall evaluate their numbers
And the nature of their leader.
I shall welcome the Emperor of Chin
And kiss the ground before his throne.
I shall see the head of the proud Kaamoos,
Compare him to Shangal and Tous.
Upon my return, I shall pick up my weapons
To wipe out the Iranians,
To once and for all consume them in smoke.
If they cannot resist our attack,

◇◇◇◇◇◇◇◇◇◇◇◇◇◇

51 Saghlaab: Land between Bulgaria and Constantinople; perhaps land of the Slavic people before they moved north.
52 Kaat: Capital of Kharazm, or Chorasmia, in ancient times, situated in western central Asia by the Aral Sea.
53 Sagsaar: East of Afghanistan.
54 Chaghan or Chaghaniyan: Land independent of Iran-Zamin or Tooran-Zamin.
55 Kahan: Land independent of Iran-Zamin or Tooran-Zamin.

I shall render dark their day and constrict their world.
I shall burden the feet and neck
Of their leaders with chains,
Send them to Afraasiyaab as war prisoners,
And I shall not rest or sleep until the deed is complete.

"With my keen blade, I shall bring down the head
Of whoever falls captive into my hands.
Then I shall burn his body, throw his ashes to the wind,
Erase his name and memory from this land.
Next I shall divide my host into three army corps
And darken the day for the King of Iran.
The first army I shall send to Balkh, to afflict our enemy.
The second army will march against Zabolestan
And obliterate the land of Kabolestan.
The third host, Tooran's bravest men and lion warlords,
I shall send to Iran, sparing no living creature,
Neither woman nor child, neither young nor old.
They will demolish and devastate the entire land.
May the hands and footmarks of Iranians be gone!
Still, until I complete the preparations,
Restrain yourself from engaging in a fight with them."

Thus speaks Piran before he takes off, heart full of hatred.
You would think the skin cracks and falls off his body.

The brave Hoomaan reassures his troops:
"Let us keep an eye on Mount Hamaavan for two days,
To prevent the Iranians from fleeing by night.
Soon river bed, valley, plain, and road
Will be covered with army troops and banners."

19 | The Emperor of Chin Approaches Mount Hamaavan

Drawing near the army, Piran sees valleys and plains
Covered with the markings and tracks of horse's hooves.
He sees the world filled with pitched tents encircled
By a line of yellow, red, blue, and purple pavilions.
Planted in the center of the compound
Is a banner of Chini brocade.

He stands astonished at the sight,
Thoughts crowding his mind:
"Is this paradise or a camp?
Is this the sublime sky or the wheeling of the moon?"

He approaches the Emperor of Chin on foot
And kisses the ground at his feet.
As soon as the emperor sees Piran,
He kisses him in return,
Admires his large breast and the strength of his arm,
Receives him graciously, addresses questions to him,
And asks him to sit by him upon a throne.

He says to him, "May praise be, O world hero,
For I witness a healthy and happy warlord before me."
Then he asks, "Which Iranian army leader bears the seal
And which the crown on whom rests the hopes of men?
Who are the Iranian warriors and the noblemen,
And why have they settled on these mountains?"

Piran replies, "O benevolent chief and ruler,
May you always be clear-sighted and young of spirit!
May the grace of the Creator rest upon your being!
Your questions gladden the heart of an aged man,
As does the sight of your happy, healthy fortune.
My heart is content with just the dust beneath your feet.
I shall answer your questions concerning the Iranians.
Not one of them possesses seal, crown, and throne.
They do not count brave and powerful men in their midst.
They came here in vast numbers in search of battle.
In the end, all they found was a steep, barren boulder.
Once they realized that their venture had failed,
They took shelter on Mount Hamaavan.
Their leader, Tous, is a brave man who fears not
A struggle against a lion in the desert.
He commands warlords Goodarz, son of Kashvaad,
Giv, and Rohaam, noble warriors.
But by the fortune of our leader, the Emperor of Chin,
Our chief commander will see no other army.
They must come into the plain to engage in battle,
For they have nothing to consume but solid rocks."

The emperor says to him,
"Remain at my side and bring forth your friends.
Today we shall drink our fill of wine
Without spending time deliberating
Or worrying about the days to come."

He asks for a tent enclosure to be dressed and decked
Like a spring garden, its colors and paints so beautiful
One may confuse it for paradise.

20 | The Iranians Hold Counsel

Once the sun rises in the celestial vault,
The hearts of Tous and Goodarz grow anxious.

Tous asks, "Why are the Turks at peace today?
They are either holding counsel or drunk with wine.
But no matter what state, troubled or jovial,
My thoughts fill my heart with sorrow.
The reinforcements received by the Turks
Will portend the start of our ill-fated days.
Be certain that the Iranian army will be wiped out.
Even if spared, it will be forced to relinquish battle.
If Rostam shows up to fight, we shall be saved.
Otherwise the Tooranian host will destroy us.
Every one of us will end up dead, heads crushed
Beneath the horses' hooves, left to rot in the dust
Instead of the shelter of a tomb or funerary chamber."

Giv says to him, "O royal commander,
What happened to you to harbor such misgivings?
There is no reason to be low-spirited.
The World Creator works in our favor,
For we have always sown the seeds of righteousness.
Besides, thanks to the fortune of the king,
World master and master of sword, crown, and throne,
The World Creator will not abandon us
To fulfill the dreams and desires of our challengers.
Rostam's arrival on the battlefield
Will surely force our afflictions to dissipate.
No one must despair of Yazdan's aid, not even

When the darkest night takes over the brightest day.
Do not afflict yourself foolishly just because
The Turks hold off their assault for one day.
They cannot close to us the doors of the firmament.
Do not allow yourself to be beaten down
By the ill will of the enemy.
If the almighty's intention is to assail us with misfortune,
Neither fear nor needless worry will deter a bad lot.

"Let us dig a trench before our army,
As ordered by custom, by law, and by the rule of war.
Tomorrow we shall grant the entrenchment.
Then we shall draw our battle swords
And kill the enemy.
We shall discover their secret plan.
Meanwhile, we shall receive news from Iran,
And the branches of the noble cypress tree
Will stretch and grow to shine anew."

21 | Goodarz Learns of Rostam's Approach

The leader Goodarz leaves the crowd
And climbs to the mountain crest.
There he hears a sentinel's cry of distress:
"The brave men of Iran are lost!"

While the shining sun descends from the dome of sky
And abandons its face to sink into the west,
There comes from the east a dust that covers the world.
In a most obscure night, the dust and flags that flutter
Upon the backs of innumerable elephants
Condense the sun's light to the deepest shades of purple.

Goodarz hears the cry of the sentinel and says
To himself, "Besides the dark and somber earth,
I can count on no other as my companion."
His cheeks turn pitch black with worry, giving him
The appearance of having been struck by an arrow.
He further reflects, "The spin of providence
Has offered me nothing but the requital of battle.
The world has delivered a most brutal destiny,

Nurturing me with bitter poison.
I had an army of sons and grandsons,
Famous across nations. Now they have
Perished in the act of avenging Siaavosh.
Good fortune, once watching over me,
Has forsaken me.
My life on this earth appears hopeless.
In the bright day, my fortune has been obscured.
O how I wish my mother had never birthed me!
O how I wish the sublime dome of sky
Would cease to wheel over me!"

Then Goodarz turns to the sentinel:
"O man of piercing sight and awakened mind,
Look at the armies of Tooran and Iran
As they take a moment to rest from combat,
And tell me the position of the Iranian leader's banner.
Look at the troops to your left as well as to your right."

The sentinel replies,
"I do not see on either side the same movement.
Over here they move and act in haste,
While over there they appear
To be unmoving or fast asleep."

These words fill the world hero with dread.
He sheds venomous tears and says with a sigh,
"Saddle my horse!
Soon, you will give me a brick to rest
My head upon instead of a pillow.
I shall once more fill my eyes with the sight of my kin,
Hold in my arms brave and proud cavaliers,
Giv and Shiddush, Bijan and Rohaam.
I shall take leave of them, kiss their cheeks,
Bid them farewell, and shed copious tears."

Once his black steed of graceful mien is saddled,
The sentinel cries out, "O world hero, be joyful!
Forget your worries, your concerns, your suffering,
For I see, on the road from Iran,
A sort of black dust obscuring the sky.
Within it, numerous banners gleam bright as the moon.

First I see a flag with the figure of a wolf,
Then another purple one with the image of the moon.
A third banner pictures a dragon.
A fourth one portrays a golden lion."

Goodarz replies, "May you live long and happy!
May the evil eye never prey on you!
If your words are accurate,
I shall reward your news with so much wealth
That you will never want for anything.
Once we return to Iran, once we show our faces
Before the king, I shall escort you to his throne,
And I shall raise your head above the assembly.
Now for the love of me, leave your post,
Report to Iran's army chief what you have told me.
Go in haste, give an account to him,
And ask for guidance."

The sentinel says to him, "I must not vacate my post
To go to camp until the earth fills with darkness,
Until I can no longer perceive from high in my tower,
Then I shall rush off, fly as swift as Simorgh
To impart the news to the Iranian army chief."

The world hero replies, "Be careful, wise man.
Look once again from the high mountaintop,
And tell me when they will reach us."

The sentinel replies, "Tomorrow at dawn
This army will arrive at the base of Mount Hamaavan."

Goodarz is as happy to hear these words
As would a dead man about to be resuscitated.

On his side, Piran swiftly
Drives his troops to the battlefield.
A messenger, carrier of good news, rides ahead of him
And reports to Hoomaan all the deeds, great and small.

Hoomaan listens to him, smiles, and says,
"It looks as if fortune unites with us."

A cry of joy resounds from the Tooranian army

And rises over the battlefield up to the clouds.
The brave men of Iran hear it, hearts full of dread.
Their cheeks turn yellow, their lips pallid.

They disperse on the mountain
To convey their last wishes.
Everywhere one looks,
One sees men sobbing for their fate:
"Alas, brave men, sons of kings,
Forgotten in the land of Iran!
The lion's maw will be their burial shroud.
The earth will be awash with the blood of heroes."

Goodarz says to Bijan, son of Giv,
"Rise and go to find out your enemy's secret.
Climb to the top of this tall boulder
And observe the army's activities,
Assess the number of its troops,
And from which road they approach us
With such numerous tents, elephants, and thrones."

Bijan leaves the gathering
And climbs to the mountaintop.
There, in the distance, he discerns the vast host.
On every side are banners, riders, elephants, and troops.

He runs back to Goodarz, heart full of concern,
Mind troubled: "There are so many men and elephants
That the surface of the earth has darkened.
One sees countless banners and spears.
The sun in the sky is black with dust.
Should you attempt to estimate the size of this army,
No number would be accurate, so great it is.
The ear is rendered deaf by the sound of its drums."

Goodarz listens, heart wrenched,
Face drenched with tears.
Overwhelmed with anguish and concern for his troops,
He gathers the army chiefs and says to them,
"I see that my destiny only doles out the burden of battle.
It has often raised me high to then at once deject me,
But never have I suffered such deep anguish.
Now, although we have few men and weapons left,

There remains for us only one last option:
To prepare for war, engage tonight in an attack,
Flood the earth with a torrent of blood
As wide as the flows of the River Jayhoon.
If we fall in this battle,
Whether we are army leader or king,
No one will have cause to say
We perished without glory and like wretched cowards.
They will regard me as a man who has
Already been wrapped in the dust of earth."

The warlord's offer is shared by those present at camp.
But when the world is covered in a sea of pitch,
When Venus, Mars, and Mercury become invisible,
And the moon raises its head under the house of Pisces
To shred its nightly robe of ebony to its navel,
The sentinel rushes to Tous, his face the color of sandarac.
He cries out, "O army leader,
The king sends troops from Iran
I spotted a banner with the image
Of a dragon of sharp claws."

The leader smiles and says to his warriors,
"O virtuous men, when challenges become
Insurmountable, the World Creator
Somehow shows you a means of escape.
Since rescue is coming our way, we need not fight now.
There is a time for haste and a time to be slow to act.
The hero of elephantine stature is coming to our aid.
With divine will and the strength given
To him by Yazdan, we shall overcome the Turks,
And our names will be lifted
Higher than the sublime sun."

No longer do they speak of a night attack.
Leader and army are as happy as the sentinel
Who is rewarded for the good news by young and old.

Tous sends night guards to the field of battle.
The din of bells resounds throughout the mountain.
All through the night, the troops do not cease to speak
Of the world hero, rejoicing with renewed vigor for life.

22 | The Emperor of Chin Reviews the Iranian Host

Once the sun drives its procession of beams
Across the dome of sky, casting out dark night,
The Emperor of Chin holds a gathering
Of celebrated warriors of Tooran-Zamin.

He says to Piran, "Today, we shall not fight.
We shall pause and rest by day.
While these brave men and riders accustomed
To carnage get a respite from their exertions
After a long and arduous journey,
We shall go to see what fate binds the Iranians
And what they are up to in their camp."

Piran replies,
"The Emperor is a wise and glorious prince.
May his wishes guide his actions,
For he is the sole ruler of this vast army!"

Clamor is heard in every tent enclosure,
Along with the sound of trumpets and timpani.

The backs of elephants weigh down
With emerald-embroidered thrones,
With coverings of sky blue silk stitched in gold,
Golden stirrups, leopard skin covers, and silver bells.
The elephant drivers are decked out
In brilliant diadems, torques, and earrings.

The air gives one the sense of a Chinese bazaar,
So numerous are the red, yellow, and purple
Billowing silk banners.

A host takes the direction of the battlefield,
A grand procession worthy of a banquet.
In the midst of the noise and color,
The splendor and the elephants,
The sounds of trumpets and cymbals,
The earth is festooned like a rooster's eye.

Princes and convoy take off
As the wail of clarions fills the air.

Spears shine, and troops stir
To darken the surface of the earth.

Once Commander Tous discerns them from afar,
He commands his troops to form the line of battle.
Brave men from Iran-Zamin seize their weapons.
Giv brings forth the Kaaviani banner.
Masses of Iranians cover the land
From field to mountaintop.

Kaamoos, Manshoor, the Emperor of Chin,
Bivard, and Shangal, the prescient, approach
Mount Hamaavan to observe rather than to fight.
The emperor is stricken with admiration
At the sight of the distant ranks formed by the Iranians.
He cries out, "There comes an army
Of proud cavaliers eager for battle.
This is what you call a host.
The leader Piran had described them to me
In other terms, but one must not
Conceal the skills of brave warriors.
If the leader covers a ditch with undergrowth,
His horse will fall during the hunt.
It is far more valuable to confound the enemy
On battle day and trample its prowess into dust.
Never have I seen riders so highbred and so valiant.
Piran had told me that it was a small,
Insignificant host, one we did not even need
To consider on the battlefield."

He turns to Piran and asks, "What plan of attack
Shall we carry out on this field of vengeance?"

Piran replies, "You have traveled far
And suffered long and hard.
You have crossed mountains and valleys.
Wait here for three days and allow your army to rest.
We shall divide our host into two parts.
We shall then put an end to days of conflict and fear.
Half of the brave men, the glory of the world,
Will attack the enemy from dawn to midday.
They will fight with javelin, dagger, mace, and bow.

The next day, from midday to nightfall,
The other army half will engage in battle.
Then, in the middle of the night, I shall launch
Those who have rested to finish the Iranians.
As for me and my riders full of passion
And covered in armor,
We shall not enjoy a moment's rest."

Kaamoos replies,
"This is not a reasonable course of action.
I do not approve and prefer to act without delay.
Why should we wait with such a vast host
Before these hard boulders? Without waiting,
Let us arm ourselves and deliver battle.
Let us constrict mountain and valley for them.
Then we shall lead our troops to Iran-Zamin,
Allowing neither throne and crown nor king to remain.
We shall fight not like heroes but as ferocious lions,
And destroy people and land.
We shall spare no one, no woman, no child,
No man, young or old, no king,
No border guard or world hero.
We shall leave standing, in all of Iran, neither
Humble abode nor palace, nor four-legged creatures.
Why should we spend a single day in misgivings?
Only a foolish man would choose to waste his time.

"Guard the paths tonight so that the Iranians
Have no way to flee the battlefield.
Tomorrow, with the first breath of dawn,
Bring the entire army, ready to move, here.
Tomorrow you shall witness, on these very heights,
A hill of enemy cadavers so lofty that no Iranian
Will glance at it without shedding copious tears."

The emperor says to him, "There is no other option.
No one is more able to equip the troops than Kaamoos."

All the noblemen agree in a common voice and
Approve the decision of Kaamoos, lion vanquisher.
They return and spend the night forming army ranks.

23 | Fariborz Arrives at Mount Hamaavan

Once the sun encloses the azure vault of sky
In a ring of golden brocade, the cry of a sentinel echoes:
"O Commander Goodarz, I see troops drawing near.
The dust they raise darkens the day."

Goodarz leaps out of his seat,
Asks for his horse of speed, mounts it with alacrity,
And takes the direction of the dust,
Devouring the road in his heart's eagerness.
Upon approaching the army,
He distinguishes the banner of leader Fariborz
Flickering over the army's vanguard.
Goodarz has affection for this young prince.

He dismounts, as does the sage Fariborz,
Captain and expert in all manner of war.
They embrace, Goodarz sheds blood tears.

Fariborz says, "O wise leader,
You feel compelled to engage in relentless battle.
The blood of Siaavosh brings you misfortune.
Alas, these able riders from the family of Goodarz,
May you receive good news from them!
May your enemy's fortune diminish!
May the master of Sun and Moon be praised,
For I find you here, alive and well!"

Goodarz sheds blood tears for the fate of the deceased,
Now swaddled in a shroud of dirt.
He says to Fariborz,
"I am continuously struck by misfortune.
This battle leaves me with neither son nor grandson,
Neither army nor banner nor drum.
I do not wish to remember past wars,
For new feuds and dangers loom.
The host that occupies this field and these hills
Converts the face of the earth into a raven's plumage.
The vast number of Tous's troops appear next to it,
Like black hair on the fur of a white bull.
They have come from Chin, Saghlaab, India, and Rum,

From arid deserts as well as populated lands.
There remains not a single creature alive
Who is not cinched at the waist and armed against us.
As long as you do not reveal Rostam's whereabouts,
I shall bend over beneath the weight of these worries."

Fariborz replies, "Rostam journeys behind me
With only thoughts of war and vengeance.
He travels at night as well as during the day,
Not stopping on the road for anything.
Now where is a temporary camp to settle my escort?"

Goodarz asks, "What did Rostam say?
For his words always dictate the path to follow."

Fariborz says, "Wise man full of experience,
Rostam forbade us to fight and said to me,
'You will remain in camp, out of sight.
You will rest on the field
Until you perceive my banner.'"

Goodarz and Fariborz resume their march
And take with great speed the road of Hamaavan.

24 | Piran Holds Counsel With the Emperor of Chin

Once he spots the army of Fariborz from his tower,
The Tooranian sentinel rushes to Piran to warn him:
"Arm yourselves for battle,
For an Iranian host appears on the field,
Marching toward Mount Hamaavan."

The leader finds the Emperor of Chin and says to him,
"There comes an army from Iran-Zamin.
I know neither its strength nor its leader's name.
What shall we do?
What remedy is there for this ailment?"

Kaamoos, skilled warrior, says,
"May you always hold a place of honor!
You command noblemen from Afraasiyaab's court.

461

Your troops are as numerous as ocean waves.
You know what you have done during a period
Of five months with these troops, on this field,
Against a weak adversary.
But now that the earth is bestrewn with our forces,
Led by such chiefs as the emperor, Manshoor, and me,
You will witness our high deeds.
You have locked the door, but we bring you the key.
Even if the brave warriors of Kabol, Zabol,
And the border of India make
The surface of earth gleam with colors,
They are powerless before my force and my skills.
You would not even need to know who the Iranians are.

"You panic at the mention of the famed Rostam,
But he is the first one I shall seek to crush.
Once I capture his head in my noose,
I shall expunge his name from the surface of the world.
You fear the army of Sistan, and your heart
Wrenches at the thought of having to fight against it.
But the force of my hand will make
Dust fly on the battlefield.
Then you will know the true meaning of a brave man.
You will witness heroic warriors in action.
You will sense how to engage in an impressive battle."

Piran replies to him, "May you always live in joy!
May your being keep misfortune's hand at bay!
May all your wishes be fulfilled!
May you never have to face your equal!"

The Emperor of Chin says to Piran,
"You have authorized Kaamoos to lead the attack.
He will act as he pledged, for he is a mountain's friend
And an elephant's companion.
The Iranians are not so mighty as they appear.
Do not instill fear in the hearts of brave men.
I shall not allow to survive a single Iranian chief.
I shall convert mountain and plain to barren land,
Send to Afraasiyaab all brave and powerful men
Loaded with heavy thrones.
I shall shackle their feet and cut off their heads.

There will remain in the land of Iran neither leaf nor tree,
Neither palace nor shah, neither crown nor throne."

Piran smiles and praises the assembled men of name,
As well as the Emperor of Chin.
He returns joyous to camp, where Tooranian heroes
Such as Hoomaan, Lahaak, Farshidvard, and others,
Lions on the day of battle, press around him to say,
"There comes an army from Iran,
Headed by a leader wielding a black banner.
One of our spies, an illustrious warrior,
Reported that it is Fariborz, son of Kaavoos,
A horseman full of pride, loyal to Kay Khosrow."

Piran says to the brave Hoomaan,
"There is no cause for worry since it is not Rostam.
We have nothing to fear from Fariborz,
Whose breath is not an antidote to poison.
Although Kaamoos, who wishes to view Rostam
As little threat on the day of battle,
Is as brave as a whale, my greatest hope
Is that Rostam abstains from pursuing war."

Hoomaan says to him, "O world hero,
Why trouble your mind with needless concerns?
This is not Rostam, it is not the army of Sistan,
And Fariborz will do more than shed abundant blood
In his hunt for a casket of dust."

Piran replies, "I have renounced throne and crown.
I have taken my fill of the light of sun and moon.
Now I despair to learn that an army of Iranians
Approaches and arrives on the battlefield.
My soul and mind are filled with worry,
And my heart expels a deep, cold sigh."

Golbaad says to him, "Why afflict yourself?
Why sob in fear of Tous and Rostam?
We have so many javelins and swords,
War elephants and troops, not even
The wind can pave a path through the mass.
What are the Iranians before us but a handful of dust?
Why fear Khosrow, Tous, and Rostam?

They have run off from here, to retire inside their tents."

On the other side, when Tous learns
That the land resounds with the sound of timpani,
That the hero of elephantine stature and Fariborz,
Son of Kaavoos, arrive from Iran with an escort,
He orders kettledrums be placed on elephant backs.
The mountain is covered with the black dust
Raised by the army.

Mount Hamaavan echoes with shouts.
The earth shakes beneath the trampling of horses.
The leader recounts at length to the Iranians
Rostam's feats in the war against Mazandaran
And his victories in the struggle against the deevs.

The brave men praise the world hero and say,
"May your heart remain vigilant and your mind serene!
Should you trade our lives for the price
Of your good news, we shall give it to you freely,
For it fills our hearts with joy.
Now that Rostam comes to our aid,
This army will not resist the whale.
We shall fight with all our might to erase
The shame weighing heavy on our hearts.
We shall risk our lives in a fierce struggle.
We shall seize the emperor's banner and crown,
Golden shields, golden belts, and ivory throne,
Golden torques, diadems of gold of elephant drivers,
Golden bells never seen in the world,
Parasol of peacock feathers inlaid with precious stones,
And many other items of wealth.
We shall fight to the death and capture everything
With great effort and strength."

The prudent Tous says to the troops, "On one hand,
We are plagued with fear, on the other with scorn.
The mountain base is brewing with warriors,
And our noblemen's heads are captured in the noose.
When Rostam arrives, he will blame us
Without bothering to enquire as to what happened.
He will say,

'You act as a wounded bird caught in a trap.
Whatever action you have taken is wrong.
Our leader and our army is the same,
Yet I do not see anyone advancing to fight.'
Now that Rostam is on his way,
Let us wash our shame away and renew our names.
Let us lead an assault like lions and chase them away."

The troops reply, "Do not be too ambitious.
Do not speak in this manner.
None of us will climb down this mountain
Unless Rostam arrives and commands us to.
We shall prostrate ourselves before the Creator,
Who is our guide on the path to joy.
By the order of the Master of Sun and Moon,
Rostam will appear on this battlefield.
Why do you despair of your lucky star?
Go ahead and distribute gold and silver to the poor."

The army's brave men shout cries of joy
Upon the mountain heights.
They cheerfully retreat to their camp,
Where they hold counsel the entire night.

25 | The Battle of Giv and Tous Against Kaamoos

Once the sun rests its fingers
On the ribs of the bull holding up the world[56]
And the lark's song rises above the desert,
A cry emerges from Kaamoos's tent,
For he is voracious for carnage
And eager to lead the way.
He assembles his troops, handing out breastplates,
His heart full of ardor, his head full of pride.

He wears a coat of mail in place of a robe,
A helmet in place of a diadem,
Armor in place of a tunic.
He selects among brave men

◇◇◇◇◇◇◇◇◇◇◇◇◇
56 Bull: Refers to the sign of Taurus, second month of spring.

A number of them decked in brocade and steel.
One can no longer discern a path
From one sea to the other due to the dust
And the forest of countless swords and shields.

The shout of the sentry warns the Tooranians
That an army approaches,
And the banner of the leader of elephant stature
Is spotted at the head of the troops.

On one side, the Tooranian host
Renders the air black as a storm cloud.
Its leader, on horseback, strong as a massive boulder,
Makes the earth shake beneath his horse's hooves.
The head of his mace is as wide as a buffalo's head.
He is preceded by riders armed with spears,
And his massive host trails behind him.
His mace, leaning against his arm and shoulder,
Appears to be searing with impatience,
His demeanor inspires one into stupor.

On the other side, the Iranian commander, Tous,
Makes the sky resound with the din of timpani.
Once he hears the cry of the sentry,
He walks in joy toward Goodarz, son of Kashvaad.
Then he sends a rider to Fariborz with a message:
"The Tooranian host advances to engage in battle.
They have formed their lines and are closing in on us.
We must not allow them to fling themselves upon us
In great numbers and destroy us by isolation.
Act in a manner that suits a man of your origins,
For you are a prince, and your father was king.
The dust rising from Rostam is visible on the road.
He will soon arrive on the battlefield."

Fariborz combines his host of bold warriors
With the hosts of Tous and Giv.
They organize their troops on the mountain heights
And adorn their sacred banners.
Once the two wings form in line and reserve soldiers,
Army core, and provisions are in place, trumpets blare,
And the host falls into motion like the starry sky.

Kaamoos, in his camp, seeing the enemy presence,
Does not stop for an instant on the plain.
He sets his troops in motion like a cascade rushing
From mountaintop to river and leads it to Hamaavan.
The air darkens, and
The earth disappears beneath the mass.

Kaamoos, approaching the Iranians,
Raises his head toward the mountain
And says to them with a smile,
"Up until now, you faced a weak opponent.
But instead of Piran, Hoomaan, and their troops,
You will soon confront a most fervent army
Led by a most zealous, fearless commander.
Who do you have in the Iranian host,
An eager warrior, to match against me?
You are about to witness my chest, arms, and stature,
My sharp sword and my mace."

At these words, Giv springs up in fury,
Draws out his sword, approaches Kaamoos, and says,
"Only a mad elephant is equal to this man."
He withdraws his arrow from its case and binds it.
He invokes the help of the Creator, Giver of joy,
And sends toward Kaamoos
A deluge of shots slung by his bow,
Like a spring cloud dropping a heavy rain.

Kaamoos protects his head with his shield
Against the force and skill of the enemy hand.
He advances through the hail of shots
Thickening the sky, a rhinoceros scrambling
Around bodies strewn on the field.
The air fills with dust and the ground with death.

Once in reach of his rival,
Kaamoos strikes him at the belt with his spear.
The force of the blow of the steel tip makes Giv
Lose his balance, and his feet slip out of the stirrups.
Yet he quickly draws out his sword from its sheath,
Hollers a shout, proclaims his name,
Flings himself madly upon the cavalier,

And, with his sword, splits his spear in two.

From the army core, Tous observes with concern.
He knows that Giv is weak next to Kaamoos
And that the latter has, in the handling of spear,
No other rival than Tous himself.
He deserts his post with a great holler, rushing
To take part in the skirmish and come to Giv's aid.

Kaamoos tightens his grip on the reins
And hurls himself between the two warriors.
He strikes the neck of Tous's horse with his blade,
Causing Tous's face to turn the color of ebony.
His horse staggers and falls to the ground.
The commander rises like a powerful lion,
Marching on foot toward the army's front line.

Two noble heroes clash against a single cavalier,
Yet the brave men from Kushan do not despair.
They fill the land with the uproar of battle
Until darkness arrives to take the place of sun.

As the shadows of night descend upon the field,
Kaamoos and Tous break apart.
The two hosts return to their respective camps.
One warrior enters his tent on the plain.
The other two trek to the mountain.

26 | Rostam Unites With the Iranians

Once the sun and moon exit the dome of sky,
Two hosts dispatch patrols to guard through the night.

An Iranian sentinel shouts from the tower:
"The desert is full of dust like a gloomy night.
The field and valley resound with the boom of chaos,
And I see torches burning in the midst of warriors.
It is the hero of elephantine stature
Who charges forth with an army from Zabolestan."

Goodarz, son of Kashvaad, hears these words

And, in the obscurity, climbs down the rocky mountain.
Soon he perceives the standard sporting the face
Of the dragon, which, despite the obscurity,
Spreads a purple glint upon the world.
His eyes make out Rostam's mien,
And tears flood his cheeks.

Goodarz and Rostam dismount and run to each other.
They embrace and kiss, and the two cry in grief
Over the deaths of Goodarz's noble sons,
Fallen in this war of vengeance.

Goodarz says to Rostam, "Wise and brave world hero,
The crown and throne borrow their splendor
From you and from your exploits.
Your words are always full of truth and wisdom.
You are, for the Iranians, more than father and mother,
More than throne and crown, gem and treasure.
You are higher and better than all of these.
Without you, we have neither head nor nobility.
You stand tall as the champion of world warriors,
Mightier than the strongest elephants and lions.
In your absence, we are fish without water,
Our heads dazed, our bodies encased in tombs.
We cherish you more than our own arms and eyes,
For you are more noble than the noblest men.
When I observe your gallant countenance,
When I hear your kind and benevolent questions,
I forget to mourn my glorious offspring.
Thanks to your good fortune, our lips constantly smile."

Rostam replies, "Calm your heart.
Free yourself of attachment to the material world.
It brings, from end to end, nothing but deceit and pain.
One person is blessed with good fortune,
While another is cursed with misfortune.
One person possesses a good name,
While another goes down in shame.
In the end, everyone must submit to death,
As there is no remedy for this spell.
May you never find yourself afflicted by pain!
May we all go now and engage in battle!"

As soon as Tous, Giv, and the brave riders of Iran
Learn of Rostam's approach toward Mount Hamaavan
And Goodarz, worldly hero, sees him in the distance,
They charge toward him, swift as wind,
Shouting cries and ringing out the blowing of trumpets.

Rostam's banner emerges as he enters camp in pitch black.
Troops and leader dismount joyfully, cinched for war.
Lamentations about the dead, buried in the dust of battle,
Resound throughout camp,
Stabbing Rostam's heart with pain.
Once again, he inhales deeply with thoughts of retaliation.

He listens to the account of the outcome of the fight.
He joins his moaning to that of the brave men
And gives much advice to army leaders:
"O noble chiefs, we are on the eve of a tremendous battle.
The fate of every fight is such that one finds in it a feast,
While another is doomed with an unyielding tomb."

The warlord, glory of the world, asks for his pavilion.
Behind him, the army of Nimrooz erects its camp
On the mountain, where it plants its leader's banner.

An ivory seat is brought,
Along with one made of teakwood.
Rostam sits on the throne
While noblemen flock around him.
On one side are Goodarz and Giv,
On the other, Tous and warrior leaders.

Rostam places burning candles before them
And speaks of various matters, great and small,
Of warriors' actions, the army's battles,
And the rotations of the sun and shining moon.

The leaders discuss at length the countless troops
Mustered by Kaamoos and Shangal,
The Emperor of Chin, Manshoor, and other warring men.
They say, "We should not speak of Kaamoos,
For we dare not glance his way.
He is a tree bearing mace and sword
Who fears not a deluge of stones falling from the sky.

He does not flee when faced with war elephants.
His head is full of hatred and his heart full of battle.
Manshoor also will not give up the place of honor,
And no one commands an army as adeptly as Karkoo.

"The entire desert is strewn with tents
And tent enclosures of Chini brocade.
From this very mountain to the waters of Shahd,
One sees nothing but banners and troops,
Helmets and armor, innumerable decked elephants.
There is not a single man whose demeanor is not fierce.
If the world hero had not arrived,
We would surely have been lost.
Praise be to the victorious Creator for ending
Our need for the oppression of worry and danger.
You are the one destined to save our lives
At the very moment we had given up hope."

The world hero sheds tears for some time,
His heart dim, saddened by the fate of the deceased.
In the end, Rostam says, "Observe the world
From the circle of the moon to the dark earth.
You will find only affliction, sorrow, and suffering.
Such is the condition of this passing world.
Such are the deeds of the revolving dome.
At times it provides us with battle and poison,
At times with honey and affection.
But whether we perish of natural causes
Or of a violent death,
Let us not worry about the how and why.
We must depart when our time is up.
Let us not blame the rotations of the skies.

"May the Creator, Master of triumph, be our support!
May the fortune of our enemy be curtailed!
We shall vengefully engage in battle,
Placing the world at the mercy of Iran-Zamin."

The brave men praise him: "May you never falter,
For you are owner of crown, sword, and ring!
May you live forever swathed in joy and glory!
May the court of the victorious king

Never find itself deprived of your being!"

27 | Preparations Made by the Hosts

Once the sun, light of the world,
Gleams over the mountain,
Once day reaches for the two curls of night,
Once it frees itself of its gloomy veil
And bites the moon's lips to the blood,
The beating of drums is heard in both camps,
And the world heroes rise from their positions of rest.

The leader Hoomaan approaches the enemy host
And says, "The Iranians must have received
Reinforcements since new tents have been pitched."

He perceives a grand pavilion of turquoise brocade,
Encircled by a great number of colorful tents.
At the sight of the banner of the world leader
Firmly planted before the tent,
A thought pollutes his mind:
The idea that their fortune is about to change.

He discerns a black tent enclosure
With a banner bright as the moon.
He sees Fariborz, son of Kaavoos,
Surrounded by elephants and timpani.
A great many tents have been erected
In proximity to Tous's encampment.

Distressed, he returns to his host and relates to Piran:
"This day brings to us a heavy burden.
We have heard this past night, in the Iranian camp,
The sound of weapons, along with the sound of cries,
An uproar greater than anything heeded on prior nights.
I have left my tent in the early morning hours
To investigate alone and to identify the enemy.
I am certain that a vast army has come to their rescue.
There is an enclosure of green brocade before which
Is planted a banner with the image of a dragon.
Around it, troops from Zabolestan are camped,

Armed with blocks and daggers from Kabolestan.
I think the king has sent Rostam as reinforcement."

Piran replies, "If Rostam, the son of a deev,
Is here to engage in battle, we are doomed.
We shall never again see the face of joy.
No one will survive against him,
Neither Kaamoos nor the Emperor of Chin,
Neither Shangal nor any other Tooranian warrior."

He exits the camp at once and nears the Iranian host
To assess its forces for himself.
Then he hurries to Kaamoos, Manshoor, and Fartoos,
And says to them, "I departed at the break of dawn
To find that they have received fierce reinforcements
And that many famous warlords have joined their ranks.
I surmise that Rostam, of whom I spoke at the gathering,
Has left the court of Iran to travel here to assist Tous."

Kaamoos replies, "O man full of caution, your mind
Dwells only on gloomy, unfavorable thoughts.
Know that even if Kay Khosrow were to come to battle,
You would not need to worry your heart so foolishly.
Why do you speak of Rostam with such dread?
Never mention again the name of Zabolestan.
If you fear the presence of Rostam,
I shall be the first to overthrow him and to execute him.
The sight of my distant banner will send pangs of terror
Into his warrior heart at the time of battle.
Go and mobilize your army. Set troops in motion.
Take your standard to the battlefield,
And when I fling myself into the scuffle
With my retinue, make haste, do not trail behind.
You will witness how brave men fight,
As the desert will soon be drenched in a sea of blood.
With a wave of my sword and my mace,
I shall strike and cut off the head of Rostam, son of Zaal."

Piran's heart rejoices at these words, and his being
Releases the anxiety spawned by thoughts of Rostam.
At peace, his heart expands with new resolve.
Dipping his soul once again in the waters of courage,

He distributes to his troops helmets and armor,
And relays to them Kaamoos's hopeful words.

Then he goes to the emperor,
Kisses the ground at his feet,
And says to him, "O King, may you live forever!
May the extent of your wisdom give comfort to all!
You have traveled long and far with a vast host.
You have renounced feast to take part in hardships.
In honor of Afraasiyaab, you have crossed
The Sea of Chin in ships and vessels.
You are the support of our army.
Act now in a manner worthy of your breed.
Adorn your elephants with bells.
Render the world deaf with the wail of your trumpets.
At the moment I engage in war, you may take over
The center line with timpani and elephants.
Keep in check the army's rear,
And help me raise my helmet as high as the clouds
The brave Kaamoos instructed me
To take the army's vanguard.
He vowed many oaths brandishing his heavy mace,
Pledging not to make use today of any other weapon,
Even if a hail of stones were to drop on his head."

The emperor listens and orders the blast of trumpets.
It appears as if the mountain is in motion
From the rising dust and, at the sound of drums,
As if the earth and sky arm themselves for battle
And shed any residual sense of mercy.
He asks for his throne to be placed on top of an elephant.
The world turns pitch black.

The emperor storms to the army's center with ceremony.
The dust covers the sky like a dark cloud,
And the sound of Indian bells
Pulsates gloom into warrior hearts.

The many turquoise thrones on the backs of elephants
Make the world shine with splendor like the River Nile.
The eyes of men are deprived of light,
Their minds deprived of a sense of peace.

The eyes of the firmament block up with dust.
You would think its once shiny face is coated with coal tar.

The Emperor of Chin emerges at the center of the host
In a grandiose manner, forcing the moon to lose its way.
Kaamoos, tall as a mountain, extends the line to the right.
His equipment is carried toward the plain.
Piran, his brother Hoomaan, and Golbaad
Quickly assume positions to the left of the mountain.

Soon Rostam notices the stirrings of the emperor.
He lays out his troops on the battlefield
And orders Tous to place the timpani
And to adorn the army like the eye of the rooster.
Rostam says, "We shall find out above
Which host the sky hovers with affection,
To which it will grant its favors,
And which of the two is destined to succumb.
I did not pause once on the road here.
My horse Rakhsh completed each day,
Three stages without the benefit of rest or sleep.
Now he is weary of the long journey.
His hooves are worn out. I dare not burden him
With the weight of my body to conquer the enemy.
Come to my aid today in this battle.
Tomorrow we shall see whose cloth of fortune
Will be drenched in the blood of combat."

Commander Tous orders trumpets and clarions
And sounds the call of war.

Goodarz takes charge of the right wing
And sends his gear and supplies to the mountain.
Fariborz occupies the left wing.
The spears of his riders give the world
The appearance of a field of reeds.

Tous, son of Nozar, settles at the army's heart.
The earth becomes covered in dust, and wind stirs the air.
The world disappears beneath the churning sands,
And brave men cannot recognize each other.

The hero of elephant stature climbs to the mountaintop

475

To identify the emperor and the Tooranian warriors.
He sees a host so vast that the sea of Rum
Appears, in comparison, like a small ball of wax.
He sees warriors from Kushan, Shakni, and Haraah,
Some from the lands of Chaghan, Chin, Saghlaab,
And India, other fighters come from Kahan,
The border of Indus, Rum, and Sindh.
Each host speaks a different language,
Raises a different banner,
And wears different garb, helmets, and armor.

The multitude of elephants and displays,
Ivory thrones, crowns, torques, and bracelets
Render the world a paradise garden,
A sight at once of great beauty and of great horror.

Rostam stands on the heights, astounded.
He begins to conceive some doubt and reflects,
"Until when will the sky smile down on us?
What game will the ancient firmament play with us?"
He wails to Yazdan, "You are higher than all things,
Creator of all the world's creatures,
Giver of light to the stars, the Sun, and Moon.
You who have need for nothing:
Give us your aid in this battle, come to our rescue.
Only with your affection and your help
Will we be victorious and will my head rise to the skies."

Then he climbs down the mountain, his courage intact.
He passes before the vanguard and before Tous,
Reflecting, "From the moment I seized weapons,
I have not taken time to rest, not for a single year.
I have seen many a host before,
But never have I come across one so vast."

He asks for the pounding of timpani.
Commander Tous sets the troops in motion
And descends upon the plain, wielding his spear
And ready to spill the blood of vengeance.
The army marches out for half a day
And forms upon the plain a line two farsangs long.

The dust rising from it makes the light disappear.

One can no longer distinguish between day and night.
The feathers and steel of spears and arrows
Further obscure the day to trouble and blur the sun.
The shouts of cavaliers and the whinnying of steeds
Pierce through the air and rise to Saturn and Mars.
The trample of horses and the beating of drums
Give wings to stones and boulders.

Swords and arms turn crimson with blood.
The heart of the earth trembles
Beneath the horses' hooves.
Cowards, stupefied, die of fright while
Brave men carve their shrouds out of coats of mail.
On all fronts, lions flee, brave eagles fly away.
The face of the sun pales, and mountain boulders jolt.

The brave Kaamoos says to his men,
"Were we to crush the sky on foot, seize your sword,
Mace, and noose, and fling yourselves into the scuffle.
The one who aims to possess the world
Must place his life in the palm of his hand
Or else his head will be lost,
To be forgotten beneath a tombstone.

28 | The Battle of Rostam and Ashkeboos

There lives a brave man named Ashkeboos,
Whose cries boom loud as the sound of kettledrums.
He comes to provoke the Iranians, hoping to fling
Into dust the head of the warrior who is his match.
He bellows, "Renowned heroes, who among you
Will dare present himself to feud with me?
Who is willing to let me make his blood flow?"

Rohaam dons helmet and armor.
Hollering a cry and boiling like the sea in fury,
He seizes his bow made of lion skin
And advances swiftly and decisively.
He sends over the head of his illustrious enemy
A raging deluge of shots.
But Ashkeboos is covered in steel,

And the arrows provoke on his coat of mail
No more impression than the wind itself.

Next, Rohaam brandishes his heavy mace.
The hands of the combatants are weary
From the weight of the struggle, but the helmet
Of the Tooranian resists the blows of mace,
And Ashkeboos's fervor only grows more intense.
He pivots to reach for his mace as the air appears
Enveloped in steel and the earth in darkness.
He hits Rohaam hard on the head and shatters his helm.

Rohaam grows fearful of the hero from Kushan.
He pulls back toward the mountainside.

Tous springs from the heart of the army
And bounds on his horse to fall on Ashkeboos,
But Rostam rushes forth and says to him,
"The cup is Rohaam's true companion,
And in feast he boasts and wears himself out.
Where did he go now, his face red as sandarac?
We have only seen his steed's spurs and hindquarters.
Is he a lesser horseman than Ashkeboos?
Remain in the army core, according to the rule of war,
And allow me to fight the enemy on foot."

Rostam hooks his bow on his upper arm,
Places a few arrows at his belt, keeping one in his hand.
With his face the color of ebony,
He advances toward Ashkeboos and cries out,
"O man eager for war, here comes an adversary.
Do not retreat before him."

The warrior from Kushan smiles in surprise.
He brings his horse to a stop and addresses Rostam
In a fit of laughter: "What is your name?
Who is the one destined to shed tears
At the sight of your headless corpse?"

Rostam replies, "O wretched one,
Why do you ask my name since you are a lost man?
My mother gave me for name your very demise.
Fate has turned me into the hammer

PART ELEVEN

Designed to crush you."

Ashkeboos says, "Without a mount,
You will only succeed in delivering your head
To an undeniable, unendurable death."

Rostam says, "O foolish man, eager to fight,
Have you never seen a man battle on foot in your land
And fling beneath the stone an overly proud head?
Have you not seen men as fierce as lions, leopards,
And whales, engage in battle with their horses?
All raging that I am, I shall, O valiant horseman,
Teach you the skills of war without a mount.
Tous has sent me on foot so that I may
Deprive Ashkeboos of the use of his horse.
The Kushani hero will soon find himself dismounted.
Both armies will then scorn him with roars of laughter.
This foot soldier is worth, on this very field,
On this very day, and in this very battle,
Three hundred riders like you."

Ashkeboos replies, "I see on you
No other weapons than deceit and good humor."

Rostam retorts, "Do you not see my bow
And my quiver of the deadly arrows
That will end your time on earth?"

Witness to Ashkeboos's dismissive manner
From high upon his horse, Rostam draws
An arrow from his belt and shoots at the horse,
At once knocking the creature down.
The hero laughs and says,
"Sit beside your noble companion.
If you wish to press your head against its chest,
I shall suspend the fight this very instant.
You are very affectionate with him,
And he has no one in life except for you."

Ashkeboos swiftly reaches for his bow,
His body shaking, his face red as sandarac.
He sends a shower of shots over
To strike at Rostam's armor. But the hero says,

479

"You needlessly tire your body and arms.
Your mind fills with evil thoughts."

Then Rostam brings his hand to his quiver, selects
An arrow of triple wood with a tip as bright as water,
Bound with four eagle feathers.
He rubs his bow made of wood from Chaadj,
Seizes by the ring the string of elk skin,
Straightens his left arm, and bends his right elbow
As the curb of the arc makes a crackling sound.
He draws back the nock of the arrow to his ear.
The string of elk skin expels a mournful wail.
Once the arrowhead's steel grazes his left hand
And the end reaches his ear, he releases the shot
To strike Ashkeboos square in the chest.

The vault of sky applauds Rostam's stroke.
Fate says, "Take." Destiny says, "Give."
The sky says, "Good." And angels say, "Bravo!"

The hero from Kushan dies on the spot.
You would think his mother had never borne him.

Both hosts intently observe the battle of heroes.
Kaamoos and the Emperor of Chin greatly admire
The Iranian's stature, strength, and fighting skills.

As soon as Rostam leaves, the emperor sends a rider
To remove the arrow from the body of the noble one.
The arrow is drenched in blood, from tip to fletching.
Once withdrawn and brought to the army ranks,
Everyone admires it with awe,
Considering it as mighty as a spear.

The emperor's young heart ages as he studies the arrow.
He asks Piran, "Who is this bold hero?
What name have the Iranians assigned to him?
You told me there is only a handful of miserable men,
Warriors of the most vile sort.
Now I come upon arrows as large as spears.
The hearts of lions who fight with them can only fail.
Whatever you told me earlier was untrue."

Piran says, "I know, among the Iranian troops,
No one with the strength of this cursed warrior
Whose shot can knock down a tree.
I have no knowledge of his goals and desires.
Among the Iranians are men such as Giv and Tous,
Who display nobility and are worthy in battle.
But my brother Hoomaan has many a time
Rendered the world dark as ebony to the leader Tous.
I have no knowledge of the origins of this man,
Nor am I aware who among us is capable of properly
Measuring himself against him. I shall go to camp,
And there we shall discover his true identity."

29 | Piran Asks About Rostam's Arrival

Piran arrives at camp full of concern,
His face a pale shade of yellow.
He addresses a number of questions
To his renowned companions:
"Who is this nobleman who arrived to battle on foot?
Is it Rostam, sent by the king to assist the Iranians?"

The bold Hoomaan says to Piran,
"A wise man does not underestimate his enemy.
Now that the warriors of Iran have reclaimed courage
And are joyous, it is as if they can split solid steel.
Their cry of war is unceasing on the battlefield."

Piran says to him, "Who is this horseman
Who comes from Iran to rescue Tous?
If he is not Rostam, I am not afraid of him.
My heart is fearless faced with Rohaam, Gorgeen,
Fariborz, or any other Iranian warrior.
No one measures up to Kaamoos except Tous.
Since a great battle awaits our brave army,
Our troops will aspire to acquire fame and glory."

He approaches Kaamoos, Manshoor, and Fartoos,
And says, "Today is a day of battle
As a wolf has emerged from this flock of sheep.
Seek a remedy to these wounds, and see

Which one of us is capable of fending off the Iranians."

Kaamoos replies, "Today's battle covers us in shame.
Ashkeboos has perished,
And his death causes Giv and Tous to rejoice.
My heart was broken in two
At the sight of this foot soldier,
Able to rush a wave of terror through our troops.
No man in the world is equal to him in stature,
And none of ours can measure up to him.
You have seen his skills in archery.
You have seen the force of his shot.
His strength is above the might of a wild elephant.
I suspect he is the warrior from Sistan
Of whom you have often spoken.
He arrived with the purpose of defending the Iranians,
Thus engaging in war on foot on this battlefield."

Piran replies, "The man from Sistan is another:
A prince who carries his head high."

The cautious Kaamoos, heart engrossed with this matter,
Asks, "Tell me how this man of lion heart acts in a clash.
Describe to me his size, his arm's muscle, his demeanor.
How does he address soldiers in the arena?
Describe to me his appearance and his character.
How shall I match up to him?
For I intend to compete with him in combat."

Piran answers, "I hope that he will never show his face.
Should a single rider dare venture to fight him,
You will witness a man of cypress stature,
Of grace and glory, and stately air.
In many a battle, Afraasiyaab himself fled
At the sight of him, eyes brimming with tears.
He is a man always ready to fight,
A faithful representative of Kay Khosrow,
Always first to reach for his weapon.
He comes to avenge the death of Siaavosh,
Whom he raised with his own hands.
Many brave men will attempt to pierce his armor,
But no one will succeed when he is girded for battle,

For his body is as strong as an elephant.
Should he let his mace drop on the battlefield,
Not even a massive whale could lift it.
The string of his bow is made of lion skin.
The tip of his arrow weighs ten sitirs.[57]
A block of granite is, in his hand, as malleable as wax
And would stand ashamed before wax itself.
When he prepares for battle, he dons a coat of mail
On top of which he fastens armor with buckles
And under which he wears a robe of leopard skin.
He gives this armor the name of Babreh Bayan,
Gauging it above the coat of mail, for it can
Neither be consumed by fire nor penetrated by water.
Thus equipped, one would think he has wings.

"He sits upon Rakhsh, a horse akin in motion
To Mount Bisootoon for the way he extracts
Fire from boulders and never ceases
To whinny for the duration of any fight.
It could be that with all these marvels
You do not count him as a man on the day of battle.
With such hands and arms, such legs and shoulders,
It is not astonishing that he is skillful and brave."

The wise Kaamoos listens to Piran,
Surrendering to him his heart, soul, and ear.
Flattered by his words and incited
By his calculated speech, he replies,
"O world hero, may your heart remain cautious
And your mind clear and serene.
Select a solemn oath, one uttered by blessed kings,
And I shall pronounce an even greater one
So that your heart and your faith can be secured.
I swear to keep my steed saddled until,
By the power bestowed upon me by the Master of Sun,
I shall ensure your good fortune and make the world
For the Iranians as constricted as the eye of a needle."

Piran lavishes praise upon him:
"O ruler of deep foresight and righteous speech,

◇◇◇◇◇◇◇◇◇◇◇◇◇
57 Sitir: Ancient form of measure.

483

Our affairs will prosper to your liking, and we shall
Have to endure the prospect of fewer battles."

He then makes the rounds of the army's camp,
Enters each pavilion and tent, recounting to troops
And to the Emperor of Chin what transpired.

30 | Iranians and Tooranians Form Their Lines of Battle

Once the setting sun spreads its veil of ruby across the world
And the night begins its march across the firmament,
The army's men of good counsel, skilled swordsmen,
Gather in the tent of the Emperor of Chin,
Hearts full of rancor and ardor for war.

Kaamoos, lion destroyer, Manshoor the valiant,
Shammiran of Shukni, Shangul from India,
Kondor from the land of Saghlaab, and the King of Sindh,
Kahaar from Kahan, brave horseman, lion warriors,
And brave leaders of Tooran and Khotan,
All unite behind the Emperor of Chin.

Each one gives his advice on the battle to be waged.
Each one speaks of the Iranians,
And everyone vows in a common voice
That they must wash their hands in blood.
Then they retire to their tents to rest,
Alone with their reflections.
But despite the strong desire, no one is able to sleep.

The moon is reduced to a slim crescent
By a succession of nights enveloping it
In the black strands of its mane.
Once it nears the sun and the latter appears
In all its splendor, face awash with golden light,
The two armies stir with much sound and clatter,
Shouts rising to the celestial spheres.

The Emperor of Chin says, "Today we must
Go to war without hesitation or pause,

As we did yesterday when Piran acted
As if he never even lived.
We mustn't start the battle without him.
We have all come here, traveled far to fight,
To come to the assistance of our allies.
But if we hesitate, as we did yesterday, we shall,
Though we seek glory, end up covered in shame.
Let us further consider that tomorrow Afraasiyaab
Will thank us, and we shall enjoy respite and peace.
Let us advance toward the enemy in great numbers,
Undivided, like a mountain,
And let us deliver a heroic battle.
We count in our midst world heroes
From ten kingdoms, and the idea is not to sit
And engage in banquet and feast."

The noblemen rise from their seats
And applaud the words of the emperor.
They say, "Today you are the army's commander.
The lands of Chin and Tooran are yours,
And you will see, on this battlefield,
Only black clouds rising from swords."

On his side, Rostam addresses the Iranians:
"The moment of determination approaches.
If we lost a few men yesterday, it is only one man
For every twice three hundred of theirs.
For this reason, there is no need to fear.
I do not wish to live deprived of splendor and honor.
The entire army of Turks retreated quickly at the sight
Of Ashkeboos's demise, their cheeks colored sandarac.
Fill your dim hearts with a keen desire for vengeance,
And you cavaliers, crease your brow in a frown.
I have reinforced Rakhsh's horseshoes with steel.
I shall mount him and render my bloody sword ruby red.
Make today a new and glorious day, and may
The entire world be the prize for Kay Khosrow.
Cinch your waists, for battle will give you crowns and rings,
And I shall offer you Zaboli gold and treasure,
As well as many shawls from Kabol."

The noblemen extol him and say,

485

"May the crown and seal prosper with your labor!
You are world hero, and we are your loyal servants.
We live, thanks to you, and you are our shelter."

Rostam dresses in his battle armor
And strides to the battlefield,
Full of confidence in his own power.
First he slips on a coat of mail,
Then his armor of Babreh Bayan.
He places over his head a brilliant Chini helm of steel,
Making his enemy reflect on death.
He pulls his belt tight around his waist
And surrenders himself to Yazdan's will.
He climbs on his Rakhsh like a wild elephant.
The sky above looks down at his stature in awe.
The earth below turns dark beneath Rakhsh's hooves.

31 | Kaamoos Kills Alvaah

The sound of clarions and timpani echoes on both fronts.
Incantations and tricks no longer hold any power.
You would think the sea is replete with waves.
The eagle of death beats its wings and takes flight.
The air stirs. Plain and mountain quiver.
The earth rattles beneath the horses' hooves.

Kaamoos occupies the right wing of the Tooranian line.
Behind him stand war elephants, bearers of the loads.
At the left wing is the Indian king, wearing a coat of mail,
Wielding in his hand a colorful Rumi sword.
At the center stands the Emperor of Chin.
The sky is dark; the earth shudders.

In the opposite camp, Fariborz, bright as the sun
Under the sign of Aries, stands at the left wing.
To the right is Giv, son of Kashvaad, braced in steel.
At the center is Tous, son of Nozar, standing on foot
With timpani and trumpets behind the troops.

The cries of warriors on all sides shred elephant ears.
Water turns to fire and smoke.

One could never dream of such a brutal battle.

The first to advance between the two hosts,
Dumping a spume of blood,
Is Kaamoos the proud leader, surrounded
By elephants, kettledrums, and troops.
He hollers like a drunken elephant,
Brandishing his bull-headed mace.
He charges onto the field and addresses his men:
"Where is this valiant foot soldier
Who defies all those who wish to fight?
Should he come forward with bow and arrow,
He will surely perish by my bow and arrow."

Brave and renowned warriors
Tous, Rohaam, and Giv discern Kaamoos,
But no one desires to contend with him.
The field is empty of Iranians,
For no one dares fight him.
Warriors appear feeble as gazelles
While he takes the stance of a mighty leopard.
Only one man from Zabolestan, a man named Alvaah,
Draws his sword, given to him by Rostam.
He is a man skilled in the handling of reins,
Able to make use of sword, mace, and spear,
His heart nourished by the labors and dangers of war.
Rostam was his teacher in the art of weaponry
And was accustomed to lending him his spear.
Alvaah charges forth to attack Kaamoos and destroy him.

Rostam says to him, "Remain vigilant.
Be conscious of the ways of this bold hero.
When the wise old man speaks, one must listen and learn.
Do not allow yourself to be dazzled
By the luster of your feats.
Maintain your footing on firm ground.
Do not foolishly merge the water of a spring
With the rushing current of a deep ocean.
Do not rely on your mace and power.
Avoid the capture of your head by the enemy's noose.
Be patient and take time to find a worthy challenger."

Alvaah takes off to battle Kaamoos, the defiant.
A sizable space is vacated for them to joust.
The hero from Kushan advances like a fierce wolf,
Strikes Alvaah with his spear, forces him to dismount,
Flings him effortlessly to the ground, stops his horse,
And makes him trample over him
With his hooves of steel until the mud,
Mixing with blood, turns a deep shade of red.

32 | Rostam Kills Kaamoos

Rostam finds himself afflicted by Alvaah's death.
He detaches his furled noose from its hook, saying,
"When you are about to challenge warriors,
You must be equipped with noose and heavy mace.
You must charge forth,
Shouting like a drunken elephant,
Noose hanging on your arm,
Mace clutched in your hand."

Kaamoos says to him,
"Do not value yourself so highly, laying your trust
On this long string rolled up sixty times."

Rostam replies, "When a lion perceives its prey,
He roars proudly. You have instigated this fight
By slaying one of our Iranian warriors.
You call my noose a string,
But you will soon feel how firm its knot can be.
Fate will turn this place into dust to cover your head,
O Kushani warrior, as this day will see your last exploit."

Kaamoos boldly charges his golden horse
Toward Rostam, finding him steady as an elephant,
Waiting for him with his noose.
Kaamoos attempts to cut off
The hero's head with a blow of his sword,
But the blade misses Rakhsh's neck,
Slashing through his armor without wounding him.

Rostam launches his noose's knot,

Captures Kaamoos at the waist, sends Rakhsh off,
Brings the end of the noose toward his leg,
And passes it in the ring of the saddle.
Meanwhile, Rakhsh appears to unfold
Feathers and wings to soar like an eagle.

Kaamoos clamps his legs around his own charger,
Releases the reins and bears down hard on the stirrups.
He attempts to rupture the noose to free himself.
He thrashes about like an insane man,
But the noose stays secure in its grasp.

Rostam slows Rakhsh down, swings around,
And, flinging Kaamoos off his horse,
Firmly tosses him to the ground.
Then he approaches him, ties him up, and says,
"From now on, you will be barred
From having a hand in evil deeds.
Magic and incantations have failed you,
And your mind has become the slave of the Deev.
Your days of battle and vengeance have ended.
You will never again set your sights
On the lands of Kushan and Chin."

He binds Kaamoos's hands behind his back,
And, taking him by the knots,
He marches on foot toward the Iranian host,
Holding his enemy under the arm.
He addresses his soldiers: "This man, eager for battle,
Wished to measure his strength against mine,
So confident he was of his skill and power.
But such is the custom of this deceitful world:
At times it elevates one; at times it brings one down.
It is the source of alternate joy and sadness,
Peaks and downfalls. It lowers one to the ground
While raising another to the highest clouds.

"Now this brave man who once held his head high,
Who claimed no one as equal, not even the lion,
Who set his mind on plundering our land,
Turning it into the dwelling of lions
By razing every palace and garden

In the provinces of Zabolestan and Kabolestan,
Who sought to rest his mace only after defeating
Rostam, now finds himself in such a state
That his armor and helmet serve him as shroud.
His diadem will be crafted out of mud
And his tunic out of dust.
What sort of death do you wish the bold
Kaamoos to suffer, for his time is imminent?"

Rostam flings Kaamoos at his troops' feet.
The army leaders emerge from ranks,
Grind his body with their swords,
Flooding the stones with blood.

Such is the custom of sky and era:
At times pain and grief, at times joy and happiness.
One must sustain worry and fear,
As not even courage will grant you immunity.
In your search for status, your body succumbs
Beneath the weight of your shortcomings,
Your heart is consumed with anxiety and suffering.
Do not count on your valor,
For fate holds out a hand for you.
Live your life, active in good deeds,
And always praise your Guide, the Creator.

The story of the battle of Kaamoos, the warrior, ends.
In his search to kill, he encountered death.
The One responsible for giving life snatched it away.

Now I shall turn to the tale of the Emperor of Chin.
I shall engage the heroes on this field of vengeance.

PART TWELVE

The Battle of Rostam
With the Emperor of Chin

1 | The Emperor of Chin Learns of the Death of Kaamoos

Listen to me, wise man.
May your tongue emit no other name
But that of Yazdan, full of wisdom and clarity,
Our inspiration when we yearn for good deeds,
Who holds up the dome of the revolving sky,
Who created spirit and wisdom,
Who alone we must worship.
Your days will end,
And another world will be your dwelling.
Listen to the poet bard's words,
Drawn from a priceless, ancient book.

Once the Emperor of Chin learns that Kaamoos
Has fallen and died on the field of vengeance,
The day turns dark and life bitter for the warriors
Of Kushan and Shakni, and for the brave men of Balkh.
They draw near each other and ask about
This daring warrior, full of passion for battle.
"What is his name, and who on earth
Would be a worthy adversary against him?"

Piran says to Hoomaan of lion heart,
"From now on, I despair of war.
How would our brave men dare battle
In view of the death of Kaamoos, a warring whale?
Never has the world witnessed a more glorious man,
Never a cavalier more deserving of the title of world hero.
The one able to tie up Kaamoos with noose on the field
Would snatch an elephant's head on the day of war
And overthrow it to fling it onto the ground."

The entire army goes to the emperor, bemoaning
The fate of Kaamoos and grieving over him.
Piran offers homage and says in a sad tone,
"O ruler, more sublime than the blue firmament,
You stood at the front of the army.

You witnessed the beginning and end of battle.
Seek now a remedy for our ailment
But do so alone, without consulting others.
Select, among the army's spies, a man able
To uncover a secret so that he may find out
Who is this hero of lion heart and who among us
Is able to measure up against him.
Then we shall expose ourselves to the fate of death,
Uniting our efforts against this single warrior."

The Emperor of Chin says to Piran,
"I sense the same worry in my heart
And the same diligence.
I wish to know who is this wicked warlord
Who captures the lion in his lasso's knots.
Furthermore, no one can avoid death.
Neither question nor prayer would serve us well.
From the moment our mothers give birth to us,
We belong to death, and we must,
Despite ourselves, lengthen our necks toward it.
No one escapes the rotations of the skies,
Even one with the strength to topple an elephant.

"Do not allow yourselves to feel discouraged
By the fate of the one who perished in the lasso's knots,
For, with my noose, I shall cast into the dust
The one responsible for the death of Kaamoos.
I shall convert the entire land of Iran
Into a sea of blood, as Afraasiyaab desires."

The Emperor gathers a throng of noblemen,
Brave warriors armed with daggers, and says to them,
"You must observe where this bold horseman stands,
So able to fling his noose and kill brave men.
We must assess whether his position is left or right.
Find out from which land he comes, what his name is.
Once we have gathered this information,
We shall be well informed to plan and execute his death."

2 | The Battle of Changgesh With Rostam

A rider full of pride, devoted to the Tooranian king,
Presents himself to attempt this feat.
Named Changgesh, he is brave and ambitious,
Ready for anything and any deed.

He says to the Emperor of Chin, "O renowned hero,
The entire world stands waiting for your favors.
Although this man is a roaring lion,
I shall deprive him of the breath of life.
As soon as I appear on the battlefield,
I shall attack him on my own and tarnish his glory.
I wish to be the first to avenge the death of Kaamoos
And to posthumously return honor to his name."

Changgesh kisses the ground before the emperor,
Who showers him with praise and says,
"If you succeed in executing vengeance,
If you capture his brilliant head,
I shall give you so many gems and so much wealth
That never again will you need to extend yourself."

At the words of the emperor,
The battle-seeking Changgesh scowls deeply.
He launches his horse to spring forth like Aazargoshasp
To the side of the Iranians.
He fastens an arrow of white poplar to his bow
And says, "This is where I wish to fight,
To hold in my hands the heads of warlords.
If the hero who defeated Kaamoos, who battles
At times with lasso and at times with arrow,
Wishes to present himself on the battlefield,
His lofty stature will disappear swiftly
From the surface of the earth."

Changgesh struts left and right, saying,
"Where is this bold lion? Let him show himself!"

Rostam springs up from his seat, grabs his mace,
Climbs on Rakhsh, and cries, "Here I am,
Vanquisher of lions and distributor of crowns,
Holder of mace and noose, bow and arrow.

I shall obliterate you, just as I did the bold Kaamoos,
End your days and deliver you to the dust of earth."

Changgesh replies, "What is your name,
What is your birth? What are you asking for?
Tell me, so that I may know the identity of the one
Whose blood I shall spill on this very battlefield."

Rostam says, "O wretched one, may the tree
That bears flowers of the likes of you be cursed!
May it never blossom and bear fruit!
My spear's tip and my name call for your death.
Your shield and helmet will soon serve you as shroud."

Changgesh rushes toward Rostam as swift as wind.
He ties the cord to the two ends of his bow.
This miscreant's bow becomes a thick cloud
That spills torrents of shots through the rising dust.

Rostam feels as if the shots will pierce through his armor.
He raises his shield level to his head
And says to the other, "Well, well, brave rider,
You will now regret your call for war!"

Changgesh examines this man of elephant build,
Whose stature resembles that of a cypress tree.
He observes his untiring horse,
Tall and steady as a mountain.
He thinks, "It is better to flee, than to risk my life."
He launches his horse to swiftly bolt around
And make his way back to his men.

The bold Rostam lunges in hot pursuit of him.
He seizes the tail of the impure Changgesh's horse
As the two hosts observe in stupefaction.
Rostam holds on to the tail for some time.
In the end, he impatiently jumps off his steed,
Taking Changgesh with him.
Changgesh falls and begs for mercy,
But Rostam flings him to the ground
And cuts off his head in a way as to sever
His wishes and worries once and for all.

The leading warriors of the land of Iran lavish
The eminent Rostam with praise and blessings.
Meanwhile, Rostam charges from one host
To the other, a shining javelin in his hand.

3 | The Emperor of Chin Sends Hoomaan to Rostam

On his side, the Emperor of Chin, grief-stricken,
And dismayed by the turn of events, says to Hoomaan,
"We are being choked by time and space.
Could you find out the name of this famed warrior?"

Hoomaan replies, "I am not an anvil, nor do I
Stand equal to this celebrated warlord in battle.
There never lived in the world a fighter like Kaamoos.
Never did a man balance such ardor with such caution.
This horseman seized him in the knots of his noose.
Do not think frivolously of him.
We shall see to whom the Creator will bestow
Victory on this field of vengeance."

He rushes to his tent, swift as wind, to fetch a helmet,
Select a different banner, horse, armor, and shield.
He approaches Rostam, observes his arms and legs,
And says, "O renowned master of noose,
O valiant horseman, I swear by the Creator
That I despair of the throne when
I witness an adversary of your kind.
In this host, no warrior is as strong and brave as you.
One must be bold to confront you, he must have
The strength and skills to annihilate a lion.
It seems as if, with your courage and your prudence,
You dare not battle us, and yet I have seen only you
In the army of Iran with the heart of a fearless warrior.
Tell me where lies your land, who are your parents,
Where is your home?
What is your lineage, what is your name?
You appear to be a man who acts like a leopard.
If you would reveal your name, land, and province,
You would grant me a huge favor, free my mind
From a rather disturbing apprehension."

Rostam replies, "O noble and discerning warrior,
Why do you not disclose your name, land, and domain?
Why do you ask me for name and lineage?
I am a noble warrior from Iran-Zamin.
I am here to engage in a vengeful battle
Against Turk and Chini fighters.
I am here to obscure the world for the son of Pashang.
Why are you addressing me with words of flattery?
If you wish peace and harmony,
We must moderate the hatred charging between us.
Search and find those responsible for spilling
The precious blood of Siaavosh, for they ignited
Within us the all-consuming flame of vengeance.
Moreover, the squandered lives of the Goodarzian
Heroes seriously added to this grievous loss.

"Where were the renowned leaders?
Why did they not fight and say anything?
We must lay our hands on the guilty one.
If you send him to me, along with the warriors
And adorned horses, the wealth and treasure
Looted from Iran, I shall end all hostility.
After that, you will be benevolent in our eyes,
As you will follow our path and our ways.
I shall deliver them to Kay Khosrow
To wash the pain from his mind.
Perhaps, in his clemency, he will forgive them.

"Now I shall proceed to punish the evil ones.
May their names be cursed,
And their desires never granted!
The principal instigator of the crime is Garsivaz,
Who inflicted such harsh blows upon Iran-Zamin.
Next, the members of Toor's family,
Whom you know foolishly troubled the waters:
Men such as Garooy of Zerreh, whose essence is unjust.
May their lineage be damned, for they slew Siaavosh!
Garsivaz's hand was the key to evil deeds.
He is the one who most affected
The heart and soul of King Afraasiyaab,
Ultimately causing such a heavy flow of blood
To spill like water upon the ground.

Furthermore, I shall punish anyone
Among the Tooranians cinched with hatred,
Bold leaders of the race of Viseh,
Who are two-faced, dishonest, and unscrupulous:
Hoomaan, Lahaak, Farshidvard,
Golbaad and lion-man Nastihan.

"If you execute what I ask of you,
You will no longer have need of armor,
And I shall close the doors of vengeance.
But if you hold a different sort of talk,
I shall revive the ancient hatred in a new war.
I swear by the head and soul of the noble Khosrow
That I shall raze and ravage all of Tooran-Zamin,
From border to border, sparing neither Shangal
Nor the Chini emperor, nor any other warriors.
I am a renowned hero from the land of Iran,
Most at ease when engaged in battles with lions.
I have severed many heads from bodies,
Heads left with no other shroud than the dark dust.
You are familiar with my blows
And my glorious deeds of war,
And such are my customs and ways.
Never have I offered an opponent a peaceful resolution.
From beginning to end, I only aim at vengeance.
Pay close attention to what I have to say.
Guard my words close to your chest."

Hoomaan listens to him, stiff to the bone with terror.
The sound of Rostam's voice, vowing vengeance
On his entire family, makes him shake like a leaf.
He says, "O man of lion heart, O warring hero,
With your mien and your tall stature,
Your seat should be the throne of Iran.
I sense you are either a brave warrior
Or a noble man from that land.
You asked me for my name and my origin,
But your mind is fixed on an ulterior motive.
My name is Kooh, I am a brave hero.
My father is Boossepaas, a man as strong as a lion.
I come, as a simple soldier, from afar with this host.
Now that you know my identity,

I wish to ask for yours
So that I may make your demands public.
If you reveal your name,
I shall return to camp content.
Everything you have told me here
I shall repeat to Manshoor and the Emperor of Chin,
To the leaders and the warriors of Tooran-Zamin."

Rostam says, "Do not attempt to know my name.
Just repeat to them what I have said.
My heart, consumed with tenderness,
Aches for Piran, the only one among the Turks
Troubled by the bloodshed of Siaavosh,
The only one poised and patient.
Send him to me in haste,
And we shall see the turns of fate."

Hoomaan replies,
"O highborn one, you wish to see Piran?
What do you know of Piran and Golbaad?
What do you know of Garooy of Zerreh and Poolaad?"

Rostam replies, "So much needless talk!
Do not seek to make the river's flow
Climb back to its source. Do you not see
That Piran is at the center of our hosts' battle?"

4 | Piran Holds Counsel With Hoomaan and the Emperor of Chin

Hoomaan takes off in haste,
Pale of cheeks and forehead.

He says to Piran, "O blessed one,
A great calamity is upon us.
This man of lion heart is Rostam of Zabolestan,
And we are left to weep over our army's fate.
Not even Eblis has the force to conquer him.
Not even the whale in the ocean
Or the leopard on dry land can overcome
This intrepid, strong-willed man.

He spoke to me and listened to my answers.
He reminded me of each person's wicked deeds.
First, O illustrious brother, he called me by my name,
And he spoke of the vengeance of Siaavosh.
He mentioned the turn of events and recalled
The pillage and destruction, the justice and injustice
Executed against Bahraam and the Goodarzian clan.
I understood that he holds affection for you alone.
He brought up your name, exposing his thoughts.

"Now, out of the entire army,
He wishes to see only you.
I do not know what his heart conceals.
Go and observe him with his spear,
A steadfast mountain. Observe him
With his armor, his helm, his Babreh Bayan,
A powerful elephant beneath him.
You will see that everything I tell you is true.
Fire borrows its sheen from his sword.
He will not take one step before you find him,
For he remains in place on your account.
When you meet him, speak to him softly.
Do not draw your sword but suppress your fury."

Piran replies, "O battle seeker,
I sense that the end of my life is approaching.
For if this man, armed with sword, is indeed Rostam,
This field will turn into a site of misery for us.
Fire and flames will consume our land.
I fear what our destiny's star holds in store for us."

He walks over to address the Emperor of Chin,
Eyes filled with tears, heart torn by worry and wrath:
"The course of my life is reaching its end
Because of this warring conqueror coming our way."

The emperor replies, "Do not weaken,
O brave Tooranian warrior.
His body is not made of steel and stone.
His thoughts alone cannot launch a war."

Piran says, "O King, do not rush to action.
Now is the time to exercise patience and care.

Once the brave Kaamoos died, I was struck
With the suspicion that this iron wall was Rostam,
That it was his noose wrapped around his victim.
Even if Afraasiyaab were to present himself
Here in his glory, not even in dream
Would Rostam turn his back on him.
The deev himself would fear a fight with him.
Whether he is confronted with one man
Or a field full of men, it makes no difference to him.
He has lived in Zabolestan in splendor and majesty.
That is where he raised and mentored Siaavosh.
His paternal instinct, driven by his grief,
Leads him to war, thus endangering our troops.
I do not know why the hero of elephant stature
Now singles me out of our vast host.
Yet I shall show up to see what he desires,
For my soul wastes away with anguish and grief."

The emperor replies, "Go to him,
And speak to him softly and accordingly.
If he desires only peace and wealth,
Then why commit this vast army to endure loss?
Go to him, and if he wishes to give you presents,
Accept them and return here,
For it is far better for us not to incite him.
But if he has donned his armor of Babreh Bayan,
Then he must be set on engaging in war.
We shall have to surrender to the Creator,
Battle like fierce lions.
As long as we enjoy the breath of life,
We shall fight to either kill or be killed.
After all, he is not made of iron, fire, and bronze,
But merely of blood, flesh, and hair.
He does not battle in midair.
Why is your heart consumed with worry?
If you believe that he eats stone and steel,
Then dagger and spear will have no power over him.
For every one man of theirs, we have three hundred.
Why do you waste time in fear and worry?
This glorious Zaboli hero is nothing more
Than a fierce elephant in the throes of a fight.
I shall then play with him a game of elephants,

And he will never wish to battle with us again."

5 | Piran Goes to Rostam

Piran departs filled with dread and grief,
His heart split over the presence of Rostam.
Once in proximity of the Iranian army, he cries,
"O battle seeker, I have heard that,
Among our Tooranian leaders,
You wish to set your sights on me.
I left my camp to find out
Why the warlord summons me."

At the news that a Tooranian warrior has arrived,
Rostam advances toward him,
Head covered with iron helm.
He says to him, "O Tooranian, what is your name?
Why are you here? What is your wish?"

The other replies, "I am Piran, leader of these noblemen.
You asked Hoomaan, son of Viseh, to summon me.
You spoke to him of me affectionately.
My heart sprang toward you, O world hero.
What is your name among brave warriors?"

The other replies, "I am Rostam from Zabolestan,
Armed with mace and Kaboli sword."

At the sound of the amazing voice,
Piran climbs down from his horse
To render homage to Rostam, who says to him,
"O noble warrior, I bring you greetings from
Our shining sun, our world famous King Khosrow,
Chief of empires and rulers, support of noblemen.
I bring you greetings from his mother,
The daughter of Afraasiyaab,
Who sees your face in her dreams every night."

Piran replies, "O hero of elephantine stature,
I greet you in the name of the Creator and my army.
May the Giver of joy bless you!

May the revolving dome spin at your command!
All benefits come from Yazdan, who is our shelter,
Thanks to whom I find you here strong and fit.
Are Zavaareh, Faraamarz, and Zaal clear-eyed,
Joyous, renowned, and in optimum health?
May the world never be deprived of their lives!
If you don't mind, I wish to air a complaint,
Though I am your inferior and your position is higher.
I have planted a tree watered by my troubled tears
That now produces bitter fruits and bloody leaves.
This tree in my garden was my life
And my most valuable treasure.
It has now become the source of my troubles
Since, instead of a remedy, it yields only poison.

"Siaavosh considered me as a father.
He raised his shield to protect me against misfortune.
Vast are my troubles and the suffering I have endured
At the hands of this king and his people.
I take Yzad as my witness, though it is not right
To invoke testimony from the Master of Justice,
That despite the lengthy time that has elapsed,
Despite the best advice given to me by wise men,
I have never acted in any manner of evil against anyone.
Yet I suffered tremendously as a consequence
Of my attempts to free Siaavosh from Afraasiyaab.
Despite my efforts, he remained within this king's reach.
As for Kay Khosrow, O noble hero,
My words and actions suffered in my attempts
To extract him from the dragon's grip.

"When he was born, my heart filled with joy.
The king himself is my witness; wisdom is my guide.
I did not utter a word to Afraasiyaab,
By day or by night, in time or out of turn.
The bold Afraasiyaab asked me,
          'Do you not wish for me to enjoy rest and sleep?
          In the end, I shall endure retribution from Kay Khosrow.
          I know such a thing is hard to believe,
          But we must behead him as we did his father Siaavosh.
          We cannot assess the extent of his actions.
          The astrologers predicted that his evil deeds will

One day be upon me and upon my kingdom.'

"I told him,
  'O highborn king, why do you listen to astrologers?
  Turn in the direction of the Creator for support.
  The Creator will guide you
  On the path to righteousness.'

"After giving him advice and by means of
A hundred more recourses, he finally bent
And shortened his reach on Kay Khosrow.
Now that your king has made his way to Iran,
He continuously blames me,
Furiously chiding me night and day, saying,
  'You are the reason for all my troubles!
  You are the reason for my sinking status in the world!'

"On his side, Kay Khosrow is aggrieved with me.
This seed of goodness that we planted
Is now bearing bitter fruit.
In the name of the pure Yazdan, the Sun and Moon,
The revolving dome, crown and throne,
My relatives did not have a hand
In the killings of Siaavosh or the Iranians.
Yet the blaze of agony continues to consume my soul.
Blood tears sprang to my eyes when I learned
Of the fate of Siaavosh, I continue to seek
A cure for my despair and despondency.
Besides anguish and pain,
I have gained nothing in this affair,
Receiving no compensation from the revolving dome.

"Once I discovered the fate of Siaavosh,
I washed my hands of good and bad deeds.
I found myself stuck between two nations
And two powerful monarchs in grief.
I found myself fallen from favor.
I saved the life of Faranguis at the risk of my own,
Since her father wished to execute her.
I secretly received her in my home,
Hiding her there and supporting her in every way.

"Now instead of rewarding me, he wants to take

505

My life away, fill my head with wicked thoughts.
I harbored deep affection for Siaavosh,
Holding him dearer than my own eyes, head, and soul.
I gave him nation and daughter to ennoble my lineage.
The gem that Siaavosh gave us, the kind Foorood,
I had to part from him body and soul.
They killed him in the most vile way.
They killed him and my dear daughter,
And you might think that I deserved it.
This is the manner in which I felt overwhelmed
And troubled as both sides protested against me.
I am incapable of escaping the grip of Afraasiyaab.
There is no corner of the world
Where I can find refuge and peace.

"I fear for my wealth, my lands, my herds,
And I do not have the means to move away.
I have sons and veiled women in my chambers
Who need me and for whom I worry deeply.
If Afraasiyaab commands us to go to war,
We shall no longer close our eyes to sleep.
I must, despite myself, take the leadership of his army.
It would be imprudent for me to disobey his demand.
Instead of planning an attack on us,
Perhaps you can forgive me and show us mercy.
If only my heart could be free of the pain and grief
I endure regarding my lineage and Pilsam's death!
Beyond them, I had other relatives who were slain,
Many young and valiant,
Who never imagined tiring of war.

"I now find myself fearing for my own life,
Yet I shall say only a few words in favor of my sons.
In the name of the Creator, Giver of victory,
I plead with you, O world hero,
That you need not worry about me.
I swear on the glorious soul of Siaavosh
That I would rather die than be forced
To seize sword, helmet, and armor.
Once the armies have engaged in battle,
You will witness mountains of corpses belonging
To men from Kushan, Shakni, Saghlaab, and India.

You will witness heaps that will cover the land
From this border to the Sea of Sindh, and countless
Troops innocent in regard to the death of Siaavosh.
Peace is more valuable to me than war.
You must not show yourself intransigent.
Reveal to me your thoughts and your leanings.
You are wiser than I am, more courageous in battle."

Rostam listens to Piran's words but does not
Answer in accordance to the other's wishes:
"Since the day I seized weapons,
Along with the king's warriors, to battle with you,
I have seen that among the Turks
You display the most righteous temperament,
Demanding from your landsmen just actions.
Even the leopard understands that war is not unfair.
Mountains and boulders know it as well.
But when the King of Kings is intent on vengeance,
One must expect a shower of shots to rain from above.

"Now I wish to offer you a two-part peace accord.
Reflect and see if the conditions suit your needs.
Firstly, you will send captive to Kay Khosrow,
Those responsible for having spilled innocent blood.
It is better for them to be absent from this battlefield.
Next, you will accompany me on a journey where
You will present yourself before the victorious king.
Whatever you leave behind and whatever its value,
The king will replace tenfold.
You will, therefore, have not the need to regret
The loads borne by the Tooranian army.
Otherwise, I shall not allow any of your men to live.
I shall kill the warriors from Shakni and Saghlaab
As well as the Emperor of Chin.
I shall devastate your mountains and plains,
Convert this place into a barren wasteland."

Piran reflects: "This is a serious affair.
He wants me to leave Tooran-Zamin
And travel to the side of his king.
In addition, he demands that we surrender
Those who committed crimes against Siaavosh.

In the name of vengeance, he wishes to execute
Afraasiyaab's relatives and the court's great leaders,
Men who possess status, honor, and wealth.
How dare he talk to me of this?
His speech holds neither head nor tail.
Goodarz is mourning endlessly because of the actions
Of Hoomaan, Golbaad, and Farshidvard.
They and everyone would have to be handed over,
And such a thing is not feasible in the world.
Such a thing would be like a wild torrent
Finding no pool or sea to rush into.
I must then rely on myself for a way out."

He says to Rostam, "O distinguished hero,
May you live long, happy, and clear-sighted!
I shall depart right away to report your intentions
To Manshoor, Shangal, and the Emperor of Chin.
I shall send to Afraasiyaab an envoy
On camelback to relay the communication
And extract him from his slumber."

6 | The Tooranians Hold Counsel on the War With the Iranians

Piran rushes to his camp, swift as wind,
To convene with members of Viseh's family
And to reveal to them his secret.
He says, "Know that this man of lion heart
Is none other than world seeker Rostam,
Whose arrival will cause us to weep mournfully.
When he battles in vengeance, when he leads
Noblemen from Zabolestan and Kabol,
All the world riders together could not withstand him.
Escorting him are Goodarz, son of Kashvaad,
Giv, and Tous, and whether we wish it or not,
We must hasten to engage in a battle
We desperately wish to avoid. He seeks
The Tooranians responsible for Siaavosh's death.
He does not wish to harm the innocent.
But we all know that Afraasiyaab

Has strong interest in those among us
Who have participated in said crime.

"Be assured that our entire nation will be destroyed,
That the Iranian warlords will do with it as they please,
And that we will be left with neither old nor young,
Neither king nor treasury,
Neither host nor crown and throne.
I advised the vile and unjust Afraasiyaab
To contain his impetuousness and his pride.
I anticipated that, one day,
This blaze would consume him,
That his mind would be expended,
And the eye of his wisdom blinded.
But the tyrant did not heed my advice.
He took it upon himself to assassinate
The noble Siaavosh without consulting
The brave and wise men of his kingdom.

"You will see that neither king nor crown will survive,
Neither war elephant nor this throne and headdress.
The King of Iran will rejoice while our brave troops
Will have to cope with pain and worry.
Alas, this vast host and these valiant men, surrounded
By pomp and power, possessors of thrones and crowns!
All will be lost before your eyes.
None of us will safely return from this battleground.
We will be trampled beneath the feet of their chargers.
The splendor of the fortune watching over us will tarnish.
My heart is troubled by the fate awaiting Hoomaan,
Consumed at the thought of Rooeen.
Rostam's face is deeply frowned with a single thought:
That of avenging Siaavosh.
I shall travel in my anguish to the Emperor of Chin
To reveal to him the menaces looming over us."

He takes off like a dust tornado toward the emperor,
Heart troubled, eyes full of bitter tears, lips full of sighs.
The emperor's pavilion resounds with laments.
An assembly of relatives of Kaamoos
Surround the Chini ruler, pleading for justice
And crying in a common voice.

The emperor, his cheeks the color of saffron, says,
"From now on, Afraasiyaab will no longer
Enjoy power, not even in a dream.
We shall return, tearful, the Kushani troops to Chin,
Hearts drumming with the urgency of retaliation.
Then we shall lead here an army from Chin
And from the coast of Barbary to avenge Kaamoos.
We shall muster troops from Bozgoosh,
Sagsaar, and Mazandaran armed with heavy mace
And impatient to contend with Rostam,
Whose cry of war should not be heard by anyone.

"If, for his part, Afraasiyaab wishes
To enter into this campaign,
He might as well renounce peace and sleep.
At the same time, the families of Changgesh
And Ashkeboos will sound the beat of war drums.
The assistants, in their compassion for these relations,
Will drench their saffron-colored cheeks with tears.

Eyes moist, he continues: "From this time on,
We shall renounce sleep and rest
Unless we set Sistan ablaze,
Fill our enemy's days and nights with bitterness.
We shall hang Rostam's head from the gallows
To exhibit our grief for the deceased Kaamoos.
We shall burn his elephantine body
And sprinkle his ashes at his palace gate."

Piran hears their cries, heart aflutter, features gloomy.
He says to them, "O wistful, anguished souls,
You are not aware that your lives will end here."

He advances toward the emperor and adds,
"A war that was meant to be short is drawn out.
A bold whale has emerged from the sea
With thick armor of leopard skin to battle with us.
He has brought with him illustrious princes
From various provinces and sundry nations.
All our efforts and exertions have been in vain.
We cannot declare unjust actions to be just.
Afraasiyaab's wrongs will be sentenced here.

The King of Tooran's head turned toward evil,
Causing Siaavosh to perish at his hand.
It was on the advice of the foolish Garsivaz
That he committed this horrendous crime.
Yet Siaavosh was a man of sense and nobility,
Nourished and raised by Rostam of Zabolestan.
Now his death brings us to war and vengeance,
As if the sky is tumbling down to earth.
Neither the leopard claw nor the elephant trunk,
Neither the lofty mountains nor the flows of the Nile
Will prevail over Rostam when he leads a host to war.
He sits on a charger that does not need a vessel
To traverse a sea of blood.
Let us not imprudently think little of this battle,
Since he was able to defeat those who attacked him.
A flame is launched from the cerulean vault of sky,
And its scorching heat smothers our dim hearts.

"Summon sages and wise men.
Let them forecast the outcome of this venture
And which man will sustain the weight of battle.
Perhaps it is better to return to our land,
Since this setback will reduce our power.
If one wishes for his affairs to prosper,
One must avoid the ambush of vengeance."

Dismayed at Piran's words,
The Emperor of Chin invokes the Creator's name
And says, "What course of action shall we take
Now that such a vast host has disembarked?"

Shangal shouts, "O highborn one,
Why waste time engaging in long discourse?
In our wish to save Afraasiyaab,
We crossed land and sea.
We received troops and presents from the king.
We rushed here, bounding like valiant lions.
If we retreat in the face of battle,
We shall return defeated, like foxes.
We did not stop on the road for one day.
And we shall now find ourselves in distress
Because a man arrives from Sistan to fight?

It is shameful to retreat before a single man,
And this is not the way to attain our goal!
Were he a mad, drunken elephant, he would not
Be able to measure himself against a lion.
Although Kaamoos buckled beneath his blows,
We must not give up hope and lose faith.

"Piran finds himself terrified of Rostam.
His anguish robs him of sleep at night.
Is there a single warrior who makes a case
For a man who raises his arms to come to rescue us?
Rostam is not a wild elephant;
He is not equal to the lion.
He is not as valiant as Piran claims.
We must come to a decision and prepare for battle,
Not allow the fear that he inspires to dishearten us.
Altogether we number more than
One hundred thousand troops, bold and eager for war.
Why are you trembling before a single warrior?
It is as if the sight of him has rendered us
Inert and lifeless as dead corpses before our time.

"Tomorrow morning, we shall unhook our maces,
Lead our valiant army into battle against the Iranians.
We shall raise into the air a spring cloud,
Send showers of shots flying down.
Our riders' blows of axes will be so sharp
That one will no longer distinguish
Between the combatants' heads and feet.
Fix your sight on me, and when I shout the cry of war,
You must strike! When I assail this Sistanian man,
You will raise the dust to the dome of sky
And will not allow a single Iranian to escape.
A fearful man is a useless, valueless thing."

Shangal's speech renews everyone's heart.
Piran says to him, "May you live in joy!
May your soul be free of trouble and worry!"

Emperor and noblemen praise Shangal, the Indian king.
Piran returns to his tent, and the warriors,
Hoomaan, Nastihan, and Baarmaan, disperse.

Some are worried; others are full of hope.

Hoomaan asks Piran, "What did you decide?
Are we assured of peace, or will the hosts battle again?"

Piran recounts to Hoomaan Shangal's speech of war,
How it was received and applauded by the assembly.

Hoomaan is afflicted, his anger flared up at Shangal.
He curses him and ends up saying to Piran,
"One can only expect a sour outcome
From the spin of the sky."

On his way out, he speaks to Golbaad
About Shangal and his foolish behavior:
"If this Rostam is as I have witnessed
And akin to the descriptions I have heard,
He will allow neither Shangal nor Kondor,
Neither Manshoor nor the Emperor of Chin,
Neither colossal elephants nor throne and crown,
Neither treasure nor wealth to prevail on the field.
We must stand somewhat to the side to find out
What can save us and what can overthrow us,
For you will see that two-thirds of these troops,
Whose heavy maces should make the world surrender,
Will soon find themselves sprawled across the ground
With their armor as shrouds
And their helmets awash with blood."

Golbaad replies, "O skilled swordsman,
Do not rush to conclude such bad omens for us.
Do not dwell in distress and disquiet,
For fate may propose a different outcome
From the one you forecast.
One will not lose courage
If one does not despair of the future."

7 | Rostam Addresses His Army

On his side, Rostam convenes his leaders
Of the likes of Tous, Rohaam, Goodarz, and Giv;
Fariborz, Gostaham, and Khorraad the warrior;
Gorgeen, skilled horseman, and Bijan, expert in battle.
Rostam addresses them properly, saying,
"O prudent, open-minded wise men,
Treasury and throne belong to the one to whom
The Creator grants opportunity and good fortune.
Such a man will be world master, victorious in battle,
Fearless when confronted by elephant, leopard, or whale.
But his hand must refrain from committing unjust acts.
Let us then devote our lives to Yazdan.
For what other purpose might we be on this somber earth?
We must turn away from the bow of evil.
Follow the divine path of Eternal Wisdom,
For in the end the world will remain for no one,
And one must not allow himself to be attached to it.

"Let us fall into the practice of humanity and virtue.
A tortuous, winding road can only lead to one's ruin.
When Piran ran to me heartbroken,
He spoke to me at length of his affection for Siaavosh,
The heartache and worry he suffered, and how,
By his words and actions, he was able to spare
Faranguis and Khosrow from the dragon's sinking jaws.
Nevertheless, I have the premonition that Piran
Will figure as one of the first to fall in this war
And that before him will die his brother, his son,
And many of his illustrious allies.

"Afraasiyaab will perish at the hands of Kay Khosrow,
For this is the vision that came to me in a dream.
None of those responsible will remain alive.
They will all succumb, trampled beneath our feet.
But I do not wish to be responsible for the death of Piran,
Since there is in him a great deal of righteousness,
Since evil thoughts are unable to find a path to his heart.
If he fulfills his promise, we must forget ancient crimes.
If he delivers to us the guilty ones, along with
Siaavosh's treasury, we must renounce vengeance,

And I shall no longer have cause to engage in war.
Nothing in the world is better than virtue.
If noblemen, masters of throne and elephant,
With their host, vast as the flows of the Indus river,
Send us wealth and tribute, I shall give up all hostility.
If they surrender to us their thrones and treasures,
You will no longer have the need to exert yourselves.
We shall cease contention and killing.
The One who bestows all that is good
Provided us with the wisdom to distinguish the path.
The world is full of wealth, crowns, and thrones,
Which should not only be the share
Of those on whom fortune smiles.
Happy is the one who lives in abundance."

At these words, Goodarz rises and says to Rostam,
"O lion, full of honor and justice,
You are the army's pillar and the court's adornment.
Crown, throne, and diadem shine through your being.
You have access to vast knowledge;
Your mind feeds on wisdom.
Without a doubt, peace is more valuable than war,
But pay heed that the bull remains
Within the confines of its leathered skin.
One does not know what the future holds.
I shall recount to you a story plucked from olden times:
          'The souls of evil men reject righteousness,
            As the neck rejects an overbearing weight.'

"If Piran, in his misery, made you a pledge,
He will attempt to elude what he rightly promised.
The Creator crafted him from a malicious seed.
You must not listen to him or believe what he says.
We are ready for battle as well; we had discussions.
Piran sent an envoy to tell us that he was fed up
With war and with the field of vengeance,
That he strapped his waist in service to Kay Khosrow,
And that he renounced his lands and his pavilions.
He listened to our advice and our demands, and replied,
          'I shall tell my men that I have no desire to battle.
            I shall go swiftly and prepare everything
            And tell my family all that has occurred.

515

I possess throne, treasury, herds, and horses,
Which I shall not abandon to Tooran-Zamin.'
We told him that if he did not agree to come here,
It will not matter that his belongings are in Tooran.
He could retire in some faraway corner
So that the king never hears of his crimes.

"After our conversation, Piran left as swift as wind
To return to his camp in the dark night.
He sent an envoy to Afraasiyaab
To report to him and urge him to mobilize troops,
As the Iranian host had arrived.
It was as if nothing had been agreed between us.
We could not make sense of this affair.
On the tenth day, he marched onto the plain,
Having deployed an army as vast as the world.
Now, O warrior, familiar only with lies and deceit,
The words he utters are shrewd and calculating,
As he wishes to play a different game.
He is frightened of your noose.
The sight of it deeply galvanized his fears.
The confidence of the Tooranians rested on
Kaamoos and on leaders Manshoor and Fartoos.

"Upon Kaamoos's death and the decline of his fortune,
Piran came knocking on the door of peace
And dared not stay longer on this field,
For he sensed his imminent demise.
Seeing no way out, he resorted to ruse and treachery.
He promised to deliver to you the offenders,
And the wealth and treasures of Siaavosh.
But you will see, as soon as we hear the beat of timpani,
As soon as Fariborz and Tous march toward the enemy,
Piran will be at the lead of his host
Eager to drive a counterattack.
His words and promises are nothing but lies,
And Ahriman alone is his ally.
If you wish to dismiss my counsel,
Consider the fate of my son Bahraam,
Whom Piran goaded in the same manner
While he was busy battling us
And converting the field into a graveyard

For the members of the Goodarzian family.
For as long as I live and breathe,
An Indian sword will be my physician."

Rostam listens to Goodarz and replies,
"May you always speak words of wisdom!
It is no secret that Piran is exactly as you describe
And that his nature is made of a different cloth than ours.
Yet I do not wish to show myself intransigent,
In view of the noble and decent deeds
He performed in favor of the King of Iran
And how he suffered for Siaavosh.
Should he retract his pledge, should he present himself
Before me ready for battle, I shall tie to my saddle's hook
My noose, able to capture the mightiest elephants.
With my positive outlook, I shall offer him the benefit
Of the doubt, for I still wish to avoid battle and war.
But if he retreats before the completion of his oath,
He will find in our midst neither regret nor pity."

Goodarz and Tous praise Rostam:
"The sun will never cease to shine upon you!
Piran's strategies, his cunning ways
And his lies would never succeed in dazzling you.
May the royal throne never be deprived
Of your support and your presence!"

Rostam says, "Night is approaching,
And our heads are weary of this discussion.
Come, let us enjoy wine for half the night
And spend the other half preparing the army.
We shall see tomorrow what secrets
The World Creator reserves for us."

Then he turns toward the Iranians and adds,
"I shall cast good fortune tonight by drinking wine,
And tomorrow morning I shall raise above my shoulder
This heavy mace that once belonged to Saam, the rider,
And which backed me up in the war in Mazandaran.
I shall lunge into the brawl in a way
That not even a massive whale could oppose me.
If I am forced to battle, I shall take tents and diadems,

Mace and crowns, war elephants and ivory thrones,
And dispense the lot to the Iranian troops."

The assembly hall echoes with noblemen's joyous cries
And their expressions of devotion to Kay Khosrow.
In the end, the lion men of Iran-Zamin retire to their tents,
Exhausted, intoxicated, and in great need of rest.

8 | The Iranians and the Tooranians Form Ranks

As the sun reveals its shining helm in the sky
And the moon takes on the appearance of a silver shield,
The moon, fearing a debate with the sun, veils her face.

The beat of drums is heard at Tous's door,
The ground disappears beneath the horses' hooves,
The earth dims to the color of indigo,
And the air stirs with dust.
Rostam dons his armor and grabs his war gear.
The Iranian host lines up,
A battle-thirsty son, a vengeful father.
Giv, son of Kashvaad, takes the right wing
Dressed in a coat of mail and armed with iron mace.
Fariborz takes command of the left wing and raises
Into the air a banner sporting the figure of a wolf.
Tous, son of Nozar, holds himself in the center of the unit.
The entire world appears covered with troops.

Rostam advances to the army vanguard
In order to better protect his warriors.

The Emperor of Chin, in the middle of his host,
Is surrounded by so many elephants
That the land turns a deep shade of blue-gray.
Kondor, vanquisher of lions, takes the right wing,
Brave horseman armed with sword and bow.
Kahaar, experienced warrior, leads the left wing,
Riding a horse whose hooves shred the ground.

Piran exits the ranks, approaches the battling Shangal,
And says to him, "O illustrious King,

Whose command is obeyed in India and Sindh,
You had conveyed to me that this morning
You would advance your troops from multiple angles,
Deny Iranians, young or old, the chance to survive,
Incite a major brawl with Rostam,
And fling into the dust his highborn head."

Shangal replies, "I do not disavow my words.
You will not see me cowardly retract my resolve.
I shall attack this conqueror of heroes,
Pierce my arrow's tip deep into him,
Thus avenging the death of Kaamoos
And reducing the Iranians to a state of despair."

Then he divides the army into three corps
And demands the rumbling drum of timpani.
Dust rises over the plain; the host falls into motion.
Escorted by war elephants, they travel for one part
Of the journey, covering a space of two miles.

The heads of the elephant drivers gleam with adornments.
They are bedecked with diadems and earrings,
Golden torques and golden belts.
The elephants are enclosed in dust covers of Chini brocade
And carry on their backs golden chests and golden thrones.
The Emperor of Chin sits on one of these white elephants,
Heart beating with hope and joy.

9 | Rostam Admonishes Piran

Shangal storms into the army core,
Clutching an Indian sword.
A man holds a parasol over his head, and a crowd
From Dambar, Margh, and Mai stands behind him.
The right and left wings move along with him,
Following his tracks.

At the sight of them shifting, Piran rejoices,
Banishing all thoughts of Rostam from his mind.

He says to Hoomaan,

"Today, the battle will conclude in our favor,
Since there are so many valiant riders, proud as lions.
Do not take your ranks to battle,
Neither today nor tomorrow.
Better to refrain from engaging in war.
Take your post behind the Emperor of Chin,
Who knows you, for if this Zaboli man sees you
With troops and banner, our venture will be halted.
Let us watch and see how our fate will unfold
And whether fortune, which watches over us,
Will work to our advantage."

Then Piran advances toward the group and the place
From which rose the imposing shadow of Rostam.
He dismounts and greets the hero numerous times,
Saying, "The glorious dome of sky
Borrows its luster from you.
May you never descend in rank!
May you never have to face troubles!
O brave warlord, after I left your side,
I reported your message to young and old.
I recounted to them your high deeds,
But who in the world could celebrate you with dignity?
I rushed to speak to them of peace and war,
To discuss all sorts of matters, great and small,
But in the end, they said,
        'How could we quench our desire for vengeance?
        It is easy for us to return treasure and jewels
        And everything else of value, but we must not
        Surrender to him those who committed the crime.
        Reflect and think about this secret.
        Do you know anyone guilty in my family,
        Which entirely consists of highborn men?
        How can I entrust them to you?
        Your longing is a good one that
        Will bring youth to aging men.
        Do not rush to speak to us.
        What Rostam asks of you is to give up our most
        Noble leaders, masters of crowns and diadems.
        Since these vast hosts have arrived to our aid
        From Chin, Saghlaab, Khotan, and Tooran-Zamin,
        Why would Afraasiyaab ask for peace,

He who summons such innumerable troops,
Both from firm land and from beyond the seas?'

"In this way, they interrupted the discussion
By reproaching me, and I rushed
To come to your side and report back to you.
They don't even know each other,
But they have heard of you
And call you 'the man from Sistan.'
The king of India wishes to fight you
With bow and arrow and with his Indian saber,
Alongside a Tooranian host vast as the flows
Of the sea and most eager to fight.
I am certain that, in the end,
The hero of elephant build will
Make this multitude of troops shed copious tears."

At these words, Rostam is shaken by a bout of fury.
He says to Piran, "O miserable man,
How could you resort to lies and deceit?
How dare you set foot on dangerous terrain?
The king spoke to me in public and in secret of your lies.
Now I stand witness to your actions and your desires.
Goodarz had mentioned to me that, from head to toe,
You are nothing but treachery,
That you rush to foolishly dip in your own blood.
Your present fate is rather wretched,
But your future fate will indeed be more dire.
Whether the earth is an abyss or a paradise to you,
Did I not advise you to leave this cursed land
And take shelter in a civilized nation?
A life such as yours has little value,
For your head is beneath the dragon's breath.

"Do you not wish to gaze at the just and generous king?
He is young, mild, and striking of visage.
Would you rather consume serpent
And wear leopard hide than dress in shiny silk?
No one will dispute you on this matter,
And you will nourish only on the fruits
Sprouting from seeds you have sown."

Piran replies, "O fortunate man, powerful and content,
You are the ornament of the throne.
What man is capable of expressing himself as you can?
May brave and noble men pay you homage!
My heart and my soul are your loyal subjects,
And my mind will always serve your will and command.
I shall spend this night in contemplation
And address the assembly of great leaders."

He returns to his army core, heart replete with lies,
Head keen on vengeance.

10 | The Battle Begins

As Piran walks away, the motion of the two hosts
Makes the world appear like a simmering volcano.
Rostam says to the Iranians,
"Here I am, cinched for battle.
May each of you fill your head with warring ardor,
Frown menacingly, and be ready to sustain
A struggle that promises to be monumental!
On this day, and on this battlefield, the difference
Between wolf and sheep will be determined.
The astrologer said to me,
        'Prepare yourself well for the impending war.
        It will be launched between two mountains
        And will wash the face of the earth with blood.
        The opposing force will consist of the entire human race:
        Experienced kings will come in multitude to fight,
        And the world will find itself bereft of its leaders.
        Vengeance will be indulged and quenched.
        A solid iron mace will lose its density
        And soften into the consistency of wax.'

"No matter who comes to fight with me, do not fear.
With the aid of the sublime dome of sky,
I shall bind his two hands in the knots of my noose.
Unite with one another and banish fear from your hearts.
If I am to perish on the battlefield,
Then I shall live tonight to feast.
Since my body belongs to death, I wish

To acquire glory and leave behind a good name.
You also assure yourselves a form of enduring fame,
And since we cannot linger on earth forever,
Let us not worry so much about our future.
Let us not attach our hearts to this transitory passage.
No matter what path we take,
It will ultimately betray us.
If our souls befriend wisdom,
It will count neither happy days nor unhappy ones.
Not even the holder of crown and treasure
Will bind his heart to this fleeting, illusive existence."

The army replies to Rostam, "Your command
Reaches higher than the sphere of the moon.
We shall fight with our piercing swords in a way
As to exalt our names until the day of resurrection."

The sound of timpani rises,
The air dims, and the earth blackens.
The hosts come together from both sides
As a fierce shower of spears and arrows
Pours down from a black cloud looming over.
The world resembles a sea of tar.
The shining face of the sun is obscured by metal tips
And by eagle feathers affixed to arrows.
One would think that the steel tips of lances
Pierce through the dust to smear stars with blood.
The metal of bull-headed maces crashes and rumbles,
As if rocks are tumbling from the sky.
Swords gleam like diamonds, causing a surge of blood.
The ground and dust are engulfed in blood and brains.
Helmets shatter on heads and fly into splinters.

The aged Goodarz says, "Since I attained
Manhood and strapped myself for battle,
Never have I witnessed or heard of such a fight.
Such is the carnage that out of two men, one perishes.

11 | Shangal Battlesf Rostam and Flees

Shangal brings forth his army, roaring and shouting,
"I am vanquisher of lions, seeker of battle.
I come to contest with the warrior from Sistan,
To measure his strength against mine."

He storms onto the field and bellows,
"Where is he, the man from Sistan?
Let him show himself and come to wrestle with me."

At the boom of this commanding voice,
Rostam looks in Shangal's direction and says,
"From the World Creator, I have never seen
Anything like this, revealed or concealed,
That a stranger from this vast host would emerge
So daringly and wish to fight with me.
I shall allow no one to survive,
Neither Shangal nor the Emperor of Chin,
Neither bold warriors nor leaders from Tooran-Zamin!"

He approaches Shangal and cries out,
"Evil offshoot of evil parents, Zaal named me Rostam.
Why do you, O wretched one, call me man from Sistan?
Know with certainty that the man from Sistan
Is your death and that your armor and helm
Will soon serve you as a shroud."

He rushes toward him with Rakhsh,
Crossing the lines of battle as swift as wind.
He strikes him with his spear, knocks him off the saddle,
And brings him down to the ground, head first.
He tramples him, not injuring him,
And seizes his sharp sword.
But the valiant men of the opposite host
Lunge into the mix with swords dipped in bile,
And everyone, Turks, Indians, and men from Saghlaab,
Lead a common attack on the great world hero,
Surrounding Shangal and plucking him away.

In this way, Shangal is able to escape Rostam's claws,
Having found protection from his coat of mail.

PART TWELVE

He runs away, scowling, to the Emperor of Chin:
"This is not a man one should contend with.
There is no one in the world that could overcome him.
He is a war elephant seated upon a colossal mountain.
Our only chance is to attack him en masse.
No one will ever emerge alive from a fight with him."

The emperor replies, "Your words said otherwise earlier.
Your countenance has changed since."
He commands his army to come together
And form a compact group, solid as a mountain,
To joust with the proud warrior and to put an end to him.
Wielding swords, the Tooranians assail Rostam
As a group, each one as steady as a mountain.

Rostam the lion brings his hand to his sword
And attacks the left wing of the Chini army.
Wherever he takes his dagger,
The plain is covered with bodies deprived of heads.
Not even a mountain could resist his attack
Nor an elephant withstand his fury.

They surround him and press him so hard on all sides
That the sun above his head dims.
So many spears, swords, maces, and arrows
Are driven at this lion vanquisher that it is as if
He is in a field of reeds, and the flowing blood
Makes the surface of the earth resemble a wine press.

In one blow, he cuts one hundred spears in half,
Bellowing and boiling with rage like a lion
In such a way as to terrify his challengers.
Behind him march the Iranian warriors,
Eager for battle, hearts desiring vengeance.

The blows of mace and the masses of weapons,
The arrows and the jolts of swords shower down on them
Like a heavy mist pouring from a cloud.
Limbs, heads, bodies, and helmets cover the field.
The lofty sky resembles the earth, so thick is the dust
Through which shots fly in all directions.
Many warriors' necks and sides are slashed and gashed.
The surviving ones lament, "Our plain has turned

Into a mountain of body parts and corpses of men
From Chin, Shakni, India, Saghlaab, and Hari."

Troops, whether on land or water, on mountain or plain,
In unison feel a deep sense of defeat and lassitude,
So injured are they at the hands of this one man.

Piran says to Golbaad, "We have lost everything here.
We have not the power to overcome this single warlord.
No one in the world can command an army of his strength.
No man of sense would believe this account,
That three times one hundred thousand renowned warriors
Found themselves powerless before a single rider.
This war will take a sour turn for Afraasiyaab,
For when will Rostam let him enjoy a moment's rest?
What I can tell you with certainty is that we will be blamed.
If we seek to soften Rostam, we will come under suspicion,
And if we anger him, we shall perish in this struggle."

12 | The Battle of Rostam With Saaveh

Rostam addresses the Iranians:
"We have not sustained many losses in this battle.
Now I shall seize wealth, elephants, throne and crown
From the men of Chin and distribute them all to the Iranians.
This day will go down as one of joy and prosperity,
And to win that, I need none of the Iranians.
I shall only require Rakhsh's legs and divine grace.
I shall never again allow a single man from the lands
Of Saghlaab, Chin, and Shakni to tread the earth.
Today is a day of victory, and the awe-inspiring sky
Lavishes us with immense glory.
Our enemy's crimes, their destructions, murders,
And evil actions have only handed them loss and defeat.
If the Creator, Donor of Justice, gives me strength,
If Rakhsh displays his fierce courage, I shall turn this field
Into a graveyard, convert fertile ground into marshland.

"Let one of you go to the army like wind, and when
I stir to advance, beat timpani and ring Indian bells.
Render the earth black as ebony with dust stirred up

By your horses' motions and the sound of instruments.
Strike hard at the masses of weapons and arms,
Like the blacksmith's hammer pounds at steel.
Do not apprehend their numbers.
You will agitate the spume on the river's flows.
Break the lines of the troops from Saghlaab and Chin
In a way as to make the sky invisible to the earth.
Maintain your gaze on my helmet of steel.
When I bellow the war cry, you will rise and strike."

Rostam takes off like a furious elephant,
Wielding his bull-headed mace.
Bellowing ferociously, he approaches the right wing
Of the Tooranian host and its leader, Kondor.
He instigates chaos among the ranks,
And many helmeted heads find themselves
Detached from the bodies that once belonged to them.

There is a relative of Kaamoos named Saaveh,
A proud and ambitious warrior.
He advances to challenge Rostam,
Clutching an Indian sword.
He swivels right, he swivels left, desperately
Wishing to avenge the death of Kaamoos.
He says to Rostam, "O wild elephant,
You are about to witness a turmoil
Fiercer than the swells on the River Nile.
I shall pay retribution for the fate of the poor Kaamoos.
This will be the last battle you will ever engage in."

At the words of Saaveh,
Rostam grabs his heavy mace,
Unhooks it, and slams it into the other's helmet
With such force that his soul instantly exits his body,
Leaving no trace of him in all the world.

The banner of the man of Kushan is lowered,
And the fate of Saaveh fills his troops with grief.
No one can overcome Rostam.
Rakhsh's hooves can convert dust and weeds into fruit.

13 | Rostam Slays Kahaar

Rostam lunges from the right wing to the left wing,
And the entire line of Tooranian troops wavers.
There he finds Kahaar from Kahan,
A warrior of lion heart, brandishing a black banner.

The sight of Rostam's helmet causes shivers to crawl
Through his body as if his heart is being ripped open.
He cries like a lion, "I shall avenge Tooran and Chin
By fighting with the warrior from Sistan on this field.
I am the only prince able to oppose him,
For I am a man of lion heart clutching a heavy mace."

He launches his horse and advances toward Rostam.
Once near, though, he pales and shrinks in fear,
Thinking, "A fight with a wild elephant
Is like drowning in the waters of the Nile.
I told myself to fight, but my mind said,
        'This thought does not conform with wisdom.'
Therefore, it is far better to run away, head firmly
On my shoulders, than to make a show of bravery
And have my head trampled beneath his feet."
He sprints to take refuge in his army's center.
On both sides, eyes are fixed on him.

Rostam's banner rises in the midst of the crowd
Like a tree on a mountain crest
As the hero chases him fast as flying dust.
The earth turns the color of ruby, and the air darkens.
With his spear, he strikes Kahaar at the waist,
Tears his coat of mail and his belt's fastening,
And flings him to the ground
Like a leaf shaken off a tree during a storm.

The black banner is lowered,
As if Kahaar of Kahan had never existed.
Everyone witnesses Rostam's feat.
The dust of battle rises left and right.
The imperial banner and timpani advance ahead.
The proud Goodarz and Tous arrive,
And the Iranians cry out in a common voice:

"The hero, our support and strength, is victorious!"

Rostam says, "Give me one hundred eminent riders,
For I shall now seize the emperor's elephant,
His ivory throne, bracelets, mace, crown, and torque.
I shall take from Chin and give to Iran-Zamin
And to the triumphant world king."

One thousand riders exit the ranks of Iranians,
Dressed in mail and armed with bull-headed mace.
Rostam says to them, "Cinch yourselves for vengeance.
I swear by the life and the head of the king,
By the Sun and the Moon, by the dust of Siaavosh,
And by the Iranian army, that if a brave leader
From Iran-Zamin flees before the King of Chin,
He will have to face the gallows
As well as the shackles and the confinement of prison.
I shall place on his head a paper headdress."

The warriors know that Rostam's nature is lion fierce
And that in battle he seizes the antelope by the hip.
They advance as one toward the emperor,
The army stirred by resentment
And the king by the desire to seize the crown.

Rostam launches the attack, releases Rakhsh's reins,
And makes blood gush forth to the sphere of the moon.
Stars look down on the battlefield in astonishment.
The dust is so thick that one no longer sees the ground.
The shock of the riders and the blows of spears
Are so intense that the distinction
Between bridle and stirrup is blurred.
You would think that the sun
Has taken shelter behind a veil,
That the earth is weary of horses' hooves.

The air is black as ebony, and one could not
Carve a path through which to pass,
So numerous are the cadavers, the helms, armor,
And heads forced to part from bodies.

The dust raised by the chargers forms a cloud
Lifting above forceful winds, and the earth

Resounds with noise and the clatter of steel.
A great number of renowned men foolishly expose
Their heads in their quest to acquire glory.

Rostam shouts a cry, as if the sea is simmering:
"This elephant, ivory throne, these bracelets,
This crown, torque, and diadem are worthy
Of Kay Khosrow, the young world king.
What need have you for crown and all this pomp?
Although you have power, skill, crown, and glory,
A better course of action is for you to concede,
To surrender your hands to our shackles
And your body to the knots of our nooses.
I shall send you to the world king,
Sparing neither Manshoor nor the Emperor of Chin.
It is enough for me to have mercy on your life,
But the crown and seal will belong to another.
And if you disagree, I shall raise dust up to the moon
By the stirrings of my charger's hooves."

14 | The Emperor of Chin Is Captured

The Emperor of Chin replies to him by insulting him
And says, "O evil man of wicked body and soul,
May curses befall the land of Iran, its king, and its host!
You will plead for forgiveness, O man of Sistan,
Vilest among all men, and you will wish to be
A simple soldier in the army of the ruler of Chin."

A deluge of arrows falls to unnerve the troops,
Like autumn wind rattles and roils the trees.
Eagle feathers abound in the air, and never has anyone,
Not even in a dream, witnessed such a raging battle.

Goodarz, observing this cloudburst of steel,
Worries and trembles for Rostam, and says to Rohaam,
"Run without delay with two hundred riders armed
With bows from Chaadj and arrows of poplar wood.
Make haste to cover Rostam in battle."

Then Goodarz says to Giv, "Launch your host.

Do not allow a single attacker to remain on this plain.
This is not the time for rest and calm,
Nor is it time to deliberate and adorn the troops.
Drive the warriors toward the right
In search of Piran and Hoomaan.
Look at Rostam, how in grappling with the emperor
He lowers the sky down to earth.
May blessing no longer glorify this family from Chin!
May curses weigh heavy on it on the day of vengeance!"

Rohaam lunges like a leopard and takes his place
Behind Rostam, who says to the lion,
"I fear that my charger Rakhsh is exhausted,
And I shall be forced to battle on foot,
Drenched in blood and sweat.
This army is like a swarm of ants and grasshoppers.
Lead an attack on their elephants and elephant drivers,
For we have to bring them back safe and sound
To Kay Khosrow when we take to him
These new spoils of war from India and Chin."

Rostam shouts, "Ahriman is the ally of Tooran-Zamin,
O miserable ones who are devoid of resource,
Overcome by grief, powerless and desperate.
Have you never heard the name of Rostam?
Is your head deprived of sense and reason?
He is a man who views the dragon as a weakling
And who attacks elephants on the battlefield.
Are you not weary of fighting me,
Whose gifts are fierce bashes of mace and sword?"
He unfastens his noose and places it, still coiled,
On the saddle's pommel, propels Rakhsh,
And hollers a cry piercing enough
To bore through a dragon's ear.

Whichever way he swings his noose, warriors disperse.
His only thoughts are of battle against Chin.
His arm holds his lasso's loops, his forehead frowns.
Time and again, he unseats leaders or mere soldiers
By capturing them in his noose's knot.

Commander Tous calls for clarions and kettledrums,

And the sound rises all the way to the clouds.
An Iranian ties up the hands of each prisoner
And then leads him from plain to mountain.

At the sight of this scene, Fartoos lurches
Toward Rostam to fight him like a leopard.
Rostam, furious, advances like a whale,
Lifts him off the saddle, and tosses him to the ground.
He ties his hands and turns him over to his troops.
Then the brave hero swiftly rushes to the vanguard,
Noose hooked on his arm, mace clutched in his hand.

Ghorcheh, witness to this brawl and its outcome,
Rushes toward Rostam to contend with him.
He sends a shower of shots on his head,
Fierce as rain falling from a spring cloud.

Rostam swings his noose and casts the loop
Around Ghorcheh's waist.
He hands him over to the Iranians
And quickly returns in the direction of Kaaloo.

At the sight of him approaching, Kaaloo grabs
His sharp Indian sword and his mace,
And, coming up behind him,
He strikes Rostam on his helm and head.
Rostam reaches for his spear, attacks Kaaloo,
Captures him in the manner
Of a polo player seizing the ball.
He flings him off the saddle
And ties him up with leopard skin.

The Emperor of Chin, from high atop his elephant,
Sees the surface of the earth
Stirring like the flows of the Nile.
He observes an elephant seated on a tall mountain
Who catches brave men in his lasso made of lion hide,
Who forces vultures to plummet from black clouds,
As stars and moon look grimly down on this battle.

At the sight, the Emperor of Chin loses all hope.
From the army, he selects a learned man,
Able to speak the language of the Iranians.

He says to him, "Go to this man of lion heart and say,
    'Cease your cruel actions of war.
    These are men from Chaghan, Shakni, Chin, and Dahr.
    They are all strangers in this war of vengeance.
    There is one king of Khotan and one of Chin.
    You should not seek retaliation against outsiders.
    Do not confuse them with King Afraasiyaab,
    Who does not distinguish water from fire,
    Who alone gathered this mass of men,
    And who, by waging this war,
    Has brought misfortune upon himself.
    No one exists who is indifferent to honor and glory,
    Yet peace is more worthy than war.
    Let us settle on a truce.
    We shall agree to your demands.
    We shall pay tribute to you every year,
    And, in addition, we shall send
    One hundred cowhides to your leaders.'"

The envoy approaches the hero of elephant stature,
Mouth full of words, heart full of guile:
"O valiant ruler, now that the fight is over,
It is time to take part in feast and banquet.
You cannot harbor hatred for bygone deeds.
The emperor is withdrawing, and you would be wise
To do so as well, for his army renounces its fight.
Since the moment Kaamoos perished at your hands,
The desire to battle has dwindled among us.
How much blood are you willing to spill?
Has your heart not grown weary of war?"

Rostam replies, "You must hand over to me
Your treasure, your elephants, stallions,
Crowns, and ivory throne.
Your intention was to invade Iran to destroy it.
Why are you now pleading and complaining?
Since the emperor recognizes that his army
Is in my hands and that mine will act
As rapidly as permits my restraint, he begs me
For mercy, unaware of my high standing.
I shall grant him life,
But his torque and crown are mine,

As well as his elephant and his ivory throne."

The messenger replies, "O master of Rakhsh,
Do not sacrifice to another
The deer sprinting across the plain.
This field is crowded with men, elephants, and troops.
The emperor, master of treasury and crown, leads.
Who knows how destiny will unfold
And who will enjoy the laurels of victory?"

At these words, Rostam launches Rakhsh, saying,
"I am Rostam, lion vanquisher, giver of crowns.
With my noose hanging on my arm, I am powerful.
Is this the time to deceive me, to wrongly advise me?
What is the Emperor of Chin next to my lasso?
What is a lion next to my steady grip?
The moment he sets his sights on me and my noose,
The moment I catch him in my loop,
He will instantly find himself weary of life."

He swings his coiled lasso to fly
And captures the leader of the riders at the waist.
He approaches the white elephant
As the Emperor of Chin despairs for his life.
The emperor strikes his elephant
With his sharpened goad and screams a scream
Akin to thunder in the month of Farvardin.
He extracts a dagger and heaves it at Rostam,
Hoping to break him and cast his head down,
But Rostam narrowly evades the dagger.

The bold hero casts his noose at the ruler of Chin
And captures the princely head in its knot.
He removes him from atop his elephant and hurls
Him to the ground, where they tie up his hands.
Then Rostam takes him to the River Shahd on foot,
Deprived of his elephant, his crown, throne, and cushion.
He delivers the emperor to Tous's executioners.
The commander asks for the beating of timpani.

Such has been the working of the revolving dome:
At times it tempts you with honey
And lavishes you with tenderness, at times

It quenches your thirst with venom and spite.
It raises one up to the magnificent heavens,
While it lowers another,
Oppressing him with grief and sorrow.
It snatches one off the moon to toss him into a ditch,
While it elevates another to the moon.
It endows one with rule and kingdom, while it casts
Another into the deep sea as a repast for fish.
O Creator, you do not act out of favor or vengeance
But out of a deep-founded wisdom.
From you originate all joy and sorrow:
The expansion of one, the decay of another.
I know not your identity, but I have a sense
That all existence stems from you.

15 | The Defeat of the Tooranian Host

Rostam grabs his heavy mace, rendering strong
And weak men equally powerless before him.
The battleground, with its field and ravines,
Soon becomes so congested that neither ant
Nor fly can carve a path to traverse it.
The corpses and the injured flood it with blood:
Heads deprived of bodies, bodies slumped down.

Once shining fortune is tarnished, day reaches for night.
A powerful wind surges, drawing in a dark cloud.
The light of sun and moon dims.
The Tooranians cannot distinguish heads from feet.
They attempt to bolt far into the desert.

Piran, observing the battlefield,
Notices that the light of the revolving dome
Has dimmed for Manshoor, Fartoos, the emperor,
And other warriors of Tooran-Zamin,
That the banners of noblemen have been overturned
And that the wounded lie miserably in the dust.
He turns to Nastihan and Golbaad and says,
"Let us cast aside our javelins and swords.
The black banner has been lowered.
Our men, trembling, have fled the battlefield."

Giv leads the Tooranians' downfall at the right wing.
He makes the field look like
The fuzz of a heather francolin.
He runs through the enemy line,
From side to side, to establish Piran's position.
In the end, unable to spot Piran,
Giv and his brave men return to join Rostam.

Their war horses are exceedingly fatigued.
They are themselves wounded and weary of fight.
They retreat to the mountain, Rostam at the lead.
Bodies spent with exhaustion, hearts exhilarated by battle,
They are happy to have attained their objective.
Such is the custom and the condition of the world,
Helm and armor saturated in blood and dust,
Their horses' coverings ripped, shredded by the axe.

They do not recognize each other before having
Washed completely their chests and swords,
For their feet and stirrups are drenched in blood,
And it is impossible to ascertain climbs from descents,
So numerous are the cadavers.

They rinse off their heads and bodies,
Free of worry, for the enemy
Is now weighed down by heavy shackles.

16 | Rostam Distributes the Spoils of War

Rostam tells the Iranians,
"The time has come to lay down our weapons,
For it is not suitable to appear
Before the Creator, Giver of victory,
With mace and arrow, spear and shield.
Lower your heads to the dark dust of earth.
Later, you shall sport crowns on your heads.
Our hearts are at peace since we have been blessed
And have not lost any of our valuable noblemen.
Once the world king received news of you,
He told me all that is revealed and concealed,
That Commander Tous withdrew to the mountain

PART TWELVE

From fear of Piran and Hoomaan.
The king's words made me lose my composure
As it simmered with a fierce warring ardor,
And my soul grew black as ebony
At the thought of Bahraam, Goodarz, and Rivniz.
I left Iran in haste and, impatient to fight,
Did not stop for anything on the road.

"But once my gaze fell on the Emperor of Chin,
On his brave and powerful soldiers,
Mainly on Kaamoos, with his mien and stature,
With his arms and legs, his hands and mace,
I could not help but feel my end draw near.
Since the day I became a man and seized weapons,
Never had I seen, in all my life, more men assembled
And a more monumental pile of arsenal.

"I saw myself among the deevs of Mazandaran,
In the dark night, threatened by their heavy maces.
Nevertheless, my courage did not bend for an instant.
Never did I surrender to the idea that my life was in peril.
But today I felt my circumstances were at stake
And my heart, which lends its sheen to the world,
Exposed to the threat of plunging into dimness.
Now it is our duty to humbly bow low to the dust
Before the pure Creator, Giver of our strength,
A favorable star, and the Support of Saturn and Sun.
May our good fortune always shine!
May we escape the anguish of adversity!
Take care to deliver, without delay,
These messages to the world king,
Who will deck out his glorious palace,
Cinch his head with Kianian crown, and distribute
Alms to the poor to collect new blessings.

"Now strip yourselves of armor,
And may your cloaks embellish your rest.
Without a doubt, the heart's delights are equally elusive.
Destiny calculates our breaths,
But better they be counted cup in hand.
Forget the dome of sky who is no one's friend.
Let us then drink wine until midnight,

Celebrate the memory of our brave men.
Let us give thanks to the World Master,
Giver of victory, valor, joy, and high deeds.
Let us not, in the midst of grief and worry,
Attach our hearts to this transitory journey."

The noblemen praise him and say, "May seal
And crown never be deprived of your presence!
May your family and your race be blessed,
As well as the mother who gave birth to you!
The one who resembles you, O world hero,
Raises his head to the whirling firmament,
Even when he is another man's subject.
You know what you have done in your affection.
May the sky rejoice at the sight of you!
We were defeated, the light of our day had dimmed.
We owe you our lives and our glory."

Rostam asks for the elephant to be charged
With ivory throne, torque, and golden crown.
He asks for royal wine and cups, and first
Raises his glass to the health of the world king.
Seeing Rostam giddy with drink,
The brave men depart blessed with happiness.

As soon as the moon tears apart the veil of night
And establishes its throne upon the turquoise skies,
Rostam dispatches sentries onto the vast plain.
Gradually, the obscurity of night dissipates,
And the bright dagger of the sun reveals itself
To render the surface of the earth as bright as a ruby.
One hears the beat of drums in the hero's tent enclosure,
And the brave army men rise from their place of rest.

Rostam says to his highborn warriors,
"Nowhere have we found traces of Piran.
You must go to the battlefield and search."

Bijan, the eager warrior, departs instantly.
He finds the field littered with corpses
And body parts, with valuable weapons, treasure,
And wounded men lying entangled in the dust.
He does not see a single man alive,

PART TWELVE

As the field is strewn with empty tents and pavilions.

At the news of the Turks' retreat,
Rostam roils with rage for the Iranians
And their cowardice, and curses them:
"Your brains are devoid of sense!
You gave the enemy the chance
To escape through two mountains.
Did I not command you to dispatch sentries,
To keep an eye on plain, valley, and ravine?
You surrendered to sleep while the invaders escaped?
The one who fails to act will acquire only misery,
While the one who exerts himself
Is recompensed with treasure.
How will I disclose to everyone that, on this day,
We abandoned ourselves to rest
And did not muster up the courage
To exert our duty toward Iran-Zamin?"

He turns toward Tous, akin to a leopard in his anger,
And says, "Is this a bedchamber or a field of battle?
From now on, it is up to you to face Hoomaan,
Golbaad, Piran, Rooeen, and Poolaad.
You are from one nation, and I am from another.
If you are so powerful, then battle yourselves.
Why would you ask me to come to your aid?
I returned victorious from this battle, but in the end
It was all for nothing, and they are gone.

"Seek to find out who were our sentinels,
Who was at the vanguard of our host,
And what was the name of his tribe.
If you encounter one of these sentinels,
Shatter his hands with a club,
Take all that he possesses, tie up his feet,
Fling him on the back of a lofty elephant,
And send him in this state to court.
Perhaps the king will sentence him to death.
Search hard for the dinars, precious stones,
Ivory thrones, bolts of brocade, diadems, crowns,
And wealth that the Iranians have seized as booty.
Many kings and important rulers have camped here,

Noblemen from Chin, Saghlaab, India, and Dahr,
All wealthy rulers of provinces.
Gather the precious lot, and from it
We shall first select gifts for the king,
Then determine my share and yours."

The leader departs to compile the spoils of war,
Which the brave men spread out on the field of battle:
Golden belts, ruby crowns, Rumi brocade,
Bracelets, ivory thrones, bows and arrows,
Horse halters, maces, and Indian swords,
All assembled between the two mountains to form
A third one that the army observes with curiosity.

A horseman and skilled archer, broad of chest,
Strong of body and valiant, who could cast
An arrow with four feathers, would not succeed
In passing through this mass of spoils.

Rostam as well is astonished at the sight.
He invokes numerous times the Creator's grace
And says, "Chance, so fickle,
At times hands us feast, at times battle.
It transfers one's wealth to give to another,
At times cursing and damning,
At times lavishing with blessings.
One amasses a treasure,
Another benefits from its fruits.
Kaamoos and the Emperor of Chin
Wished to set fire to the land of Iran,
Bringing war elephants and gold,
Their hosts and their abundant wealth.
They rejoiced over their vast numbers,
Their treasures and possessions,
Casting aside the memory of Yazdan,
Who created the sky, space, and time,
The visible universe, as well as
Everything that exists beyond our sight
And beyond our scope of knowledge.

"We must give thanks to the Creator of all things,
Whom the wise man trusts unequivocally.

Who gave us strength and power, joy and prosperity.
Their host is destroyed, their wealth is lost,
For their schemes and strategies were unjust.
Since they did not call the name of the Creator,
They did not reap the benefits
From the turning dome of sky.
I shall send to the king these great men and
Chosen princes among the elite of many kingdoms.
I shall sit them on war elephants, hand them over
With their golden thrones and golden diadems.
I shall load up fiery camels
With everything worthy of the king.
I shall seize the world with my arm's force,
Purify it of every evil person
With my sword's edge, mercilessly.
Then I shall promptly march on Gang,
For a sensible man avoids losing time.
It would be a shame for any criminal to survive.
We shall wash our hands in the blood of each of them.
I shall fling into dust the heads of idol worshippers
And allow the cult of Yazdan to flourish."

Goodarz replies, "O wise man,
May you live in joy to the end of time!
May you fulfill the king's wishes!"

Rostam seeks Fariborz to take
The news to the imperial king.
As the son of Kaavoos,
He is suitable because of his ancestry.
Rostam says to Fariborz,
"O illustrious prince, you are of royal lineage.
You are prudent, wise, noble, and cheerful.
You are much like Siaavosh to the king;
You bring joy to all. No one exists
With your courage and heroism in the world.
Undertake this arduous journey.
Take my letter to the new king.
Take with you prisoners, camels, and this wealth:
Diadems, torques, bracelets, maces, crowns,
War elephants, and ivory throne."

Fariborz replies, "O valiant lion,
Here I am, ready to depart."

17 | Rostam's Letter to Kay Khosrow

Rostam summons a skilled scribe
And dictates a letter written with amber on silk,
As one writes to kings, opening in praise of the Creator:
"The One whose existence has no beginning, no end,
Who created Saturn, Moon, and Sun,
Who gives its sheen to power, crown, and courage,
Who created the earth, time, space, wisdom, and faith.
May the Creator bless the King of Kings!
May the time never be upon us
When only his memory lingers!

"I arrived as you commanded between two mountains,
Where I found assembled the armies of three kingdoms,
Where the enemy had gathered on the field of battle
More than one hundred thousand sword-bearing riders:
Men from Kushan, Shakni, Chin, and India.
Troops spread from Chin to the Sea of Sindh
And covered with tents, elephants, and litters
The land from Kashmir to the base of Mount Shahd.
I had no fear, thanks to the king's good fortune,
And I proceeded to kill his enemies on the field.
We battled for forty days, and it appeared
That the world was constricting for them.
They were leaders of important kingdoms,
Owners of crowns, thrones, and diadems.
We now find ourselves unable to cross
Between the two mountains, through plains
And ravines, for the space of forty farsangs
Because of the vast number of corpses.
The ground is saturated with blood and mud.

"Finally, if I wished to reveal everything
Relating to this important battle,
My letter would extend to infinity.
I executed thirty thousand sword-wielding men.
I shackled kings, notable rulers of the likes

Of Fartoos, Manshoor, and the Emperor of Chin,
Whose ferocity made the earth tremble
Beneath his horse's hooves.
I plucked them off their elephants with my noose.
I send them now to you with vast treasure and jewels.
I shall continue to battle here
In the hopes of encountering Garooy of Zerreh
And confronting him with my sword.
I shall stick his head on the tip of my blade
As a crown, bring him among our assembly
In retaliation for the death of Siaavosh.
May all the world tongues bless your being!
May the dome of sky revolve
On the ground beneath your feet."

Rostam affixes his seal to the letter
And hands it to the brave and noble Fariborz,
Along with captured kings, elephants, and three
Thousand camels loaded with the spoils of war.

Fariborz, son of Kaavoos, takes off happily
In the direction of the royal court.
Rostam accompanies him for a short while
With his army's noblemen, then he kisses him
And takes leave of the prince, who sheds tears.

Rostam returns to his camp just as
The two curls of night's mane unveil.
The brave and fortunate men sit joyfully in feast,
Reveling with song and music.
Some are drunk on lute, some are drunk on flute.
In the end, they retire to their respective tents,
Taking with them riches beyond their desires.

As the golden sun pulls apart the indigo folds of night,
The sound of trumpets rises from Rostam's pavilion.
The hero dresses in his battle armor,
Sits on his charger reminiscent of a mountain,
And commands the army to load the provisions.
They set off on an arduous and exhausting march.

Host and leader take the long road of the plain,
Ready once again to engage in war.

Rostam says to Tous and Giv,
"O illustrious warriors, I begin warfare,
Eager to reduce our enemy to despair.
Perhaps this cunning one will bring back fresh troops,
Drawn from the lands of Chin, Saghlaab, and India.
I shall render him a drunken man, deprived of reason,
And reduce his body to dust
Sprawled across Siaavosh's tomb so that
The peoples of India, Saghlaab, Shakni, and Chin
Will never again have the chance to praise him."

He asks for the blare of trumpets.
Dust stirs the air, the earth swarms with troops,
And their clamor reaches the clouds.

For two days, they march away from the battlefield,
Encountering the land black with corpses.
Finally, they arrive at a forest where Rostam halts.
They settle for some time at the river's edge,
Resting from the exertion of the long march.
They drink wine and listen to singers.
Some are joyous, others inebriated.
And in the end, they fall asleep.

Kings and noblemen from various provinces
Send messengers to Rostam to offer him
Many precious gifts: tribute, gold, and silver.

18 | Kay Khosrow's Reply to Rostam's Letter

During these developments,
The magnificent dome of sky ceaselessly turns
And brings the news to the Iranian king
That Fariborz, son of Kaavoos, is approaching.

Kay Khosrow advances to meet the prince
With trumpet and drums and a procession
Composed of leaders and governors of provinces.

Upon nearing Kay Khosrow, Fariborz dismounts,
Kisses the ground, and offers homage to him.

He declares, "O blessed and fortunate king,
The lofty firmament gains its joy from your being.
The world flourishes beneath the shelter of your justice."
He hands over the hero's letter to the King of Kings,
Who stands astonished at the account within,
Tales of war and battlefield, of triumph and victory.

Khosrow examines the prisoners,
The camels, the elephants, and the wounded.
Then he turns his horse's bridle, pulls away
From the road, takes off his royal crown, dismounts,
And bends down in the dust before the Creator:
"O holy World Master, I was oppressed
By an unjust man who deprived me of my father
And overwhelmed me with grief.
You liberated me from anguish and hardship.
You raised me up to crown, empire, and good fortune.
Time and space are my slaves.
The world is replenished with my treasury's bounties.
I give thanks to you alone, O Creator,
And beseech you to keep Rostam alive and well!"

Khosrow returns, covered in dust,
And reviews the elephants and the hostages,
Whom he orders to be dragged to prison
And placed at the side of other wretched men.
Anything that remains of the spoils of war
He entrusts to his treasurer.
They restore and design a section of the palace
In which they place the loot
Captured from the Emperor of Chin,
Thus planting a new tree in the garden of nobility.

At court, Khosrow composes a reply to Rostam.
He begins in praise of the Creator
From Whom originates victory in war,
Master of Sun and revolving dome,
Who dictates wars, alliances, and friendships.
"The One who built the vault of sky, who makes
Night for rest and day for earning a living,
Who spawns one to endure a miserable fate
And another to be blessed with crown and glory.

Joy and pain, courage and fear, come from Yazdan."

He continues, "O world hero, may your body
Remain pure and your soul shine bright!
Everything you collected during your battles has arrived
At my palace to benefit pleasure and feast:
Prisoners, elephants, ivory thrones, and golden crowns;
Chinese brocade, Taazian steeds,
Torques, and diadems; numerous camels
Loaded with bolts of silk, weaves, and carpets;
Wardrobes, attires, and other items to be distributed.

"The person who dares contend with you will be
One whose time is up and who is disheartened by life.
I have spent night and day with thoughts of you,
Of your struggles against such a vast Tooranian host,
All the while refraining from opening my mouth
To speak to a single stranger. Night and day,
I remained prostrate before Yazdan, the Pure,
Despairing, pleading with divine will to favor you.
My brow was deeply furrowed in worry.
I now find myself relieved that you
Successfully captured the Emperor of Chin
And defeated him with the knot of your noose.
I do not wish to execute him; I would rather detain him.
A noble sage once told me that when you capture
A prisoner, do not kill him expeditiously.
For that reason, I find it wise to wait.
His life is in your hands,
And you can always kill him at a later time.
But if you do so now,
You can never bring him back to life again.
No one is capable of reversing the course
And converting the dead back to living.

"Let us wait then, and keep him captive and alive.
Bound up, the emperor can no longer commit evil acts.
Furthermore, it is wrong to kill a ruler defeated in war.
Do not rush to action in any way, O blessed man.
Do not spill needless blood,
Which would be an insurmountable obstacle.
This is the way Afraasiyaab killed my father in haste,

May he be cursed! O noble warlord,
Whenever you capture an adversary, be content
With merely weighing him down with shackles.
The one who has a world hero such as Rostam
Must always remain youthful, for the sky
Has never witnessed a more loyal servant.
May fortune never deprive you of its favors!"

The scribe completes the letter; Khosrow affixes his seal.
He prepares gifts for Rostam: Golden halters and reins,
One hundred curly-haired women with golden belts;
One hundred noble steeds with golden saddles;
One hundred camels loaded with brocade from Chin;
One hundred mules with bolts of fabric and rugs;
Two shiny ruby rings and one golden crown;
Many lush golden robes, bracelets, belts, and torques.

An array of gifts is arranged for the leaders,
Taken from the royal treasury: a mace for Fariborz,
A golden crown, a purple sword, and golden boots.
Then the king commands him to depart, to take
The road back to Rostam, to whom he is to say,
"Khosrow will not rest in this battle with Afraasiyaab.
He will neither eat nor sleep until the powerful head
Of this king is captured in the knot of your noose."

Fariborz marches off, just as the king has commanded.

19 | Afraasiyaab Learns of His Army's Defeat

Afraasiyaab is handed the news that a flame
Has emerged right out of the sea surf.
He learns that misfortune has befallen Tooran-Zamin,
That Kaamoos, Manshoor, and the Emperor of Chin
Suffered an insurmountable fight and a dreadful defeat.
He learns that a vast host arrived from Iran-Zamin,
Making the rotations of the sky recede
In a battle lasting forty days, during which time
One could not distinguish between day and night
As the dust rising from the riders concealed the sun.

In the end, it appears that the fortune that once
Watched over Afraasiyaab succumbed to sleep
And that there remained, in this vast host,
Not a single horseman able to carry on the war.
Many brave men and eminent rulers
Have been shackled, flung disgracefully
Upon the backs of elephants
In the midst of a host that extended two miles.
He learns that thousands of influential Tooranians,
Including the Emperor of Chin, were taken to Iran;
That the battlefield was so encumbered with corpses
That a path could not be cleared to cross to the other side;
That Piran is on his way to Khotan escorted by a procession;
That troops from Kushan, Chin, and India dispersed;
That everyone surrendered to Rostam's sword;
That the tent dwellers, in border cities, absconded;
That they left the area drenched in blood
For a distance of more than two miles;
That the earth emptied of leaders and elephants;
That an Iranian host was approaching
Led by Rostam, eager for vengeance,
Ready to reduce the mountain into plain.

Afraasiyaab's heart fills with concern,
His head with anguish. He summons his wise men
And at length relates all that occurred:
How a warring host marched against their valiant leaders,
And how they were defeated, although so well-equipped,
So well-armed, and so numerous their troops.

He laments, "I feel as if the grief I endure over the fates
Of Kaamoos and the Emperor of Chin has disarmed me.
Now that such a host has been destroyed or injured,
While two-thirds of our brave men are held captive,
Dragged to Iran-Zamin on elephant backs,
Filling the land with blood for miles and miles,
What shall we do? What remedy shall we find?
We cannot remain inactive after this downfall.

"If Rostam takes the field against us, there will
Remain in this land neither ground nor grass,
Especially if he stays as strong as I witnessed

Numerous times when he forced me to flee.
He was still so young, like a reed,
When I led my army to the city of Rey.
He assailed me with blows, removed me from the saddle
In a way as to astonish both armies.
My belt and my tunic's fastenings snapped,
And I fell from his hands, head first, to his feet.
Such legendary power, such skills, which I had heard
From my spies, I witnessed in person, on the battlefield.
I was aware of the way he dealt with the deevs
Of Mazandaran with only the use of his heavy mace.
I was aware of the ailments he accumulated
On the field of vengeance.
He dismembered the White Deev, severed his side,
And pierced the hearts of Poolaad, Ghondi, Beed."

The noblemen rise to voice a common reply,
"If the rulers of Saghlaab and Chin wished to attack
Iran in revenge, they are the ones who suffered.
No one perished on our side. We did not lose soldiers,
Neither is this land basted in our blood.
Now is our time to campaign, fight like leopards.
Why are you fearful of Rostam?
Why do you extol your adversary's name?
Our mothers gave birth to us so that we ultimately die.
We are firmly cinched at the waist, ready for battle,
And shall not loosen our warrior belts.
If he dares trample our land beneath his feet,
He will have cause to sorely repent.
If we cinch our waists in retribution,
Not a single Iranian will survive our assault."

The king listens to the noble warriors' words,
Selects from his troops the most eloquent ones,
Summons the bravest, the most distinguished men,
Renounces rest and food, and opens his treasury door.
He liberally distributes dinars and gold.
His mind communicates to appease his seething heart.

Such is the clatter of the troops filling the world that
You would think the sky is in search of a new reckoning.

20 | Rostam's Battle Against Kaafoor, Man-Eater

On their side, the Iranians strap for vengeance.

While the evil man's plan is developing,
Fariborz makes his way back to Rostam, heart joyous,
Bearing the load of presents, a crown, and earrings.

Rostam of elephantine stature receives him happily.
Noble leaders gather and bless the world hero,
Saying, "May the earth flourish in your care!
May the king's eye rejoice at the sight of you!
May our land prosper under your protection!"

Rostam leads his army swiftly to Soghd,
Where they stay for two weeks,
Hunting onager and drinking wine.
They revel in this way for some time.

Then Rostam takes the road, and after a day's ride
He finds himself at the edge of the city of Bidaad.[58]
He perceives a fortress inhabited by men
Who feed only on human flesh and before whom,
At every moment, disappears a fairy-faced slave.
At their untamed ruler's table, they only serve
Young people not yet touched by maturity.
Every day, a group of young, beautiful maidens
With perfect figures prepares the ruler's meals.

Rostam commands three hundred armored riders,
Mounting chargers barded with steel,
To lead an assault against the fortress,
Under the command of Gostaham, escorted
By two prudent warriors always at the ready:
Bijan, son of Giv, and Hojir.

In the castle is a valiant man, ruler
And master of the land, named Kaafoor,
Who possesses the city through an investiture.
The moment he learns of the approach

◇◇◇◇◇◇◇◇◇◇◇◇◇
58 Bidaad: Meaning unjust.

Of an Iranian host led by a famed, vengeful chief,
He dons his war armor and exits with his subjects.
They take on the manner of leopards
Skilled in the handling of the noose,
Warriors who fight as strong as stone and anvil.

Kaafoor lunges at Gostaham.
The two hosts soon intermingle,
Attacking each other like lions pouncing on deer.
A great number of Iranian soldiers are killed.
The bravest of them feel discouraged by their losses.

As soon as Gostaham sees his host in such a state,
As soon as he sees the world about to fall
Into the hands of the nefarious deev,
He orders his men to send a shower of shots
And to crush the enemy with a charge of riders.

Kaafoor, on his side, says to his proud warriors,
"The points of arrows do not leave traces on steel.
Seize your heavy maces and strike enemy heads.
Act like furious lions and leopards on this battlefield.
Exhibit your valor, trample them beneath your feet."

They immediately engage in such a fierce fight
That flames emerge from the water's swells.
They kill many a foe, and the sphere of misfortune turns
Against the Iranians, who grow weary of battle,
Somber at the sight of so many of theirs deceased.

Gostaham brusquely says to Bijan,
"Swing your reins in the direction of Rostam.
Gallop at high speeds and urge him to rise
And to rush here with two hundred cavaliers."

Bijan, son of Giv, departs as swift as wind.
He relates the words to Rostam,
Who instantly leans on the stirrups,
Unimpaired by either steep climb or descent.
He arrives on the battlefield
Like a violent storm out of a dark mountain.
He sees many Iranians sprawled dead on the ground
And a number of them returning from war.

He says to Kaafoor, "O unskilled, evil man,
I shall put an end to this battle at your expense."

Kaafoor attacks the royal tree laden with fruit.
He deals him a blow of his blade,
Quick as the flight of an arrow, hoping
To pierce through to the hero, lion vanquisher.
But Rostam buffers the blow with his shield.

Kaafoor directs his noose at the son of Zaal.
Again, Rostam dodges the assault
And taunts him with mockery.
He hollers as loud as an elephant,
A cry that sends Kaafoor into a state of shock.

Rostam pulls out his spear and strikes him hard,
Shattering his head, helm, shoulders, and neck.
His brains spurt out of his nose, and this man,
So eager for battle, plummets to his death.

Rostam then attacks the castle gates,
But the inhabitants, weak and strong, resist him.
They bolt the doors and continue to fight
By firing shots from atop the ramparts.
They cry, "O powerful, prudent man,
O elephant dressed in leopard skins,
What name did your father give you at birth?
Are you merely a man able to skillfully cast his noose,
Or are you the firmament of battles?

"You are wasting your time attacking this city
That wise men call the City of Battle.
Once Toor, son of Fereydoon, left Iran,
He called to his side skilled men and built
This wall of stone, wood, mortar, and reed.
He constructed it with the aid of magic
And hard labor, covering himself
With sweat and depleting his wealth.
Many a warrior has attempted to seize its walls
And to destroy the fort, but no one was able
To successfully besiege it and rule over it.
The fortress is well-stocked with supplies and weapons.
An underground passageway allows us to access more.

Even if you were to exhaust yourself and assail it
Over the course of many years,
You would only instigate more quarrel.
Toor's magic spells and the breath of the priest
Protect and guard this wall from war apparatus."

Rostam finds himself troubled by these words.
His brave soldiers' souls cloud with worry.
They see a battle that does not smile down on them.
Nevertheless, he advances his army
Toward the city's four corners.
On one side Goodarz, on the other Tous,
Supported by Giv with timpani.
On one side Zaboli troops, on the other men dressed
In coats of mail and brandishing Kaboli swords.

The warriors receive a shower of stones on their heads
Cast from mangonels, and arrows shot from bows.

The hero, full of experience, seizes his bow
And sends the defenders of the fort into a stupor,
For at the moment a head appears behind the rampart,
He strikes him with an arrow and instantly kills him.
The points of his arrows precisely enter enemy brains,
And the victims become one with woe.

Then Rostam begins to mine the rampart walls,
To rush the defenders to jump off the heights.
Beams, coated with black naphtha,
Are placed beneath the mined parts.

Once half of the wall is mined, they set fire to the beams,
And Toor's fort crumbles down to the ground.
Rostam's troops approach from all sides,
And he commands them to launch an attack,
Making use of bows and arrows of poplar wood.

The besieged expose their heads to death
In order to save treasure, children, land, and ally.
A better thing would have been for them
To have never been born from their mothers.

The Iranian riders set foot,

Grab their shields, bows, and arrows,
And advance with spear-wielding infantrymen,
Bijan and Gostaham at the head.
The defenders of the fort can no longer
Resist the breath of the burning fire
And the shower of shots that assails them.
Weeping, they bolt out of the castle
And take cover on the plain.

Rostam closes the castle gates,
And the workings of death and destruction
Begin as a great carnage ensues. They kill many,
Take countless prisoners, old and young.
The Iranian troops seize much gold and silver,
Gems and horses, slaves, male and female,
And carry the loads to their camp.

Rostam appears, washes his head and body,
And turns to the Creator with praise and prayers.
Then he says to the Iranians,
"One should always secretly worship Yazdan.
Give thanks for this victory and for the joys granted."

The leaders bring their foreheads to the ground.
They pray and extol the noble Rostam:
"The one who cannot contend with you is better off
Staying quiet and still than seeking fame and glory.
You have the body of an elephant,
The force and claws of a lion.
You never tire from fighting."

Rostam replies, "This power and strength
Are bestowed upon me by the Just Giver.
You can all have a part of it. None of us
Should ever complain about the Creator's deeds."

He commands Giv to seize ten thousand riders,
Armed with shield and riding steel-barded stallions,
To rush to the border of Khotan swiftly
Before the Tooranians have a chance to gather.

As soon as night displays its black curls
And worry bends the moon's back,

Giv departs with his valiant horsemen.
He remains absent for three days.
On the fourth day, at the moment the sun displays
Its golden crown and sits upon its ivory throne,
The proud Giv returns from Tooran
With a great number of proud and bold prisoners,
Fair-faced idols from Taraaz,
Stallions of noble race, and all sorts of wealth.

Rostam dispatches a part of the booty to the king
And distributes the remainder to the army
And to Goodarz, Tous, Giv, Gostaham, Shiddush,
The valiant Rohaam, and Bijan, son of Giv.
The leaders rise and lavish him once again with regard.

Goodarz says to him, "O highborn hero,
The world craves your benevolence.
We shall from now on, by day or by night,
Never open our lips without celebrating you.
May you continue to live on forever, happy,
Gifted with the wisdom of an old man
And the strength of a youth!
Yazdan brought you forth from a pure race,
And never did a holy mother
Give birth to a more worthy offspring.
May the succession of fathers to fathers
And sons to sons continue in your family!
You are above all need. Your star shines bright.
You are the leader of all the earth's rulers.
May the World Creator continue to be your haven!
May time and space work in your favor!
May your name live on forever!
May the world prosper in the shelter of your throne!
The man who measured the length of the earth's
Surface with his feet, who has seen the world,
Seen war and peace and vengeance,
Has never heard of such a vast and united host.
So many kings and elephants, ivory thrones and men,
Stallions and all sorts of crowns.
And yet, once the stars looked down on the plain,
This army found itself reduced to defeat.

"We turned at length around this fortress
Without finding anyone to come to our aid.
We shouted beneath the dragon's breath
When you showed up to free us with your shots.
You are the crown of Iran, the army's support.
You hold your head high, and we are your subjects.
May the Creator reward you for all your feats!
May you always have a smile on your face!
We cannot reward you, but our tongues will forever
Exalt you, which is all that is in our power to do."

Rostam is delighted to hear these words.
He returns the praise, his mind freed from worries:
"O noble princes, your minds are vigilant.
You govern many provinces.
I draw my strength from you,
And my heart, in its joy, bears witness to this fact.
My face renews its adornments from your features.
My soul shines brighter from your affection."

Then he adds, "Let us stay here for three days,
To revel and to render the world bright with our feast.
On the fourth day, we shall march against Afraasiyaab
And incite fire to emerge from water.
We shall lead our host to turn this land upside down."

The noblemen obey his command
And surrender to wine, music, dancers, and feast.

21 | Afraasiyaab Receives News of Rostam's Arrival

Afraasiyaab receives the news that Rostam
Has ravaged and destroyed his kingdom.
His robe's satin feels as rough as brambles on his skin.
His heart afflicted, he thinks,
"Who will shoulder the burden of fighting this man?
I hold many troops, but who will rise as their leader?
Who will dare contend with this brave warrior
Who rendered the earth black with his burning sword?"

He writhes and squirms, and further reflects,

"There is no one among the Turks able to defeat him."

The army replies to Afraasiyaab,
"Do not concern yourself so much with Rostam.
You have the ability to make blood gush up
From the dust of a battlefield to the moon.
You have weapons, valiant men, and treasure.
Why would your heart clamp at the thought of Rostam?
Do not fear a fight with this rider.
Look around you at these illustrious heroes.
Even if he were made of steel, no matter
How brave he may be, Rostam is a lone man,
And we are talking at length of him.
Mobilize your troops to free yourself of him.
Bring his head out of the clouds and down to the dust.
What do you have to fear of the king and of Iran?
Neither Kay Khosrow nor his throne will prosper,
Neither Iran-Zamin nor a single branch of the tree.
Cast your sight on your renowned warring army,
On these young men ready for battle.
We are ready to plunge ourselves
Into the throes of death in favor
Of nation, sons, women, children, and allies,
Rather than surrender our land to the enemy."

These words propel Afraasiyaab
To forget earlier conflicts.
He contemplates his ancestors' kingdom
And his wealth with renewed confidence.
He replies, "I shall distribute weapons.
I shall not allow Khosrow to rejoice on his throne.
I shall not glorify his happiness.
On the day of battle, I shall cast into dust
The head of the Zaboli man, after a long struggle.
Once Rostam is sacrificed, I can engage in a joust,
Fight and slay Khosrow with my sword,
And erase all thought of my grandson from my mind."

He commands his leaders to muster forces
And to prepare to engage in new wars of vengeance.
The noblemen acclaim him,
And highborn warriors rise to the conflict.

There is a man of lion heart named Farghaar,
Who has seen more than one cage in his life
But has always been able to free himself from traps.
The king had often witnessed his feats in battle
And always approved of his skills and actions.

Afraasiyaab dismisses the visitors from the hall
And says to Farghaar, "O prudent man,
Go right away to the Iranian host.
Attempt to observe this Rostam, eager for vengeance,
To assess the scope and quality of his troops,
To learn which men from our land serve as spies.
Report to me their strategies and plans,
And how many brave leaders escort them.
Count the number of illustrious riders
Armed with noose and spear,
The number of war elephants and men of lion heart.
Appraise their good fortune and tribulations in war."

As Farghaar takes the road to spy on the Iranians,
The ambitious king finds himself troubled.
He prevents visitors from entering his audience hall
And summons his son Shiddeh,
Whom he engages in a secret conversation
About the present circumstances: "O wise son,
When will your troops come to your aid?
Know that this vast host of innumerable riders
That crossed our border is led by Rostam of lion heart,
Whose sword converts dust into mud.
The fortune of this lion vanquisher has allowed him
To either kill or take captive Kaamoos, Manshoor,
The Chini emperor, Kahaar, and the worthy Fartoos,
Kondor, the Indian ruler Shangal and his troops,
Which extended from Kashmir to the border of Sindh.
The struggle lasted forty days,
At times full of battle, at times in truce.
But in the end, Rostam removed the emperor
From atop his elephant with his noose,
Flung him to the ground, and enchained him.
He sent noble prisoners from various lands
To Iran with extensive spoils of war: weapons,
Camels, elephants, crowns, and an ivory throne.

"Now we receive news that Rostam has invaded
Our land with his illustrious and proud companions.
Since the turns of fortune take this path,
I shall depart with treasure and throne.
I shall send all that I hold of value to the Almas River:[59]
My crowns, belts, golden torques, and golden shields.
This is not the moment to surrender
To weakness, music, and song.
I truly fear Rostam of sharp claws,
For who is at ease in the maw of a whale?
He does not resemble a human being in battle.
Blows do not provoke him to bend,
And pain does not incite in him a single complaint.
He fears neither spear, nor mace, nor sword.
When the clouds send down a deluge of arrows,
It is as if he is made of stone or steel,
As if he is Ahriman rather than a mere mortal.

"On the day of battle,
The weight of him causes a dent in the earth,
For he layers an unyielding suit of armor,
Consisting of chain mail, cuirass, and Babreh Bayan.
His cry is as loud as thunder launched from a cloud.
The war elephant has no power to alter his purpose.
A vessel would not be sturdy enough
To carry his weapons on the flows of the River Nile.
He sits on a mountain that runs as fast as wind.
You might think the firmament has birthed this stallion,
As speedy as a deer and as strong as a lion,
Always valiant, whether on land or on the sea.
In short, I shall say that, if you ask me,
He is able to cross the waters like a ship.
I have faced his mount in many challenges.
His armor of leopard skin is so thick and strong
That no matter my efforts with my shots and battle axe,
Never did I succeed in piercing his covering.

"Now that he has launched an attack on us,
We must prepare ourselves for all sorts of occurrences.
If the Creator favors us, if the glorious sky turns

◇◇◇◇◇◇◇◇◇◇◇◇◇
59 Almas River: Perhaps beyond the borders of Tooran-Zamin.

To our will, I shall destroy the land of Iran and its king.
I shall, decidedly, conclude this war.
But if Rostam wins on the day of battle,
I shall not remain here.
I shall travel all the way to the Sea of Chin
And surrender to him this border of Tooran-Zamin.
O dear son, I deeply fear the deeds
Of this disloyal, capricious wheel of time."

Shiddeh replies, "O wise king,
May you live as long as crown and throne!
In you dwell royal majesty and splendor,
Knowledge, high birth, valor, and power.
You need not heed the counsel of an advisor.
You only have to observe the turns of fortune.
Piran, Hoomaan, Farshidvard, Golbaad, and Nastihan
Ended up with broken weapons and broken hearts.
Fear and worry paralyzed them and continue to do so.
Cast aside your concerns.
Summon your leaders, renew their courage,
Motivate them to drive their troops
Once again to pounce on the enemy.
Mighty rulers celebrate your glory.
You know the world; you have gained experience.
I swear by the life and head of the Tooranian king,
By Sun and sword, throne and diadem,
That the fates of Kaamoos and the Emperor of Chin
Fill my heart with unending grief
And my head with a deep longing for vengeance.
We must lead troops to Gang
And refrain from deliberating.
Call your hosts from Chin and Maachin;
Prepare for combat."

Having thus spoken, Shiddeh returns to his palace,
Heart full of hatred, head full of fury.

The dark night opens its gloomy eyes.
Worry bends the back of the moon.
The world becomes as black as musk,
And Farghaar returns from the Iranian camp.

He presents himself in the dark night to Afraasiyaab
At the moment of rest and sleep and reports to him:
"After leaving the court of the powerful king,
I marched toward Rostam, deev-binder.
I witnessed a huge horseman akin to a wolf.
A black banner with the image of a dragon
Rose as if it were able to graze the moon.
Tent pavilions were set up before the enclosure,
And a great number of noble banners
Were rooted into the ground.

"In the main pavilion, I saw a fierce elephant covered
In Babreh Bayan before whom stood a dappled horse,
Who appeared unable to remain still, not for an instant.
The bridle was cast over the saddle's knob,
And on its hook hung a rolled up noose.
The leaders of this army are Tous, Goodarz, Giv,
Fariborz, Gorgeen, and the valiant Shiddush.
Goraazeh commands the stars with Gostaham,
Who is now joined by Bijan, son of Giv."

The king is afflicted by Farghaar's words.
He sends for army leader Piran and elite warriors,
Who rush to court, as fast as dust.
The king conveys Farghaar's report to them and asks,
"Whom do we have able to fight and beat Rostam?"

Piran says, "What do we care of battle and glory?
We shall fight for our land, our children, our family."

This response confirms Afraasiyaab's resolve
To prepare for war without delay.
He commands Piran to march off with his host
In the direction of the vengeful Rostam.

The noblemen take leave of the king
And march toward the plain to rally for battle.
Soon the desert resounds with the blare of trumpets
And the clatter of men.
The dust renders the world as black as ebony.
The troops are so numerous that you would think
The earth is hiding beneath the horses' hooves.
The drumbeat of war is heard,

And the long line of elephants rolls off.

22 | Afraasiyaab's Letter to Poolaadvand

Afraasiyaab exits his palace and goes to the field,
Eager to execute vengeance.
After giving Piran necessary directions,
He retires to the side, dismisses all visitors,
And summons an experienced scribe,
To whom he says, "We must not hide these secrets.
Write a letter to Poolaadvand, open your heart to him.
Begin in praise of the Creator, Giver of life and death,
Master of Saturn, Venus, Sun, and revolving sky.
Then pay tribute to the triumphant Poolaadvand,
So skilled is he in the capture of our enemy.
Recount to him the dangers menacing us
From Rostam, illustrious hero of dim beliefs,
And his leaders full of courage:
Tous, Goodarz, and many other Iranian warriors.
Relate to him the story of my grandson,
Master of victory, king of the Iranian people,
Whom I raised with such care
That not even the wind could affect him.

"If the sublime sky wishes to grant me favors,
Poolaadvand would rush to my land
Where a large host of Turks,
Warriors from Saghlaab and Chin,
Have been vanquished and have had to bend,
Where so many provinces have been razed by Iranians.
They have taken captive an entire host,
Converted the land of Tooran into a sea of tar.
Their army resembles a mountain in motion.
Their leader is world hero Rostam.
Their commanders are Goodarz, Giv, and Tous.
Their timpani resound up to and through the clouds.

"Once Rostam perishes, no other army
Will ever take the road of Tooran-Zamin,
For our distress originates solely from him.
Play the role of my savior in this war.

Once he receives death at your hands,
The entire world will infallibly fall subject to me.
I shall take only half of my rich empire,
And the other half, consisting of throne,
Crown, and treasure, I shall impart to you,
Since you are the one who endures
The agonizing challenges of battle."

The king affixes his seal to the letter,
And at the moment when the moon
Displays its face in the house of Cancer,
Shiddeh cinches himself before his father
In the role of messenger charged with relaying
To Poolaadvand the expressions of the king's concerns.

Shiddeh departs right away, swift as a flame,
Propelled by his fears.
He soon arrives at the side of Poolaadvand,
Who has no equal in valor in the land:
A ruler whose head reaches above the firmament.
He dwells in the mountains of Chin,
Possesses a vast host steered by a whale-like leader
And eager warriors fierce as leopards.

Shiddeh greets him, remits the letter to him,
And relays Rostam's feats and exploits.
He says, "He came from Iran-Zamin to fight us
And has destroyed our beautiful land.
May divine grace never seek to touch him!
He has encumbered Kaamoos, the Emperor of Chin,
And Fartoos with heavy chains.
He holds his rolled-up noose around his arm.
His body is dressed in lion skin,
And he never tires of combat.
He is able to drag to Iran the ground of Tooran.
What can be said of this impure hero?
He has ruined our prosperity, tarnished our splendor!"

Poolaadvand summons his border guards
And wise men, speaks to them at length
And reveals to them the contents of the letter.
He is a young, ambitious, and reckless man.

He prepares the timpani and sends his tents to the plain.
He mobilizes troops that appear fierce as deevs,
And a great clamor emerges from his warriors.

Poolaadvand walks at the head of his troops,
Armed with shield, quiver, and noose,
His banner brandished behind him.
In such a way, he marches from mountain to plain,
Crosses the River Jayhoon, and before long
Approaches Afraasiyaab's royal court.

The beat of drums is heard at the royal palace gates.
The entire Tooranian army advances toward Poolaadvand.

The king embraces him and reminds him of past events,
Disclosing to him the identity of the man
Who incites such dread in the hearts of the Turks,
And relating the goals and the means necessary
To bring this venture to a favorable conclusion.

With a grand entrance into the royal palace,
They hold counsel and remain open to new ideas.
Afraasiyaab makes a case for both options:
Whether to make haste or to delay the course of battle.
He speaks of the murder of Siaavosh, the wars,
And the reprimands he drew as a result of his actions,
Of the fate of the Emperor of Chin,
Manshoor, and the valiant Kaamoos.
He then adds, "All my troubles arise
From a single man who wears leopard skin.
My weapons are ineffective against
His Babreh Bayan, helmet, and Chini shield.
You have crossed the desert,
Traveled a long and arduous road.
Now find a way to preserve us
From danger and from Rostam."

Poolaadvand reflects on ways to unravel this affair.
In the end, he replies to Afraasiyaab:
"We must not rush to action.
If Rostam is the same Rostam who destroyed
And conquered Mazandaran with his heavy mace,
Who ripped apart the flank of the White Deev

And the hearts of Poolaad, Ghondi, and Beed,
I shall not have the force to contend with him.
Furthermore, I shall not dare provoke his anger.
Body and soul, I am devoted
To the execution of your command.
May reason be your mind's constant guide!
I shall make use of deception to defeat him.
I shall circle around him like a leopard.
You rouse your host to provoke his troops.
Let him stand astonished at the numbers of our men.
Perhaps this way we shall be saved.
Otherwise, our misfortune is certain, for we do not
Have the strength to break his chest and his limbs."

Rejoicing at these words, Afraasiyaab
Summons shining wine and string instruments.

Once inebriated, Poolaadvand shouts furious cries:
"I successfully removed the craving to eat, sleep,
And rest from Fereydoon, Zahaak, and Jamsheed.
The noblemen trembled at the sound of my voice
And at the sight of my proud warriors.
I shall carve the body of this Zaboli man into tiny
Pieces with my sharp sword, on this very battlefield!
Rostam to me is nothing more than a handful of dust,
Not to mention how meek are Khosrow, Giv, and Tous."

23 | Poolaadvand Battles Giv and Tous

As the shining sun reveals its banner, the somber,
Violet satin of night assumes a shade of saffron.
The sound of drums is heard at the king's door,
And the uproar of the army rises to the clouds.

Poolaadvand resumes the vanguard of his host.
He is strong of body, with a noose hanging on his arm.

The two hosts form their lines of battle.
The air dims purple, and the earth turns black.

Rostam dons his Babreh Bayan, mounts Rakhsh,

His war elephant, shouts a cry, and attacks
The right wing of the Turks, killing many a brave man.

Poolaadvand, angered by this move,
Detaches his rolled-up noose from his saddle's hook
And charges at Tous like a drunken elephant,
Noose on arm and mace in hand.
He grabs him by the belt, lifts him up effortlessly
From the saddle, and flings him to the ground.

At the sight of this struggle, at the sight of Tous,
Son of Nozar, being overthrown,
Giv lunges on his horse, Shabdeez,
And prepares to fight body and soul.
This brave man, like a lion, leads an attack
Braced in mail and armed with bull-headed mace.

Poolaadvand the deev makes his noose fly
And captures Giv's head in its knot.

From afar, Rohaam and Bijan observe the force,
The stature, and the skills of Poolaadvand.
They rush to tie up his hands with their nooses.

The prudent Poolaadvand launches his horse and speeds
Toward them, and soon, before all the fighters,
He overturns and tramples as vile things the two heroes
So often victorious, two noble, highborn men.
To the horror of the Iranian troops, he lunges and
Slashes through the Kaaviani banner, splitting it in two.
Not one of the warriors wishes to remain on the battlefield.

At the sight of the deeds of the courageous deev,
Fariborz and Goodarz, valiant heroes, say to Rostam,
"Poolaadvand unseats all our leaders
And hurls them into the dust.
Not one of them is able to firmly hold on to the saddle.
He flings them down with mace, sword, arrow, and noose.
The entire field is a scene of devastation.
Only Rostam is able to come to our rescue."

New cries rise from the army's core
And from the right and left wings.

The aged Goodarz assumes that Rohaam and Bijan,
His two sons, have been killed.
He addresses new lamentations to Yazdan, Justice Giver:
"I had so many sons and grandsons
Whose existence lifted my head above the sun.
But now they have all been slain right before my eyes.
My star of good fortune, once shining, has tarnished.
They died young while I endure in my old age.
I feel ashamed to wear helmet and belt.
Alas, these young heroes, members of my family!
Alas, my fortune once so bright
Has turned frightfully sour and sad!"

He unfastens his belt, removes his helmet
To cry and complain loudly.

24 | The Battle of Rostam and Poolaadvand

Rostam, deeply saddened by the news,
Shakes like a leaf on a tree.
He approaches Poolaadvand, noticing that
He assumes the stance of an imposing mountain.
He worries about the fate of the four Iranian heroes,
Meek as gazelles before their lion-like adversary.
He sees that his army has suffered greatly
And that the battle is being carried out across the line.

He thinks, "This day dims for us.
The heads of our warriors are troubled.
I fear that the circle of life comes to an end here
And that the fortune watching over us
Is languishing in a state of slumber.
Today I feel listless, as if I need to resume my sleep.
This belligerent deev is a colossal and skilled rider."

Rostam braces his horse with his legs
To launch him as he assumes the stance of battle.
He cries, "O miserable deev,
You will soon witness the turns of fortune!"

The hero's voice strikes the warriors' ears.

Rostam perceives them on foot and says,
"O World Creator, you are above everyone
And everything, visible and invisible,
Give me the strength to annihilate this enemy host
And to eradicate this army-destroying deev.
It would have been better for me to be blind
Than to perceive this day of limitation and defeat
When the warriors of Tooran, such as Piran,
Hoomaan, and this valiant deev shout cries of victory,
When I find Giv, Rohaam, Tous, and Bijan,
Heroes who mock lions on foot,
Wandering around aimlessly because their horses
Have been assailed and knocked down by arrows."

He falls on Poolaadvand, casts on him his noose.
The brave horseman is seized by fear
But is able to steal away his head from the knots.

Poolaadvand says to Rostam,
  "O brave, worldly man, O illustrious lion
Before whom the war elephant turns away to flee,
You will hear the roars of the surge of the River Nile.
You will see the blaze of my battle, my noose, my courage.
You are about to experience the force of my blows.
Renounce, from now on, any hope to set your gaze
On the court's great men and on your king.
You will never again enjoy your power,
Not even in dream, and I shall
Surrender your host to Afraasiyaab.
I shall stitch your body through and through
With my arrows in such a way that your eyes
Will no longer rest on the figure of your aging father."

Rostam replies to Poolaadvand,
"How far will you lead your threats
And your desires to intimidate me?
May there never be braggarts among men of war!
If there is one, he is sure to lose his head to the wind.
No matter how brave you are, no matter
How highborn, you are neither Saam
Nor Garshaasp of high stature."

Poolaadvand remembers the old proverb:
"Whoever seeks unjust battle will return heartbroken.
Whether you suffer misfortune from enemy or friend,
It is best to execute justice with regard to good and evil."

Poolaadvand reflects further on the fact
That Rostam conquered Mazandaran
With his heavy mace in the middle of the night.
He says, "O hero, you have been tested in battle.
Why do we foolishly stand inactive?"

They circle each other; dust stirs the air above the field.
These two brave men resemble two warring lions.
Rostam strikes Poolaadvand on the head
Such a blow of his heavy mace that echoes reverberate
And send tremors through the battlefield.
The eyes of Poolaadvand dim, his hand releases the reins,
And a shooting pain makes him lean to the right.
He reflects, "Today is indeed a day of adversity."

Rostam expects Poolaadvand's brains to gush forth
From his two ears and flood his side,
But when he sees him remain in the saddle,
He addresses the Creator: "O World Creator,
You are above the capricious turnings of destiny.
You contain the world. You maintain all that exists.
You observe all beings and all things.
If this battle is undeserved,
I shall no longer find joy in this world.
But if Afraasiyaab is an unjust man, do not deprive me
Of my life, my strength, and the power to act.
If I die at the hands of this Poolaadvand,
If my soul liberates itself from my body's bonds,
There will remain alive in the land of Iran
Neither warrior nor farmer nor artisan, neither land
Nor nation, for the ground itself will withdraw."

Then Rostam turns to Poolaadvand and says,
"What wounds did our warriors' mace inflict?
Your hands do not handle the black reins.
Dismount, O deev, and plead for mercy!"

Poolaadvand replies,

"Your mace did not affect me in any way!"

The combatants exchange words and hateful glares
As they face each other in vengeance.

Poolaadvand draws a purple sword of forged iron
To strike the head of Rostam, crown-giver,
But the blow falls powerless on Rostam's Chini helm.

The warring Poolaadvand is in a state of shock,
Seeing his sword fall short of the target.
His deev heart swells with worry.
He draws a dagger as sharp as diamond
And, with spells and incantations, strikes Rostam,
But the Babreh Bayan is unaffected and untouched.
His wicked heart seethes with blood.
He curses fate, for he greatly fears the limbs
And shoulders of Rostam, son of Zaal.
He addresses him once more:
"Bequeath this Babreh Bayan and dark helmet to me.
Don another suit of armor, and I shall do the same."

Rostam replies, "Such a thing is impossible.
Our waters' flows do not mix in the same river.
I shall not change this battle armor,
So you might do well to keep yours."

The two heroes resume their fight,
But weapons and heavy maces
Remain powerless against either coat of armor.
In the end, the combative Poolaadvand says,
"Only in a wrestling match
Will the strongest one be determined.
If you wish, we can prepare to fight like wild lions,
Encircle each other, grapple and grab each other
By our leather belts to see which one of us
Will be favored by divine grace to shine victorious."

Rostam replies, "O miserable deev, you find
Yourself unable to resist the blows of brave men,
And every minute you make use of artistry
And machinations like a cunning fox, but to what end?
Your head is meant to be caught in my noose's knot."

They agree and solemnly promise each other that
No friend from either host will come to their aid.
Once this is settled, they dismount and remain
For some time on foot to catch their breath.

25 | Rostam and Poolaadvand Fight Hand to Hand

After having first stipulated that no warrior
Would come to their aid, the two heroes,
Eager for battle, begin to wrestle.

Between the two hosts is a span of half a farsang.
The stars watch the battle of two furious lions
Who first rub their hands together,
Then grab each other by the belts' straps.

At the sight of Rostam's chest and arms,
Shiddeh sighs deeply and says to his father,
"This powerful man whom you call binder of deevs
Is superior to the other and will sever his deev head.
Expect certain decampment from your army troops.
Do not foolishly contend with the rotating skies."

Afraasiyaab replies,
"My mind is quite troubled by this affair.
Observe the way Poolaadvand grasps his opponent.
Give him sound advice in the language of Turks,
Show him how he can lift the hero of elephantine build,
Overthrow him, and end this quarrel with his sword."

Shiddeh says to him, "Your command does not
Conform with the covenant the king and Rostam
Agreed to in the presence of both hosts.
If you fail to keep your promise,
If your anger provokes you to act rashly,
Nothing will ever again prosper in your hands.
Do not trouble these limpid waters and tint them black,
For those who seek fault will blame you."

The king, furious, curses his son and tells him,
"If Poolaadvand succumbs to the enemy,

None of ours will remain alive,
Thanks to you whose only talent is in your tongue."

At these words, the valiant Shiddeh shakes the reins
And, swift as a lion, lunges into the melee.
He observes the struggle of two elephants,
Two bold men who roar like thunder
And fervently fight with bare hands.
He says to Poolaadvand, "O valiant horseman,
If you succeed in defeating him,
Cleave his stomach with your dagger's blade.
One must act and succeed in one's actions
Rather than congratulate oneself."

Giv watches Afraasiyaab speaking harshly
To his son Shiddeh, he watches Shiddeh's race
And the apparent breach of promise.
He springs on his horse, rushes to Rostam,
And says to him, "O famous warlord,
Command me, your humble subject.
Pay attention to what was agreed in the pact.
Afraasiyaab, impatient, seeing the time is here to act,
Has approached to encourage Poolaadvand
And to advise him to make quick use of his dagger."

Rostam replies, "I am a warrior,
A tireless, winning conqueror.
Why do you all tremble so?
Why do your heartbeats pause in fear?
In a moment, I shall take Poolaadvand's head
From the lofty sphere of sky
And sink it into the low dust of earth.
This is a battle I am fighting with my bare hands.
Why are you discouraging my heart so impudently?
If this foolish sorcerer violates
The agreement sworn to before Yazdan,
It is not for us to feel trepidation, for the deev
Would only scatter dust upon his own head."

Rostam then extends his hand like a lion,
Seizes the shoulder of the war-whale Poolaadvand,
And, with all the might he can muster, plucks him

Off the ground as if uprooting a sycamore,
Raises him to his neck's height,
And flings him down, giving thanks to the Creator.

A loud roar emerges from the Iranian host.
The beating of drums, the blare of trumpets,
The clang of cymbals, and the jingle
Of Indian bells rise to the clouds.
Everyone jubilantly shouts that Poolaadvand is dead,
That he squirms helplessly like a serpent in the dust.

It is as if all the bones on Poolaadvand's skeleton
Have been smashed and crushed.
The deev's cheeks turn a pale yellow,
Like the flower of fenugreek.
His body is now still, but he remains alive.

Rostam thinks that his contender's joints are severed.
Triumphant, the hero climbs on the valiant Rakhsh
And leaves the dragon's body sprawled on the ground.

As soon as the vanquisher of lions reclaims his host,
His eye catches sight of Poolaadvand rising to his feet,
Mounting his steed, and taking off to flee.
So fearful is he of Rostam that he appears to roll
The ground beneath his horses' hooves.

He takes shelter at Afraasiyaab's side,
Heart full of blood, cheeks flooding with tears,
His body's bones shattered.
After a while, he loses consciousness.
He falls into a long slumber on the dark dust.

When Rostam observes Poolaadvand alive
And the entire field covered with scattering troops,
His heart swells, as he commands his army to advance.
He summons the experienced Goodarz
And calls for a shower of shots
To fall down like rain from a spring cloud.

On one side is Bijan, on the other is Giv,
The worldly Rohaam, and warrior Gorgeen.
You would think that they ignite a huge blaze,

That they consume the world with their swords.

Poolaadvand says to his troops,
"Our fortune, treasures, and fame are lost.
Why should we surrender our heads to the wind?
Why should we wear ourselves out in fight?"
He sends away his host, and he leaves in great despair.
He feels as if his arteries have been ruptured by Rostam,
His bones smashed, and his heart's cords burst.

26 | Afraasiyaab Flees Before Rostam

Piran addresses Afraasiyaab,
"The surface of the land is a sea.
Did I not tell you that we could not safely
Stay here and face the cursed Rostam?
By inexorably spilling the blood of Siaavosh,
You pierced our dim hearts and wounded us.
Now what will happen to you?
No one remains by your side.
Even Poolaadvand left, taking his host with him.
More than one hundred thousand Iranian riders
Soar on strong, barded stallions.
At their head marches Rostam, lion conqueror.
The ground is drenched in blood;
The air is replete with shots. We united our troops
From sea, land, desert, and mountain.
When men did not suffice, we summoned deevs.
This is how we were able to engage in battles,
To generate immense chaos throughout the world.

"But now that Rostam has arrived,
You stand no chance against him.
The only option left for you is to escape,
To retire to the opposite shore of the Sea of Chin
If you are meant to subsist on the earth.
Abandon your host here mobilized for war,
And take the road to the seashore with your escorts."

The king obeys Piran's advice, for he determines
That a battle would bring overwhelming defeat.

He leaves his banner in place and departs on his own,
Swiftly taking the road to Chin and Maachin.

Meanwhile, the two hosts advance toward each other.
The world begins simmers and swells into a dark cloud.

Rostam cries out,
"Put down your spear, bow, and arrow.
Fight with your sword and mace,
And strike with the skills of your high standing.
The leopards will satiate their raging thirst,
For the prey will come to find them in their den."

The entire host responds with a shout.
The cavaliers wield their spears above the mountains.
Soon the battlefield is so encumbered with corpses
That one cannot find a trail to pass through.

Half of the Tooranians come to plead for mercy.
The other half rush to flee on the roads leading away,
Dispersing like a herd of sheep deserted by its shepherd.
The plain becomes a mass of cadavers deprived of limbs.

Rostam says, "Enough carnage!
Every act requires proper timing.
Fortune gives us downfalls and peaks,
At times the share of one,
At times the share of another.
One moment we are fed a venomous fruit,
In another its antidote.
Strip yourselves of armor and be at ease.
Endeavor to occupy yourselves with good deeds.
Why attach ourselves to this transitory dwelling?
Not even the wisest, most learned is privy to its secrets.
At times we are assailed by the wrath of Ahriman.
At times we revel in enticing feasts where everything
Is resplendent with music, color, and scent.
Be content with living in obscurity.
Honor and praise others.
Always refrain from abusing your fellow men."

Rostam marches into the field to collect the spoils of war.
He sends slaves, stallions, swords, and helmets to the king.

He reserves for himself diadems, amber, and musk,
Abandoning to the troops the balance of the goods.

Then he asks whether anyone knows
Of the whereabouts of the Tooranian king.
They search for him on all sides, on roads
Traveled or deserted, and in faraway corners,
But no one can find a trace of him
In mountains or plains, deserts or rivers.

The Iranians destroy the palaces and royal residences.
Rostam consumes with fire all the inhabited cities,
Making the flames illuminate the world.

27 | Rostam Returns to the King's Court

They pack their loads to depart from Tooran-Zamin,
Taking with them precious weapons, gold, and thrones.
Rostam compiles countless treasures, then takes off
In haste with his army toward Iran-Zamin,
Having secured so many camels and horses
That his troops have no cause
To complain of the lack of beasts.

One hears on the plain the racket of men,
The blare of trumpets, and the din of Indian bells.
This army, resplendent in wealth, color, and scent,
Makes its way toward the land of Iran.

Once king and kingdom hear of Rostam's approach,
The city and palace echo with cries of joy.
The beating of drums rises all the way to the clouds,
For the master of mace and armor is on his way home.

All men, noble or not, rejoice throughout the world.
The king's heart resembles the sublime heaven,
And he offers the Creator acts of giving and grace.

He orders elephants and leaves his residence.
The population prepares grand, extravagant feasts,
Summoning wine and meals, music and musicians.

The sound of drums and trumpets echoes all around
As the world king exits his palace.
Elephants are drenched in a mix of wine, musk, and saffron.
Drivers sport diadems on their heads and rings in their ears.

A scattering of silver is tossed to the crowd,
Wine and saffron, a blend of musk and amber.
The entire land echoes with the chant of musicians
Stationed everywhere from border to border.

Once Rostam spots the noble king's crown,
Once he hears the clamors emerging from the world,
He dismounts to properly acclaim Kay Khosrow.

The world king asks about his long journey,
Enfolds him in a tight embrace and holds him at length.
He extols the renowned hero of lion heart,
Orders him back on his horse, and holds
On to Rostam's hand for the duration of the way.
He says to him, "Why have you been absent for so long?
Why did you cast on my head the flames of worry?"

Rostam replies, "One cannot enjoy a moment of happiness
When deprived of the sight of your noble being."

They advance thus on the road to the royal palace.
Shah Khosrow sits on his golden throne, while Rostam,
Illustrious hero, takes a seat of honor next to him.

Tous, Fariborz, Goodarz, and Giv,
Farhaad, Gorgeen, and the valiant Rohaam
Enter the palace to take their respective
Places among men of worth and nobility.

Kay Khosrow addresses many questions to them
Relating to campaigns, battles, wins, and losses.

Goodarz replies, "O King, an account of these battles
Would be a lengthy one that would require cups of wine.
We shall need some time to rest and mend from our efforts.
Then you may inquire, and we shall gladly enlighten you."

Banquet tables are dressed, and the king, laughing, says,

"It seems as if your travels have triggered your appetite."
He summons wine and musicians, and resumes
His questioning from beginning to end
On matters relating to Afraasiyaab,
To Poolaadvand and his wrestling match
with Rostam and his coiled noose.
He wishes to know everything about the events
Involving the emperor, Kaamoos, Ashkeboos,
And their vast hosts, elephants, and timpani.

Goodarz says to him, "O King, never will a mother
Give birth to another horseman the likes of Rostam.
Whether deev, lion, or dragon,
Not a single creature escapes his prevailing hand.
May the king be blessed a thousand times
And as many times the noble hero!"

The master of crown is so pleased by these words
That you might think his head rises above Saturn.
He replies, "O lofty warlord, world conqueror,
Vigilant and clear-minded, the revolving dome
Protects any man who adopts
Divine wisdom as his master.
We must deeply reflect on these occurrences.
May the evil eye never strike the world hero!
May his entire life pass in amusement and feast!"

For one week, the assembly remains, cup in hand,
Rejoicing in the presence of king, throne, and royal court.
Many times they recount and sing of Rostam's exploits
In heroic songs complemented by the melody of a lute.

28 | Rostam Returns to Sistan

Rostam remains one month at the side of the king,
Goblet in hand. Then he says to him,
"O illustrious and valiant ruler, master of throne,
You are full of wisdom and compassion, but I miss
My father Zaal, and I feel the urge to see his face again."

The king opens the doors to his vast treasury,

PART TWELVE

Withdraws hidden wealth, and distributes to Rostam
Rubies and crowns, rings and brocade,
Clothing woven in luxurious silk. He also gives him
Maidens decked with diadems and earrings,
One hundred horses, one hundred camels
Saddled and loaded with gold dishes
Filled with aloe and musk, a pair of golden shoes
And two maces inlaid with jewels,
Worthy of a monarch and as suits a noble hero.

The king escorts Rostam the length of two days.
When Rostam sees him grow weary of the journey,
He sets foot on the ground, offers him homage,
And takes leave of him, departing from Iran-Zamin
To take the road in the direction of Zabolestan.
The entire world submits to Shah Khosrow's will.

At this point, I shall end the story of Kaamoos,
A long and detailed account.
My soul would find itself much afflicted at the knowledge
Of having withheld a single word of this adventure.
My heart is satisfied with the outcome of the battle
Of Poolaadvand, pleased that the deev did not
Succeed in clasping new bonds onto the world.

Now, would you lend your ear to another story?
A fascinating tale of the battle between
The glorious Rostam and the wicked Akvan Deev.

PART
THIRTEEN

The Story of Akvan Deev

1 | The Beginning of the Story

The Creator of Soul and Eternal Wisdom
Is most deserving of your worship.
Consider, O sage of clear mind,
If it is possible to properly honor Yazdan.
Knowledge and science are powerless, and we are left
To shed bitter tears over the fate of the hapless.
O philosophers, you speak endless nonsense.
I shall not follow the path you carve ahead.
No single doctrine is worth the unity of Yazdan,
And whether we admit it or not,
There exists only one divine being.

You blend in your head what passes before your eyes,
With your mind's deductions, you prove such existence.
Know that Yazdan, author of all that is virtuous and kind,
Is above anything you may discern with your eyes' vision.
The way of the heart is much grander than the perceived.
Do not allow yourself to drift away from this path.
If you are a thoughtful man, follow wisdom's way.

Notwithstanding, discussions on this matter
Will never reach a definite conclusion.

You view yourself as a powerful being, but a breath
Will cause the death of your body and your soul.
Your days will pass, another world will be your dwelling.
Reflect above all else on the Creator,
And may your worship be founded on this thought,
For the revolving vault of sky turns at Yazdan's will,
And it is Yazdan who is our Guide to good deeds.

If you wish to ponder this, you will witness
A world filled with marvel. You will realize
That no one can enter into a feud with the Creator.
The soul is full of wonder, the body is a miraculous thing,
And one must first grow to deeply know oneself.
The sky revolving above shows us a new face

Every moment of every day.

Perhaps you will not acknowledge the truth
Buried in the tale of the poet bard, according
To the account of our ancient forefathers.
Upon hearing it, the wise man examines it
Through the lens of Knowledge and does not give it
Easy credence until he is able to decipher the meanings.
He will find himself at peace and will cease his arguments.

Listen now to the words of the aging poet bard.
Listen, even if this story's outcome fails to entertain you.

2 | Kay Khosrow Asks Rostam to Battle Akvan Deev

The poet bard recounts this ancient tale:
In the early morning hours,
In a garden blooming like spring with fresh roses,
Kay Khosrow holds court with his noble leaders:
Goodarz, Tous, Gostaham;
Borzeen, son of Garshaasp, heir of Jamsheed;
Giv, Rohaam, skilled warrior;
Gorgeen; and Khorraad the worthy.
They recall the war against Kaamoos,
The Emperor of Chin, Manshoor, and Fartoos.
They raise their cups to the king's health,
And the wine renews their dim spirits.

On the ninth hour of the day,
A shepherd presents himself at the palace gates.
He approaches the royal throne,
Bends low to kiss the ground,
And says to the king of celebrated birth,
"A deer has appeared amidst my band of horses.
He resembles a deev liberated from chains.
One may take him for a lion, the way he takes a breath,
The way he breaks my horses' necks.
His color matches the sun exactly.
You may think the sunset sky
Has washed him in its golden waters.
A musk-black stripe stretches from his mane to his tail.

If one is to assess his hefty haunches and limbs,
One would take him for a fierce and powerful horse."

Khosrow surmises that this is not a deer:
First, because a deer is not more powerful than a horse;
And second, because Khosrow is a worldly king.
He has heard from wise men the tale of Akvan Deev
And his dwelling near the fountain, the site where
The shepherd allows his herd to roam free.
Akvan is a wicked deev who sends cries of terror
And distress throughout the world.

Kay Khosrow says to the shepherd,
"This being you describe is not a deer.
I am familiar with this matter.
You may be dismissed."

Then he addresses the renowned heroes
Enveloped in glory and power:
"I have need for a brave man, an indomitable lion,
Who is willing to strap himself for war."

For a long time, Kay Khosrow glances around,
But none of those present appears strong enough
To withstand the sort of danger Akvan Deev displays
Save for one warrior, Rostam, son of Zaal.
Only he is suitable for such a feat.
Only he can save them from the most terrifying threat.

He writes him a friendly letter full of compliments
And hands it over to Gorgeen, son of Milaad.
The fortunate ruler says to his messenger,
"Take this letter at this opportune time to Rostam.
Travel swiftly by day and night, like a swirl of fire,
And stop only once you have reached Zabolestan.
Convey to him a thousand greetings from me,
Wish him a long life, and once he has read my letter,
Tell him that he is the one who enfolds my reign
In a wrap of glory, and implore him to come to me,
To leave without delay upon reading my letter."

Gorgeen departs like a hurricane
Or a deer running for its life.

Once in Zabolestan, he encounters Rostam,
The salvation of heroes, on foot.
He approaches him, gives him the letter,
Showers him with praise, while
Rostam questions him on his long journey.

At the order of the king,
Rostam sprints off in the direction of court.
He arrives, kisses the ground at the foot
Of the throne, utters blessings, and says,
"O King, you have summoned me.
Here I am, ready to execute your plans!
Here I am, strapped to accept your command!
May happiness and might always be your consorts!"

Khosrow receives him in friendship, asks him to sit
Beside him, and says, "O eminent world warrior,
May you live forever in joy and clarity!
The day turns bright when my sight rests on you.
Your watchful mind is the source of my happiness.
I shall relate the affair for which I have called you,
Since no one else at court, O mighty hero,
Is suitable for the task, and since you do not
Recoil in the face of hardships.
I shall impose on you to take up arms
To win crown and treasure.
A shepherd has told me that a wild deer
Has appeared in the midst of his band of stallions."

He recounts to Rostam, from beginning to end,
The words of the shepherd, and then he adds,
"Confront for us the dangers, one more time.
Be vigilant, for I fear Ahriman seeks vengeance."

Rostam replies, "Thanks to your good fortune,
Your throne's most loyal slave dwells not in fear.
Neither a leopard nor a lion,
Neither a dragon nor a wild deev will find
Means to escape the speed of my sword."

3 | Rostam Searches for the Deev

Rostam takes off for the hunt like a brave lion,
Noose in hand, seated upon a dragon.
He takes the direction of the countryside
Where the shepherd looks after his herd
And where the unleashed deev made an appearance.

He searches for three days, hunting and wandering
Through plains and pastures, around the band of horses.
On the fourth day, he spots the beast
Dashing across the meadow.
Rostam bolts to pounce on him like the north wind.

He perceives a creature in a robe the color of bright gold,
But within its frame squats an ugly, malicious deev.
He launches Rakhsh, but once he is near,
He changes his mind and thinks, "I must not kill him.
I shall capture him in my noose's loop.
I do not wish to bring him down with my sword
But rather lead him to the king, bound up and alive."

He flings his Kianian noose to capture
The creature's head in the knot,
But the valiant deer spots the lasso and, like wind,
Vanishes right before Rostam's eyes.
Rostam bites the back of his hand,
Dismayed by his failure to capture him.

The world hero is convinced this being is not a deer
And understands that he must be defeated
By trickery rather than by his biceps' strength.
He reflects, "This creature can only be Akvan Deev.
I must strike him as sharp and quick as wind.
I have heard from wise men that he resides in these parts.
I have heard that he hides beneath deerskin.
I must then trust my sword
And stain with blood his golden robe."

At this very moment, the deev reappears in the desert.
The leader launches his horse of speed once again,
Binds his bow, and, like Aazargoshasp, shoots an arrow

While galloping with all the speed of his mount.
But just as he draws out his royal bow from its case,
The deer once again disappears.

Rostam makes his horse run the length of the vast field.
After riding back and forth for one day and one night,
He grows thirsty and hungry, and his head,
Heavy with sleep, bumps against the saddle's pommel.

He rushes to find some fresh water to drink.
At that very moment, a source appears
Right before him, fragrant as rosewater.
He dismounts, allows Rakhsh to drink his fill,
And, eyes weary, prepares to give in to sleep.
He unties the strap of Rakhsh's poplar wood saddle
And makes use of the leopard skin as a pillow.

Rakhsh settles in a corner to graze.
Rostam drops the quilted saddle by the side
Of the spring at a spot he selects for his rest,
For he is weary from the day's riding.

4 | Akvan Deev Tosses Rostam Into the Sea

Akvan Deev, spying on him from afar,
Finds Rostam fast asleep.
He rushes to him as swift as wind,
Digs into the ground around him,
Lifts the plot of earth on which the hero reclines,
And raises it to the sky.

Rostam abruptly awakens, much disconcerted
And growing increasingly fearful.
He says to himself, "This despicable deev
Has designed a murderous trap.
Alas, farewell to my courage, my strength, my limbs.
Farewell to the sharp blows of my sword and mace.
Should I perish, the world will be laid to waste,
And all the wishes of Afraasiyaab will be fulfilled.
No one will remain, neither Goodarz nor Khosrow,
Neither Tous nor throne and crown,

Neither elephants nor kettledrums.
Who will avenge me on this hideous deev?
Alas, never will there be an adversary like him.
My venture brings misfortune
And takes a downward turn."

As Rostam trembles for his life, Akvan says to him,
"O mighty hero, tell me where and how you wish
To die as I dump you from high above the clouds.
Would you like me to toss you into the waters?
Or would you prefer to crash against the mountains,
Where you will descend far from men?"

Rostam reflects on these words, coming to the realization
That the world is in the hands of this infamous deev.
He thinks, "If he casts me onto the mountain,
My body and bones will surely be crushed.
But I sense that he will do the opposite of what I ask.
He knows nothing of oaths and will renege on his promise.
If instead I select the waters
Where the crocodiles' maw will serve as my coffin,
This abominable deev will, at that moment,
Cast me down to the mountain,
Where I shall be broken into tiny pieces and be gone.
I must then come up with a clever ploy
To convince him to drop me into the sea."

Rostam replies, "A wise man from Chin once told me
A story that applies to this situation quite fittingly:
It is that the soul of those who perish in the water
Will not be greeted by Sooroosh at the portal to paradise.
They will hover miserably on the earth without
Ever finding a place of rest in the other world.
Do not cast me into the sea where
The ribcage of a fish will serve me as coffin!
Instead, fling me to the mountain, so that tigers
And lions witness the hands of a bold warlord."

At these words, Akvan Deev roars like a raging sea
And says to him, "I wish to send you to a place
Where you will remain hidden between two worlds,
Where you will roam miserably on the earth

And will never find rest in the heavens."

Akvan Deev acts contrary to Rostam's request.
He rushes him into the deep sea with the intent
Of making the bowels of fish serve him as coffin.
But as soon as Rostam drops into the water,
He draws out his battle sword, and the whales,
Seeing his combative stance, glide away shyly.

He navigates with his left hand and foot,
Defends himself with his right hand and foot,
Without pause or without wasting a moment.
This is the way of the true man of war, if it is at all
Possible for a man to keep death at bay forever.
Never could fate allow Rostam to perish.
But such is the turning of destiny, that one day
It nourishes you with honey and the next with poison.

Rostam struggles so bravely against the rolling surf
That he finally reaches the seashore.
He pulls himself onto firm land
And thanks the Creator for safeguarding
His servant from the grip of the evil being.
Then he rests for a while after having unfastened his belt,
Placed his Babreh Bayan by the spring,
And cast to the ground his wet noose and armor.

Once these are dry,
The bouncing lion dresses in his coat of mail.
He approaches the spring
Where the Deev lifted him while asleep.
The brilliant Rakhsh is nowhere to be found.
His ambitious master curses providence.
In a rage, he grabs saddle and reins, and follows
The hoofprints of Rakhsh until the early morning light.

Such is the custom of this cruel world:
At times it places you on the back of a saddle,
At times it places the saddle on your back.

Rostam walks in this way, searching for game,
When he spots before him a meadow
Through which runs a freshwater spring.

It is carpeted by treading woodcocks and doves.
He spots a band of horses belonging to Afraasiyaab
And, sleeping nearby in the woods, its guardian.
In the midst of the band is Rakhsh,
Running wildly like a deev and whinnying madly.

As soon as Rostam spots his stallion, he flings
His Kianian noose, captures his head in the knot,
Draws him in, and wipes the dust from him.
He tosses the saddle over him,
Expressing thanks to the Creator.
With the noose around Rakhsh's neck, Rostam
Climbs on him, places his hand on his sword's hilt,
And starts to push the entire herd before him
While invoking the name of Yazdan on his sword.

At the sound of the horses, the guardian lifts his head.
He calls the cavaliers who answer to him
And asks them to mount their noble stallions.
Each one grabs noose and bows to assess the adversary
Who dares venture into this meadow
And approach such a numerous guard.

The riders pursue Rostam heatedly,
Hoping to tear apart this lion's skin.
But Rostam, who watches them approach,
Takes his sharp sword out of its sheath,
Roars like a lion, and calls out his own name,
Exclaiming, "I am Rostam, son of Zaal, son of Saam!"

He kills two-thirds of them with his blade,
And the guardian of the herd, witness to this,
Turns his back on him and takes off swiftly.

Rostam pursues him, bow hanging at his arm.

5 | Afraasiyaab Arrives to Observe His Horses, and Rostam Kills Akvan Deev

At this very moment, Afraasiyaab arrives unexpectedly,
Like a blustering wind emerging out of a crevasse.
He brings music and wine, an escort of daring leaders,
And hopes to engage in revelry and forget his worries.

Once on this field, where every year
Its guardian allows his Tooranian herds
To roam along the water's edge, Afraasiyaab
Fails to see signs of either horses or guardian.
But suddenly a loud sound reaches him from the plain,
And soon a number of steeds come into view,
Charging and trying to outdo one another.
Above these spirited beasts,
The figure of Rakhsh looms through a veil
Of dust rising from beneath his hooves.

The aging guardian approaches the King of Tooran
And recounts to him his astonishing adventure,
How Rostam injured him with his arrow
And captured the horses all by himself;
How he slew a great number of them
And passed over others.

At these words, Afraasiyaab recalls the old days.

The Turks raise their voices to complain:
"This brave man once again dares come alone to battle.
We must shelter ourselves with armor
Or this affair will bring us immeasurable shame.
Are we so weak, so vile, so despicable
That a lone man is able to spill our blood?
Are we going to tolerate our herds to be seized shamefully?
No, we shall not allow this sort of act to go unpunished!"

The leader, with his escort and with four elephants,
Goes in pursuit of Rostam, but once near him,
Rostam reaches for his bow and advances in great fury,
Overwhelming the adversary with a shower of shots
And countless blows of his sword.

PART THIRTEEN

After having killed sixty warriors in the manner of a lion,
Rostam launches an attack with his mace
And kills forty more noblemen.
The world master, distressed, fearfully runs away.
Rostam captures his four white elephants,
And the Turkish army absconds, hopeless of the outcome.

Rostam pursues them for two farsangs,
Like a spring cloud raining on them
A vicious hail of his mace's blows, sending bits
Of their shattered helmets high into the air.
Then he returns, gathering the elephants, the loot,
And all the herds that fall into his hands.

Rostam's combative heart reflects on future wars.
The deev Akvan accosts him at the source
And says to him, "Are you not yet weary of battle?
You have evaded the sea as well as the whale's claws.
You have thrown yourself
On the desert like a roaring leopard.
But now you will see your end,
As this is surely your last battle.

Rostam replies to the deev's words with a lion growl.
He unhooks his rolled-up noose from its knob,
Flings it, and captures the deev midriff
While teetering on the saddle against the lurching deev.
He raises his heavy mace as if it were a blacksmith's hammer,
Strikes the head of the deev like a war elephant,
And smashes his skull, brains, and legs in one blow.
Then he sets foot to ground, draws out his sharp sword,
And slices off the head of the fearless deev.

Rostam gives thanks to the Creator,
Who grants victory on the day of battle.

Know that a wicked man is a deev, as is an impious man
Who neglects to worship Yazdan and show gratitude.
One must add to the class of deevs, and not to that of men,
Anyone who deviates from the path of humanity.
Your wisdom may reject the truth of this account
But only because it may not absorb
The depth of its implication.

A hero must be strong and brave, formidable
In his upper arm and soaring in his stature.
Only then can he be given the name of bold warrior.
But do not assign such a title to Akvan Deev.
Speak only of heroic deeds.

What do you say, my aged master,
Who has endured the heat and chill of worldly life,
Who knows the highs and lows of a long life?
The shortest existence makes use of elephant strength.
No one knows what the rotating vault of sky
Will settle upon to confer to us of feast and battle.

6 | Rostam Returns to Iran-Zamin

After Rostam beheads the wicked deev,
He climbs on his mountain-like steed,
Gathers the herds of stallions
And the loads abandoned by the Turks,
And begins his march with loot and elephants.
The world is embellished by the sparkle of his deeds.

Kay Khosrow hears that Rostam, who had left
To capture the dreadful deer in the knots of his noose,
Is about to march on the road
As he returns from his feats, in pomp and glory.
Kay Khosrow also learns that he conquered deev
And elephants on firm land, and whales in waters,
And that neither lion nor deev,
Neither men nor heroes searching for battle,
Survived the strokes of his sword.

The king makes arrangements.
Noblemen place diadems on their heads.
The imperial banner is lifted,
The indomitable elephants are decked in bells,
And this procession, with the host at the lead
And the king, world master, perfectly happy trailing,
Marches on the road to meet Rostam, world hero.

Rostam discerns the banner of the noble king from afar.

He dismounts, touches his glorious forehead
To the dust, and kisses the ground. The sound
Of voices, troops, elephants, and timpani rises.
Army leaders set foot on the ground before the hero.

The King of Kings steadies himself in the saddle.
He commands Rostam, giver of crowns,
To climb back on Rakhsh. The hero obeys,
And in this manner they travel the distance to court,
Hearts full of joy, with a sense of goodwill for each other.

Rostam says, "O renowned Khosrow,
A king of your stature must not exert himself
To meet his most humble subject on the road.
I am merely the servant of the Kianian king's servant."

Khosrow showers him with blessings and praise:
"May the sky remain loyal to your sword!
Never will there exist an epic tale
To celebrate a man of your caliber!
May my heart always rejoice in your presence!"

Rostam distributes the stallions to the Iranians,
Wishing to keep for himself no other mount but Rakhsh.
He sends the elephants to the king's stables.
Lions cannot block their path,
For the king is master of throne and crown.

For one week, feasts overtake the palace.
Wine is summoned with music and musicians.

Rostam drinks and recounts to the king
His adventures and the story of Akvan Deev:
"Never have I seen a more colorful, strong, majestic deer.
Since my sword tore up his flesh to shreds,
Neither friend nor enemy may gain profit from him.
His head was as large as that of an elephant;
His fur long, his mouth full of claims,
Like those of a boar; his eyes white,
His lips black; one dared not glance his way.
There exists no camel so strong for the carnage he caused.
He converted the field into a sea of blood.
Once I cut off his head with my sharp sword,

A torrent of blood spewed into the air."

Khosrow is astonished to hear this tale.
He sets down his cup and gives thanks to Yazdan
For having created a heroic warrior like Rostam,
A marvelous man as never described before,
A hero with no equal in valor, stature, or beauty.
He adds, "If the Creator had not granted me this favor,
I may not have a subject like you in all the world,
A bold hero able to turn deevs and supplicants into prey."

They pass two weeks in joy, in drinking,
And in tales of wine, battle, and conquest.
At the start of the third week,
Rostam expresses his desire to joyously return home:
"It would not suit me to hide the deep longing I bear
To set my eyes on home and on Zaal, son of Saam.
I shall depart without delay to my father's court,
Where I have made preparations for war.
One must not renounce the vengeance due Siaavosh,
Who was killed for a vile loot of horse and herd."

Kay Khosrow, world king, opens his treasury,
Holding within magnificent jewels.
He withdraws a cup filled with pearls
And five royal sets of apparel woven in gold.
He offers Rostam Rumi slaves with golden belts,
Women decked in golden necklaces,
Carpets, brocade and silk, an ivory throne,
A turquoise crown, and dinars.
He presents these to Rostam and says,
"These gifts are for you to take to Sistan,
But let us still enjoy each other's company.
Tomorrow we shall consider your departure."

Rostam obeys the king and empties his cup of wine.
But once night descends, he can think
Of nothing else but his journey home.
The king escorts him the distance of two farsangs,
Then kisses him as Rostam continues on the road.

The king takes the opposite direction back to court.
He devotes himself to restoring order throughout

PART THIRTEEN

The realm, and the world turns at his will.

Thus rotates this aged vault of sky:
At times like a bow, at times like an arrow.

I end here the tale of the battle
Between Akvan Deev and the mighty Rostam,
The noble, valiant hero who overcame the deev
Like a mosquito conquers an elephant.
I pay tribute to the pure Yzad, Giver of sight and speech.

I shall now address the story of Bijan, a story
That will move the reader to shed copious tears.

PART
FOURTEEN

The Story of Bijan and Manijeh

1 | The Beginning of the Story

The night, jet black, washing its face in tar,
Rendered Mars, Saturn, and Mercury invisible.
The moon, decked for better times, mounted on her throne,
Was ready for her voyage across the heavens.
She grew darker in the midst of this bleak world,
Her body slimmer, her heart constricted.
Three-fourths of her crown eclipsed as she sailed
Through space, the air thick with rust and dust.

The procession of the dark night projected
On plains and valleys a spread of crow's plumage.
The sky appeared to be a sheet of steel,
Corroded and weather-beaten as if enfolded in tar.

On all sides, I could see Ahriman, a giant serpent
With gaping jaws, with every cold breath,
An ominous man blowing out a spark of coal.
The garden and river's edge were black,
Like waves lurching on a sea of tar.
The sky halted its rotations,
And the sun's feet and hands were paralyzed,
Powerless to make the slightest shift.
You would have thought the earth
Was asleep beneath a black veil.
You would have thought the world feared itself
And the night watcher held jiggling bells.
One could hear neither the gentle chants of birds
Nor the long howls of wild beasts.
There was complete silence:
The world did not utter a word, neither good nor bad.
You could see neither high nor low,
And my heart pulled at the length of the situation.

I rose in anguish.
I had a kind friend living with me in the house.

I called her[60] and asked her for a lamp.
My friend, who resembles an idol, came to the garden
And asked, "Why do you need light?
Does not sleep visit you in the dark of night?"

I answered her, "O fair-faced idol, I have no use for sleep.
Bring me a candle as bright as the sun's face.
Place it before me; prepare a feast,
Take your lute, and let us drink."

My divine friend left the garden and returned to me
With a bright candle, along with wine, pomegranate,
Orange, quince, and a shining cup worthy of a king.
She drank and in turn played the lute.
It was as if I were bewitched by the angel Haaroot.[61]
With my heart's desires thus appeased,
My dark night turned into a bright day.

Listen to what my tender mate, my sun-faced moon,
Said to me as we befriended the cup of wine.
"May the sky rejoice with your life!
Drink while I read to you a story from an ancient book.
As soon as your ear grasps the first words of my tale,
You will find yourself confounded
With the workings of the heavens.
It is a story full of ruse, love, magic, and treachery,
One worthy of being heard by sensible men.
Perhaps you can adapt it to poetry
In your book written in the language of Pahlavi."

I said to this lean and tall cypress tree,
"O moon-faced idol, prepare to read your story,
Which will surely increase my love for you.
Dear cypress tree full of grace, I owe you my talent,
And by divulging this hidden secret, you will
Awaken my dormant mind in this dark night.
I shall convert this story into verse
Just as I hear it from your mouth.
I shall thank the Creator,

◇◇◇◇◇◇◇◇◇◇◇◇◇
60 Perhaps Ferdowsi is referring to his wife.
61 Haaroot: Angel, who along with another fairy Maaroot, came to earth to teach
spells; they lost access to heaven because of their sins and were imprisoned in Babel.

Who is familiar with the just and the virtuous."

Then the cherished idol read me the story
Written so long ago.
Listen now to the beginning of my song.
Collect your mind, and pay attention.

2 | The Armanians[62] Ask Kay Khosrow for Protection

Once Kay Khosrow draws on vengeance,
He organizes the world affairs on a new order.

Glory and honor are removed from Tooran;
The throne of the Iranian king is lifted higher than the sun.
The sky wraps its favors around the earth
And around the noble Iranians.

World beauty is restored to its essence of eternity
As Khosrow is purified by the waters of loyalty.
But the wise man does not take for granted
A place already carved by a river.
Two-thirds of the world submits to the rule
Of Kay Khosrow, avenger of Siaavosh.

One day a gathering sits in joy, drinking wine
To the health of the army's brave warriors.
The imperial palace is decorated in brocade.
The king sets on his head a jewel-inlaid crown,
Holds in his hand a ruby chalice filled with wine,
And abandons his heart and ears
To the playing of the lute.

Noblemen sit and listen to the music:
Fariborz, son of Kaavoos; Gostaham;
Goodarz, son of Kashvaad; the bold Shahpur;
Farhaad, Giv, and Gorgeen, son of Milaad;
Tous, the leader of princes, born of Nozar,
Army destroyer; Khorraad; and Bijan the warrior.
These brave heroes, devoted subjects of Kay Khosrow,

◇◇◇◇◇◇◇◇◇◇◇◇◇
62 Armanian: Resident of Arman, region on the border of Iran and Tooran.

Sit in the midst of tulips and narcissus.
They drink royal wine the color of Yemeni carnelian.
Fairy-faced slaves stand before the throne,
Their curls, black as musk, frame their jasmine cheeks.

The banquet room is full of fragrance, color, and paint.
The grand palace master stands ready to serve the king.
A chamberlain, guarding the entrance curtains,
Slowly nears the palace master to announce to him
The approach of the Armanians from the border,
Their long journey to regain security,
And their presence at the gates
Asking for a royal audience in the name of justice.

The cautious palace master listens,
Then takes a step toward the famed throne
To relate the message and await royal command.

Then he receives the Armanians with ceremony.
They drag themselves before the king, arms crossed,
Faces against the ground, shedding tears,
Hollering cries of distress and begging for help:
"O victorious king, may you live forever,
For you prove yourself earnest and worthy!
We have traveled far and wide in the name of justice.
We arrive from a land that sits between Tooran and Iran,
A land called Arman, whose leader sent us to you.
O King, may you live in joy
And protect the world against evil.
You are the ruler of the seven regions.
You must come to the aid of any place
Stricken by hardship and misfortune.
Our city touches the border of Tooran-Zamin,
And the Tooranians submit us to constant misery.

"Now there is a forest on the side of Iran,
The cause of all our troubles.
We grew a great many crops
And a great many fruit trees.
We allowed our herds to graze there,
And our city's fortune depended
On the bounty we reaped from this forest.

PART FOURTEEN

O King, protect us, for innumerable boars
Charged at the forest and at the river's edge.
Their teeth's strength is as mighty as elephant teeth;
Their bodies as large as mountains.
They have reduced the city of Arman to its last resort.
So many wrongs have they done to us,
Our four-legged creatures, and our crops.
Finding it a fun game, they preoccupy themselves
With chopping in half, with their teeth,
Trees planted from time immemorial.
Not even a rock can resist their bite, and we fear
That good fortune has decidedly abandoned us."

The king listens to these men imploring his help.
His heart wrenches in pain; he takes pity on them.
He addresses his noble heroes:
"My brave and illustrious leaders,
If someone among you wishes to acquire a name,
To stand higher than the others,
Let him go to this forest devastated by boars.
Let him combat in glory
While uttering the name of Yazdan the powerful.
Let him slice off their heads with his sword.
I shall not be close-fisted with such a hero.
I shall offer him vast treasure and many gems."

He asks for a large golden platter,
Which the treasurer places before the throne,
And pours onto it all sorts of gems, mixing them up.
Ten horses are brought with golden bridles
Marked with the name of Kaavoos,
Each with a covering of Rumi brocade.

The eminent council members are called upon.
The world king says to them, "O glorious heroes,
Who will dare attempt the deed I suggest
And assume my distress as his distress
While my treasure becomes his wealth?"

No one in the assembly replies
Except for the glorious Bijan, son of Giv.
He emerges from the leadership rank,

Conjures up the divine on the king, and says,
"May your palace never be deprived of you!
May your wish formulate the law of the realm!
I have heard your command and your promise
For protection extends throughout the world.
I shall depart to carry out this deed,
For I exist body and soul merely to serve you."

At the words of Bijan, on the other side of the hall,
Giv feels a pang of worry.
He utters a blessing to the king and advises his son:
"From where do you draw this lightheaded courage?
From where comes this strength and confidence?
A young man, no matter how well educated,
No matter how high his birth,
Cannot accomplish great deeds
Before having first acquired vast experience.
He must feel good fortune
And bad in their various facets,
He must, at times, taste the bitterness of life.
Do not go down a path never trampled
Before by your feet, and do not make
Foolish claims to glory before the king."

The clever young man, on whom fortune shines,
Is indignant at his father's words and replies,
"O victorious father, do not underestimate me.
Accept my offers. I may be young in my deeds,
But I am mature in my ruling and decision-making.
I shall fearlessly cut off the heads of these wild boars.
I am Bijan, son of Giv, destroyer of armies."

The king rejoices at these words.
He praises and blesses Bijan,
Granting him permission to go: "O skilled warrior,
You offer yourself as a shield against ill deeds.
A king, lucky to have a subject such as you,
Would be deemed weak were he to fear the enemy."

Then he says to Gorgeen, son of Milaad,
"Bijan is young and unfamiliar with the road.
Go with him with horses and loads.

Serve him as companion and guide."

3 | Bijan Fights the Boars

Bijan arms himself and prepares for departure.
He tightens his belt, places his helmet on his head,
And, accompanied by Gorgeen, son of Milaad,
His equal in strength and courage,
He takes leave of the court with cheetahs and falcons
To assist them as they hunt on the journey.
Bijan departs like a fiery lion toward the desert.

Bijan seizes the heads of deer in his noose
And tosses them aside.
Their chests are left to be stripped by cheetahs' claws.
One might wonder whether this man
Is Bijan the warrior or Tahmures Deev-Binder.
Pheasants are captured in the talons of falcons.
As a result, beads of blood plummet from clouds
To stain the blooming, sweet-smelling jasmine.

In this way the two warriors carry on.
The plain is to them nothing but a playful field.

In the end, Bijan discerns a forest,
And his blood boils with impatience.
The boars roam inside, unaware that warriors
Are close by, saddled upon their chargers.

The two advance and dismount at the forest's edge.
They set ablaze a massive fire, sit around it,
And stoke it with tree trunks.
They have a flask filled with wine.
They take a fleshy female deer, cut it into pieces,
And roast its bits over the fire.
After eating their fill, they bring their hand
To the flask to drink and soon become jovial.
Once their faces exhibit signs of intoxication,
Gorgeen expresses his wish for a place to sleep.

Bijan says to him, "I am not tired.

607

Do not seek to rest yet, my brother.
Remain standing so that we can better execute
What we have been charged with and free,
By our efforts, the king's heart from worry.
Go near this pond while I shoot at the boars.
When you hear sounds in the forest, seize your mace.
Pay close attention, and if a boar escapes me,
Bring it down with one blow."

The valiant Gorgeen replies,
"This is not the way we agreed with the young king.
You have taken jewels, gold, and silver.
You assumed this battle.
I can only show you the way."

Bijan listens with astonishment.
You would think the world turns black before his eyes.
He enters the forest as brave as a lion, and, binding his bow,
He shouts out like spring thunder, shaking leaves on trees
To make them tumble down like rain.
A shining sword in hand,
He follows the boars' trail like a rutting elephant.

The boars rush forward to attack him, thrusting dirt
Into the air with tusks from which sparks fly out.
One would think they are about to set the world ablaze.

A boar charges at Bijan as if it were Ahriman.
He tears apart his coat of mail,
Sharpens his tusks with tree trunks
Like one files a steel blade with solid stone.
From the forest rises the smoke of battle.

In the end, Bijan strikes the boar's side
With his sword, splitting his massive body in two.

The dauntless wild beasts run off like foxes,
Bodies wounded by sword and weary of battle.

Bijan cuts off their heads and hangs them
On the saddle strap of his powerful horse Shabrang.
He hooks the tusks around the horse's neck,
For he wishes to present them

Before the king upon his return.
As for the headless bodies, which are to display
His hunting skills to the brave leaders of Iran,
He piles them up on a cart,
The heap large as a mountain, to be dragged
With much effort by a powerful buffalo.

4 | Gorgeen Betrays Bijan

Meanwhile, the malicious, resentful Gorgeen
Quietly makes his way to the outskirts of the woods.
The entire forest appears black to his eyes.
Still, he receives Bijan under the pretense of joy
And congratulates him.

He feels ashamed and fears that he will be met
With considerable embarrassment and ill repute.
Ahriman stirs his heart
And inspires him to turn against Bijan.
But his wishes are not in accordance with what
Was written, for he harbors no thoughts for the Creator.
A man who digs a deep ditch on the road
Is certain to stumble and fall into that ditch.

Gorgeen, spurred on by the hope of growing his fortune
And acquiring vast popularity, begins to set a trap.
After drinking wine joyfully two or three times,
He says to Bijan, "O world hero,
You are all insight and wisdom.
With the help of the Creator
And your invincible good fortune,
You have the ability to perform tremendous feats.
I shall now speak to you of things that are worth
Listening to, for I have often come here
With Rostam, Giv, and Gostaham,
With Tous, son of Nozar, and with Gojdaham.
Often have we proved our courage on this vast plain.
Much time has passed since we received
Glory and honor in the eyes of Kay Khosrow.

"Nearby, on the border of Tooran-Zamin,

Within a journey of two days,
There is a site reserved for feasts.
You will find there a red and yellow field,
The delight of a warrior's heart.
The woods, the gardens, and the springs
Make it a place worthy of a brave hero.
The ground is as soft as silk,
The air carries the scent of musk,
And the rushing spring flows with rosewater.
The stems of jasmine bend low with the weight of flowers.
The rose is an idol, and the nightingale its worshipper.
The pheasant runs around the roses while
The nightingale sings loud on the cypress branch.
The river's edge will soon appear like paradise.
Mount and field will populate with fair women,
And a joyous crowd will gather there.

"Manijeh, Afraasiyaab's daughter,
Will turn the garden as bright as the sun.
She will pitch her tent in the meadow,
Surrounded by one hundred young girls,
Each as beautiful as a painting;
One hundred Tooranian maidens of cypress height,
Hair black as musk, with rosy cheeks, pining eyes,
And lips like cups of rosewater-scented wine.
The entire plain will be decked like a Chini temple,
With an abundance of precious objects.
Let us now go to this place of feast.
Let us quickly travel the distance in the span of a day.
Let us seize some of these women and take them
To Kay Khosrow, to cover ourselves with glory."

In this way speaks Gorgeen.
Bijan's heroic and youthful blood on the boil,
He replies, "Let us leave right away!
Let us take joy in this enchanting place!"

Most often, Bijan seeks glory, but in this moment,
He can think of nothing but pleasure.
His time is of youth, and he acts impulsively.

5 | Bijan Sees Afraasiyaab's Daughter Manijeh

They take the road,
One man clutching greedy intentions,
The other meditating on treason.

Bijan, the army's support, stops between two forests
After one day of travel, and for two days
He and his companion enjoy the hunt
With cheetah and falcon on the Armanian fields.

Once Gorgeen is aware that the young lady
Has arrayed the field with color
And scent like the eye of a rooster,
He speaks to Bijan of feast and music.

Bijan says to Gorgeen,
"I shall walk ahead of you to the Tooranians,
Observe and assess how they revel in feast.
From there I shall rattle my horse's reins
And stir the dust into the air.
We shall then discuss and agree on a plan of action.
Our hearts will lighten at the sight of them."

He addresses his treasurer and asks for the golden,
Shining headdress his father wears in times of feast,
For its sparkle illuminates any banquet hall,
The torque and earring offered by Kay Khosrow,
And Giv's bracelet inlaid with precious stones.

The treasurer obeys and brings the items to Bijan,
Who dons his tunic of shining Rumi silk
And inserts a feather from Homa in his headdress.
Once Shabrang is saddled, he demands his jeweled belt.
Dressed and ready, the brave hero mounts his steed and,
Full of confidence, swiftly takes the road to the forest.

As he penetrates deeper into the woods,
His heart feels constricted by the force of his desires.
He takes shelter from the sun beneath the shade
Of a tall cypress tree, protecting his horse as well.
He approaches the tent of the fair maiden,

Glancing furtively at the Tooranian women.
He instantly feels affection invade his heart.

He sees young women, as beautiful as dolls from
Kandahar and decked like fresh, gay spring.
The entire field resounds with music and song.
The beauty of the world ravishes every heart present.

From her tent, the beautiful Manijeh
Perceives the face of the army warrior,
As bright as the star of Canopus in Yemen,
Like a violet, white in its center.
On his head is the diadem of the world hero,
And his chest is covered in plush Rumi silk.

Immediately, the veiled woman's heart
Stirs with longing and tenderness
For this love-seeking man.
She sends him a message by way
Of her court attendant, to whom she says,
"Go, swift as wind, to the tall cypress tree.
Find out the identity of the moon-faced man,
Whether it is Siaavosh reborn or a fairy, and tell him,
          'How do you explain your presence here?
          Who and what brings you to these parts?
          Are you born of a fairy or of Siaavosh?
          You fill dim hearts with affection.
          Will the day of resurrection come,
          Since you have ignited the fires of love?
          For years I have celebrated spring here,
          But never have I seen you in this land of delights.
          I have eyes only for you, O free cypress tree.
          Tell me if you are a man or a fairy.
          Join us; take part in our feasts.
          Never have I seen a being of such beauty.
          Tell me who you are and where you come from.'"

The young lady's attendant takes off in a quick stride,
Approaches Bijan, praises him and bows at his feet
To repeat to him her mistress's message.

Bijan's two cheeks blossom like a rose,
And he replies, "O envoy of sweet appearance,

I am neither Siaavosh nor the son of a fairy.
I come from Iran, the land of free men.
I am Bijan, son of Giv, here to battle the boars.
I cut off their heads and flung them on the road,
Wishing to return to the king and hand him their tusks.
After hearing of your feasts,
I failed to hurry to Giv, son of Goodarz.
Instead, I hastened my way down the forest road.
I have come in the hopes that my fortune
Grants me the wish of seeing in dream
The enchanting face of Afraasiyaab's daughter.
I find a field decked and filled
With jewels like a Chinese temple.
Well then, if you wish to act in my favor,
I shall give you a golden crown, earrings, and a belt,
And you will take me to the fair-faced beauty
And fill her heart with love for me."

The court attendant returns
To whisper the reply in Manijeh's ear
And to describe to her Bijan's appearance
And the perfect attributes given to him
By the World Creator on the advent of his birth.

Manijeh immediately sends a message to Bijan:
"Your wishes have been granted. Come to me!
Light up my obscure heart with the sparkle of your being.
My eyes will shine at the sight of you, and I shall plant
A rose garden in this field now covered with tents."

The envoy delivers Manijeh's reply.
Bijan listens to it with a pounding heart.

6 | Bijan Presents Himself at Manijeh's Tent

Having nothing more to say, Bijan emerges from
Beneath the shadow of the cypress tree and, on foot,
Takes the direction of Afraasiyaab's daughter's tent.
He raises the tent's curtains and enters,
Like a tall cypress tree, strapped in a golden belt.

Manijeh rushes over, holds him close to her breast,
Unfastens his royal belt, and asks him about his journey
And his escort of warriors on the day of battle.
She adds, "O man of handsome face,
How weary you must be after making use of mace!
How weary your body, so beautiful, so noble, so svelte!"

Someone washes Bijan's feet with musk and rosewater,
Then a banquet is set up for him,
A table dressed with various dishes,
More numerous than one's mind can imagine.

Musicians and wine are summoned,
And all the visitors are dismissed from the tent.
Slaves stand by, singing or playing lute and harp.
The ground is sprinkled with gold coins.
Vibrant silk carpets are spread on the ground,
The colors of peacock feathers.
The tent enclosure is perfumed in amber and musk,
And woven with rubies and gold.

Aged wine, poured into crystal cups, revives Bijan.
They rejoice in this way for three days and three nights,
Until the hero succumbs to sleep and intoxication.

7 | Manijeh Takes Bijan to Her Palace

When the time comes for Manijeh's departure,
She finds it hard to part company with Bijan.
Determined to act in her favor, she calls her slaves
And commands them to mix with honey a drink
That would make him unconscious.

The slaves give the mixture to the youth, who,
Though inebriated, cannot resist another drink.
He loses consciousness; his head rolls to the side.

Manijeh asks for a litter, places Bijan,
Asleep, next to her, and they take off.
She sprinkles camphor over the bed of her inert companion
And drops of rosewater over sticks of sandalwood.

Once near the town, she covers him with a veil
And enters the palace secretly at night,
Without saying a word to anyone.

A bedroom is prepared for Bijan.
Manijeh, eager to see him awaken, brings a balm meant
To dissipate sleep and to prompt him to open his eyes.
Once awake, Bijan gathers his senses,
Finds himself in the arms of a woman
With a figure nicely fragranced and white, like lilies.
He finds himself in Afraasiyaab's residence with
A moon-faced beauty whose head rests on his pillow.

He fears his position and pleads with Yazdan
For help against Ahriman, saying, "O Creator,
Nothing can save me from this grave danger!
Help me get even with Gorgeen.
Grant my wishes against him and his deeds.
He is responsible for my shameful state.
He uttered a thousand magic spells on me."

Manijeh says to him, "Surrender your heart to joy.
View events that have not yet come to pass,
As the wind's breath. Men must endure all sorts of trials.
At times they are given a feast and at times a battle."

They sit down to eat. Bijan weighs the outcome.
Either he will win or he will lose his head in the gamble.

From another tent, they call a girl of rosy cheeks,
Who dresses them in robes of Chini silk.
These fairy-faced women produce sweet music,
And thus they spend some days and nights in joy.

Some time elapses.
A man occupied in pointless discourse,
Eager to shake the tree of ill,
Spies on others' secret positions.
From the onset, he observes this curious affair,
Probing to find out who is this stranger,
What region he is from,
And why he has entered the land of Tooran.

In the end, this man discovers the affair,
And fearful for his life, he rushes to the chamberlain.
The latter thinks his only course of action
Is to expose the deed.
He abandons the guard of Manijeh's chambers,
Appears before the King of Tooran, and tells him that
His daughter has picked a mate from the land of Iran.

The world-seeking king pronounces
The name of the Creator, World Master.
You would think him a willow tree shaken by the wind.
Blood spills from his eyes, filling his eyelashes and cheeks.
In his wrath, the old man says, "Miserable is the star
Of the man who has a daughter in his chambers,
Even if he makes claims to be owner of crown."

He remains confounded by Manijeh's actions.
He calls the palace's grand executioner
And says to him, "Give me wise advice
On the way I am to act with this impure woman!"

The executioner replies, "First you must make
A more exact inquiry in the palace.
If the affair is as recounted to you,
I have nothing more to say,
But seeing is better than hearing."

As soon as Afraasiyaab receives the killer's reply,
He rushes to follow his counsel,
Addressing Garsivaz: "So many ills
Have we suffered from the land of Iran.
How much more must we endure?
Has there ever lived in the world
A man more despondent than me
Or one burdened with added afflictions,
All caused by Iran-Zamin
And by my depraved offspring?
Go, escorted by prudent riders.
Occupy gates and palace rooftops, and search
The interior chambers until you find this man.
Then bind him up with chains and drag him to me!"

8 | Garsivaz Takes Bijan to Afraasiyaab

As Garsivaz approaches the chamber's door,
He hears clatter inside and sounds of a banquet.
Afraasiyaab's palace resounds with the strum of lute.
The king's riders occupy the gates and rooftops
And block access to the exits.

Garsivaz, seeing that the entry to Manijeh's pavilion
Is sealed and that wine is poured in abundance,
Breaks the locks without hesitation and rushes inside,
Where, from the threshold, he spots the outsider Bijan.
The sight of the Iranian makes his blood boil with rage.

In this dwelling, he sees three hundred slaves
Holding string instruments and goblets.
Bijan sits in the midst of these women,
Joyfully sipping red wine.

Garsivaz shouts from afar,
"O presumptuous man of impure breed,
You have fallen into the clutches of the wild lion!
How will you now safeguard your life?"

Bijan trembles within and thinks,
"How shall I defend myself without weapons,
Without either Shabrang or another stallion?
I fear my star has dimmed today.
Where is Giv? Where is Goodarz, son of Kashvaad?
Why must I needlessly surrender my head here?
I see no one in the world who can come to my aid
Except for Yazdan, the Savior."

Bijan always hides a sharp dagger in his boot's leg.
He reaches for it, draws it out of its scabbard,
Takes his place behind the chamber's door,
And declares, "I am Bijan, grandson of Kashvaad,
Leader of warrior heroes and noblemen!
May none of you attempt to touch me
Unless his body is weary of bearing his head!
Even if the earth were to shake on resurrection day,
No one will ever witness me taking flight!"

617

Then he turns to Garsivaz:
"Misfortune has drawn this trap before me.
You know my ancestors, you know my king,
You know my place among warrior heroes.
If you wish to fight me, I shall not hesitate
To soil my hands in blood and, with this dagger,
Cut off the heads of a great number of Tooranians.
But if you wish to take me before the king,
I shall tell him of this adventure, ask him for mercy.
You will be his guide on the road to happiness.
It is in your favor to show him
The way to good deeds."

Garsivaz, seeing how quick he is to engage
In battle, refrains from attacking him.
He knows that Bijan is telling the truth and that
He will not hesitate to wash his hands in blood.
He guarantees his life under oath
And gives him much advice.
With flattery, he convinces Bijan to surrender his dagger
And allow him to tie him up without a show of resistance.

Garsivaz thus succeeds in confining Bijan in chains,
Like one ties up the limbs of a cheetah.

Alas, what good is courage when fortune is opposed to it?
Such is the rotation of the sky, which treats you harshly
At times and at times delights you with its favors.
In this manner, Bijan is beguiled and taken
To Afraasiyaab, cheeks pale, eyes full of tears.

As soon as he is at the king's side, hands tied up
And head bare, he says, "O King, it would be wise
For you to take the path of wisdom and justice.
I have not come to this palace of my own free will.
No one is to blame for this affair.
I left the land of Iran with servants
And a procession to destroy the boars.
I came across this festival in the land of Tooran
As we were in pursuit of a falcon gone astray.
Now I have annihilated my land and my family.
I fell asleep beneath the shade of a cypress tree.

"A fairy came and spread her wings,
Carried me in her arms while I slept.
She lifted me from the side of my horse
And flew me to the side of the royal daughter.
Riders covered the plain, litters passed on all sides.
An Indian palanquin was drawing close,
Surrounded by Tooranians on horseback.
In the midst of this crowd was a litter of aloeswood,
Its satin curtains drawn, holding within it
A sleeping beauty whose diadem rested on a pillow.
At once, the fairy recalled Ahriman.
She flew as swift as wind in the midst of the riders,
Put me down abruptly inside the litter, and
Whispered a magic spell over the fair woman.

"Once at the royal palace, I slept for some time,
But once I awakened, I trembled and shed tears.
I have not committed a crime.
The purity of Manijeh has not been compromised.
But surely the fairy has troubled my fortune as
She sought to tempt my fate with the power of her spells."

Afraasiyaab replies,
"Your day of misfortune has too soon arrived."
You are the one who left Iran-Zamin
With bow and noose to seek battle and fame.
Now here you are before me,
Hands tied like a woman, and telling me
Befuddled stories like a drunken man.
But no matter how much you lie to me, you will not
Save your head from the wrath of my hands."

Bijan says, "O King, lend me your ear, listen to me.
The boars with their tusks, lions with their claws
Are always assuming a stance of defense.
Heroes, with their sword and bow and arrow, can fight.
But when one's hands are tied and one is disarmed,
While another man dons an armor of steel,
How can this be deemed a fair contest?
How could a lion, deprived of his claws, tear apart its prey?
No matter how valiant his heart, if the king wishes for me
To make a show of courage in the middle of this court,

May he provide me with a steed and a heavy mace.
May he select a thousand Tooranian warriors.
If a single one of these men survives,
May I no longer be counted among formidable men!"

Afraasiyaab sends Bijan a furious glare
And allows his rage to explode.
Turning to Garsivaz, he says,
"You told me we should not sentence him to death.
But do you not see that this vile, despicable man
Is plotting new crimes against us?
He is not satisfied with the injuries he has caused us
And asks to be allowed to engage in an honorable battle.
Take him away as he is, feet and hands tied up,
This very moment, and rid us of his presence!
Set up a gallows before the palace gates
In a spot accessible from all sides.
Hang this miserable man alive at the gallows
And never speak of him to me again
From now on, may no Iranian ever dare
Turn his eyes toward the land of Tooran!"

Bijan is dragged away from Afraasiyaab's hall,
Heartbroken, eyes flooding with tears.
He arrives at the palace door troubled,
His feet colored like a rose with the blood
Dripping from his lashes. He says,
"If the Creator rules that I must die miserably,
I do not fear the idea of the gallows and death.
But I tremble at the thought of Iran's mighty men
Considering me a coward for being executed
Without suffering a single wound.
I will be cursed forever after my death,
Cursed before people at the royal court,
Before my father and my grandfather.
Alas, my enemy will rejoice,
And all that he has plotted against me will occur!
Alas, I shall never set my sights on Giv or on the king!
Alas, I am so far from the heroes full of valor!
O early morning winds, please go to the land of Iran.
Take a message from me to the noble Kay Khosrow.
Tell him that Bijan is in grave distress.

Tell him that his body has fallen prey to lion claws.
Tell Goodarz, son of Kashvaad, that Gorgeen
Is the one responsible for my tarnished glory,
That he plunged me into a calamitous situation
With no hope for either rescue or survival.
Tell Gorgeen, 'O foolish warrior,
How will you answer me in the other world?'"

9 | Piran Asks Afraasiyaab to Have Mercy on Bijan

Yazdan takes pity on Bijan,
Attributing his transgressions to the idiocy of youth.
While the workers dig a hole to insert the gallows,
Chance wishes that Piran, son of Viseh, appears.
He finds the road covered with girded Turks.
He discerns the ominous post from which
Hangs a noose and asks the Tooranians,
"What is the meaning of these gallows?
Who has crossed the king so badly
That he must now face an execution?"

Garsivaz replies, "His name is Bijan.
He has come from Iran to prove
To be the king's vilest enemy!"

Piran urges his horse forward
And finds a despondent Bijan, his torso bare,
His two hands tightly bound behind his back,
His mouth dry, and his face devoid of color.
He asks him, "How is it that I encounter you here?
Have you come from Iran in search of bloodshed?"

Bijan recounts his adventure and how his ill-intended
Cohort turned against him to betray him.

Piran, son of Viseh, feels compassion for Bijan,
And his eyes' tears flood his cheeks.
He gives the order to suspend the execution
And says to Bijan, "Wait until I see the king's face
And guide him down the road to righteousness."

He bestrides his horse, swiftly taking the direction of court.
He humbly enters the palace, like a slave, and appears
Before Afraasiyaab, arms crossed at his chest.
He invokes divine grace before the royal seat,
As suits a virtuous man of good counsel.

At the sight of the noble Piran standing expectedly,
The world ruler smiles and says, "What is your wish?
There is no one in the world I respect more than you.
If you wish gold and jewels, if you wish to rule
Or to lead troops, I shall not be stingy with you.
I shall offer you my treasure,
For I cannot bear to see you in a state of affliction."

At these words, Piran, loyal subject,
Kisses the ground, rises, and says,
"May you always maintain sovereignty!
May joy select your glorious throne as dwelling!
All the rulers of the earth sing your praises,
And the shining sun pays homage to you.
By your grace, I own vast treasure and horses,
Warriors and the power of my arm.
None of your subjects is reduced to begging.
I have no other desire; it suffices for me to see you rule.
Eminent men are my support.
My work is my most valued treasure, glory is my essence.
My only concern comes from another man suffering
While I live in peace and splendor.
Long ago, I often gave the king valued advice,
But since he never heard me out,
I chose to abstain from providing further counsel.

"I begged you not to kill the son of Kaavoos,
But you effectuated the deed and further incited
Enmity between us and Rostam and Tous.
Siaavosh, of Kianian lineage, stood at your side,
Cinched to serve you with affection and amity.
I predicted that the Iranians would trample
Our troops beneath their elephants' feet,
That they would break the bonds that tied us.
But still, you foolishly sent Siaavosh to his death.
By doing so, you mixed honey with poison.

Have you forgotten Giv
And the brave Rostam, leader of warrior heroes?
Have you not witnessed the damage and devastation
The Iranians have brought upon Tooranian cities?
Their chargers' hooves squashed two-thirds of the land.
With our fortunes eclipsed, the tip of Rostam's sword
Has not since found its way back to its casing.
He will surely seize it once again to make
Countless heads fall and roll on the ground,
Blood gushing and flowing all the way to the sun.

"Why should we, in peacetime, revive the urge for battle?
Why perceive, in your foolishness, the lethal rose?
If you spill the blood of Bijan, the dust of destruction
Will rise above the land of Tooran.
You are a sensible king; I am merely your subject.
Open your wisdom's eyes and assess carefully.
Think of how much you have suffered
From the vengeance of the Iranian Shah,
Whom you provoked in the first place.
Do you now seek retribution, wishing
To bring new fruit to the tree of misfortune?
O famous world master, we cannot survive a second war.
No one is better acquainted than you with Giv
And the brave Rostam, a formidable whale,
Not to mention Goodarz of Kashvaad, with his hand
Of steel, who will come to avenge his grandson."

Piran attempts to toss water on the ardent blaze.
But Afraasiyaab replies, "Do you not see
What deeds Bijan dared carry out against my being
And how he covered me in utter shame
Before the lands of Iran and Tooran?
Do you not see how my daughter
Has dishonored my head?
Bijan has spread among the crowd
The names of all the veiled women of the palace
So that troops and subjects will continue
To laugh at my expense as they pass my gates.
If I spare his life, a loud clamor will rise against me.
I shall remain forever under the light of shame,
And my eyes will grow weary from shedding tears."

623

Piran showers him with blessings:
"O King of fortunate star and genuine speech,
What you say is the truth,
And you only wish to safeguard your honor.
However, I beg my thoughtful and wise master
To carefully ponder my prudent counsel,
Which is to burden Bijan with chains so heavy
That he would prefer to die at the gallows.
Then he will serve as example to the Iranians,
And they will no longer dare to strap themselves
And invade our realm to do us harm.
Whoever remains captive in your prison,
His name is never uttered again
Until it is written in the book of the dead.

The king decides to follow Piran's advice,
For he deems his words true and sincere.
A virtuous counselor of sound guidance
Brightens royal throne and majesty.

10 | Afraasiyaab Sends Bijan to Prison

Afraasiyaab gives the order to Garsivaz:
"Prepare heavy chains and a dark dungeon.
Bind the hands of Bijan with iron bands.
Restrict him from head to toe with a Rumi chain,
As strong as the cable of a bridge,
And fasten the chains with large nails.
Then toss him into the pit, head first,
So that he never again sees the light of sun and moon.
Go with elephants and find the stone of Akvan Deev,
The one extracted from the Creator's deep sea, the one
Which Akvan, long ago, flung into the forest of Chin.
Use this stone to serve my vengeance against Bijan.
Have the elephants carry this stone to Arjang's ditch
And place it at the opening to seal the entrance.
You will keep him confined until reason parts with him.
Then you will take a number of riders and enter
The dwelling of Manijeh, who dishonors my family.
Destroy everything, dispossess this miserable,
Errant being of honor and diadem, and say to her,

'O wretched one, you are unworthy of majesty.
You have reduced your family to the dust.
You have humiliated me before world rulers.'
Drag her uncovered to the dungeon and say to her,
'Look at the man who once sat in a palace.
Now you find him deep in a narrow pit.
You were once his spring.
Now be his sympathizer and servant.'"

Garsivaz departs, ready to execute the king's orders.
Bijan, son of Giv, is dragged to the dungeon.
Garsivaz commands that he be shackled with iron chains
From head to toe and his body wrapped with Rumi links
To be affixed with nails by blacksmiths' hammers of steel.
Lastly, he is to be thrust head first into the pit,
Its opening to be blocked and secured by Akvan's stone.

From there, Garsivaz leads his troops to the royal
Daughter's palace, where he submits her jewels
And treasure to plunder, plucks out from one
A bag full of gold and gives to the other a crown.
He hands a veil to Manijeh
And makes her walk barefoot, head uncovered.
Thus, he drags her to the pit's entrance,
Heart full of pain, cheeks flooding with tears.

Garsivaz says to her, "Here is your dwelling
To which you will be forever bound as a servant."

Manijeh remains there, troubled and afflicted.
Drops of her heart's blood streak her cheeks.
She wanders in the plain, around the well,
Lamenting, and thus passes one day and one night.
She approaches the well, shouting and crying,
And finds an opening large enough for her hand.

From this day on, as soon as the sun
Reveals its face above the mountain, Manijeh begs
For bread, and after a long day collecting food,
She passes it into the opening to share with Bijan.
In this sort of misery, she continues to live,
Pining and bemoaning day and night,
And ceaselessly guarding the pit.

11 | Gorgeen Returns to Iran and Lies About Bijan

Gorgeen remains on the road for seven days.
Seeing that Bijan does not reemerge,
He looks for him left and right,
His cheeks flooding with blood tears.
He now repents of his actions and the setbacks
He poured upon his companion's head.

He travels quickly to the field of banquets
And searches the grounds for his friend,
Traversing the forest from end to end,
Finding no one there.
The place is silent and deserted,
Absent of any sound, even birdsong.

He roams the meadow back and forth.
Then, all at once, he spots from afar
Bijan's horse returning from the river's edge,
Its bridle torn to pieces, its saddle dragging,
Its lip hanging low, its demeanor forlorn.

At this moment, Gorgeen realizes that Bijan is lost
And that he will not be returning to the land of Iran.
He suspects something bad has happened to him
At the hand of Afraasiyaab:
Either he has been hung at the gallows
Or is held captive somewhere in a dungeon.

Gorgeen lets his noose drop and looks away,
Deeply remorseful and longing
To cast his eyes on his friend once again.
He grasps the bridle of Bijan's charger
And leads him away from the verdant meadow
To his tent, where he remains for one day.

Then he takes the direction of the land of Iran,
All the while reproaching himself for what he has done.
But since he cannot predict the future,
He renounces food and sleep, day and night.
He repeats to himself, "What shall I say when I arrive?
How will I dare look the king in the eye?"

Upon learning of Gorgeen's solo approach,
Kay Khosrow refrains from telling Giv that Bijan is missing,
Hoping to have the chance to first interrogate Gorgeen.

But Giv soon finds out
About the disappearance of his brave son.
He exits the palace and rushes to the road,
Heart wounded, face flooding with tears.
He says, "Will Bijan not return?
I do not know why he remains in Arman-Zamin."

Giv orders his horse be prepared
And decked with a saddle of poplar wood.
Heart full of rage, he bestrides the mount
With which he often charges to the rescue of men.
Swift as wind, he gallops to meet Gorgeen
On the road, to enquire about Bijan,
His whereabouts, and what occurred.
He says to his heart,
"I fear that Gorgeen has committed a crime,
Unexpectedly and secretly, and if I see him arrive
Without my son Bijan, I shall cut off his head!"

As Gorgeen sees Giv galloping toward him,
He dismounts and runs to him.
He rolls in the dust, bare-headed,
And tears at his cheeks with his nails.
Then he asks Giv, "O brave army leader,
O guardian of throne, what are you doing?
Why do you show yourself, eyes full of blood?
My poor heart was afflicted,
But now it is far more wretched.
My eyes are too ashamed to glance your way,
And my face is flooding with burning tears.
But do not be worried, for he remains alive,
And I shall show you the signs."

At the sight of his son's horse being led by Gorgeen,
The animal full of dust and stumbling as if drunk,
At the sound of Gorgeen's words,
Giv falls unconscious off his steed.
He thrusts his head onto the ground,

Tears apart his warrior clothes, pulls out
His hair and beard, and scatters dust on his head.
All the while, he cries, "O Creator of sky,
You have placed in my heart sense and tenderness.
Since my son has been seized from me,
I wish that you break the bonds that tie me to life
And that you take my soul into its blessed sojourn,
For you know the pain of my heart.
I had in all the world only one son
Who was for me a sympathizer and a support.
Now misfortune has taken him away, and I find
Myself caught inside the dragon's ferocious jaws."

Then he turns once again to Gorgeen and asks,
"What happened since your departure?
Has fate taken him all at once,
Or did you lose sight of him?
Tell me what hardships befell him
And who burdened him with the chains
Handed to him by the dome of sky.
Tell me which deev he has fallen prey to,
Who has put an end to his life, O brave man.
How did you find his horse, and when
And how did you get separated from Bijan?"

Gorgeen replies, "Take charge of your senses.
Listen to my words. Open your ears.
O illustrious hero, know what happened
And how we battled the boars in the forest.
May you forever render bright the king's throne!
We left this place in order to fight the boars.
Once in Arman-Zamin, we spotted a forest,
Bare like the desert. Trees had been chopped down,
And the woods had been razed and converted
Into a field where one could only see a boar's den.
The entire spread of land was desolate.
We raised our spears for battle;
We cried out in the forest.
The boars arrived, large as mountains,
Not one after the other but from all sides.
They charged at us in massive herds.
We fought like lions, and the light of day dimmed,

PART FOURTEEN

Yet we did not grow tired of battle.

"We overturned them as if we were elephants.
We plucked out their tusks with our nails.
Joyfully, we then entertained ourselves with the hunt,
And we took, once again, the road to Iran-Zamin.
But then a deer arrived near us on the field,
More beautiful than in a painting.
His fur resembled the robe of Golgoon,[63]
Goodarz's steed, its head the color
Of Shabaahang, Farhaad's white horse.
Its wings were as swift as the wings of Simorgh,
Its feet shaped in hooves like Poolaad Deev's hooves.
Its head and tail looked much
Like those of Bijan's horse Shabrang.
Its neck was like a lion's neck,
Its sprint as quick as wind. You would think
He was born from the lineage of Rakhsh.

"He approached Bijan like a powerful elephant.
Bijan flung over his head his undulating noose.
At the same time, the deer took off galloping,
And Bijan lunged to chase after him.
The race of the deer and the dust from Bijan's horse
Spread a mist over air and field.
The earth raged like the sea.
The hero who flung the noose, along with his prey,
Both disappeared before my eyes.
I followed them through mountain and field,
Until my horse grew weary of the race.
But I found no trace of Bijan except
For his staggering horse, its saddle trailing behind.
My heart was on fire from such intense worry.
What happened in the battle between Bijan and the deer?
For a long time, I searched the field for Bijan.
In the end I left, despairing and convinced
That the wild deer was indeed the White Deev."

After hearing this artificial discourse,
Giv feels all is lost.

◇◇◇◇◇◇◇◇◇◇◇◇◇◇
63 Golgoon: Meaning of reddish color; the name of Goodarz's horse.

He sees a discomfited Gorgeen, his eyes clouded,
His cheek pale from fear of the king,
His body shaking, and his heart guilty.

Coming to terms with the fact
That his son has disappeared,
Giv understands that Gorgeen is lying
To cover his guilt and that he allowed
Ahriman to conquer his heart.
He feels the urge to kill him on the road,
To avenge the death of his beloved son,
Though he would dishonor himself by doing so.

He continues to ponder, unable to shed light on the matter.
He thinks, "How will this murder serve me
But to give in to the wishes of Ahriman?
What use would the death of Gorgeen be to Bijan?
I must find another solution, a remedy for my despair.
It would be easy for me to punish the one culpable,
For there is no wall before my spear.
But it is better to request an audience with the shah
And allow Gorgeen's words to be proof of his crimes."

Then he says to Gorgeen with a voice of thunder,
"O vile, evil man, sullied by your transgressions,
You have taken from me my love and my moon,
My son, my selected horseman, and my king!
You have flung me into the depths of anguish.
You force me to turn the earth over,
To find a remedy to my endless misery.
I shall find neither rest nor sleep nor patience
In the midst of your deeds, lies, and deceit.
I shall not allow you to enjoy any hints of freedom
Until I am in the presence of the king.
Then I shall seek retribution with my sharp dagger
And avenge the loss of my beloved son,
For you stole from me the light of my eyes."

12 | Giv Takes Gorgeen to Kay Khosrow

Giv takes the direction of the king's palace,
Eyes full of blood tears, heart full of vengeance.
He greets Khosrow and says, "O fortunate King,
O world master, may you live eternally!
Your star showers you with good fortune.
Do you know what calamity has befallen me?
I had in all the world only one son, a young man
For whose life I trembled, day and night,
Consumed by the fear of losing him.
I shook at the thought of parting from him.
Now, O King, Gorgeen has returned,
His mouth full of absurd tales, his soul full of sin.
He brings bad news of my glorious young prince.
He returns with a horse, its saddle dragging behind,
And that is all he brings back from my dear son, Bijan.
If the king wishes to arrive at the truth of this matter,
Let him look into it with his deep gaze,
And may he avenge me on Gorgeen,
Who has filled my life with bitterness."

Giv's sorrow deeply aggrieves the king.
He places the crown of justice on his head
And remains on the throne, cheeks pale,
Heart tight with worry for the fate of Bijan.
He asks Giv, "What has Gorgeen told you?
Where did he part ways with his virtuous companion?"

Giv repeats to Kay Khosrow Gorgeen's account
And the fate of his noble son.

Khosrow replies, "Do not despair.
Rest assured that Bijan is alive.
Be hopeful that he is only lost somewhere.
I have agreed with illustrious sages of vigilant mind
That I shall depart without delay, with riders
From Iran, to deliver battle to the Tooranians.
I lead my army to avenge the death of Siaavosh.
I shall destroy the land of Tooran with my elephants.
Bijan will be freed to fight with us like an Ahriman.
Go, and do not trouble yourself about this affair.

I wish, as much as you, to see Bijan once again."

Giv takes leave of the king, heart full of worry,
Cheeks pale, eyes brimful of tears.

Once in the presence of the king,
Gorgeen finds the royal court empty of warriors.
Concerned over Bijan's fate, they decided
To remain close to Giv, to comfort him.

Gorgeen crosses the palace threshold
And advances toward the king,
His ill-willed heart filled with shame.
He kisses the ground at the feet of Kay Khosrow,
Invokes the grace of Yazdan on the king,
And places before the throne the boars' tusks,
Sharp as diamonds. He greets the king befittingly:
"May Khosrow be victorious in every battle!
May every day be for him a new Nowruz!
May he continue to live in joy, free of concern!
May his enemies' heads fall beneath the shears of death
And be severed like the heads of the boars!"

The king observes the tusks, then asks,
"How was your journey?
Where did Bijan part ways with you,
And what evil deed did Ahriman inflict on him?"

Gorgeen is rattled and discomfited.
His tongue tied by nonsense,
His heart guilt-ridden for his crimes,
His cheeks pale, his body shaking from fear,
He speaks vaguely of forest, field, and deer.
Since his words are contradictory and illogical,
The king becomes irate and dismisses him abruptly.

Kay Khosrow realizes that this man is deceptive
And witless but refrains from cursing him:
"Have you not heard, from the mouth of Rostam,
This saying, that if a lion seeks retribution
With the family of Goodarz,
He will unquestionably perish?
If I wished for you to obtain a bad name,

If Yazdan reserves for you a miserable end,
Then I would ask the executioner
To cut off your head as one chops off a bird's head."

Khosrow commands a blacksmith
To prepare a heavy chain and large nails
And, at the very moment, to enchain Gorgeen,
Iron to feet, so that this evil man learns how to think.

Then he says to Giv, "Regain your peace of mind.
Make every attempt to search for your son.
I will send troops, hardened riders, from every
Province in the hopes of tracking Bijan's trail.
I shall make every effort and exert great care in this task.
Even if news from him reaches us late,
Do not allow your heart and mind to despair.
Wait until spring, when the sun,
Object of our devotion, will regain its luster;
When gardens will shine bright with their array of flowers;
When the wind will send
A shower of roses upon your heads;
When the earth will reclaim its fresh, green veil;
And the gentle breeze will sigh
Above the blushing rosebush.
I shall address Ormazd[64] with my pious request,
And the prayer will lighten my heart.
I shall ask for a chalice representing the world.
I shall present myself before the divine, stand up,
And look into the chalice to discover the seven lands.
I shall scrutinize every nation of every zone of earth.
I shall invoke Yazdan's grace on the souls
Of our ancestors, the elected, the powerful, the saints.
Then I shall reveal to you Bijan's position,
For the chalice will clearly reveal his location."

Giv rejoices as these words quell his concern for his son.
He smiles and praises the king: "May space and time
Never be deprived of your presence!
May the glorious firmament be at your command!
May the eye of ill-intentioned men never reach your being!

◇◇◇◇◇◇◇◇◇◇◇◇◇
64 Ormazd: Another name for the Creator.

May the Creator of righteousness praise you,
For you are blessed with the glory of crown and seal!"

As soon as Giv takes leave of the king,
He expedites able riders to search for Bijan.
They cross every land from Tooran to Iran
But do not find a single trace of the son of Giv.

13 | Kay Khosrow Sees Bijan in the World-Reflecting Chalice

Once the joyous feast of Nowruz arrives,
Giv senses the need to consult the chalice of fortune.
The aged hero, his back bent by worry for his son,
Strides to the palace, his heart hopeful.

When Khosrow sees the pale cheeks of Giv,
When he observes how pain devours his heart,
He rushes to dress in his Rumi tunic
And leaves to present himself before the World Creator.
He raises his voice, invokes grace upon the bright sun,
Asks for help from Yazdan, the Savior,
And the execution of justice on Ahriman, the wicked.

Then he returns to his palace,
Lowers the blessed crown onto his head,
Takes the chalice in his hand, and gazes into it.
He sees, reflected within the seven lands, the actions
And plans, great and small, of the sublime sky.
He sees a picture of the world,
From Pisces to the sign of the Ram.
He sees Saturn and Mars, Jupiter and the Lion,
Venus and Mercury, and, above it all, the Moon.
In this way, the world master, with the help of mystic arts,
Discerns in the chalice the entire future
And all that has been manifested and created.

He looks into the seven lands for a sign of Bijan.
He arrives near the land of Gorgsaran.
At Yazdan's command, he sees Bijan in the well,
Restrained by heavy chains,

Desiring death to escape the hardships of his fate.
Next to the dungeon, he sees a young woman,
A woman of royal race yet braced like a servant.

The shah turns to Giv with a smile
That illumines court and palace and says,
"Rejoice, for Bijan is alive.
Banish from your heart all hints of worry.
Do not be afflicted by the fact that he is in prison,
For his life has been spared.
Bijan is tied up in Tooran-Zamin, where a young
Woman of illustrious birth serves him well.
The solicitude that I felt for him filled me with sadness.
Fate has treated him so cruelly
That his servant ceaselessly sheds tears.
He despairs of ever catching sight
Of his family and allies again.
He is consumed by grief, shakes like a willow branch.
His two eyes are filled with blood, his heart full of pain,
And his tongue invokes the names of his kin.
He sheds bitter tears that tumble down like a spring cloud.
In his dark, confined prison, he longs for eternal rest.

Khosrow lifts his eyes to face Giv and wonders,
"Now who will strive to undo this misfortune?
Who will rise, ready for action, ready to plunge himself
Into the dragon's jaws to free Bijan of his misery?
Only Rostam, quick of hand, can accomplish the deed,
Rostam, who wrestles dragons in the deepest seas.
Strap your belt. Leave for Nimrooz.
Travel by day and night. Take my missive to Rostam,
And keep from speaking of this matter to anyone.
I shall summon the mighty hero
And recount to him what has occurred.
Let us quickly end Giv's anguish."

14 | Khosrow's Letter to Rostam

The king calls a scribe, tells him what has happened,
And orders him to write a letter to Rostam, the virtuous:
"O brave warrior of heroic race,

You lift your head above all warriors in the universe.
You are for us a memory of your ancestors.
Always cinched for battle, you are the heart of the king,
The support of Kianians, at the ready to lend a hand.
Your power rivals that of a leopard.
The whale in the sea cries in fear at the sight of you.
You washed the world from the presence of deevs
In Mazandaran and severed the heads of evil men.
So many times have you seized crowned heads
And plucked them off thrones and seats of honor.
So many adversaries have perished at your hands.
So many lands have been devastated by you!

"O leader of heroes, O refuge of magicians,
You have shattered the heads of witches
And sorcerers with the end of your mace.
With your power, you returned its luster to the crown.
Next to you, who is Afraasiyaab?
Who is the Emperor of Chin?
They all wear your name engraved on their seals.
No man has the power to untie your bonds.
You alone can effortlessly free captive men.
You are the sky of happiness for the Kianians,
But if Yzad bestowed you with the strength
Of an elephant and the heart of a lion,
With wisdom and a noble birth, it is so that
You take by the hand the one who cries for help
And drag him out of a dark abyss.
Only in your competence can we rely,
For only you can accomplish the impossible.

"An incident has ensued worthy of your intervention,
An incident beyond understanding and conception.
Never has the family of Goodarz suffered such grave injury
At the hands of the Tooranians of deev countenance.
Only in you do Goodarz and Giv hold any hope,
For you are today the champion of all the lands.
You know their standing in my court and how,
In frankness, courage, and wisdom, they have no equal.
If you wish to agree to this arduous mission,
Ask of me all that you want in men and in treasure.
Never have I seen this family, the most glorious one,

So afflicted with misfortune.

"Giv has only this sole child, both his son and his support.
Giv is a man I hold in high esteem.
He is my friend and my grandfather's friend,
Always by my side in times of need,
Whether in good or ill fortune.
You are well aware of the high deeds
Performed by members of the Goodarzian family,
Both in times of peace and in times of war,
How its members contributed to our triumphs
And the personal afflictions they endured
As a result of our losses in battle and war.
Once you have read this letter, do not delay.
Immediately rise and journey to me escorted by Giv.
Come so that we can hold counsel and, in caution,
Discuss matters relating to Bijan and to finding a solution.
I shall hold men, treasure, and all that your heart desires
At the ready to present to you.
I promise, by your glorious footsteps and by your fame,
That you will be victorious in the land of Tooran.
Make swift preparations for your departure so that
We can save Bijan and return to him his freedom."

15 | Giv Carries Khosrow's Letter to Rostam

Khosrow seals the letter and hands it over to Giv,
Who praises the king, prepares for the journey,
And mounts his horse of speed,
Taking with him horsemen from his family.
He calls the name of Yazdan, asks for divine support,
And advances into the desert on the road of Hirmand.[65]

He travels as a messenger, charging like a wild beast,
Capturing the distance of two days in one.
He rushes forth, a man with a wounded heart
Who devours road, mountain, and plain.

From high in his tower, the sentinel spots Giv.

◇◇◇◇◇◇◇◇◇◇◇◇◇
65 Hirmand: On the border of Iran and Afghanistan.

His voice echoes toward Zabolestan:
"From Hirmand advances a cavalier with an escort.
He brandishes a shiny banner and a Kaboli sword."

Zaal, son of Saam, hears the guard's call
And orders his horse to be harnessed.
He charges his mount toward the stranger
To assess whether he is friend or foe.

Once he spots Giv, pale of countenance,
He rushes to him, surprised, and says to his heart,
"Something serious must have happened,
For Giv is the one who is sent my way."

The brave hero and his procession approach Zaal
And stand in front of him in greeting.
Zaal asks the Iranians for news of king and noblemen.

Giv greets him in the manner of a highborn leader,
In the name of the shah and heroes of noble birth.
Then he confides in him his heart's worry
And the anguish he feels for the loss of his son.
He adds, "It is for this reason that I look so worn
And that the top of my feet are spotted,
Like leopard's fur, with blood."

Zaal's face pales, his heart pained as he wails.

Giv asks, "Where is world warrior Rostam?"

Zaal replies, "He is busy hunting deer,
But he will return by sundown."

Giv says, "I shall find him
So that I may hand him Khosrow's letter."

Zaal says, "Do not go too far,
For the hero will soon return from the hunt.
Remain at my side, pass the time with me,
So that I may celebrate your presence."

Together they ride to Zaal's palace, conferring.
At the moment they reach the gate, Rostam returns.

Giv gallops up to him on the road
And dismounts to properly greet him,
Heart full of emotion, face discolored,
Cheeks flooding with torrents of tears.

At the sight of Giv's wounded heart
And drenched face, Rostam assumes
That some calamity has fallen on Iran.
He jumps off his horse, embraces Giv,
And asks him for news of Khosrow, master of crown,
As well as news of Goodarz, Tous, Gostaham,
And warriors, great and small, such as Shahpoor,
Farhaad, Bijan, Rohaam, Gorgeen, and others.

Once Bijan's name strikes Giv's ear,
He cries out in pain and praises Rostam:
"O glorious hero, elected from among
The earth's most able leaders,
I am so happy to lay eyes on you
And to receive your warm greeting.
Your words have the power to bring life
To the lifeless and convert old age into youth.
Those you have mentioned in name are well.
They greet you and are your friends, O noble hero,
Except for Bijan, whose fate has led him
To be enchained at the bottom of a deep, dark well.
You cannot imagine the depth
Of the misfortune my aging head must bear.

"I had in all the world only one child
Who was for me not only a son but a wise advisor.
He disappeared right before my eyes.
The family of Goodarz never suffered such setbacks.
Since then, I am like the shining sun,
Never stopping on its journey.
I am seated on my charger, galloping day and night.
Day and night I spend searching like a foolish man,
Traveling the world on the hunt for Bijan.
In the end, the day of the Kianian feast,

Ormazd day during the month of Farvardin,[66]
The king presented himself before the Creator,
Holding in his hand the world-reflecting chalice.

"He cried in pain, he pronounced prayers,
Then he returned from the fire temple to his palace,
Dressed in royal robes, climbed on his throne,
Placed before him the shining chalice, and looked
For a long time at the image mirrored within.
Finally, he announced to me
Bijan's presence in the land of Tooran, burdened
With heavy chains and condemned to adversity.
Upon this revelation, Kay Khosrow urged me
To leave in haste to find you, O world hero.
Here I am, heart full of hope, cheeks pale, eyes dull.
I have witnessed you emerge as the savior many times.
I have witnessed you cinch yourself to help those in need."

He speaks thus, eyes brimming with tears,
Sighing deeply. He hands the letter to Rostam
And recounts to him Gorgeen's awful deeds.

His heart full of hatred for Afraasiyaab,
Rostam cries out in pain for the fate of Bijan.
Blood tears drip onto his chest.
He has been, for a long time, ally to the family of Goodarz.
Giv's wife is the proud daughter of Rostam.
He himself married one of Giv's sisters and has,
From this noble wife, a son, the valiant Faraamarz.
Furthermore, Bijan, hero of noble birth,
Is the son of Rostam's daughter.

The hero says to Giv, "Do not worry, for Rostam will not
Unsaddle Rakhsh before having seized Bijan's hand,
Broken all his bonds, and destroyed his prison.
With the strength given to me by Yazdan and
In obedience to my king, I shall draw him out
Of his deep, dark well and out of his detention!"

◇◇◇◇◇◇◇◇◇◇◇◇◇
66 Farvardin: First month of the solar calendar and the first day of spring. Ormazd day is the first day of any month.

16 | Rostam Prepares a Feast for Giv

From there they make their way to Rostam's castle,
All the while deliberating on their future departure.

After reading the king's letter, Rostam finds himself
Bewildered on matters relating to Khosrow's request.
He calls divine grace on the king,
World master and glorious warrior.
Then he says to Giv, "I know how to proceed.
I shall liberate Bijan, as the king commands.
I know all you have suffered and all you have done.
I have always regarded you with utmost respect,
For you have been present, eager to fight, on all battlefields.
Whether in the war to avenge Siaavosh or in Mazandaran,
You emerged at the head of warriors, cinched and armed.
Now you have endured the fatigues of the long voyage.
You have covered difficult terrain.
I am happy to see you but sad for the fate of Bijan.
I did not like to see you so wretched, so despairing of life.
I shall be on my way as ordered by my king,
My heart overcome with pain for you.
I seize weapons to rescue Bijan, make every attempt
To save him, even at the risk of my soul being
Snatched out of my body by Yazdan, the pure.

"For Bijan's sake, I shall give it all up: flesh, treasure, army.
I shall strap my belt with blessed divine grace,
Pluck him out of the deep, dark well,
Hand him over to the victorious king,
And place him at the side of the royal throne.
Stay in my house for three days.
Let us engage in feast.
Let us drink and free our hearts of worry.
Do not dwell in sadness, for our homes are the same
As are our treasures, our bodies, and our hearts.
We shall sit in this residence for three days in joy,
Talk of the king, our relation to him, and our heroes.
On the fourth day, we shall depart for Iran
And for the court of the King of Kings."

After Rostam's words, Giv rises abruptly,

Kisses his hands, head, and feet, and praises him:
"O noble man, may you continue to enjoy
The strength given to you by Yazdan!
O illustrious hero, may you shine
With power, good fortune and indomitable skill.
You exhibit the grandeur and the courage
Of an elephant and the insight of a wise man.
You are blessed with all sorts of joys, since
You have wiped off the rust that veiled my heart!"

The sight of Giv somewhat appeased
Nurtures a sense of hope in Rostam's heart.
He summons his chamberlain and tells him,
"Come and spread the banquet; invite the noblemen."

Zavaareh, Faraamarz, Zaal, and Giv take their seats.
After eating their fill, a splendid festival is prepared
In the bejeweled palace, with music and musicians.
Every face shines like rubies from the ruby-colored wine.

For three days, Rostam lingers at his court,
Drinking wine, with no intention of speeding away.

17 | Rostam Travels to the Court of Kay Khosrow

On the fourth day, they rise to take their leave,
For the time has arrived.
Rostam orders loads be placed and preparations
Be made for their journey to the land of Iran.
His kingdom's highborn riders convene at his gate,
Armed and ready.
Dressed in a Rumi tunic, Rostam emerges,
Sitting high on Rakhsh, his belt strapped.
With his grandfather's mace on the saddle hook,
His heart is full of ardor for battle, his head full of strategy.

Rakhsh's ears seem to touch the sky,
And the hero, distributor of crowns,
Rises higher than the sun.
Weapons and supplies are loaded.
Rostam bids farewell to his son, Faraamarz,

Who remains in Zabol, and marches off toward Iran
With Giv and a hundred riders, armed for war,
Impatient to exact justice, hearts full of vengeance.

Approaching the throne of Kay Khosrow,
A soft breeze gaily touches the hero
With affectionate greetings from the firmament.

Giv addresses Rostam and says,
"I shall speed ahead of you, O valiant leader,
To announce that the incomparable Rakhsh
Is transporting the mighty Rostam
To his royal highness."

Rostam replies, "Go in joy, talk to the king,
And banish all signs of worry."

Giv takes leave of the hero to make his way to court.
Once there, he honors him accordingly by bowing low
Before the one whose heart is pure, whose voice is holy.

Khosrow greets Giv happily and asks,
"Where is Rostam? How did you fare in your travels?"

Giv replies, "O noble King, by your good fortune,
Rostam is bound to your command so steadfastly
That he will never deviate from it.
Once I handed him the king's letter,
He rubbed it on his eyes and forehead.
He tied Rakhsh's reins to those of my horse,
As is the duty of a servant of Kay Khosrow.
I marched ahead of him to relay news of his approach."

The king asks Giv, "Where is Rostam's position?
He is the support of power, the example of loyalty.
It is my duty to honor him, for he is a man
Whose virtue shines as his devotion to the king binds."

Giv replies, "O King, you are worthy of supremacy.
I came ahead of him to announce his arrival."

Khosrow commands his advisors,
His family's princes and noblemen to form

A procession and to meet Rostam on the road.
They summon Goodarz, son of Kashvaad;
Tous, leader of Nozar's family; and Farhaad;
Two-thirds of the horsemen and highborn leaders;
Mace-bearing warriors and enemy-destroyers.

They instantly rise, as dictate the royal rituals,
And form a convoy to advance toward the hero.

The world turns purple from the dust of riders.
Chargers whinny; banners sparkle.
At the sight of Rostam, they dismount to greet him.
The world hero dismounts as well
And inquires after their hardships.
He addresses each questions on the matter of the king
And the fate given to them by the spin of Sun and Moon.

Rostam and the leaders climb back on their steeds,
Each like the brilliant flame of Aazargoshasp,
And gallop to the king's palace
With Rostam marching at the lead.
Once in proximity of the subject-loving ruler,
Rostam rushes to him and pays him revered tribute,
For Khosrow is worthy of blessings and love.

Then the hero raises his head and says,
"May you always find yourself on the throne!
May Ormazd keep you in your dignity
And Bahman be your crown's guardian.
May the three divine values,
Ordibehesht, Bahraam, and Teer, be your protectors.
May Shahrivar give you victory,
A noble name, splendor, and valor.
May Esfand protect you from harm.
May Wisdom be your mind's clear dwelling.
May Deh and Farvardin spread favors upon you
By closing all the doors of evil before you.
May Aazar make your days and nights shine,
And may you always live in joy,
Your crown illuminating the world.
May Aaban help you succeed in all things,
And may the sky turn to your will.

PART FOURTEEN

May Mordaad guard your herds,
And may your body and destiny always flourish.
I wish for your lineage to be eternally glorious.
May Khordaad cause your land to prosper
And your fortunes to grow."[67]

After having lavished the king with blessings,
Rostam is assigned a seat of privilege
Next to Kay Khosrow, who says to him,
"You are welcome, O warrior hero!
May danger be deterred from reaching you!
You are the champion of world kings.
What others hide is no mystery to you,
While what you expose is a mystery to them.
You are the elect of the Kianian race.
You are the army's support.
You are the guardian of Iran-Zamin,
The shelter of brave men.
I am pleased to see you so valiant, so vigilant.
What news have you of Zavaareh, Faraamarz, and Zaal?
Are they well and in good health?"

Rostam bends low to the ground, kisses the throne,

◇◇◇◇◇◇◇◇◇◇◇◇◇
67 The Persian calendar:
Based on the solar calendar, the months are named after twelve divinities and
correspond to nature's cycles and the signs of the zodiac:
Spring:
Farvardin – Aries; the first month of the year begins with the first day of spring and
with the spring equinox.
Ordibehesht – Taurus; spans the months of April and May.
Khordaad – Gemini; third month of the year.
Summer:
Teer – Cancer; Mercury; the fourth month begins with the summer solstice.
Mordaad – Leo; fifth month of the year.
Shahrivar – Virgo; sixth month of the solar year.
Fall:
Mehr – Libra; the seventh month begins with the fall equinox.
Aaban – Scorpio; eighth month of the year.
Aazar – Sagittarius; ninth month of the year, ends with the winter solstice or Yalda.
Winter:
Deh – Capricorn; tenth month of the year.
Bahman – Aquarius; eleventh month of the solar year.
Esfand – Pisces; twelfth month of the year.

And says, "O renowned King to whom fortune
Assigns victory, by your grace,
The three warriors are happy and in good health.
Blessed are those whom the king deigns to remember!"

18 | Kay Khosrow Celebrates With the World Heroes

The master chamberlain opens the doors to the king's
Gardens, where he is to spread a lavish royal feast.
The throne and golden crown are placed
Beneath a tree towering over a rosebush.
Priceless carpets of brocade are stretched on the ground,
And the rose garden shimmers with color and light.

Next to the king's throne, they plant a tree
To shade the throne and golden crown.
Its trunk is silver; its branches are gold and ruby
Inlaid with clusters of various precious gems.
Its leaves are the color of emerald, and from every branch
Hang fruits bright as carnelian earrings,
Golden oranges and quinces hollowed
And filled with musk dissolved in wine,
Their entire surface pierced like reeds.
Whoever sits on this throne, by the order of the king,
Is perfumed by musk drifting to him in the wind.

The king arrives, sits on the golden throne.
Musk drips from the tree onto the heads of guests.
Wine stewards line up before him wearing diadems
Of precious stones and tunics of Chini and Rumi silk.
They stand before the king's throne, dressed
In gold-stitched robes and decked in torques and earrings,
Finery worthy of kings, their faces shining like silk.
Dim hearts fill with joy, hands hold cups,
Cheeks are flushed the color of ruby,
But no one is yet intoxicated.
They burn aloe before the king,
And musicians delicately pluck at their lutes.

The king orders the captain of the guards
To summon Goodarz, Tous, and all the warriors.

He invites Rostam to approach,
To sit beneath the tree where he address him,
"O noble friend, you are the shelter of my fortune.
Your presence is a shield around Iran-Zamin.
You spread your wings over us like the glorious Simorgh.
Many times have you endured the trials of war
In your battles for the sake and safety of our land,
Always with the goal of saving its kings from trouble.
You are familiar with the hardships
Endured by the family of Goodarz.
You have known them in peace and war,
In prosperity and misfortune.
They hold themselves before me,
Waists strapped and ready to serve.
They are my constant guides to all that is good and pure,
Especially Giv, who always intervenes in all matters,
Acting as a barrier between me and danger.
Never has this family suffered so much pain as today,
For who knows a heavier grievance than the loss of a son?

"If you do not cinch your waist to take charge,
I see no other hope in all the world to save Bijan.
The Tooranians are torturing him,
Leaving him overcome with pain.
Think and come up with a solution.
Take what you need in terms of horse and weapon,
Men and treasure, and do not refuse this service."

At these words, Rostam kisses the ground
And, rising quickly, blesses Kay Khosrow and says,
"O glorious King, so alike to the sun,
Your dominion has a wide reach.
May you keep distance from greed, fury, and need!
May your enemy's hearts be consumed
By the blaze of adversity!
You are the King of Kings, master and leader,
And the earth's princes are the dust beneath your feet!
Never have kings, dazzling sun, or revolving moon
Witnessed a throne shine brighter than yours.
You separate the worthy from the wicked.
You vanquished the dragon with magic spells.

"My mother bore me so that I might live in service to you.
Your right is to enjoy rest and happiness.
I have heard the king's command.
I shall follow the path dictated by your guidance.
I have plucked out the heart of the White Deev
In the land of Mazandaran with the help
Of Kianian grace and my valuable mace.
Now, were the sky to flood my head with fire,
I would not pay attention to it but march to rescue Bijan.
Were the tip of my spear to pierce through my eyes' lashes,
I would not retreat from executing the king's command.
I shall conclude this venture, trusting your good fortune,
And have need for neither leader nor warrior."

Rostam finishes his speech.
The noble army leaders, Goodarz, Giv, Fariborz,
Farhaad, and warrior Shahpoor,
Praise Rostam and the World Creator.
They raise their cups, thinking of Zaal.
The king drinks joyfully with them,
Heart blooming with joy like fresh spring.

19 | Rostam Asks the King to Pardon Gorgeen

Once aware of Rostam's arrival,
Gorgeen senses the imminent end of his sorrow.
He sends Rostam a message thus conceived:
"O renowned warrior of auspicious path,
Glorious tree of power, treasure of loyalty and royalty,
You are the door to the savior of righteous men,
For you bind the hand of ill will.
If you do not reject my words,
If you wish to allow me to extend my deeds,
Reflect on the destiny handed to me by the sky,
A misfortune that abruptly smothers my heart's light
And drives me down an obscure path.

"This is the way it has been written.
I am ready to set fire to myself before the king
If only he wishes to forgive my crimes.
I hope that he will revoke the poor opinion he has of me,

For it is a bitter end he reserves for me in my old age.
If you wish to ask the world king to show mercy,
I shall leave with you, bounding like a mountain goat.
I shall appear at Bijan's side, roll in the dust,
In the hopes of recovering my honor and innocence."

Rostam sighs deeply at Gorgeen's message.
His grief and laments genuinely trouble him,
And this reckless demand gives him a twinge of pain.
He says to the messenger, "Return and tell Gorgeen,
        'O foolish, impure man,
        Have you not heard the story of the leopard
        Who battled the whale in the deep sea?
        If pleasure closes the door to wisdom,
        No one escapes its claws. But if a man of sense
        Is able to quench his appetite for pleasure,
        His story will be the story of a valiant lion.
        You have been cunning as an old fox,
        But you have not perceived the hunter's trap.
        I do not wish to utter your name before Kay Khosrow,
        Like you ask of me so impudently,
        And yet I find you in such a state of despair,
        So despondent from this blow,
        That I see myself, in the end,
        Begging the king to have mercy on your life.
        I shall make shine once again
        The light of your eclipsed moon.
        If Bijan is able to free himself from his bonds,
        By the will of the just Creator of the universe,
        Then you too shall be liberated from your chains.
        Then you shall resume your free life,
        And the heroes' vengeance will cause you no harm.
        But if the sky reserves another fate for Bijan,
        You will be left feeling sorry, heart and body.
        I shall find Bijan and avenge him at the king's command
        And by the strength given to me by Yazdan's will.
        But if I do not take action, the skillful Giv will take
        Vengeance on you for the fate of his noble son.'"

Rostam waits one day and one night
Without uttering a word to the king.
On the second day, as the sun displays its crown

And sits on its ivory throne like a ring of silver,
Rostam appears before the victorious king,
Spreads out his arms like a supplicant, and speaks
Of Gorgeen, of his fate and his misadventures.

The king says, "O army leader, you wish to break
The bonds that unite us and reject my protection?
I have sworn by my throne and crown,
By Mars and Venus, by Sun and Moon,
That Gorgeen will witness trials from me
Unless Bijan is liberated from chains.
Ask me anything you want except for this one thing.
Ask for throne, sword, seal, or diadem."

Rostam says to the noble king,
"O illustrious, noble master, if he acted wrongly,
He pays for it dearly by sacrificing his life.
But if he does not obtain pardon from the king,
His heart will remain broken, his faith shaken.
Whoever drifts from the path of reason will end up
Trembling at the consequences of his crimes.
May it please you to remember his previous service,
His high deeds in battles and wars,
When he held weapons before your ancestors, when
He fought on every battlefield at the side of bold men.
If it pleases the king to pardon him for my sake,
May fortune shine on him once again!"

The victorious king agrees, surrenders Gorgeen to Rostam,
And frees him of the chains and of his somber dungeon.

20 | Rostam Organizes His Procession of Troops

The monarch then says to Rostam,
"How do you wish to proceed on this matter?
What are your needs in terms of troops and treasure?
Tell me whom you wish to take as your escort.
I fear this vile Afraasiyaab is eager to spill Bijan's blood,
For he is an arrogant being who travels with the wind,
An impure, malicious deev, educated
And coached in trickery and the arts of magic.

Ahriman will excite his heart in a moment
And push him to send our hero to a sudden death."

Rostam replies to the world king,
"I shall make preparations in secret.
The key to unlock this affair is deception,
And one must not act in haste to engage in war.
I shall pretend to be a merchant and disguise myself as such.
Now is not the time to use sword, spear, or mace.
One must instead rattle the reins to travel
To Tooran-Zamin with patience and strategy.
I shall need an abundance of jewels
And a great deal of gold and silver.
We must depart guided by a sense of hope
But spend the time there in a state of fear and caution.
We shall need carpets and rich, lush fabrics
To serve as exchange in the trade of goods and gifts."

Khosrow calls for cases of ancient treasures,
Containing within all variety of possessions.
The king's treasurer opens the crates
And piles up gold and precious stones in the hall.

Rostam selects what he needs for the venture.
He loads up ten camels with dinars,
One hundred more with fabrics and provisions.
Then he orders the palace master,
"Select one thousand men among the army's greats,
A number of renowned heroes strapped for war:
Leaders such as Gorgeen and Zangueh of Shaavaran;
Gostaham, conquering lion; Goraazeh, army commander,
Guardian of heroes and of throne and crown;
Rohaam and Farhaad, brave warriors; and the lion Ashkesh.
These are the seven heroes I shall need, along with weapons
And gear, to protect our escort and our treasure."

They complete their tasks to ready for departure,
Leaving behind any unnecessary supplies.

21 | Rostam Visits Piran in Khotan

Rostam says to his mace-bearing,
Enemy-destroying men, "Once the captain
Of guards appears at the palace doors
At dawn, you must reach for your weapons
And cinch your waists, dressed in full armor."

At the first call of the rooster and the first light of day,
They load up the elephants with supplies and timpani.

Rostam appears like a tall cypress tree, belt strapped,
Hand clutching his mace, noose hanging on the saddle.
He exits the king's palace with his host,
Uttering blessings on his land and nation.
The warrior heroes lead the way while troops
Trail behind, each one placing his life in the palm
Of his hand as if he had washed it in blood.
Spears and arrows guide the procession, pointing the way

Once near the Tooranian border,
Rostam addresses his army leaders:
"Remain here. Be patient and vigilant.
Do not budge from this place unless Yazdan,
The holy, deprives me of the breath of life.
Prepare yourselves for battle and bloodshed!"

He leaves the troops at the border while he takes
The road of Tooran with his most loyal men.
He dresses in full merchant garb and removes his belt.
The warriors unfasten their silver belts as well
And conceal their true nature beneath woolen robes.
In this manner, they enter Tooran-Zamin as a caravan,
Rich with abundance, and full of color and scent.

They take with them eight noble chargers,
Rakhsh counting as one of them.
The others are mounted by the disguised warriors.
They take many camels loaded with jewels,
One hundred more camels bearing war supplies.

The plain booms with the cry of men and the sound of bells,

Echoes resounding like the trumpets of Tahmures.
Rostam advances deeper into the plain,
Approaching the city of Khotan, where Piran rules.
Men and women run out to observe the caravan curiously.

The noble Piran, son of Viseh, is absent from town
And occupied in the hunt, his palace empty.

Rostam catches sight of him just as he makes his way back.
The hero wraps a veil around his head
And lifts a golden cup full of precious gems.
He takes two noble horses bearing
Golden saddles lavished with ornaments
And hands them over to Piran's servants,
At the head of which he places himself.

In this way, he enters the palace, praising Piran:
"O illustrious world hero, the tales of your fortune
And high deeds fill the lands of Tooran and Iran!
No one is as worthy as you of power and diadem.
You are the king's advisor and the pride of the throne."

By the grace of the Creator, Piran does not recognize him.
He asks, "Who are you? Where do you come from?
Why have you traveled here in such haste?"

Rostam replies, "I am merely your devoted slave.
The Creator guided me to your town to quench my thirst.
I have traveled long and hard on the road from Iran
To engage in commerce in Tooran-Zamin.
I sell and buy merchandise, trade all sort of goods,
Trafficking back and forth. The image of your splendor
Fills my heart with hope and affection.
If it pleases the hero to give me shelter beneath his wings,
I shall buy horses and sell my jewels.
Your justice will protect me from harm,
And the cloud of friendship will shower me with pearls."

Rostam places before Piran a cup of jewels
Worthy of a king and begs him to accept it
Along with noble stallions of Taazian breed
Of such refined hide that the dust,
Rising beneath, does not cling to their fur.

He hands over these gifts invoking Yazdan's grace
On the leader Piran, thus concluding the affair.

At the sight of the jewels held in the brilliant cup,
Piran calls divine blessings on Rostam,
Compliments him, receives him graciously,
And offers him a seat on a turquoise throne.
He says, "Go in peace, enter the city in full security.
I shall prepare a dwelling for you next to mine.
Do not concern yourself for the safety of your assets;
No one will dare seek to quarrel with you.
Go and bring all that you have of value,
And feel free to find your buyers in every corner.
Make yourself comfortable in my son's palace.
We shall treat you as one of our relatives."

Rostam replies, "O world hero, I prefer to reside
Outside the palace, close to my caravan.
Wherever we are from here on, all will be well.
I have with me all sorts of jewels and gems,
And I must not allow a single one to go astray.
By your good fortune, let us remain outside."

Piran replies, "Select your dwelling as it pleases you.
I shall place guards nearby to protect you."

Rostam rents a house, establishes himself,
And sets up his loads and merchandise in the store.

Rumor spreads through town
Of the arrival of a caravan from Iran.
On all sides, buyers sharpen their ears
To the sound of the merchant and his jewels.
Those in need of silk carpets and gems set out
On the road in the direction of Piran's court.

As the sun reveals itself to launch its ascent across the sky
And spread beauty throughout the world,
A shining market is established next to the residence.

22 | Manijeh Arrives at the Side of Rostam

Manijeh receives news of the arrival of the caravan
And instantly runs to town.

The daughter of Afraasiyaab, bare-headed,
Eyes full of tears, appears before Rostam, wiping off
With her sleeves the blood overflowing from her lashes.
She praises Rostam, asks questions, and says,
"You have enjoyed life's fineries.
May you never have cause to repent for your labors!
May the sublime sky act in accordance with your will!
May the evil eye be powerless before your being!
May the pains you have endured, and continue
To endure, yield to the hope linked to your heart!
May reason always serve you as guide!
May Iran-Zamin be joyous and its fate fortunate!

"What news have you from the king's army leaders?
What news have you of Giv, Goodarz, and troops?
Has a report of Bijan's fate reached Iran-Zamin?
Does his grandfather not wish to seek a way out for him?
Must a young man of his stature, a member
Of the Goodarzian family, perish in such a wretched way?
His feet are bruised by heavy chains, his hands
Are bound up in knots, fastened by large nails.
He is surrounded by shackles, burdened with metal,
And his clothes are drenched with blood.

"The concern I feel for him allows me no sleep,
And the laments he exhales fill my eyes with tears.
O world hero, when you go back to Iran-Zamin,
The lands where Giv and Rostam sit at court,
Tell these illustrious men that Bijan
Has been confined to a narrow pit
And that he will perish if they delay in coming."

Rostam finds himself frightened by her discourse
And calls for someone to take Manijeh away.
He says to her, "Leave my sight!
I have knowledge of neither king nor young warrior!
I know nothing of Goodarz and Giv!

Your words have cause to trouble my mind!"

Manijeh gazes at him, all the while crying bitterly,
And in her distress, she floods her breast with tears.
In the end, she says, "O powerful, wise man,
This harsh response is not worthy of your standing.
If you wish to refrain from speaking to me,
At least do not banish me from your side,
For my poor heart is shattered with grief!
Is this the custom of Iran, to reject news of the downcast?"

Rostam replies, "O woman, what is wrong with you?
Has Ahriman shown you the day of judgment?
You disrupted my commerce, so I treated you rudely.
Do not hold my wrath against me,
For I was preoccupied with my business affairs.
In any case, I do not reside in the city of Kay Khosrow.
I have never heard of Giv or Goodarz.
I have never even crossed the border of their land."

He asks for all the food available in the dwelling
To be brought before the poor woman.
Then he addresses her with questions:
"Why do you despair so?
Why do you speak of heroes and of the king's throne?
Why do you look in the direction of Iran?"

Manijeh responds, "Why do you question me
On my affairs, my misery, and my worries?
I left the dungeon, heart wounded, and have run to you,
O noble man, so that I may obtain from you
News of Giv and of the brave Goodarz.
But you shout at me as one hollers in battle.
Do you not fear the all-powerful Master?
I am Manijeh, the daughter of Afraasiyaab.
The sun itself has never beheld my unveiled face,
And now with tearful eyes, afflicted heart,
And pale cheeks, I travel door to door
Collecting coarse barley bread.
Such is the fate imposed on me by the Creator.
Does anyone know a more dismal life?
May Yazdan have pity on me and end these calamities!

The poor Bijan, in his cell, distinguishes
Neither day nor night, neither sun nor moon.
Restrained by a neckpiece, by nails and heavy chains,
He beseeches the Creator to grant him death
Instead of such a pitiful, despicable existence!

"I am burdened with increasing grief;
My eyes ceaselessly shed tears.
Are you able to receive news from Goodarz?
Perhaps you will find Giv
Or the valiant Rostam at court.
Tell them that Bijan is in a state of utter misery,
And if they delay in coming, he will certainly perish.
If they wish to see him, they must not lose time,
For a boulder is above his head
And solid metal beneath his frame."

Rostam replies, "Fair-faced woman,
Why do you shed tears of affliction?
Why do you not ask intervention
From your father's noblemen?
Perhaps Afraasiyaab will take pity on you,
And his affection will revive.
Perhaps remorse will seize his heart.
If I did not fear his wrath against you,
I would give you riches beyond measure."

Then he orders his cooks
To bring food for Manijeh.
He asks for warm roasted poultry,
Which he wraps with soft bread,
And, with a hand as swift as a fairy's hand,
He conceals a ring inside the meat.

He hands the fowl to Manijeh, saying,
"Take this to the dungeon,
O protector of troubled souls."

23 | Bijan Divines Rostam's Approach

Manijeh returns to the pit,
Pressing against her chest
The cooked chicken packaged in a napkin.
She drops it down to Bijan as it was given to her.

The hero observes the offering with astonishment.
He calls from his pit: "O sun-faced Manijeh,
My kindhearted friend, where did you find this?
So many pains and fatigues you suffer,
And how you stir on my account, day and night!"

Manijeh replies, "It is a gift
From a wealthy merchant, who arrived here
With a caravan full of pricey merchandise.
He is a famed trader from Iran,
An honest, prudent man, full of grace.
He has loads to trade, a great variety of jewels
He occupies a counter and a large residence
In front of which he has set up a store.
He asked me to pray for him.
He gave me this food and napkin to take to you
And to return for new provisions."

Bijan uncovers the bread around the chicken,
Heart stirring with a mix of hope and fear.
In the midst of his troubles, he begins to eat
And discovers the ring hiding within.
He examines its seal, reads the name on it,
And smiles widely with awe and joy.
It is a turquoise seal on which
The name of Rostam is etched in iron,
The writing as fine as a strand of hair.

With this offering from the tree of loyalty,
Bijan realizes that the end
To his term of hardship is drawing near.
He roars with a laughter that echoes outside the shaft.

Confounded at the sound of this mirth coming from
The dark, hollow well, Manijeh thinks to herself,

"Only an insane man would laugh in this manner."

Still astonished, she says, "O blessed man,
Why do you holler such cries of joy?
You can distinguish neither day nor night.
How can you open your lips to laugh?
What secret do you behold? Tell me, entrust it to me.
Has fortune finally turned its face toward you?"

Bijan replies, "You have given me the hope that
Destiny will soon end the trajectory of my ill fortune.
If you wish not to betray my confidence,
Bind yourself by an oath.
I shall tell you everything as soon as I hear your pledge.
But no matter how one sews together a woman's lips,
Her tongue will refuse to be restrained."

At these words, Manijeh sobs violently and says,
"What new calamity does fate hold for me?
Alas, my days have passed, my heart is broken,
My eyes are in tears, for now he suspects me!
I have sacrificed everything for Bijan:
My body, my soul, my legacy,
My wealth, my gold, my crown and jewels.
I have surrendered it all to looting.
I have flung into despair my father and my family.
I have walked unveiled in the midst of crowds.
Now that Bijan is hopeful, I find myself losing hope.
The earth turns black for me,
And my eyes are wanting of clarity,
For Bijan hides from me a deep, dark secret.
O World Creator, only you know the truth."

Bijan says to her, "O fair-faced beauty, you are right.
You have lost everything on my account.
O my sweet and wise companion,
Now is the time to speak of this matter
For which I need your advice.
My misfortunes have troubled my mind.
The merchant of jewels who gave you the roasted bird
Has come from Iran-Zamin on my account.
Thanks to him, the Creator has forgiven me.

I shall once again perceive the face of the world.
This man will liberate me
From the calamities I endure day and night.
He will spare you these hard errands you run
For me that make you wither away.
Go now to him and tell him in secrecy,
        'O protector of world kings,
        You are soft of heart and a great rescuer.
        Tell me, are you the warrior, master of Rakhsh?'"

Manijeh departs as swift as wind and, with ingenuity,
Takes responsibility for Bijan's message.

Rostam hears the words of the fine woman
Who in haste made the long excursion.
He understands that Bijan entrusted
This tall cypress tree with his deepest secret.
He says, "O fair-faced woman,
May the Creator never deprive you of Bijan's love!
You are a woman in the heights of her beauty.
You have suffered at length innumerable difficulties.
Because of your affection for him, you have
Endured hatred, oppression, and banishment.

"Tell him that Yazdan, the Savior, has sent to him
The master of Rakhsh, who has traveled for him
The long road from Zabolestan to the land of Iran,
And from Iran to the land of Tooran.
Once you have relayed this message,
You will not speak of this matter to anyone.
You will listen at night for the slightest sound.
You will bring wood from the forest during the day.
Once night descends, you will light a huge blaze
So that I may discern the location of the dungeon
And take the light of the flame as my guide."

Manijeh rejoices at these words
As her heart finds itself free of anguish.
She returns at a run to the well
Where her beloved is held captive.
She says to Bijan, "I have faithfully taken your message
To this pure man of bright path and glorious name.

He said to me,
      'I am precisely the man Bijan recognized
      From my name and my emblem.
      You have walked so far with a wounded heart,
      You have flooded your cheeks with blood tears.
      Tell him that we have tired our horses' reins
      And our hands searching everywhere for him,
      Mountain and plain, like leopards chasing prey.
      But now that we have found certain hints
      Of his whereabouts, he will have a chance
      To see the tips of the spears of brave men.
      We shall make the earth shake with our battles!
      We shall cast the stone that weighs on his cell
      High into the sky to graze the Pleiades!'

"Then he commanded me to light a fire as tall as a mountain,
As soon as day is dark and night escapes the grasp of sun,
A blaze that glows like daylight on the desert and
On the entrance of your well, so that he may perceive
Your prison and direct his march toward the flames."

Hearing this message in the depths of his well,
Bijan is pure joy. He turns to the World Creator
And says, "Merciful Yazdan, Master of Justice,
You will liberate me from these worries.
You will strike my enemies' eyes and hearts.
Avenge me on these unjust ones, for you know
What I have endured of pain and sorrow at their hands.
I hope to set my sight once again on the face of the world.
I hope that I can bury, deep in the ground, my doomed star.

"As for you, young woman, you have strained yourself,
Suffered greatly to tend to me and to come to my aid.
You have surrendered your soul, your body,
Your heart, and all of your possessions.
In the midst of your efforts and the love you bear for me,
You have looked upon your losses as gains.
You have sacrificed your crown, throne, and belt,
Your treasure, your family, and your father and mother.
If I am able, still young, to be freed from
The dragon's clutches, I shall stand before you,
Spread out my hands toward you,

As do pious men in worship of the Creator.
I shall stand before you as a slave stands before the king,
Ready to serve you to compensate for your suffering.
Now take on one last burden,
Which will mean for you treasures of all sorts."

Manijeh rushes to the forest.
She climbs on tree branches like a supple bird
And brings back armloads of wood.
Eyes cast on the sun, she anticipates the instant
Night reveals its head above the mountains.

Once the sun disappears and the dark night
Covers the desert with the panels of its robe,
At the time when the world prepares to rest,
And the earth disappears beneath darkness,
At the time night sets its army in motion against day
And the sun diverts its shining head,
At this hour, Manijeh ignites a massive blaze
That burns the dark eye of night.
She sits and waits, heart pounding like kettledrums,
Listening for the arrival of Rakhsh,
The steed who treads the earth with hooves of steel.

24 | Rostam Pulls Bijan Out of the Pit

Rostam dresses in Rumi armor and fastens its clasps.
He appears before the Creator of Sun and Moon,
Worshipping and begging for shelter and protection.
He says, "May the sight of evil men dim!
May my force suffice to successfully rescue Bijan!"

He commands his escort to strap for vengeance.
Horses are saddled in leopard skin,
And everyone keenly prepares for battle,
Spreading out their sharp claws.

Rostam takes the direction of the blaze in haste,
Guided by its flames.
He arrives at the side of Akvan's stone,
The site of burning, suffering, and decay,

And says to the seven heroes,
"We must dismount and find a way
To clear the well's opening, free it of the stone."

The army leaders alight and attempt
To remove the rock from the entrance of the well.
They struggle with it at length,
But their arms' strength is powerless,
As the boulder does not budge one bit,
And they strain themselves in vain.

The bold lion witnesses the brave men's backs
Bent with sweat and quite unable to move the rock.
He jumps off his horse,
Tucks his armor's panel inside his belt,
Asks the World Creator for might and power,
And grabs the boulder to remove it.
He tosses it into the forest of Chin,
Making the earth shake violently.

Then he asks Bijan, all the while sighing,
"How did you find yourself in this predicament?
Your share of the world was all sorts of delights.
How did you seize a cup filled with poison?"

Bijan replies from his dark well,
"How does the warrior hero
Find himself after such long travels?
As soon as my ears perceived your cries,
The bitter poison that was my lot
Quickly converted into honey.
You are witness to my dwelling,
With metal as my ground and rock as my sky.
My heart renounced all hope for this passing world,
So grave were my pains, worries, and misfortunes."

Rostam says to him, "The gracious World Master
Took pity on your life, O wise and noble friend!
I still have a request to make of you:
Have mercy on Gorgeen, son of Milaad.
Pluck from your heart any notion of hatred."

Bijan replies, "You do not know how hard I fight.

You do not know, O lion man,
The calamities brought down on me by Gorgeen.
If my gaze falls on him, my vengeance will be clinched."

Rostam returns, "If you are so spiteful as to have
No consideration for my friendship and my words,
I shall leave you, feet bound, in this dark well,
Climb on Rakhsh, and take my leave."

Bijan cries out from his trapped confinement:
"I am the most wretched being among my family's heroes,
Perhaps among all the world's noblemen.
I must then, on this day, forget the wrong, no matter
How great, afflicted upon my head by Gorgeen.
Well then, I shall forget it; forgive and forget.
My heart will renounce all notions of retaliation."

Rostam drops the end of his noose down into the abyss.
Bijan takes a tight grip on it, allowing the hero
To heave him up out of the dark depths.

Rostam hollers at the sight of him,
Feet bound, head bare, hair and nails long,
Body thinned out by worry, suffering from destitution,
Cheek tone yellowing, skin slashed
And bloodied by shackles, the chains rusting deeply.

Rostam quickly unfastens the bonds
And removes the rings around his neck and feet.

Together they take the direction of Rostam's home.
On one side of the mighty warrior is Bijan,
On the other side, the one who devotedly serves him.
The two young ones recount to Rostam their story
And the events leading to their hearts' affliction.

Rostam orders Bijan's head and body to be washed
And to have him dressed in a fresh set of clothing.
Gorgeen approaches Bijan, prostrates himself before him,
And, face in the dust, asks forgiveness for his crimes,
Repenting for his foolish words and actions.

Bijan's heart renounces vengeance,

And Gorgeen's transgressions are exonerated.

Camels are loaded; horses are saddled.
Rostam dons an armor of choice and climbs on Rakhsh.
The illustrious heroes draw their swords,
Prepare their weapons and heavy maces,
And depart in order of battle, their venture complete.

The cautious Ashkesh, always watching over
The army's welfare, takes the road with the loads.

Rostam says to Bijan, "Leave with Ashkesh and Manijeh,
For tonight I shall take vengeance on Afraasiyaab,
Allowing myself to indulge in neither rest nor food
Until I deliver to him, in his own palace, an insult
That will render him the army's laughingstock.
You have intensely suffered in the well;
You need not participate in this battle.
I shall turn the light of his day black.
I shall cut off his head and present it to Kay Khosrow."

Bijan rejects Rostam's counsel
To leave with Manijeh and return to his land.
He replies, "I shall take the lead
In this new act of vengeance."

25 | Rostam Leads a Night Attack on Afraasiyaab's Palace

Rostam and the seven heroes depart while Ashkesh
Transports the provisions and merchandise.
They fling the reins on the horses' saddles
And draw out their swords of vengeance.
They dash to Afraasiyaab's residence,
Reaching it at the time of rest.
Rostam grabs the door handle with his hands
And effortlessly extracts the locks.
He forces his way in like a raging lion.

The scene develops into an assault of blows received
And blows delivered, swords gleaming, flashing,

A shower of shots falling, dropping.
Severed heads of great men roll on the ground,
Hands filling with dust, mouths with blood.

Beneath the portico of the king's chambers
Rostam cries out, "May your sleep be sweet
And your head full of wind!
You rested peacefully on the throne
While Bijan crouched in a well.
Did you think of him as a wall of iron
On the road to Iran-Zamin?
I am Rostam from Zabolestan, the son of Zaal.
Now is not the time to sleep or lie about in bed!
I have shattered the doors and prison chains
You had entrusted to the guard of a boulder.
Bijan is now freed from his bonds.
This was not a proper way to treat a son-in-law.
The war you deserved by causing the death of Siaavosh
Was not enough for you, O worthless man!
I have spread around you enough ruins,
And yet you dare further ask for Bijan's life?
But I see that your heart is evil, your mind adrift."

Bijan cries out, "O stupid, ignoble Tooranian,
Remember that it is on this throne
And in this site of honor that you once sat
When you held me standing captive before you.
I asked to fight like a leopard,
But you restrained my hands in bonds hard as stone.
Look at me now on the plain, free and full of air,
And such as no mad lion would dare assail me."

These words awaken Afraasiyaab's ancient fears,
And he begins to holler in his own palace:
"My brave men, are you bound by sleep?
Rise and seize the enemy.
May the heroes who have their hearts set on seal
And diadem cut off our rivals in their retreat."

From all sides resound shouts and brisk footsteps.
Spilled blood flows in waves at the king's door.
Any Tooranian who presents

PART FOURTEEN

Himself at court is instantly killed.

While the Iranians rush to retaliate,
Afraasiyaab flees his dwelling.
The master of Rakhsh enters the palace,
Trampling beneath his feet silk carpets,
Furnishings, furniture, and fairy-faced women.
Slaves of the king seize the hands of heroes,
They kidnap the noble steed of poplar saddle covered
In leopard skin and embroidered in precious gems.
Then they exit the palace taking with them the loot,
Wishing not to linger in the land of Tooran.

Rostam speeds up his horse's gallop
Because of the loot they carry and from fear
That the adventure will take an unfavorable turn.
So weary is he from the race
That his helmet weighs heavy on his head.
The riders fought so fiercely
And the horses galloped so speedily that the artery
Coursing through their bodies ceases to pump.

Rostam sends his troops a message thus conceived:
"Draw from its sheath the sword of battle,
For I have no doubt that Afraasiyaab will soon
Cross the river with a vast host.
Horses will trample the east and make it black.
The tips of their spears will conceal the face of the sun."

The riders leave altogether, eager to spill enemy blood.
A sentinel arrives from afar who spied
The march of the Tooranian horsemen,
Holding gleaming spears of steel, having joined
The two reins, ready to engage in combat.

Manijeh is seated beneath the tent with slaves
And a guide at the ready before her.
Rostam addresses her and says,
"If one spills musk on the floor, its scent will linger.
Such is the custom of this furtive world.
At times it gives you cuddles and honey,
And at times pain and worry."

26 | Afraasiyaab Attacks Rostam

At the moment the sun gradually
Unveils its head over the mountain crests,
The Tooranian horsemen prepare for departure.
They show up at Afraasiyaab's palace gates
To await his commands.

The city resounds with cries and the clatter of weapons.
You would think the earth is in a simmer.

The brave leaders of Tooran bow down before the ruler,
Belts fastened and foreheads to the dust.
They say, "We have spoken at length of this affair,
But now is the time to take action.
We must go to war to wash away
Bijan's insulting stains upon the king's honor.
Never again shall we be counted
Among men and warriors in the land of Iran.
They will call us women cinched at the waist."

The furious king orders preparations for battle.
He orders Piran to place timpani on elephants,
For he is both confounded and incensed
At the turn of events and the humiliation
Brought down on them by the Iranians.

Brazen clarions ring out before the palace gate.
The Tooranian city echoes with the racket of troops.
Brave troops form ranks according to Afraasiyaab's dictates.
The hollers of men are heard amid the blare of trumpets.
The host departs from Tooran-Zamin
To march toward the border, a host so numerous
The surface of the earth resembles a vast sea.

Once the sentinel spots from his tower
The ground moving like a sea on the boil,
He runs toward Rostam and says, "Prepare yourself!
The world turns black as dust rises
From the stride and sprint of warrior steeds."

Rostam replies, "We do not fear war.

We are the ones who are certain
To scatter dust upon our enemies' heads."
He bids Manijeh to leave with baggage and loads.
He dresses in battle armor, climbs on some heights,
Observes the Tooranian army,
And roars like a mad lion, "What is the weight
Of a fox next to the force of a lion's claws?"

Then he hollers to his men full of pride:
"The hour of battle has arrived.
Where are your swords?
Where are your steel-piercing javelins?
Where are your spears, your bull-headed maces?
Now is the time to exhibit courage.
Now is the time to vengefully rush to battle!"

Trumpets boom. Rostam climbs on Rakhsh
And leads his troops from mountain to plain.
Soon the enemy host appears, advancing rapidly.

The two armies line up on this large battlefield,
Rising like fortifications of steel.

Rostam forms his line of battle,
And the dust, stirred by the horses' motions,
Renders the world eerie.
At the head of the right wing, he places Ashkesh
And Gostaham with a great number of riders.

Rohaam and Zangueh, in war armor, take the left wing,
The war, in their eyes, insignificant.
Rostam and Bijan, son of Giv, occupy the center line,
A point from which they can observe and support the army.

Mount Bisootoon stands behind the Iranians,
Who form a line, a thick barricade of swords.

Afraasiyaab, at the sight of this army, with Rostam
Shining above, is seized by a wave of despair.
He dons his coat of mail dedicated to battle
And orders his army to halt its forward movement.

They line up, fitting to the rules, in front of the Iranians.

The air turns black, the earth disappears.
He entrusts the left wing to Piran,
Sends the valiant Hoomaan to lead the right wing.
At the core are Garsivaz and Shiddeh.
And for himself, he reserves the overall supervision.

Rostam, covered in steel from head to toe,
Resembling a black mountain,
Spurs toward the Tooranian host.
He cries out in a frightful voice,
"You wretched Turk, disgrace
Of your land, of your throne and crown,
You have not the courage to fight as suits a cavalier.
Have you no shame before your army's men?
Is this how you come to battle?
You cover the earth with men and horses,
But once my army advances, eager to reach its end,
You cower back, presenting me
With the sight of your charger's hindquarters!

"Have you never heard the ancient proverb?
It says that a lion fears not an entire field of deer;
That a cluster of stars will not shine as bright as one sun;
That the heart and ear of a wild goat shred to bits
At the scratching sound of a wolf's claws;
That when the eagle spreads its wings to fly,
The partridge trembles in fear;
That the fox does not show courage
By attempting to be brave
And that the deer does not intentionally
Rub himself against a lion's nails.
May a man as weak as you never appear on the throne!
Such a man will surrender his kingdom to the winds.
You will undoubtedly perish, body and heart,
In the battle you wage against me on this very plain."

27 | The Iranians Defeat Afraasiyaab

At these words, the fierce Tooranian
Shudders and exhales a deep sigh, shouting in anger,
"Mighty Tooranians, is this a battle or a feast?

Fight with all your might, and I shall
Satisfy your desires with a vast fortune.
Prepare for war and constrict the world for our enemy."

The Tooranian troops reply with a war cry.
Dust dims the sun in a way as to make one think
That the world is about to drown in water.

Brazen kettledrums are attached to elephants.
Clarions and trumpets ring out.
The warriors in armor form a wall of metal
On the surface of the earth, causing the field to tremble.
Echoes respond to the cries of the men.
Arrows and swords shine in the midst of dust,
Like the sun in the midst of fog on Resurrection day.
A vicious hail of blows of mace rains down on helm.
The shining face of the sun pales
Into a shade of amethyst before Rostam's
Banner sporting the image of a dragon.
The dust rising from elephants conceals the sky,
As if it masks the sun in a layer of tar.

Everywhere Rostam launches Rakhsh, he cuts off heads.
Like the camel who has burst its halter,
He flings himself out of his army core,
Brandishing his bull-headed mace.
Like a wolf, he makes Tooranian troops disband,
Scattering heads like the wind scatters leaves.
The Tooranians' fortune turns.

Rostam says to his men,
"Display your prowess in battle.
Let us fight together,
Place laurels of blood upon our foes' heads.
Today is a day of vengeance,
A day to cleanse the world of Ahrimans.
You must act as bold men.
Act in haste to keep the world safe for posterity.
Make every effort so that our victory is recorded
For as long as the world exists."

At the words of Rostam, Ashkesh rushes forth
From the right wing, impatient and as swift as wind,

Wishing to confront sword-wielding Garsivaz.

Gorgeen, Farhaad, and the brave Rohaam
Bend the left wing of the Tooranian army.
In the center, Bijan, swift of hand, as if in feast,
Unable to contain his ardor for battle,
Makes the heads of famed warlords
Fall like leaves plucked off a tree by a fierce wind.

The arena is a torrent of blood.
The banner of Tooranian leaders
Is knocked down to the ground.
Afraasiyaab, seeing fortune abandon him,
Seeing his men perish left and right,
Casts down his Indian sword,
Climbs on a fresh horse, and flees the scene.
In this way, he deserts his remaining troops,
Who are left to fight without their leader.
He gallops fearfully in the direction of Tooran
Before having crushed the Iranians
And before having avenged himself.

Rostam, vanquisher of lions, pursues him
For two farsangs, showering him and the Tooranians
With blows of mace and shots of arrows, like a dragon
Aflame who would burn men with its breath.

One thousand valiant riders from the land of Tooran
Are taken captive as a result of this clash.
Rostam leaves the battlefield to return to camp
To distribute the loot to his troops.

Once distribution is complete,
He asks for the goods to be loaded,
And he departs triumphant,
Taking the direction of the king's court.

28 | Rostam Returns to Kay Khosrow

News of the lion's victorious return from the forest,
And of the liberation of Bijan from his confinement
And from his bonds of steel reaches the brave king.
At the report of Rostam's victory over the enemy host
And how he reduced its plans to nothingness,
Kay Khosrow presents himself before the Creator
And remains a long time, face turned downward,
Joyful and grateful, forehead grazing the ground.

Goodarz and Giv rush up to the triumphant king.
Troops arrive, drums fill the streets,
The blare of trumpets resounds
At the palace gates, and the army clamors.

The enormous square disappears
Beneath the horses' hooves.
The city fills with the shrill call of clarions.
Warriors take off and proceed in joy.
Elephants work the ground with their tusks.

An elephant bearing kettledrums leads the procession.
Goodarz is next, with Commander Tous
Marching behind, trailed by his banner.
On one side are lions and leopards bound in chains,
On the other army cavaliers. This grand procession
Receives the brave hero in royal fashion.

The convoy, a mass of marching men organized
By divisions, covers the earth like a mountain.

Arriving in sight of Rostam's fearless army,
Goodarz and Giv set foot to ground.
Iranian brave men follow suit and run
To meet the hero, praising and blessing him.

The world hero in turn dismounts
And addresses questions to the leaders
Who exerted themselves to come to his approach.

Goodarz and Giv offer him homage and say,
"May Yazdan never cease to protect you,

O renowned and valiant army leader!
May the Sun and Moon spin only to your will!
Lions borrow courage from you.
May the sky never tire from circling over you.
The members of our family stand as your slaves
Since you are returning to us our lost son.
You have freed us from worry and pain,
And Iranians are strapped to best serve you."

The noblemen climb back on their steeds
And rush to appear before the world king.
But once Rostam, the army's shelter,
Approaches the city of the world master,
Khosrow himself, leader of heroes,
Supporter of troops, crown of noblemen,
Marches toward him to personally receive him.

At the sight of the imperial banner,
Rostam dismounts and prostrates himself,
Confounded by the fact that the king went through
The trouble of advancing toward him on the road.

Kay Khosrow holds Rostam close to his breast
And says, "O bold warlord, you are the strength
Of our feats, the support of all courage.
Your manner of acting resembles that of the sun.
Everywhere are the marks of your high deeds."

Rostam takes Bijan's hand, as he stands there
In awe of the king and his father.
The hero walks him to them and, in this way,
He straightens the backs of those bent by misfortune.

Then he offers the king
One thousand Tooranian prisoners.

Khosrow blesses Rostam and says to him,
"May the sky always act according to your wishes!
You are a mighty world hero,
A prince of the highest value.
You are the shield safeguarding us
Against harm and hatred.
May your head remain young

And your heart joyous, for without you,
I wish not to be master of earth and era.
Fortunate is Zaal, who will leave, like you,
A memory of himself in the world
Once his time has passed.
Fortunate is the land of Zabolestan,
Whose milk nourishes such brave heroes.
Fortunate is the land of Iran and its warriors,
Who are blessed with a leader like you.
But the most fortunate of all is the king
Whose throne is served by a hero
Of your ability and high standing.
May the world never be devoid of your blade!
May you always be ready to fight!
You are the crown of Iran and the support of nobles.
We shall not wish to live in your absence.
May Nimrooz always enjoy your being,
For no one recalls a warrior of your competence!"

Then the world ruler turns to Giv and says,
"The mysterious designs of the Creator
Work in your favor, for your cherished son
Is returned to you by Rostam's hand."

Giv kisses the ground and says,
"May you continue to live in joy
For as long as the world endures!
May Rostam prolong his youth to the end of days!
May Zaal's noble heart never cease to be cheered by him!"

29 | Khosrow Celebrates With a Feast

Khosrow orders banquet tables
To which he summons noblemen full of pride.
They dine and feast, and after they rise
They go into a hall set up with wine.

There stand slaves whose beauty dazzles.
The cascading sound of harps rushes
Beneath the fingers of players,
Fairy daughters arrayed with earrings,

And each wearing heavy golden diadems inlaid
With gems, their cheeks colored like Rumi silk.

Golden trays are filled with pure musk,
A basin overflows with rosewater.
Khosrow shines in imperial splendor akin to
A two-week-old moon above a tall cypress tree.

At the end of the night, the world heroes,
Servants of King Khosrow, retire home, inebriated.

At dawn, Rostam arrives at the palace,
Heart full of joy, belt strapped tight
To ask permission to return home.

Khosrow asks for a chalice filled
With jewels fit for a king and a full attire,
With tunic and diadem inlaid with stones.
He asks for one hundred saddled horses,
One hundred camels bearing one hundred women,
Fairy-faced strapped slaves,
And one hundred servants of golden diadems.

This wealth is collected before the king.
He transfers it to Rostam, who kisses the ground.
As he rises, he places on his head
The Kianian headdress and fastens
Around his waist the imperial belt.

Then he exits, praising the king,
And engages in making preparations
For his departure back to the land of Sistan.
He distributes gifts according to rank
To the brave warriors who shared
His battles and fatigues, his joys and worries.
They depart cheerfully,
Leaving behind the royal palace.

Once the heroes have left,
Kay Khosrow sits on his throne in peace.
He summons Bijan, who speaks to him at length
Of the pains and anguish he endured,
Relating his misfortunes shackled in the dungeon,

PART FOURTEEN

His liberation, and the ensuing battle.

Khosrow feels a deep sense of compassion
For the unfortunate daughter of Afraasiyaab,
For the weariness and troubles
To which she was forced to submit.
He asks for one hundred robes of Rumi silk,
Embroidered with precious gems,
With the finest golden threads;
A crown, and ten pouches filled with dinars;
Slaves, horses, and much more wealth.
He says to Bijan, "Take this present
To the virtuous woman who has suffered acutely.
Never allow her to hurt,
Never address her with cold words.
Think of the wrong you have caused her.
Live your life together in happiness
And reflect on the way in which fate turns,
Raising one to the clouds only to be later brought
Down precipitously to a tomb below the ground."

The revolving dome is a place of dread and terror,
For it flings brusquely into a pit
The same man it raised tenderly at its breast.
It takes one from a dungeon,
Brings him to the throne, and places above
His head a diadem of precious stones.
Destiny does not blush from wrongdoing.
It holds affection for no one.
Eternal master of happiness and misfortune,
It demands friendship from no one.

Such is the custom of this passing world,
Guiding us down the path of good and ill.
As long as you abstain from the worry of wealth,
Your noble heart will remain trouble free.
If you can refrain from gazing at the outside world,
You will live your days in joy and serenity.

I have now told in full the account
Of this adventure as I have heard it related
According to ancient tradition.

Having completed the story of Bijan and Manijeh,
I shall now turn to new exploits:
These will be the ones of Goodarz and Piran.

 End of Volume Two

APPENDIX

Glossary of Names

The Kianian Kings: Line of Succession

The Iranian Heroes: Line of Succession

The Tooranian Kings and Warriors:
Line of Succession

Glossary of Geographical Markers

Map of the World of Shahnameh

Glossary of Persian Words

The Persian Calendar

Glossary of Names

Aabteen: Fereydoon's father; killed and served as a meal to Zahaak's snakes. (Vol. 1)

Aarezooy: Daughter of Sarv, King of Yemen, and wife of Salm, son of Fereydoon. (Vol. 1)

Afraasiyaab: King of Tooran-Zamin and son of Pashang (son of Zaadsham). (Vols. 1-2)

Aghriras: Brother of Afraasiyaab and Garsivaz and son of Pashang. (Vol. 1)

Ahriman: Dark spirit whose goal is to promote division and chaos.

Ajnaas: Tooranian warrior in Afraasiyaab's army. (Vols. 1-2)

Akhvaast: Tooranian warrior in Afraasiyaab's army. (Vol. 2)

Akvan Deev: A threatening creature that resembles a deev with a black stripe across its back. (Vol. 2)

Alkoos: Tooranian warrior in Afraasiyaab's army. Killed by Rostam. (Vol. 1)

Alvaah: Zaboli warrior in Rostam's retinue. Killed by Kaamoos. (Vols. 1-2)

Andariman: Tooranian warrior and brother of Afraasiyaab. (Vol. 2)

Arjang: Deev and army commander in Mazandaran. Killed by Rostam. (Vol. 1)

Arjang: Son of Zerreh and brother of Garooy; Tooranian warrior in the army of Tajov. Killed by Tous. (Vol. 2)

Arjasp: Tooranian leader in the army of Afraasiyaab. (Vols. 1-2)

Armail: With brother Garmail, saves intended victims of Zahaak's serpents. (Vol. 1)

Arnavaaz: Daughter or sister of Jamsheed; concubine of Zahaak then wife of Fereydoon and mother of Iraj. (Vol. 1)

Ashkeboos: Ally of Afraasiyaab from Kushan who fights Rohaam and Rostam. Killed by Rostam. (Vol. 2)

Ashkesh: Of the family of Ghobaad and leader in the Iranian army under the rules of Kay Kaavoos and Kay Khosrow. (Vols. 1-2)

Aspanooy: Slave under the command of Tajov, Afraasiyaab's son-in-law. (Vol. 2)

Baanoogoshasp: Rostam's daughter and Giv's wife. (Vol. 2)

Baarmaan: Tooranian warrior, son of Viseh. (Vols. 1)

Baarmaan: Tooranian warrior. (Vol. 2)

Baazoor: Tooranian sorcerer. Killed by Rohaam. (Vol. 2)

Bahraam: Son of Goodarz and Iranian warrior who serves under the rules of Kay Kaavoos and Kay Khosrow. (Vols. 1-2)

Barteh: Iranian warrior and leader of the family of Tavaabeh under the rule of Kay Khosrow. (Vols. 1-2)

Beed: Deev in the army of Mazandaran. (Vol. 1)

Behzaad: Siaavosh's horse, then mastered by Kay Khosrow. (Vol. 2)

Bijan: Son of Giv and Baanoogoshasp, Rostam's daughter; Iranian warrior under the rule of Kay Khosrow. (Vols. 1-2)

Bivard: Ruler of Kaat and ally of Afraasiyaab in war. (Vol. 2)

Boossepaas: Father of Kooh; Hoomaan pretends to be Boossepaas when he meets Rostam. (Vol. 2)

Borzeen: Iranian warrior and son of Garshaasp. (Vols. 1-2)

APPENDIX

Caesar of Rum: Title assigned to various Rumi leaders, often allies of Afraasiyaab. (Vols. 1-2)

Changgesh: Ally of Afraasiyaab who fights Rostam and is killed by him. (Vol. 2)

Damoor: Tooranian warrior who lends a hand in the slaying of Siaavosh. (Vol. 2)

Deev: Child of Ahriman, also referred to as Eblis; represents the material or physical embodiment of Ahriman; a fragment of the dark spirit.

Eblis: Name synonymous with Ahriman and deev. Eblis is one of the many physical manifestations of Ahriman.

Emperor of Chin: Or Faghfoor of Chin; title assigned to the ruler of Chin or China, often an ally of Tooran-Zamin. (Vol. 2)

Faghfoor: Title assigned to the Emperor of Chin, or China, who governs under the authority (jurisdiction) of Afraasiyaab. (Vol. 2)

Faraamarz: Rostam's son and Iranian warrior under the rules of Kay Kaavoos and Kay Khosrow. (Vols. 1-2)

Faraanak: Fereydoon's mother and Aabteen's wife. (Vol. 1)

Faranguis: Afraasiyaab's daughter, wife of Siaavosh, and mother of Kay Khosrow who later marries Fariborz, son of Kaavoos. (Vol. 2)

Farghaar: Skillful warrior who defends Afraasiyaab. (Vol. 2)

Farhaad: Grandson of Goodarz and Iranian warrior under the rules of Kay Kaavoos and Kay Khosrow. (Vols. 1-2)

Fariborz: Son of Kaavoos and brother of Siaavosh. (Vols. 1-2)

Farshidvard: Tooranian warrior and leader in Afraasiyaab's army. (Vol. 2)

Fartoos: Ruler of Chaghan and ally of Afraasiyaab. (Vol. 2)

Fereydoon: Sixth king and son of Aabteen and Faraanak; father of Salm, Toor, and Iraj; great-grandfather of Manoochehr. Dies of old age. (Vol. 1)

Five Chambermaids: Rudaabeh's servants. (Vol. 1)

Foorood: Son of Siaavosh and Jarireh (Piran's daughter). Killed by Bijan. (Vol. 2)

Garmail: With brother Armail, cook in Zahaak's kitchen. (Vol. 1)

Garooy: Son of Zerreh, descendant of Toor; Tooranian warrior responsible for Siaavosh's death. (Vol. 2)

Garshaasp: Son of Nariman and father of Saam and Borzeen; warrior in Manoochehr's army. (Vol. 2)

Garshaasp: Son of Zu and tenth King of Iran who rules for nine years. (Vol. 1)

Garsivaz: Pashang's son and Afraasiyaab's brother, responsible for Siaavosh's death. (Vols. 1-2)

Garzam: Tooranian warrior in Afraasiyaab's army. Killed by Giv. (Vol. 1)

Ghaaran: Son of Kaaveh; brother of Kashvaad; Iranian warrior and chief. (Vols. 1-2)

Ghobaad: Son of Kashvaad (son of Kaaveh); Iranian warrior in Manoochehr's army; not to be confused with Kay Ghobaad. Killed by Baarmaan. (Vol. 1)

Gholoon: Tooranian warrior in the army of Afraasiyaab. (Vol. 1)

Ghorcheh: Tooranian warrior in the army of Afraasiyaab. (Vol. 2)

Giv: Son of Goodarz, grandson of Kashvaad, husband of Baanoogoshasp, and father of Bijan and Goraazeh; Iranian leader and warrior who serves under Kay Kaavoos and Kay Khosrow. (Vols. 1-2)

Gojdaham: Iranian warrior; defender of the White Castle; and father of Gostaham, Gordaafareed, and Hojir's wife. (Vols. 1-2)

Golbaad: Tooranian warrior killed by Zaal. (Vol. 1)

Golbaad: Tooranian warrior and leader in the army of Afraasiyaab. (Vols. 2)

APPENDIX

Golgoon: Goodarz's horse. (Vol. 2)

Golrang: Fereydoon's horse. (Vol. 1)

Golrang: Fariborz's horse. (Vol. 2)

Golshahr: Piran's wife and mother of Jarireh. (Vol. 2)

Goodarz: Iranian leader who serves under Kay Kaavoos and Kay Khosrow; son of Kashvaad (son of Kaaveh); has 78 sons and grandsons. (Vols. 1-2)

Goraazeh: Son of Giv (son of Goodarz); Iranian warrior under the rules of Kay Kaavoos and Kay Khosrow. (Vols. 1-2)

Gordaafareed: Iranian female warrior who fights with Sohraab; daughter of Gojdaham (of the family of Goodarz). (Vol. 1)

Gorgeen: Son of Milaad and Iranian warrior in the armies of Kay Kaavoos and Kay Khosrow. (Vols. 1-2)

Gostaham: Son of Nozar; brother of Tous (different from Gostaham, son of Gojdaham). (Vol. 1)

Gostaham: Young son of Gojdaham and brother of Gordaafareed (different from the son of Nozar). (Vols. 1-2)

Haaroot: Angel who along with the fairy Maaroot comes to earth to teach spells. They lose access to heaven because of their sins and are imprisoned in Babel. (Vol. 2)

Hirbad: Sudaabeh's servant. (Vol. 2)

Hojir: Son of Goodarz; Iranian warrior and Gojdaham's son-in-law. (Vol. 1-3)

Homa: Large and powerful bird in Persian mythology, symbol of happiness; similar to the griffin or the phoenix. (Vols. 1-2)

Hoomaan: Tooranian leader, son of Viseh (son of Zaadsham). (Vols. 1-2)

Hooshang: Second King of Iran and son of Siaamak who rules for forty years. (Vol. 1)

Hormozd: Or Ormazd, another name for Creator. In the ancient Persian solar calendar, each day had the name of a deity instead of a number. Each name evoked a concept. The division then was not based on a seven-day week but on a thirty-day month.

Iraj: Youngest son of Fereydoon and Arnavaaz; brother of Salm and Toor and grandfather of Manoochehr. Killed by his brothers. (Vol. 1)

Jahn: Tooranian warrior and Afraasiyaab's son. (Vol. 2)

Jamsheed: Son of Tahmures and fourth King of Iran who rules for 700 years. Killed by Zahaak. (Vol. 1)

Jandal: A wise envoy selected by Fereydoon to find three sisters to marry Toor, Salm, and Iraj. (Vol. 1)

Jarireh: Siaavosh's wife and Foorood's mother; eldest daughter of Piran. (Vol. 2)

Jooyaa: A warrior leader in the army of the King of Mazandaran. (Vol. 1)

Kaafoor: "Man-eater" Tooranian who dwells in the city of Bidaad. Killed by Rostam. (Vol. 2)

Kaakooy: Descendant of Zahaak who battles Manoochehr. Killed by Manoochehr. (Vol. 1)

Kaaloo: Tooranian warrior in the army of Afraasiyaab. (Vol. 2)

Kaamoos: Ruler of Kushan and Afraasiyaab's ally in war. Killed by Rostam. (Vol. 2)

Kaaveh: Father of Kashvaad and blacksmith who leads the opposition against Zahaak. (Vol. 1)

Kaboodeh: Servant of Tajov, ruler of Gorooguerd. Killed by Bahraam. (Vol. 2)

Kahaar: Ruler of Kahan;ally of Afraasiyaab. Killed by Rostam. (Vol. 2)

Kalaahoor: Warrior in the army of the King of Mazandaran. (Vol. 1)

Karkoo: Warrior and ally of Afraasiyaab. (Vol. 2)

Karkooy: Salm's grandson and a relative of Zahaak on his mother's side. (Vol. 1)

Karookhan: Tooranian warrior in Afraasiyaab's army and relative of Viseh; Afraasiyaab's minister. (Vol. 1)

Kashvaad: Son of Kaaveh and brother of Ghaaran; father of Ghobaad, Garshaasp and Goodarz; Iranian warrior and soldier. (Vols. 1-2)

Kay Aarash: Son of Kay Ghobaad. (Vols. 1-2)

Kay Aarmin: Son of Kay Ghobaad. (Vol. 1)

Kay Ghobaad: Descendant of Fereydoon and eleventh King of Iran who rules for one hundred years; father to four sons: Kay Kaavoos, Kay Aarash, Kay Pashin, and Kay Aarmin. (Vol. 1)

Kay Kaavoos: Son of Kay Ghobaad and twelfth King of Iran who rules for 150 years. (Vols. 1-2)

Kay Khosrow: Son of Siaavosh and Faranguis and grandson of Kay Kaavoos and Afraasiyaab. (Vols. 2-3)

Kay Pashin: Son of Kay Ghobaad. (Vols. 1-2)

Khazarvan: Tooranian warrior in the army of Afraasiyaab. Killed by Zall. (Vol. 1)

Khojabr: Tooranian warrior in the army of Afraasiyaab. (Vol. 1)

Khorraad: Iranian warrior in the army of Kay Kaavoos. (Vols. 1-2)

Kiaanoosh: Fereydoon's brother. (Vol. 1)

King of Egypt: Ally of the King of Haamaavaran. (Vol. 1)

King of Haamaavaran: Father of Sudaabeh, wife of Kay Kaavoos. Killed by Rostam to save Kay Kaavoos. (Vol. 2)

King of Mazandaran: Ruler of a kingdom of deevs who captures Kay Kaavoos and is then killed in Rostam's epic seven-stage quest. (Vol. 1)

King of Shaam: King of Syria and ally of the King of Haamaavaran. (Vol. 1)

King of Sindh: Ally of Afraasiyaab. (Vol. 2)

Kiumars: First King of Iran who rules for fifty years. (Vol. 1)

Kohram: Tooranian warrior. (Vol. 2)

Konaarang Deev: Guardian of the rocky, desolate place on the way to the White Deev's dwelling. (Vol. 1)

Kondor: From the land of Saghlaab and an ally of Afraasiyaab in war. (Vol. 2)

Kooh: Assumed name used by Hoomaan to trick Rostam; son of Boossepaas. (Vol. 2)

Kundrow: Zahaak's minister. (Vol. 1)

Lahaak: Son of Viseh (son of Zaadsham); Tooranian warrior and leader in the army of Afraasiyaab. (Vol. 2)

Maah Aafareed: One of Iraj's wives and Manoochehr's grandmother. (Vol. 1)

Maah-e Aazaadeh Khooy: Daughter of Sarv, King of Yemen, and wife of Toor, son of Fereydoon. (Vol. 1)

Manijeh: Afraasiyaab's daughter and Bijan's wife. (Vol. 2)

Manoochehr: Seventh King of Iran who rules for 120 years; he is the grandson of Iraj and the son of Pashang and *Nameless*. (Vol. 1)

Manshoor: Ruler of Chin and ally of Afraasiyaab. (Vol. 2)

Mardaas: Zahaak's father, ruler in Mesopotamia. Killed by Eblis. (Vol. 1)

Mardooy: Tooranian warrior in the army of Tajov. (Vol. 2)

Mehraab: Ruler of Kabol and father of Rudaabeh; descendant of Zahaak. (Vols. 1-2)

Milaad: Father of Gorgeen and Iranian hero in the army of Kay Kaavoos and Kay Khosrow. (Vols. 1-2)

Nahel: Tooranian warrior. (Vol. 2)

Nameless: Daughter of Maah Aafareed and Iraj; granddaughter of Fereydoon; wife of Pashang, mother of Manoochehr; Ferdowsi does not assign her a name. (Vol. 1)

Nameless: Wife of Kay Kaavoos and mother of Siaavosh; granddaughter of Garsivaz. (Vol. 2)

Nariman: Great Iranian warrior in the army of Manoochehr; Saam's father and Zaal's grandfather. (Vols. 1-2)

Nastihan: Tooranian warrior and leader in the army of Afraasiyaab; son of Viseh (son of Zaadsham. (Vol. 2)

Nastooh: Son of Goodarz and Iranian warrior. (Vol. 2)

Nozar: Son of Manoochehr and eighth King of Iran who rules for seven years; father of Tous and Gostaham. Killed by Afraasiyaab. (Vol. 1)

Palaashan: Tooranian warrior and Afraasiyaab's army leader. Killed by Bijan. (Vol. 2)

Pashang: Iranian warrior from the seed of Jamsheed; Fereydoon's nephew (his brother's son), selected by Fereydoon to marry Fereydoon's *Nameless* granddaughter; father of Manoochehr. (Vol. 1)

Pashang: Son of Zaadsham and father of Afraasiyaab, Aghriras and Garsivaz. (Vols. 1-2)

Pilsam: Tooranian leader, son of Viseh (son of Zaadsham). Killed by Rostam. (Vols. 1-2)

Piran: Tooranian leader, son of Viseh (son of Zaadsham). (Vols. 1-2)

Poolaad: Of Ghondi; ruler deev in the army of Mazandaran with hooves as feet. Killed by Rostam. (Vol. 1)

Poolaad: Tooranian warrior. (Vols. 2-3)

Poolaadvand: Fierce Tooranian warrior who dwells in the mountains of Chin. Defeated by Rostam. (Vol. 2)

Pormaye: Cow that nurses Fereydoon. (Vol. 1)

Pormaye: Fereydoon's brother; same name as the cow that nurses

Fereydoon. (Vol. 1)

Rakhsh: Rostam's horse. (Vol. 1-3)

Rezvan: Keeper of paradise. (Vol. 2)

Rivniz: Tous's son-in-law and Zarasp's brother-in-law; Iranian warrior who has forty beautiful sisters. Killed by Foorood. (Vol. 2)

Rivniz: Son of Fariborz and grandson of Kaavoos. (Vol. 2)

Rohaam: Son of Goodarz and Iranian warrior under the rules of Kay Kaavoos and Kay Khosrow. (Vols. 1-2)

Rooeen: Son of Piran (son of Viseh) and Tooranian warrior. (Vol. 2)

Rostam: Iranian world hero and son of Zaal and Rudaabeh; marries Shahrbaanoo; father of Faraamarz and Baanoogoshasp. (Vols. 1-2)

Rudaabeh: Daughter of Mehraab and Sindokht, wife of Zaal and mother of Rostam. (Vol. 1)

Saam: Iranian warrior and head of Manoochehr's army; Nariman's son and Zaal's father. (Vol. 1)

Saaveh: Relative of Kaamoos and warrior ally of Afraasiyaab. Killed by Rostam. (Vol. 2)

Sahi: Daughter of Sarv, King of Yemen, and wife of Iraj, son of Fereydoon. (Vol. 1)

Salm: Son of Fereydoon and Shahrnaaz; brother of Toor and Iraj. Killed by Manoochehr to avenge Iraj's death. (Vol. 1)

Sanjeh: One of the deevs serving Mazandaran; guardian of the mountain path leading to the White Deev. (Vol. 1)

Sarv: King of Yemen and father of the three maidens who marry Fereydoon's sons Toor, Salm, and Iraj. (Vol. 1)

Sepahram: Brother of Afraasiyaab and Tooranian warrior. (Vol. 2)

Shaavaran: Father of Zangueh. (Vols. 1-2)

Shabaahang: Farhaad's white horse. (Vol. 2)

Shabdeez: Mehraab's horse. (Vol. 1)

Shabdeez: Ghobaad's horse (Vol. 1). Giv's horse. (Vols. 1-2)

Shabrang: Bijan's horse. (Vol. 2)

Shahpoor: Iranian warrior who serves the kings from Fereydoon to Kay Khosrow. (Vols. 1-2)

Shahrnaaz: Daughter or sister of Jamsheed; concubine of Zahaak before she weds Fereydoon and gives birth to Salm and Toor. (Vol. 1)

Shahrbaanoo: Giv's sister and Rostam's wife; mother of Faraamarz. (Vol. 2)

Shamaasaas: Tooranian warrior in the army of Afraasiyaab. Killed by Ghaaran. (Vol. 1)

Shamiran: From Shakni, an ally of Afraasiyaab. (Vol. 2)

Shangal: From India, an ally of Afraasiyaab. (Vol. 2)

Shiddasp: Minister under the rule of Tahmures. (Vol. 1)

Shiddeh: Afraasiyaab's son and Tooranian leader. (Vol. 2)

Shiddush: Son of Goodarz (son of Kashvaad) and Iranian warrior serving the kings from Manoochehr to Kay Khosrow. (Vols. 1-2)

Shirui: Warrior in Toor's army. (Vol. 1)

Shiruye: Iranian warrior and general in Manoochehr's army. (Vol. 1)

Shitarakh: Tooranian warrior. (Vol. 2)

Siaamak: Son of Kiumars and father of Hooshang. Killed by the deev. (Vol. 1)

Siaavosh: Son of Iranian Kay Kaavoos and descendant of Tooranian Garsivaz. (Vol. 2)

Simorgh: Bird of knowledge that rescues and raises Zaal. (Vol. 1)

Sindokht: Mother of Rudaabeh and wife of Mehraab. (Vol. 1)

Sohraab: Son of Rostam and Tahmineh. Killed by Rostam. (Vol. 1)

Sooroosh: Archangel able to hear and relay divine messages. (Vol. 2)

Sorkheh: Afraasiyaab's son and Tooranian leader. Killed at the order of Zavaareh. (Vol. 2)

Taazi/Taazian: Bedouins or tribes living in the land of Arabia or Mesopotamia (between the Tigris and the Euphrates), also "field of warriors" or "field of spear-riders"; worshippers of the Black Stone or Kaaba, as given by the prophet Muhammad; symbolic rather than cultural, national, or geographical.

Tahmineh: Wife of Rostam and mother of Sohraab; daughter of the King of Samangan. (Vol. 1)

Tahmures: Son of Hooshang and third King of Iran; Deev-Binder who rules for thirty years. (Vol. 1)

Tajov: Ruler of Gorooguerd, a province of Tooran-Zamin; of Iranian lineage, but also Afraasiyaab's son-in-law. (Vol. 2)

Taliman: Iranian warrior in Nozar's army. (Vol. 1)

Tarkhan of Chin: Title assigned to rulers of Chin, allies of Tooran-Zamin. (Vol. 1)

Tavaabeh: Name of a family of warriors loyal to Kay Khosrow, led by Barteh. (Vol. 2)

Tevorg: Sentinel who watches over Afraasiyaab's city. (Vol. 2)

Tokhaar: Warrior in Foorood's army and Foorood's advisor. (Vol. 2)

Toor: Son of Fereydoon and Shahrnaaz; brother of Salm and Iraj. Killed by Manoochehr. (Vol. 1)

Tous: Son of Nozar, brother of Gostaham, and commander of troops under Kay Khosrow; bearer of the Kaaviani banner and the golden boots. (Vols. 1-2)

Turkish boy: Servant of Zaal. (Vol. 1)

APPENDIX

Turks: The Turks of *The Shahnameh* are nomadic tribes moving through the lands east of Iran with no relation to today's Turkey, which sits west of Iran and which was established in the 11th century upon the conquest of the Turks by the Byzantines. (Vol. 1-2)

Ulaad: Landowner in the fifth stage of Rostam's epic quest. Ultimately, Rostam makes him ruler of Mazandaran. (Vol. 1)
Ulaad's guardian: Unnamed guardian of the field owned by Ulaad.

Varaazaad: King of Sepijaab and warrior who fights for Afraasiyaab. Killed by Faraamarz. (Vol. 2)

Viseh: Father of Piran, Pilsam, Baarmaan, and Hoomaan; Tooranian army leader and Afraasiyaab's minister. (Vols. 1-2)

White Deev: Leader in Mazandaran. Killed by Rostam. (Vol. 1)

Witch: Woman who conspires with Sudaabeh to avow her innocence. (Vol. 2)

Yazdan: Plural of Yzad (divine), encompasses all of divinity, Creator of all that is manifested, unmanifested, and all that is yet to come into existence.

Yzad: Singular of Yazdan, Divine Creator.

Zaadsham: Afraasiyaab's grandfather and Pashang's father. (Vol. 1-3)

Zaal: Saam's son; Rudaabeh's husband and Rostam's father; also called Dastan-e Zand by Simorgh and Zaal-e Zar by Saam. (Vols. 1-2)

Zahaak: Son of Mardaas and fifth King of Iran who rules for 1000 years. Captured by Fereydoon. (Vol. 1)

Zangueh: Son of Shaavaran and Iranian warrior under the rules of Kay Kaavoos and Kay Khosrow. (Vols. 1-2)

Zarasp: Son of King Manoochehr and brother of Nozar. (Vols. 1-2)

Zarasp: Son of Tous (son of Nozar) and brother-in-law of Rivniz. A warrior under the rule of Kay Khosrow. Killed at the hands of Foorood. (Vol. 2)

Zavaareh: Rostam's brother. (Vols. 1-2)

Zerreh: Father of Garooy and Arjang; Tooranian warrior. (Vol. 2)

Zhendehrazm: Son of the King of Samangan and brother of Tahmineh, uncle of Sohraab. (Vol. 1)

Zirak: An interpreter of Zahaak's dream of Fereydoon. (Vol. 1)

Zu: Son of Tahmaasp, descendant of Fereydoon, and ninth King of Iran who rules for five years. (Vol. 1)

THE KIANIAN KINGS: LINE OF SUCCESSION

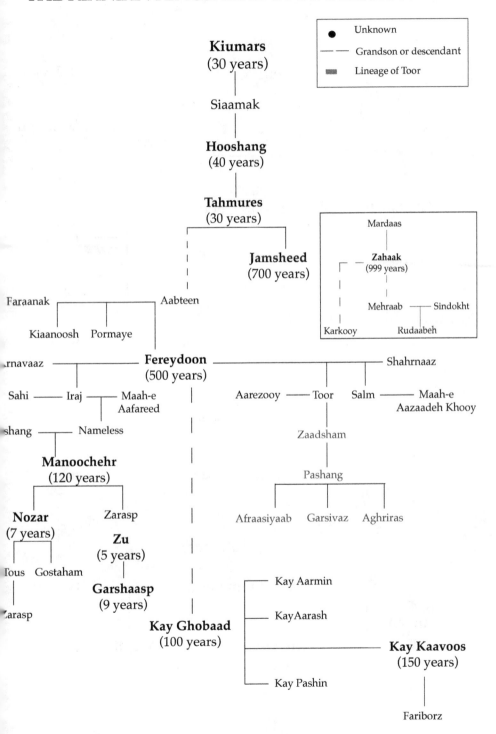

Kiumars
(30 years)

Siaamak

Hooshang
(40 years)

Tahmures
(30 years)

	Unknown
●	Unknown
– – –	Grandson or descendant
▬	Lineage of Toor

Jamsheed
(700 years)

Mardaas

Zahaak
(999 years)

Faraanak   Aabteen

Mehraab ——— Sindokht

Kiaanoosh Pormaye

Karkooy   Rudaabeh

..rnavaaz ——— **Fereydoon** ————————— Shahrnaaz
(500 years)

Sahi ——— Iraj ——— Maah-e   Aarezooy ——— Toor   Salm ——— Maah-e
Aafareed   Aazaadeh Khooy

..shang ——— Nameless   Zaadsham

Manoochehr
(120 years)   Pashang

Nozar   Zaraasp   Afraasiyaab Garsivaz Aghriras
(7 years)

Zu
(5 years)

Tous Gostaham

Garshaasp
(9 years)

Zarasp

— Kay Aarmin

— Kay Aarash

Kay Ghobaad
(100 years)   ——————— **Kay Kaavoos**
(150 years)

— Kay Pashin

Fariborz

THE IRANIAN HEROES: LINE OF SUCCESSION

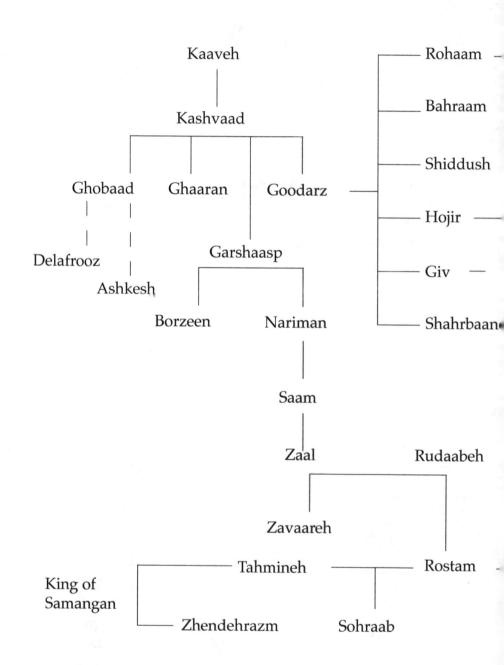

Farhaad

Gojdaham

Gostaham   Gordaafareed

Shiruye

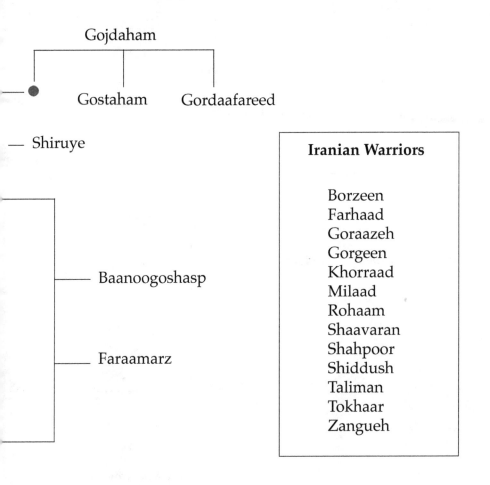

Baanoogoshasp

Faraamarz

Iranian Warriors
Borzeen
Farhaad
Goraazeh
Gorgeen
Khorraad
Milaad
Rohaam
Shaavaran
Shahpoor
Shiddush
Taliman
Tokhaar
Zangueh

Giv   Baanoogoshasp

Goraazeh   Bijan   Manigeh

THE TOORANIAN KINGS AND WARRIORS: LINE OF SUCCESSION

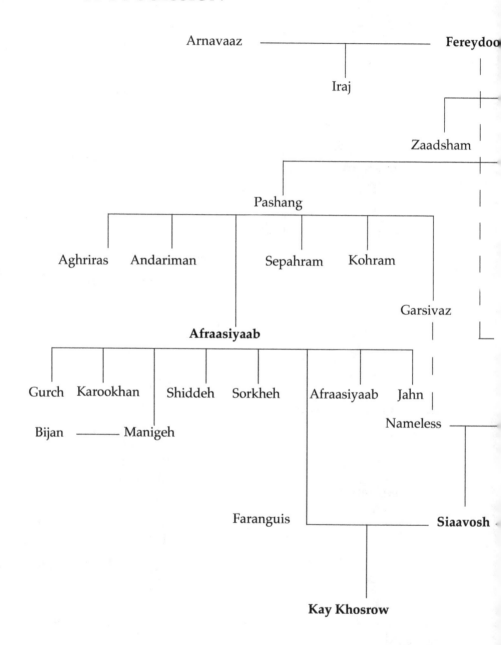

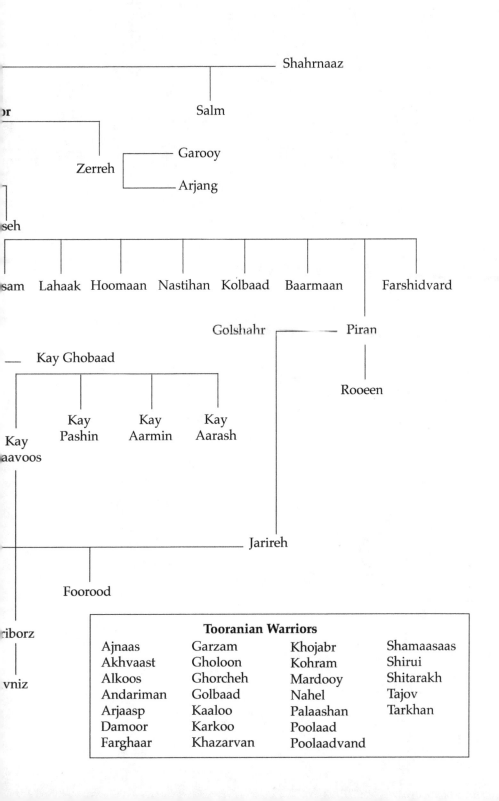

Shahrnaaz

ɔr

Salm

Zerreh

Garooy

Arjang

seh

sam Lahaak Hoomaan Nastihan Kolbaad Baarmaan Farshidvard

Golshahr ——— Piran

Kay Ghobaad

Rooeen

Kay
aavoos

Kay
Pashin

Kay
Aarmin

Kay
Aarash

Jarireh

Foorood

riborz

vniz

Tooranian Warriors			
Ajnaas	Garzam	Khojabr	Shamaasaas
Akhvaast	Gholoon	Kohram	Shirui
Alkoos	Ghorcheh	Mardooy	Shitarakh
Andariman	Golbaad	Nahel	Tajov
Arjaasp	Kaaloo	Palaashan	Tarkhan
Damoor	Karkoo	Poolaad	
Farghaar	Khazarvan	Poolaadvand	

Glossary of Geographical Markers

Aarman or Aarman-Zamin: On the border of Tooran-Zamin and Iran-Zamin.

Ahvaz: A city in southwest Iran; capital of the province of Khuzestan.

Alaanan: Region in northwest Iran, north of the Aras River.

Alborz, Mount: Regarded as a holy mountain in myths and legends. In geographical terms, it stands in northern Iran.

Almas River: Perhaps beyond the borders of Tooran-Zamin.

Amol: A city in Iran where Fereydoon resides before taking residence in his capital city of Tammisheh. Situated in the Mazandaran Province, near the Alborz mountains.

Ardabil: An ancient city in northwestern Iran.

Arvand: A river also known as the Shatt al-Arab River. It begins at the confluence of the Tigris and Euphrates rivers.

Asprooz, Mount: Perhaps a mythical mountain on the road to Mazandaran where Kaavoos is blinded by the deevs.

Azerbaijan: A region situated in northwestern Iran.

Badakhshan: In today's northeast Afghanistan; southeast Tajikistan.

Baghdad: Capital of Iraq.

Bait-Al Moghaddas: Jerusalem; meaning pure city.

Balkh: A city in Iran-Zamin, situated in today's Afghanistan.

Baluchistan: A province in today's Iran bordering Pakistan and Afghanistan.

Bidaad: Meaning unjust, also referred to as "city of battle"; a city built by Toor with spells and magic in Tooran-Zamin, and populated by man-eaters.

Bost: A city and river east of Sistan; situated in today's Afghanistan and now named Lashkargah.

Borz: Another name for Mount Alborz.

Bozgoosh: Area on the way to the dwelling of the White Deev.

Bukhara: An ancient town in Tooran-Zamin; a city in today's Uzbekistan.

Chaadj: A city in Tooran-Zamin; near today's Tashkent in Uzbekistan.

Chagal: A city in Tooran-Zamin, in today's Turkestan region.

Chaghan: Or Chaghaniyan, land independent of Iran-Zamin or Tooran-Zamin; a region in Afghanistan north of the River Jayhoon; ruled by an ally of Afraasiyaab.

Chalus: A seaside town on the Caspian Sea; may refer to Mount Koos or Caucasus.

Chin: China; generally refers to lands to the east of Iran, as Rum represents the lands to the west.

Daghooy: Hunting plains near the border of Tooran-Zamin.

Dahestan: Presently located in Turkmenistan and Iran.

Dahr: Land outside the borders of Iran-Zamin or Tooran-Zamin.

Dajleh: Arabic for Tigris River.

Damavand, Mount: The highest peak on the Alborz mountain range.

Dambar: A place in today's eastern Afghanistan.

Damghan: A city east of Tehran.

Eram, garden of: A Persian garden located in Shiraz, Iran; also heavenly garden in the desert said to appear to the traveler like a mirage.

Estakhr: An ancient city in southern Iran in the Pars Province, north of Persepolis; seat of Kashvaad's palace.

Fort Bahman: A fortress on the border of Iran-Zamin and Tooran-Zamin.

Gang: May be an ancient city on the edge of the Sayhoon River (Syr Darya); seat of Afraasiyaab.

Gang-Behesht: Same as Gang-Dej, the city built by Siaavosh.

Gang-Dej: A fort city built by Siaavosh past the Sea of Chin.

Ghaaf, Mount: A mythological mountain often depicted in images as encircling the world.

Ghajghaarbaashi: A town in Tooran-Zamin, situated in today's Turkey.

Ghatan: A city located in present-day Afghanistan.

Ghennooj: A city near or in India.

Gholoo, Mount: Unclear of the location, but in Tooran-Zamin.

Gholzom, Sea of: The Red Sea, between Egypt, Saudi Arabia, Sudan, and Yemen.

Ghom: Or Qom, a city between Tehran and Isfahan.

Ghoor: A province in Afghanistan.

Gilan: A province in today's northwestern Iran bordering the Caspian sea; Iranian warrior shields often come from this region.

Gilan, Sea of: Caspian Sea.

Golzarioon: A fictional river in Tooran-Zamin.

Gorgan: A city in northern Iran; capital of the Golestan Province.

Gorgsaaran: Meaning "land of the wolf," marks the border separating Iran-Zamin from Mazandaran.

Gorooguerd: A province of Tooran-Zamin.

Guraabeh: Burial site of Saam, the hero.

Haamaavaran: Perhaps a fictional land; perhaps a reference to Yemen.

Hamaavan, Mount: Site of retreat for Iranian warriors in Tooran-Zamin.

Haraah: A region ruled by an ally of Afraasiyaab; perhaps al-Harrah, in today's western Saudi Arabia, near Jordan.

Hari/Herat: A city in Iran-Zamin, situated in today's Afghanistan.

Hirmand: On the border of Iran and Afghanistan.

Hirmand River: Flowing through Sistan and through today's Afghanistan.

Iran-Zamin: Land of Iran.

Isfahan: A city in Iran, south of Tehran; the seat of Giv, where he receives Kay Khosrow upon his arrival in Iran-Zamin.

Jaram: A city situated in today's Afghanistan.

Jayhoon River: Also known as Oxus River and Amu Darya; located in present-day Afghanistan.

Kaasseh Rood: Perhaps a fictional river in Tooran-Zamin.

Kaat: Capital of Khaarazm, or Chorasmia, in ancient times, situated in west-central Asia, south of the Aral Sea.

Kabol: A city in today's Afghanistan.

Kahan: Land independent of Iran or Tooran; its ruler is Kahaar, ally of Afraasiyaab.

Kalaat: A city in present-day Afghanistan.

Kandahar: A city in today's southern Afghanistan.

Kashaf: A city in northeastern Iran.

Khargaah: A border town or area near the Jayhoon and part of Tooran-Zamin.

Khataah: A city near Chin.

Khazar Sea: Caspian Sea.

Khorasan: Region in today's northeastern Iran.

Khotan: A town on the southern side of the Silk Road between China and the west; situated in Tooran-Zamin and ruled for some time by Piran.

Khotlan: A city in Maavaronhar.

Kooch and Baluch: Kooch is a village in today's Iran; Kooch and Baluch are two tribes near Baluchistan, Iran.

Koos: Caucasus.

Kushan: A mountainous region in today's China.

Laadan: In present-day Ukraine; site of a battle where the Iranians lost heavily to the Tooranians under Kay Khosrow.

Maachin: Comprises greater China.

Mai: An area in today's eastern Afghanistan or Indian subcontinent.

Margh: A city in today's south Khorasan Province of Iran.

Marv: A city in Iran, situated in today's Afghanistan.

Maavaranhar: An area near the Jayhoon and part of Tooran-Zamin.

Mayam: A fictional river or sea.

Mazandaran: Residence of the deevs and the White Deev in *The Shahnameh* including Gorgsaaran; a non-geographical realm that in no way references the present-day province in northern Iran bordering the Caspian Sea.

Naarvan: An area in Northern Iran, perhaps in present-day Mazandaran.

Navand: A village in northwestern Iran where shines the flame of Barzeen.

Nile River: A river in northeastern Africa.

Nimrooz: Capital of Zabolestan or Sistan; served as the prime meridian until Europe gained strength and made the switch to Greenwich, England.

Nishabur: A city in Iran-Zamin, situated in today's Afghanistan.

Pars: A province in southern Iran with Persepolis as capital.

Pashan: Perhaps in present-day India; site of a battle where the Iranians lost heavily to the Tooranians under the reign of Kay Khosrow.

Paykand: Or Baykand; a city in Tooran-Zamin, near today's Bukhara (Uzbekistan).

Rey: The oldest city in the province of Tehran, today it is part of the capital city.

Rum: Name of regions west of Iran; Byzantium, eastern Roman Empire.

Rumi: Adjective meaning from Byzantium.

Saghlaab: Land outside of Iran-Zamin and Tooran-Zamin; land of the Slavic people; ruled by Kondor, ally of Afraasiyaab.

Sagsaar: East of Afghanistan.

Sagsaaran: Or Sistan, is in today's eastern Iran and southern Afghanistan, near Baluchistan; also named Sakastan.

Samangan: Land in ancient times and a province in present-day Afghanistan.

Samarkand: A city in Tooran-Zamin, a destination on the Silk Road, and in present-day Uzbekistan.

Sari: A town in present-day Mazandaran; once the capital of Iran.

Saroj, Desert of: Region in Iran-Zamin; unclear of the location.

Sea of Chin: Reference to a body of water in the Far East.

Sea of Sindh: May refer to the Gulf of Oman, south of the Sindh Province, or perhaps the Sindhu (Indus) River.

Sepad, Mount: Appears to be a fictional mountain in Kalaat.

Sepand, Mount: Meaning sacred, holy.

Sepijaab: Land in Tooran-Zamin close to the river Jayhoon.

Shaam: Syria.

Shahd, Mount: Unclear location, perhaps in India.

Shaheh: A city in today's Khuzestan Province of Iran.

Shahd River: May be a reference to the Arvand River also known as the Shatt al-Arab (in today's southern Iraq).

Shakni: Land outside of Iran-Zamin and Tooran-Zamin ruled by Shamira.

Shirkhan: An area in Damavand in western Iran.

Siaavosh-Guerd: A city built by Siaavosh in Tooran-Zamin on land given to him by Afraasiyaab.

Sindh: A province in the southeastern part of India.

Sindhu River: Indus river in India.

Sistan: A province in today's eastern Iran and southern Afghanistan, part of Baluchistan; same as Zabolestan.

Soghdi: A region in Tooran-Zamin.

Sughd: A town in Tooran-Zamin; perhaps in northern Mongolia, near the Chinese border.

Taleghan: A city in the Alborz mountain range.

Tammisheh: Fereydoon's capital in northern Iran; in Mount Koos (meaning Caucasus.)

Taraaz: Or Taraz, a city in Turkestan famous for its beautiful women; also a river in today's Kazakhstan.

Tarmaz: A town on the edge of the Jayhoon River, on the border between Iran-Zamin and Tooran-Zamin.

Tehran: Present-day capital of Iran since 1786.

Tooran-Zamin: Land of Toor and his descendants Pashang and Afraasiyaab; also referred to as Turkestan.

Transoxiana: Also referred to as Maavaran-nahr (Arabic). It is in the land of Tooran beyond the Jayhoon (Oxus) River and covers the region in today's Uzbekistan and Tajikistan, and parts of Kyrgyzstan and Kazakhstan.

Turkestan: Land of Turks east of Iran; also referred to as Tooran-Zamin.

Viseh-Guerd: A city in Tooran Zamin named after Piran's father, Viseh; ancient city in northern Afghanistan.

White Castle: A castle defended by Gojdaham and his children in Iran-Zamin, near Tooran's border.

Zaabeh, Mount: Perhaps a mythical mountain in the Alborz mountain range.

Zabol: Capital of Sistan or Zabolestan; a province in today's eastern Iran, part of Baluchistan.

Zabolestan: Also Sistan; land ruled by Nariman and his descendants Saam, Zaal, and Rostam; in today's southern Afghanistan.

Zam: A city on the border between Iran-Zamin and Tooran-Zamin.

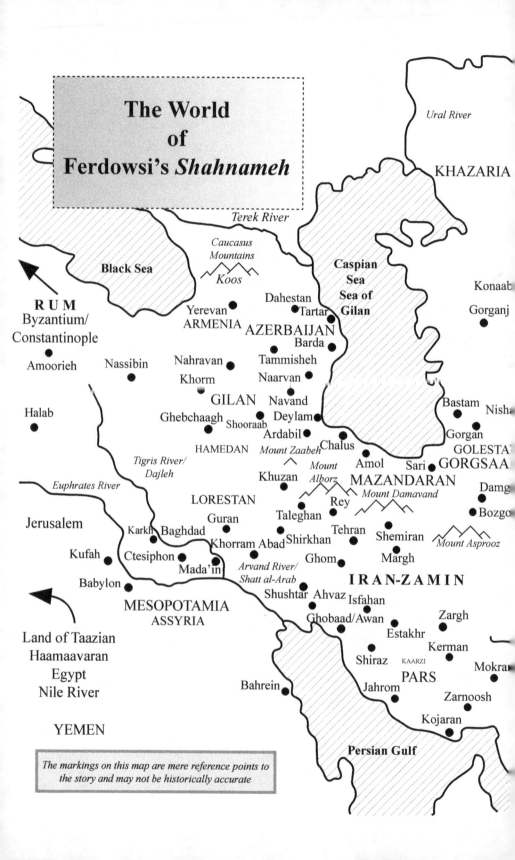

The World of Ferdowsi's *Shahnameh*

Ural River

KHAZARIA

Terek River

Caucasus Mountains

Black Sea

Koos

Caspian Sea

Sea of Gilan

Konaab

Dahestan

Tartar

Gorganj

RUM
Byzantium/
Constantinople

Yerevan
ARMENIA   AZERBAIJAN

Barda

Amoorieh   Nassibin   Nahravan   Tammisheh

Khorm   Naarvan

GILAN   Navand

Bastam   Nisha

Halab   Ghebchaagh   Shooraab   Deylam

Ardabil   Gorgan

HAMEDAN   *Mount Zaabeh* Chalus   GOLESTA

Tigris River/ Dajleh   *Mount Alborz*   *Mount* Amol   Sari   GORGSAA

Euphrates River   Khuzan   MAZANDARAN   Damg

Mount Damavand   Bozgo

LORESTAN   Rey

Jerusalem   Guran   Taleghan   *Mount Asprooz*

Karkh Baghdad   Tehran   Shemiran

Kufah   Khorram Abad Shirkhan   Margh

Ctesiphon   Ghom

Babylon   Mada'in   *Arvand River/ Shatt al-Arab*   IRAN-ZAMIN

MESOPOTAMIA   Shushtar Ahvaz Isfahan

ASSYRIA   Ghobaad/Awan   Zargh

Land of Taazian   Estakhr   Kerman

Haamaavaran   Shiraz   KAARZI   Mokra

Egypt   PARS

Nile River   Bahrein   Jahrom   Zarnoosh

Kojaran

YEMEN

Persian Gulf

The markings on this map are mere reference points to the story and may not be historically accurate

RUS/RUSSIA

Mazandaran
Residence of the deevs and the White Deev
in *The Shahnameh* including Gorgsaaran;
a non-geographical realm which in no way
references the present-day province in northern Iran
bordering the Caspian Sea.

Dambar

Syr Darya/
Sayhoon River

Khalkh

Aral
Sea

Khotlan

Farab

MAAVARANHAR

SOGHDI

Kaat   Paykand   Samarkand

Soghd

Bukhara

Taraaz

Mai   Khargaah   Chagal

TOORAN-ZAMIN

Kushan Mountains

Amu Darya
Jayhoon/Oxus   Chaadj

Khataah

Maimargh

ARMAN-ZAMIN

COSHMAIHAN

CHIN/CHINA

Amoy

Marv   Bukhara   Samangan   Ghabchaagh

Tous   Tarmaz

Balkh   Andaraab   Khotan

Badakhshan

Kashaf   Baamian   Dambar

Faariaab   GHOOR   Kabol

KHORASAN   Ghaznein

Herat/Hari   Ghatan

Hirmand   Chaghan   Jaram

Nimrooz   Zam

Bost

Zabol

BOLESTAN   Kalat   Kandahar

SISTAN   *River Hirmand*

Firozabad

Sorsan

BALUCHISTAN

Sindhu River/
Indus River

INDIA

Ghennooj

SINDH

Sendal

Milad

Sea of Sindh

Glossary of Persian Words

Aab: From aaberoo, meaning honor, nobility, and integrity; code of honor.

Aazargoshasp: Divine, holy, eternal flame of the Zoroastrians; a revered fire temple for kings and warriors during the Sasanian times in Azerbaijan.

Andisheh: Thought.

Ard: The 29th day of any month is the day of Ard in ancient Iran.

Arrash: Unit of measurement corresponding to the length of the forearm, from fingertip to elbow.

Ayeen: Divine principle or code of human life; path and purpose that reflects all that encompasses the divine, free of barriers set by culture, geography, dogma, or religion.

Babreh Bayan: Armor that is worn only by Rostam. Uncertain about its meaning. Literally refers to leopard skin. Other interpretations refer to beaver skin or dragon skin. It is meant to be waterproof and impenetrable.

Bahraam: Mars.

Barzeen: Zoroastrian fire temple with an ever-burning flame situated in Khorasan, in northeastern Iran.

Bidaad: Meaning unjust.

Daad: Infinite justice; justice that is non-judgmental and unchangeable for it is divine, constant, eternal; different from human justice that is encompassed by a strict set of laws.

Dehghan: Farmer; keeper of land and crops, of rain and sun, and all that grows; keeper of ancient wisdom, poet, and bard.

Dinar: Gold coin.

Dirham: Silver coin.

Esfand: Twelfth month of the Persian solar calendar; begins in February and ends in March; also the name of the plant and herb rue; also meaning sacred or holy, as in *Sepand.*

Esfand: Rue; meaning sacred or holy, as in Sepand; also twelfth month of the Persian solar calendar; begins in February and ends in March.

Farr: Divine grace; state of consciousness holding infinite grace of light and life.

Farsang: Ancient unit of measure equivalent to 6.24 kilometers or 3.88 miles.

Gohar: Essence

Jaan: Life force, soul, spirit.

Kaavian: Belonging to Kaaveh, the blacksmith, who leads the opposition against Zahaak. The Kaaviani banner is made of the cloth of blacksmiths with the colors red, yellow, and purple representing the two ends of the color spectrum as well as the center color.

Kamand: Ancient unit of measure.

Kay: King.

Kherrad: Wisdom; Eternal Wisdom; absolute, pure consciousness.

Kianian: Royal; from kian, meaning royalty.

Mahn: Reference to a form of weight measurement in ancient Middle East, around 3 kilograms or 6.6 pounds; so 600 mahn is equivalent to 1,800 kilograms or 3,968 pounds

Mehr: Complex word that includes deep eternal love, affection, compassion, mercy; also the seventh month of the Iranian calendar.

Mehregan: A festival and memorial to Fereydoon, still celebrated

716

today on the Mehr day of the Mehr month of the year. Iranian fall festival during the month of October.

Naam: Divine essence, what is contained in space; also defined as "name."

Nowruz : New Day, the Persian New Year, still observed today by Iranians of all religions during the spring equinox on or around March 21.

Pahlavan: Noble hero, paladin, warrior, fighter for the cause of mehr; guardian of crown and throne, soldier of light.

Pahlavi: Or middle Persian; literary language during the Sasanian rule until the advent of the modern Persian language.

Pishdaadian: Meaning the era prior to the rule of law. The dynasty comprises the first Persian kings: Kiumars, Hooshang, and Tahmures.

Raai: Will or thought (andisheh); intellect or knowing that works in favor of universal time, not human or chronological time.

Saddeh: Festival to celebrate Hooshang's discovery of fire in The Shahnameh; meaning one hundred, it marks one hundred days before the start of spring, or Nowruz; it is a celebration of overcoming darkness.

Sepand: Same as esfand, meaning sacred or holy.

Sitir: Ancient form of measure equivalent to 75 grams.

Sokhan: Divine Word, ultimate truth.

Teer: Mercury.

Yazdan: Creator of all that is manifested, unmanifested, and all that is yet to come into existence. Plural of Yzad (divine) encompasses all of divinity.

Zamin: Land of; for instance, Iran-Zamin means land of Iran.

The Persian Calendar

Based on the solar calendar, the months are named after twelve divinities and correspond to nature's cycles and the signs of the zodiac:

Spring:
Farvardin – Aries; the first month of the year begins with Nowruz, the first day of spring and the spring equinox.
Ordibehesht – Taurus; spans the months of April and May.
Khordaad – Gemini; third month of the year.

Summer:
Teer – Cancer; Mercury; the fourth month begins with the summer solstice.
Mordaad – Leo; fifth month of the year.
Shahrivar – Virgo; sixth month of the solar year.

Fall:
Mehr – Libra; the seventh month begins with the fall equinox or Mehregan.
Aaban – Scorpio; eighth month of the year.
Aazar – Sagittarius; ninth month of the year, ends with the winter solstice or Yalda.

Winter:
Dey – Capricorn; tenth month of the year.
Bahman – Aquarius; eleventh month of the solar year.
Esfand – Pisces; twelfth month of the year.

This translation would not have been possible without the selfless and unwavering dedication of Soudabeh Araghi who spent countless hours with me revising the entire final manuscript. I am immensely grateful for her truly heroic contribution, which played an instrumental role in completing this significant work.

Printed in the USA
CPSIA information can be obtained
at www.ICGtesting.com
LVHW041624041123
762611LV00007B/6